WORLD POLITICS 83/84

Suzanne P. Ogden, *Editor*
Northeastern University

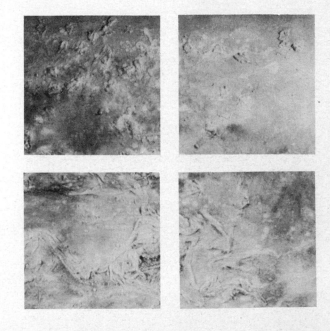

Cover Credit: "Place of Many Mansions," Russo, Alexander; Courtesy, Corcoran Gallery of Art.

ANNUAL EDITIONS

The Dushkin Publishing Group, Inc. Sluice Dock, Guilford, Ct. 06437

Volumes in the Annual Editions Series

Abnormal Psychology
● Aging
● American Government
● American History, Pre-Civil War
● American History, Post-Civil War
● Anthropology
Astronomy
● Biology
● Business
● Comparative Politics
● Criminal Justice
Death and Dying
● Deviance
● Early Childhood Education
Earth Science
● Economics
● Educating Exceptional Children
● Education
● Educational Psychology
Energy
● Environment
Ethnic Studies
Foreign Policy
Geography

Geology
● Health
● Human Development
● Human Sexuality
● Macroeconomics
● Management
● Marketing
● Marriage and Family
● Microeconomics
● Personal Growth and Behavior
Philosophy
Political Science
● Psychology
Religion
● Social Problems
● Social Psychology
● Sociology
Twentieth Century American History
● Urban Society
● Western Civilization, Pre-Reformation
● Western Civilization, Post-Reformation
Women's Studies
World History
● World Politics

● Indicates currently available

©1983 by the Dushkin Publishing Group, Inc. Annual Editions is a Trade Mark of the Dushkin Publishing Group, Inc.

Copyright ©1983 by the Dushkin Publishing Group, Inc., Guilford, Connecticut 06437

Fourth Edition

Manufactured by George Banta Company, Menasha, Wisconsin, 54952

Library of Congress Cataloging in Publication Data
Main entry under title: Annual Editions: World Politics.
    1. International relations—Addresses, essays, lectures.   2. United States—Foreign relations—Addresses, essays lectures.   I. Title: World politics.
ISBN 0-87967-474-1   327.09

CONTENTS

1

The US in an Interdependent World

2

Revival of the Cold War: The US and the USSR in Confrontation

3

Allies of the US: Western Europe and Japan

4

Socialist States: Allies and Adversaries of the USSR

5

The Third World: Areas of Conflict, Crises, and Problems

6

The International Political Economy: Aid, Investment, Trade, and Finance

7

The Arms Race, Arms Control, Nuclear Freeze, and Arms Sales

8

International Organization and International Law

9

Problems and Prospects for the Future

TOPIC GUIDE

This topic guide can be used to correlate each of the articles in *Annual Editions: World Politics 83/84* to one or more of the topics normally covered by textbooks used in World Politics courses. Each article corresponds to a given topic area according to whether it deals with the subject in a primary or a secondary fashion. These correlations are intended for use as a general study guide and do not necessarily define the total coverage of any given article.

TOPIC AREA	TREATED AS A PRIMARY ISSUE IN:	TREATED AS A SECONDARY ISSUE IN:
Diplomacy and Obstacles to the Peaceful Settlement of Disputes	8. Excerpts from *Whence the Threat to Peace* 14. French Diplomacy 25. US Policy and Africa 29. The Tragedy and the Hope 30. Moscow's Middle East 44. Limits and Cuts	16. America and Japan 48. Law of the Sea
Domestic Politics' Linkage to Foreign Policy	2. Concepts and Communications 9. Changing of the Guard 14. French Diplomacy 21. China's Split-Level Change 22. Sino-American Relations	6. Human Rights 13. Is NATO Obsolete? 14. French Diplomacy 23. Central America's Bitter Wars Spread 34. Foreign Aid
Dominance and Dependence as Aspects of World Politics	12. A New Course for Britain and Western Europe 17. Japanese Perception of America 18. Stability in the Warsaw Pact 20. The German Democratic Republic 26. Zimbabwe Is a Success 28. The Strategic Significance of South Asia	3. Chain Linkage in American Foreign Policy 19. East Europe Instability 29. The Tragedy and the Hope 35. The US Caribbean Basin Initiative
Economic Aspects of World Politics	16. America and Japan 17. Japanese Perception of America 19. East Europe Instability 20. The German Democratic Republic 33. The North-South Dialogue 34. Foreign Aid 35. The US Caribbean Basin Initiative 36. Conditionality Reflects Principle That Financing and Adjustment Should Act Hand in Hand	13. Is NATO Obsolete? 15. West Germany's New Chancellor 17. Japanese Perception of America 32. Development Strategy Distorted by Western Propaganda

TOPIC AREA	TREATED AS A PRIMARY ISSUE IN:	TREATED AS A SECONDARY ISSUE IN:
Economic Aspects of World Politics (cont'd)	37. Thirty-Two Years of World Trade Developments 38. De Larosiere Stresses No Monetary System Can Substitute for Sound Economic Policies 39. Trade Relations Between Industrialized Countries in Times of Crisis 49. Sea Law Convention Battle	
Ideological Aspects of World Politics	4. Human Rights and the Refugee Crisis 5. Outmoded Assumptions 6. Human Rights 10. Reagan's Foreign Policy 13. Is NATO Obsolete? 20. The German Democratic Republic 32. Development Strategy Distorted by Western Propaganda 43. Practice and Theory on Soviet Arms Control Policy 49. Sea Law Convention Battle	1. Defining the National Interest 8. Excerpts from *Whence the Threat to Peace* 26. Zimbabwe Is a Success 33. The North-South Dialogue
Interdependence of States	3. Chain Linkage in American Foreign Policy 25. US Policy and Africa 27. Sino-American Relations 39. Trade Relations Between Industrialized Countries in Times of Crisis 47. The Common Heritage 50. Global Future	5. Outmoded Assumptions 11. The Russian Connection 26. Zimbabwe Is a Success 38. De Larosiere Stresses No Monetary System Can Substitute for Sound Economic Policies 48. Law of the Sea
International Law and Organization	45. The Falklands and the Law 46. The UN 47. The Common Heritage 48. Law of the Sea 49. Sea Law Convention Battle 51. The Establishment of a World Authority 53. US Nuclear Strategy and World Order Reform	

TOPIC AREA	TREATED AS A PRIMARY ISSUE IN:	TREATED AS A SECONDARY ISSUE IN:	TOPIC AREA	TREATED AS A PRIMARY ISSUE IN:	TREATED AS A SECONDARY ISSUE IN:
Military Aspects of World Politics	2. Concepts and Communications 7. Changing Soviet Conceptions of East-West Relations 13. Is NATO Obsolete? 15. West Germany's New Chancellor 16. America and Japan 17. Japanese Perception of America 18. Stability in the Warsaw Pact 23. Central America's Bitter Wars Spread 24. Central America 28. The Strategic Significance of South Asia 40. Russian and American Capabilities 41. Pushing Arms 42. Conventional Arms Transfers in the Third World 43. Practice and Theory on Soviet Arms Control Policy 44. Limits and Cuts	12. A New Course for Britain and Western Europe 21. China's Split-Level Change 30. Moscow's Middle East	**National Security and National Interest**	1. Defining the National Interest 7. Changing Soviet Conceptions of East-West Relations 12. A New Course for Britain and Western Europe 13. Is NATO Obsolete? 16. America and Japan 24. Central America 28. The Strategic Significance of South Asia 39. Trade Relations Between Industrialized Countries in Times of Crisis 40. Russian and American Capabilities 43. Practice and Theory in Soviet Arms Control Policy	4. Human Rights and the Refugee Crisis 5. Outmoded Assumptions 6. Human Rights 21. China's Split-Level Change

PREFACE

This collection of readings is aimed at filling a void in materials for the teaching of introductory level world politics and foreign policy. Specifically, amidst the dozens of textbooks and readers, there does not exist an accessible compilation of readings that brings together the major current problems concerning relations among nations in easily understandable language and to which students can relate.

This collection is addressed to those students who are new to the study of world politics. The objective of these selections is to stimulate the student's interest in learning to understand what often seems to be foreign, remote, irrelevant, and boring, but which indeed has consequences to their economic well-being, security, and even survival.

International events are proceeding at a rapid pace. The events of the fall, 1982, made innumerable articles concerning international events in the earlier part of the year hopelessly out of date. International relations should, therefore, be seen as a constant flow of actions and reactions that produce new situations calling for further actions. In addition, the readings in this volume should convey to the student a sense of the complexities and the interdependence of international problems confronting the world at this time. The interdependence of relationships means that events as far away as Zimbabwe, Japan, Poland, South Africa, or Central America affect the United States, just as our actions, and inactions, have profound repercussions in other states. The United States can hardly afford to be smug, aloof, or incautious in its policies when so much may be at stake.

It is hoped that students will come away from these readings enlightened, angry, questioning, excited, wanting to learn more about complex world developments as they unfold during the course and, perhaps more importantly, long after the course is over.

Annual Editions: World Politics 82/83 went to press amidst the great uncertainties created over the East-West conflict (as manifested by the deadlock over strategic and tactical nuclear weapons between the USA and USSR, and over such crises as Poland, El Salvador, Nicaragua, and Afghanistan), and the North-South conflict (as manifested by the Third World's insistent demands for a New International Economic and Information Order, and for total sanctions against South Africa for its apartheid and denationalization policies); the Arab-Israeli conflict (the latest incident being Israel's annexation of the Golan Heights); and the political, economic, and military tensions within the Western alliance.

As *Annual Editions: World Politics 83/84* goes to press, momentous problems, hence momentous opportunities, face the world. The re-emergence of the cold war with a vengeance in the late 1970s has resulted in the worst Soviet-American relationship in well over a decade. But a change in the Soviet leadership and its initiatives to break the deadlock on strategic arms limitations provide an opportunity to improve this deteriorating situation. The American-Japanese partnership is being undermined by actions on both sides, but new proposals by the Japanese on economic and defense matters could turn the relationship around. The Third World countries continue to suffer from consuming poverty, and face diminished aid from the industrialized states. In response to this, however, they are initiating among themselves self-help measures that may not only improve the economic situation but also diminish their dependence on, and domination by, aid-donor industrialized states. The Soviet and the Chinese confront each other along thousands of miles of borders, but the possibility of their coming to the bargaining table now may bring more than 20 years of acrimonious feuding to an end—an eventuality which need not be seen as detrimental to American interests in world peace. And while the Middle East continues in seeming turmoil, negotiations between the Israelis and the concerned Arab states may eventuate in a more stable situation in at least one part of the Middle East.

Despair concerning the future continues, however, not only because of the numerous areas in the world suffering from ongoing and potential conflicts, but also from the utter poverty of so much of the world. At this time there seems little to comfort those who are evaluating international trends as the world economy moves further into economic recession—a recession fueled not only by economic problems in the industrialized states and in the most advanced of the developing states (such as Brazil, Mexico, and Korea), but also by protectionist measures that will further foster international economic recession in response to those very problems. This situation indicates once again the highly interdependent nature of the international system. It is not a "zero-sum game" where some state can "win" in any absolute sense of the word. No country can expect to remain rich in a sea of poverty, as some of the following articles so amply indicate. The importance of the structure of the international economic order to world peace cannot be overstated.

The structure of the contents of this edition has been amended in several different areas. Allies of the US, including Western Europe and Japan, have been grouped together, while the Eastern European states and the People's Republic of China appear together in the section called Socialist States: Allies and Adversaries of the USSR. Since the bulk of the Middle Eastern states are Third World states according to most criteria, the section on the Middle East has been added as a subsection of The Third World: Areas of Conflict, Crises, and Problems. Finally, all issues of the international political economy, whether they include North-South, East-West, or West-West relationships in aid, investment, trade, and finance have been integrated into a single chapter.

Many thanks are owed to Chau T. Phan, the former Editor of this compilation of readings, who has built it into such a highly successful text. And many thanks also to all those colleagues who have taken time to write useful comments concerning *Annual Editions: World Politics.* I hope to hear from many more of you.

Suzanne P. Ogden
Editor

The US in an Interdependent World

The US remains today the most powerful country in the world, but this does not mean that the US is able to achieve its goals in any given situation. Indeed, while maintaining overall preponderant "power," the US at present probably has less power to influence the actions of others than at any time in the post-World War II era. Our strongest partnerships and alliances from that era are slowly being eroded: Western European countries no longer follow us in foreign policy, and even cause us considerable embarrassment by challenging American objectives abroad; and our great Asian ally, Japan, questions both our economic and security goals. Third World countries are, in part because of what we term our "national interest," able to put pressure on us to obtain military and economic aid, even when by any definition they are ignoring American goals and ideals, including the violation of the human rights of their citizens. But such American foreign policy ideals as pursuing human rights abroad and "making the world safe for democracy" are in constant tension with what is in our "national interest," as well as with what is within our national power to achieve. During the Reagan Administration, in the name of these ideals, a new version of the Cold War objectives of containment and isolation of communism throughout the world has resulted in contorted rationalizations of our foreign policy, as well as both inconsistent and indecisive actions. This is distressing to our allies and ineffective against our enemies.

Part of the explanation of our diminished power over recent decades resides in the rise of our allies to new positions of economic, financial, political, and military power. But our national power has been further eroded by the growing interdependence of American foreign policy with the foreign policies of so many other states. As a global power, in both economic and military terms, the US is often affected by whatever happens in the rest of the world. It is not that other states necessarily design their policies for the purpose of thwarting our objectives, or limiting American power. But often this is the result. And of course there are many states that consciously reject the leadership of the US, while others actively oppose US policies. Such a situation has provided for a dynamic, rapidly

1

evolving system of international relations, in which any given action, often in a very unpredictable fashion, may serve to augment or diminish American power. Actions taken that seem to be in America's national interest today may turn out to be detrimental to it tomorrow. One need only mention the Vietnam War or the pipeline controversy to suggest how difficult it is to take a foreign policy action that will not prove harmful to American leadership because of all the unanticipated reactions to that policy.

The following articles are meant to suggest some of the complex interrelationships that the US has to consider in making foreign policy, as well as some of the philosophical and psychological assumptions underlying American foreign policy values and policies. It is hoped that these articles will highlight the difficulties the US often assumes when making foreign policy decisions, and the difficulties of predicting the outcome of any given action the US takes in the international system. One thing is clear: there is rarely a simple "I win, you lose" situation in international affairs.

Looking Ahead: Challenge Questions

Does America's "national interest" require that we diminish our efforts to spread our ideals and morality abroad, or at least that we limit these efforts to a few specific regions?

What have been the effects of an inconsistent human rights policy on the effectiveness of America's world leadership? What problems have been encountered when the US has implemented an "evenhanded" human rights policy?

Is the US becoming more militaristic or is it simply responding defensively to the offensive actions of others? What are some of the world problems that are immune to military intervention?

What kinds of priorities should be used to rank and reconcile the conflicting aspects of America's national interests in the 1980s and beyond?

What kind of an international system is in the American "national interest"?

Is it possible, or likely, for the US to regain primacy in world military and economic matters? What would be the benefits and costs of being the predominant world power?

Defining the National Interest

Anthony Lake

A balance among self-interest, idealism, and power has defined successful American policy since the earliest days of the Republic. But when proclamations of grand goals run ahead of capabilities or when economic, political, and military power is allowed to wither, there is posturing, not policy. When the pursuit of American ideals is not perceived both at home and abroad as rooted in American interests, the result is confusion and suspicion. When American policy is seen to be defined solely in the terms of realpolitik, it loses much of its natural character, strength and appeal.

Debate about American foreign policies has traditionally revolved around how the balance among ideals, interests, and power is to be struck. Much of this debate has been unnecessarily complicated by the assumption of a stark separation of interests and ideals. Until the end of the nineteenth century, interests and ideals were largely in harmony, and the United States's pursuit of both was generally commensurate with its power. But since the Spanish-American War, characteristic American idealism and impatience have helped produce alternating periods of illusion and disillusion, euphoria and gloom, expanded and contracted definitions of interest, perceptions of the world as friendly and hostile, and perceptions of the United States as triumphant and beleaguered. The pendulum has constantly been swinging: from the fervor of the war against Spain to the anti-imperialist revulsion at the start of the century; from Wilson's moral crusade during and after World War I to the disillusion and narrow anti-idealism of the following decades; from the great effort during and after World War II to the bitterness and questioning during and after the Vietnam war.

Since the mid-1970s it has swung again, to a new assertiveness. Will this assertiveness provide, over time, a broadly based approach that encompasses all of the United State's interests? Or will there be only another spasmodic shift, containing the seeds of a new reaction?

The formulation of foreign policy is much more difficult today than it was thirty-five years ago. The Soviet threat remains, indeed in an intensified form, but in a changed world of multiple challenges and interests. While a foreign policy designed to meet a single threat would include necessary defense measures and could provide an easy and popular coherence, it would be at the cost of incompleteness when measured against the full range of the United State's interests.

In the past, the nation's periodic waves of disillusion and retrenchment have been characterized by distrust of pursuing American ideals and a redefinition of American interests in more limited ways. Yet ideals of individual freedom were not necessarily inconsistent with the pursuit of national interests. The failures that created disillusion were more often failures to keep power and commitments in balance.

Formulating Foreign Policy

There are, of course, shifts in foreign policy emphasis and priority when there are shifts in American opinion and political leadership. But until new administrations learn to reject the temptation to emphasize the new at the expense of the enduring, until the press ceases to dramatize every "new beginning," and until the public ceases to expect more than any American government can deliver in a world of diffused power, the cycles of illusion and disillusion will continue. A consistent American foreign policy must allow the flexibility demanded by international change and a domestic democratic system. But it must also be grounded in general agreement on national interests and how they are consistent with American ideals.

The most realistic measuring stick for American foreign policy interests, or any nation's international interests, is the effect foreign events may have on the lives of individual citizens. Nations are not markers on an international chess board, yet the abstractions of conventional foreign policy analysis too often treat them as such. Nations are, of course, collections of people, and it is in their fortunes that the fortunes of nations are told.

"Defining the National Interest," Anthony Lake, *Proceedings of the Academy of Political Science,* Vol. 34, No. 2, 1981.

From this perspective, the relative importance of different kinds of interests becomes most clearly defined. Involvement in a foreign war provides the most dramatic and deadly damage to the welfare of a nation's citizens. Especially in the nuclear age, primary attention must therefore be given to the maintenance of power balances, the prevention of political coercion, and the work of peaceful diplomacy. But international economic events have the most immediate effect on people's lives. The quiet economic decisions of a friendly nation can affect real American interests far more than a dramatic revolution in a country of little economic or strategic interest, yet they are likely to receive less attention in the daily headlines.

A central question is whether economic and military interests can be separated. In perhaps the most interesting and thoughtful foreign policy document produced in the 1980 electoral campaign, the Libertarian party urged such a separation through a return to the policies of the Founding Fathers. Political and military nonintervention abroad and concentration on territorial defense, coupled with an active and free international trade, "would do far more to advance the legitimate aims of American foreign policy than has the interventionism of the past thirty-five or forty years," and would be more consistent with domestic American institutions.[1] While couched in terms familiar to those who learned the most from the Vietnam experience, the intellectual origins of this argument are more precisely found in the conservative views of the 1930s.

Yet the economic welfare of American citizens, and perhaps their political freedom, cannot be broadly separated from maintaining an active American diplomacy and the use of military power abroad. The necessity of intervention in World War II provides the most important evidence of this fact. The need to keep open the Strait of Hormuz and the flow of most Persian Gulf oil provides the most recent example. The question is one of balance and proportion. Where, and to what degree, are the interests of American citizens so involved that American diplomacy must become deeply engaged and American military power readily available?

Based on their importance to the United States, their power and political orientations, and the United States's previous commitments, a priority for different geographic regions can be roughly sketched: (1) America's allies in Europe and Northeast Asia, with the importance of Asia constantly increasing; (2) the Persian Gulf; (3) the Western Hemisphere and the rest of East Asia, including Australia and New Zealand; and (4) Eastern Europe, Africa, and the Asian subcontinent.

The caveats against creating such priorities are as important as the priorities themselves. Relations with important countries within one area, such as Nigeria and India, may matter far more than relations with smaller nations in crucial regions. It is also difficult to segregate, even analytically, the United States's interests in one area from its interests in another. For example, the United States's relations with its European allies and with Japan increasingly involve events far beyond the region of the formal alliance. In addition, the act of drawing lines around regions can, in itself, be dangerous. It could imply that nations of genuine importance lie beyond the lines of interest or could tempt adversaries to believe that the United States is ceding them new spheres.

The point of thinking about regional priorities is not to draw arbitrary defense perimeters. Its importance lies in making the distinctions necessary to keep the United States's commitments and tactics proportionate to its interests and power. A tendency toward undifferentiated thinking—equating, for example, Soviet and Chinese support for North Vietnam with a Communist move in Europe or a Soviet adventure in the Persian Gulf—has clouded American foreign policy debates since the 1950s. The United States certainly has an interest in "containment" everywhere, but it must realize that different degrees of interest allow different approaches to the problem.

Where the most important interests of the United States would be jeopardized by an attack, as in alliance areas, a commitment to immediate military action is necessary. But where its interests are less immediately involved, it can rely more on other instruments and the workings of time—on the use of economic leverage, determined efforts peacefully to resolve international disputes, patient efforts to expand United States political influence, or even careful support for the nationalism of those populations under the control of the Soviet Union or its allies. Indeed, in areas where American military power is limited, it must turn to these more subtle means if it is to avoid disaster. Paradoxically, the United States competes best with the Soviets in most Third World nations by deemphasizing global competition. Treating such nations as pawns in a larger game, interpreting "socialist" domestic institutions as allegiance to the Soviets, and insisting on alignment with either the United States or the Soviet Union offend Third World nationalism and thus limit American influence. The United States competes best in the Third World by pursuing policies that respond primarily to Third World concerns: economic development and national independence.

While current American interests and Third World realities call for such an approach, three trends increase the likelihood that American military force could be required to defend vital interests in nonalliance areas: the expansion of American economic interests in and political ties to Third World nations; the precedent of the Soviet invasion of Afghanistan and more assertive Soviet global policies; and the enhanced military capacities of Third World nations themselves. The lesson of Vietnam is not that the United States should never use force when there are new challenges to American interests. Such thinking smacks of the earlier absolutist rigidities that resulted in the Vietnam intervention.

1. THE US IN AN INTERDEPENDENT WORLD

Vietnam

The lesson should be the injunction to ask careful questions before undertaking new military actions or commitments that could force such actions. To what extent are American interests involved? What would be the impact on the lives of American citizens, current and future, of a failure to take military action? Is there a legitimate request for assistance by a nation under external attack? Is there an assault on the international legal rights of the United States or its allies? What is the degree of effort by the government requesting assistance? By its allies? Will the government requesting assistance become dependent on American intervention for its survival against the wishes of its own people? What are the prospects for military success? Is the cost of military failure acceptable? Even with congressional support, will the American public support the venture? If such questions are not adequately answered, the consequence will be policies of dangerous bluff and bluster or defeat.

Conclusion

Beyond the defense of immediate interests in various regions of the world, complete United States foreign policies must also address a range of long-term interests that are largely synonymous with American ideals, such as the pursuit of limitations on the spread of armaments, the economic well-being of other nations, and human rights. These are not idealistic luxuries, but investments in a safer and more prosperous future for America. American interests are immediately affected by the decisions of the governments of other nations. American values call for concern about what happens to individuals within those nations. In the long run, the two come together, for the needs and hopes of those individuals will define the actions of their governments—most quickly in democracies but in time even in authoritarian societies. As Hans Morgenthau has written, "the greater the stability of society and the sense of security of its members, the smaller are the chances for collective emotions to seek an outlet in aggressive nationalism, and vice versa."[2]

Recent events in Iran and Central America make clear the ways in which American interests can be damaged when nations fall into turmoil because repressive governments have lost legitimacy with their people. The United States's interest lies in encouraging an early balance of popular political, social, and economic reforms, not on America's terms but in the terms of the local society. If repression is allowed to drive out moderate alternatives, sooner or later the United States will face an unpleasant choice between support for further repression (resulting in international obloquy) and acquiescence in the triumph of radicals.

Extending the ideals and protections of the Constitution throughout the United States has generally enhanced internal stability. Similarly, pragmatic support of human progress abroad—within the limits of United States influence—constitutes an investment in future moderation. At home and abroad, humane reform opposes rather than invites radicalism. Economic progress does not guarantee political peace either among or within nations. But economic adversity does produce both frustration and short-sighted decisions by individuals and governments to serve the present at the expense of the future. Current trends in global population growth, environmental degradation, and resource development clearly presage further political instabilities.

There is no doubt that meaningful attention to such concerns as human rights and nuclear nonproliferation complicates both American diplomacy and the task of presenting coherent foreign policies to the American people. But shying away from complexity and relegating such concerns to the realm of "idealism" disregards long-term American interests. Moreover, a policy that does not reflect American values and that does not address America's humanitarian and self-interested stake in the progress of hundreds of millions of people in the world who live lives of terrible desperation will fail to touch the hearts of Americans. Appealing to a fear of communism will always mobilize support for a policy, but it will not sustain it.

Concern for issues like human rights also strengthens the American position abroad. Mere defense of the status quo leaves the initiatives to others, diminishes American prestige, and damages the country's alliances. As Robert Osgood wrote in 1953, "no coalition can survive through a common fear of tyranny without a common faith in liberty. If the leader of the Western Coalition ceases to sustain that faith, then who will sustain it?"[3]

American ideals must always be evaluated in terms of interests. Only thus can foreign policies be made sustainable in domestic politics and American behavior made more explicable to others. National interests are well understood. Claims of altruism are instinctively mistrusted.

There will always be ample room for debate about the paths and priorities the United States should pursue in defending its security, advancing its interests, and pursuing its ideals. It is long past time, however, for Americans to accept a broadened conception of their interests that includes their ideals—and to pursue both with a realistic sense of the possible. Only then will the pendulum cease its swings between idealism and anti-idealism.

Notes

[1] Libertarian Party, "White Power on Foreign and Military Policy," Washington, D.C., 1980, pp. 4-5

[2] Hans Morgenthau, *Politics Among Nations* (New York: Alfred A. Knopf, 1963), p. 106

[3] Robert Osgood, *Ideals and Self-Interest in America's Foreign Relations* (Chicago: The University of Chicago Press, 1953), p. 450

Concepts and Communications in American Foreign Policy

Dante Fascell

Dante B. Fascell, the Democratic congressman from Florida's 15th district, has served on the Committee on Foreign Affairs since 1957.

The foreign affairs situation of the United States is at its most dismal point since World War II. This is not President Reagan's fault. It is not even President Carter's fault. In a sense, we have done it to ourselves, and to restore the effectiveness of our nation abroad, our determined effort will be required.

To be sure, there have been grim moments before in that period. The Berlin blockade, Korea, East Germany, Hungary, Cuba and the missile crisis, the Viet Nam years, Czechoslovakia, Iran, Afghanistan, Nicaragua, Poland, El Salvador, the running series of flash points in the Middle East—the list is by no means complete, but it serves to acknowledge a valid point: we have seen difficult and even dangerous times before, and we have survived them.

To make clear what is different now, what has changed over the years since the halcyon days immediately following World War II, we need to recall the underpinnings of our strength and capabilities at the time. To begin with, we had just emerged victorious from a war marked by high moral purpose and broad, fervent popular support at home. Alone of the developed countries we were virtually undamaged within our boundaries at war's end, and in many ways our economy had in fact benefited from the war effort. Our political prestige around the world was exceptionally high; our economy was by far the largest, strongest, and healthiest in the world; our military superiority, both qualitatively and quantitatively, was not only unchallenged but unquestioned; our enemies were few and weak; and our friends were ready to join us whole-heartedly in an enterprise we all believed we saw the same way.

Adding to the effectiveness of our foreign policy effort was the perceived consensus at home about our purposes and policies abroad. Little serious disagreement, except from the fringes, was heard regarding what we were about, what challenges we faced, or how we had to respond. There was indeed an aura of broad, bipartisan consensus. Commentators both then and now have also pointed to the excellent state of Executive-Congressional relations at the time. Extensive mutual consultation and cooperation were the watchwords, facilitating a foreign affairs effort rare in our history for its cohesion of view and ease of execution.

In discussing the undisputed decline since that time, many people have cited the difficulties of U.S.-style presidential democracy, and in the foreign affairs context the particular difficulty of establishing long-term, reliable goals and commitments. Rather, we are told, our political leadership is unable to focus beyond the next election, and for the sake of its own political survival is obliged to favor short-term expediency over the long-term national interest.

On this last point let me make clear first that I propose no important change in our political system. Further, I submit that the underlying problem is not democracy, periodic elections, or the right of a U.S. president to seek a second term. The basic problem is in ourselves, that we have lost our shared sense of the point and purpose of the United States in the world.

The contrast between our current outlook and the far-happier prospects of the late 1940's of course flows from some developments for which we cannot fairly blame ourselves. Leaks of critical information and exports of important goods and services have occurred, but I believe in any case we would have experienced one of the most important changes: the emergence of the Soviet Union as a military peer prepared to commit a significant proportion of all its resources to its world-wide effort to expand its influence.

Furthermore, the development of Soviet military parity has been accompanied by an increase in that country's ability to challenge both our scientific supremacy, at least in certain areas, and to contest the once-unmatched appeal of our political system to people around the world. In all these areas, we can be justly proud of our accomplishments, and we should not be blind to persistent Soviet shortfalls and failures. The

1. THE US IN AN INTERDEPENDENT WORLD

point is that where we once stood alone as a giant on the earth, we have acquired a rival able to look us in the eye, if only in certain areas or respects.

Similarly, our economy has, understandably in my view, not maintained its pre-eminent condition. If others, from their disadvantaged departure points, were bound to grow faster than we could, it still seems clear that we have failed to make proper use of the advantages with which we began. Others could be expected to catch up, but in too many ways we have lost the lead—and this was not inevitable.

In any case, the point once again is the contrast between then and now. Where once we were seen as the economic model and the source of economic guidance and assistance, we are now a source of dismay and complaint. Having been viewed as the solution, we are now one of the problems.

My contention is that the changes in all these conditions—political, economic, and military—underlie many of the other complaints and concerns. When we were, in effect, supreme, our task was easy. Executive, Congressional, and party leaders had no trouble reaching agreement on foreign policy questions, partly because the issues seemed clear, and partly because the breadth and reach of our power and resources enabled us to structure actions and programs to cover all important concerns. Where a range of views existed, we had the wherewithal to toss enough into the pot to satisfy every view that mattered. The result was called consensus.

Clearly, both the consensus and the conditions which made it possible are gone for good. Replacing them is out of the question. Calling for a bipartisan approach and urging better Executive-Congressional relations are understandable, and improvement in these areas is indeed essential. It is particularly important that the Executive branch overcome its natural institutional tendency to develop its plans fully, and then present them to the Congress as accomplished fact, blessed by the President and not subject to Congressional modification.

But I fear we will see no improvement, at least nothing like a return to the confident, comfortable days of the late 1940's, until we have found a way to establish a new set of conditions which will provide the basis for a renewed sense of national purpose and national possibility. The task before us, then, is to establish a new national structure of concepts and resources which will make possible a consensus and a confidence that will endure through the 1980's, the 1990's and beyond.

Regarding the resources, I believe the point is not to seek some sort of impossible resurrection of our former economic supremacy. Certainly, a major effort should be made to strengthen and energize our economy. Since that effort must be borne principally outside the foreign affairs sector, however, I will not address it further here. Suffice it to say that the goal in the foreign affairs context must be the development of an economy able to provide the resources and sustain the effort deemed

necessary and desirable. Similarly in the military field, we must now ensure that our defense capability remains unquestionably equal to the challenges before it.

Efforts in both economic and military areas are in any case being made. It is in the other principal part of the equation, the policy side, that a special and well-conceived effort must be focused, for it may be in that area that we have become most deficient. Old beliefs and assumptions regarding the benevolence of our purposes, the inexhaustibility of our resources, and the broad international acceptance of our political views have fallen away, and have not been replaced by any effective and reliable set of guiding principles and beliefs. We have a far less clear, and less agreed upon, idea of what we are about in the world.

It may be argued that the reigning concepts of U.S. foreign policy in the late 1940's were neither subtle, far-reaching, nor profound, amounting essentially to containing Communism and helping our friends rebuild their shattered economies. Such a view does no justice to the high idealism with which we approached the birth and infancy of the United Nations, even if we acknowledge that the organization was at its beginning a far more comfortable place for us than it is today.

But in any event I do not base my case for conceptual rebuilding on any particular role ascribed to concept at that or any other time in our history. Rather, a conceptual framework combining broadly-agreed national principles and interests seems to me the best starting point for reforging the collective sense of shared purpose that is required if we are to become effective once again in supporting our ideals and pursuing our interests around the world. I acknowledge the difficulty of long-term planning and commitment under our system. If we cannot count on the longevity of any particular administration to provide continuity and consistency in foreign policy, we must look elsewhere—and I can think of no better place to begin with than the fundamental national principles on which there already exists a broad national consensus.

"Liberty and justice for all" does not, admittedly, take us very far by itself; but it is not a far leap from there to agreeing that preserving liberty requires an effective defense capability that reaches beyond our shores; nor to agreeing that a respect, even a passion, for justice is a legitimate and essential part of any American foreign policy worthy of the nation. We do not believe, as a people we have never believed, that we are the only ones with "certain unalienable rights."

These formulations quickly cover one of the basic dichotomies in our country today, i.e. the split between those who for the sake of security at home are prepared to acquiesce in close relations with repressive regimes abroad, and those who find such an approach both morally unworthy and in the long run self-defeating. My purpose here is not to argue for one side or the other, nor to attempt to elaborate a complete set of principles, but rather to make the point that such a set, enjoying broad national support, is possible; and that as a starting point, fundamental beliefs make for a solid foundation.

Principles—moral standards—may seem admirable but impractical. In fact they are important not only in and of themselves, and not just as expressions of beliefs deeply held among the American people, and not even simply for the advantage they give us over rival systems which provide far less room for individual human beings and their "unalienable rights." These principles are important also because they endure, because our belief in them is not temporary, not subject to revocation at the next election. They therefore constitute a reliable basis for a consistent long-term approach to foreign policy.

In the conceptual structure which is our goal, we must combine principle with interest—that is, include with the list of agreed moral standards and beliefs another list which will enumerate abiding national interests. Principles alone will prove an inadequately specific guide to actions and policies. We have national interests, as all nations do, and we have a right to identify, protect, and pursue them.

Broad national agreement on just what those interests are may be harder to achieve, particularly as they get more specific. But agreement on national defense, for example, leads quickly to agreement on a whole list of specifics involving limits in the oceans and in the air, cooperation with friends, maintenance of a lead or of parity in arms technology, etc. Maintaining and strengthening the domestic economy, enhancing our foreign trade, improving international travel and communications—interests across a broad spectrum of human activity come readily to mind, and each involves a subset of more specific interests.

In most cases it will not be a far distance from obvious truism to contentious issue; but the important goal is not to reach definite agreement on a list of highly specific interests which we must ever after pursue without further thought. The important goal is to engage in the process of defining our interests, and to make that process a continuing reality for enough people so that our conceptual reach is long enough, and that at any given moment there exists a domestic political basis for defining our long-term goals.

The elaboration of such a structure—a reliable framework of principles and interests, goals not subject to daily revision, is absolutely essential if we are to overcome the difficulties with which we are now beset.

With the Soviet Union, we swing wildly from confrontation to collapse, blustering one day and selling butter the next, basically because we have never defined in any sustainable way what we seek, what we will accept, and what we will not tolerate in that combination of competition and cooperation which perforce constitutes our relationship. With no far star to steer by, we yank the tiller with every wave, retreating into rhetoric whenever blandishments seem to fail, and rushing back to cooperation when confrontation begins to seem counter-

productive. Adherence to principle and a strong definition of our own interests could spare us the buffeting. Our allies, no less than our principal rival, would welcome greater reliability and consistency from us. But how are we to tell them what we want and what we will do if we cannot tell ourselves?

Perhaps the greatest need for enhanced national awareness and agreement regarding our long-term goals is exemplified in the current crisis of El Salvador. It is also an example of how apparently divergent views within the U.S. can actually come together. As of this writing, the situation in El Salvador appears desperate, and it is being questioned whether the Salvadoran government can hold off its guerrilla opposition without the introduction on its side of U.S. troops. Clearly, we should not have let matters develop to the point where this issue even arises.

How did we get here? I am not interested in scapegoats. It should only be clear that if the location of El Salvador gives it a national security value to us, that fact should not have been discovered last week or last year. And once it was recognized, we should have applied ourselves to the problem in a consistent way from the outset, with long-term objectives in mind. To oversimplify, if we wanted a secure and reliable neighbor, and if we had thought the problem through, we might have anticipated the basic problem of pro-West dictatorships. They may endure for decades, but they can vanish quickly and with little warning, and they tend not to leave well-founded democratic structures and practices in their wake. I hardly need cite examples.

In the specific case of El Salvador, I wholeheartedly applaud President Duarte's sincere and dramatic reform efforts, and he is not to be blamed that those efforts have come so late. Are we? We do not need to agree on an answer to that question to agree at least that timely economic assistance, focused within a well-conceived socio-political framework, is greatly to be preferred to emergency military assistance and the commitment of American combat troops.

In effect, as in too many cases in the past, we slid through inadvertence and lack of foresight into a situation so far advanced in decay that there were no longer any attractive options. We will continue to do so until we have consciously and carefully worked out a broadly-based, internally-cohesive set of principles and interests which will enable us to look down the road, set our route, and stick to it.

International communications and information policy presents another, much knottier, foreign policy problem which nonetheless gives us the opportunity to exercise foresight and avoid the pitfalls we face with problems like El Salvador—provided we reach a national awareness, define our interests and pursue them in a rational manner. Few have grasped the magnitude of the revolution which has occurred and is occurring in communication and information resource technology, yet the effects will transform lives and institutions on this planet much faster than did the Industrial Revolution. Every facet of life will be affected, from the home to the workplace, from policy-making to policy execution, from the developing world to the industrialized world. The response that the United States makes to the challenges presented will determine our place in the world—our political power, our economic position, our social and cultural influence—for decades to come.

Among the effects of this communications and information revolution are the following:

- Satellites now orbit in the atmosphere to search for uranium in Zimbabwe, oil in Mozambique, and manganese in Paraguay.
- Transborder data flows raise issues of personal privacy protection, national security, taxation and customs valuation.
- In recent years, computers, satellites and television have linked to provide new avenues for education and entertainment.
- Remote sensing is now a practical means of surveying resources and forecasting crop production.
- The U.N. system has pressured the media and the communications industry to study the implications of information saturation and to regulate the free flow of information.
- Airlines, financial institutions, and multinational corporations rely on computer-to-computer data for future growth.
- The information industry is now the second largest export enterprise in the United States.

Information today increasingly travels from one point to another by means of digital bits in computers. This digital information travelling through space or by cable will ultimately include such things as telephone conversations, banking transactions, television shows, stock market transactions, agricultural estimates, and personal data, among others. Since this information is essentially a stream of electrons all mixed together, the distinctions among transmissions carrying news, financial data, political information, entertainment, or personal phone calls are vanishing. Thus, the regulation of any of this information for whatever purpose is daunting and difficult. Indeed, dealing with the technology and its problems is impossible if the terms are not defined and the technology not understood by more people than our scientists.

Such awareness and understanding are vital, because rights and opportunities both are at stake. New technologies are evolving at a rate which makes last year's computers antiques. The potential benefits are great—if innovation is to flourish. The potential dangers are equally great—if the free flow of information is unnecessarily impeded or if personal privacy is unprotected.

The concepts underlying any workable, coherent national communications and information policy already

exist. The First Amendment to the U.S. Constitution guarantees freedom of speech and of the press. Competition is a necessary component of a viable, productive, and growing economy. Merging those concepts with the inescapable realities of complex new information technologies and the finite nature of the electromagnetic spectrum is a challenge which must be met if growth is to be sustained—be it intellectual, economic, political, social, or cultural growth. We must also remember that these concepts of freedom and competition are minority views in the international community, a fact which presents another significant challenge.

It is one thing to engage in policy disputes over the kind and amount of assistance to provide El Salvador. It is quite another to fail to reach consensus on the conditions for global communications. Any country in the world, regardless of economic condition or political power, can dump enough electronic garbage into the spectrum to defeat activities vital to the well-being of millions—creating interference with authorized radio or television broadcasting, or impeding the transmission of vital, instantaneously-needed financial data.

Never before has the old saying, "Information is power," been as true as it is today. Furthermore, communications and information activities are significant elements of both foreign and domestic policy and do not lend themselves to neat categories. The attempt to control the flow of information, in any form, across national boundaries has serious implications for the international economic system, national security, and, ultimately the interdependence of nations. The challenge is clear. If we abdicate our responsibility and our leadership, we hand the future to others whose concepts of political and social equality do not match ours. If we accept the challenge and meet it, we will ensure the future for ourselves and generations to come.

In essence, my appeal is for a broadly-based, national effort to look deep into ourselves and come up with a set of far-reaching, forward-looking principles and interests to serve as a constant guide to our foreign policy and its conduct. We should begin with the principles and convictions on which our country was founded and which inspire us still.

The effort must involve the people, the Congress, and the administration. Reagan must meet his responsibility by taking the lead, for there will be no bipartisan foreign policy unless he truly wants one. Similarly, the effort must include a commitment to full and timely consultations between the Executive branch and the Congress if evolving policies are to have the broad support they require to be clearly understood. Only then will we have the steady and reliable long-term strategy we need to regain our effectiveness abroad.

Chain Linkage in American Foreign Policy

Hoyt Purvis

Mr. Purvis, associate professor of political science and journalism, University of Arkansas, Fayetteville, previously served as a foreign/defense policy advisor to then-Majority Leader Robert Byrd in the Senate and, earlier, as an aide to Sen. J. W. Fulbright (D.-Ark.).

FOR some years, we have been hearing that the U.S. has entered "a new era of foreign policy" or, at least, that an old era has ended. This refrain has been particularly prevalent since the end of the Vietnam War.

Various analysts have offered their views of how American foreign policy has evolved. Some argue that the period of detente with the Soviet Union in the 1970's was really only a mirage and that the U.S.-Soviet rivalry simply entered a new phase. Others look upon the 1970's as a period of missed opportunities. Still, there is some general agreement that, however significant or insignificant the detente period may have been, we have moved beyond that.

The 1970's ended with American hostages in Iran and Soviet troops in Afghanistan. In 1980, there was evidence of national frustration with foreign policy. The Carter Administration was criticized for inconsistency and incoherence—charges that came not only from political opponents, but were echoed by some more objective observers at home and abroad. Ronald Reagan appealed very successfully to this widespread frustration. He offered the prospect of a more assertive, more confident American role in the world and talked of restoring direction, credibility, and strength to the American position. Underlying the Reagan foreign policy approach was the premise that somehow the U.S. could act unilaterally; or, if the U.S. simply cast itself in a "leadership" role, other nations would quickly follow. However, those notions are far from today's international realities—where careful and subtle strategies are often needed; where prior consultation with allies may be essential; where sweeping symbolic gestures may occasionally be important, but where overblown rhetoric can undermine prospects for real success; and where a keen understanding of interrelationships is critical for deft geopolitical maneuvering.

A primary emphasis of the Reagan foreign policy was to be linkage, particularly in regard to the Soviet Union. Our policy toward the U.S.S.R. would be "linked" to Soviet actions elsewhere in the world; our policies toward other countries would be similarly linked. To back up this linkage, we would use leverage, making more effective use of our moral, political, technical, economic, and military resources to influence events.

Events have unfolded somewhat differently, however. The Reagan Administration has experienced its own frustrations and has been subjected to some of the same charges it leveled against its predecessor—inconsistency and incoherence. Some of these problems relate to management and decision-making weaknesses in the Administration, but others are tied to the governing reality in today's world—reality that any American administration has to deal with. It is a world full of nations not necessarily inclined to follow the lead of the U.S., nations that may apply their own "linkage" toward this country.

There has to be some awareness of the constraints under which the U.S. now operates. Although there is the desire for a stronger, more assertive nation, getting beyond the Vietnam syndrome requires restraint as well as resolve. The kind of patience, skill, and spirit of give-and-take required in today's diplomacy lies, in the words of pollster Daniel Yankelovich, "at the opposite ends of the pole of emotions from those that thirst for bold, simple actions in the name of national honor."

The fact is that we are in a new era, even though it is not clear what our policy for this era may be. Indeed, broad doctrine or policy may be inappropriate, although there are certain fundamental principles which could guide policy. A foreign policy for the 1980's must not be limited to increased military spending and tough talk, as satisfying as that may be on the surface. We must recognize the folly of unilateralism. We must understand the world in which we live. When we think of linkage, we should see its full implications. When we think of leverage, we should recognize the limits of such leverage and not deceive ourselves, for we are operating in a world of complex interrelationships and interconnections which might be described as a kind of chain linkage, and this could well be the era of chain linkage.

As Pres. Lopez Portillo of Mexico has stated, "Everything is part of everything else." U.S. policies toward one nation or on a particular issue may have a major bearing on our relations with another nation, even though that nation is not directly involved. Other nations have their own agendas, their own policies, their own priorities.

Examples

There are abundant examples of chain linkage at work. They can be found at home as well as abroad, and often they involve domestic as well as foreign policy. An obvious instance is the Carter-imposed Soviet grain embargo, which Reagan lifted because of its unfairness to American agriculture. Yet, Reagan has consistently been critical of the Soviets and, indeed, has tended to try to fit everything that happens in the world into the framework of the U.S.-Soviet rivalry. Reagan maintained that the embargo was not very effective anyhow, which simply underlines the limits of U.S. leverage with the Soviets, and he said that American farmers and grain traders were the ones being hurt most by the embargo. One of the reasons for this is another ironic demonstration of

1. THE US IN AN INTERDEPENDENT WORLD

chain linkage. The Argentines, supposedly strongly anti-communist, quickly stepped in to sell wheat to the Soviets when the U.S. cut off sales. Yet, one of the Reagan Administration's earliest moves was to proclaim Argentina as a friendly nation and to declare its intention to develop a strong relationship with Argentina, which was heavily criticized during the Carter years for its abominable human rights record.

Reagan thought more emphasis should be given to building up American military strength *vis a vis* the Soviets, and he had strong Congressional support. While there was consensus on the concept, there has been no meeting of minds on the particulars. Reagan wants a massive military spending increase, which is fine, except that it means taking money away from some important domestic programs and increasing a budget deficit that was not supposed to be there in a tax-cutting administration.

Throughout his campaign, Reagan emphasized the need to close the "window of vulnerability" in U.S. strategic capability. A key to doing this was deployment of the MX missile. Reagan, along with almost everyone else, belittled Carter's plans to deploy the missile in the "race track" or "shell game" mode. After months of delay, the Reagan Administration came up with its own scheme, which, in fact, was not responsive to the vulnerability issue at all; after a short time, that scheme had to be altered. One of the constraints affecting MX deployment is that, while many support it, no one wants it in his backyard. This includes some strong defense supporters from the Western states, who also happen to be strong Reagan supporters. Their states were prime possibilities for deployment, but they did not want any major deployment in their states. The net result is that the window of vulnerability has been shrouded by a curtain of confusion.

The Middle East. An early tipoff to the Reagan Administration's difficulties in coming to terms with chain linkage occurred in the Middle East, and this, too, related to the Soviets. Secretaries Haig and Weinberger made early trips to the Middle East in search of what they termed a "strategic consensus." This was to be the basis of American Middle East policy—built around shared opposition to the Soviets, with a greater U.S. military presence in the region, including the stationing of American troops. Yet, for all their avowed anti-communism, Haig and Weinberger found that the consensus among the Arab nations was not directed against the Soviets, but was centered on Arab-Israeli issues and the future of the Palestinians.

Next, the Administration got involved in a costly battle over the sale of the AWACS planes to Saudi Arabia. The Saudis, as major oil suppliers, are of unquestioned importance to the U.S. and the U.S.-Saudi relationship is one that has to be given a high priority, but the Reagan Administration allowed the Saudis to make the AWACS sale a "litmus test" of that relationship. Although the President managed to stave off Congressional disapproval of the sale, the no-win melee troubled many in Congress, added to Israeli apprehension, and has not made a noticeable difference in Middle East peace prospects. Later, the Administration found itself issuing conflicting statements about possible sales of missiles and planes to Jordan, which again set off a storm in Israel and in Congress. The Administration has consistently hinted that Jordan was going to join the peace effort; in fact, King Hussein has consistently steered clear of the Camp David process and has felt that the U.S. has not been sufficiently appreciative or understanding of his country's position. He has even been talking of buying arms from the Soviets.

Meanwhile, Reagan, who had promised to strengthen the U.S. special relationship with Israel, has frequently been at odds with the Begin government. Israel has gone its own way in military moves in Lebanon and against the Iraqi nuclear reactor, as well as in action on the Golan Heights and the West Bank, disdaining consultation with the U.S. and disregarding U.S. policies.

Europe. European-American relations have also foundered over varying views of how to deal with the Soviets. U.S. statements on the neutron warhead and strategic policy which failed to take into account the European perspective seemed to scare the Europeans more than the Soviets. (The forceful U.S. position on the neutron warhead clouded the environment for the more important theatre nuclear force modernization program.) Even the NATO alliance, the centerpiece of U.S. international security policy, has been called into question. The Europeans simply have differing interpretations of their needs and priorities and see different political imperatives. Even the Polish crisis failed to really unite the West, and the U.S. has expressed dismay, after the events in Poland, at the European willingness to go ahead with the Yamal gas pipeline from the Soviet Union. Completion of the pipeline would undoubtedly result in greater West European dependence on the Soviets, adding to the growing East-West economic ties—which many Europeans see as being in their interests, regardless of what the U.S. thinks. Ironically, the Europeans quickly point to Reagan's lifting of the grain embargo as evidence of U.S. willingness to put its economic interests above principle.

China. With arms sales having become a major component of American foreign policy, U.S. policymakers are increasingly involved in difficult decisions about such sales, and these proposed sales often invoke chain linkage situations. This has been dramatically illustrated in the controversy over possible U.S. sales to Taiwan. To have sold to Taiwan the advanced FX fighter planes it sought would have resulted in a serious rift in U.S. relations with the People's Republic of China, undercutting what has been one of the most significant U.S. foreign policy advances of the past decade. Relations with the PRC will be troubled enough if the Administration goes ahead with plans to sell Taiwan military spare parts plus more of the less-sophisticated F-5E planes it already has.

Early in his campaign, Reagan left the impression that he might reverse the course of U.S. relations with China, which had been steadily developing since the Nixon years, and return to a formal relationship with Taiwan. Once in office, however, he recognized that such a move would be clearly contrary to the national interest and that the Beijing government was entirely serious in claiming that any steps in that direction would sabotage Sino-American relations. To the PRC, this is a matter of principle which overrides even the desire to cooperate with the U.S. in other areas. If the U.S. pushed its relationship with Taiwan, this would be a blow to the PRC pragmatists who have favored closer relations with the U.S.

Thus, the U.S.-Taiwan-China triangle is another example of chain linkage, and the bearing on U.S.-Soviet relations of U.S. dealings with China is another. Secretary of State Haig has talked of selling combat arms to the Chinese, but, if the U.S. plays the China card too forcefully, it would almost certainly further complicate the troubled U.S.-Soviet relationship —probably making it even more difficult to bring the arms race under control and to limit military spending.

A brief tour of the horizon points out numerous other cases of chain linkage:

- Greece is using U.S. cooperation with Turkey to stir discord in NATO, just as Turkey has often cited U.S.-Greek relations as an obstacle to U.S.-Turkish cooperation.

- The Reagan Administration has given signs at times of seeking a closer relationship with South Africa, but key African nations such as Nigeria and Kenya condition their relations with the U.S. on this country's policies on Southern Africa.

- Japan and the U.S. have a number of differences over trade-related issues and an additional problem results from Japan's extreme reluctance to bow to the heavy U.S. pressure to increase significantly its defense budget. Japan does not see itself seriously threatened by the Soviets. The Japanese are more concerned about Middle East tensions because of their dependence on imported energy.

X ● The Reagan Administration is intent on lavishing arms and military aid on Pakistan, primarily because of its proximity to Afghanistan and the desire to discourage any more Soviet adventures in Southwest Asia. However, in addition to putting the U.S. behind an unpopular and previously unfriendly government in Pakistan, it seems likely to push India, a larger and more influential nation, into a closer relationship with the Soviets.

X ● Nearer home, the Reagan policy on Central America and the Caribbean has had to take into account the differing perspective of Latin American nations, particularly Mexico. Because of its oil riches, its strong economic ties with the U.S., and because it is a bellwether of Latin relations with the U.S., Mexico has been belatedly recognized as being an important factor in U.S. foreign policy, but Mexico has had an entirely different view of Central America than the alarmist interpretation and confrontational approach advocated by the Administration. The position of Mexico and other key Latin American nations, plus some strong Congressional and public resistance, has served as a brake on U.S. actions in Central America.

The Reagan Administration hopes to make its Caribbean Basin initiative the showcase of its foreign policy. It is a potentially admirable effort, but, in order to be credible, it had to have the support of Mexico and Venezuela and it had to be steered away from an initial military orientation toward an economic emphasis, which is probably a more meaningful approach to "security" in any case.

The list of chain-linkage situations could go on. Many of the problems are related to arms transfers and, with such transfers constituting a major element of U.S. foreign policy, there are going to be recurring difficulties in balancing international relationships. It is one thing to provide economic assistance to a nation, and quite another to provide modern weaponry. Obviously, there are situations where, because of Soviet-supplied nations in an area, or clear-cut threats from outside forces, it may be important for the U.S. to make arms transfers. Frequently, however, they not only contribute to escalation of regional arms spirals and complicate U.S. relations with adjacent nations, but contribute to internal difficulties within recipient nations as well.

This rapid global tour points out some of the factors which weigh on American foreign policy, limiting options and making unilateral action difficult and often unwise.

U.S. foreign policy has to recognize the chain linkage in current-day international relations. We have to acknowledge that there is a Third World. It is by no means cohesive on all issues, and many of the key nations have moved beyond the Third World in certain respects, but it is clearly in the U.S. interest to lessen the potential sources of destabilization in the world and to help create a stable international environment. A key to attaining such an environment is sustained economic progress in the Third World.

We have to recognize the political and economic importance of these developing nations and their significance for our own economy and security. The fastest-growing U.S. export markets are in the Third World, and the Third World is a major source for critical raw materials needed to support U.S. economic activity and national security.

Obviously, we need to concentrate on strengthening our own economy, which is the real basis for national power and security. A major element in this process must be better management of energy policy. It would be tragic if a period of more plentiful supply enabled us to forget how fragile and volatile the energy situation can be.

Strengthening the economy will, as much as anything—and more than misguided military bravado—restore our national confidence. In turn, this will help reduce the compulsion to "do something" which plagues American presidents in times of national despondency.

As a very nationalistic nation, we need to try to understand and come to terms with nationalism in other nations. We have to recognize that other nations have their priorities and their agendas and to take this into account in formulating our policies. We need to identify areas of mutual interest.

We need to strengthen the American "presence" in the world and to have the ability to act to protect our interests, not through intervention, but by working to build and develop mutual interests.

Human Rights and the Refugee Crisis

Elliot Abrams

Address before the Tiger Bay Club in Miami, Florida, on June 2, 1982. Mr. Abrams is Assistant Secretary for Human Rights and Humanitarian Affairs.

As you know, I am in charge of the Bureau of Human Rights and Humanitarian Affairs. As you may not know, in that capacity I am charged with overseeing for the State Department the granting of asylum to people from all around the world who seek asylum in the United States. Both responsibilities—human rights and the asylum aspect of U.S. immigration policy—obviously give me a great deal to do with Latin America and the Caribbean. What I want to do today is talk about our human rights policy and our foreign policy, and, I hope, help explain our views on a number of problems which face south Florida.

Our human rights policy is, basically, easy to explain: We try to improve the respect for human rights in countries around the world, so that we can improve the lives of the people who live there and so that we continue to make clear America's historic commitment to the cause of liberty. Of course, this is easier said than done, for the problem of human rights violations around the world is profoundly complex. The causes of human rights problems vary from race (as in South Africa) to religion (the Ba'hai in Iran), to factional strife (as between Christians and Muslims in Lebanon), to a wide variety of usually military dictatorships. And the kinds of human rights violations vary from denial of free elections to elimination of the free press or freedom of religion, to arbitrary arrests, to torture and murder.

Needless to say, each situation calls for different tactics for an American effort in the area of human rights. Furthermore, our tactics will vary depending on our relationship with the country in question: whether it is a friend or foe, whether there exists between us distant relations or a dense network of ties. The tools we use range, of course, from straight diplomatic discussions, to public denunciations, to U.N. votes, to denial of economic or military assistance, and so on. Often this Administration is accused of doing too little for human rights or of "coddling" friendly regimes while we attack enemies. In fact this accusation is false. We use whatever we think will be the most effective tactic. Where we have good diplomatic ties, common sense tells us to use them. Where we do not have friendly relations, but a regime is very sensitive to its public reputation, we find that public discussions and criticisms are most effective, and we use them—as in the case of the Soviet Union. Our goal, in every case, is to be effective, not to give good speeches but to have a good effect in the real world.

If we are to achieve our human rights goals, it is clear that American power and influence are essential. Few governments around the world are greatly moved by preaching from the United States or anyone else. They change their behavior when American power, American assistance, American commitments, persuade them that it is in their interest to do so. Above all, the intangible force of the American example as a successful example inevitably affects the willingness of other countries to pay attention to our concerns on human rights. The Reagan Administration has, it is correctly noted, improved relations between our country and such countries as South Africa and South Korea. It is our view that isolating these countries, driving them away from us, would do nothing but decrease our influence there. Our ability to obtain our goals, including our human rights goals, is sufficient only when America is understood to be an important force.

Role of Communism and Soviet Power

Thrown into the many complexities I have mentioned is another major one—the role of communism and Soviet power. Why do I single out communism and the Soviet bloc countries, among all the world's dictatorships?

First, because once a Communist government is established, the Soviets make sure that it endures permanently. No efforts by the people of that country will be allowed to win them freedom, as we have just seen in Poland. Unlike Greece or Spain or Portugal, which were dictatorships but are now free, today Communist countries are not permitted to leave the grasp of the Soviet Union and seek freedom.

Second, Communist dictatorships are aggressive. Compare Paraguay and Nicaragua, or Haiti and Cuba, or North Vietnam with the now disappeared South Vietnam. Communist countries not only destroy the human rights of their own population but threaten to export repression to their neighbors and around the world. Most recently we have seen this in Afghanistan, and even now Cuba and Nicaragua are engaged in a massive supply of arms to fuel subversion in Central America.

   "Human Rights and the Refugee Crisis," Elliot Abrams, *Department of State Bulletin*, Vol. 82, No. 2066, September 1982.

Third, Communist regimes are incredibly brutal. Let me take but one example. The French group, Doctors Without Frontiers, has sent doctors to Afghanistan to help injured Afghans. They have reported, and these items have been published in several of the leading journals in Paris, that the Soviets drop small mines from planes. They don't explode on landing, but only when picked up by a passerby. They are made to look like matchboxes, and some to look like children's toys. The French doctors report that much of their work in hospitals on the border of Pakistan is surgery performed on children who have lost limbs. And of course, even now the Soviet Union is providing chemical and biological weapons to its proxies and allies in Afghanistan and Southeast Asia—the infamous yellow rain which is outlawed by international treaty and by any sense of human decency.

Obviously, we must take care in our human rights policy to make situations better and not worse. South Vietnam under General Thieu, or South Korea today, present serious human rights problems, but they are as nothing compared to the Communist alternatives. We want to be very sure that in a situation such as El Salvador, we do not trade the serious but solvable human rights problems of today for a permanent Communist dictatorship. Resisting the expansion of communism is a key human rights goal.

And here again, American influence in the world is essential to our goals. A strong, confident, vigorous America will be able to help countries resist Soviet subversion. And it will provide a powerful alternative model of a successful, confident people whose freedom leads to prosperity and unity. Needless to say, economic and military strength are essential elements in this picture, which is why President Reagan is determined to restore both.

Relevance to Refugee Flows

Now the relevance of all this to the refugee flows you have seen here in south Florida, and to the greater ones you may fear is, I think, clear. People do not flee free, prosperous countries. The largest refugee flows of recent years have come from Indochina and Afghanistan, where, quite simply, people are fleeing communism. The same is true of Cuba. Perhaps the greatest source of refugees throughout history has been, not natural disasters, but misgovernment. When governments have destroyed people's rights and freedoms, and have destroyed the economy, people have voted with their feet.

Our response to the refugee problem of today and the potential problems of tomorrow is necessarily complex. Neither we nor any other wealthy country can accept all of the refugees and immigrants who come to our borders. Neither can we accept immigrants who will constitute a servile class, a class of permanently unequal people such as exists in many countries around the world. Yet our response must have in it a substantial amount of humanitarianism, and we are bound (by international treaty and our own law) to grant asylum to genuine refugees who reach our shores.

But humanitarianism alone will not enable us to deal with a ruler such as Fidel Castro, who with unbelievable cynicism uses his own people as a weapon against foreign countries. He shoots streams of refugees at nearby countries in the way a cannonball is shot out of a cannon. Think of the cynicism, think of the viciousness, of a ruler who would take mentally retarded people and drag them off and shove them into boats to be sent away from their home country. Our foreign policy must make it clear that such behavior is simply unacceptable to us and will not ever again be tolerated.

It is obvious, of course, that this country has many immigration problems that have nothing to do with communism, such as the problem of Haitian migrants you face here in south Florida. But our experience has shown that the most serious refugee problems have political causes and—even more important—that these refugee problems develop much more suddenly than those that have their origin in poverty. Compare the steady flow of migrants from Haiti to the sudden waves from Cuba. Thus they present us with a challenge that the international community has trouble preparing for ahead of time.

In fact, it is Communist rule that has caused the greatest refugee flows of recent years. We can, therefore, have a very firm notion of what the expansion of communism to El Salvador and Guatemala would mean. It has the potential to create a Southeast Asian refugee crisis right here on our doorsteps. Indeed, we have every reason to think that the expansion of communism in Central America would create this kind of incredible problem. I am always amazed when people come to me to voice their concern about refugees from El Salvador, yet who oppose the Administration's effort to avoid enlargement of that problem by giving El Salvador the aid it needs to defeat Communist-led guerrillas.

Addressing the Problem

Obviously, the problem of migration and refugee flows is enormously complex, and we must address it in a number of ways. One way is economic assistance. It will help in cases such as Haiti, where poverty leads people to leave home, and it will help in the long run to reduce the opportunities that those seeking political disorder can exploit.

FOREIGN POLICY
OUTMODED ASSUMPTIONS

Henry Steele Commager

Henry Steele Commager, noted historian and educator, has taught at many universities here and abroad. He is now at work on a fifty-volume work, The Rise of the American Nation.

"*W*HEN SOCIETY REQUIRES *to be rebuilt, there is no use in attempting to rebuild it on the old plan.*"

" *No great improvements in the lot of mankind are possible, until a great change takes place in the fundamental constitution of their modes of thought.*"

John Stuart Mill's admonitions are still valid. Since the Truman Doctrine of 1947—perhaps since Hiroshima and Nagasaki—the United States has been locked into a Cold War whose temperature has fluctuated over the years, and now threatens to become incandescent. The origins of that war have fascinated a generation of historians whose disagreements are by now irremediable, perhaps because the explanations are not to be found so much in unraveling the tangled skein of history as in probing the philosophical and psychological assumptions that were uncritically adopted at the beginning of hostilities, and that have not yet been subjected to serious re-examination by those in power.

How are we to explain our obsession with communism, our paranoid hostility to the Soviet Union, our preoccupation with the Cold War, our reliance on military rather than political or diplomatic solutions, and our new readiness to entertain as a possibility what was long regarded as unthinkable—atomic warfare? Can we avoid the "unthinkable" and rebuild a world of peace and order without a change in the "fundamental consti-

tution of [our] modes of thought"—modes of thought themselves largely responsible for the crisis that glares upon us with relentless insistence from every quarter of the horizon?

Some of those assumptions have long enjoyed the dignity of official endorsement; some have been eroded in principle but linger on in official ideology—and are held together by passionate emotional harmony; some are sustained by interests so deeply entrenched that they seem invulnerable to criticism. As a body, the catechism of assumptions resembles in many respects that of the Moral Majority: it is rooted in emotion rather than in reason; it is negative rather than positive in its objectives; it is inspired by fear rather than by confidence; it is inconsistent and even contradictory in logic.

Consider some of those assumptions that have proved most tenacious.

First is the assumption that the world is divided between two great ideological and power groups, one dedicated to freedom, the other to slavery. History appointed the United States to represent and defend the first. The Soviet Union, whether by appointment or not is unclear, represents the second. These two worlds have been, for thirty years, locked in fateful combat.

This simplistic picture has, over the years, been badly distorted by developments that do not fit its logic: the conflict between China and Russia; our own almost nonchalant rapprochement with China; the emergence of a new power bloc in the Middle East; and the growing reluctance of many members of the "free-world" coalition to respect either the freedom or the morality to whose defense we are committed. None of these

developments has as yet persuaded many Americans to modify their original conviction that communism is the inveterate enemy.

A second assumption is implicit in the first: that communism, especially the Soviet variety, is not only dedicated to the enslavement of men but is godless and deeply immoral. Therefore the Soviet Union can never be relied upon to keep its word; it is engaged in ceaseless aggrandizement; it makes a mockery of international law and human dignity, and trusts only force. From all this it follows that for us to substitute diplomatic negotiations for military power would be to fall into a trap from which we could not extricate ourselves.

This assumption, to be sure, has deep roots in our history and our psychology. Though perhaps no other nation of modern times has had such spectacular success at the diplomatic table as the United States, Americans have long deluded themselves with the notion that their diplomats—invariably virtuous and innocent—have been consistently seduced and betrayed by wily Old World diplomats. This is, needless to say, fantasy. The Treaty of Paris of 1783 represented a spectacular triumph of American diplomats over both the British and the French, and the new nation found itself not thirteen independent states hugging the Atlantic but a vast empire. Twenty years later Jefferson intended to secure no more than New Orleans, but found that, thanks to Napoleon's impatience, the Treaty of 1803 doubled the territory of the United States without war and almost without cost. No one really won the War of 1812, but American diplomats won the negotiations at Ghent, and after that treaty, and the Battle of New Orleans, Europe left America alone. In 1871, the United States collected substantial awards from Great Britain for her violations of neutrality during the Civil War—violations of international law that were tame compared with those we now commit as a matter of course. In 1898, we dictated our own terms to Spain; and if in 1919 Wilson was not able to get all the Fourteen Points into the Treaty of Versailles, he did get his associates to set up a League of Nations, which we subsequently scuttled. Certainly we were in command in 1945, dictating terms not only to Germany and Japan but to our allies as well—terms characterized on the whole by magnanimity. Yalta, which most Americans have been led to believe a diplomatic defeat, was no such thing: in the military circumstances of February, 1945 (when American forces had not yet crossed the Rhine), it constituted an American success.

As for violation of international law, treaties, and agreements, and of the territorial integrity of weaker nations, the record of the Soviet Union is indeed deplorable. Whether it differs greatly from the American record depends, no doubt, upon the point of view. Little need to rehearse that record: suffice it to say that the CIA has at least tried to be as subversive as the KGB in many parts of the globe, that intervention in Cuba, the Dominican Republic, and Guatemala was no less in violation of law than the Soviet invasions of Hungary and Czechoslovakia, and that a ten-year undeclared war in Vietnam, with casualties of some two million, both military and civilian, and bombardment with three times the tonnage dropped on Germany and Japan in World War II contrasts unfavorably with the much-condemned Soviet invasion of Afghanistan.

Nothing surprising about all this except that a people brought up, for the most part, on the New Testament should so readily ignore the question raised by Matthew: "Why beholdest thou the mote that is in thy brother's eye, but considerest not the beam that is in thine own eye?"

A third assumption is rooted in the second: that the Soviet Union is the mortal enemy of the United States and that her animosity is implacable. This assumption, implicit in innumerable statements by President Reagan and Secretary of Defense Caspar Weinberger, dictates most of our current political and military programs. The term "dictates" is appropriate, for we no longer appear to be masters of our own destiny or even in control of our policies, but react with almost Pavlovian response to the real or imagined policies of the Soviet Union. Clearly, our reaction to the Polish crisis is animated more by hostility to the Soviet Union than by compassion for Poland.

In all this we rarely ask ourselves what the Soviet Union has to gain by destroying the United States. In the past neither czarist nor Communist Russia has been an "enemy" of the United States, and in the twentieth century Russia was allied with or associated with the United States in two major wars. Nor do many Americans pause to acknowledge that the Communists have more ground for fearing the United States than we have for fearing them: after all, American military forces invaded the Soviet Union at Archangel and Vladivostok to prevent the Bolshevik takeover and remained on Russian soil for well over two years: had Communist forces invaded the United States in, let us say, Alaska or Florida, we would not be quite so forgetful.

That the ideological conflict between the Soviet Union and the United States is deep and perhaps irremediable cannot be denied. It is sobering to recall that during the early years of the nineteenth century—and, indeed, again during our Civil War—much of Europe looked upon the United States as we now look upon the Soviet Union, and with more justification. The new American republic did indeed threaten the peace and security of Old World nations. Republicanism, democracy, constitutionalism, and social equality challenged all Old World monarchies and class societies. That challenge was practical—millions of Europeans found refuge in America—and it was philosophical, as well. Listen to Prince Metternich, the greatest and most powerful European statesman of his generation, excoriate the United States for proclaiming the Monroe Doctrine:

These United States . . . have suddenly left a sphere too narrow for their ambition, and have astonished Europe by a new act of revolt, more unprovoked, fully as audacious, and no less dangerous than the former [against Britain]. They have distinctly and exactly announced their intention to set not only power against power, but, to express it more exactly, altar against altar. In their indecent declarations they have cast blame and scorn on the institutions of Europe most worthy of respect. . . . In permitting themselves these unprovoked attacks, in fostering revolutions wherever they show themselves, in regretting those which have failed, in extending a helping hand to those which seem to prosper, they lend new strength to the apostles of sedition, and re-animate the courage of every conspirator. If this flood of evil doctrines and pernicious examples should extend over the whole of America, what would become of our religious and political institutions, of the moral forces of our governments, and of the conservative system which has saved Europe from complete dissolution?

Nor was this paranoia confined to spokesmen of autocratic countries. Here is what the leading British journal of its day—*Blackwood's Edinburgh Magazine*—had to say of Lincoln's Emancipation Proclamation:

Monstrous, reckless, devilish. . . . It proves . . . [that] rather than lose their trade and custom, the North would league itself with Beelzebub and seek to make a hell of half a continent. In return this atrocious act justifies the South in hoisting the black flag . . . And thus . . . we are called upon to contemplate a war more full of horrors and wickedness than any which stands recorded in the world's history.

The exacerbation of anti-Russian paranoia by this administration is not in fact in the mainstream of American experience. We have had less excuse for it than any other major nation, for since 1815 we have never been threatened by external aggression by any nation except Japan nor, except for the Civil War, by serious ideological conflicts.

Our current crisis dramatizes the wisdom of President Washington's warning, in his Farewell Address:

. . . nothing is more essential than that permanent, inveterate antipathies against particular nations . . . be excluded; and that in place of them just and amicable feelings towards all should be cultivated. The nation which indulges towards another an habitual hatred or an habitual fondness is in some degree a slave. It is a slave to its animosity or to its affection . . . Antipathy in one nation against another disposes each more readily to offer insult and injury . . .

1. THE US IN AN INTERDEPENDENT WORLD

IT IS PERHAPS THIS enslavement to our own animosity that explains a fourth major assumption—one we might call the Dr. Strangelove syndrome: that we could fight and "win" an atomic war, that the loss of 50 million to 100 million lives would be "acceptable," that the Republic could survive and flourish after such a victory. An atomic war is no longer "unthinkable"; perhaps it never was: after all, we are the only nation ever to use the atomic weapon against an enemy. Now spokesmen of both our parties have declared that in an "emergency" we would not hesitate to use it again. In all this we are reminded of the moral of slavery: when a "necessary evil" becomes necessary enough, it ceases to be an evil.

This philosophy is a product, or a by-product, of a fifth assumption: that the most effective way, and perhaps the only way, to counter the threat of communism is neither political, economic, nor moral but quite simply military, and that the mere threat of overwhelming military might will persuade all rivals to abandon the field.

This is, to be sure, a familiar maxim: it was Voltaire who observed that God is always for the big battalions. But there is an older wisdom. More than three centuries ago Francis Bacon wrote, "Walled towers, stored arsenals, and armories, goodly races of horse, chariots of war, elephants, ordnance, artillery and the like—all this is but a sheep in lion's skin, except the breed and disposition of the people be stout . . ."

That is still true, though we must rephrase it to comport with modern weaponry. The futility of reliance on superiority in nuclear arms should have been clear as early as 1949, when the Russians astonished most of the "experts" by detonating their own atomic bomb a decade earlier than had been expected. Certainly it should be clear by now that the Russians can produce anything that we can produce, and that the notion of "winning" an arms race is fantasy. The hope—perhaps the only hope—of avoiding a nuclear war lies not in adding another $1,500 billion to the $2,000 billion we have already spent on the military since the close of World War II but in mutual abandonment of that race, and a cooperative program of systematic reduction of existing nuclear arms.

As for security, that is indeed to be found in the "stoutness" and the disposition of the people—in their courage, intelligence, and resourcefulness, and in the preservation and nurture of that common wealth with which Nature has endowed them. The most serious threat to national security is in the wastage of human and the exhaustion of natural resources. It is in permitting our industrial and technological enterprises, our transportation system, our financial health, to deteriorate, our cities to decay into slums, our schools to fail of their primary functions of education, our society to be ravaged by poverty, lawlessness, racial strife, class hostilities, and injustice. It is in a leadership that lacks prudence, wisdom, and vision. It is in a society whose leaders no longer invoke, and whose people no longer take seriously, those concepts of public virtue, of the pursuit of happiness, and of the fiduciary obligation to posterity that were the all-but-universal precepts of the generation that founded the Republic.

A sixth assumption is a by-product of the fifth: that the security of the United States is bound up with and dependent on whatever regimes throughout the globe are ostentatiously anti-Communist. Our record here is a dismal one, yet instead of repudiating that record, the present administration seems determined to outstrip it. We persist in regarding South Korea and Taiwan as not only friends but allies; we practically forced Pakistan to accept billions of dollars for arms; we have abandoned all pretense of holding aloof from the tyrannical regimes of Chile and Argentina; we even conjure up a distinction between "authoritarian" and "totalitarian" regimes, whose only real distinction is whether they are authoritarian on our side or not. The vocabulary of this administration, as of Nixon's, inevitably conjures up what Thucydides said of the corruption of language in the Athens of his day: "What used to be described as a thoughtless act of aggression, was now regarded as the courage one would expect to find in a party member . . . fanatical enthusiasm was the mark of a real man . . . anyone who held violent opinions could always be trusted . . . and to plot successfully was a sign of intelligence."

To many of the peoples of the Third World, and even of the European world, the United States appears to be what the Holy Alliance was in the early nineteenth century. The analogy does not favor the United States, for while the Holy Alliance, for all its interventions in Spain and Italy and Greece, had the good sense to keep out of distant continents, the United States does not. What our interventions throughout the globe—Vietnam, Cambodia, Angola, Nicaragua, El Salvador, and Iran—have in common with those of the Holy Alliance is their failure.

MUCH OF OUR NEW "imperialism" is rooted in a seventh assumption: that the United States is not only a Western but an African and an Asian power.

That the United States is a world power is incontestable. Clearly, too, it is by virtue of geography an Atlantic power and a Pacific power, and it is by virtue of history something of a European power—a fact convincingly vindicated by participation in two world wars. But the United States is no more an Asian power than China or Japan is an American power. We have never permitted an Asian power to establish a military presence in the American continents. We bought Alaska from Russia, and the 1912 Lodge Corollary to the Monroe Doctrine extended that doctrine to "any Government, not American." It was the illusion that we could control the internal politics of China that distracted us from a recognition of reality for a quarter-century: certainly the greatest blunder in the history of American diplomacy. Even now, notwithstanding the commonsense reversal of that misguided policy by Nixon and Kissinger, we have not yet wholly rid ourselves of the purblind notion that we can, and should, "play the China card"—a notion that in its arrogance and in its vulgarity must represent the low-water mark of American foreign policy.

Another corollary of our reliance on the military for security is dramatized by an eighth assumption: that to achieve security it is proper for government to conscript science and scholarship for the purposes of war, cold or not; that, in short, the scientific, philosophical, and cultural community should be an instrument of the State for secular purposes.

This principle was not embraced by those who founded the Republic nor, for that matter, by the philosophers of the Enlightenment in the Old World. During the American Revolution, Benjamin Franklin joined with the French minister of finance, Jacques Necker, to decree immunity for Captain Cook because he was "engaged in pursuits beneficial to mankind." In the midst of the Napoleonic Wars, the French Institute conferred its gold medal on the great British scientist Humphrey Davy, and while the war was still raging, Sir Humphrey crossed the Channel to accept that honor. "If two countries are at war," he said, "the men of science are not." Napoleon himself shared this view: during his victorious campaign in Germany, he spared the university city of Göttingen from bombardment because it was the home of the greatest of classical scholars, Christian Heyne. And it was Napoleon, too, who, at the request of Joseph Banks of the Royal Society, freed the great geologist Dolomieu from the dungeons of Naples. Edward Jenner, the discoverer of the smallpox vaccine, put it for his whole generation: "The sciences are never at war. Peace must always preside in the bosoms of those whose object is the augmentation of human happiness."

It was Thomas Jefferson who stated this principle most clearly and most eloquently, and this at a time when he himself had abandoned his study and his laboratory to serve in the Virginia legislature. In 1778, he addressed a letter to the scientist David Rittenhouse, then serving as treasurer to the Commonwealth of Pennsylvania:

> Your time for two years past has . . . been principally employed in the civil government of your country. Tho' I have been aware of the authority our cause would acquire with the world from its being known that yourself and Doctr. Franklin were zealous friends to it, and am myself duly impressed with a sense of arduousness of government, and the obligation those are under who are able to conduct it, yet I am also satisfied there is an order of geniuses above that obligation, and therefore exempted from

it. No body can conceive that nature ever intended to throw away a Newton upon the occupations of a crown. It would have been a prodigality for which even the conduct of providence might have been arraigned, had he been by birth annexed to what was so far below him.

A NINTH ASSUMPTION, PERHAPS the most intractable of all, is that any of the fundamental problems that confront us—and other nations of the globe—can be resolved within the framework of the nation-state system. The inescapable fact, dramatized by the energy crisis, the population crisis, the armaments race, and so forth, is that nationalism as we have known it in the nineteenth and much of the twentieth century is as much of an anachronism today as was States Rights when Calhoun preached it and Jefferson Davis fought for it. Just as we know, or should know, that none of our domestic problems can be solved within the artificial boundaries of the states, so none of our global problems can be solved within the largely artificial boundaries of nations—artificial not so much in the eyes of history as in the eyes of Nature. Nature, as the dispenser of all resources, knows no boundaries between North and South Dakota or Kansas and Nebraska, no boundaries, for that matter, between Canada, the United States, and Mexico, and very few between the two Americas, Europe, Asia, and Africa. Every major problem that confronts us is global—energy, pollution, the destruction of the oceans and the seas, the erosion of agricultural and forest lands, the control of epidemics and of plant and animal diseases, famine in large parts of Asia and Africa and a population increase that promises to aggravate famine, inflation, international ter-

rorism, nuclear pollution, and nuclear-arms control. Not one of these can be solved within the limits of a single nation.

Even to mitigate these problems requires the cooperation of statesmen, scientists, and moral philosophers in every country. Americans should find it easier to achieve such cooperation than did the peoples of Old World nations, for they are the heirs and the beneficiaries of a philosophy that proclaimed that *all* men were created equal and endowed with unalienable rights to life, liberty, and the pursuit of happiness.

Of all the assumptions I have discussed, that which takes nationalism for granted is perhaps the most deeply rooted and the most tenacious. Yet when we reflect that assumptions, even certainties, no less tenacious in the past—about the very nature of the cosmic system, about the superiority of one race to all others, about the naturalness of women's subordination to men, about the providential order of a class society, about the absolute necessity of a state church or religion—have all given way to the implacable pressure of science and of reality, we may conclude that what Tocqueville wrote well over a century ago is still valid:

> The world that is rising into existence is still half encumbered by the remains of the world that is waning into decay; and amid the vast perplexity of human affairs none can say how much of ancient institutions and former customs will remain or how much will completely disappear.

If some of our ancient institutions do not disappear, there is little likelihood that we shall remain.

HUMAN RIGHTS: THE BIAS WE NEED

Alan Tonelson

ALAN TONELSON, *associate editor of* The Wilson Quarterly, *is on leave to write a book about political leadership in American history.*

Once simply the passion of scattered humanitarian activists, the protection of human rights worldwide has become a full-blown dimension of American foreign policy, complete with its own State Department bureau. And the stakes involved in formulating U.S. human rights policies have grown correspondingly large.

A human rights policy, after all, can profoundly affect national security. Arms control negotiations, for example, have been delayed and complicated both by the imposition of martial law in Poland and by recent Soviet campaigns to stamp out the dissident movement. The need to preserve U.S. interests in politically unstable developing countries has turned human rights into a dispute between Washington and several strategically and economically important countries. Further, human rights is increasingly the standard by which Americans judge the legitimacy of their country's avowed interests, particularly toward the Soviet bloc and the Third World.

Thus a human rights policy that does not enhance national security is unjustifiable. But a policy that is not supported by the American people is unsustainable. The last several U.S. administrations can point to policies that have satisfied both criteria. Yet despite—or perhaps because of—the mounting salience of human rights issues, such successes have been few and far between, either under the Nixon and Ford administrations, which generally tried to lock human rights out of American foreign policy; the Carter administration, which aspired to respond evenhandedly to human rights violations by friend and foe alike; or the Reagan administration, which has generally adopted a double standard that favors friendly "authoritarian" regimes of the right over hostile "totalitarian" regimes of the left.

Inept or inconsistent implementation frequently sabotaged each of these three strategies. But their built-in flaws are too deep for even the shrewdest execution to overcome. An alternative course, however, does exist. The criteria for a successful human rights policy can only be met by reserving America's harshest criticisms and sanctions for those authoritarian regimes that President Reagan has favored, while responding to repression by totalitarian governments with a mixture of quiet diplomacy and economic incentives. The obstacles to success will be formidable. It will require a break from traditional ways of thinking about human rights policy goals. It will require a precision of rhetoric American policy makers have rarely displayed. And it will require the recognition that an effective human rights policy may be expensive, at least in the short run.

At the same time, this tilt can establish the balance of power and commitments journalist Walter Lippmann identified as the hallmark of a successful foreign policy. It can turn human rights violators closely tied to the United States into stabler and more reliable allies. It can win the United States good will and long-term influence with the populations of regimes that resist American pressure. It can moderate the foreign policies and internal repression of governments with which the United States currently has little leverage. And it can furnish the moral foundation a human rights policy needs, while avoiding the arrogance to which Americans have often succumbed.

The Principle of Evenhandedness

Two kinds of goals will enable human rights policy to strengthen America and attract popular support: changing the repressive practices

Reprinted with permission from *FOREIGN POLICY*, 49 (Winter 1982-83). Copyright 1982 by the Carnegie Endowment for International Peace.

of foreign governments and convincing foreign and domestic audiences of Washington's commitment to freedom—whether the policy achieves visible results or not. A third important goal is often overlooked, although it was emphasized by congressional human rights legislation during the 1970s—the frequent need to distance the United States publicly from repressive regimes. Washington can aim such dissociation primarily at the voters at home. But far more important audiences are the downtrodden citizens of and organized opposition to foreign dictatorships, particularly those with extensive ties to the United States. The right combination of diplomatic frost, critical rhetoric, and possibly sanctions may prevent an anti-American backlash should any of those dictatorships fall.

In a world ideal except for human rights violations, the United States would respond to all comparable abuses with equal vigor, regardless of the violator's political leanings. Even in the real world, compelling reasons militate for evenhandedness. Still-sketchy polling data indicate that a majority of Americans do not favor preferential treatment for pro-Western autocrats. The principle of evenhandedness also commands the support of most political and opinion leaders.

In addition, evenhandedness appears to be a tactical necessity for a human rights policy seeking either foreign support or even only modest change abroad. Pro human rights diplomats generally seek to press a universal principle on governments that feel forced by ideology, paranoia, or genuine—and sometimes justified—threats to abuse their people. These efforts will go nowhere if they seem part of an opportunistic campaign to advance U.S. interests or to embarrass U.S. adversaries.

Yet the Carter administration's experience indicates that a popular and effective policy of evenhanded actions is a pipe dream. Despite the charges of bias and inconsistency leveled at the Carter human rights record, nothing stands out as strikingly as its scattershot, almost random nature. The contention that U.S. officials picked on friendly authoritarian regimes such as Iran's or Nicaragua's has no foundation. So evident was the concentration on the Soviet bloc in 1977 that Soviet dissident Valery Chalidze reminded the administration in print that human rights violations were not confined to communist countries. After 1977 only the frequency of such public statements declined.

Between 1977 and 1980 Washington regularly sought resumptions or increases in aid to or military cooperation with South Korea, Indonesia, the Philippines, Guatemala, Argentina, Chile, Uruguay, and Brazil. And substantial U.S. aid to Iran and Nicaragua continued up through 1978—scant months before the ousters of Shah Mohammad Reza Pahlavi and President Anastasio Somoza Debayle.

A clear imbalance in the Carter human rights performance did exist in the realm of punitive or dissociative action. The victims of such measures were nearly always pro-Western—countries with which the United States had extensive trade, aid, or political ties. Yet the United States does not enjoy such relations with all countries. This variety of relationships prevents a human rights policy that transcends words from ever being evenhanded in practice. America can withhold aid only from aid recipients, deny weapons only to arms clients, embargo trade only to trading partners. Thus any peaceful human rights policy involving deeds must fall most heavily on countries linked most closely to the United States. Every concession to this reality, no matter how well explained, sabotages the claim of evenhandedness and compromises the credibility of U.S. policy the way each leak compromises the credibility of a dam.

The problems of explaining evenhandedness are staggering as well. A policy that effectively singles out friendly countries for criticism and punishment seems to defy strategic common sense. This practice will, as some charge that it did under Carter, seem to reflect a soft-headed desire to atone for past sins and make Americans feel good about themselves.

The Politics of Human Rights

If double and even triple standards are inevitable, then a human rights minded administration must choose a pattern of preferential treatment that enhances national security and attracts widespread support. Reagan has tried to apply just such a bias to human rights diplomacy. He and his top aides have drawn principally on two now well-known analyses of the politics of human rights by U.S. Ambassador to the U.N. Jeane Kirkpatrick and Ernest Lefever.[1] These articles and related writings have been so important in shaping the human rights debate that they are worth reviewing in some detail.

Kirkpatrick and Lefever urge basing Ameri-

[1] Jeane Kirkpatrick, "Dictatorships and Double Standards," Commentary, *November 1979*; Ernest W. Lefever, "The Trivialization of Human Rights," Policy Review, *Winter 1978*.

can policy on the clear differences between dictators they classify as "traditional authoritarians" and "revolutionary totalitarians." As Kirkpatrick explains, authoritarian regimes are "less repressive" than their totalitarian counterparts. Their leaders, she has written, "leave in place existing allocations of wealth, power, status, and other resources which . . . maintain masses in poverty." They leave untouched "habitual rhythms of work and leisure, habitual places of residence, habitual patterns of family and personal relations." Adds Lefever, authoritarian regimes "often allow opposition parties to operate and a restrained press to publish. . . ."

Further, in Kirkpatrick's words, "right wing autocracies do sometimes evolve into democracies," given enough time and certain economic, social, and political conditions. She also characterizes authoritarian regimes as "more compatible with U.S. interests."

Totalitarian rulers, however, "become the arbiters of orthodoxy in every sphere. . . . The ruling party even usurps the place of God," argues Lefever. Philosopher Michael Novak, who served as U.S. representative to the 37th and 38th sessions of the U.N. Human Rights Commission for the Reagan administration, adds another dimension. The distinguishing crime of totalitarianism "is not the total physical barbarity or total range of State control . . . but the total ideological claim, against which there is no appeal."

Finally, writes Kirkpatrick, virtually all totalitarian regimes existing today are hostile to American interests, and the contamination of most national liberation movements with Marxists practically assures that newcomers to their ranks will be equally anti-American. The challenge of Soviet-inspired subversion all but guarantees that strong pressure on pro-Western authoritarians will lead to disaster for the United States. As Lefever states, the choice between the lesser of two evils is "inescapable."

This emphasis on external subversion comprises the bottom line of the Reagan administration's original policy. Explicit objections to the claim that most authoritarian rulers battling popular revolutions are doomed to be overthrown are its corollary. Kirkpatrick openly condemns as a Carter administration fantasy the view that the Third World is "in the grip of an extraordinary process of transformation which [is] deep, irresistible, systemic. . . ." Though violence and instability are "integral, regular, predictable" elements of Latin American politics, she contends, only the recent appearance of "the unfamiliar guerrilla

violence of revolutionaries linked to the Soviet Union and to Cuba has threatened to decisively transform the status quo."

Meanwhile, the brutality, staying power, and hostility of totalitarians justify strong, public U.S. criticisms. As Assistant Secretary of State for Human Rights and Humanitarian Affairs Elliot Abrams explained during his Senate nomination hearings in November 1981, "The Soviet Union is a country where we have very little diplomatic leverage. . . ." Consequently, Washington must "make sure at the very least that everyone in the Soviet Union knows that we in the West are watching those events with the greatest attention."

The Reagan administration dutifully followed these prescriptions in its early months. In his first postelection press conference, President-elect Reagan criticized withdrawing U.S. support from "basically friendly" countries because of disagreement over "some facet of human rights" when that action would help destroy "all human rights in that country." And former Secretary of State Alexander Haig, Jr. argued in an April 1981 interview on French television that "one establishes a dialogue with historic friends . . . in an atmosphere of normal relationships, not by the creation of paranoia. . . ."

In fact, the president and his top aides took every opportunity to pile extravagant praise on pro-Western human rights violators, a practice typified by Vice President George Bush's toast to Philippine President Ferdinand Marcos during a visit to that country: "We love your adherence to democratic principles and to the democratic process." Scant weeks after his inauguration, the president himself raised his glass to visiting South Korean President Chun Doo Hwan and gushed, "In the short time you've had . . . you've done much to strengthen the tradition of 3,000 years' commitment to freedom."

More important, the new administration reversed the Carter policy of opposing multilateral aid to Chile, Argentina, Paraguay, and Uruguay on human rights grounds. After specifically denouncing the Carter policies and assuring Buenos Aires that all criticisms would henceforth be made privately, it strove to restore military aid to Argentina and Guatemala, first reduced and then banned by Congress during the Carter years. Meanwhile, the administration suspended $15 million in loans to Nicaragua to protest the Sandinistas' aid to guerrillas in El Salvador.

Although the totalitarian-authoritarian analysis was dropped from American rhetoric

24

after November 1981, it still tyrannizes American policy. To be sure, administration officials have sporadically recognized the need to demonstrate more sensitivity to human rights. On separate trips to South Korea last spring, both Bush and Secretary of Defense Caspar Weinberger publicly discussed the Chun regime's human rights record. Bush even met with South Korean dissidents. U.S. officials have also urged the new Salvadoran government to continue the land reform program begun under former President José Napoleon Duarte and encouraged Salvadoran leaders to seek negotiations with rebel forces. Yet Washington is still trying to resume aid to Chile and Argentina by attesting to a significant relaxation of repression by each government, although little independent evidence corroborates this view. The president certified to Congress in July that El Salvador has reduced political violence, but he remained silent when the number of killings surged in August.

The Features of Dictatorships

Not surprisingly, the administration's policy is still unpopular and still vulnerable to the weaknesses of the totalitarian-authoritarian analysis. Contrary to the suspicions of today's liberal human rights activists, this conduct was not originated by conservative apologists desperate to justify their affinity for right-wing dictators. It was invented by such esteemed political theorists as Hannah Arendt and Carl Friedrich, as they groped in mid-century to conceptualize the technotyrannies of Adolf Hitler and Joseph Stalin.

Yet this distinction has not aged well enough to guide U.S. foreign policy. Virtually all dictatorships today display both totalitarian and authoritarian features. Reagan's sketch of the archetypical authoritarian ruler, content to amass personal wealth and the trappings of power while leaving traditional patterns of life and limited freedoms intact has simply been mocked by former Ugandan President Idi Amin, Latin American tyrants who nearly exterminated their Indian populations, and the Salvadoran officers who crushed a 1932 revolt by killing some 30,000 peasants.

Even short of killing, authoritarian regimes' harassment of ordinary citizens often approaches totalitarian levels. Although some authoritarian governments—such as the shah's monarchy and the Somoza regime—have sanctioned political parties, many others, notably in the southern cone of South America, have banned all organized political activities for varying lengths of time. Authoritarian governments in countries such as El Salvador, the Philippines, and South Korea have systematically denied the right to form labor unions and have assaulted universities with a vengeance. According to Kurt Gottfried of the American Physical Society, the southern cone governments "have all but destroyed science, intellectual life, and educational systems."

Moreover, all-embracing claims of total political power appear with surprising frequency in the statements and constitutions of authoritarian governments. Brazil's labor code, for example, was modeled on Benito Mussolini's *Carta del Lavoro* and dates from the 1930s, when dictator Getulio Vargas tried to create an *Estado Nôvo* inspired by interwar European fascism. South Korea's National Security Law of 1961 refers specifically to "anti-State organizations" and mandates felony punishment for "any person who has organized an association or group for the purpose of . . . disturbing the State."

Indeed, many scholars contend that a sophisticated structure they call "bureaucratic authoritarianism" has replaced the individual *caudillo* in several Latin American countries. This structure, they assert, strives "to destroy permanently a perceived threat to the existing structure of socioeconomic privilege by eliminating the political participation of the numerical majority."[2]

Totalitarian regimes persistently defy their stereotypes as well. While communism does indeed claim jurisdiction over all aspects of life, tens of millions throughout the communist world cling to family loyalties, to their livelihoods, to their faiths, and even to their vices, despite determined indoctrination programs. On occasions they have risen in revolt against their rulers. Since Stalin's death, limited degrees of free expression have been tolerated in Eastern Europe and even in the USSR. And as the Reagan administration has asserted, even China is moving "slowly toward a more culturally diverse and open society."

Supporters of the Reagan stance consider the potential for liberalization of different autocracies dubious as well. The list of durable traditional despots is long and includes Francisco Franco, who ruled Spain for nearly 40 years, and the Central American oligarchies, which have kept power for many generations despite a parade of revolving door governments. Only in their last ruling years did

---

[2] *Lars Schoultz,* Human Rights and United States Policy Toward Latin America *(Princeton: Princeton University Press, 1981), pp. 19-48.*

any of them even inch toward representative government.

Moreover, the history of numerous communist regimes reveals significant political turmoil, even before the founding of the trade union Solidarity in Poland: the Hungarian revolt in 1956; the "Prague Spring" in Czechoslovakia in 1968; the Polish labor upheaval that first brought Edward Gierek to power in 1970. Clearly, the main obstacles to change in the Soviet bloc have not been inherent properties of communist systems but Red Army tanks.

The totalitarian-authoritarian dichotomy fails on theoretical grounds as well. The "history of this century provides no grounds for expecting that radical totalitarian regimes will transform themselves," Kirkpatrick has written. Right-wing autocracies, however, sometimes do evolve into democracies—although the process can take "decades, if not centuries." Yet a clever double standard is at work here. The world's oldest totalitarian regime has been in existence only 65 years. The rest of the totalitarian communist world did not come into being until after World War II. Clearly these countries cannot be written off already. For they too deserve the hundreds of years that it took Britain and other West European countries to democratize and that Kirkpatrick has granted to existing authoritarian regimes.

This fundamental misjudgment contributes greatly to the untenable belief that the status quo in most strife-torn authoritarian countries can—and should—be preserved. Kirkpatrick, for instance, disparages the view that insurgency "is evidence of widespread popular discontent." Yet she refers repeatedly to the chronic "lack of consensus on legitimacy" throughout Latin America, to the "vulnerable," "dependent" economies of the region, and to rising popular expectations—the same historical forces whose prominence in Carter administration rhetoric she derided.

Finally, the correlation between totalitarian governments and anti-American policies is far from perfect. On several occasions, totalitarian governments have supported U.S. interests by design and by coincidence—witness Angola's overall cooperation in the talks seeking independence for Namibia and its excellent relationship with Gulf Oil Corporation, and Yugoslavia's successful rearguard action to contain Soviet and Cuban influence at the 1979 Nonaligned Movement meeting in Havana.

Meanwhile, the friendship of many authoritarian regimes may be questioned. The shah was a leader of the Organization of Petroleum Exporting Countries' so-called price hawks throughout the 1970s. Argentina ignored Carter's embargo and sold the Soviet Union 7.6 million tons of grain in 1980; Moscow has become Argentina's largest trading partner.

A Reasonable Guideline

One dichotomy exists, however, that can serve as an intelligent, politically sustainable guide for a human rights policy: the difference between countries with which the United States boasts extensive economic and political relations and countries with which it does not. And this distinction points to a policy that purposely and openly focuses its public actions on countries closely tied with the United States and that relies on behind-the-scenes persuasion and incentives for good behavior to achieve human rights goals in countries not so linked.

U.S. leverage with closely related countries makes them logical targets of a human rights diplomacy seeking to ease repression abroad. Even critical rhetoric will probably have more effect on countries that consider themselves U.S. allies than on countries that the United States has treated as neutrals or adversaries.

Critics of the Carter human rights policy have raised numerous objections to such a tilt. Several analysts have attacked basing U.S. policy on the different kinds of relationships established by Washington with foreign countries as unfair or incomprehensible. Thus, Kirkpatrick describes as "curious" Carter's focus on U.S. aid recipients. And in February 1982 the Reagan administration argued that keying actions to leverage would not "fairly represent the distribution of human rights abuses in the world." But differences in leverage are precisely what make the goal of basing U.S. actions on the geographic distribution and the severity of repression unattainable. Lefever proposed a far better guideline: U.S. responsibilities should be "commensurate with our capacity to influence external events."

Some also claim that public criticisms of and sanctions against pro-Western governments frequently backfire. In 1977 and 1978 they note, several Latin American countries renounced varying amounts of U.S. aid following disapproving American actions.

Yet the United States has successfully and publicly twisted the arms of pro-Western dictatorships in the past. From 1948 to 1965 both Democratic and Republican administrations regularly used their enormous influence in South Korea to curb the worst excesses of Presidents Syngman Rhee and Park Chung Hee. During the Carter years American diplomacy helped achieve many important successes. Starting in early 1977, thousands of political prisoners were released throughout Latin America and Iran. Most striking, a series of strong public warnings helped deter incumbent Joaquin Balaguer and his generals from overturning the election of Antonio Guzman as president of the Dominican Republic.

The failures of public pressures—particularly sanctions—are explained in large part by examining resource flows to some representative Third World countries. Argentina, for example, rejected only $15 million in American military aid in 1977. But during the Carter years 1977 through 1980, Argentina's multilateral aid receipts ranged from $388.7 million to $495.4 million. The year-end book value of American private investment climbed from $1.5 billion to $2.4 billion. And the year-end value of U.S. private bank claims soared from $2.6 billion to $6.9 billion. Argentine trade with the United States rose steadily as well.

Multilateral and private resource flows also dwarf U.S. bilateral aid to poorer Latin American countries where Washington would seem to wield extraordinary clout. From 1977 to 1978 total American assistance to Guatemala declined from $21.3 million to $10.6 million. But multilateral aid rose from $84.3 million to $108.7 million. The Commerce Department pegged U.S. private investment in Guatemala at $250 million as of 1977, and from December 1977 to December 1980 U.S. private bank claims on Guatemala increased from $226 million to $321 million.

With all of these flows rising steadily, the Carter administration could hope to accomplish little by trimming small sums of foreign aid. In addition, the cuts could not convey serious U.S. concern as long as the Carter administration both refused to politicize the international aid organizations by imposing mandatory human rights standards on all aid recipients and maintained its opposition to restricting American private bank loans on human rights grounds.

The stipulation that the multilateral aid banks heed "only economic considerations" is contained in their charters, and it may be convenient for a country that believes in the free flow of trade, finance, and investment to insist on a distinction between politics and economics. But in practice politics and economics inevitably taint each other. The aid banks, after all, were established by Western countries and are consistently defended by Western leaders as effective institutions for winning and keeping friends in the Third World.

During the 1970s American representatives frequently abstained from or opposed loans on human rights grounds, and circumstantial evidence suggests that in the past bank leaders have succumbed to U.S. pressure to reward or punish certain countries with their lending policies. As Representative Tom Harkin (D.-Iowa) has observed, Chile under the leftist government of Salvador Allende Gossens received an average of $6.4 million in multilateral aid from 1971 to 1973. From 1973 to 1975, after his overthrow in a military coup, such aid skyrocketed to $77.6 million annually, a 1,112 per cent increase. Latin American loans increased by 65 per cent during the same period. Multilateral aid to the Philippines before and after Marcos declared martial law in 1972 followed a similar pattern.

In fact, the bank charters contain major actual as well as potential human rights loopholes. The incidence of civil strife in a country must give pause to bankers who follow the sound business principles alluded to in the banks' charters. In March 1982 the World Bank reportedly suspended its operations in El Salvador to protect loan officers. The United States has contended that in Afghanistan security concerns prohibit effective U.N. aid.

A Dissociative Policy

The machinery for placing restrictions on business activity is also in place. The 1969 Export Administration Act, for example, empowers the president to impose "foreign policy controls" on any product headed for any destination. And America's traditional distaste for politicizing trade notwithstanding, Washington has curbed or embargoed trade with every communist country, the Dominican Republic, and Uganda since the 1920s. Moreover, Congress has tied human rights strings on Export-Import Bank and Overseas Private Investment Corporation (OPIC) activities.

American businessmen have complained bitterly that such restrictions have cost them millions in overseas sales, and in a period of large U.S. trade deficits and persistent unemployment, no effort to inhibit exporters appears promising. But so far, the restrictions have been applied sparingly, and the total costs have been very small. In 1978 only 23 out of the 1,000 export license applications reviewed for human rights concerns were refused. And despite the focus on a handful of lost contracts, U.S. trade with Latin America actually expanded during the Carter years.

Although the percentage of American trade, investment, and loans accounted for by many individual pro-Western human rights violators is very small. American business is vital to their economies. The U.S. share of Guatemalan, Salvadoran, Nicaraguan, and Bolivian imports and exports has hovered around the 30 per cent mark for most of the past decade. U.S. private capital has been critical to the economic development these countries have achieved.

American leverage on larger countries with more extensive economic ties to the United States, such as Brazil, Argentina, Chile, South Korea, and the Philippines, is frequently considerable as well. The larger prospective losses to American business make sanctions that much more costly—but not necessarily prohibitive—especially in the absence of cooperation from Japan and Western Europe. Yet prospective short-run losses must be balanced against possible long-term exclusion from a national market ordered by a government resentful of U.S. support for its predecessor. Further, sanctions against these countries are far more likely to effect change than measures against countries with which U.S. economic relations are relatively insignificant.

The Jackson-Vanik amendment to the 1974 Trade Reform Act, for example, linked U.S. extension of most-favored-nation (MFN) status to the Soviet Union with the increased emigration of Soviet Jews. Changes in the annual levels of such emigration are difficult to interpret because Soviet policy is based on many considerations. Two conclusions, however, do seem reasonable: Emigration increased markedly during the height of détente diplomacy and during the two years before the SALT II treaty was signed and submitted to the Senate; and emigration fell during periods of strain. Indeed, during the first year and one-half of the Reagan administration, emigration plunged to a new low. And clearly no evidence suggests that the amendment per se has helped more Soviet Jews depart for the West.

Yet the most important argument made by critics of pressure on authoritarian regimes holds that such policies hurt U.S. national security by damaging America's reputation as a reliable ally and sometimes by destabilizing and toppling friendly governments in strategically important countries. Iran and Nicaragua are cited as prime examples. Unfortunately, both arguments assume that the United States can sustain embattled authoritarians with the right amount of diplomatic support and resources. Yet the utility of American power in these cases is at best arguable. And plainly the American people had no stomach for military intervention in either country.

In fact, how well do tottering dictatorships —so-called one-bullet regimes—serve U.S. interests over the long run or at times when the United States needs them the most? For nearly 30 years the shah's government anchored U.S. policy in the Persian Gulf, permitted Washington to station vital intelligence facilities on Iran's border with the Soviet Union, and provided a secure environment for lucrative American business ventures. But when the Soviets invaded Afghanistan and when the SALT II treaty came before the Senate, virulently anti-American Islamic fundamentalists controlled both Iran's military and the listening posts that the United States counted on to help verify the arms control pact. Nor is it clear that the United States bolsters its international credibility by committing massive resources to besieged governments. To most of the world, U.S. involvement in Vietnam signaled nothing but an inability to identify genuine threats to U.S. interests.

Recent administrations have insisted that friendly relations with autocracies did not constitute endorsement of human rights violations. Yet foreign populations frequently receive just the opposite message from U.S. actions. In Nicaragua, members of Somoza's National Guard often dressed in U.S. fatigues and drove American-made vehicles with U.S. Army markings, and a U.S. ambassador's portrait long adorned Nicaraguan currency. The hostility of Iran's Moslem government and the hostage crisis attest to the Iranian people's bitter resentment of U.S. support for the shah. And South Korean and Philippine dissidents increasingly blame Washington for human rights violations by their governments.

Suspending or curtailing aid or commerce during a period of serious political upheaval or even after crackdowns on dissent by an apparently stable government may win the United States influence or at least good will with opposition groups should they prevail. Moreover, such action runs little risk of permanently antagonizing incumbents, whose political views would make entering the Soviet orbit extremely difficult and who would remain heavily dependent on U.S. resources. Dissociation should be seen as a form of preventive medicine. As Lefever has said, "We should have started many years before to have moved away from the kind of identification we had with the shah and the army and so on."

Behind the Scenes Pressure

In countries where the United States has little leverage, dissociation does not come into play. Washington is not linked in any way with repression in these countries. The best hope for reducing abuses in such countries lies in conducting quiet diplomacy and inducing offending governments to improve by offering them carrots. U.S. economic relations with countries such as Vietnam, Cuba, North Korea, and Cambodia are either minuscule or nonexistent. Resource flows to avowedly leftist but noncommunist nations such as Tanzania, Guyana, and Mozambique are somewhat larger. But most seem able to limp along without U.S. help. Trade with America runs as high as 20 per cent of imports or exports with only Guyana, for example.

The Soviet bloc presents a perplexing combination of risks and opportunities. Like other industrialized Western countries, the United States provides members of the Soviet bloc with important margins of capital and high technology goods. The Soviet Union itself appears to possess enough valuable raw materials to sustain even joint Western pressures for the foreseeable future. Other Warsaw Pact economies, however, are much more vulnerable and already drain Moscow's resources. Yet the great volume of Western loans to and trade with the East has exposed major banks and entire countries to serious injury should economic war break out. In addition, as the Siberian gas pipeline controversy demonstrates, American policy today is tripping over an obstacle frequently cited by opponents of sanctions against friendly regimes—the alternate supplier problem. Still, the calculus of Soviet and Western economic power and political resolve can change and should be reviewed continually. For now, the best results will most likely come from exploiting the acute desire of the Warsaw Pact countries for Western resources and by pressing for human rights improvements behind the scenes.

Problems of history and politics also dim the prospects of using sticks to beat open societies where the United States has little clout. These countries are instinctively suspicious of all U.S. words and actions. They recognize no American right to judge their domestic policies, and they are not inclined to follow American leads. The problem is not how to use leverage, but how to get it; not what to say, but how to gain a hearing. Haig defended quiet diplomacy toward "historic friends" that abuse human rights by arguing that progress is impossible in "the glare of public bludgeoning" or in an atmosphere of "paranoia." Yet this reasoning makes even more sense for countries in which the paranoia and the suspicion already exist.

Preferential treatment for these countries may also enhance U.S. national security by drawing communist and left-leaning countries in the Third World away from the Soviet orbit. Past failures to achieve rapprochement with Cuba and Vietnam demonstrate the difficulties involved. But a policy that writes such countries off must be very comforting to the Kremlin. Implacable hostility to postrevolutionary regimes in Cuba in 1960 and in Vietnam during the late 1940s at the least handed Moscow two effortless political victories.

Within the context of quiet diplomacy, U.S. leaders should take every opportunity when communicating with those countries to affirm the value of the freedoms Americans enjoy. But only a foolish consistency would prevent the United States from expressing its displeasure in votes over distantly related countries' human rights violations taken in the U.N., where Washington has few special powers—none in the General Assembly—by dint of its size and strength; where Washington generally casts just one vote and can easily slough off the primary blame for condemnatory resolutions; and where no action short of the unusual step of imposing sanctions can materially harm a human rights violator. As a rule, however, publicly threatening and reprimanding individual, distantly related countries can only push them back into shells of suspicion and hostility.

A human rights policy that discriminates against friends and allies also flows from an important moral consideration. An avowedly amoral posture would seriously undercut the credibility of American diplomats and undermine their efforts to gain international agreement on the need to respect human rights. Polls suggest that Americans want their leaders to stand periodically for the values of decency and liberty, regardless of realpolitik considerations.

However, opinions on how specifically to carry out this moral mandate range from advocacy for condemning all abuses and for aiding all victims of repression to the belief that any action that strengthens America even indirectly passes the test of morality. Still, one kind of obligation seems more compelling and less easily brushed aside than the others: the obligation that flows from America's responsibility for repression in certain countries.

This suggestion has drawn contemptuous responses, especially from supporters of the administration's human rights policies. Yet on several occasions, the United States has helped to install repressive regimes—in Iran in 1953; in Guatemala in 1954; in Chile in 1973. And from 1962 to 1975 the Agency for International Development's Office of Public Safety and similar programs spent tens of millions of dollars not only on riot and surveillance equipment for authoritarian police officers but also on providing instruction in censorship and handling mass rallies. Finally, many of the world's most brutal governments rely heavily on American aid, business, and defense commitments. One need not consider America the scourge of freedom to acknowledge special U.S. obligations to their populations.

At the same time, this focus on America's political wards may well defuse a critical peril of active human rights policies—the possibility that a resolve to promote freedom will degenerate into an arrogant crusade to impose American ways on other nations. As philosopher Reinhold Niebuhr once noted, "a deep layer of Messianic consciousness" runs through "the mind of America." A policy that continually highlights the results of interventionism run riot may keep these sentiments submerged. The emphasis placed during the last presidential campaign on restoring American strength suggests that American public opinion might not support a human rights diplomacy that focuses on friends and allies. At the same time, the revival of interest in human rights during the mid-1970s stemmed from public concern over U.S. responsibility for repression in allied countries. Given apprehension over even the current level of U.S. involvement in El Salvador and the likelihood of continued unrest elsewhere in the developing world, it is easy to see how such sentiments might surface again. The rapid growth of the nuclear freeze movement in recent years shows how suddenly opinion can shift. Yet more so than the alternatives, such a change in human rights policy, with its bias against friends and its humbling stress on responsibility, must be carefully and systematically explained to the public.

Leverage with Responsibility

Recent American history demonstrates that nothing will destroy public backing for U.S. foreign policy faster than rationalizing support for certain dictators by touting them as paragons of even modest virtue, whether they are described as "moderately repressive" or as "standing on the right side of history." These assessments flow from personal preferences not from dispassionate analysis and are unlikely to change any time soon. A policy based on one position is bound to provoke

heated and effective opposition from the other faction.

Nevertheless, even a leverage-based policy will be open to charges of hypocrisy and ineffectiveness. The United States has extensive ties with Saudi Arabia, for example, but is in no position to scold the Saudis for their failure to establish a parliamentary democracy. The benefits of dissociative policies may not become apparent for many years, despite the demands of Americans for quick results. And the policy must be able to respond to less than epochal but significant shifts in national policies—for example, liberalization by gross violators or new repression by countries with relatively good human rights records.

Curbs on multilateral aid present further problems. An administration with an eminently shakable commitment to the multilateral banks and to multilateral aid in general could use this policy as a ploy to paralyze or reduce these institutions' operations or cite leverage factors as an excuse to acquiesce in congressional attacks on the banks.

The costs businesses have suffered until now from human rights restrictions have been grossly overstated, and a leverage-based policy can preserve long-term U.S. access to a national market. But cutoffs of trade, loans, and investment cannot be implemented cavalierly. They should be seen as last resorts, to be invoked only after private suasion has failed. And business sanctions could still unfairly penalize companies that deal with target countries for perfectly valid business reasons.

Several measures may remove or shrink some of these obstacles. Washington should continually explore alternate means of safeguarding U.S. security interests. If close military ties with persistent human rights violators are unavoidable in the short run, the diplomatic relationship should be conducted in a low-key, businesslike manner.

Diplomats and elected officials alike should continually articulate and explain the goal of dissociation, both for American audiences and for foreign governments, to help counter charges of faintheartedness and to detail the pragmatic reasons for withdrawing support for dictatorships incapable of controlling insurgencies. Washington should make clear its reluctance to take sides in so volatile a situation and its willingness to work with any victor able to govern with popular consent. Despite the belief that the key to halting Soviet expansionism lies in defeating avowedly radical or communist-armed insurgents, few, if any, such groups are or have been irremediably pro-

Soviet. It is difficult to imagine one with the ideological backbone to abjure U.S. resources for the sake of doctrinal purity—to conceive, in short, of a country that does not have its price. Only a takeover by a genuinely fanatical or barbarous force such as Cambodia's Khmer Rouge or Uganda's Idi Amin would warrant U.S. hostility.

Presidents frequently stress the risk of politicizing the international financial institutions (IFIs) but tend to ignore the even greater dangers of pretending that official repression and brutality have no impact on economic development. This posture deprives the United States of one means of demonstrating the seriousness of its human rights intentions. It ignores a flow of Western resources always capable of mitigating the impact of unilateral U.S. sanctions. And it robs Washington of a valuable means of expressing its human rights concerns before imposing business sanctions.

Further, the attempt to insulate the banks from human rights issues damaged the credibility of the Ford and Carter administrations and may be thwarting the reconstruction of a pro-IFI coalition in Congress. After all, the votes that tipped the congressional balance against the banks during the 1970s came not from conservative human rights advocates but from otherwise sympathetic liberals angered by the IFIs' seeming indifference to human rights. Serious executive branch efforts to close this loophole could overcome such suspicions.

Other major donors appear increasingly willing to consider human rights in loan decisions. Nations such as Sweden regularly, if not frequently, oppose loans to Chile and other gross violators. On December 10, 1981, West Germany, Denmark, Canada, and other donors opposed or abstained on a proposed Inter-American Development Bank loan to El Salvador to support land reform. Bonn argued that the Salvadoran government could not implement the loan properly. The high proportion of negative West European votes aimed at Latin American human rights violators suggests that vigorous U.S. lobbying and consulting could periodically win support for limiting aid to closely tied repressive regimes. A focus on such friendly countries and the short-term sacrifices this approach entails would go far toward reassuring other major donors that America's prime concern is human rights and not simply carrying political vendettas into the aid banks. Finally, it must be remembered that unsuccessful public U.S. efforts to block multilateral aid will have valuable dissociative effects.

An administration committed to a leverage-based human rights policy can also distribute the domestic economic costs of sanctions more equitably. The Export-Import Bank and OPIC already offer American firms insurance against unjust, precipitous acts by foreign governments, such as expropriation and nonpayment of bills. It follows that Washington has an even greater obligation to compensate companies for losses incurred because of U.S. actions. Where possible, the federal government could give victimized companies preferences in the awarding of contracts. And the United States could cut its future losses and expenses by continuing to include human rights considerations in subsidy and insurance programs and by offering this aid for commerce with closely tied human rights violators with more discretion.

American diplomats and legislators can use the entire range of actions with which they register approval or disapproval of foreign actions to fine-tune the leverage-based policy. Praise and criticism and changes in levels of U.S. representation are useful because all can be easily extended, withdrawn, or moderated on short notice. But turning aid and business spigots all the way on or off weekly would destroy the predictability and political certainty development planners and businessmen legitimately demand.

Fortunately, there exist partial measures and widely accepted political review processes able to cushion or prevent human rights shocks. Foreign aid levels, which are set annually, may be raised or lowered rather than cut entirely. In fact, Congress already requires that the administration certify an improvement in El Salvador's human rights policies biannually before aid can be approved. This practice should be extended to cover other extreme, persistent violators. Before embargoing commerce, presidents could terminate or reduce such government benefits as export credits, import preferences, and MFN status, after a suitable period of notice.

With these policies, the United States emphasizes that its primary concerns are less with particular regimes than with the people they should serve; its primary loyalties are to the populaces that may prosper or suffer under the rule of those regimes. When foreign policy concerned only affairs between states, a policy that ran roughshod over friendly regimes when necessary might have been indefensible. Now that developments within countries crowd the international agenda, a leverage- and responsibility-based human rights policy for the United States has become imperative.

Revival of the Cold War: The US and the USSR in Confrontation

Soviet-American relations have sunk to their lowest level since the Cuban missile crisis of 1962. The principle of détente has received a constant battering from both sides since the late 1970s. Mutual distrust and anger plague the Soviet-American relationship and make negotiations on even trifling matters difficult. The rapid substitution of cold war ideological rhetoric and military competition for détente suggests that détente had inadequate foundations, and that the Cold War was only in abeyance, never eradicated.

What made détente work in an earlier period that is not working now? In general, the basis for détente was the "thickening" of the Soviet-American relationship. Americans presumed that if the Soviets were offered a vested interest in ties with the US, through credits, trade, economic incentives (including the sale of wheat and advanced American technology), scientific cooperation, and other mutually beneficial intertwinings of American and Soviet national interests, the Soviets would see that the benefits to be gained from cooperation would greatly outweigh any advantages acquired by destroying the relationship, much less destroying the US. The complement to these incentives was a guarantee from both sides that they would not seek strategic superiority. Where would the Soviets buy their grain if the US was in smoking ruins? And what would be left of the Soviet Union itself? To the extent that both sides believed that "mutual assured destruction" was the most probable outcome of conflict, each side would find it in its interest not to push conflict anywhere in the world to the point at which it might mean confronting the other superpower directly. Détente failed because the incentives were inadequate to enmesh the Soviet Union in a cooperative relationship with the US. In particular, the hoped for most-favored-nation trade benefit was never granted to the Soviets, and grain sales, scientific cooperation, and trade in advanced technology all became political weapons in the hands of America to stop the Soviets from doing what they felt was their legitimate right to do. In the meantime, the Americans developed a relationship with the People's Republic of China that, from the Soviets' perspective, was tantamount to an alliance. From the perspective of both sides, the other side was seen to be attempting to gain military superiority. And from the perspective of the US, the Soviets were pursuing their own aggressive goals in the Third World, Afghanistan, Vietnam, and Poland—all while parading the ideas of détente.

On the American side, much of the hope for improvement of relations with the Soviet Union has hinged on the long anticipated leadership change. Until Brezhnev's death in November 1982, it seemed as if America's policies toward the Soviet Union had come to a standstill. And similarly, on the Soviet side, Brezhnev exercised an implicit veto over any initiative in Soviet foreign policy, regardless of his weakened capacity for leadership, as long as he lived. Thus Soviet-American relations faltered, and finally became stalemated in the early 1980s as leaders shifted (Carter to Reagan, Haig to Schultz, and Brezhnev to Andropov). Since these changes, both sides have been hoping for a softened stance from the other side.

As the articles in this Section and Section Six indicate, the Soviets have already responded to Reagan's "zero option" on strategic weapons with a plan of their own—a compromise plan on strategic nuclear weapons aimed at Western Europe. While at first the Reagan Administration seemingly rejected the proposal out of hand, there are now signs indicating that it is being viewed as a bargaining position. Compromise on both sides now seems possible. This year's negotiations on arms control and disarmament, as well as events involving any of the superpowers in Asia, Africa, Latin America, and Europe will be critical in determining whether the door to détente slams shut or remains ajar.

Looking Ahead: Challenge Questions

What kinds of incentives could the US offer the Soviets that the Soviets would not want to risk losing?

Do you think that an American "position of strength" is the only factor that really will count in getting the Soviets to back down from their militant stance? Does nothing matter more to the Soviets than spreading Moscow's control over more and more governments and territories?

Are there internal political and economic factors that will drive the Soviets to the bargaining table to discuss strategic arms limitations?

What could be the consequences of a greatly weakened Soviet economy? Is it necessarily to America's advantage to have the Soviets feel they are in a vastly weaker position than the US?

Changing Soviet Conceptions of East-West Relations

Paul Marantz

Paul Marantz, associate professor of political science at the University of British Columbia, Vancouver, is the author of several articles on Soviet foreign policy.

To what extent and in what ways does contemporary Soviet foreign policy differ from that of the Stalin years? This has long been one of the most controversial and vexing questions confronting students of Soviet foreign policy. With the recent deterioration in East-West relations, it has taken on increased practical relevance; for any sound investigation of the origins of détente, of the reasons for its collapse by the late 1970's, and of the implications of this for Western policy in the 1980's must be grounded on a firm sense of just what has and has not changed in the Soviet approach to international politics.

Given the direct policy implications of this debate, it is not surprising that the argument has often been quite spirited.[1] Some analysts believe that present-day Soviet diplomacy differs little from Stalin's, and they argue therefore that the central task of the West is to preserve its strength, act with firmness, and avoid self-defeating illusions about its highly manipulative and tactically adroit enemy. In contrast, others perceive a "learning process" which has resulted in a major evolution in Soviet perspectives on international politics, and on this basis they call for flexible policies designed to encourage and facilitate further changes in the Soviet outlook.

Over the past quarter of a century the West has become so accustomed to fervent Soviet professions of fidelity to peaceful coexistence that it is easy to forget just how sharply the post-Stalin conception of East-West relations diverges from the view that prevailed until 1953. The Stalinist framework for viewing East-West relations was bleak in the extreme, so much so that it is hard to imagine a view that could have been more negative, pessimistic, and fatalistic. The Stalinist world view was based upon a series of mutually reinforcing propositions which all pointed to the same gloomy conclusion: the Soviet Union was confronted by implacable enemies with whom no real cooperation was possible because they were resolutely dedicated to the destruction of the world's first socialist state.[2]

The distribution of power between East and West was depicted not as one of parity or balance, but as one characterized by capitalist encirclement. The Soviet Union was said to be ringed by hostile states bent upon utilizing every means at their disposal to undermine and weaken it. The need for vigilance was constantly emphasized, based upon the contention that the primary goal of the Soviet regime—ensuring the continued survival of socialism in the Soviet Union—had not been secured and indeed was very much in jeopardy. This view was expressed by the ideological formulation that the "final" victory of socialism—by which was meant the achievement of sufficient security to rule out any possibility of the restoration of capitalism in the Soviet Union—had not been won and could not be attained as long as the capitalist governments of West Europe and North America continued to exist.

Soviet insecurity was further heightened by a deep sense of fatalism in that it was explicitly argued that there was relatively little that the Soviet Union could do to alter the international environment in which it existed. Right to Stalin's last days it was dogmatically asserted that world wars remained an inescapable feature of international politics under capitalism. Just as World War I had prepared the ground for the Second World War, so World War III would inevitably break out some years hence. Intense strife was the norm, and the interlude between wars was but a temporary lull. Until the day when capitalism ceased to exist in the major Western countries, there was nothing the Soviet Union or its allies could do to alter this unhappy situation.

---

[1]For example, see the exchange between Charles Gati and William Zimmerman in Stephen F. Cohen et al., eds., *The Soviet Union since Stalin* (Bloomington, Ind.: Indiana University Press, 1980), pp. 279-311.

[2]The discussion of the Stalinist world view that follows draws on: Frederic S. Burin, "The Communist Doctrine of the Inevitability of War," *American Political Science Review*, vol. 57 (June, 1962), pp. 334-354; Elliot R. Goodman, *The Soviet Design for a World State* (New York: Columbia University Press, 1960); Paul Marantz, "Prelude to Detente," *International Studies Quarterly*, vol. 19 (December, 1975), pp. 501-528; Robert C. Tucker, *The Soviet Political Mind* (New York: W. W. Norton, 1963), pp. 20-35.

Arms control and disarmament were specifically rejected as feasible goals for Soviet policy. It was argued that the basic nature of capitalism, which bred a furious struggle for markets and profits, precluded any significant limitations on the means by which that struggle was waged. As long as capitalism held sway in the world, disarmament was a meaningless utopia. From time to time, it might be useful for the Soviet Union to make sweeping proposals for disarmament, but Soviet writings explicitly stated that this was to be done for the sole purpose of exposing the predatory nature of imperialism.

It was for these reasons that, during the Stalin years, Soviet spokesmen depicted international relations as a zero-sum game. In their conception, there were only two players, the socialist camp and capitalist camp, locked in direct conflict. The gains of one side were inevitably losses for the other. Moreover, the stakes of the game were nothing less than one's ultimate survival. *Ktokogo,* who would destroy whom, was constantly being put to the test.

Given this perspective, it clearly made no sense to advocate—as is now so frequently done by Soviet spokesmen—"the relaxation of international tension." Quite the contrary, such a goal was viewed in Stalin's day as a dangerous illusion. Far from advocating the goal of a lessening of international tension, Stalin's main concern was to preserve a high level of tension so that vigilance toward the class enemy would not be relaxed. For Stalin, not unlike some people in the West, a state of détente was vastly more threatening than a state of acute tension, for tension had the advantage of making clear just who was the enemy. There is clear evidence that by the late 1940's some influential Soviet officials were cautiously leaning toward a new, more optimistic conception of international relations. But these impulses to change were decisively stifled.

KHRUSHCHEV: OPTIMISM AND INNOVATION

Stalin's conceptual rigidity is all the more apparent when it is contrasted with the remarkable innovativeness—and even iconoclasm—of his successor Nikita Khrushchev. Within just four years, from 1956 to 1960, Khrushchev decisively transformed Soviet conceptions of East-West relations.

In February 1956, at the twentieth party congress, Khrushchev forthrightly declared that the time-honored theory of the inevitability of war was no longer valid. In announcing this position, he specifically endorsed many of the arguments that Stalin had rejected just a few years earlier. Khrushchev contended that the growing strength of the socialist camp meant that new opportunities existed for creative diplomacy and for real efforts to prevent the outbreak of war. In 1959, at the twenty-first party congress, Khrushchev carried this new position one step further and provided additional grounds for a more optimistic and open-ended view of the world. He proclaimed that it was fully possible, even while capitalism still existed in the West, to create an international system in which world war would cease to be possible.

A further impetus toward regarding East-West diplomacy in a new light was provided by the repudiation of the traditional Leninist proposition that disarmament was impossible to achieve under capitalism. Khrushchev took the lead in proclaiming that disarmament was a practical, realizable goal. It was argued that only one segment of the ruling elite in capitalist countries had a direct economic stake in military production. Other powerful capitalist groups were said to be harmed by the militarization of the economy, and for this reason their economic self-interest would lead them to oppose an arms race and to join with the Soviet Union in the constructive search for genuine arms control.

Soviet optimism was also reflected in Khrushchev's declaration at the twenty-first congress that capitalist encirclement no longer existed and that the "final" victory of socialism had been achieved in the Soviet Union. This repudiation of Stalinist dogma was more than symbolic. It meant that the survival of the Soviet regime was no longer viewed as hanging in the balance. The Soviet leadership could now approach East-West negotiations with a new feeling of confidence, with a broader agenda of issues in mind, and without a paralyzing fear that they would be manipulated, outmaneuvered, or overwhelmed by a vastly more powerful opponent. A more normal process of diplomatic give-and-take could now be envisaged.

A NEW CONCEPTION

In this context, one of Khrushchev's greatest contributions—one that has often not been sufficiently appreciated in the West—was to provide a fundamentally new basis for the conceptualization of Soviet-American relations. Lenin and Stalin automatically regarded the most powerful imperialist state as the leader of the imperialist forces hostile to the Soviet Union. What was lacking in the traditional view was any conception suggesting either the possibility or the utility of long-term Soviet cooperation with its most powerful capitalist adversary.

Khrushchev provided this bridge. First of all, it was argued that in the nuclear age the Soviet Union and the United States, as the world's only two superpowers, had a special joint responsibility to work together to avoid a nuclear holocaust and to regulate conflict anywhere in the world.

Second, and more significantly, a new view of foreign policy decision-making within the capitalist countries was developed during the Khrushchev years. Soviet spokesmen, including Khrushchev, embraced the proposition that there were two very different tendencies or groups within the ruling capitalist elite. One was portrayed as bellicose and virulently anti-Soviet,

35

while the other was said to be sober, moderate, possessed of a healthy appreciation of the consequences of nuclear war, and sincerely interested in improved relations with the Soviet Union. These two very different factions of the ruling bourgeoisie were locked in a sharp struggle for power, whose precise outcome was an open question. The final result was not preordained and would be decided not just by immutable economic forces, but by the interplay of complex and uncertain political factors as well. There was, according to Khrushchev and his colleagues, a very real possibility that moderate forces would triumph in many of the leading capitalist countries, including even the United States.

This rather unorthodox view had important implications for the Soviet conceptualization of East-West relations. It suggested that there was a real basis for genuine and sincere cooperation even between the Soviet Union, the world's most powerful socialist state, and the United States, the leading force in the imperialist camp. The significance of Khrushchevian innovations was further enhanced by bringing them together in a newly expanded doctrine of peaceful coexistence. The more Khrushchev's conception of peaceful coexistence came under attack (by hard-line elements in the Soviet Union such as Foreign Minister Vyacheslav Molotov and by militant parties within the Communist movement such as that of China), the more Khrushchev and his spokesmen expanded and broadened its meaning. It was argued that the avoidance of war (not social revolution) was *the* central goal of contemporary Soviet foreign policy. Peaceful coexistence was said to consist not merely of the absence of war, but of the establishment of economic, political, and cultural links between East and West, and it was claimed that increasingly the main focus of East-West rivalry was shifting to the arena of peaceful economic competition between the two systems.

In focusing on Khrushchev's innovations and on the ways in which they departed from earlier Soviet conceptions of East-West relations, the positive side of the ledger has been stressed. But these favorable developments were vitiated by the maintenance of ideological elements reflecting a more traditional outlook. Thus throughout Khrushchev's reign, it also remained official orthodoxy that: capitalism is doomed; the Soviet Union has an obligation to promote capitalism's demise; the Communist party alone is the authentic spokesman for the working class; Marxism-Leninism is a science; peaceful coexistence is a form of class struggle; peaceful coexistence precludes military conflict, but not a sharp political, economic, and ideological struggle between capitalism and socialism; ideological coexistence between East and West is impossible; and so forth. Soviet spokesmen remained unwilling to acknowledge openly that Soviet policies might have been partially responsible for the cold war. They attributed changes in Western policies solely to growing Soviet strength which "compelled" these countries to abandon their evil schemes, and they applied a double standard which endorsed Soviet "ideological struggle" against Western policies, but condemned Western criticism of Soviet behavior as impermissible "cold war propaganda."

Some of the traditional elements of Soviet doctrine were no doubt retained simply as part of the ideological baggage necessary to legitimize the Communist party's continued monopoly of political power within the Soviet Union, and thus they need not be taken too seriously. But others were of greater importance, and as long as they remained unaltered, they hindered the improvement of East-West relations. Khrushchev presided over a remarkable amount of ideological and conceptual innovation. Even though the job of refashioning the Soviet world view was far from complete, a promising beginning had been made. A firm foundation upon which to build was bequeathed to his successors.

What, then, has been the response of Leonid Brezhnev and his colleagues to the Khrushchevian legacy? To what extent have official Soviet conceptions of East-West relations continued to evolve and to moderate? The record of the post-1964 period makes it apparent that the forward movement of the Khrushchev years has not continued. On the contrary, there is not just the absence of further conceptual innovation but in some areas an actual retreat. The hopes that many in the West had in the mid-1960's for a gradual de-radicalization of Soviet foreign policy perspectives have been disappointed. However, the circumstances producing this situation are multiple and diverse. There is no single factor at work (for example, one cannot simply speak of a "hardening" of Soviet foreign policy).

On the negative side of the ledger, there has been a complete absence of any further modification of traditional Marxist-Leninist ideological categories in the years since Khrushchev's ouster. Whereas Khrushchev repudiated such concepts as capitalist encirclement, the inevitability of war, and the impossibility of disarmament under capitalism, his successor has not taken any similar steps. There has been a complete disinterest in any further doctrinal change.

Second, there has been not just an absence of further forward movement in regard to the concept of peaceful coexistence, but a definite de-emphasis. Under Khrushchev, peaceful coexistence was frequently defined as the general line of Soviet foreign policy. When the goals of that policy were listed, peaceful coexistence was often ranked ahead of all other priorities. With Khrushchev's departure, there was a distinct change. For the first time, authoritative spokesmen issued stern warnings against giving too much weight to peaceful coexistence, and they cautioned against neglecting the role of other fundamental principles, especially that of proletarian internationalism. When the goals of Soviet foreign policy were listed in Brezhnev's speeches, peaceful coexistence was generally ranked last, behind such objectives as building communism in the Soviet Union, strengthening the socialist camp, and supporting the forces of national liberation in the third world. Peaceful coexistence was still viewed as combining elements of both competition and cooperation, but under Brezhnev it was given a harder inflection. The side of the equation dealing with "struggle" was clearly stressed.

A third negative development of the Brezhnev period has been the severe downgrading of the importance attached to economic competition. Beginning most prominently at the twenty-first party congress in 1959, Khrushchev increasingly portrayed economic competition between the two systems as the central focus of East-West relations. War, violent revolution, and direct confrontation were all de-emphasized, and it was argued in the strongest possible terms that the Soviet Union was fulfilling its international obligations to the world proletariat by defeating the capitalist world in a battle of economic indices. The claim was made that the Soviet Union, by constantly improving the standard of living of its people and by working to surpass the United States in industrial production, would graphically demonstrate the superiority of socialism and thereby hasten its worldwide victory. Unfortunately, the post-Khrushchev leadership has had no such faith in economic competition. It has been de-emphasized and relegated to a minor place in the Soviet conception of East-West relations.

How, then, should the lack of further conceptual innovation under Brezhnev, the downgrading of peaceful coexistence, and the de-emphasizing of economic competition be evaluated? Clearly the hoped for de-radicalization of Soviet international perspectives has not occurred. It would nevertheless be a mistake to see these developments as constituting some sort of re-radicalization of the Soviet outlook or as signifying a decisive rejection of the Khrushchevian conception of East-West relations.

More than anything else, these developments are a manifestation of those same traits in Brezhnev's political style that are so apparent in most other policy areas in the post-1964 period: a determination to reject Khrushchev's impulsiveness, wishful thinking, and incautious experimentation, and to substitute instead caution, realism, and patient incrementalism. Khrushchev's enthusiasm led to a one-sided emphasis on his panacea of the moment (be it the virgin lands or the improvement of Soviet-American relations) to the detriment of other Soviet interests. The Brezhnev period has been characterized by the pursuit of carefully framed policies which sought to avoid a one-sided thrust in any direction and attempted to address simultaneously a wide range of basic concerns. This, in turn, was coupled with a hard-headed appreciation of the ideological and political costs associated with a too-eager public embrace of peaceful coexistence with the imperialist world.

A major reason, then, for the post-1964 upgrading of the principle of proletarian internationalism and the corresponding downplaying of peaceful coexistence has been the wish to reduce some of these costs (for example, to undercut Chinese and third world charges of Soviet-American collusion and to avoid ideological de-mobilization at home). However, while the prominence of peaceful coexistence in Soviet pronouncements has been reduced somewhat and it has been given a more balanced formulation, peaceful coexistence has certainly not been abandoned. It continues to occupy a highly visible place in Soviet discussions of East-West relations. The Soviets pushed it in the 1972 Soviet-American agreement on "Basic Principle of Relations," and an explicit endorsement of peaceful coexistence is contained in the new Soviet constitution adopted in 1977. Similarly, all the other doctrinal and conceptual innovations introduced by Khrushchev have been retained by the Brezhnev regime.

A second factor influencing the present leadership's conservatism is its awareness of just how successful Khrushchev was in refashioning the Marxist-Leninist world view. He left his successors with a new set of propositions and principles which enables them to conceptualize in their own minds—and to legitimize in the eyes of their followers—a broad range of policies toward the capitalist world. Khrushchev's doctrinal innovations provide them with an ideological carte blanche to pursue far-reaching détente if they so choose, and hence there is no compelling need—especially when the potential costs are kept in mind—to engage in the further revision of Lenin's legacy.

A third factor contributing to the absence of continuing conceptual innovation is the Brezhnev regime's declining interest in questions of ideology and doctrine. For example, Brezhnev's speeches to the four party congresses over which he has presided have exhibited growing pragmatism and realism. There is a heightened concern with concrete issues and an increased tendency to address East-West relations in terms of the specific interests of the Soviet Union.[3] Thus the de-emphasis of the role of economic competition under Brezhnev, which in one sense is a retreat from Khrushchev's position, can be viewed from another perspective simply as a pragmatic response to compelling realities (that is, the Soviet economy's failure to outperform those of the West). Brezhnev's more sober recognition of the complexities of the

[3] A careful content analysis of Brezhnev's speeches to the twenty-third, twenty-fourth, and twenty-fifth party congresses is contained in Franklyn Griffiths, "Ideological Development and Foreign Policy," in Seweryn Bialer, ed., *The Domestic Context of Soviet Foreign Policy* (Boulder, Col.: Westview Press, 1981), pp. 19-48.

world, the competing considerations that affect any decision, and the constraints on Soviet power can thus be a positive force even if it does lead to a toning down of some of the earlier grandiose claims made on behalf of economic competition and peaceful coexistence.

The general approach of the Brezhnev regime, even at the height of détente, was to proceed with concrete measures to expand political and economic cooperation with the West, but to avoid calling undue attention to this process through sweeping ideological pronouncements. Thus the absence of ideological change is not automatically evidence of rigidity. The prolonged retention of past ideological formulations may be a sign of dogmatism, as was the case under Stalin, or it may be evidence of a declining interest in ideological matters coupled with a realistic recognition of the value of retaining an existing ideological rationale which is now broad enough to allow the unhindered pursuit of a wide range of practical policies.

Related to this is a fourth point: the absence of dramatic change at what might be called the summit of Soviet ideology (that is, formulations concerning the inevitability of war or the final victory of socialism) does not preclude the amending and revision of middle level propositions of much importance. This process, which began under Khrushchev, has clearly continued throughout the post-1964 period. There has been a development in Soviet knowledge and sophistication concerning the processes of foreign policy formulation in the West, the workings of capitalist economies, the role of public opinion and interest groups, and such.[4] Here the clock has not been set back or stopped. The Soviet perception of its capitalist adversaries has evolved and broadened.

It is true, of course, that greater knowledge of the West facilitates Soviet efforts to influence political developments beyond its frontiers, such as the West European peace movement. But this knowledge also brings home more vividly to the Soviet leadership the costs of particular actions and hence imposes a greater degree of restraint than otherwise might be the case.

Last, in evaluating the receptiveness of the Brezhnev regime to cooperation with the West, account must be taken of the actual policies followed. Despite the recent deterioration of East-West relations, one must not overlook the complex negotiations that were begun in the past 15 years, the number of high-level meetings that have taken place, and the variety of agreements that were worked out. Even more important was Brezhnev's support for a number of policies which would have been inconceivable a few years earlier, such as allowing the emigration of over a quarter of

a million Soviet citizens, vastly expanding the Soviet Union's reliance upon trade with the West, and time and again bowing to Western protests concerning the treatment of specific dissidents or would-be emigrants. Small as these policy changes may seem in the grand scheme of things, they are evidence of a capacity to innovate, and they suggest that in the area of practical policy the Brezhnev regime has been willing to move beyond the confines of past practice.

Several conclusions emerge from this examination of Soviet perspectives on international politics. First, since Stalin's death there has, indeed, been a fundamental change in Soviet conceptions of East-West relations. The Soviet view of international politics has been transformed. Thus the adversary that the West confronts today differs significantly from that of the pre-1953 period. The extent of the change under Khrushchev provides a basis for cautious optimism that some time in the future—perhaps during the post-Brezhnev period—a further evolution of Soviet perspectives may occur.

A second conclusion is that the changes that took place in official Soviet conceptions of East-West relations were not just a matter of abstract ideology. On the contrary, they had very real consequences affecting the nature and texture of relations between the Soviet Union and the West. Without these changes, even the limited progress that has been made would not have taken place, and the degree of tension in times of worsening relations—such as the present—would have been much more severe.

A third and more somber conclusion, however, is that while Soviet conceptual change may have been a necessary condition for lessening the cold war, it clearly has not been sufficient, in and of itself, to bring about a fundamental change in East-West relations. It is unfortunate that as Soviet ideology has receded as a root cause of East-West conflict, new complicating factors have come into play. These include the greatly increased military capabilities of the Soviet Union; the tendency of Brezhnev and his colleagues to attach much more importance to military might than did Khrushchev and to regard military prowess as the one viable substitute for the growing Soviet inability to compete with the West in the realms of economics, politics, or ideology; and the Soviet desire to enjoy all the worldwide prerogatives that it believes its new-found global superpower status should confer upon it.

The times ahead will not be easy. There is abundant fuel for present and future conflicts. However, the fact that Soviet perspectives and policies are not immutably fixed should encourage Western policymakers to seek a balanced policy which combines firmness aimed at discouraging Soviet adventurism with conciliation designed to foster a climate conducive to the further evolution of Soviet perspectives.

---

[4]Alexander Dallin, *The United States in Soviet Perspective*, Adelphi Papers, no. 151 (London, 1979), pp. 13-21; Alexander Dallin, "The Fruits of Interaction," *Survey*, no. 22 (summer/autumn, 1976), pp. 42-46; Jerry F. Hough, "The Evolution in the Soviet World View," *World Politics*, no. 32 (July, 1980), pp. 509-530.

Excerpts from the Book "Whence the Threat to Peace?"

January 18, 1982

It was recently reported that the Military Publishing House of the USSR Ministry of Defense has issued in five foreign languages a book entitled "Whence the Threat to Peace?"

In the introduction the authors refer to the pamphlet "Soviet Military Power" brought out by the Pentagon several months ago and widely advertised by the U.S. mass media. The Pentagon's pamphlet is clearly designed to frighten the public, above all in Western countries, with the military potential of the USSR and convince it of the necessity to further build up U.S. and NATO military strength.

The book "Whence the Threat to Peace?" prepared by competent Soviet quarters, contains authoritative factual data, including comparative data, which give the reader an opportunity to gain an objective picture of the components and the actual state of the balance of armed strength between East and West. It contains detailed and objective information on the magnitude of the military potential on which the U.S. Administration relies in its policy from "positions of strength," of attaining military superiority.

The book "Whence the Threat to Peace?" consists of an introduction, four sections and a conclusion.

The first section—"They Call This Objective"—shows that the appraisals of the military potential of the USSR, its foreign policy and military strategy made by members of the U.S. Defense Department are unobjective and biased and that the authors of the U.S. pamphlet were anything but impartial in selecting data related to the Soviet Armed Forces.

To determine impartially who really challenges whom, who initiated the arms race, notably in mass destruction

weapons, who has been pursuing it at an ever increasing rate for more than three decades and who is building up military power without restraint, creating a menace to peace and the security of nations, the authors of the book "Whence the Threat to Peace?" have turned to facts.

These facts show convincingly that initiative in developing new weapon systems through all the postwar years has always come and continues to come from the USA (See the following table):

Type of Weapon System	Time of Development	
	In the USA	In the USSR
Nuclear weapons	Mid-1940s	Late 1940s
Intercontinental strategic bombers	Mid-1950s	Late 1950s
Nuclear-powered Submarines	Mid-1950s	Late 1950s
Nuclear-powered aircraft carriers	Early 1960s	None
Multiple independently targetable re-entry vehicles	Late 1960s	Mid-1970s
Neutron weapons	Late 1970s-Early 1980s	None

The book also cites data on who initiated buildup of nuclear-powered ballistic missile submarines (SSBNS), ballistic missiles and nuclear warheads.

Year	USA		USSR	
	SSBNS/ Launchers	Nuclear Warheads	SSBNS/ Launchers	Nuclear Warheads
1960	3/48	48	None	None
1967	41/656	1152	2/32	32
1970	41/656	2048	20/316	316
1975	41/656	4536	55/724	724
1981	40/648	5280	62/950	2000

Excerpts from WHENCE THE THREAT TO PEACE, Military Publishing House, USSR Ministry of Defense: Moscow, 1982.

2. REVIVAL OF THE COLD WAR

These and other factual data have enabled the authors of the book to conclude that the Soviet Union initiated no new types of weapons throughout postwar history. In building its armed forces, it only reacted to dangers created by the West. The USSR has never aspired to positions of military superiority and has always confined itself to measures that sufficed to ensure dependable security for itself and its allies.

The book goes on to say:

In its "Soviet Military Power" pamphlet, the U.S. Defense Department says the Soviet Union has 1,398 ICBM launchers, 950 SLBM launchers and 156 heavy bombers with a total payload of nearly 7,000 nuclear weapons. These figures taken out of context sound impressive. But the authors of the Pentagon pamphlet make no mention of the 10,000 nuclear weapons of the U.S. strategic offensive forces, which have 1,053 ICBM launchers, 648 SLBM launchers and more than 570 heavy bombers, plus 65 medium bombers. In addition, the United States has thousands of nuclear-capable aircraft in its forward-based forces in the proximity of Soviet territory in Europe, the Far East and the Indian Ocean.

It should also be borne in mind that the Soviet Union is confronted not only by the United States, but also by two other Western nuclear powers and that the threat of China's nuclear forces is, for the time being, more serious for the Soviet Union than for the United States. Furthermore, the book goes on to say, the Pentagon is trying to frighten the world public with the growth of the Soviet Navy and its now greater capability in distant regions of the world. This is said to "challenge the West's traditional dominance of the open oceans." The U.S. President, indeed, went so far as to say that the USA is faced with a naval "window of vulnerability."

The appearance in the Soviet Navy of air-capable ships, the *Kiev* and *Minsk,* and of a nuclear-powered missile cruiser, the *Kirov,* is portrayed as a grave threat to the West. Yet, for these two ships the United States has 20, and for the one nuclear-powered missile cruiser the United States has nine. In the 60s and 70s alone, the United States built in quick succession seven of the world's largest aircraft carriers, including three nuclear-powered, with 80,000 to 90,000 tons displacement and 90 aircraft each. The construction of a fourth nuclear-powered carrier is in the stage of completion. Its cost is four billion dollars.

It may be proper to recall, too, that in this period the Soviet Union was building nuclear-powered icebreakers for the peaceful development of Soviet arctic regions.

A deliberately one-sided appraisal is also given of the armaments of the ground forces of the USSR. The U.S. Defense Department pamphlet says, for example, that the Soviet Union has adapted some of its 203-mm and 240-mm artillery systems to nuclear shells. Yet it makes no mention of the self-propelled 203.2-mm nuclear-capable howitzers which the armies of the USA, the FRG, Great Britain, Italy, Belgium, Denmark and the Netherlands have had in service for dozens of years. The 155-mm howitzers that the troops of all NATO countries have in their arsenals are also adapted to firing nuclear shells. It is only fair to note, too, that more than 600 American, British and Canadian artillery systems adapted to nuclear shells are stationed in the territory of the FRG.

To back up the trumped-up claim of an "alarming Soviet military buildup," various deliberately exaggerated figures are cited in the West about the military expenditures of the USSR. Contrary to the facts, the public is being told that these expenditures are continuously rising. That they have really been practically the same over the recent years is withheld.

The military budget of the United States, on the other hand, has been rising steadily from year to year. Its rate of growth in 1978-1980, and this according to official U.S. figures, was in excess of 13 percent, and as much as 19 percent in 1981. And still higher growth rates of U.S. and NATO military spending are envisaged in the years to come. In 1985 alone, the United States is planning to allocate more than 340 billion dollars for military purposes, and a total of 1.5 trillion dollars in the coming five years.

There is no trace of objectivity in the conjectures that the authors of "Soviet Military Power" make concerning the Defense Industry of the Soviet Union. They declare that the Soviet Union has 135 munitions factories. Yet not a word is said by them that in the United States arms and materiel are produced by 146 government-operated plants and nearly 4,000 large-scale private enterprises.

The U.S. Defense Department alleges that the Soviet Union seeks a "global projection of Soviet military power." Here again, however, the Pentagon is at loggerheads with the facts and indeed with its own statements. For does it not admit that the Soviet Union has military contingents in the territory of only some of its East European allies and in neighboring Mongolia and Afghanistan, and this, moreover, strictly in conformity with treaty provisions? At the same time, U.S. military units are deployed in dozens of countries all over the world, and there are more than 1,500 U.S. military installations and bases overseas, chiefly in the proximity of Soviet borders.

U.S. nuclear-capable aircraft carriers, nuclear-powered missile submarines and squadrons of surface warships are on continuous patrol near the shores of Europe, the Far East and in the Indian Ocean. The more than 200,000-man Rapid Deployment Forces are ready to be moved many thousands of kilometers from the United States of America.

No less one-sided and tendentious is the account of Soviet arms shipments to developing countries. The USSR is portrayed as the biggest exporter of military hardware, though the United States accounts for nearly 45 percent of the world arms trade. And since other NATO countries account for more than 20 percent of the arms trade, it ought to be clear from whence comes the bulk of the arms flow. It is common knowledge that U.S. arms go to shore up reactionary and dictatorial regimes, to suppress revolutionary and national liberation movements and to consolidate the U.S. military presence in the recipient countries.

At the end of the first section of the book the authors conclude: 'The above shows how lacking in objectivity the authors of the pamphlet 'Soviet Military Power' were in evaluating the so widely advertised but, in fact, nonexistent Soviet threat to the strategic interests of the West.'

"It is impossible to get the correct idea of whence the threat to peace emanates without a concrete examination of the armed forces, the scale of military production, the substance of the military strategy and the foreign policy orientation of the United States."

All these questions are examined in detail in the second and largest section of the book—"The U.S. War Machine."

The U.S. War Machine

To implement its global aggressive designs, the United States maintains the largest and technically best equipped armed forces in the capitalist world. In strength and armaments, they surpass the combined armed forces of Great Britain, France, the FRG and Italy. The total strength of the U.S. Armed Forces is close to three million servicemen and one million civilian employees.

Administratively, the U.S. Armed Forces, like those of many other countries, consist of three services— Army, Air Force and Navy. The services are, in turn, divided into regular troops (naval forces) and organized reserves.

In addition to the administrative structure, the U.S. Armed Forces, unlike those of other countries, have an operational structure under which all manpower and equipment are distributed among five unified and three specified commands. These commands have been set up in peacetime to direct and prepare definite military groupings for war and to draw up advance plans of theater strategic operations suiting adopted U.S. global policy.

In accordance with the provisions of U.S. military doctrine to prepare and fight aggressive wars in overseas territories, the manpower and equipment of four out of the five unified commands are already deployed outside the United States in peacetime: in the European zone, the zones of the Atlantic and Pacific oceans and in Central and South America. The two strongest groupings are stationed in the West and in the Orient, in the immediate proximity of the Soviet borders.

Each grouping has strategic nuclear weapons systems, diverse theater nuclear weapons systems and Army, Air Force and naval formations equipped with

the latest armaments and brought up to wartime strength.

By purpose and nature of mission, the U.S. Armed Forces are divided into strategic, general-purpose and strategic mobility forces and reserves.

The backbone of the U.S. military power and nuclear potential is the strategic offensive forces. These include intercontinental ballistic missiles (ICBMs), strategic aircraft and nuclear-powered ballistic missile submarines (SSBNS). That is the so-called American strategic triad.

The combat units of the U.S. strategic offensive forces have 2,112 nuclear delivery vehicles, including 1,053 ICBM launchers, 411 bombers and 648 ballistic missile launchers installed in 40 nuclear submarines. These can lift about 10,000 nuclear warheads of 50 kilotons to 10 megatons each at one launch/sortile.

All in all, including reserve and mothballed heavy bombers, the U.S. strategic offensive forces have 2,338 nuclear delivery vehicles, including 2,273 vehicles of intercontinental range and 65 medium-range bombers specially designed for action on the European continent.

The ground-based strategic missile forces have 550 Minuteman III missile launchers, 450 Minuteman II launchers and 53 Titan II launchers. At one launch, the U.S. ICBMs can lift 2,153 nuclear warheads of 170 kilotons to 10 megatons each. These forces the political-military leadership of the United States consider to be means of delivering a pre-emptive nuclear strike.

The sea-based strategic missile forces consist of 40 nuclear submarines armed with Trident I (216 launchers), Poseidon C-3 (304 launchers), and Polaris A-3 (128 launchers) missiles carrying over 50 percent of the total strategic nuclear force load. More than half the nuclear-powered missile submarines are on continuous combat patrol in areas ensuring delivery of nuclear strikes at targets inside the Soviet Union from different directions.

Units of the strategic bomber force have 346 B-52 heavy bombers and 65 FB-111A medium bombers. The strategic bomber force is based in the continental United States and partly on Guam in the Pacific.

Apart from their basic purpose of delivering nuclear strikes the U.S. political-military leadership relies on strategic aircraft in other missions. They are being used in peacetime as an essential means of demonstrating force. For this purpose, B-52 bombers engage in regular flights, including flights with nuclear arms on board, to regions of U.S. "vital interests"—the Middle East, Western Europe, Australia and elsewhere.

The strategic defense forces of the United States consist of the manpower and equipment of the Army, Air Force and Navy operationally subordinated to the Aerospace Defense Command. These forces augment the potential of the strategic offensive forces, continuously inform the U.S. political-military leadership

2. REVIVAL OF THE COLD WAR

of the global aerospace situation and are intended for use in organizing strategic nuclear strikes.

The U.S. general-purpose forces include ground troops, the tactical Air Force and Navy (less nuclear-powered ballistic missile submarines). They are the chief component of the U.S. Armed Forces in overseas territories and are designed, even in peacetime, to secure the global political aims of the United States. The general-purpose forces are intended for independent operations or joint operations (with troops of U.S. allies) in land and ocean war theaters, for reinforcement of armed forces in overseas territories, for show of force and for use in crisis situations, the armed support of reactionary regimes and the suppression of the national liberation movement.

The ground forces have some 200 tactical missile launchers, 11,400 tanks, 12,000 field guns and mortars, including 155-mm and 203.2-mm nuclear-capable howitzers and 16,600 antitank guided missile launchers. They also have more than 5,000 anti-aircraft guns and some 8,600 Army planes and helicopters.

The general-purpose Air Force has more than 8,700 aircraft of different types.

The U.S. Navy has 848 warships and other vessels (including the Reserve), of which 386 are major warships, including 79 multipurpose nuclear submarines, 20 aircraft carriers (three nuclear-powered) and 287 other ships and over 5,000 planes and helicopters, of which more than half are combat aircraft.

Meeting the requirements of the officially adopted strategic "forward base" concept the main general-purpose groupings are, already in peacetime, deployed and maintained outside the territory of the United States of America.

The most powerful overseas group of U.S. general-purpose forces is stationed in Europe. Its total strength is 336,200 men, and it is armed with the latest offensive weaponry and other military hardware, has great firepower and is, along with the FRG Army, the main strike force of the Allied NATO Armed Forces spearheaded against the USSR and the other Warsaw Treaty countries.

The group in Western Europe accounts for nearly 30 percent of the personnel of the regular U.S. Army and has up to 150 tactical missile launchers (three-quarters of the U.S. total), 3,000 tanks, 2,500 field guns and mortars, more than 5,000 antitank guided missile launchers and over 1,000 helicopters.

The U.S. Air Force in Europe has some 850 aircraft, including 660 combat planes, of which two-thirds are nuclear-capable. Its more than 400 F-111 and F-4 fighter-bombers are medium-range aircraft and can deliver nuclear strikes against the entire territory of the European socialist countries and the western regions of the USSR.

The Pentagon is planning a considerable reinforcement of U.S. Armed Forces in the European zone with Army and tactical Air Force manpower and equipment stationed in the continental United States. To ensure the rapid buildup of the group, heavy equipment for four army divisions is prepositioned in Europe.

For combat in NATO's zone of responsibility, first of all the European zone, the U.S. Navy maintains its Sixth and Second fleets in the Mediterranean and Atlantic, consisting, all in all, of some 180 warships, including multipurpose aircraft carriers and up to 50 nuclear submarines and over 800 combat aircraft, of which at least 240 are carrier-based nuclear-capable attack aircraft that can reach the territory of the USSR.

More than 7,000 nuclear warheads are sited in Western Europe for use by the general-purpose forces. In addition, the Commander-in-Chief of U.S. Armed Forces in Europe has at his disposal a few hundred Poseidon C-3 strategic missile nuclear warheads.

The general-purpose group that is second in importance is deployed in the Pacific. It has a complement of 465,000 men, 140 warships and over 1,100 combat aircraft.

A considerable portion of this group is stationed in the Western Pacific, including South Korea and Japan, that is, in the immediate proximity of the Soviet Far East. A special role is assigned to the naval force, notably the Seventh Fleet. Reinforcement of the naval group in the western Pacific is provided for with forces of the Third Fleet.

A large U.S. naval force is deployed in the Indian Ocean. Its backbone consists of two carrier task forces (nearly 20 combat ships) of the Sixth and Seventh fleets. Up to 180 combat aircraft are based on the carriers, including 80 nuclear-capable attack planes. Reinforcement of this group is planned chiefly through shipment of the interventionist Rapid Deployment Forces to the Middle East region. To reduce the buildup time of the task force in the Indian Ocean zone, seven depot ships with heavy equipment for an expeditionary brigade of the marines are permanently berthed at Diego Garcia.

The U.S. Armed Forces in the zone of Central and South America are maintained to secure U.S. control over the Panama Canal, ensure the U.S. military presence and counteract any national liberation movement in this region.

The general-purpose forces in the continental USA are a strategic reserve intended chiefly to reinforce U.S. Armed Forces overseas, notably in Europe. The bulk of their manpower and equipment comes under the Readiness Command (RC), whose prime task is to organize rapid transportation of units and formations to overseas theaters of operations.

For purposes of direct armed intervention outside NATO's zone of responsibility, first of all the Middle East, the United States has activated a Rapid Deployment Force (RDF). Its total strength stands at 200,000 regulars and 100,000 reservists. The regular Army, Air

Force and Navy have assigned to the RDF 4 divisions, several separate brigades and special-purpose and logistical ground units; 5 tactical air wings (some 350 combat planes), 28 strategic bombers, airborne command posts, tanker-aircraft, reconnaissance and AWACS planes of the USAF; and 2 or 3 carrier task forces, 3 expeditionary marine brigades, and an air wing of the U.S. Navy.

To secure the "world leadership" claims publicly voiced by Defense Secretary Caspar Weinberger, the United States devotes special attention to the development of strategic mobility forces ensuring movement of troops from its continental part to any region of the globe that it may declare a sphere of its "vital interests."

The strategic mobility forces come under the USAF Military Airlift Command (MAC) and the U.S. Navy's Military Sealift Command.

The MAC has some 1,000 planes and helicopters of various types, including more than 600 heavy and medium military transport planes. Provisions have also been made to use over 400 reserve aircraft of civil airlines, including 340 of the latest transport and passenger planes and 350 military transport planes of the USAF Reserve for troop airlifts.

The centralized global system of command and control consists of something like 130 top-level government and military agencies. It is called upon to ensure reliable and uninterrupted command and control of armed forces in both a protracted war, including one with massive use of strategic nuclear arms and military operations on a smaller scale.

(A map in the book shows the number and location of major U.S. military bases on foreign territories and also the number of national military bases, airfields and ports used by U.S. Armed Forces).

U.S. military installations overseas include large-scale air and naval bases, Army and Marine garrisons, positions of tactical and surface-to-air missiles, ground weapons, ammunition and other supplies, aerospace observation posts, shore-based sonars, radio interception posts, communications centers and other diverse installations.

At present, the United States has more than 1,500 military bases and installations on the territory of 32 countries. More than half a million U.S. servicemen are stationed there permanently.

The greater number of U.S. military bases are located in the immediate proximity of the Soviet Union and the other countries of the socialist community, first of all in Western Europe. In the FRG alone, whose territory the Pentagon regards as a military springboard against the Warsaw Treaty countries, there are nearly 200 large-scale military installations. Something like 60 U.S. military installations, including seven large bases, are located in Turkey, which borders on the Soviet Union. The Pentagon has cast Turkey as a staging area for military operations against the Soviet Union in Transcaucasia and the socialist countries in the Balkans

and, indeed, as a transit base for Rapid Deployment Forces routed to the Middle East.

Large U.S. allocations and funds out of the joint NATO infrastructure program are being made available for the construction of new bases in connection with the planned stationing in Europe of new weapons systems (ground-launched cruise missiles, Pershing II ballistic missiles and others), and for expanding facilities for the reception of additional large contingents of ground forces, marines and aircraft from the United States.

The authors of the book show how, throughout the postwar period, the United States has been building up its strategic nuclear potential, especially strategic offensive forces, rapidly developing the general-purpose forces, chiefly the nuclear theater weapons, and, steadily and in contravention of international treaties and agreements, producing and stockpiling new weapons of mass destruction to people and other living things.

In early October 1981, President Reagan announced his "strategic program" for the 80s, containing provisions for a further buildup of the strategic nuclear potential. For 1982-1987 alone, the White House estimates expenditure under the program at 222 billion dollars.

A special place in Reagan's "strategic program" is accorded to a plan for deploying MX intercontinental ballistic missiles. The MX, now in its final stage of development, is designed as a first-strike weapon. It will have ten warheads of 600 kilotons each.

Having confirmed earlier construction plans for Ohio-class SSBNS, the Reagan Administration authorized as obligatory a program for building and deploying from 1989 on a new submarine-launched ballistic missile, Trident II (D-5), considerably more powerful and effective than the Trident I. According to the tactical and technical specifications of the U.S. Defense Department, the missile will have practically the same combat capability as the MX ICBM, that is, it will be a first-strike weapon.

In addition to the earlier planned 172 B-52G bombers, Reagan's "comprehensive" program also provides for fitting out B-52H bombers (there are 96 such aircraft in the USAF SAC) with ALCM-B cruise missiles.

The earlier rejected plans of building B-1 bombers have been readopted, this time on a qualitatively new level. A new B-1B carrier of cruise missiles is to be developed on the basis of the B-1 and will be put in service with the strategic air force in 1986. Before 1988, in addition to B-52 bombers, it is planned to build and put in service 100 such aircraft, each capable of lifting up to 30 cruise missiles.

At the same time, it is planned to develop a fundamentally new strategic bomber called Stealth, an aircraft which, as conceived by the Pentagon, will not be detectable by the existing air defense means. Hence, it is usable for surprise strikes.

On completing the deployment of air-launched cruise missiles, the new strategic bombers, the MX ICBMs,

2. REVIVAL OF THE COLD WAR

and the Trident system of SSBNS and SLBMs, the Pentagon will have raised the total deliverable number of strategic nuclear weapons in one launch by at least 50 percent in just this decade.

As part of the buildup of general-purpose forces, the U.S. military leadership attaches great importance to expending the so-called theater nuclear forces, especially in Europe. Ever since 1960, the delivery vehicles and nuclear ordnance of the U.S. Armed Forces deployed in Europe have undergone substantial qualitative change. Their range, accuracy and kill effectiveness have been heightened.

The nuclear-capable artillery of U.S. forces in Europe has been substantially modernized. At present, all 155-mm and 203.2-mm artillery pieces can fire nuclear shells. Their range has gone up from 15 to 30 kilometers. From 1983 on, it is planned to begin siting new U.S. medium-range nuclear systems (108 Pershing II missile launchers and 464 ground-launched cruise missiles) in Western Europe. They are to be deployed in Great Britain (160 cruise missiles), the FRG (108 Pershing II launchers and 96 cruise missiles), Italy (112 cruise missiles), Belgium and the Netherlands (48 cruise missiles each).

Mass production of neutron weapons started in 1981 in accordance with President Reagan's decision. The neutron munitions for the Lance missiles and 203.2-mm howitzers are designed for use outside the United States, first and foremost in Europe. The placing of these weapons in Europe or any other region will considerably lower the so-called nuclear threshold and will increase the probability of nuclear war. Moreover the neutron weapon is in itself an offensive rather than defensive weapon (though the Pentagon is trying to prove the opposite to the layman), since it is designed to destroy personnel in shelters and permits offensive operations immediately after its use.

The plans and practical measures taken by the USA for building up the nuclear capability of general-purpose forces and above all the medium-range nuclear weapons in Western Europe, aim at changing the existing balance of forces in favor of the United States, preparing the material basis for a "limited" nuclear war in Europe and thus averting the danger of nuclear retaliation against the United States.

The building, training and technical equipment of the Army is oriented to preparing it for operations outside the United States. It is trained and equipped for offensive operations with nuclear and chemical weapons.

The American command envisages a number of organizational and technical measures to enhance the combat readiness and mobility of tactical air units so that by 1986 up to 80 tactical fighter squadrons (up to 1,900 planes) can be moved from the USA to Europe within 10 days.

U.S. military leaders attach great importance to raising the capability of the Navy, which is assigned a special role not only in war but in carrying out their global policies, as an instrument for demonstrating force and direct military intervention.

The program for the present decade envisages raising the number of ships in the regular Navy to a total of 600 (not counting the considerable number of vessels kept in mothballs).

In addition to the massive equipment of the armed forces with nuclear weapons, the U.S. military and political leadership devote ever greater attention to developing, improving, deploying and stockpiling other mass destruction weapons for use against man and living nature in general.

With the coming to power of the Reagan Administration the U.S. Armed Forces have intensified direct preparations for chemical and biological warfare. The Joint Chiefs of Staff are planning to have at their disposal five million units of chemical munitions. Chemical weapons are stored not only in the United States, but also in other countries: There are more than 2,000 tons of American toxic agents in the FRG alone.

The authors of the book analyze in detail how the policy of achieving military superiority is finding expression in the steady expansion of the scale of financing U.S. militarist preparations.

During the past 20 years (1960-1980) U.S. military spending under the national defense program has tripled—from 45 to 135 billion dollars. An even sharper increase in military spending is planned for the 80s. In the period between 1981 and 1985 alone, expenditures on war preparations will increase by more than 120 percent, reaching 303.9 billion dollars a year by the end of 1985. Average annual rates of increase in military spending in the first half of the present decade will be higher than at the peak of U.S. aggression in Southeast Asia. Allocations for the national defense program in fiscal 1986 are earmarked at 342.7 billion dollars.

The book cites data about the exports of American arms and military equipment to other countries and also information on the industrial base of U.S. militarism. This data indicates that the USA is the biggest exporter of military hardware and that the U.S. military-industrial complex plays a decisive role in planning military, political and economic measures, working out military strategy and concepts, drafting programs for building the armed forces and developing new weapons systems.

During the past 10 years U.S. arms exports more than quadrupled to a total of 17.5 billion dollars in 1980.

The U.S. share in world sales of arms and military equipment is 45 percent; that of the other NATO countries is over 20 percent.

Between 1950 and 1980 the USA exported overseas: 26,800 planes and helicopters; 32,300 tanks; about 50,000 APCs and armored cars; 31,900 warships and other craft; 29,700 field and antitank artillery pieces; around 240,000 missiles of various types.

All in all the USA exported weapons and materiel in 1970 to 131 countries to the tune of 4.33 billion dollars, and in 1980 to 126 countries to the tune of 17.5 billion dollars. Between 1971 and 1980 the USA delivered weapons and materiel worth 123.5 billion dollars to other countries.

Twenty-five thousand contractors and more than 50,000 subcontractors are engaged in fulfilling the Pentagon's orders. The principal weapons and equipment systems are manufactured at 146 state-owned plants and some 4,000 major enterprises owned by private firms.

In fiscal year 1980, the Pentagon placed contracts with various branches of the economy for over 83 billion dollars' worth of arms, military equipment and other military supplies. Nearly half of this sum will go to the 25 biggest arms and materiel manufacturers, including the McDonnel Douglas, United Technologies, General Dynamics, Boeing and General Electric corporations, which specialize mainly in producing offensive systems such as nuclear missiles, aircraft armaments and nuclear-powered ships.

To meet the needs of its own armed forces and its export commitments to other countries, the U.S. war industry is manufacturing several hundred types of weapons, including 47 basic systems at a total cost of over 310 billion dollars (in 1974, 40 basic systems costing 150 billion dollars).

Simultaneously, the Reagan Administration has decided on a drastic reappraisal of its policy for preparing a rapid switchover of the arms industry to a war footing. Its aim is to raise the capacity of the war industry to such an extent that it should be able to mass-produce armaments, with nearly a half of the gross national product allocated for military requirements.

The book analyzes the USA's present military strategy, which is overtly aggressive and which provides for the United States using military might as a tool to assert worldwide dictation by U.S. imperialism and safeguard Americans' "vital interests" in various areas of the world, including access to sources of strategic raw materials and energy resources. This strategy incorporates all the provisions of the notorious Presidential Directive 59.

The U.S. military strategy embodied in multi-scenario plans for waging aggressive wars to satisfy the global aspirations of U.S. imperialism and the large-scale preparations of material facilities for war, including one with unlimited use of nuclear weapons, are a danger to peace and are pushing humankind to the brink of catastrophe.

The East-West Military Balance

The first paragraph from the third section of the book says: "One indisputable fact must first be emphasized:

An approximate military balance has arisen and is being steadily maintained between the USSR and the USA and between the Warsaw Treaty and NATO, both in the world at large and in Europe, where the most powerful concentrations of armed forces confront each other. This plain fact has been stressed on many occasions by the most authoritative Soviet leaders."

This section also deals in detail with the balance of the strategic nuclear weapons of the USSR and the USA, the balance of the medium-range nuclear systems in Europe and the balance of the general-purpose forces of NATO and the Warsaw Treaty. Significant data is also given there on the naval forces of NATO and the Warsaw Treaty.

Appraising the Soviet Navy, the Pentagon leaders claim that: "The Soviet Navy has been transformed from a basically coastal defense force into an ocean-going force designed to extend the military capability of the USSR well out to sea."

During the past two decades the USSR has undoubtedly improved the technical equipment and combat capability of its navy. But the U.S. Navy has not marked time either and has continued to increase its combat potential.

The strike forces are the chief component of the U.S. and NATO navies. They have 25 aircraft carriers and air-capable ships (including 20 of the USA), whereas the Soviet Navy has only 2 air-capable ships designed principally for antisubmarine warfare.

Thus the objective facts show: In all cases—in strategic nuclear weapons, medium-range nuclear weapons in Europe or conventional forces of NATO and the Warsaw Treaty—there is approximate parity between the sides. Neither the United States nor NATO has ever "lagged behind." There is parity and it exists in practice, not on paper. The United States has no need to "rearm" because it has never lagged behind the USSR. Rearmament under the pretext of achieving parity is, in effect, a desire to achieve military superiority.

Two Trends in World Politics

This section of the book contains facts illustrating the approach of the governments of the USSR and the USA to the treaties they signed and to the arms control and reduction negotiations.

The authors of the book write that in recent years two opposite trends have stood out more and more sharply in the approach of the United States and that of the Soviet Union to the solution of international problems. The determining line in the Soviet Union's foreign policy always was and still is the struggle for peace and security of the nations, for detente and curbing the arms race.

United States policy is going the other way. Instead of seeking agreement on the basis of equality and equal security, it gives priority to achieving military superiority. Instead of curbing the arms race, it talks about rearmament and development of new, still more powerful mass destruction weapons.

The Soviet Union, on the other hand, prompted by its desire to ease tensions in international relations and ensure that they follow the road of detente and cooperation, in its desire to curb the arms race and lessen the danger of a nuclear war, is countering the militarist efforts of Western reactionary circles with a balanced, restrained and confident approach to the solution of international problems by negotiation and by a search for mutually acceptable agreements. This policy is not prompted by considerations of momentary advantage. It is a built-in feature of socialism, which is fundamentally opposed to any policy of expansion and recourse to war or the threat of force as an instrument of foreign policy, to interference in the affairs of other nations and to imposing one's will on them.

It has been universally acknowledged that the Soviet Union and the United States, like the countries of Europe belonging to the opposite military alliances, are at a point of relative equilibrium in military capability, and this is confirmed by the aggregate of facts and figures on the armaments and armed forces of the two sides. This equilibrium is objectively a factor stabilizing the international situation and was, indeed, the starting point in the relaxation of tensions.

It is more than obvious that in the present conditions no one will succeed in upsetting the existing military-strategic equilibrium and winning superiority.

We, in the Soviet Union, would like to hope that those who formulate U.S. policy take a more realistic approach. Unrestrained intimidation of peoples with the spurious "Soviet military threat" is no longer effective. People in the West will be able to see for themselves where the threat to peace really comes from.

CHANGING OF THE GUARD

ADAM B. ULAM

Adam B. Ulam is Gurney Professor of History and Political Science at Harvard University, where he is also director of the Russian Research Center. Mr. Ulam's Dangerous Relations: The Soviet Union In World Politics, 1970-1982, *was published by Oxford University Press.*

"**I** MUST NOT die now. It would be the greatest mistake I ever made," the first Lord Rothschild was reputed to have observed when, following the outbreak of World War I, British inheritance and income taxes were substantially increased. Similar sentiments must have agitated Leonid Brezhnev during his last months. His longtime closest friend and collaborator, Konstantin Chernenko, was being challenged for the role of heir apparent, and several members of the ruling oligarchy evidently decided that their ailing chief should not be allowed to appoint his successor. It was a clear indication that Brezhnev's grip on the main instruments of power was becoming shaky when, after the death of Mikhail Suslov early in 1982, his place on the Central Committee Secretariat was filled by Yuri Andropov—who, in view of his longstanding membership in the Politburo (since 1973) and his relative youth (67 years old then, 68 now), immediately became a contender for its highest post.

Two years ago, after the resignation of Prime Minister Alexei Kosygin, Brezhnev still had the clout to guarantee that the new occupant of the post, traditionally the second most important in the Soviet Union, would not be a contender for the top job. He did this by the simple expedient of arranging the appointment of the 75-year-old Nikolai Pikhonov, a relatively marginal figure. And so toward the end there were just four oligarchs in the running, those who combined full membership in the Politburo with a Party secretaryship. Of the four, Andrei Kirilenko was older than Brezhnev and even more ill, and Mikhail Gorbachev's extreme youth— he is 51—was bound to make him unacceptable to his septuagenarian colleagues. Quite possibly Brezhnev contemplated, just before his demise, some maneuvers and personnel changes that would have

offset the influence of Andropov and strengthened that of Chernenko. But before any such schemes could be put into operation, Brezhnev died, and the Politburo hastened to choose Andropov over his rival.

Brezhnev had other reasons to cling desperately to his post, despite his increasingly obvious physical infirmity. Change of leadership in the Soviet Union, no matter how smooth the process of transition appears to be, is bound to send tremors throughout the entire structure of the Party and society. Political power in the Soviet system is exercised in a conspiratorial as well as an authoritarian manner. Normally, some twenty-odd people—full and alternate members of the Politburo, plus perhaps a few of the highest military officials—are the only ones who know what the regime's real goals and fears are, how it actually views the dangers of a nuclear war, the current state of the Soviet economy, the country's future relations with China and the United States, and so on.

The secrecy of the decision-making process, which gives the impression of unanimity and self-assurance on the part of the rulers, is rightly prized by the regime as one of its strongest assets in dealing with foreign and domestic problems. In foreign affairs, it keeps the Soviet Union's rivals from clearly discerning what is bluff and what is seriously meant by those ritualistic threats the Kremlin is prone to issue in just about any international crisis: "The gravest possible consequences will follow unless. . . ." In domestic politics, the aura of awe and iron resolve surrounding the Soviet Olympus inhibits such groups as the military or the industrial managers from developing any idea of challenging the Party's domination, and contributes to the average citizen's feeling that it is not only dangerous but useless to voice his grievances or indulge in fantasies about alternative political systems.

Any change in the Soviet Union's top leadership is bound to affect this picture. The curtain of secrecy surrounding the Kremlin is, if only momentarily and slightly, lifted. The world sees that behind that curtain are not demigods, but quite ordinary politicians, fearful of each other, of their own people, and of what might happen in the outside world. The rhetoric of the new leaders bespeaks such fears. They protest too much: let no one think that the terrible loss suffered by the Soviet people can affect their unity and loyalty, or swerve the government and the Party from the path laid down by Lenin; let our foreign ill-wishers rest under no illusion that our loss has made us any less resolute or capable of defending the honor and interests of the Soviet Union, as well as those of socialism and national liberation, etc., etc.

For all such reassurances, the disappearance of the leader, the man built up for years by official propaganda into a paragon of political wisdom and iron determination, has made the ruling group as a whole feel less secure and more nervous. To be sure, with Soviet politics now on a more orderly course, Brezhnev's death, unlike Stalin's, did not throw the ruling elite into a veritable panic. A student of Party history, however, could not miss some unconventional features attending the enthronement of Andropov as General Secretary. According to custom, the meeting of the Central Committee to approve formally the decision of the Politburo should have been open, and it should have been presided over by someone other than the nominee—normally by the senior man with the title of Party secretary. Yet it was Andropov himself who unabashedly took the chair. And it was the defeated rival, Chernenko, who placed Andropov's name in nomination. After describing Andropov—with perhaps conscious irony—as Brezhnev's "closet associate," Chernenko stressed that from now on it will be especially important that the leadership be exercised collectively. Well, such assurances have been given by each successive leader, starting with Stalin. Yet experience has shown that these assurances have usually run against what might be called the logic of the Soviet system. Those who could not impose their domination over the Politburo, like Georgi Malenkov (or Khrushchev during his last two years in power) bit the dust. But by 1970 Brezhnev had managed to elbow aside his Politburo rivals and to start quite a "personality cult" of his own.

The somewhat unusual procedure that was followed in the election of Andropov forcibly suggests that the Politburo intended to convey two messages to the Central Committee and the Soviet establishment in general. First, the Politburo was saying that this time leadership will in fact remain collective in character, with the new incumbent prevented from building up his personal power in the way Brezhnev managed to do (a point strengthened by the fact that Andropov is eleven years older than Brezhnev was when he assumed the office of the General Secretary). And second, by stressing *its* collective rule insofar as decision-making was concerned, the Politburo seemed to convey a warning that it would not tolerate a repetition of the situation that had arisen occasionally under Khrushchev, when the Central Committee as a whole was called upon to resolve a conflict within the top elite. In brief, the oligarchs do not propose to acquiesce to a personal dictatorship or

anything close to it, nor to permit those scandalous practices of 1956-1964, when hundreds of Central Committee members—and, toward the end, even some outsiders—became privy to the inner workings of the Party and state apparatus.

Whether and to what extent these desiderata of the current leaders will prevail is another matter. Given his age, Andropov cannot afford to move slowly if he wants to establish clear authority over the Party and the government rather than simply remain first among equals. But it is only the first phase of succession that has ended. There are at least three vacancies to be filled on the Politburo, and one on the Secretariat.

A clue to Andropov's disposition and skill in political infighting will come with the filling of Brezhnev's other job, that of the Chairman of the Presidium of the Supreme Soviet (i.e., head of state), a position which by itself is mostly ceremonial in nature, but which is of some political importance when held by a top Party leader. In 1967 Brezhnev succeeded in removing Nikolai Podgorny, a potential rival, from the Central Committee Secretariat by foisting the Presidency on him. Will Andropov try the same maneuver vis-à-vis Chernenko? Will the General Secretary attempt to solidify his position by something that undoubtedly would be very popular with broader Party circles if not with his present colleagues: a kind of youth movement, bringing into the Politburo, the Secretariat, and the Council of Ministers some youngsters in their 50s or even their 40s? We probably will not see or hear of such maneuverings for some time, but they may already be going on. It is only when new appointments and resignations are announced that we shall be able to gauge the strength of the new General Secretary's position.

What of the man himself? The veil of secrecy covers not only the operations of the Politburo as a whole, but also the political personality of its members—until they reach the summit. Who in the 1930s or 1940s would have envisioned Nikita Khrushchev, then a faithful executor of Stalin's policies, as a future reformer and a man given to impulsive political improvisation and pyrotechnics? Similarly, it is only now that the real Andropov is likely to emerge from behind the notoriety of his fifteen years' stint as head of the K.G.B., and from behind his more recent—and, one suspects, somewhat contrived—image as a man of cosmopolitan tastes who is not unfriendly to the capitalist West. In post-Stalin Russia, Andropov's K.G.B. past is bound to create some ever-so-slight embarrassment. Since Andropov's elevation to a secretaryship last May, Soviet travelers have taken pains to assure their hosts that he was not "a real" K.G.B. man, but had been delegated by the Party to supervise the secret police and prevent it from abusing its powers. Still, the leadership of the secret police is hardly a job to be given to, and held for so long by, a highly sensitive or squeamish individual.

AS TO ANDROPOV'S cosmopolitan image, it is fair to say that it is highly improbable that a liberal, "closet" or any other variety, could survive for long in the highest echelons of the Soviet hierarchy. Plainly, though, the new leader must be a man of great intelligence and political acumen. None of his predecessors as police chief had held that highly ticklish assignment for so many years. Only two went on to higher things, and not for long: Lavrenti Beria was shot, and Aleksandr Shelepin, after a period of political prominence, was dismissed from the Politburo. And so Yuri Vladimirovich had to be quite an agile politician to have made it to the very top of the slippery political pyramid from a position that in the past had eventually led, if not to a firing squad, then to political oblivion. Being an intelligent man, Andropov must realize that the regime cannot continue as it has, during the latter part of Brezhnev's reign, to sweep the most urgent domestic problems under the rug. If allowed by his senior colleagues, he will undoubtedly attempt to shake up the Party and state bureaucracy, and to impart new dynamism to the Soviet economy, now dangerously close to stagnation. Perhaps he will try to compensate for his background by some liberal-sounding pronouncements and gestures. (One remembers how Beria, after Stalin's death, made his short-lived bid for power by becoming a fervent proponent of "socialist legality.") But Andropov would not have been selected in the first place had his associates thought him inclined to tamper with the fundamental elements of the system.

BREZHNEV'S DEATH, the Kremlin must feel, was also particularly inopportune from the point of view of Soviet foreign policy interests. Again, no matter how strenuous Moscow's warnings that the U.S.S.R.'s position in world affairs has in no way been affected by the event, the changing of the guard is bound to create a feeling of uncertainty and apprehension among the Soviets' friends, and bring fresh hope to their antagonists. It is no accident that the Warsaw regime decided to release Lech Walesa after it received the news of Brezhnev's death. All over Eastern Europe the Communist satraps must be wondering whether their new boss will be as solicitous of their interests as the old one, and whether their people, counting on uncertainty and disarray in the Kremlin, might now give vent to their long-suppressed longings.

As for the main lines of Soviet foreign policy, it would be foolish to expect that the new leadership (or, to be more precise, up to now the new leader) will initiate basic changes in such areas as the Soviet Union's attitude toward the United States, China, and its own arms program. From the point of view of the Soviet oligarchy, Brezhnev's foreign policy must have been seen as the most successful aspect of his reign. It helped widen the breach between the West and its European allies, it expanded Soviet influence to new areas in the third world, and, toward the end, it made considerable progress papering over the dispute between the U.S.S.R. and China. Eschewing Khrushchev's missile-rattling while expanding Moscow's prodigious nuclear arsenal, Brezhnev succeeded in convincing most of the world (including many in the U.S.) that it was not the Soviet Union but America that has been the chief villain in the arms race.

And yet, on Brezhnev's foreign policies, as on his domestic policies, the future historian's verdict might well be that he failed to tackle the most serious problems and thus left a particularly heavy burden for his successor. Has the Soviet Union over-committed itself by trying to subvert and replace the influence of the West in practically every part of the world? Can Moscow reach a real rather than a superficial reconciliation with Peking if it does not constrain its imperialist striving in Southeast Asia, Afghanistan, and elsewhere? And if a genuine Sino-Soviet detente is possible, can the U.S.S.R. afford to wait until China becomes a major industrial and hence nuclear power, as it is bound to become in time? How long can the present pattern of Soviet domination over East Europe endure, with the Red Army being the sole guarantor of Communist rule over some 110 million people, the great majority of whom detest their regimes? Will the ailing economy be able to bear indefinitely the heavy burden of increasing outlays of expenditures and resources that go for armaments?

For the immediate future we may take the new leadership at its word: it will try to continue the foreign policies of its predecessor. To do otherwise would be, in its opinion, a sign of weakness and vacillation that would be noticed both in the Pentagon and in Poland. But in the longer run, the pressures and constraints of the still unfolding process of succession might well force Andropov and company to alter their tactics. At the same time, as long as the present oligarco-bureaucratic system endures, it is unwise to expect Russia's rulers to change their basic philosophy of international relations. And so the West would be foolish to hope that its own burdens could be lifted by some miraculous change of heart on the part of the current and any future prospective leaders of the Soviet Union.

Reagan's Foreign Policy: New Dangers

Roy Bennett

ROY BENNETT is the U.S. correspondent for the London Tribune *and associate editor of* Social Policy.

In his election campaign President Reagan pledged to wage an unremitting hard-line confrontation crusade against the Soviet Union. He kept his promise to the point of overkill.

The Administration's attack was cacophonous. In the supercharged atmosphere created by Iran and Afghanistan, and coincident with the waves of Solidarity strikes in Poland, the President and his aides unleashed a cold-war barrage not seen since the most acute days following World War II.

In the first 12 months of Reagan's Administration three different periods unfolded. The first dramatized an alleged huge Soviet military arms build-up; projected an unprecedented image of America's military vulnerability; and obtained passage of the spectacular record-breaking five-year, 1.5 trillion dollar arms budget. The second unveiled the American plan to deploy new nuclear missiles in Europe; witnessed a European peace movement explosion; and, paradoxically, saw the opening of formal talks with the Soviet Union on limitation of European theater nuclear weapons. The third began clamorously late in December with the Polish government's imposition of martial law; the outlawing of Solidarity; and the unilateral imposing of sanctions on the U.S.S.R. by the United States.

The President personally took the lead in his very first press conference, setting the tone for the ideological drive that was to color the year. In coarse, undiplomatic language he denounced Soviet leaders as willing to "commit any crime, to lie and cheat," as people who would do anything to conquer the world, and vowed to punish them for their evil deeds.[1]

Echoing the President, his aides trailed only a step behind. Alexander Haig, in a Senate confirmation hearing, charged that growing Russian military prowess could "eventually paralyze Western policy altogether" and portentously warned, "There are more important things than maintaining peace."[2] Even lesser officials joined in. A national security adviser, Richard Pipes, for example, was quoted in a rather startling statement warning the Soviets that they must consider changing their policies or face World War III.[3]

The concerted campaign continued without letup even during the period of the President's recovery from an attempted assassination. Defense Secretary Weinberger took control of the campaign after then Secretary of State Haig had clumsily and unconstitutionally attempted to establish himself as second in command. On April 4 Weinberger characterized the Polish situation as "serious";[4] on April 7 he warned that "invasion by osmosis" was taking place with Soviet forces "filtering" into Poland;[5] on April 8 he charged the Soviets with continuing their arms buildup,[6] and on April 12 stated that in the event of a Russian invasion, the United States would supply arms to China.[7]

Upon returning to the White House, the President lifted the 15-month embargo on grain shipments to the U.S.S.R. that was established after the Afghanistan invasion. This appeared a contradictory act, but in reality was forced by the fierce pressure he had been under from the farm lobby, who vigorously objected to being the main economic group sacrificed to the cold war.

The President, however, rejoined the drumfire campaign in May. In a major address at Notre Dame's commencement, he stated that the West will not contain communism but "transcend it" as a "sad, bizarre chapter in human history whose last pages are being written."[8] Late in the month, the Soviets responded by attacking the Notre Dame speech as "alarmist and warlike."

However, from the beginning of the President's term, the Russians' counterpropaganda stressed the need for negotiation. Rather than match the United States in polemics, they uncharacteristically and repeatedly underlined the desirability of negotiations and a summit between Brezhnev and Reagan.

Stanley Hoffman saw the Soviets' behavior in this period as "relatively prudent." They were skillful, and evidently concerned to reassure the Islamic world after Afghanistan and not tempt Washington to move from rhetoric to action.[9] The approach worked. It appeared that the Russians, merely by exercising caution, were winning the propaganda battle. Washington was seen as overreaching, at least in contrast to the relative calm in Moscow.

The Administration opened the second phase with the announcement of their decision to produce the neutron bomb and to deploy in 1983 the medium-range theater nuclear missiles—Pershing II's and Cruise missiles—in Germany, Great Britain, Belgium, the Netherlands, and Italy. These, the Administration charged, were to counter the new Russian SS medium-range mobile missiles, the SS 20s, already

From *Social Policy,* Summer 1982. Social Policy published by Social Policy Corporation, New York, New York 10036.

partly deployed. In 1979 NATO, in a "two-track" decision, had agreed to accept the Pershings and Cruises subject to prior negotiation with the Russians to limit the deployment of all theater missiles.

An explosive reaction took place in Europe. The moribund peace movement burst into life. The six months of cold-war campaigning and the popular revulsion to the neutron bomb—a weapon seemingly uniquely designed to destroy people but not property—fanned an unprecedented campaign. All over Western Europe huge demonstrations flared, in Bonn (300,000), London (250,000), Brussels (300,000), Madrid (400,000), and in Paris and Rome. In all, a survey in *Newsweek* estimated, several million people had demonstrated or marched by the end of November.[10]

Against this background, President Reagan made a most remarkably inappropriate diplomatic blunder at a Washington press conference, which blew the lid off the European missile controversy. Asked if he thought an exchange of nuclear weapons between the United States and the Soviet Union would be limited, or if escalation was inevitable, he replied, "I could see where you could have the exchange of tactical weapons in the field without it bringing either one of the major powers to pushing the button."[11]

This was precisely what the Europeans had feared. Their response was not only a reaction against the presidential slip, it was a backlash against the missile policy as a whole.

Under enormous popular antinuclear pressure, the President decided to make his first major foreign-policy address on medium-range nuclear missiles in Europe just before the planned Geneva negotiations with the Soviet Union. He was also reacting to a startlingly friendly meeting between Brezhnev and Chancellor Schmidt of West Germany, just prior to his address. In it the Russians established Schmidt as an acceptable mediator between Moscow and Washington. The extremely cordial meeting marked a new stage in Moscow-Bonn relations.

In his address President Reagan unveiled his view of a "zero option": withdrawal and dismantling of all SS 20s in exchange for the United States' canceling deployment of Pershings and Cruises. There was no mention of America's "forward-based" nuclear weapons, the Russians' *bête noir*. Although it appeared his proposal would be unacceptable to the Russians, the President did not employ the bellicose tone characteristic of his earlier period.

The Geneva negotiations opened, and for a brief moment there emerged a feeling of relaxation in the year-long cold war.

However, the third period in foreign policy began with an explosion. The timid shoots of a nascent détente were shattered. Polish authorities declared martial law in the middle of December, opening a new, heightened phase in the cold war.

The development caught the West, especially the United States, by surprise. After predicting a Soviet invasion for most of the year and after dismissing the possibility of Polish use of force because of the unreliability of Polish armed forces, the unexpected happened. Moreover, by any standard the army-militia take-over was accomplished with apparent ease. Although some 5,000 people were interned, actual clashes and deaths—so far as it could be ascertained—were minimal.

The Administration's reaction was electric and unilateral. Interpreting the Polish government's action as if it had been the predicted Soviet invasion, Washington imposed a series of economic sanctions against the Soviet Union. These sanctions quickly came under fierce criticism from Administration hawks as "soft" and "ineffective." It was true that they were less than fatal. They banned high-technology exports when American exports of this type had disappeared years ago; they postponed grain talks until 1983, but did not embargo current shipments; and they made a number of nuisance restrictions, such as banning Russian plane landing rights in the United States and limiting use of U.S. ports.

Washington's reluctance to cut off all future credits to Poland and its refusal to discuss a rollover of current debts, as well as its hesitation to clamp a solid embargo on all grain shipments to the Soviets, had a rational basis. Grain is available to the Soviet Union from a number of other countries. An embargo would be a very serious blow to American farmers in a year when bumper crops have markedly lowered prices. The political connotation in a bi-election year is obvious.

A credit embargo would have been highly unwelcome to European governments and banks, which hold most of the Polish debt and are in the process of working out a solution to prevent default. West Germany in particular, but Europe in general, made clear they would not go along with the American sanctions policy. After almost a month of arm-twisting, the NATO Council agreed only to criticize the Soviet Union. This created the most serious split that has taken place between Europe and the United States in years.

Of course much more than Polish martial law was involved. But before considering the larger meaning of this new, unexpected inter-Western conflict, it would be useful to look at some aspects of the origin of U.S. foreign policy and consider their current application.

DEFINING U.S. FOREIGN POLICY

Out of these wide-ranging events of 1981, three major strands of U.S. policy emerge:

- Assertion of a "new containment" of the Soviet Union.
- Achievement of military superiority.
- Management and control of the superpower balance of power.

Containment

It has been the U.S. position since 1945 that the Soviet system by its inherent nature has to expand to survive, and that an effective policy of quarantine would in consequence lead to its "breakup" or "mellowing." (This, of course, compares with Lenin's description of imperialism, which, he charged, likewise had to expand to survive.)

The old containment aimed at preventing a Russian thrust into Western Europe. Europeans, however, have never shared this fear and remain unconcerned—to Washington's dismay—to this day. The new containment has been most visible in the assertion of American vital interests in ever-widening areas of the globe, but more particularly up to the borders of the Soviet Union. The claim of vital interest has extended to the Soviet bloc's Western borders; to the Persian Gulf and Turkey and, until recently, Iran to Russia's south; and to Russia's Eastern borders in the United States' quasi alliance with the Peoples' Republic of China.

2. REVIVAL OF THE COLD WAR

While the new containment aims to demonstrate the power of American global reach, the reality of geography proves its weakness. The Soviets are from ten to a few hundred miles from most contested areas; America is 5,000 or more miles away. And the "Rapid Deployment Force"—neither a force nor rapid—is more rhetorical than real.

The exaggerated reaction to the Afghanistan invasion—of negligible importance to the West in strategic or political terms—resulted more from the dramatic image of American power totally at bay than from the claimed threat to the Persian Gulf and the Indian Ocean.

In sum, the assertion of this new containment is, in reality, a defensive response to the national humiliation of Vietnam and Iran, and to America's frustrating inability to have a material effect on the Afghanistan or Polish situations.

Superiority

Paradoxically, the Administration's graphic and mythological claim of military weakness, enshrined in Pentagonese as a "window of vulnerability," contrasts with its boastful objective of superiority. The dubious campaign—against a nonexistent military imbalance—was necessary, in the short term, to secure passage of the proposed massive escalation in the military budget. Ironically, the talk of military weakness required that Defense Secretary Weinberger, among others, assure the country that America's objective was still military superiority.

Thus, on August 14, he presented publicly a plan that he said guaranteed superiority by the end of the decade.[12] This superiority objective came under fire at a Senate Foreign Relations Committee hearing. Senator Glenn of Ohio charged, "The new Administration . . . would opt for superiority rather than parity . . . . They have indicated an unwillingness to continue with the SALT talks until some new level of superiority is achieved." Paul Warnke, former chief SALT negotiator, outlined the absurdity of escalating the arms race: "History shows that if we continue to raise the number of forces . . . the Soviets will do the same thing, and we will again have parity . . . but at a higher level of cost and risk."[13]

At the end of the year ambiguity on strategic policy surfaced. The President let it be known that, on principle, he had no objections to a Summit meeting and a possible resumption of talks on a new SALT. Since SALT's purpose is parity, it became difficult to square Weinberger's (and his supporters') continuing campaign for superiority and the President and Secretary of State Haig's tentative approval of negotiations on arms limitations. It suggests that the President and his Secretary of State were more conscious of America's critical allies and the continuing popularity of the policy of negotiations than the Defense Secretary.

The Balance of Power

Spheres of influence and balance of power are not unknown to American policy. The late Hans J. Morganthau wrote extensively on the subject.[14] F.S. Northedge, in *Foreign Policy of the Powers*,[15] saw historical American foreign policy this way: "The pattern has consisted, first, of an assertion of U.S. dominance in the Western Hemisphere comprising North and South America, the Caribbean, and the Pacific as far as Hawaii. Further, it has been traditional American policy to support a general balance of power in Europe in order to prevent any one superpower there which would be capable of exercising a huge threat across the Atlantic." It was in implementing this role that America entered both World Wars in Europe, to prevent Germany on both occasions from becoming the feared dominant power when the allied powers could no longer assure victory.

After World War II, America's standing changed fundamentally from the role of last-resort participant in the European balance of power. Great Britain, throughout the nineteenth century, was not only a part of the European balance, it was, by virtue of its military and economic preeminence, the manager, manipulator, and controller of the balance. World War II saw an end to this dominating role, corresponding to the decline of British power. But America emerged undamaged physically, militarily powerful, and overwhelmingly the strongest economic power in the world.

Not surprisingly, America saw itself as the heir to the British role. The balance of power, which now included the Soviet Union, would be managed and controlled by the United States. As long as Western Europe and the Soviet Union were weaker components in the balance, American de facto domination prevailed.

By the 1960s the emergence of Western Europe as a powerful economic community, a rival of the United States in economic affairs as much as a political ally, changed "the correlation of forces," as the Russians call it. In addition, the Soviet Union, stung by its humiliating defeat in the Cuban missile crisis, decided to redress the strategic military imbalance. The Vietnam war was the turning point. While the United States poured in endless resources and severely weakened itself economically, the Soviet Union, Western Europe, and Japan prospered with the biggest gains in growth since the end of the Second World War. By 1972 the Soviet Union had achieved parity in strategic arms and most probably, apart from naval forces, in overall arms as well.

Former Defense Secretary Harold Brown stated, "We and the Soviets are now, in fact, in a position of rough equivalence. Moreover, the present relationship is rather stable. . . . Neither can count on gaining permanent advantage by adding to or changing its forces, since there are countering force changes readily available to the other."[16]

ILLUSION AND REALITY

It was to this new situation that the United States had the most difficulty in adjusting. It is never easy to revise long-held judgments even when the circumstances that produced them have changed. Acknowledged as the preeminent superpower for so long, the relative suddenness of the emergence of the Russians as an economic giant, equal in military power, made recognition of parity impossible to accept.

To some extent America was a victim of its own propaganda. The raging anti-Soviet campaign portraying the Soviet state as a crippled, staggering giant, virtually incapable of feeding its own people, hardly contributed to clarity about what was happening in the real world.

We can judge the rapidity of this economic change, to which Washington paid less than rapt attention, from two eminent American specialists on the Soviet Union. These sources do not suggest that the Soviet system is a great success. Clearly it is not. However, it is true that if the Russian economy is not the wave of the future, neither is it unstable, crippled, nor in the throes of disintegration, as the media too often depict it.

By 1980 the Soviets had moved into first place in the world in the production of steel, petroleum, coal, iron ore, pig iron, cement, tractors, combines, diesel locomotives, machine tools, and housing units. They were a close second in mineral fertilizers and natural gas.[17] Professor Thomas B. Larson (former Chief of Russian Research on Soviet Affairs for the State Department) has pointed out:

- The U.S.S.R. in 1950 produced about 30 percent of U.S. production; by 1975 this was in the neighborhood of 75 percent [higher in 1980].
- In 1975 output of oil, gas, electrical, chemical products, and machinery was 8 to 12 times 1950 output.
- Housing units per 1,000 population reached 80 percent of the American level in 1975. [In 1980, with the collapse of the U.S. housing market, Soviet unit production, 2.2 million units annually, was double that of the U.S.]
- In 1950 Soviet agriculture produced 60 percent of output production in the United States; *a quarter century later it was 80 percent.*[18]

In his book *Stalin's Successors,* Professor Seweryn Bialer, Director of Columbia University's Institute on International Change, pointed out that the decisive sphere in any regime's stability is its domestic economy. "By this standard," says Bialer, "the Brezhnev era can be judged a success."

Furthermore, behind the aggregate figures there was a steady and significant increase in food production and a noticeable improvement in the population's diet. According to Bialer, "Per capita consumption of high-quality food rose 100 percent [from 1961 to 1975]." This paralleled "a significant improvement in the supply of clothing and shoes . . . and . . . personal consumer services for the first time [and] demonstrated a rapid visible growth. . . . [There was] . . .

remarkable progress in the supply of durable consumer goods . . . [including] . . . large-scale construction of new housing units," "The major conclusion," says Bialer, ". . . from our present data of Soviet performance in the Brezhnev era is that the Soviet regime has by and large been able to deliver the goods; it has generally been able to satisfy popular expectations for higher standards of living."[19]

It is worth noting that the charges of inefficiency, bureaucracy, rigidity, and nepotism as characteristic of the Soviet economy are undoubtedly true, as all serious observers, including the two quoted here, have observed. But the striking fact, and the one American policy-makers have difficulty swallowing, is that Soviet achievements were obtained despite these acknowledged structural weaknesses.

We know that politburo hard-liners like Boris Ponomariov and the late Michael Suslov argue that détente will lead to dissolving ties with Warsaw Pact members. We also know that the opposite argument is made in Washington that an overall détente settlement between the Soviet Union and the United States will lead to the end of NATO and the neutralization of Europe. This is, as the hawks see it, the first step in its Finlandization—that is, the establishment of Soviet suzerainty over all Europe. This is the spectre that really haunts Washington when it drops the hobgoblin fiction of Red hordes invading Europe.

The concept of Finlandization is a red herring that needs little refutation. The Soviet Union, even if it wished to, is incapable of dominating Europe, with its more than one quarter billion population. The Russians' problems with their own bloc, less than one-third the size of Western Europe, are illustrative. Western Europe as a whole exceeds the Soviet Union in gross industrial output, gross national product, and population. It is a powerful independent bloc that is technically still well ahead of the Russians. The possibility of an active but neutral Europe is feasible. And this worries the United States almost as much as its potential Finlandization.

THE COLD-WAR CAMPAIGN

The most exceptional aspect of Ronald Reagan's foreign policy is its archaic character, for he is doing no less

than trying to move the clock back over three decades to the period when America was, without question, the strongest power in the world.

At that time the scale of the world balance of power was never more unbalanced. America towered over Europe and the U.S.S.R. Virtually undamaged by the war, its industrial plant had more than doubled in size in five years. It had broken all records for industrial and agricultural output, while Europe and the Soviet Union were nearly prostrate, with tens of millions dead and up to half their prewar economy in rubble.

Today, 35 years later, Western Europe and Japan have caught up to and in some cases (Germany and Japan) passed the United States in efficiency and per capita output. The Soviet Union's military establishment, always a few years behind but finally catching up, matches the American war machine. In economic affairs they have remained behind Western Europe and the United States, but the margin in industrial output, as distinct from total goods and services, by now has become less than decisive. Essential equivalence of the three economic worlds is becoming close.

By his refusal to recognize that 1980 cannot be transformed into the world of 1945, it seems the President believes that by rhetorically invoking the language, style, and polemics of an era long past, he will bring the nation into that period once again.

The ground was fortuitously prepared for Reagan's figurative flight to the past. He came into office on a wave of virulent anti-Sovietism not seen since the late 1940s, caused by events in Iran, the invasion of Afghanistan, and the turmoil in Poland. The crisis in Iran, in which the Russians had no part, in particular produced a spillover of heightened patriotism, humiliation, and even antiforeignism.

Observers' judgments on the results of the President's first year were harsh. In a major New York *Times* summary, Hedrick Smith, former Moscow correspondent, noted that "President Reagan has found it hard to translate the tough anti-Soviet oratory . . . into a consistent foreign policy and had to moderate, reshape, and even defer some early objectives because of frustrating realities abroad."[20]

2. REVIVAL OF THE COLD WAR

Stanley Hoffman, in a review of Reagan's "year abroad," made an essentially similar analysis. Charging that Reagan had produced an ideology but not a policy, Hoffman contended, "This ideology turned out to be utterly deficient as a strategy because it fails to address many real problems, it aggravates others, it provides no priority other than anti-Soviet imperatives and precious little guidance even in connection with the cold war."[21]

The Administration's policy served little better in the Middle East. In a contradictory position, the United States tried to win support from both the Arabs and Israel by using the Russian threat. Saudi Arabia, on this basis, demanded an 8.5 billion dollar arms program, including high-technology AWAC planes. Israel, in turn, demanded billions in aid and arms as the only force in the Middle East capable of defending the area against the Russians. Yet the world knew that neither feared the Russians; the Arabs feared Israel and Israel feared the Arabs.

Washington's unstated aim in this triangular chess game was to secure an American military presence in the Arab Middle East, which up to now the Arabs have refused without resolution of the Palestinian state issue. The President's great Congressional victory, permitting delivery of AWACS to the Saudis, was answered by Israeli annexation of the Golan Heights. This act potentially healed the split between the moderate and militant Arabs, with the probable ultimate destruction of the tottering Camp David accords.

This political schizophrenia is duplicated in place after place. Militarist-ruled Turkey, the only NATO ally on Russia's southern border, demands and receives a 3 billion dollar arms deal from the United States. The result: Greece, victim of Turkish occupation of Greek Cyprus, draws further away from the United States, refusing even to go along with NATO's pallid critique of Poland. And on the basis of the Russian aggression in Afghanistan, militarist-ruled Pakistan obtains a multibillion dollar military aid program, pushing India closer to the Russians than they have ever been.

The White Paper entitled "Communist Interference in El Salvador,"[22] the opening gun in the cold-war campaign, was also its first fiasco. Planned as a "bombshell," it claimed evidence of clandestine military support given by the Soviet Union and Cuba to the Salvadoran guerrillas. Shown to be a tissue of inaccuracies and outright fabrication in a front-page story in the *Wall Street Journal*,[23] the State Department admitted in July it was "possibly misleading and overembellished."[24] The campaign that opened with such vigor quietly disappeared as a major focus. But instability and civil war in Central America remains. And early in 1982 the campaign was resumed with the President's promise of arms and economic aid.[25]

But if the record is bleak in these areas, the most important development of the year was the sharpest break ever between the United States and NATO over the American reaction to martial law in Poland.

The ultimate resolution of the Poland crisis is likely to be long in development. Whether the repression of martial law will lead finally to a conservative Czech type of solution or to a more liberal Hungarianization, only time will tell. In the interim, Europe—particularly West Germany—is unalterably opposed to exploiting the crisis.[26]

To Europeans the issue of Poland was part of the 35-year division of Europe. As much as they deplored martial law, they continued to respect formal agreements of noninterference in one another's internal affairs. To Europeans living on the borders of Eastern Europe, this understanding has a profoundly different meaning than it does to ideologically involved Americans.

But Poland is far from the whole of the Western problem. As the *Wall Street Journal* once put it, "East-West crises are acquiring the distressing habit of becoming West-West crises."[27] Dividing the allies are issues of defense spending (too much, says Europe; too little, says the United States); East-West trade (too much, says the U.S.; too little, says Europe); arms control (too little, says Europe; too much, says the U.S.). On top of this is Europe's overriding fury at the American economic policy that has led to hitherto unheard of interest rates. These rates pulled huge sums of capital out of the European countries, slowing down already depression-weakened economies.[28]

Nor could Europe ignore American efforts to use the Polish situation to scuttle the Soviet-European natural-gas deal through the use of economic sanctions against the Soviet Union. After failing to convince Europe earlier in 1981 that American coal was a viable substitute for Soviet gas, the United States used the Polish events as a useful ploy to try to accomplish the same end by other means.

The gas pipeline is the largest single East-West project in European history. This 250 billion dollar, 25-year deal would supply Europe with a lower-cost substitute for petroleum and immediately place 10 to 15 billion dollars in capital goods orders in countries very much in need of this business.

The United States objected to the enormous gain accruing to the Soviet Union. With a virtually unlimited supply of gas, the Russians would receive on an average 10 billion dollars a year in hard currency up to the year 2005.[29] (For a frame of reference, total foreign imports of grain in a very poor year cost the Soviet Union approximately 4 billion dollars.)

While emphasis has been laid on the materialistic motivation of the Europeans, much less attention is given to their assessment of the Soviet Union and its intentions—one that diverges widely from Washington's. Europeans do not see the Soviets as the aggressive, ideologically driven revolutionary regime that obsesses the Reagan Administration. On the contrary, their view is of a cautious, conservative group of markedly ageing men whose attention is turned inward on a series of seemingly intractable economic problems. These problems are a product of the Soviet economy's reaching a level of maturity that now requires sophisticated technological and managerial restructuring. The Russians are finding that this hurdle is far more complex than they believed and has come at an inconvenient time, when the current leadership is about to pass from the scene. Succession has always been the worst aspect of a sclerotic political system. Taken together, the Europeans feel that these problems explain why the Soviets in recent years, when they are concerned at all, are almost exclusively focused on their borders (Afghanistan) or bloc (Poland) problems.

Thus, Washington's aggressive cold-war campaign, with its out-of-date perception of a rabid Soviet Union determined on world conquest, is so far from Europe's that it is not surprising that it has deepened the already great discord between Europe and America.

Unfortunately a working out of a more rational policy is made more difficult by a conflict within the Administration. From the beginning Alexander Haig and the State Department tried an approach combining the cold-war campaign with accommodation to some of Europe's détente views. In this more conventional Eastern financial establishment position, the former Secretary of State from time to time had the President's support. However, a virulent group of fundamentalist hardliners led by Defense Secretary Weinberger fought for a direct onslaught against what they perceived as European cowardly and neutralist attitudes.

This group's constituency, often referred to as the Westerners, are the original supporters of Ronald Reagan, and may still be a majority within the party. The President and the more traditional Eastern base of the party are not only more pragmatically sensitive to Europe's views but are more aware of the growing complexity of domestic economic problems that the drive for military superiority is making worse. If these economic problems increase, as they are likely to, this conflict between the hawks could become exacerbated by attacks on the swollen military budget from within the party.

Continued conflict within the chaotic foreign-policy establishment exploded in late June with the resignation of Alexander Haig. The precipitating reason was a difference in approach to the British/Argentine war over the Falkland Islands. The deeper cause, however, was the Administration's continued determination to pursue aggressively the cold war, even if it meant an unprecedented open clash with our NATO allies—a policy about which Haig had cautioned.

The Reagan-Weinberger embargoing of several billion dollars of pipeline equipment ordered by the Soviet Union from British, French, and West German firms raised a serious question of interference in the sovereign affairs of other nations. The dubious grounds for this embargo were claims that the original license under which the products were manufactured gave the United States the right to prohibit a foreign firm from producing them. Even Margaret Thatcher was openly outraged. Whether European refusal to accept the commercial dictate will lead to more serious trade problems remains to be seen, but it is clear the schism threatens to become a chasm.

The new Secretary of State George Schultz, former president of the huge multinational Bechtel Group, is seen by some as another California hardliner. He is no dove. But one should remember he has significant Eastern financial connections, and, more important, there is a limit to how far one can carry crude ideology when it conflicts with a reality that threatens to isolate the United States from every major grouping in the world.

The outlook is therefore not promising for an Administration under attack from its allies as well as its domestic opponents and beset with conflict within its own ranks.

In the next period, three scenarios seem possible. The first would be a continuation of the dominant character of the first year—uninterrupted cold war. Although it conforms most with the thinking of both factions now in power, it is likely to be the most difficult to sustain, unless exogenous events or further Soviet blunders take place. The second, neither peace nor war, is more likely. It does not require hauling down the crusade's flag, but it permits some retreat when the going against the world and domestic tide gets too heavy. The third is the most desirable and least likely—that is, a retreat from the hawklike warmongering campaign of the Administration's first year.

In other Administrations Presidents campaigned as fierce cold warriors who would establish American control of the balance of power, only to discover that reality was stronger than ideology. This was true in the two Eisenhower Administrations. John Foster Dulles's brinkmanship opened the Administration's campaign, but Eisenhower's last year saw the first breaking of the ice of cold war at his Camp David meeting with Khrushchev.

Similarly, John Kennedy campaigned on the "missile gap," invaded Cuba, and faced down the Russians in the Cuban missile crisis. Never-theless, he ended his regime with the first major arms control agreement, the Limited Nuclear Test Ban Treaty of 1963.

The most spectacular turnaround, however, was Richard Nixon's détente agreements of 1972. An architect of the cold war and an anticommunist almost without peer, Nixon became the author of the most far-reaching arms control, trade, and cultural agreements ever made with the Soviet Union.

All this is not to suggest that Ronald Reagan will repeat these experiences. They are cited simply to suggest that such changes in policy are not impossible.

Credence that just such a change might come about was heightened in the spring of 1982 when an unexpected, spectacular, explosive upsurge took place in the American peace movement. This outpouring of sentiment had its effect on the President. In April at Eureka College in Illinois, in a major foreign-policy address, he announced in a comparatively conciliatory tone that the United States was ready for negotiations that could lead to "significant reductions" in strategic missile warheads.[30]

Despite this apparent but qualified retreat, a high degree of dubiety greeted Reagan's new approach, for the ideological fever reemerged shortly thereafter during the President's European tour, particularly in his London and Bonn Parliament speeches.[31] Nevertheless, one cannot dismiss this clear change in tactics as inconsequential. The awesome size of the grass-roots negative response in Western Europe and the United States to the nuclear arms buildup and the saber-rattling that accompanied it are political phenomena of considerable importance.

However, it is not possible at this juncture to forecast the direction the Administration will take or may be forced to take. In an important sense Reagan's revised cold-war crusade may have produced its own dialectic. Having scared the West Europeans and Americans half to death with Armageddon for over a year, he may have produced the forces for his own negation.

In the meantime, for the next few years, the three divided world economies—the United States, Europe, and the Soviet Union—will be working their way laboriously out of their respective economic crises. These years of the Damocles sword of massive nuclear overkill will probably be the most decisive of the last 50, and their outcome may well set the tone for the next century.

NOTES

[1] Jan. 29, 1981, Press Conference, Facts on File (1981).

[2] Jan. 9, 1981, Facts on File (1981).

[3] Thomas Hughes, *Foreign Policy* Magazine (Fall, 1981).

[4] The New York *Times* (Apr. 4, 1981).

[5] The New York *Times* (Apr. 7, 1981).

[6] The New York *Times* (Apr. 8, 1981).

[7] The New York *Times* (Apr. 12, 1981).

[8] The New York *Times* (May 15, 1981).

[9] *New York Review of Books* (February 4, 1982).

[10] The demonstrations reflected a majority European opinion. Polls taken before the demonstrations by the official U.S. International Communication Agency in "major selected European countries" showed: Belgium 66 percent opposed to 19 percent in favor of missile emplacement; Holland 68 percent opposed to 28 percent in favor; Great Britain 50 percent opposed to 40 percent in favor; Germany 39 percent opposed to 29 percent in favor, young Germans 70 percent opposed. France in a March, 1981, poll regarding a U.S.-Soviet war voted 63 percent to stay out, 22 percent to side with the U.S. *The Economist* (Oct. 31, 1981), pp. 52–58.

[11] Washington *Post* (Nov. 1, 1981).

[12] The New York *Times* (Aug. 14, 1981).

[13] Senate Foreign Relations Committee Hearing: Strategic Weapons Proposals, Nov. 9, 1981.

[14] Hans J. Morganthau, *Politics in the 20th Century* (Chicago: University of Chicago, 1958).

[15] F.S. Northedge, *Foreign Policy of the Powers* (New York: Oxford University Press, 1968).

[16] University of Rochester Speech, Release, Office of Secretary of Defense, Apr. 13, 1977.

[17] Val Zabrijaka, U.S.S.R. Affairs Division Bulletin, U.S. Department of Commerce. (Advised in conversation; figures supplied by CIA.)

[18] Thomas B. Larsen, *Soviet–American Rivalry* (New York: W.W. Norton, 1978).

[19] Seweryn Bialer, *Stalin's Successors* (New York: Oxford University Press, 1980).

[20] The New York *Times* (Jan. 22, 1982).

[21] *New York Review of Books* (Feb. 4, 1982).

[22] "Communist Interference in El Salvador," White Paper, U.S. State Department, Feb. 23, 1981.

[23] Jonathan Kwitny, *Wall Street Journal* (June 8, 1981).

[24] *Ibid.*

[25] President Reagan, Press Conference, Feb. 20, 1982.

[26] "Chancellor Helmut Schmidt said today that West Germany would hold to its policy of restraint and cooperation with the Soviet Bloc despite criticism from some Western countries." Reuters (Jan. 16, 1982). Also see NATO Foreign Ministers' Declaration on Poland, The New York *Times* (Jan. 12, 1982).

[27] *Wall Street Journal* (Dec. 29, 1981).

[28] See *Solvency, the Price of Survival,* ed. James Chase (New York: Random House, 1981).

[29] For full discussion see Norman Crossland, "Pipeline Diplomacy," *Europe* (January-February, 1982).

[30] Address at Eureka College Commencement. The New York *Times* (May 10, 1982):

"At the end of the first phase of the Start reductions, I expect ballistic missile warheads—the most serious threat we face—to be reduced to equal ceilings at least one-third below current levels. . . . I would ask that no more than one-half be land-based.

"I am confident that together we can achieve an agreement of enduring value that reduces the number of nuclear weapons, halts the growth in strategic forces, and opens the way to even more far-reaching steps in the future."

[31] Text, London Parliamentary address. The New York *Times* (June 9, 1982). Although repeating his offer of negotiations, the President attacked the Soviet Union for almost every crime on record. He saw a "decay of the Soviet experiment" and "a revolutionary crisis in . . . Marxism-Leninism." He charged repression at home, enslavement and aggression abroad, the use of chemical warfare, and the sponsorship and training of international terrorists. One wondered why he wanted to negotiate at all.

THE RUSSIAN CONNECTION

Lester R. Brown

Lester R. Brown is director of Worldwatch Institute. He wrote the Worldwatch report, U.S. and Soviet Agriculture: The Shifting Balance of Power, *from which this article is excerpted.*

Each day two 20,000-ton freighters loaded with grain leave the United States for the Soviet Union. The flow of grain between the two adversaries, something neither country had planned on, is influenced by economic considerations, such as the size of the Soviet grain deficit, the U.S. capacity to supply, and the Soviet ability to pay. Political considerations include the risk to both trading partners associated with being heavily dependent on each other.

Soviet grain purchases during the late Sixties and early Seventies were intended largely to offset poor harvests in the marginal rainfall areas of the virgin lands. More recently, grain imports have offset the consistently large differences between planned production and actual harvests.

Because of the massive size of Soviet food imports the United States necessarily figures prominently as a source of food. No country has ever dominated world grain trade as the United States does today. Its 55 percent share of world grain exports in 1981 easily overshadows Saudi Arabia's 24 percent share of 1978 world oil exports. And while the amount of oil traded internationally has been falling since 1979, grain shipments are continuing to grow.

By the early Eighties, U.S. grain exports dwarfed those of the other principal suppliers—Canada, Australia, Argentina and France. Annual grain exports from each of these countries now typically range from 11 million to 24 million tons compared with over 110 million tons from the United States.

From 1972 until 1980 the United States supplied on average 61 percent of Soviet grain imports. With a partial export embargo imposed by the United States in early 1980, following the Soviet invasion of Afghanistan, the U.S. share of Soviet imports fell to 24 percent. As the Soviets were forced to seek grain elsewhere, Argentina emerged as the leading Soviet supplier in 1980. When the U.S. embargo was lifted in April 1981, Soviet imports began to rise again, nearly doubling the 8-million-ton flow permitted under the partial embargo. At 17.8 million tons, the 1982/83 estimated U.S. grain shipments to the Soviet Union rival those going to Japan. If Soviet imports continue to be heavy and if the U.S. share of the market continues to expand, moving toward the preembargo level, the flow of food from the United States to the Soviet Union will become the largest between two countries in history.

The U.S. embargo distorted normal grain trade patterns, as the Soviet Union turned to other suppliers, all quite small compared with the United States. Tying up the lion's share of exportable supplies from countries such as Argentina, the Soviet Union forced Japan and other major importers to rely even more heavily than usual on the United States. As a result, U.S. restrictions on grain shipments to the Soviet Union effectively altered not only Soviet sources of supply but the entire world pattern of grain trade. The partial embargo did not measurably reduce the amount of grain imported by the Soviets, but it did make grain imports more difficult and somewhat more costly. It also let the Soviets know that food would be used as an instrument of foreign policy.

The current flow of grain from the United States to the Soviet Union operates within the framework of the U.S.–Soviet Grains Agreement, signed in October 1975, a five-year pact that ran from October 1976 to September 1981. It was extended for one year in August of 1981.

The Grains Agreement requires that the Soviet Union annually purchase a minimum of 6 million tons of corn and wheat in roughly equal quantities. It also allows the Soviets to purchase up to 8 million tons if needed, but purchases over 8 million tons require consultations between the two countries and special permission by the U.S. government. In any year that the U.S. Department of Agriculture estimates the combination of U.S. production and carry-over stocks to be less that 225 million tons, the United States may reduce the amount available to the Soviets below the minimum called for.

The United States delayed negotiations, scheduled to begin in early 1982, on a new long-term grain agreement, in response to the Soviet Union's role in Poland.

2. REVIVAL OF THE COLD WAR

In late July 1982, the United States offered another one-year extension of the agreement rather than a new one, expressing its displeasure over martial law in Poland. After pondering the proposed one-year extension for a few weeks, the Soviets decided to accept it, even though they would have preferred the security of a multi-year agreement.

The original agreement was made when the Soviets were far more hopeful about their long-term food prospects than they are today. As a result, purchases have invariably greatly exceeded the 8-million-ton maximum automatically permitted in the agreement, requiring numerous consultations from 1976 on. Nonetheless, the agreement has helped stabilize the world grain market.

Ultimately, constraints on Soviet food imports may hinge on the country's ability to earn foreign exchange. The Soviet Union now depends heavily on export earnings from oil, natural gas and gold. Eventually it will lose its exportable surplus of oil and gold, and with it, key sources of hard currency. Unless the Soviet Union develops a competitive industrial capacity, something it has not yet done on any meaningful scale, foreign exchange shortages could ultimately limit its food imports.

This limited capacity to earn foreign exchange is more likely to restrict Soviet food imports than the U.S. ability to supply. The yield-raising technologies on which U.S. agriculture depends to boost food output are advancing, though more slowly than in the early postwar decades. In addition, there is an extensive potential for double cropping that farmers are now systematically exploiting.

Of the various long-term constraints on U.S. food exports, soil erosion is perhaps the most serious. As the world market for U.S. grain expands, the resulting intensification of agriculture, particularly continuous row cropping on sloping lands in the Midwest and Southern states, is leading to a national soil loss that may match or exceed that of the Dust Bowl Era. The Soil Conservation Service has identified 17 million acres of land now in crops (over 4 percent of the total) losing topsoil so fast they should be converted to grassland or trees before they are rendered worthless. Without government programs to convert this land and to help farmers adopt terracing, strip cropping, minimum tillage or other conservation measures on the rapidly eroding lands, farmers, facing the severe cost-price squeeze imposed by the market, may not be able to arrest the loss of topsoil and maintain the inherent productivity of their land. In the absence of effective Washington leadership on this issue, U.S. farm exports to the Soviet Union amount to a subsidy of Soviet farm inefficiency paid with U.S. topsoil.

Freshwater shortages may also restrict long-term growth in U.S. farm output. For example, in the southern Great Plains, depletion over the next few decades of the Ogallala Aquifer, an underground source of freshwater stretching from southern Nebraska to northern Texas, will force a conversion from irrigated agriculture back to dry-land agriculture. As this conversion progresses, land productivity in this region will decline accordingly.

These threats to agricultural productivity notwithstanding, U.S. export capacity is likely to expand further in the years ahead as land productivity increases and as the double-cropped area expands. If the Administration does not respond to the threat of massive soil erosion, Congress may take the initiative. In addition, the growing popularity of minimum tillage, a practice designed to reduce fuel use, is inadvertently reducing soil erosion.

In the new commercial food relationship between the two superpowers, dependence is mutual but it is not symmetrical. Soviet dependence on U.S. supplies, directly or indirectly, is greater than U.S. dependence on Soviet markets. Whether or not the Soviets import directly from the United States, U.S. export capacity makes Soviet imports possible. For the United States, an embargo on grain exports to the Soviet Union would eliminate direct shipments but would not likely have much affect on total U.S. exports. If Canada and Australia were to join the embargo, as they might in an emergency, then Soviet imports would be reduced, as would overall U.S. grain shipments. In this event, the United States government could idle cropland by supporting farm prices. This technique has been widely used since World War II and was reintroduced on a limited scale in 1982.

The new food connection between the United States and the Soviet Union may represent the most important change in the relationship between the two countries since the cold war began a generation ago. It demonstrates in clear economic terms that the United States and the Soviet Union need each other. This is particularly true now, when the productive capacity of U.S. farms continues to climb while growth in grain markets outside the Soviet Union has slowed because of a sluggish economy worldwide. The record grain deficits of the early Eighties in the Soviet Union show more than ever its dependence on U.S. agriculture.

Although American farmers are the most outspoken advocates of trade with the Soviet Union, the higher level of farm exports that Soviet imports make possible benefits the entire U.S. economy. As the U.S. oil-import bill soared after 1973 price increases, the enormous growth in farm exports paid much of the bill. Traditional export industries, such as automobiles, have sagged in international competition. Even high technology exports, such as commercial jet aircraft, are suffering. In a stagnant economy, the productivity and ingenuity of American farmers have helped the United States balance its international payments.

Great as the benefits of this expanded farm trade are for the United States, the Soviet Union has even more to gain. One can only imagine how long the lines would be at Soviet meat counters had it not been for U.S. grain. The Soviet Union is in deep trouble economically because it must import so much food, but it would be in even deeper trouble politically if food were not available.

Both superpowers at times feel uneasy with their new trade dependency, because it complicates a traditional adversarial relationship. The food connection does not ensure peaceful relations between the two countries, but it does make massive arms spending more difficult to justify. The American people and Congress may increasingly doubt that a country depending on the United States for so much of its food could be as dangerous as commonly portrayed. Hardliners in the Soviet Union may be unable to convince Kremlin colleagues that the country that feeds them is indeed a mortal enemy.

The evolution of U.S.–Soviet agricultural trade is a reminder that in the long run, economic forces tend to override political considerations. With another bumper grain harvest in 1982,* the United States will need Soviet markets more than ever. Indeed, U.S. Secretary of Agriculture John R. Block, eager to bolster farm income, has implored the Soviets to buy more U.S. grain.

Internal stability within the Soviet Union, as well as in the Soviet bloc, may depend more on grain imports than any other external factor. If the Reagan Administration is serious about putting pressure on the Soviet Union, it should urge a joint embargo with U.S. allies Canada and Australia of all grain shipments to the Soviet Union. This would provide real and immediate economic pressure, but no such effort has been made. Instead, President Reagan has promised American farmers that the Soviets this year will receive the biggest shipment ever of U.S. grain.†

In the absence of such an effort to press the Soviets, the Reagan Administration arguments against the Yamal gas pipeline from northern Siberia to Western Europe sound insincere and unconvincing. In the short run, forgoing the pipeline would deny the Europeans industrial exports and employment, much as a grain embargo would deny American farmers a market. In the long run, failure to build a pipeline would deny Western Europeans needed energy and a more diverse supply.

Arguing against the 3,500-mile gas pipeline, Reagan notes that U.S. grain sales drain the Soviet Union

of hard currency, while the pipeline will boost Soviet money supplies. But if the United States is unwilling to wield grain as an economic weapon against the Soviets (and face the consequences at home), its pipeline stand is unfair to Western Europe. Pipeline opposition also ignores eventual advantages to the United States. For U.S. farmers, earnings from the pipeline will eventually allow the Soviets to buy more U.S. wheat, feed grain and soybeans than they otherwise could. If U.S. agriculture seeks foreign markets in the late Eighties as eagerly as it does now, the pipeline is a welcome development, something the United States should support rather than oppose.△

The key decisions affecting the long-term fate of this new economic relationship between the superpowers are more likely to be made in Moscow than in Washington, as the Soviets endeavor to improve their agriculture. Soviet officials may not yet realize that the agricultural modernization they want is incompatible with centralized planning and management. If not, they will keep tinkering with the system, trying to make it work. One inevitable consequence will be declining morale among farm workers as frustrations with the inherent defects of the system mount. More broadly, shortages of high quality foodstuffs, especially livestock products, will lower worker morale throughout Soviet society. Without corrective action, the Soviets face continued food shortages, rationing and longer waits at the market.

A second Soviet option is to begin economic reforms similar to those in Hungary, where managers in both industry and agriculture are relatively free of central control and have wide latitude to make independent decisions. No modest adjustments the Soviets can make, however, such as giving private farm plots more support, will arrest the broad-based deterioration. Only fundamental reforms, perhaps as great as any since the Communist party came to power in 1917, will be adequate.

There are signs that the Soviet leadership is looking carefully at the Hungarian experience. Hungarian poultry producers are now aiding their Soviet counterparts, using techniques the Hungarians acquired from the West. Soviet Premier Nikolai A. Tikhonov visited Hungary to examine firsthand the Hungarian successes and, in so doing, gave an implicit stamp of approval. Whether this interest will translate into Soviet decentralization along Hungarian lines remains to be seen.

For the United States, policy options are less clear-cut. The shift in the agricultural power balance in favor of the United States provides an opportunity to reshape the relationship with the Soviet Union. When two powers are evenly balanced it is difficult for either

---

†In October, President Reagan offered to sell 23 million tons of grain to the USSR in 1982—nearly three times the amount already agreed to.

*In the corn- and wheat-belt states, farmers are running out of space to store their grain.

△On November 14, President Reagan announced a policy change: Sanctions against American and other companies participating in the Soviet gas pipeline were being lifted.

Why

In one major natural resource—area of arable land—the Soviet Union enjoys a wide edge over the United States. The Soviets currently plant over 500 million acres, exceeding by nearly half the 350 million acres planted annually in the United States. Measured only by its cropland area, the Soviet Union is in a class by itself among world food producers.

The Soviet cropland advantage of 150 million acres, however, is partly offset by climatic differences favoring the United States. Whereas most U.S. cropland lies between 34 and 45 degrees north latitude, Soviet cropland lies farther north, mostly between 48 and 55 degrees. In much of the Soviet Union, as in Canada, which is similarly situated, winter grain crops cannot survive the harsh winters. Over half of the wheat, the crop dominating Soviet agriculture, is spring wheat—wheat planted in May and harvested in September. This northerly location also means that the Soviet Union has much less potential than the United States for double cropping winter grains, such as wheat and barley, with summer crops such as soybeans.

Rainfall differences also offset the Soviet advantage in arable land. The geographic distribution of rainfall in the United States is better than in the Soviet Union, where heavier rainfall is in the north while the cropland with a longer growing season is in the semiarid south. Indeed, the south central Soviet Union is largely semiarid, similar to the southwestern United States.

. . . .

Contrasting approaches to agricultural management in the Soviet Union and the United States are obvious when their respective agricultural structures are compared. In the Soviet Union, 500 million acres of cropland are divided in roughly equal amounts between 20,800 state farms and 26,000 collective farms. Each state farm averages just over 13,000 acres and each collective farm about 9,000 acres.

In the United States, where 2.4 million farmers cultivate some 350 million acres, each farm averages 144 acres of cropland. Including grazing and forest land, the typical farm has close to 400 acres. As is often the case, however, these averages conceal a wide range of farm sizes. The 1974 census reported 225,000 farms with fewer than 50 acres of land. At the other end of the spectrum, there were 150,000 farms with 1,000 acres or more. The vast majority of U.S. farmers—some 2 million—were in the 50 to 1,000 acre category.

The Soviet Union employs a farm labor force of 26.1 million. Of this group 46,800 are the managers of the state and collective farms. Even allowing for numerous assistant farm managers and other supervisory personnel, the bulk of the 26 million farm labor force are farm workers directed by the 46,800 farm managers, who in turn are directed from Moscow. By contrast, the U.S. farm labor force totals 3.7 million, only a small fraction of that in the Soviet Union. Of this total, 2.4 million are managers of family farms, mostly owner-operators, and fewer than 1.3 million are hired workers.

In the highly competitive U.S. market economy these farm managers must excel to survive. The market is heartless in weeding out poor managers.

—L.R.B.

side to take major initiatives. Now that the balance has been decisively altered in the strategically important food sector, the United States can proceed from a position of strength.

While unfortunate for the Soviets, the deterioration of their agriculture does present a timely opportunity to lessen tensions between Washington and Moscow. An obvious beginning for the Reagan Administration would be to slow down the arms race. Identified in the U.S. public mind as a Soviet hard-liner, President Reagan is well positioned to engage the Soviets in serious discussions of reductions in both nuclear and conventional weapons. Just as hard-liner Richard Nixon was able to reopen the door to China and in so doing ensure a place in history, Ronald Reagan can lead U.S.–Soviet relations into a new era.

Conditions within the Soviet Union suggest that the Soviets will respond to U.S. initiatives that would lessen international tensions and permit the Soviets to focus on internal reforms. In his missile-freeze speech in early 1982, President Leonid I. Brezhnev said, "We have not spent, nor will we spend, a single ruble more for these purposes than is absolutely necessary." As Soviet analyst Marshall Goldman notes, this departs from past statements, since Soviet leaders normally omit cost considerations when discussing military matters, and it may well reflect a Soviet interest in reordering priorities.

For the United States the question is how to use this new advantage most effectively to reduce tensions between the two countries. Using food as a lever in U.S.–Soviet relationships requires an understanding of its limitations. While a joint grain embargo by the United States, Canada and Australia could check more radical Soviet military actions, access to the U.S. exportable grain surplus cannot easily be put on the arms-reduction negotiating table along with tanks in Europe and nuclear warheads. For the Soviets, it is embarrassing enough to import four times as much grain as India imported after its worst monsoon failure. To spotlight this shortcoming by directly linking it to arms reductions would be an unacceptable affront to Soviet national pride.

The Soviets have already indicated that they will

resist the U.S. use of food for political purposes. In his May 24, 1982, address outlining the new "food program," President Brezhnev noted, "The leadership of certain states is striving to turn ordinary commercial operations such, for example, as grain sales, into a means of putting pressure on our country, into an instrument of political pressure." This preemptive rhetoric shows that the Soviets are fully aware of their dilemma, but will not easily bend to pressure. Brezhnev's successor is hardly likely to change this posture.

The potential benefits of massive U.S. food shipments to the Soviet Union are not limited to the U.S. economy. These shipments are an important commercial transaction for the United States, but they may also provide insurance against a Soviet nuclear attack. Although the prospect of destroying its principal source of imported food will not necessarily prevent a Soviet nuclear attack, it is certainly a deterrent.

The importance of the dramatic shift in the agricultural balance of power lies less in the potential it provides for using food as a political lever than in the psychological effect new commercial ties will have on the political relationship between the two countries. The long line of grain-laden ships linking U.S. farmers to Soviet consumers represents a major new economic tie between the two countries, one that could transform long-term political relationships as well.

Allies of the US: Western Europe and Japan

For many years the growing tensions and problems within the Atlantic Alliance and the American-Japanese alliance have been remarked upon. Recently, however, the relationships of the US with its major allies have taken on near-crisis proportions, causing genuine concern for the future. The sources of the present tensions are many, but if one factor were to be singled out, it would be the change in the relative power of Western European countries and Japan to the power of the US. Americans have found it difficult to acknowledge that since World War II, European and Japanese children have grown up to become adults with ideas of their own. It is not that they wish to harm their American friend, but only that they want to act in a manner that enhances their own national interests. Unfortunately, this has given rise to serious conflicts between their interests and ours.

Much of the difference in their world view may be attributed to their particular histories—far removed from the American experience—and geopolitical considerations. Both Western European countries and Japan are faced with the presence of the Soviet military on or not far from their borders. The effect of such a factor on our allies is, on the one hand, to confront the Soviets with equal forces but, on the other hand, to accommodate the Soviets wherever possible. This does not imply a "neutral" position between the US and USSR. Indeed the Europeans are deeply concerned about Europe's defense becoming "decoupled" from the US. But their position does reflect their living with the reality of war spreading to their territories if the Soviets should perceive their foreign policies as too threatening. Of course, our allies' perception of the "Soviet threat" has often been at variance with the American assessment, resulting in many of the present tensions over the emplacement of American Pershing II and cruise missiles in Western Europe for "defense," and tensions with the Japanese over their refusal to increase their defense budget to higher levels.

The varying strategic assessment of the Soviet threat frequently spills over into the economic arena and becomes part of the economic tensions eroding the relationship of the US with its allies. The basic question of "who is to pay for the allies' defense" weaves itself into unbalanced budgets; but the source of this problem goes far beyond defense to questions of the relative productivity of our competing economies, protectionist regulations, and unfair trade practices. The gas pipeline controversy bares testimony to the interdependence of economic and military issues with the differing assessments of Soviet intentions. It also demonstrates that in a conflict of "national interest," the US no longer possesses adequate power to get its

way. Similarly, Japanese Prime Minister Nakasone's visit to the US in January, 1983, led to little more than a statement of commiseration on his part with the plight of unemployed American workers, allegedly because of nefarious Japanese business practices. But as the leader of Asia's most successful democracy, Nakasone must always keep in mind that he cannot sacrifice the interests of powerful domestic groups, both industrial and agricultural, without severe repercussions on the strength of the ruling Liberal Democratic Party. Indeed, the problem of having allies that are democracies is precisely the problem of having governments that can listen to the US with only one ear, while the other ear must listen to domestic pressure groups, popular opinion, and political parties.

As the following articles demonstrate, agreement upon the existence of a Soviet military threat does not mean that Western Europe's or Japan's interests are identical to those of the US on all related issues. In addition, the articles indicate the splits between, and within, the European countries over not only the Soviet threat, but also the German threat, the Japanese (economic) threat, the nature of the European Economic Community, policies toward Third World countries, and policies toward Israel and the Middle East. As shall be seen in this and subsequent chapters, many of these conflicts are being brought to a head because of the delicate negotiations between the Soviets and Americans over Reagan's "zero option," and by the Soviet "peace offensive."

Looking Ahead: Challenge Questions

What can be done to lessen the tensions between the Western Europeans and the US? Are the divisive forces ones over which we have little or no control? Would a mere change in American attitudes help diminish the tensions?

To what extent can the problems in the American-Japanese relationship be attributed to basic cultural and geopolitical differences? What can be done to salvage the US-Japan partnership in the light of so many built-in constants? If Japan were to end all protectionist legislation, would this necessarily lead to an improvement in the US balance of payments deficit?

What would be gained, or lost, if NATO were dissolved? What are the possible alternatives to "Atlanticism" in the strategic area? Does a European defense, without American support, presume a united Europe? What would be Germany's role in a solely European defense strategy?

What do the increasing number of socialist governments among America's allies tell us about the nature of "nationalism" and "international socialism"?

A New Course for Britain and Western Europe

Hedley Bull

Hedley Bull has been Professor of International Relations at Oxford University and Fellow of Balliol College since 1977. He taught previously at the London School of Economics and the Australian National University and has held visiting appointments at a number of American universities. His most recent book is The Anarchical Society: A Study of Order in World Politics *(New York: Macmillan and Columbia University Press, 1977).*

The policies being pursued by the United States under the Reagan administration seem to me so dangerous and misguided that it is now vitally important that Britain and her Western European partners should take steps to reduce their dependence on America and defend their own interests and points of view more vigorously.

In the United States today it is widely held that the Western European allies have failed to awaken to the threat posed by the Soviet Union to the world balance of power. While the United States has taken steps to restore the military balance that was neglected during the 1970s and to oppose Soviet encroachments around the world, the Europeans are said to have failed to give it the support it is entitled to expect. In Europe, where the United States has responded to an initially Western European request to balance a Soviet nuclear thrust directed specifically at Western Europe, this has been greeted with demonstrations of public hostility so great that it has been possible to proceed with plans for a new theater nuclear force deployment only by returning to the very path the United States has wanted to forswear: making the deployment of new weapons conditional on the outcome of negotiations with the Soviet Union. In the Third World—and especially in the Middle East,

where the interests of the West are everywhere threatened by Soviet advances—the European allies are said to be dragging their feet, where they are not actually (as in the case of the European Community's attitude to the Palestine Liberation Organization) giving aid and comfort to the West's enemies. Western European countries are said to be doing all these things because they have sunk into a slothful state of mind, in which they prefer economic gain and a comfortable life to facing their responsibilities.

The growth of Soviet military strength does indeed pose a threat to the world balance of power on which our whole system of international relations rests, and it is in Western Europe's interest that the United States should not allow a Soviet global preponderance to come about. It does not follow from this, however, that Western Europe's interests are to be identified with those of the United States, wherever Washington and Moscow clash around the globe.

For one thing, it is an interest of Western Europe's (one shared, perhaps, with all mankind) that the superpowers conduct their competition with one another in such a way as to keep at bay the risk of nuclear war. Some of the recent actions of the United States, and rather more of its rhetoric, have given the impression, even if wrongly, that the commitment to do this has weakened in Washington. The effect has been to mobilize against America one of the most powerful emotions at work in Europe today, the fear of nuclear war.

For another, Western Europe has no particular interest in the preservation or restoration of an American preponderance or superiority in world affairs (even though it would be bound to prefer an American preponderance to a Soviet one, if this were the only choice). We need to remember that from 1945 until at least the end of the 1960s it was not the Soviet Union but the United States that was closest to being the preponderant world power, able to play, in some respects, the role of an imperial or suzerain power rather than that merely of a leading participant in a balance-of-power system. Even today, it is only if we compare the military statistics for the Soviet Union and the United States in isolation from other factors that we can persuade ourselves that the former has overtaken the latter in power terms. If we allow for the gross economic inferiority of the Soviet Union, the loss of its ideological appeal, the weakness and unreliability of its Eastern European allies as compared with America's NATO allies, and the quasi alliance that exists between the United States and China, it is difficult to conclude that the Soviet Union is within reach of dominating the world.

The Americans, who in their domestic affairs have given such a central place to the theory of checks and balances, have in their approach to international affairs found it difficult to grasp that checks to their own excessive power are necessary; they have tended to believe that their virtue in exercising this power is a sufficient safeguard of the interests of others. In fact, the power of the United States has made dependents or mendicants of others, while inevitably, in some measure, corrupting those who have exercised it in Washington. The decline of the United States as the result of the economic growth of Western Europe and Japan in the 1960s, the rise of the Soviet Union as a military power in the 1970s, and the series of reverses suffered by the United States at the hands of Third World countries, disastrous as it has sometimes been for America's clients, has been a liberating experience for much of the rest of the world.

Western European countries still look to the United States to maintain its position as a viable great power and to uphold the central balance against the Soviet Union. But they have no interest in seeking to reverse the redistribution of power that has taken place, even supposing this were possible. They do not share the patriotic or jingoistic emotions that lead some Americans to seek a restoration of American primacy. Nor is there much belief in Western Europe in the idea that America's struggle with its adversaries is a moral contest of Light with Darkness, especially at a moment when some of the goals that Washington now appears to stand for in the world are morally distasteful to most Western Europeans.

Western Europeans cannot be expected to regret the increase in their own stature in world affairs vis-à-vis the United States, which is a basic cause of the present tensions in the alliance. Moreover, although the increased capability of parts of the Third World to act independently creates problems for Western Europe, just as it does for the United States, it also helps to increase Western Europe's own freedom of maneuver: the European Community's dialogue with the Arab states, its special relationship with black Africa, symbolized by the Lomé II agreement, Britain's continued interest in exploiting its Commonwealth connection with Third World countries, France's cultivation of Mexico—all demonstrate Western Europe's present tendency to align itself more closely with Third World countries than with the United States, and, in so doing, to frustrate its policies.

Nor is the rise of Soviet power—for, after all, that is what concerns Western Europe most in the world—wholly negative from a Western European point of view. It is the Soviet Union that provides the principal check to the power of the United States. The support given by the Soviet Union to Third World movements for "national liberation" has provided a basic condition for the success of these movements in Southeast Asia and Africa during the 1970s. The dialogue that Western Europe, and above all Western Germany, now has with the Soviet Union, strengthens its own diplomatic position vis-à-vis the United States.

The core of NATO is the common interest perceived by the United States and the Western European members in resisting any possible Soviet military threat to Western Europe, and in providing Western Europe with a sense of security against any such threat. Most West European opinion continues to recognize this common interest, but Western Europe's security is also thought to rest upon arrangements that have been arrived at with the Soviet Union: territorial settlements that have removed some of the causes of conflict, networks of trade and technical cooperation in which both sides have a stake, and a habit of coexistence that makes the behavior of both sides predictable. All this now seems to have been placed in jeopardy by U.S. policies that subordinate the preservation of these arrangements to the requirements of a global struggle with the Soviet Union for objectives (such as American primacy, or the primacy of America's ideology) in which Western Europeans have no interest.

Western Europeans, moreover, still recognize that the security of Western Europe against Soviet attack cannot be provided without the cooperation and the military presence of the United States. But the advantages the allies derive from this cooperation and military presence have always had to be weighed against the disadvantages that follow from it; i.e., the possibility that the American alliance will involve Western Europe in a war begun over interests that are not its own, or in a war conducted in such a way that its own interests are treated as subordinate. The United States has always held the leading position in the decision-making structure of the alliance. The American nuclear weapons on which the strategy of the alliance chiefly rests, apart from those tactical nuclear weapons subject to the "double-key system," are controlled by the United States alone, and the proposed deployment of Pershing II and cruise missiles in Western Europe will extend this

3. ALLIES OF THE US

American control further. Given the Reagan administration's belligerent posture toward a Soviet Union that is still faithful to the idea of détente, at least as this term is understood in Europe, and given the shallow and insensitive talk of nuclear war-fighting that it has fostered, it is hardly surprising that a Western Europe more conscious of its increased capability to act independently should have become more conscious of the disadvantages, as against the advantages, of the partnership.

Almost as alarming is the approach of the Reagan administration toward the defense of the common interests of the West in the Third World. In the Middle East it is indeed true that Europe's interests regarding oil are even greater than those of the United States, but it is difficult to believe that these can be effectively upheld by threats to coerce Arab oil producers, intervention to prevent political change in Arab countries, and partnership with a now overtly expansionist Israel. In Africa the whole basis of the West's carefully constructed accommodation with black African states is now threatened by an American policy of "constructive engagement" with South Africa. In South Asia the United States is again engaged in a policy of arming Pakistan and, therefore, antagonizing India, thus repeating John Foster Dulles' errors of the 1950s and making more remote than ever the goal of fruitful cooperation with the one stable democracy in that part of the world.

In Central America, toward which American public attitudes today display the same, almost unconscious, presumption of a right to paramountcy that the British public had toward the Middle East a generation ago, the United States, by its determined hostility to the forces of change, appears to be headed for a terrible storm—perhaps not a storm wholly of its own making, but one whose adverse consequences for itself and the West will be magnified by the policies now being followed. In its approach to this as to other problems in its relations with the Third World, U.S. policy apparently is governed by the proposition that the main source of these problems is the Soviet Union's penetration of the Third World. It is scarcely credible, and deeply undermining of one's confidence in the United States, that with all its specialist knowledge of the Third World countries, with the intellectual resources of its matchless universities and research institutions, and after its long and tragic experience in Asia since 1945, it should now choose to found its policies on ideas that can only be described as infantile.

What, then, is to be done? In my view it is imperative that Britain and her Western European partners should seek to disengage themselves at least from the present extent of their dependence on the United States and of commitment to its policies. There are three reasons that point to this conclusion. First, Western Europe's interests in the preservation of the nuclear peace, in détente with the Soviet Union, and in accommodation with the

Third World are placed in jeopardy by the policies being pursued in Washington today. Second, some move in this direction has become a domestic political necessity in Western European countries, where disenchantment with American policy is now widespread, even if more so in some countries (Germany, Britain, the Low Countries, Scandinavia) than in others (France and Italy). The European nuclear disarmament movement represents only a minority view, even in those countries in which it has most support, but the sentiments of concern about American policy and the desire for a louder European voice in world affairs—which among other things it expresses—are much more widespread. European governments of whatever political complexion will have to take account of these sentiments. Third, such a step is necessary for the health of the alliance itself. The tensions that are at present so evident in the alliance are likely to endure, and if NATO is to contain them and survive, some radical rethinking will have to be done about its structure.

It is true that neither the Reagan administration nor the American public mood that brought it to power will last forever, and that part of the present tension derives from America's psychological difficulties in adjusting itself to a diminished position in the world, which in the long run it will overcome, as Western European nations in their postimperial phase have perhaps now done. It is true also that NATO has faced and survived divisive conflicts of policy before: in the 1950s the Suez crisis, in the 1960s the conflict between Atlanticism and Gaullism, in the 1970s the oil crisis and the October war.

But the present tension has an underlying cause that may outlast particular governments and, if not attended to, could prove fatal to the alliance. NATO has not yet adjusted itself to the shift in wealth, and to a lesser extent in power, from North America to Western Europe. The NATO of the 1950s and 1960s was far more unbalanced than the NATO of today. The United States overwhelmingly contributed the most to an alliance in which Western Europeans were the chief beneficiaries, and in return the United States claimed a position of leadership that the European member-states freely accorded. Now that the inequality within the alliance has been redressed, new arrangements must be made.

The Europeans, as the Americans naturally insist, should be ready to shoulder more of the common burdens, especially the defense of Western Europe itself, commensurate with the increase of their wealth. The Americans, on the other hand, need to recognize that in an alliance in which burdens are shared more equally, they cannot expect to maintain the same position of unquestioned leadership that they have been accorded in the past. To the great credit of American leaders of an earlier generation, the United States has never opposed the recovery of European prosperity and power and the growth of its political unity; on the contrary, both are in very considerable measure the fruit of America's own postwar efforts.

Americans, however, have been inclined to assume that European power, once recovered, would be harnessed to the service of America's own objectives—assumed to be the proper objectives of the alliance as a whole. The United States has been slow to recognize that the increased power of European states would cause them to define goals of their own more sharply, and to provide the resources with which to pursue them more resolutely.

There is a tendency in Western Europe for the debate about security policy to become polarized between what we may call the Atlanticist position of the governments, seeking to rally support for the old arrangements of the alliance, and the neutralist position of the dissidents, stressing withdrawal from the alliance, renunciation of nuclear weapons, and trust in the Soviet Union. The neutralist position, I believe, carries the implication that Western Europe, essentially disarmed and cut off from American protection, would lapse into subservience to the Soviet Union, even if not immediately or totally. This outcome is not compatible either with its liberty or with its dignity. The Atlanticist position, as I have argued, does not take account of the changed circumstances of the alliance.

The course that the Western European countries should now be exploring may be called the Europeanist one. It requires the countries of Western Europe to combine more closely together, increase their defense efforts, and take steps toward reducing their military dependence on America. It means that European institutions—either established organizations such as the European Community, the Western European Union, or the Eurogroup, or groups that have yet to be created—should take on functions in the security field that they have previously eschewed. It means that NATO itself will cease to be the only international organization concerned with Western European defense.

The member-states of the European Community have already gone some distance in coordinating their foreign policies, and it is possible to speak of a European voice in world affairs not only in matters of trade, but also in relation to certain key issues concerning the CSCE (Conference on European Security and Cooperation), the Middle East, and Afghanistan. It is possible to speak of an emerging concert or entente of Western European states, however tentative and incomplete, based less on the institutions of the Community than on the perception of common and distinct interests by the major Western European governments, especially France, West Germany, Britain, and Italy. But the basis of all independence in foreign policy is the ability to provide for one's own security from one's own resources, and until this is attempted we can hardly expect that a West European voice will ring forth loud and clear.

The countries of Western Europe are superior to the Soviet Union in population, wealth, technology, and military potential, and the idea that Russia is the naturally dominant power in Europe, against which Europe itself can construct no counterbalance without importing help, is a very recent one. This axiom should not remain unquestioned during the next thirty-five years of European politics, as it was during the last. It remains unassailable only if we assume that the Soviet Union will retain its present cohesion, that Germany will remain militarily emasculated, that Western Europe is without any effective political and strategic unity, or that its public opinion remains unwilling to shoulder defense burdens comparable to those carried by the superpowers.

For the present, however, these are the assumptions that we still have to make, and it is idle to imagine that Western Europe's security can be assured without an American contribution to the European balance. Two elements in that contribution remain essential: the deterrent role of U.S. strategic nuclear forces to neutralize a Soviet strategic nuclear threat to Western Europe, and the presence of a substantial body of U.S. conventional forces in Western Europe as a guarantee of U.S. involvement in a local conflict. The question is how much of the burden of defending Western Europe (and, along with it, the authority to make decisions within the alliance) can be shifted from American to European hands.

First, the countries of Western Europe need to take steps toward providing themselves with nuclear deterrent forces that will in due course assume the United States' function of neutralizing any Soviet nuclear threat, and in the short term take a greater share in it. The present basis for such forces is provided by Britain and France, and the most urgent need is for nuclear collaboration between them. It is most regrettable that the British government, in opting to purchase the Trident missile from the United States, has turned its back on cooperation with France, and embarked on a course that can only increase London's dependence on Washington.

Public opinion in Western European countries other than Britain and France has been unwilling in the past to regard the British and French forces as affording them protection, or as an effective substitute for the protection afforded by the United States. There are signs that, in present circumstances, this mood is changing, and to change it further, some form of strategic authority will have to be devised, in which all Western European governments and peoples will feel that they are given some role.

We should not assume that a Western European nuclear force must duplicate the forces available to the United States and the Soviet Union; its purposes would be not to enable Europe to dispute world primacy with the superpowers but rather to provide what used to be called, in the language now so despised by strategic analysts in Washington, a minimum deterrent against the extreme and highly improbable contingency of a

3. ALLIES OF THE US

direct Soviet nuclear threat. There would be a need to develop it in such a way as to indicate to the Soviet Union that it would have the effect of lessening, rather than of increasing, the tension in Europe.

More immediately, there is a need for European action to reduce the role played by nuclear weapons of all kinds in the defense of Western Europe, and to assert Western European control over those weapons still judged to be necessary. This issue of control is missing in the debate over the deployment of Pershing II and cruise missiles in Western Europe. The proposed theater nuclear weapons to be deployed will be American weapons, controlled by the United States alone and, thus, wholly contrary to the spirit of what I call a Europeanist policy. Such a policy must insist on some measure of European control over any new nuclear weapons that are deployed, and also take up the issue, so strangely neglected for many years (except by France), of control over existing U.S. nuclear forces in Europe, such as the U.S. bomber forces in Britain, in whose use European governments have, in effect, no voice whatever.

Second, the countries of Western Europe should make greater efforts to increase the size and improve the quality of their conventional forces in Europe. The Americans have been asking the Europeans to do this throughout the history of the alliance. They have been right to do so, and the shift in the distribution of wealth from America to Europe gives added weight to their arguments. It will not be accomplished without a radical change in public attitudes to defense in Western Europe, and I do not pretend that such a change can be brought about easily. It is, however, more likely to be achieved if defense is less associated in the public mind with support for the United States and its policies, and more exclusively connected with the need of European peoples to be ready to defend their own homelands. The desire to lessen reliance on nuclear weapons in Western European countries may also be pressed into the service of a campaign for conventional rearmament.

An increase in the proportion of Western Europe's contribution to the defense of Western Europe should lead to an increased European voice in the decision-making machinery of NATO. It should mean a European SACEUR (Supreme Allied Command in Europe). It would mean, at least if present political trends continue, that European countries would be not more, but less willing to facilitate the kind of military preparations to which the United States is committed outside the NATO area, and, thus, Washington's own reaction to it would be ambivalent.

Third, a Europeanist policy is not possible unless West Germany plays a more positive role. Germany is the largest and richest country in Europe, and it is only on the basis of West German power that a West European counterpoise to the Soviet Union can be constructed. This means that West Germany needs to play some role, even if at first a small one, in the control of

European nuclear forces: that West Germany's already considerable preponderance in conventional land forces in Western Europe must increase; and that West Germany must take more of a lead in making political and strategic decisions.

This cannot be done unless steps are taken to allay the inhibitions felt by the Russians and East Europeans, by the Western allies, and not least by the West Germans themselves, about Germany's return to a more "normal" status in world affairs. Even apart from these inhibitions, West Germany's continuing interest in the restoration of German unity, to which the Soviet Union holds the key, raises a persistent doubt about the permanence of its alliance with the West.

But this nettle, sooner or later, will have to be grasped. It will soon be forty years since the end of the Second World War. West Germany is an exemplary social democracy. The broad lines of its foreign policy enjoy a wide measure of support in Western Europe as a whole. Its chancellor is Europe's most experienced and respected statesman. The legitimization of West Germany's eastern frontiers has removed some, if by no means all, of the sources of its neighbors' anxieties. There can be no sudden change, but a continued evolution toward West Germany's assumption of a normal role is still desirable.

Fourth, Western Europe cannot make itself more self-sufficient in defense without developing some viable form of political unity. Although the countries of Western Europe are more united today than they have ever been before, they are still essentially a group of nation-states with a long history of conflict. Their recent habit of cooperation, moreover, has been formed against the background of American protection and the American presence. We are not entitled to assume that if this protection or presence were withdrawn or drastically reduced, the habit of cooperation would survive. Even if it does, it is scarcely sufficient at present to provide the common policies—as distinct from mere coordination of different policies—which a European strategic entity might be thought to presuppose.

The European Community at present has no defense function, and moreover includes one member (Ireland) that is outside NATO. The efforts of its member-states to coordinate their foreign policies have provided a valuable step forward, but they have to proceed on the basis of unanimous agreement among a group of states that is already politically and strategically diverse, and will become more so as the process of enlargement to include Mediterranean states is taken further.

The basis of Western European unity at present is, in fact, provided not by the institutions of the Community but by cooperation among the major nation-states. The precedent of the abortive European Defence Community of the 1950s, when the revival of European nation-states had not yet taken place, cannot be followed today. Nevertheless, some form of machinery will have to be devised that will take account of the reality of major-power leadership, the need to ensure the participation of the smaller states, and the desirability of giving a role to the European Community.

Fifth, a Europeanist policy will have to be executed with careful attention to its effect on the United States. There are good reasons why American opinion should be gratified by the emergence of a Western Europe that is more willing to shoulder the common burdens of defense, and is more united and more relaxed about its relationship to the United States because of its increased independence. On the other hand, this Europe is likely to disappoint some traditional American expectations. It would be less willing to follow the American lead, more capable of working against American policies should it wish to do so, and more of a risk as an ally of the United States. The "dumbbell alliance" of equal partners, beloved of Atlantic visionaries, is in theory the fulfillment of an old American dream, but America, in fact, has little experience with allies of equal stature.

If Western Europe has an interest in reducing its dependence on America, it also has to remember that it will need America's strategic support for a long time to come, and that a neo-isolationist mood in the United States, fed by European neutralism and anti-Americanism, may lead to a premature withdrawal. If Western European countries follow this Europeanist course, the United States is bound to regard its interests in European defense more cautiously and critically. Europe must ensure that this interest is perceived strongly.

Finally, the most important question of foreign policy that presently faces Britain is whether to persist in its chiefly pro-American orientation, or to begin regarding its neighbors in Europe as its principal partners.

There are many factors causing Britain's reluctance to move in what I have called a Europeanist direction. Britain is the principal foreign architect of the American commitment to Western Europe. It has been in many ways a favored beneficiary of this relationship. Its reliance on America in defense matters is older than the alliance itself. It has persistently championed the idea that defense is the preserve of the Atlantic Alliance and is persistently unfriendly to the organization of defense on a European basis, although it is true that both the Western European Union and the Eurogroup, which

alone today give Europe some personality in matters of defense, are mainly British creations. There is a deep fear among the older generation in Britain (in great contrast, I should say to the younger) that American withdrawal would mean a return to a pre-1941 situation, when Britain was uncomfortably alone in a Europe without America. There is the known antagonism of a majority of ordinary British people toward membership in the European Community, carefully kept at bay by the elite who feel (rightly, as I think) that they know better. There is the uncomfortable realization, even among those who are committed to the Community, that Britain is not the equal of France or West Germany in European affairs, as it was assumed to be when Britain joined. Among that very substantial section of the British public that is deeply uneasy about the American alliance, many are drawn toward the alternative offered by a neutralist, nuclear-free Scandinavia.

The present British government appears to have something of a split personality on these issues. Mrs. Thatcher's government has given the Reagan administration's foreign policies rhetorical support, reflecting both the prime minister's own community of ideological outlook with it, and the old British game of courting favor in Washington. On the other hand, the foreign policy establishment is well enough aware that Britain's interests in peace, in European détente, and in accommodation with the Third World are endangered by some of Washington's policies, and is politically much closer, *e.g.,* to Chancellor Schmidt than to President Reagan. The Foreign and Commonwealth Office under Lord Carrington has been keen in its support of European political cooperation and has played a prominent role in the shaping of what may be called (with some exaggeration) the European foreign policy line.

But Lord Carrington's Europeanism stops short of the crucial issue of defense. British defense policy, as the Trident decision shows, remains stodgily Atlanticist, and there is no sign that any attempt has been made to spell out the relationship between this policy and Britain's professions of European partnership. If Britain and Western Europe are to have a world policy distinct from that of America, they must first constitute themselves a strategic identity distinct from America's. Who will draw a bow at this venture?

Is NATO Obsolete?

LAWRENCE FREEDMAN

Lawrence Freedman is Professor of War Studies at King's College, London. His report is excerpted from the quarterly "International Affairs" published by the Royal Institute of International Affairs of London.

It is easier to describe the malaise that afflicts the Atlantic alliance than to explain its origins. It is also unclear whether this is a temporary phenomenon or the symptom of a deeper crisis that is unsettling the assumptions that have governed Western policy over the past three decades.

The disarray in the alliance at the start of 1980, caused by the Iranian seizure of American hostages and the Soviet invasion of Afghanistan, stimulated a surge in seminars, conferences, and publications that has yet to subside and was given added stimulus by differences over the imposition of martial law in Poland. Much of the comment assumes that the Atlantic alliance is the most fragile and delicate of international relationships. Yet the North Atlantic Treaty Organization has survived a stormy three decades in international affairs and many internal arguments. Nevertheless there are elements of the current situation that distinguish it from previous crises.

Some people maintain that the source of the problem is the decline of a sense of Atlantic community that followed World War II. It was a legacy of the relationships developed during the war, sustained in the years of the Marshall Plan, the Berlin airlift, and the creation of NATO and nurtured on a vision of cooperation between the Western democracies as the road to peace and prosperity.

It is important not to overstate the ideals and cohesion of that generation. The commitment of those present at the creation of the alliance was largely a function of the political battles waged against those who questioned the propriety of alliance. Defenders of NATO still see their antagonists as direct descendants of the first opponents. The fear is of isolationism in the U.S. or neutralism in Europe. Insofar as the arguments against alliance always stress the risk of being drawn into something dangerous or foolish, a certain continuity in the forms of opposition is to be expected.

Opinion polls, however, have not detected any groundswell in anti-NATO sentiment in the member states. But there is a hazy notion as to what NATO actually is. In the U.S. the lack of media coverage of European affairs has been reinforced by a loss of interest in these matters, evidenced by the decline in European studies in the universities. The European language most favored is Spanish rather than French or German, reflecting preoccupations with Latin America.

Europeans often suspect that American lack of interest in them is matched by an increasing interest in the Pacific region, a result of the shift in power and population in the U.S. from the East to the West and the increase in American trade with Pacific countries. Yet the Japanese claim not to be aware of any surge of interest in their affairs. The change may be not so much a switch of attention from the Atlantic to the Pacific as a preoccupation with domestic affairs and an interest in foreigners only to the extent that they impinge on domestic matters.

Introspection is not unique to the U.S.; the same phenomena can be observed throughout Europe. Moreover the economic troubles of the past decade have rendered political activity less predictable. National policy has become correspondingly less coherent and consistent. This turns into a vicious circle; introspection and instability at home have a negative effect on foreign policy, and cooperative endeavors falter. The effect of this is to make domestic problems less tractable.

The problem facing the Atlantic alliance is therefore nothing so simple as active hostility led by the twin evils of isolationism and neutralism. Such a view may assume far too much interest in the structure of international relations. The real risk may be of a drifting apart, fueled largely by indifference and introspection, rather than some dramatic and decisive break.

For our earlier generation of policymakers the Atlantic alliance provided a point of reference for all international issues. The politics of the rest of the world was an extension of the politics of the U.S. and the old European powers (including the old outsider, Russia). Over the past twenty years other powers have intruded into this framework. The end of the empires has meant that the former colonies have had to be dealt with on their own terms, and the old powers find themselves competing to gain footholds in each other's former colonies.

Japan has emerged as a world economic power and other small Asian nations have become industrial trendsetters; the Arab states have been attempting to buy political muscle with oil. Thus the quality of the Atlantic relationship can no longer be the determinant of a stable world order. Policymakers have to cope with more complex linkages than in the past.

In these conditions it is not surprising if the U.S. and the Europeans de-

From *World Press Review*, November 1982. Excerpted from International Affairs, published by the Royal Institute of International Affairs of London. Reprinted by permission from World Press Review.

velop dissimilar approaches to the international system, or if their views of each other become less generous. Whether or not different attitudes have actually emerged on each side of the Atlantic is difficult to say, but in any given trouble spot it is unlikely that American and European interests directly coincide. The major divergence is the priority given by the U.S. to opposing Communism as a major foreign policy objective.

Inevitably, economics enters into NATO's disarray. In the early days of the alliance the U.S. dominated the international economy. The relationship between the U.S. and Western Europe is now quite balanced. The U.S. is still the largest economic unit in the world and the role of the dollar as a reserve currency has not yet been seriously challenged. But in trade terms the U.S. has become more dependent on Western Europe, the only major region with which it enjoys a consistent surplus, thereby offsetting deficits with OPEC and the industrial countries of Asia.

The U.S. and Europe are in different positions when it comes to raw materials. In neither oil nor nonfuel minerals is the U.S. as close to self-sufficiency as it once was, but the dependence is still less than that of Western Europe. Thus trouble in the resource-rich areas of the Third World has graver implications for Europe than for the U.S.

With the relative decline of America's economic power and the slowing of its economic growth, the Europeans feel that the U.S. ought to be more willing to cooperate on an equal footing and that they are no longer obliged to accept whatever economic pressures flow across the Atlantic. Transatlantic arguments are therefore likely to be frequent and substantial. The particular sources of controversy may vary — high inflation one moment, high interest rates the next. The only comfort is that while the two sides may blame each other for part of their economic woes, they are likely to blame Japan and OPEC more. International economic problems cannot be solved on a transatlantic basis.

Although the Atlantic alliance is essentially about security, it is impossible to isolate the military side of the member countries' relationship from the economic side because of the high cost of defense. The economic troubles of the past decade ended the surge in public expenditure that had marked the 1960s. Now defense spending either has to be made a special case (with a potential for arguments based on guns versus butter) or else it is necessary to tolerate a diminution in the overall defense effort. The Reagan Administration's attempts to combine increased defense spending with lower taxes resulted in higher interest rates and a setback to European economic hopes. It is unlikely that the Europeans will be able to respond to calls for increases in defense spending comparable to those planned by the U.S.

There is another more fundamental sense in which economic changes influence security. The diffusion of economic power over the past two decades — largely away from the U.S. — means that Western Europe is now in a stronger position vis-à-vis the U.S. but has to take account of other important groups, of which the oil producers and the East European economies are politically important while the newly industrializing countries play an increasingly prominent trade role. The U.S. imports proportionately less of its oil from the Middle East than does Western Europe and conducts remarkably little trade with the Soviet Union and Eastern Europe. Western Europe has much more at stake in its economic relations with both regions than has the U.S. This puts a cloud over all NATO diplomacy.

The debates with NATO accentuate the importance of defense spending and of the relative dependence of the U.S. and Western Europe in the international economy. If the alliance can hold together and project a serious military capability, it probably can keep the Soviet Union in check. But the asymmetrical relationship between the U.S. and Western Europe ensures continual tension. The Europeans will always be nervous about being sold out or subjected to undue risk, and the Americans will grumble about shouldering disproportionate burdens. Nevertheless, it is unlikely that any party to a NATO debate would feel that its security position would be improved by the breakup of the alliance.

The basic problem is that NATO has put at the center of its strategic doctrine the dubious proposition that an American president would authorize first use of nuclear weapons in response to a Warsaw Pact conventional-weapons invasion of Western Europe that looked as if it might succeed. West European dependence on this myth has become one of the more unsettling features of U.S.-European relations. Although it is intellectually unconvincing in that it requires the U.S. to threaten suicidal action on behalf of its allies, it is politically viable in that the Soviet Union is unlikely to try to call America's bluff.

It is an act of faith for the U.S. to offer, and the West Europeans to accept, a nuclear guarantee that can be sustained as long as both sides engage in an elaborate process of mutual reassurance. Because of this, alliance doctrine has acquired a heavy overlay of symbolism. It is one reason why discussions of Atlantic relations soon get down to fundamentals, for every security move is immediately treated in symbolic terms.

It is common to blame the confusion in NATO strategic doctrine on the Soviet Union's achievement of nuclear parity with the U.S. But the prospect of a nuclear stalemate has figured in alliance calculations since the first Soviet atomic test in 1949 and the mutual state of assured destruction was proclaimed in the mid-1960s. It has certainly become more evident in a strictly numeric sense, but the real change is in the judgment of the consequences of parity.

During the 1970s, in part a result of the loss of confidence in détente, American strategists became preoccupied with the question of what will happen if deterrence fails. Unless a satisfactory answer can be found, it has been argued, the whole edifice of deterrence will collapse because the threats upon which it depends will be exposed as worthless. To remedy this position either American superiority must be regained or NATO's position at the lower levels of the escalation ladder reinforced. Otherwise accommodation to Soviet power has to be accepted.

In 1981 the new Reagan Administration soon discovered that the allies would not be reassured by American displays of military preparedness. When Secretary of Defense Caspar Weinberger spoke about the likelihood of the neutron bomb being reinstated, he thought this would be welcomed by the Europeans and must have been surprised by their reaction, which conveyed the impression of an appeasing and neutralist trend. A likely explanation for the European — particularly the West German — position was that accommodation was under way. Attempts to shore up nuclear deterrence had failed to convince the Europeans.

West European leaders found themselves accused by Americans of succumbing to Soviet power because of their inability to accept what was necessary to make deterrence work, and accused by many of their own people of succumbing to American power by accepting, via nuclear weapons, the risks of a hawkish American foreign policy. To argue that the likelihood of an allout war in Central Europe is too remote to warrant all this tension hardly seemed adequate. It might be possible to restore some faith in deterrence by effective measures of arms control, but it is difficult to be optimistic.

There is no reason to believe that the present disquiet in Europe on American security policies will quickly evaporate. Part of the anti-nuclear movement is a response to the combative approach of the Reagan Administration to its foreign policy problems. This might be remedied by a less assertive American diplomacy or by developments that might convince the public of the need for toughness.

The anti-nuclear movements in Europe gained credibility from American behavior during 1980 and the election of Mr. Reagan with his entourage of zealous hawks. If East-West relations improve these movements may subside, even if the objects of their protest remain. The long-term implication of these movements is the growing influence of activists who developed their beliefs during the days of student radicalism and anti-Vietnam War protest in the late 1960s. The generation whose Atlanticism was based on the cooperation of World War II and postwar reconstruction is giving way to a generation with an inbuilt suspicion of American foreign policy.

This has clear implications if the centerpiece of American foreign policy over the coming decades is going to be an indiscriminate stance against all manifestations of Communism. The new European activists' critique of NATO military doctrine gains force because of their prior critique of American foreign policy in the Third World. If deterrence fails, it will not be because of a political breakdown in Central Europe but because of superpower conflict in the Third World that will spill over into Europe.

In the episodic crises of the past decade there is a recurring theme of an effort by European leaders to encourage the U.S. to keep a sense of perspective about left-wing successes in various parts of the world. They recall how the rise of Euro-Communism and the Portuguese revolution was going to lead to the collapse of NATO's Southern flank; then Angola and Zimbabwe were going to be the means by which the Soviet Union could control the Cape Route; next the invasion of Afghanistan was the first stage en route to the Gulf; and more recently insurgency in El Salvador was adding to the Communist outposts.

From an American viewpoint such an impression is exaggerated. It is arguable that had Washington not made a fuss there could have been a drift into a dangerous situation because of the cumulative effects of developments that might individually appear to be of only marginal importance. The American complaint was that Europeans had lost their global vision and were unwilling to see the links between their security and events outside Europe.

Much of the questioning in Europe of the advisability of close links with the U.S. stems from concern over the consequences of what is perceived to be recklessness by the U.S. in its dealings with the Third World. The disagreement over security challenges in the Third World has three main causes. First, there are so many parties involved and the issues are so complex that the potential for miscalculation is enormous. Second, the differential dependence on key raw materials, notably oil, means that the Europeans are willing to take fewer diplomatic risks. Third, the incentives for low-risk policies are intensified by the decline in European ability to project significant military power outside the continent.

There has been a debate within NATO over whether it is appropriate to prepare for large-scale military intervention in the Third World — the Gulf in particular — to counter any Soviet adventure. The Europeans prefer to keep out of local controversies and concentrate on what is believed to be the Western interest in preserving steady markets and raw material supplies by encouraging regional stability. This may be fine as a general inclination but it leaves little scope for active diplomacy. It becomes risky to offend key states by talking too loudly about their more dubious internal practices or external adventures.

This may mean that disputes which once might have been dealt with by traditional diplomacy backed by threats of military force will now be played out in the economic sphere. In each of the recent crises — Iran, Afghanistan, Poland, El Salvador — the lack of credible military options led to demands for economic sanctions or, if the recipient was not too large, generous offers of aid. Even with the Falklands crisis, where military options seemed more appropriate, the first instinct of many was to seek economic pressure.

The Atlantic alliance remains a crucial feature of the structure of international relations, but its relative importance has declined. The challenge therefore is for the alliance to organize itself so that it may influence the forces shaping the rest of the structure. To some extent this has already been recognized in calls for alliance-wide consultations (including Japan) to coordinate responses to crises in the Third World.

Such institutional improvements are difficult when the international conditions that make them necessary create an indifference toward and impatience with multilateral diplomacy. They are also insufficient unless those involved operate with a clear sense of what is at stake and where they stand. Only by doing this can the alliance be turned into a more mature relationship between countries aware that traditional ties and common interests require them to stay together.

French Diplomacy:
A Two-Headed Sphinx

Franz-Olivier Giesbert

Franz-Olivier Giesbert is Political Editor of Le Nouvel Observateur, *a French weekly. His biography of François Mitterrand won the Prix Aujourd'hui for the best political book of 1977. This article was translated by Steven B. Kennedy, who received his M.A. in International Relations from Yale University that same year.*

Since de Gaulle, America has had a problem with France. Recent French presidents have not been easy partners for Washington. First, they have sought to maintain a special relationship with Moscow; in the Gaullist conception, after all, Europe extends "from the Atlantic to the Urals." The second reason is that these presidents have all been unpredictable and elusive—a question of ambition. Henry Kissinger hits the nail on the head when he writes in the second volume of his memoirs that "the traditional goal of French diplomacy during the Gaullist Fifth Republic" was to "give at least the impression that France had shaped events, whatever they were." Things can go well only if the United States allows Paris to play the leading role.

If François Mitterrand's accession to power signaled a break on the economic front, it has changed practically nothing in the diplomatic arena. The chief of state has slipped easily into the robes of president de Gaulle, Pompidou, and Giscard d'Estaing.

Americans who had tagged Mitterrand as the apostle of union on the Left and who feared a turn toward the Soviet Union were wrong. But those who foresaw a very pro-American turn were also wrong. After practically a year of Mitterrand's diplomacy, a number of broad lines are emerging, which enable us to understand better what Raymond Aron has called "the Socialist Sphinx."

The Socialist party (PS) has spoken with two voices for quite some time. On the one hand, in a 380-page long-range plan adopted by party leaders in 1980, the party played its anti-American card. Simultaneously defending the principle of France's membership in the Atlantic Alliance, the plan exalts French-Soviet friendship, asserting that "our security and European peace hinge on Moscow." In this view, the United States, and not the U.S.S.R., is imperialist. On the other hand, during the 1981 presidential campaign Mitterrand reproached Valéry Giscard d'Estaing for his concessions to the Soviet Union, and particularly for his Warsaw meeting with Leonid Brezhnev following the Red Army's invasion of Afghanistan. Moreover, several months after his election Mitterrand took a clear stand in favor of the deployment of Pershing missiles in Europe—a decision adopted by NATO in 1979—whereas his predecessor had been consistently evasive on this question. Need one speak further of a split personality?

Like Jimmy Carter, Mitterrand has never been troubled by the confrontations amongst his advisors. Cohabiting the Elysée are economist Jacques Attali, an ardent supporter of Israel, and the pro-Palestinian, Régis Debray (who was with Ché Guevara in Bolivia). Around the Council of Ministers' table each Wednesday one finds all sorts: Atlanticists like André Chandernagor, minister of European affairs; neutralists like Jean-Pierre Chevènement, minister of research and technology; Third Worlders like Jean-Pierre Cot, minister of cooperation and development; and Soviet-leaning Communists like Charles Fiterman, minister of transportation. They talk . . . and Mitterrand decides. To date this has produced diplomacy that is often flamboyant, sometimes windy, and imbued with several contradictions. It is a mixture of audacity and realpolitik that is not so far from Giscardism.

Why this continuity? Because France does not enjoy a great deal of room to maneuver. Economically, these are serious times, if not yet desperate. There are more than two million unemployed in the country. The trade deficit has tripled in eight years. This calls for a certain prudence, and President Mitterrand has shown that. Following a period of grand statements in defense of human rights and in condemnation of arms merchants, Mitterrand has returned to the stock-in-trade of "Giscard, Inc.," in which France may sell arms to Ethiopia for use in crushing the Eritrean national liberation movement, which is still supported by the PS in its official texts. And France continues its past practice of littering Third World countries with military hardware.

3. ALLIES OF THE US

This provides jobs and exchange. Apparently, the Socialists have discovered *raison d'état*. Sounding the trumpets of neorealism, Lionel Jospin, first secretary of the PS and militant Third Worlder, began suddenly to sound like Ronald Reagan in declaring that "the rights of man must not be confused with economic logic."

With regard to the Middle East, Mitterrand is the first sincerely pro-Israeli statesman that France has had for some time. Fascinated by the Jewish spirit, the French president fervently defends Israel's right to exist and maintains friendly relations with portions of the leadership of the Labor party. Here, too, however, matters become complicated in the exercise of power, since France's hands are not entirely free. Importing 75 percent of its energy needs each year, the country is dependent on the Arab world.

So it was not by chance that Mitterrand paid one of his first official calls on Saudi Arabia, France's leading source of oil. Nor is it chance that Paris and Jerusalem have exchanged sharp words these past few months. Overall, however, the French president has pursued a more balanced Middle East policy than did Giscard. Not long ago, *Al Baas,* organ of the ruling Baath party in Syria, accused France of having come out in favor of a "Zionist entity" by participating in the international peacekeeping force in the Sinai. The newspaper invited Arabs to "review their relations with France, since President Mitterrand is the first European head of state and the first French president to visit Israel since its creation."

Mitterrand's positions on Israel were expected. On this question he has never wavered. It is in the area of East-West relations that he has caused the most surprise. During the presidential campaign, for example, he was extremely cautious on the matter of the Pershing missiles. However, in one of his first political acts as president, he positioned himself unreservedly behind Helmut Schmidt in the missile quarrel, disavowing Willy Brandt and the left wing of the German Social Democratic party, with which he had until then been closely identified within the Socialist International. Poland completed the rupture with Brandt. The day after Jaruzelski's putsch, the ex-chancellor redoubled with conciliatory statements, showing an astonishing leniency toward the U.S.S.R. At worst, these statements reinforced journalist Jack Anderson's contention that Brandt was in cahoots with Moscow. At best, they shocked French Socialists.

Sincerely moved, Mitterrand was among those Western heads of state who virulently denounced the black winter in Warsaw. Although he likes to place himself in the vanguard, the French president did not go as far as Ronald Reagan. Isolated in Europe, he even ended up beating a strategic retreat.

On January 10, 1982, Minister of Foreign Relations Claude Cheysson explained that the fundamental characteristic of the East-West conflict was "the struggle against totalitarianism." According to Cheysson, the "terrible event" in Poland should be seized upon for purposes of "dismantling" the machinery and exposing the "true nature" of the Soviet system. Bold words. In uttering them, Cheysson was merely returning—with a bit of added emphasis—to the statements made by the chief of state in his New Year's message. Nevertheless, the president fiercely disavowed them.

Twelve days later France signed a natural gas agreement with the U.S.S.R. Each year for twenty-five years, France is to receive eight billion cubic meters of Siberian gas, over and above the four billion it already receives. By 1990 a third of the gas consumed in France will come in from the cold. The French government, in short, has committed itself to furnishing billions of dollars in exchange to the U.S.S.R., while at the same time providing the latter with a new means of intimidating France. The Agreement was not well timed, coming less than two months after the Warsaw coup, and it irresistibly called to mind Giscard's capitulations following the invasion of Afghanistan.

Mitterrand did not lack economic reasons for approving the accord. Like his predecessors, he is seeking to diversify France's energy sources. In addition, the contract is drawn up in French francs, so that Siberian gas will not be subject, as is oil, to the wild fluctuations of the dollar. And since France is not at war with Moscow, the president concluded, there could be no question of embargo. In the end, Mitterrand acted as if there were nothing between détente and the cold war.

This analysis does not clash with Schmidt's, a fact that has made possible the maintenance in Europe of a Paris-Bonn connection which one might have thought doomed by the victory of the Left in France. Schmidt, who had hoped for the reelection of Giscard, has never concealed his mistrust of Mitterrand and the strategy of the Union of the Left. Today, the two men find themselves on approximately the same wavelength on East-West questions. Both worry about the neutralist wave sweeping Europe, a movement encouraged and infiltrated by Moscow. And both wish to avoid a worsening of tensions between the superpowers.

Of course, President Mitterrand has more latitude than Schmidt, and he aims to make the best of it. The neutralist movement does not count for much in France. The forces of Finlandization are being organized by the Communist party, which represents no more than 15 percent of the electorate. Moreover, the party's prospects are not good. In power, it has weakened and has begun to lose some of its zeal. George Marchais, its leader, is France's least popular political figure, according to the polls. The party is further faced with insurmountable contradictions. Totally committed to an orthodox pro-Moscow line, the PC mimics attacks by the Soviet press on Solidarity, an entity enthusiastically supported by the French government, of which the Communists are, of course, a part. Nevertheless, President Mitterrand does not wish his own rhetoric to make Communist participation in the government impossible.

In his view, such participation will keep the PC from capitalizing on conceivable failures in the future. Consequently, he will not provoke them.

President Mitterrand readily admits that "anything that helps us to leave Yalta behind will be to the good." But, for him this seems more in the nature of a pious vow than a long-term design. He has no more of a liberation plan for Eastern Europe than do Schmidt, Thatcher, or Reagan. Giscard, the Soviets' favorite in the 1981 presidential election, bought social peace and the tacit support of the Soviets by offering them diplomatic pledges, because (and this cannot be said often enough) the U.S.S.R. is a weighty presence in French politics, thanks to the PC, which Moscow uses at will. It was Brezhnev's ambassador to Paris who announced to Giscard on July 28, 1977, that the then high-flying Union of the Left would break apart. At that time, the Socialists did not even suspect that such a break was possible. It came two months later. This probably accounts for Giscard's softness toward Moscow in the years that followed.

President Mitterrand appears to have decided to make fewer pledges to the U.S.S.R. than his predecessor. Jacques Huntzinger, foreign secretary for the PS, emphatically asserts the necessity of "vigorously denouncing the regimes of the East." And the minister of foreign affairs declared last summer that French relations with the Soviet Union "cannot be the same as long as there are Soviet troops in Afghanistan. It's as simple as that." Of course it was not so simple.

After the Communist party's[1] crackdown in Poland, the same minister stated weakly, "We will do nothing." He was reprimanded by the president for having spoken the plain truth. France has taken no retaliatory measures, symbolic or economic, refusing even to cancel the visit of two French representatives scheduled to take part in a Soviet space experiment. But this did not stop the chief of state from speaking out loud and clear about crucified Poland.

The great change from recent years is that anti-Soviet proclamations, far from shocking the Left, are now approved by a larger and larger school of Socialist thought. Dailies close to the government, such as *Le Monde, Le Matin,* and *Libération,* no longer show any indulgence toward Soviet expansionism. Many reject any connection between El Salvador and Poland, viewing the two dictatorships as being of different natures. The gas contract with the U.S.S.R. has been sharply criticized by a number of Socialists, and by Edmond Maire, leader of the French Democratic Confederation of Labor.[2] "A stab in the back of Solidarity," was Maire's reaction. At the same time, of course, CERES,[3] the small pseudo-Leninist stream within the PS, has criticized the administration for its "essentially Atlanticist" foreign policy.

If this policy does, in fact, add up to an Atlantic orientation, it is because President Mitterrand is, on the whole, an Atlanticist. In 1966, for example, he voted in the National Assembly against the French withdrawal from NATO engineered by de Gaulle. Since his arrival to power he has made decisions that belong unmistakably in the Atlanticist camp. Thus, his leftist administration appears more concerned than its conservative predecessors with halting exports of "sensitive" technology to the East. To this end, it has created a commission under the authority of Prime Minister Pierre Mauroy to screen trade accords, and has supported the reactivation of the Coordinating Committee for Multilateral Export Controls (COCOM).[4] In the same vein, it is unreservedly supporting the admission of Spain into NATO and has condemned more strongly than ever the occupation of Afghanistan. The Socialist party even committed itself recently to "making available those means it could to the Afghan resistance."

President Mitterrand's Atlanticism has limits, of course. And the honeymoon with the United States will probably never take place, for two reasons. The first is economic: Along with Saudi Arabia, the United States, is at the heart of France's large trade deficit. The United States, furthermore, forces France to keep interest rates high. "The United States must realize," declared the president on June 9, 1981, "that there can be no true solidarity which is not founded upon just economic cooperation."

The second reason is the Third World. On this point, President Mitterrand could have communicated with Andrew Young and Jimmy Carter. With Ronald Reagan, the lines are closed. The French president believes that poverty and hunger, and not the Soviets, fuel movements of national liberation. And he condemns U.S. aid to the dictatorships of Latin America. Last August 28 he chose guerrillas over junta in El Salvador when, with Mexico, he "recognized" the revolutionary fronts. In the same way, France has sold antiguerrilla weaponry to Nicaragua. A number of Socialist leaders, with a sort of naive candor, even maintain excellent relations with the Castro dictatorship. In the Third World, therefore, it would appear that the breach between Washington and Paris may widen, while the two capitals continue to move closer together on East-West matters.

The "Socialist Sphinx" is, in the end, not a mystery at all. If it is intriguing, it is simply because it has two faces, one turned toward the Atlantic, the other toward the Third World. It is Reaganite in its East-West relations, Carterite in North-South affairs.

NOTES

1. Official name: Polish United Workers' Party—TN.
2. The CFDT (Confédération Française Démocratique du Travail) is France's largest non-Communist labor union.—TN.
3. The Centre d'Etudes. de Recherches et d'Education Socialistes was founded in 1966 by Jean-Pierre Chevènement, presently minister of research and technology.—TN
4. Based in Paris, COCOM regulates Western sales of military, nuclear, and "sensitive" industrial equipment to the Communist world.—TN.

WEST GERMANY'S NEW CHANCELLOR

The thoughts of Helmut Kohl

Helmut Kohl is West Germany's first Christian Democratic federal chancellor for 13 years. Not an English-speaker, he is more of a stranger to outsiders than were either of his Social Democratic predecessors. Here is Mr Kohl's first interview outside West Germany. Our questions were aimed at German policy towards east and west. Mr Kohl's answers show a clear head—and a man who has not yet had to make the hard choices ahead

You have said that you will not yield to pressure against deployment of Nato's new nuclear weapons, that you would be prepared to have Pershing-2 and cruise missiles stationed in the Federal Republic of Germany if the negotiations in Geneva do not yield satisfactory results. Will you be in a position to do that?

Those are two questions. I said that we must keep to both parts of the Nato twin-track agreement of 1979. The two parts are mutually dependent, they condition each other. The first part deals with the modernisation and deployment of new medium-range nuclear systems on the western side in response to the previous Soviet build-up of such systems. The second part states that we want the limitation of intermediate-range nuclear weapons on both sides to be discussed seriously and earnestly in Geneva. We shall do everything we can, in conjunction with our friends in Europe, to help our friends in America to do this. I have stressed again and again both to the American president and his ministers in Washington, and again to his secretary of state here in Bonn, that we expect the Americans to tackle this seriously, to make every effort in the negotiations in view of the threat to our existence posed by the Soviet superiority in intermediate-range nuclear weapons. I have every reason to believe that the Americans will negotiate seriously and earnestly.

I am firmly convinced that our chances of reaching a positive result in Geneva will be so much better the clearer the position taken by the west is. For instance, if we, the federal republic, give way beforehand to the temptation not to deploy the Pershing-2 and cruise mis-

siles—this is the principle of the stick and the carrot—America's negotiating position in Geneva will be weakened. If the Soviet Union succeeds in getting West Germany to withdraw from the Nato agreement on deployment of medium-range missiles it will not need to negotiate seriously or intensely in Geneva. The clear and firm will to accept both parts of the agreement is the precondition for success in the negotiations. Anyone who proclaims the slogan "peace without weapons" in advance (ie, unilateral disarmament) undermines the negotiations in Geneva and is programming their failure.

The federal republic is the seam between east and west: 17m Germans are living in the east. We are, to change the metaphor, a seismograph—any worsening of the political climate, any drop in the temperature in east-west relations, is immediately felt in Berlin, the divided city, and here. Yet our position is absolutely clear: we are a part of the west, we are not equi-distant from Moscow and Washington, we are members of the alliance, and without the presence of American soldiers here, the British army of the Rhine, the French, the alliance, you wouldn't be sitting here with me in the federal chancellor's office.

On the last part of your question—will I be able to achieve deployment if negotiations fail? Yes, I am sure I will. The great majority of our people understand the issue and share my conviction that we must not be open to blackmail and pressure.

If the Dutch and Belgians refuse to accept the weapons, do you think it will be

sufficient for you if only the Italians accept them?

I have no reason to believe that Holland and Belgium will finally refuse their consent. I assume that we will give our consent jointly.

Assuming the Italians were to refuse, what then?

That is a purely academic question. I have no reason to doubt that they will stick to their decision. The new Italian prime minister, Fanfani, is a close friend of mine; I have many close and valuable friends in Italy's Christian Democratic party and their position is absolutely clear. They are highly experienced politicians. The Italian Socialists have also taken a very clear stand. There is a definite majority in Italy in support of Nato's position.

Some Americans talk of doubling up, by supplying "reloads", the number of Pershing missiles to be deployed.

We had a very clear discussion on this in Washington. We want to be a reliable and serious partner, calculable for both sides. If we are to be calculable, we have to keep to the timetable and the number agreed on. We are not going to discuss other figures. The number agreed on remains. The Americans understand perfectly what our position is.

Wouldn't reloads be sensible in any case? Would you not be prepared to accept more?

We are going to keep to the number agreed. I am dependent on the support of my fellow citizens, and I can only keep their confidence if I keep my word. That is my capital investment.

Do you think you can hope for any help from the Americans before the elections in March by way of their modifying their zero-option proposal before then?
No. I don't want American aid for a German election. I don't use guests of the state as propaganda for elections, it is my job to represent German interests and German policies. I don't need help as far as the German general public are concerned on the matter of our readiness for defence. Others, who are moving away from views they used to hold, are the ones who need help just now.

You were reported when visiting the army at Koblenz as saying that you were rather optimistic regarding the outcome of the Geneva negotiations—that you had signals of this from both west and east.
The report was not quite correct. I simply put forward a consideration, and I don't mind repeating it: I said, the American president will be facing an election in two years time. Two years before you have to fight an election is a very good position to be in. We have just had a change of leadership in the Soviet Union: Andropov is a new man. He has come to power at a certain age—he is 68. He will try, in the time he has left, to leave his mark on history. And so he will have to make his decisions now.

When I was in Washington I suggested that in this situation the gesture President Reagan, when he was in hospital after the assassination attempt, made to Secretary General Brezhnev should be repeated to the new man at the top of the Kremlin. The president wrote a hand-written letter to Brezhnev, a very moving letter, not only in his capacity as president of the United States but as father of a family, as a man. It was an appeal to the other man in Soviet Russia, not only on a political level but on the human level. Brezhnev never replied individually to the letter. Only months later a bureaucratic answer was sent.

I suggested to President Reagan that he should stretch out his hand again. I suggested that it should be done not as a propaganda measure but again as a human gesture. I was asked whether it would be a good idea that the two could meet on that level, and I said, yes I do. Optimism regarding a successful summit is of course to a certain extent optimism regarding Geneva.

General Rogers [supreme allied commander Europe] has said that more should be spent on conventional weapons: do you think that is a good idea?
General Rogers has certainly raised a worthwhile long-term question. Let me

answer for the present moment. The economic situation is very bad at present. We have more than 2m unemployed, more than ever before in the history of the federal republic. We are having serious problems with our public budget. I was elected chancellor by the Bundestag only in October and it is now early December: I have had to force through a huge number of decisions in a very short time, I have had to cut expenditure to an extent never experienced before—I put back the date for pensions adjustment, cut school money, and I am facing a federal election in the spring.

What I am trying to say is that we have done in a few days and weeks everything possible to put forward and implement a programme of financial reforms. As a first step we have also made money available for Nato infrastructure. We also have problems with what we call a "backlog of claims" on certain items for the army, and we have made a positive move here. This will benefit precisely those groups in the army who have to deal with young soldiers and this should improve motivation. We are also facing serious demographic problems. We will have discussion on this in the election campaign and it will take a major effort in the next legislative period: if we want to keep up our manpower quota in Nato on a falling birth-rate we will be facing the question of lengthening military service along with other measures. Look at the debate that has erupted in America over conscription.

Specific promises have been made, eg, that Nato countries should spend in real terms 3% a year more on defence—do you think you will manage that? General Rogers has suggested that 4% will be necessary.
We have had a good record on this in previous years. We will have to see how it turns out next year. Then you have to ask, what is 3%? What does it include? All these percentages have their own significance—you can do anything with statistics. If the Nato supreme commander says he needs 4% that doesn't mean that the Germans—the two chambers in parliament, the government, business and so on—will all meet and declare that this will be carried out. I am a partner in an alliance, and in my view a partnership means that you talk to each other and not about each other. I may add that from my talks with General Rogers I gained the impression that he sees the matter in exactly the same way.

That raises a philosophical question: how can western countries increase their Nato commitment and defence expenditure when they are facing such economic diff-

iculties, with choices necessary between social and military spending?
That is an important question, an elementary political question, and it needs a political answer. This has to be very drastic: the German chancellor must do all he can to stimulate the economy. I must do all I can to reduce unemployment, youth unemployment above all. But it would all be a waste of time if I could not guarantee peace and freedom for our country.

But then the question arises: how do you set which is your priority?
You have to do both. I cannot say: I am going to cut down the army and cut down military service because I have to combat unemployment first. You have to take the middle route.

But there is only so much in the kitty.
Yes, of course, and so I have to spread the sacrifices as best I can. I don't really see this as a problem. Perhaps I am rather old-fashioned. Politicians have to behave as people do in their private lives; in my view a bad housekeeper makes a bad politician. You can't simply eliminate certain areas of expenditure altogether. We must remain capable of defending ourselves. And we will not do that if we adopt a policy of "either-or". Our young people must realise that there is a point in what they are doing, when they are being asked to defend our country. They must come to see that they are defending freedom and peace. It must be a freedom that appeals to them, that makes sense to them. The principle of social justice and the will to defend are closely related.

Do you believe that Andropov's accession to power means that we can expect a more co-operative foreign policy from the Russians?
I am not a Kremlin astrologer, and Kremlinologists have anyway often been wrong.

The new general secretary is facing a multitude of problems: in the economy; in supplies; there is the war in Afghanistan, which is like a cancer on the Soviet Union's reputation abroad, especially in Islam; he has the problem of Poland, which is symptomatic of the whole situation in eastern Europe. After 35 years the communist party has burnt itself out, the workers have gone underground or run away, tens of thousands of young people, students, the intelligentsia have turned away from the party. You may suppress the people but you don't win their hearts.

The Poles are streaming to the Black Madonna at Czestochowa although in the Leninist view that is all rubbish. The Poles have retained all the fervour of their nationalism. You can seal the border hermetically. But thoughts are free, they pass through the air, through the pores of the walls, and here in the west we have no reason to say time is against us: it is working for us.

Soviet policy is always a continuation of Russian policy. If you don't know anything about Russian history you won't understand Soviet policy. The Soviet leaders see themselves as part of a long continuous line. They have always seen themselves in that way. Their country does not have a natural frontier to the west. It is quite incomprehensible to me, to the Germans, to hear the Russians say they feel threatened by the west. Who do they believe can attack them? The Bundeswehr? Nato? Nato is a defence alliance. Nobody here wants a war. But, historically, the Russians have experienced invasion from the west from Napoleon through to Hitler and that experience is reality to them, whether we understand it or not. I feel that in this phase especially it is important to hold talks with the Soviet Union, but the talks will be all the more serious if it is clear that we are partners who do not shirk their obligations, who keep to their word, even if they are saying "no".

Andropov will be the leader of a group which existed before, although of course now it will be re-profiled. Changes won't all happen overnight. We should see what can be achieved, step by step, and, if the steps prove positive, we should be positive in our reaction, not as propaganda but calmly.

We have nothing to get uptight about, nothing at all. I can't see that time is against us. A falsifying "culture-pessimism" is generally propounded by people who live very well on it. They are well paid—in university jobs, the media and so on. I can see no reason for such pessimism. We need patience and a calm, sensible and reliable policy.

Whether or not we expect it, should we not at least behave in the west as though we expect a more conciliatory line from Andropov than from Brezhnev?
What will help peace best—and preserve it—is "Realpolitik". I think we should wait and see how Soviet policy develops. President Reagan has put forward concrete proposals. It is now up to the Soviet Union to answer. Then we can see.

Under what conditions should Reagan meet Andropov? Should such a meeting be absolutely dependent on results of the Geneva talks?
Talks of that nature are only meaningful if there is a real chance of success. There must be good will on both sides as well as thorough preparation. There must be no attempt to make propaganda out of it.

Can West Germany, as your predecessor used to say, play an interpreter's role between America and Russia?
I think the whole concept is wrong. Anyway the federal republic never played any such part.

But it was seen like that.
It was represented like that. But we are talking about policy, not propaganda. I think the cobbler should stick to his last, and the saying "Am deutschen Wesen soll die Welt genesen"—the German character can heal the world—dates from the nineteenth century: it is nonsense in the twentieth. It is not a part of my vocabulary, I have crossed it out. Being an interpreter in politics means being a referee. That is a role we last played at the Berlin Congress under Otto von Bismarck—it didn't do us much good, and this is a case of people here using concepts without a very good knowledge of history.

My hair stands on end when I hear comparisons of that kind. What are we Germans? A medium-sized power, an industrial state, a divided country. The existence of our old capital, Berlin, now cut in half, depends on the powers which guarantee it—the United States, France and Britain (so I was particularly pleased when Mrs Thatcher went to Berlin a few weeks ago). We are a firm part of the western world, we have not moved on to the dead-end track of neutralism—neutralism doesn't stand a chance in the federal republic of Germany.

If the American president really has anything to discuss with Andropov, he doesn't need a three-cornered relationship with us, he doesn't need help from the chancellor of the federal republic. He is capable of picking up a telephone and talking direct to Andropov. And that has been happening all these years, regardless of propaganda to the contrary. That is a very good thing. I hope it will stay that way. There is no reason for us to intervene and pretend we Germans are the umbilicus of the world. What we are, or what is important for us, is that we have very particular interests, we are the most advanced post in east-west relations, the border goes right through our country, we have Berlin, we are particularly sensitive to many issues. It is our particular duty to make it clear to our friends in the United States what the impact of east-west relations is here in Europe. But that is not an interpreter's role. I am not talking about detente in a vacuum: there isn't any water between us and the Soviet Russians. In a few hours' travel by tank from this room you will meet the first Soviet tank division. We are not in a well-equipped interpreter's cabin, we are in the direct line of fire of world politics.

And relations with the German Democratic Republic?
This is not an academic issue for me. Whether someone lives on this side or the other side of Germany—families are split—often it was just the result of chance. The brother is now here and the sister in the east—these are real experiences, it is hard for the British to understand the real impact of that. If someone applies for a government job here he is first of all given a security check-up. The first question is: Do you have close relations—brother, sister, father, mother—in the GDR?

The consequences of the division of Germany are very real to us, and we are going to hold firmly to the concept of one indivisible nation: self-determination is one of the basic rights of our people. Being realistic means accepting that that is not at present attainable. It may be possible in a peaceful world for future generations.

. . . in the plural?
Perhaps for the next generation, or the one after that. But the obligation to see Germany as one indivisible nation remains for me. It is something we have to reconsider every day—and this brings us back to Geneva, to Andropov and world politics. It is no use hoping that we can improve relations between the two halves of Germany in a bad world political climate. That will only be possible if the climate improves.

It is believed abroad that the federal republic has to pay a certain price for relations with the GDR—you finance the "swing", subsidise the motorways and so on. How far are you prepared to go on with that?
When we buy off political prisoners—and we do—it is a question of humanity. You cannot decide academically, or in a leading article, you have to decide by the human face; you have the man's relations there, in the room with you, his mother, sister etc. The answer is obvious. I cannot support the concept of one nation and pursue a policy which would intensify the division. The decisive principle is reciprocity. We cannot have a one-way track, with one side giving everything and the other only taking. It may be that it is not 50/50, but *The Economist* should pause for a moment and ask what you would do if London were divided along the Thames.

Part of the price for such detente and the open door is German banks giving major credits to eastern Europe.
Not only the German banks—British and French banks too. . .

German banks more than others.
Well, we have a commercial banking system—our banks are not nationalised. I cannot give orders to the Deutsche Bank. Certainly there will be more than purely commercial considerations behind this. It is not a development I would encourage.

Would you drop sanctions against Poland if martial law were lifted but there were no concessions on free trade unions?
We have 100 years of ambivalent relations with Poland—periods of fine co-operation and periods of terrible hatred. In the twentieth century atrocities, especially under the Nazi regime, have predominated. The Germans committed terrible crimes in Poland but the Polish revenge has been terrible too. One should make clear to non-Germans that the psychological climate has changed in Germany especially among the young. An enormous amount of aid is flowing out of private funds from West Germany to Poland—more than from any other European country. Jaruzelski has promised much, and some things have been eased—Walesa has been freed, martial law eased. It is up to the Polish government to keep promises, not up to us to start saying what we would do if. . .

If American and European interests were to diverge, where would you stand?
We have to represent German interests. There are questions of principle which dominate everything, and for us peace and freedom for the federal republic is the dominant issue. Everything else takes second place. And so we must do everything we can to keep the alliance intact. But there can be no question of taking orders from the Americans. But this is not the issue anyway. We are a free people in a free country and the Americans are our friends. So are the British and the French. These are not empty phrases. It means that we must discuss our differences with each other. There is also the emotional issue. I am the first chancellor of the postwar generation, I was 15 when the war ended. I have not forgotten the semi-starvation in Germany after the war and American generosity. Nor have other Germans. But, for instance, I could not support a policy of protectionism in trade. We have interests to represent.

The Americans are a world power, and they have two coasts, the east and the west. The people on the Pacific coast do not look to Europe, they look west, to Asia. America is not just a big country, it is a continent, the whole structure of interests is different. We expect the Americans to play the role of chairman in world politics and look after our interests—we expect them to intervene in a case of conflict on the Persian Gulf, where 60% of our oil comes from. If we feel we have to represent German interests, we cannot blame the Americans for representing their own. It is not my job to go to America and lecture them on European expectations—but I differ here from many others.

A friendly tone helps. France is a good example. We currently have a number of trade problems with France, but calm and friendly discussion is better than public recrimination, and I have close and friendly personal relations with Mitterrand.

Could such good relations be used to prevent further French protectionism within the EEC?
I hope that will prove possible, but here too one must be fair. I think before anyone starts accusing another country of protectionism he should draw up a very careful list of what is going on in his own country. The French have some criticism to make of us. We shall have to see what we can do about it. The French will co-operate, that is in their interests. The discussion on protectionism is not a purely European affair.

But relations in the EEC are particularly close. . .
It is French policy to see the European community as one trading area.

How about Japan then. . . ?
The Japanese cannot have it both ways, they cannot participate in free world trade but exercise protectionism for home markets. I am sure the new Japanese prime minister will visit Europe and America very soon and that will be the major subject for discussion. It is again like private life—you cannot accuse others of doing what you are doing yourself.

Will you continue the old line about Germany's financial contribution to the EEC?
We are facing the major problem of the entry of Spain and Portugal into the EEC. I strongly support their entry. The European idea has played a major part in the recent return to democracy in Portugal and Spain: again this is a case where we gave a promise and must keep it. There are very considerable problems, as you know, between France and Spain, less with Portugal: I do not believe we can solve these by arranging different dates for entry for the two countries. There are problems with wine, fishing.

All these things together add up to a financial issue. It is not my business to suggest solutions here. We must see what is in the kitty. I definitely did not coin the phrase "The Germans are the paymasters of Europe". We all need Europe and we must work for European integration. We must also ensure that Europe is a free trade area. I am sure that we will have lost our political weight in the world if we have not made very decisive progress here by the end of this century. But mutual aid is essential. I went into an election with the slogan:"Every D-mark invested sensibly in Europe is an instalment for peace" and I am sure that we in West Germany need Europe perhaps more than the others do. A new mentality, a communist nationalism, has evolved in the GDR. I do not believe that we can offer democratic nationalism as a meaningful alternative: we must offer the European idea.

And money?
It does not mean that I can say now that certain items will be increased. But you may take it that this government is the most actively engaged for Europe the federal republic has had for some time.

How do you see European foreign policy?
When the Rome treaties were concluded it was never assumed that the common agricultural policy would dominate everything, it was always taken that there would be general development towards unity and integration. We have not progressed very fast towards this end yet. But much has already been done. If we look back on 300 years of European history it is quite incredible to see how much has been changed in the 25-30 years of existence of the community: simply the fact that we now have European political parties.

Does the attempt to reach a common European policy inhibit relations with America?
Not at all. If the Americans look after their own interests, they must stick to the concept of the bridge across the Atlantic. A bridge needs pillars on both sides. These must be solid.

When American and European interests diverge, and when attempts to reach a common European foreign policy mean that the effort of reaching a European view takes precedence over what that view actually is, Europe sometimes seems to move at the speed of the slowest ship in the convoy.
Well, yes, but that is essential in an alliance. You have to expect that. And sometimes the Europeans have to ask themselves in some amazement—"What is American policy?"

America and Japan:
A Search for Balance

Stephen J. Solarz

Representative STEPHEN J. SOLARZ *(D.-New York) is chairman of the Subcommittee on Asian and Pacific Affairs of the House Foreign Affairs Committee.*

Growing tensions over trade and defense disputes threaten the successful relationship forged by the United States and Japan since World War II. These conflicts would be difficult to resolve under any circumstances, but unfavorable economic trends in both countries and a deteriorating international security environment have exacerbated the situation. A continuation of these developments would make it more difficult, but also more important, for the two governments to solve these disputes before they undermine the basis for U.S.-Japanese cooperation.

On the defense issue, Americans believe that Japan spends much less than it should. They are convinced that Japan lacks the military strength necessary for its own defense at a time when the Japanese could easily afford to do more to meet the Soviet threat. The Japanese believe, given the nature of the threat they face, that their defense spending and defense forces are adequate for Japan's needs.

U.S. frustration over Japan's low level of defense spending is heightened by the major sacrifices the American people are making to strengthen their own military forces. Americans may differ about whether U.S. defense spending—now about 6 per cent of gross national product (GNP)—should increase by 5 or 7 per cent annually in real terms, but virtually no one has any sympathy for a prosperous Japan's insistence on keeping its defense outlays below 1 per cent of GNP.

On the trade issue, Americans worry about the U.S. trade deficit with Japan of nearly $16 billion in 1981 and believe that Japan protects its market with a web of nontariff barriers involving quotas, regulations, customs procedures, and entrenched buy-Japanese attitudes. They argue that it is far more difficult for an American company to penetrate the Japanese market than for a Japanese firm to sell to Americans. The Japanese are convinced that their country has substantially opened its markets to foreign goods. They contend that foreign firms still unable to sell in Japan have not put sufficient effort into making high quality products at a competitive price and into marketing those goods in ways attractive to Japanese buyers. Japan maintains that even if it eliminated all its trade barriers, its trade surplus with the United States would not decline significantly and that Americans are blaming Japan for their own economic failures.

These contrasting perceptions substantially increase the difficulties the United States and Japan face in dealing with defense and trade disputes. The U.S. trade deficit with Japan increased from $9.9 billion in 1980 to $15.8 billion in 1981, and it could rise to over $20 billion in 1982. Large deficits may be acceptable in a period of rapid economic growth and full employment. But they become a contentious issue at a time of recession and growing unemployment, especially when there exists a widespread American perception that Japan is not fair in its trading practices. The growing support for legislation designed to force other countries to open their markets or face restrictions on their exports to the United States is aimed principally at Japan and is causing apprehension and anger among Japanese.

Fortunately, these growing strains have not undermined the awareness in both countries of the importance of continued U.S.-Japanese cooperation. Japan both relies upon the United States for military security and benefits from the U.S. nuclear umbrella. U.S. bases in Japan are essential to America's military position and strategy in Asia, especially the U.S. ability to defend South Korea. The 45,000 U.S. troops in Japan are a key component of the American strategic reserve in Asia. The two countries have benefited enormously from their mutual trade, which reached almost $60 billion in 1981. This amount was nearly one-half of U.S.

total trade with Asia, which has surpassed U.S. trade with Western Europe.

Japan's increasing strength and its greater willingness to take an active role in international affairs has also led to Japanese support for and cooperation with the United States on such key issues as Afghanistan, Vietnam, Iran, and Poland. Unlike some of America's West European allies, Japan boycotted the 1980 Moscow Olympics and adopted sanctions against the Soviet Union following the latter's invasion of Afghanistan. Tokyo also halted its aid program to Vietnam in response to Hanoi's military action against Cambodia.

Japan and the United States have similar policies toward the People's Republic of China, the Korean peninsula, the Association of Southeast Asian Nations (ASEAN), and South Asia. Japan's foreign aid program has increased substantially in recent years, and it now provides substantial economic assistance to such politically important countries as Turkey, Egypt, Sudan, Oman, and Pakistan. Tokyo's Official Development Assistance is scheduled to be $21.4 billion in the 1980-1984 period, twice the level spent during the previous five years.

Important mutual interests and shared values—a stable but flexible world order, maintenance of an East Asian balance of power, an open international economy, and a commitment to democracy—have enabled the two countries to forge a unique relationship despite great differences of history, geography, and culture. Nonetheless, the current disputes over trade and defense could erode the trust and confidence necessary for the maintenance of U.S.-Japanese cooperation, which is essential for the peace and stability of Asia.

Inadequacies and Shortages

Japan's 1982 defense budget amounts to approximately $10 billion, the eighth largest defense budget in the world. The Japanese point out that real defense spending increased by an average of more than 7 per cent annually during the 1960s and the 1970s. The Japanese also stress that defense spending, which grew by 7.61 and 7.75 per cent in fiscal years 1981 and 1982 respectively, is increasing more rapidly than nearly all other types of government spending. They frequently mention that Japan contributes about $1 billion annually in support costs for U.S. military forces in Japan. Japan points out that its armed forces of approximately 250,000 men are now acquiring modern equipment—for example, F-15 fighter

aircraft and P-3C antisubmarine planes. The Japanese navy has 34 modern destroyers and 16 frigates, more than twice as many as the U.S. Seventh Fleet. The Japanese maintain that the adoption of the 1978 Guidelines for United States-Japanese Defense Cooperation has encouraged closer and more meaningful cooperation between U.S. and Japanese military forces and that periodic joint exercises have enhanced the ability to work together in time of crisis.

Yet the real test of any country's level of defense spending and of the capabilities of its military forces is not whether spending has increased but whether the military can adequately protect the country's security. Japan's defense spending has risen more rapidly than that of NATO in recent years, but the Japanese began from an extremely low base. Although Japan's present equipment is more modern than in the past, improved equipment capabilities are unlikely to deter a potential adversary if they remain inadequate to the task at hand.

Japan's military forces cannot now contribute substantially to the defense of their own territory against any realistic threat. Its air force lacks the number of planes needed to counter even a moderate-sized attack. Unprotected radar sites and air bases and inadequate repair facilities would force Japanese planes out of action in a few days. Much of the equipment of the ground forces is obsolete. The naval forces lack adequate electronic equipment, antisubmarine weapons, surface-to-surface and surface-to-air missiles, and mine-laying capabilities. All of the Japanese forces suffer from shortages of ammunition and spare parts and from poor logistics. Command and control capabilities are seriously inadequate. Reserve units and mobilization procedures virtually do not exist. It does no service to U.S.-Japanese relations to ignore these problems. The United States and Japan must now examine security issues in a realistic manner. Both countries need to appraise the nature and extent of the Soviet threat, the scenarios that might trigger an active menace to Japan, the military forces needed to counter those dangers, and the respective responsibilities of Japan and the United States to provide these capabilities.

An increase in Japanese military strength is required for several specific reasons. For one, the United States and Japan must counter the steady expansion of Soviet military power in the western Pacific in order to maintain a military balance there. A shift in the regional balance in favor of the USSR would leave Japan vulnerable to Soviet intimidation. The United

3. ALLIES OF THE US

States will use most of the increased strength that will result from the planned American military build-up to counter the Soviets in other parts of the world. The task of maintaining an adequate military balance in the western Pacific will thus rest largely with Japan.

Another reason for an increase in Japanese military capabilities is that Japan must be able to respond to a crisis if one develops. The real danger is not an isolated Soviet attempt to invade Japan, but the possibility of an outbreak of hostilities elsewhere that would require the diversion of some U.S. naval and air forces now in East Asia, thus leaving Japan in a relatively weak position.

The United States has in recent years undertaken to defend the Persian Gulf. Japan recognizes that it benefits from this undertaking. It also realizes that some U.S. naval and air forces probably would have to move from the Pacific Ocean to the Persian Gulf in the event of a crisis in the chronically unstable Middle East. With the United States preoccupied elsewhere and its naval and air forces stretched thin, North Korea could move against South Korea. Moscow might then threaten to cut the sea lanes that are Japan's lifeline unless Tokyo refused to let the remaining U.S. forces use their bases in Japan or abandoned its security ties with the United States.

To reduce any Soviet temptation to threaten Japan does not require a major military build-up. Japan does, however, need an air defense system adequate to defend its own skies. It must also develop the naval and air capacity to protect its sea lanes in conjunction with U.S. forces remaining in the area. Finally, Japan—together with the United States—should develop the capability to close the Tsushima, Tsugaru, and Soya straits to Soviet ships, which must pass through these waters to reach the Pacific Ocean and to return to their home ports. This task would require a sharp increase in mine-laying capacity. Control of the straits is necessary to keep the sea lanes open.

Tokyo accepts the first two requirements in principle, and while still in office former Prime Minister Zenko Suzuki stated that Japan would develop the capability to defend the sea lanes for 1,000 nautical miles east and south of Japan. Specific U.S. and Japanese responsibilities and force levels necessary to assure sea lane security are still being developed.

The Japanese government is considering setting 1987 as the date for reaching the targets of the 1976 Defense Outline. But the government would only order the necessary weapons and equipment rather than actually acquire them by this target date. If defense spending continues to rise at the present rate of only 4-5 per cent annually in real terms, Japan would still lack the capabilities needed to carry out the three missions set forth above until early in the next century. By contrast, if real defense spending were to increase by about 10 per cent annually—an increase of little more than $500 million a year above what is presently planned—Japan could acquire these capabilities in about a decade, and defense spending would remain below 2 per cent of GNP.

Japanese officials cite several obstacles to such an increased effort. Japan's budget deficits have been running at about one-third of total spending in recent years. Japan's rate of economic growth has also declined significantly. Increasing defense spending is difficult in such conditions and raising taxes is always politically painful. Yet it would require an annual increase in taxes of only one-half of one per cent—or an annual reduction of planned non-defense outlays of three-quarters of one per cent—to increase defense spending by about 10 per cent a year in real terms. The lack of public consensus and political will are the real obstacles to such a program.

There are a number of underlying reasons why a consensus in favor of a more rapid defense build-up has not yet developed. The trauma of defeat in World War II still exerts a powerful influence on Japanese thinking. Many Japanese fear that a military build-up would develop a momentum that could get out of hand, leading to a resurgence of military influence within Japanese society. A more rapid military build-up would be viewed by many Japanese as violating the ethos, if not the letter, of Japan's antiwar constitution and thus poses substantial political and psychological problems. Japan also argues that a significant military build-up could cause increased tensions with its Asian neighbors. Some Japanese acknowledge that most countries now friendly to Japan, including China, have indicated that they would have few problems with a greater Japanese capacity to defend its own territories and the surrounding seas, as long as the United States retains its military presence in the area. Finally, Japan is naturally reluctant to change a policy that has successfully protected the country's security at very little cost.

Japanese are concerned about rising Soviet military strength in the area and about Soviet use of Da Nang and Cam Ranh Bay in Vietnam, which increases the range and capabilities of the USSR's naval and air forces. Yet most Japanese still doubt that the Soviet Union poses a direct danger and are unwilling to spend more to protect themselves against a threat they regard as improbable.

The Japanese tend to focus on Soviet intentions rather than capabilities when analyzing defense matters. Specifically, they believe a Soviet invasion of Japan is improbable unless prompted by a crisis elsewhere in the world. In such a case the Japanese conclude that the Soviet threat is minimal and that the United States could adequately deter such an attack or protect Japan, especially since the USSR lacks significant amphibious capacity. If the United States failed to protect Japan, the Japanese see little their own country could do in view of the USSR's overwhelming power. Therefore, they support increased defense outlays more to placate Washington than to deter Moscow.

Japanese arguments about the constraints on a military build-up do not apply to a more rapid increase in Japan's foreign aid program. Many Japanese urge that both countries adopt a "comprehensive security" concept and consider foreign aid and other contributions as well as defense spending when evaluating a country's effort. Yet Japan's combined defense and foreign aid spending amount to only about $15 billion, or 1.5 per cent of its GNP, while West German, French, and British outlays amount to 4-5 per cent of their respective GNPs. Japanese per capita GNP is now approaching that of the United States, but America spends about $800 per capita on defense and foreign aid, while Japan spends only about $135 per capita.

In groping for a solution to these issues, the United States must recognize the changes in Japanese thinking and attitudes on defense issues that have taken place in recent years. Military matters, once virtually off limits in public discussion, are now debated openly. A broad public acceptance of government policy has superseded the polarization between the supporters and the opponents of the U.S.-Japan security treaty, American bases in Japan, and Japan's self-defense forces that characterized the postwar period. The centrist Democratic Socialist and the Komeito (Clean Government) parties now basically support the government's policy on these issues. Growing strains over defense issues have also developed within the country's strongest opposition party, the Japan Socialist Party, which officially advocates a policy of unarmed neutrality.

These shifts are substantial. But Americans should not exaggerate the significance of these changes in attitude. The defense debate has shifted from one between those advocating unarmed neutrality and those supporting a minimal defense capability to a debate between those in favor of the present policy of slow expansion and those calling for a more rapid but still moderate increase in Japan's military strength. Virtually no Japanese favor a rapid, large-scale military build-up, and public opinion is opposed to such a course. The aversion to nuclear weapons remains strong, and little support exists for changing Japan's policy against sending military forces abroad.

The United States should reiterate publicly and emphatically that it does not want Japan to become a nuclear power, a major military power, or even a regional military power. Indeed, given the anxieties such a development would generate among U.S. allies in the region, not to mention the likelihood of increased tensions with the Soviet Union, a major Japanese rearmament program is clearly not in the U.S. interest. All the United States asks is that Japan acquire the military capabilities necessary to defend its territories and to resist Soviet pressures and threats—in cooperation with remaining U.S. forces—if some U.S. military units now in the western Pacific have to be shifted elsewhere in an emergency. This commitment would not require renegotiation of the U.S.-Japan security treaty or revision of the Japanese constitution. Just as the United States is not in a position to defend Western Europe without West European cooperation, the United States is unable to defend Japan without Japanese assistance.

To persuade the Japanese people that it is in their interest to rearm more rapidly, a broadening of the U.S.-Japanese defense dialogue is required. It should include not only the defense and foreign affairs officials of the two governments but also economic and financial officials, Diet—Japanese legislature—members and U.S. congressmen, and interested and influential elements of the U.S. and Japanese publics. One way to maintain this dialogue would be an annual parliamentary exchange program with Japan. Members of Congress and the Diet need to engage in serious, sustained discussions to bring their views together. Such a structured program could provide a more constructive basis for a continuing U.S.-Japanese dialogue than ad hoc exchanges between congressional and Diet members.

Another way to broaden the dialogue would be to include officials from the Japanese Ministry of Finance and from the U.S. Treasury and the Office of Management and Budget in the meetings of the U.S.-Japanese Security Consultative Committee and its Security Subcommittee. These latter organizations are not well known to Americans, but they have become important bodies in the effort to coordinate U.S.-Japanese military strategy and cooperation in the Pacific.

Even with such new approaches, rapid increases in Japanese defense outlays are unlikely in the next few years. If a consensus develops, Japan will move rapidly and effectively to develop the defense forces it needs. If no significant increase in the pace of the Japanese defense effort occurs by the mid-1980s, however, those in the United States arguing for stronger pressures on Japan or for reducing the U.S. contribution to Japanese defense will gain influence.

Trade Imbalances

Economic conflict between the United States and Japan has reached a level that now threatens to undermine the U.S.-Japanese relationship. Trade between the two countries has increased dramatically, rising from $5.7 billion in 1967 to $58 billion in 1981. Unfortunately, the U.S. trade deficit with Japan has risen even more rapidly—from $.3 billion in 1967 to $15.8 billion in 1981, when it was nearly 60 per cent of the total U.S. trade deficit. Preliminary indications are that the deficit could increase to $20-25 billion in 1982 and 1983.

From one perspective, bilateral trade imbalances have little relevance. The United States, for example, has large surpluses in its trade with Western Europe, but this fact has not been a major issue in transatlantic economic relations. And if a country has a large enough surplus in its exports of services—transportation, insurance, tourism, and investment income—to offset its trade deficit, it will have a current account surplus. In 1981 the $41 billion worldwide surplus in the U.S. services account provided the United States with a $14 billion current account surplus despite its $27 billion trade deficit. America's 1981 surplus in services with Japan was only $2.8 billion, however, and offset only a small part of the bilateral trade deficit.

Japanese stress that their country needs time to overcome its historic sense of isolation and vulnerability and to remove the residue of trade barriers erected to protect its industries while they recovered from the ravages of World War II. They also argue that their lack of natural resources requires them to import large quantities of foodstuffs, raw materials, and petroleum.

The only way for Japan to pay for such imports—which amounted to over $105 billion in 1981—is to maintain a large export surplus in its trade in manufactured goods. Finally, Japanese point out that even with a $20 billion trade surplus in 1981, their $15.2 billion deficit in services reduced their current account surplus to only $4.8 billion. Japan had current account deficits of $8.7 billion in 1979 and $10.7 billion in 1980. The absence of large current account surpluses, they argue, demonstrates the unfairness of charges that Japan seeks only its own short-term interests.

Such perspectives, however, overlook many specific problems. Japan's practice of targeting specific industries in its export drives creates serious economic problems for major sectors of the U.S. economy. Imports from Japan of products such as steel, machine tools, and consumer electronics account for between 10 and 60 per cent of the U.S. market, and in 1981 Japan captured over 20 per cent of the U.S. automobile market. Yet with the single exception of airplanes, no manufactured civilian product imported from the United States has as much as 10 per cent of the Japanese market. About 14 per cent of Japanese defense equipment is purchased in the United States.

Japanese point out that their average tariff level is as low as that of the United States or the European Economic Community. They also stress that Japan has reduced the number of foreign imports limited by quotas from over 400 in the 1960s to only 27 in 1982. Japanese assert that unequal market access can hardly account for the growing U.S. trade deficit since the Japanese market is more open and the American market more closed than in the past. Penetrating the Japanese market for manufactured goods may be more difficult than selling to other countries, but the records of such firms as Du Pont Company, Bendix Corporation, Borg-Warner Corporation, and National Cash Register Corporation demonstrate that it can be done. Japanese conclude that U.S. complaints overlook more rapid Japanese productivity gains, knowledge of foreign markets, and persistence in providing high quality products attractive to foreign buyers at competitive prices—traits they claim are conspicuously absent in most American firms seeking to sell to Japan.

Americans recognize the need to improve U.S. productivity and to devote more effort to penetrating the Japanese market. Nevertheless, they see matters in a quite different light from the Japanese. If the Japanese market is substantially more open than in the past,

Americans ask, why has the ratio of imports of manufactured goods relative to GNP not increased in Japan as it has in other major industrial countries that have lowered their barriers to trade? Between 1960 and 1980, for example, this ratio increased sharply for the United States, West Germany, France, and Great Britain—doubling or much more in every case. For Japan alone the ratio, which is at 2 per cent, has shown no increase during the 20-year period. Such a unique pattern suggests that unusual barriers exist. Taiwanese and South Koreans know Japan and work hard to sell to it, but they have had only limited success. Indeed, Taiwan temporarily banned the importation of 1,500 Japanese products in 1982 in retaliation for what it claimed were Japanese barriers to imports from Taiwan.

American businessmen also point to many specific examples of Japanese nontariff barriers. There are very stringent quotas on beef and some citrus products and sharp restrictions on imports of foreign cigarettes. Complicated customs procedures, product standards established by Japanese trade associations to which foreigners cannot belong, a refusal to accept foreign safety certification of products, and a wide variety of restrictive business practices and attitudes have hindered foreign penetration of the Japanese market. Underlying all of these barriers and constraints is a deeply ingrained attitude that selling abroad and buying at home whenever possible is the appropriate Japanese behavior.

No one has yet discovered a method of determining with precision the relative openness of the markets of two such different countries. The available evidence, however, indicates that the Japanese market is not as open as the American. Many Japanese businessmen and officials reluctantly acknowledge that this comparison remains true despite important reforms.

Japan has responded to U.S. and West European complaints by adopting one series of measures in December 1981 and another in May 1982 that Tokyo claims will remove many foreign complaints concerning Japanese trade barriers. Both sets of measures involved implementing some planned tariff cuts ahead of schedule, although only a few of these cuts affect items important to the United States. The 67 changes announced in December 1981 included the removal of certain burdensome product testing and customs procedures, and in January 1982 Tokyo announced the establishment of an ombudsman to deal with foreign business complaints. The May 1982 measures included giving foreign firms access to standards-setting procedures and to government-sponsored research and development efforts in some areas. Suzuki also publicly called on Japanese firms and individuals to end discrimination against foreign products and to assist foreign firms in their efforts to sell, invest, and do business in Japan. The pledge by the prime minister to use the influence of the government to persuade Japanese firms to buy foreign products is potentially the most important of all the announced reforms.

These specific measures, which are a tacit admission that barriers to foreign products have existed, represent steps in the right direction. The real test will be how Tokyo's powerful and protectionist-minded bureaucracy implements these policy changes, and American officials and businessmen remain understandably skeptical that a basic shift regarding nontariff barriers has begun.

No one knows what effect on the U.S.-Japanese trade balance the further reduction of Japanese tariffs and the elimination of nontariff barriers would have, but estimates range from several hundred million to several billion dollars annually. Even assuming that within a few years such actions would lead to increased U.S. exports to Japan of $5 billion, this growth would only reduce the current and projected trade deficits by one-third to one-fourth. Japanese argue that the major beneficiaries of tariff reductions would be the newly industrialized Asian countries and are puzzled about the reasons behind U.S. policy. But even if other Asian countries were the direct beneficiaries of such action, the increased foreign exchange they earned could be used to purchase American goods. The United States has demonstrated in recent years that it can compete successfully with Japan in many Asian markets, especially in fulfilling the rapidly growing demand for high technology products. U.S exports to the five ASEAN countries increased at an annual rate of 22.4 per cent during the 1970s, while Japanese exports to these countries increased by 20.3 per cent. Thus U.S. businessmen can adapt to non-Western markets.

From a political point of view, the administration has created the unfortunate impression that opening the Japanese market will greatly reduce the trade imbalance. A stronger argument against Japanese trade barriers is that they fuel protectionist pressures in the United States. Japan must recognize that Americans believe that fair trade is a condition for free trade. The complete elimination of trade barriers by both Japan and the United States might conceivably increase rather than reduce the trade imbalance. Yet a greater imbalance in the context of equal access probably would be less threatening to the basic U.S.-Japanese relationship than the present U.S. deficit in the context of unequal access. Japan has more to lose from an outbreak of protectionism than most major countries, and it would be tragic if Japan undermined its future by clinging to outmoded policies.

In reality, neither Japan nor the United States will completely eliminate its trade barriers. Some situations, such as the Japanese insistence on producing a substantial part of their rice needs, will have to be accepted. The United States must also recognize that other important Japanese agricultural quotas will be difficult to terminate because of the power of rural constituencies in Japan. The United States cannot allow the auto industry—in which employment has fallen from 760,000 in 1978 to about 500,000 in 1982—to be irreparably damaged, especially since a recovery of the U.S. economy can hardly occur without a revival of the automobile industry.

No single solution to the U.S. trade conflict with Japan exists. Nonetheless, the United States could adopt several measures that would alleviate the current conflict. The United States should press for an expansion of the authority of the General Agreement on Tariffs and Trade (GATT) so that it may assure its members equal access to one anothers' markets. Pending GATT's acceptance of such a role, the United States should enact its own reciprocity legislation. The International Trade Commission (ITC) could then determine whether the United States has access to the markets of Japan and other countries equal to the access those countries have to the U.S. market. Such legislation would provide the U.S. president with the authority to take retaliatory action if the ITC concludes that the United States has not received equal market access. Since it would be best to deal with this problem in a multilateral context, this legislation should stipulate that the president's authority to retaliate will terminate if and when GATT assumes international responsibility for this issue.

The United States should also offer the Japanese guaranteed access to U.S. agricultural products provided they open their markets further to American goods. Such an offer could help eliminate the lingering resentment over the 1973 U.S. soybean embargo, which inflicted great psychological damage on Japan.

Even if the issue of unequal market access

were resolved, the undervalued yen—or overvalued dollar—would hamper Washington's efforts to decrease its trade deficit with Tokyo. Normally a trade imbalance of this magnitude would result in a stronger yen, which would make Japanese goods more expensive in the United States and American goods cheaper in Japan. Most specialists who have studied this issue conclude that a yen-dollar rate of between 180 and 200 to 1 would appropriately reflect the basic economic conditions and trends in the two economies. Yet high interest rates and a large budget deficit in the United States together with low interest rates and a falling deficit in Japan have led to a flow of capital from Japan to the United States. The flow has recently amounted to nearly $2 billion per month. These factors have pushed the value of the dollar to more than 275 yen, which accounts for much of the surge of imports from Japan.

Both countries need to change their policy mixes. The United States must reduce its budget deficits so that interest rates will decline further. Japan, whose economy has slowed down substantially during the past two years, needs to move in the opposite direction. A slower move toward reduced budget deficits in Japan would spur economic growth there and would lead to somewhat higher interest rates, which would have a beneficial effect on the exchange rate.

Equal Partners

In recent decades Japan and the United States have demonstrated an impressive ability to surmount the specific disputes that have periodically strained their relationship—the security treaty riots of 1960, the Vietnam war, the reversion of Okinawa to Japan, the "Nixon shocks" of the early 1970s, and earlier differences over trade and defense issues. The ability of the two countries to overcome the resentment generated by a bitter and bloody war demonstrates the possibility of reconciliation.

How serious the current tensions in U.S.-Japanese relations become will be a function of two factors: economic developments in the two countries and changes in the international environment; and the skill the leaders of the two countries show in settling their differences. Large trade deficits would be easier to accept and deal with in the context of improving economic conditions. But depressed U.S. economic conditions and growing unemployment are generating bitter resentment and intense political pressures to curtail such deficits by resorting to protectionist measures. Similarly, a growing Soviet military threat would increase U.S. resentment over Japan's limited contribution to common security interests at a time of rapidly rising U.S. military spending. A less threatening international environment would lead to greater American acceptance of Japan's low level of defense spending. But there is no assurance that economic trends in the United States and Japan will improve or that the international environment will become more favorable.

The changes occurring in the relative power of the two countries will require Japan to assume larger responsibilities in the areas of defense and foreign aid than it has in the past. This shift will not be easy for Japan in view of the domestic constraints facing its government and its tendency to adapt to the international environment rather than try to modify it. The posture and policies that were understandable and appropriate for a weak Japan must change to reflect its great economic strength. Indeed, its remarkable economic progress has raised expectations throughout the world regarding Japan's potential contribution to a better future. Yet if the United States expects Japan to do more to strengthen the international system that has brought it security and prosperity, the United States must be prepared to accept Japan as a more equal partner. The United States could, for example, defer on some Asian economic and political issues where Japanese interests are much more directly involved than America's.

The key issue facing the United States is how it should influence Japan to strengthen its defenses and to open its market. Firm American pressure will be necessary, though heavy-handed threats would be counterproductive. The whining tone that has come to characterize many American statements is neither effective nor dignified. At the same time, the United States can hardly remain silent about a basically unfair division of efforts in the defense field and unequal market access in the economic sphere. The United States must continually press Japanese officials to act on the basis of their country's overwhelming interest in maintaining an open international economic system, and their responsibility for supporting it in the difficult times that lie ahead.

On defense, most Japanese believe that the United States overemphasizes military matters and neglects diplomatic means when addressing international security issues. The Japanese also maintain that the United States should stress the need to prevent military conflict rather than its ability to wage one when it occurs. Given such views, Japan is more likely to respond to American calls for a greater defense effort if it thinks the United States is pursuing a balanced policy. Ultimately, a consensus in Japan favoring a greater defense effort will depend on Japan's belief that such a policy is in its own interest. The United States can influence the development of such a consensus. But without far-sighted and courageous leadership in Japan, little progress can be expected.

When two such large and dynamic societies as Japan and the United States are so closely involved in so many ways, friction and frequent adjustments are inevitable. Making sure that such adjustments take place constructively will require both countries to accord a higher priority to their mutual long-term interests than to their individual short-term interests. Americans and Japanese alike need to recognize that either country can, through shortsightedness or intransigence, undermine the relationship. Maintaining balanced U.S.-Japanese relations will require vision and sacrifice on the part of both. If Japanese and American leaders and peoples act in this spirit, the U.S.-Japanese relationship will benefit the two countries and the entire world as much in the 21st century as it has in the second half of the 20th century.

Japanese Perception Of America: Evolution From Dependency To Maturity

Toshikazu Maeda

Summary

Japan's perception of America has undergone several distinct phases in the post-war period, from extreme dependency immediately following World War II to what can be termed mature friendship today. After America's image plummeted to an unprecedented bottom during the early 1970s, it recovered following the end of the widely reported Vietnam War and racial and social disturbances in the United States. Recently, the lessening of the gap in economic strength between the two countries seems to have placed the relationship on more or less an equal footing. The economic disputes with the United States today are putting further strains on U.S.—Japan relations. In spite of some Japanese who are becoming increasingly vocal in their concern about what they perceive as American scapegoating of Japan, most still seem to perceive America as their major friend and partner in the world.

***

Japanese perceptions of relations with the United States are currently undergoing a major readjustment. It is too early to tell how the wrangling over trade and security issues will ultimately be reflected in the public mind. Various positions are still being debated in the government and the media and a variety of internal issues must be settled before public opinion begins to emerge more clearly. It is possible, however, to gain some insight into the future evolution of opinion by looking at changes that have occurred in the past.

Since 1945 Japanese perceptions of relations with the United States have been influenced by politics, economics and the international environment. In order to ascertain their perceptions, public opinion polls conducted over the last 35 years have been extensively utilized. From these surveys one can categorize the change in perception into three general periods: dependency, breaking-away and mature friendship. This essay will describe how Japanese opinions evolved during these periods and will examine briefly Japan's perception of the current debate over trade issues in light of this analysis.

Dependency: 1945-early 1960s

Japanese-American relations from 1945 to the early 1960s were characterized by Japan's heavy dependence on the United States. The war left Japan's economy shattered and totally reliant on American help. Furthermore, seven years of military occupation and unprecedented changes in government and other basic institutions combined to influence Japanese perceptions of America. Military defeat also had an enormous impact on the Japanese psyche. Propagandists before and during the war had stressed Japanese racial superiority and the inferiority of the "fiendish Americans". Since people had little contact with Americans and little information about America it was easy to create a negative image. Defeat and occupation, however, produced great confusion. Because the negative image of America was based on so little understanding, it quickly changed in the opposite direction. The Japanese way of thinking and behavior was considered a vice and Americans were regarded by many as symbols of all that was good and just. Many Japanese singlemindedly set out to learn all they could about American thinking and behavior.

The positive view of America was immediately apparent in early opinion polls. In a poll conducted by *Yomiuri Shimbun* in 1949, 66 percent of those questioned answered positively to the question "Do you like America?". Similar questions continued to show that over 60 percent of the Japanese people had strong, positive attitudes toward America until the early 1960s. To a certain extent the general positive image of America must have resulted from a sense of Japanese appreciation of what the United States did for them both economically and politically during these years.

When the occupation began, in 1945, the production of consumer goods had fallen to 30 percent of prewar levels and producer goods were down to 10 percent. American aid during the occupation was seen as vital. According to a poll conducted in 1949 by the Jiji Newspaper Service almost half of the Japanese people felt they could not operate their economy without American support. In contrast, only 12 percent thought they could do without help. After its wartime isolation, General MacArthur appeared like another Commodore Perry, reawakening Japanese interest in the outside world. Dependence on outside aid was accompanied by a growing fascination with American products. Slogans from this period included: "The fastest car is the Jeep", "The strongest fiber is nylon", and "The most effective medicines are DDT and penicillin". Everything seemed to be "Made in U.S.A.".

Breaking Away: Early 1960s-mid 1970s

The parent-child dependency relationship between post-war Japan and America soon evolved into a period that more closely resembled adolescence. From 1960 to 1975 Japanese perceptions of America became less positive. The United States had serious domestic problems during this time and was fighting an unpopular war. In Japan, on the other hand, the economy recovered from its post-war devastation and began a period of rapid growth. These events led the Japanese to break away from their former relationship of one-sided dependency and develop a more reciprocal dependency.

Political events in the 1960s put a severe strain on U.S.-Japanese relations. Ratification by the Diet of the revised U.S.-Japanese Security Treaty in 1960 led to massive public protest in Japan and a major post-war crisis in relations between the two countries. According to a poll conducted in 1960, 42 percent of the people were opposed to the treaty while only 27 percent favored it; 38 percent of the people were afraid that Japan would be led into war by the treaty.

The growth and spread of the mass media also enabled the Japanese to learn more about America. The assassination of President Kennedy, for example, was televised directly by satellite for the first time and was watched with great interest in the 10 million homes with television sets. The assassinations of other American leaders and the race riots in the middle and late 1960s tarnished Japan's image of America.

As the Vietnam war escalated in the late sixties it became one of the hottest issues in the Japanese mass media. Throughout this period the percentage of people who indicated an interest in the war ranged from 61 to 78 percent (1965-1972, Institute of Statistical Mathematics). In an opinion poll conducted by NHK in 1971, 31 percent of those questioned agreed with the statement "America is intervening and threatening other countries", while only 17 percent felt that "America is fair and full of life". In short, negative feelings about American foreign policy were becoming more common.

In the economic field, similar changes occurred. Affirmative answers to the earlier question, "Can the Japanese economy operate without American support?", surpassed negative answers for the first time in 1960. As indicated by an NHK survey, many people still believed "America has strong economic power and a very high standard of living" (41 percent) rather than "America has a problem with recession and unemployment" (31 percent). The vast differences in economic strength were no longer apparent; i.e., the Japanese no longer worried about catching a cold when America sneezed.

As mentioned previously, more than 60 percent of the Japanese people expressed positive attitudes toward America in the post-war dependency period. This percentage decreased rapidly during the 1960s, and by 1974 hit its lowest point when only 18 percent of the public had a favorable impression of America. This decline, however, was not matched by an increase in dislike or a realignment. The increase in dislike of America was only 6 percent between 1965 and 1973, and, favorable answers about Communist countries, for example, did not increase in number. Liking seemed to increase only for Switzerland, which was a symbol of neutrality and peace. Like an adolescent who begins to see his parents' faults, the Japanese began to see America in a different light. In short, political and economic changes during this period did not lead to antipathy toward America, but seemed to have resulted in a more balanced impression.

Mature Friendship: Mid 1970s-Present

U.S.-Japanese relations after the Vietnam war were marked by greater harmony and mature friendship. That is, before the trade imbalance and pressure to increase defense expenditures had begun to receive wide coverage in the Japanese press, ordinary people believed that U.S.-Japanese relations were quite positive. Favorable answers to questions about America increased rapidly from 1975 to 1980. For example, more than 39 percent of the people answered affirmatively in 1980 to the question, "Do you like America?", a higher percentage than before the Vietnam War. Furthermore, 69 percent felt that the United States set a high value on U.S.-Japanese relations, while 18 percent of the people did not think so. In regard to future U.S.-Japanese relations, 41 percent of the people said that they wished to strengthen the relationship, while 20 percent of the people wished to weaken it.

The reasons for increasing positive perceptions can be traced to improvements in political and economic relations. In addition, changes in the international environment produced by crises in Iran and Afghanistan reinforced the importance of good relations between America and Japan.

3. ALLIES OF THE US

Current Opinion

Current opinion about relations with the United States appears to be in a state of flux. The most recent Yomiuri-Gallup poll found that 40 percent of the Japanese questioned agreed that relations between Japan and the United States were "good", a four percent drop since the question was first asked in 1978. There have been no more polls on public perceptions since that time, but opinion articles in the newspapers and white papers issued by the various government ministries provide some indications of the factors that will influence Japanese perceptions in the next several years.

To many Americans, the current Japanese restrictions on agricultural imports must seem like a simple protectionist issue. Closer analysis, however, reveals a more complicated problem involving Japanese agricultural interests, consumers and the mass media. Japanese agricultural interests oppose unrestricted imports of American beef and citrus fruit since the cheaper imports will certainly have a negative impact on the agricultural sector. Although the number of beef and citrus fruit producers is rather small, they traditionally have wielded a great deal of power in the Liberal Democratic Party. In addition, they have drawn the support of a number of other agricultural interests.

In essence, the beef and citrus fruit producers are arguing that the lifting of restrictions on beef and citrus will lead to a domino effect that will soon destroy other domestic agricultural products. In recent years they have seen domestic lemons and black tea swept away by imports and predict that beef, citrus fruit, and rice will soon follow. They believe that rice occupies the central position in Japanese agriculture and any threat to rice production would have profound implications for Japan's economic and political security as a whole. Finally, they feel that they have sacrificed in the past for the growth of the industrial sector and that they are unwilling to sacrifice for further growth in that sector.

The issue is complicated by consumer reactions. A poll of housewives in 1980 found that over 60 percent wanted more imported beef; many were dissatisfied because such beef always sold out so quickly. Consumers, in general, insist on open markets for agricultural products and increased imports of beef and oranges. They also believe that agricultural interests have too much power in Japanese politics.

Editorial comments expressed in the media on these issues tend to support the consumer viewpoint. In general, these commentators or press reporters represent the majority of critical, urban white-collar workers as expected, for they themselves have such socio-demographic characteristics. The media supports the principle of free trade, but they also believe that restrictions on imports should be withdrawn step-by-step because they feel that the Japanese political system cannot deal with a crushing blow to the farmers. They feel that such an adjustment should be completed gradually in order to reduce the burden of adjustment in a given period, say, one year, and that such a gradual approach would be easier for society as a whole. This position reflects a typical exercise of Japanese logic. Instead of deciding on the basis of a principle what is right or wrong, a decision is made to change in a way that will "share the burden" among the various parties. No one is likely to be happy with such an approach but it has the advantage of doing the least damage to the social system in the short-run.

Japanese exports are another problem. During the 1970s the threat of U.S. protectionist measures against Japanese textile exports was a very serious issue. Since more than five million Japanese households would have been affected by such measures a strong consensus developed against them. The Japanese economy is richer now and opinions on export controls appear to be more moderate. The 1981 Yomiuri-Gallup poll found that 18 percent of those questioned were in favor of reducing exports and 32 percent argued for Japanese plants built and operated in the United States, while approximately one-quarter expressed opposition to American import controls.

Comments in the press have also been moderate. There is a recognition that the United States is Japan's best trading partner and that the deterioration of the U.S.-Japan relationship would be a disadvantage to Japan. Although it could probably survive without America, Japan's well-being is still seen as tied to American prosperity. On the other hand, the media has been paying close attention to problems in the American economy. It is difficult for the Japanese people to see how the essentially protectionist response of voluntary export restraints by Japanese exporters is beneficial to the long-term strength of the American economy. The Japanese White Paper on Economic Cooperation, for example, notes a general decline in the American economy due to a number of factors, including high labor costs and union problems. Japanese voluntary restraints tend to discourage Americans from taking measures to correct these problems.

There is also the feeling of many Japanese analysts that American criticism of Japan is in some part motivated by politicians and others who wish to blame their problems on the Japanese. Overall, there continues to be concern about further restrictions against Japan.

Summary: Sharing the Burden

Relations between the United States and Japan have reached a mature state. The Japanese are no longer politically or economically dependent as much as in the 1950s or 1960s and they have a good understanding of the American way of thinking. What people desire now is the improvement of each country's economic well-being through the principle of free trade. There is some evidence that the Japanese people are willing to make sacrifices to ensure their partner's economic well-being. Yet the perception of a Japan unwilling to take initiative on its own behalf to strengthen the international trading framework is still deeply rooted in the American mind. Therefore, the U.S. government persists in its traditional negative negotiating style of exerting pressure on Japan, sometimes harshly, in order to achieve its goals.

In some ways current U.S.-Japanese relations have come to resemble a card game where only one player wins continuously. The loser, unwilling to accept the full blame for a poor showing, asserts that the rules of the game are unfair, while the winner is intent on explaining why the old rules are reasonable. Obviously, if it is mutually beneficial to continue the game, the rules will have to be changed with mutual agreement. U.S.-Japan relations are now at the point where new rules must be sought and it is probable that both sides will be forced to make sacrifices. Under these conditions U.S.-Japan relations may be entering a new period that will be marked by "sharing the burden."

Socialist States: Allies and Adversaries of the USSR

The verbal haze created by cold war rhetoric often obscures the fact that the socialist bloc is not a servile monolithic group of states in the iron fist of Moscow. The old saw that the Soviet Union is paranoid about its security because it is the only state surrounded by hostile communist countries reveals one dimension of the problems plaguing the socialist bloc. Two major issues are at the core of the tensions in the relationship of the Soviet Union with other socialist countries: nationalism, which affects Party and ideological relations, as well as attitudes toward Soviet military dominance; and economic development. Nationalism fuels the irritations over Soviet control, not only in Eastern European countries such as Poland and Rumania, but also in China, Vietnam, and even within the Soviet Union itself. What is in the interests of "the larger socialist community" (a moral cloak for the interests of the Soviet motherland), has not necessarily been in the national interests of the various socialist states. The Sino-Soviet split can be attributed largely to nationalist animosities, and to China's fear that "international socialism" could be used to justify Soviet hegemony over China, as it did in Hungary and Poland in 1956, and in Czechoslovakia in 1968. In addition, Party to Party relations have foundered on nationalism. Indeed, the Communist Parties of Poland and Rumania, which have little national support, could not survive at all without the Soviet linkage. The Communist Parties of Yugoslavia and China, on the other hand, did survive precisely because they were nationalist parties with roots deep among the people; but they asserted independence from Soviet dominance early on.

Eastern European economies, which the Soviets tightly controlled during the Stalinist period, much to their own benefit, have turned into liabilities. Now the Soviet Union, which used to get goods at little cost from their Eastern European satellites, must pour in money to prop up their industries and keep them producing. The Polish rebellion by Solidarity has challenged the socialist economic system directly, and has highlighted the Soviets' refusal to accept either social or economic reforms that are not under its tightly controlled system. (In some sense, Hungary is an exception to this, however.) Economic developments outside the socialist bloc are also threatening Eastern European economies, which have come to depend on a growing amount of trade with and investment from the West. Even East Germany, whose economy is subsidized by West Germany and by de facto membership in the European Economic Community (EEC), has recently met with serious economic problems.

In spite of these economic difficulties, pressures from Moscow for greater contributions to higher defense budgets mount. Part of the Soviet defense effort must, however, still go to defending the Soviet Union against a presumed Chinese threat to the East.

With both socialist countries paying for close to a million troops to guard their more than 4000 miles of common borders (the Soviet Union's Asian defense constitutes 25% of its military budget), critical choices must be made between defense and economic development. The Chinese thus far seem to be winging their defense, hoping for the Soviet inbuilt fear of a two-front war to keep Soviet troops out of China. On their side, the Soviets seem anxious to improve their relationship with the Chinese, to counterbalance Chinese ties with the US. But the Soviets could hardly welcome a return to their own 1950s style of close bonds with the Chinese: a renewed alliance would undoubtedly mean a certain level of Soviet aid for Chinese economic development, but the Soviets have little with which to help. In any event, nationalism and ideological righteousness on both sides, combined with Soviet support for Vietnamese expansionist efforts, make it difficult for the two communist powers to come to terms. Thus, with the Soviets' own capacity for economic development thwarted, with their resulting inability to help out the other troubled socialist economies, and with their efforts to gain complete control over Afghanistan, the new Soviet leadership will face many challenges to its authority in the years ahead.

Looking Ahead: Challenge Questions

If the Soviet Union in the years to come is unable, because of its own economic problems, to satisfy the energy needs and other economic demands of its Eastern European satellites, what will be the likely consequences?

What would the Chinese hope to get out of an improved relationship with the Soviet Union? Would a better relationship between the Chinese and Soviets necessarily affect the world strategic balance in an adverse way?

What are the risks for the US and its Western European allies if the Soviet postwar empire threatens to disintegrate? What kind of dilemma is posed for the West by such situations as the suppression of Solidarity in Poland?

Is it in America's best interest to see the Polish crisis resolved?

What kind of power does the West have at its disposal to get concessions from the Soviet Union in terms of its relationship with the Eastern European socialist states?

Stability in the Warsaw Pact?

JOHN ERICKSON

John Erickson, Director of Defense Studies, University of Edinburgh, is the author of numerous books and articles on Soviet and East European military history and military affairs. His latest book is Road to Stalingrad: Stalin's War with Germany, *vol. I (New York: Harper and Row, 1975).*

FOR all the animosity that prevails between East and West, there is at least one thin thread of mutuality: the alliance systems of both sides, NATO (North Atlantic Treaty Organization) and the Warsaw Pact, are in visible disarray. Distress signals are flying in several directions, and statements designed to reassure do little or nothing to dispel the sense of strain. Senator Charles Percy (R., Ill.), chairman of the Senate Foreign Relations Committee, emphasizes that "NATO is not now in a crisis" but somberly adds that it could easily be pushed into one. The "two-way street," intended to spread the economic benefits of rearmament, has become a highway for recrimination and reproof. European attitudes irritate and even antagonize the United States Congress, which duly responds with proposals whose net effect is merely to promote further alienation or misgivings on the part of the Europeans.

The issues cannot really be accounted new, although the guises in which they appear have a hint of the novel.[1] The credibility of the United States commitment to Europe, a perennial debating point, has again been highlighted as American global perspectives and commitments appear to clash with European regionalism (indeed, some might say, parochialism). Thus the notion that the United States should implement a global strategy based on sea power and utilize power projection from the sea, recently expounded by Senate Armed Services Committee consultant Jeffrey Record and retired Admiral Robert J. Hanks, has as its inevitable corollary United States troop withdrawals from Europe and Asia alike.[2] Unsettling though that prospect may be, in paradoxical fashion the very elaboration of American warfighting capabilities in the European theater—surely one earnest of American

commitment—has generated more acrimony and obloquy. Further, the modernization of theater nuclear forces, undertaken initially at the behest of worried Europeans, has also become a source of friction and tortuous negotiation, not to mention bruised feelings over the relative advantage (or disadvantage) in arms production, the "two-way street" that appears to many to have become an unpromising cul-de-sac.

Looking eastward to the Warsaw Pact, the problems of alliance cohesion do not seem to be appreciably easier. Again, long-standing discrepancies and discriminations rather than radically new issues have induced unsuspected difficulties. Both alliance systems are apparently subject to a singular strain: their predominant powers, the United States and the Soviet Union, are embarking on what is at least a shake-up in their strategic concepts if not a thoroughgoing revision of strategic preferences. For the United States, the choice is relatively clear; there is within NATO as it presently stands no alternative to American leadership, the cost being some 40-60 percent of the American defense budget ($133 billion as of October 1, 1982).

The Soviet predicament is of a different order, because of the distinctive structure of the Pact (itself largely a Soviet artifact) and because the Polish crisis—ripping a huge gash in the political and military facade of the Pact—has far-reaching implications. This is not to raise the cry that the Warsaw Pact is on the point of actual disintegration but to affirm that the Polish debacle, combined with the Soviet emphasis on "larger-scale forms of military operations," operations on a strategic scale within given theaters of military operations (TVD's), brings into sharpest relief the question of furnishing and sustaining the main effort, either by beefing up the Soviet component or by spreading part of the load among the non-Soviet elements.[3]

The structure of the Pact is informative, although a table of organization does not disclose the nature of the system. Since 1969 and the "Budapest reforms," the highest military organ of the Pact has been the committee of defense ministers. The Warsaw Pact commander in chief (Marshal Viktor G. Kulikov) and the chief of staff/joint armed forces (Army General

"Stability in the Warsaw Pact?" John Erickson, *Current History*, November 1982. Reprinted by permission.

Anatoly Gribkov) are members supported by the chiefs of staff of the national military establishments. Designed to give non-Soviet states a greater say in military matters, the ministerial committee is supplemented by the military council, another body freshly created in 1969 under the permanent chairmanship of the Pact's commander in chief, who is assisted by the Pact chief of staff and is attended by non-Soviet deputy commanders. The Pact high command consists, in formal terms, of a Soviet commander in chief assisted by these consultative organs, the ministerial committee and the council, both of which appear to concern themselves mainly with training and organization in general.[4]

Serving in direct subordination to the commander in chief, the joint staff, established in 1969, consists of the chief of staff assisted by deputy chiefs of staff from the member nations, plus a Soviet political officer. The joint staff is officially designated as the administrative organ of the commander in chief and is responsible for organizing the meetings of the defense ministers council and the military council. It is, therefore, a headquarters staff in a formal sense, and its headquarters functions include the coordination of the various Soviet military missions and "Soviet Representatives" distributed throughout East Europe, with Soviet officers "co-located" in the national Ministries of Defense. In addition, the Pact has its own inspector general (again, a Soviet senior officer) and a military-technical committee (with a Soviet general at its head) to regulate both military research and development and military production within the Pact, linked with the military-industrial committee of East Europe's COMECON (Council for Mutual Economic Assistance).[5]

Viewed historically, this is simply an extension and expansion of the arrangements that have prevailed since the early 1950's, when the tenth directorate of the Soviet general staff was charged with the supervision of the bilateral Soviet-East European treaties (and with a watching brief over East Germany). The net result over the years has been the development of a large multinational staff attached to the Soviet Ministry of Defense.[6] A certain elaboration came with the creation of the Pact proper, when in 1955 a political consultative committee was formed, together with a joint command of joint (Pact) forces, the latter comprising the Pact commander-in-chief and East European Defense Ministers as deputy commanders. In addition, a place was found automatically for the head of the Soviet PVO Strany (Homeland Air Defense) within the joint staff. The subordination was obvious, and it appears to have been injurious to national feeling. Defense Ministers were accountable to a commander in chief holding only the position of a Deputy Defense Minister. A certain leveling out came in 1969 when East European Deputy Ministers replaced the Defense Ministers.[7]

The principle of joint armed forces was also established at the time of the signing of the Warsaw Treaty. Article Five signified the assent of the contracting parties to the assignment—by agreement—of national units to the joint command, which would in turn "function on the basis of jointly established principles"—a vacuous formulation which could mean anything. What has transpired in practice is of a different order; even if the term joint is rendered as unified, this does not signify integrated forces, since on both Soviet and non-Soviet (Pact) testimony these assigned or earmarked contingents remain under their own national deputy commander and are responsive to national control. In effect, as Pact commander in chief Marshal Kulikov has direct control over only the 30 divisions of the four Soviet groups of forces (GSFG, Northern, Central and Southern) plus the *Nationale Volksarmee* (NVA) of the German Democratic Republic, although here national control is once more asserted at divisional level and below.

It is obvious that we must look elsewhere for the operational command structure of the Warsaw Pact. Integration in any real sense can be said to exist only with respect to air defense, both for early warning and defense of air space. It remains to be seen whether the recent Soviet reorganization of the *PVO Strany* (Homeland Air Defense) into Air Defense Troops (*Voiska PVO*) will affect non-Soviet systems, but since the Soviet move foreshadowed an expansion of air defense capability it is likely that the Pact will be similarly affected. Attack helicopters on the battlefield and cruise missiles penetrating at low altitude are not likely to respect national sensitivities.

Specialization rather than integration within one Soviet-directed system—as in the case of strategic air defense—is more the hallmark of the Pact's non-Soviet air forces, equipped as they are with Soviet aircraft and trained in Soviet operational doctrine. The modernization of the non-Soviet tactical air force is proceeding (costly though it is), with the MiG-23 going to East Germany and Czechoslovakia.[8] Nor is it likely that the non-Soviet air forces will remain unaffected by yet another Soviet reorganization, changes in the Soviet air force that include the displacement of the "air army" (like the Sixteenth Air Army in GSFG) in favor of what look increasingly like theater or sector strike commands, a move greatly facilitated by the rapid introduction of multipurpose aircraft with appreciable improvements in performance.[9]

Last but by no means least in this sphere of specialized forces or specialized integration are the East German and Polish naval forces, admirably fitted to provide support (such as minesweeping and amphibious forces) to overall Soviet naval activity in the Baltic and in European coastal waters.[10]

4. SOCIALIST STATES

That an operational command structure does exist (as might have long been suspected) is borne out by recent disclosures of command positions held by senior Soviet officers. Commander in chief Marshal Kulikov continues the unbroken tradition of a Soviet officer as overall commander; Army General Gribkov is chief of the joint staff, assisted by Lieutenant General N.N. Tereshchenko as his immediate deputy (plus Lieutenant General Merezhko); Air Marshal Aleksandr Koldunov is head of *Voiska PVO* in command of the integrated strategic air defense system; Aviation Colonel General V.V. Katrich commands the Pact air forces; and Admiral V.V. Mikhailin commands joint naval forces.

Modernization in weapons systems has evidently been accompanied by an uprating of professional competence and experience. Tereshchenko, for example, came from his post as Chief of Staff/Belorussian Military District, which is no sinecure. A noteworthy arrival is Lieutenant General G. Khoreshko to the post of Assistant to the Commander in Chief for Rear Services/Logistics. These appointments cannot really be described as command cosmetics, a tart phrase used to describe the effect of the 1969 reforms in the Pact.

FORCE MAKEUP

What, then, do these senior commanders command? Before the onset of the Polish crisis, that question could have been answered with a relative degree of certainty, assuming that the Joint Armed Forces included the four Soviet Groups of Forces deployed forward, the six divisions of the NVA (which could be brought up to eight divisions with the operational activation of the East German border troops) and the operational component of the Polish armed forces, sometimes estimated as the equivalent of three field armies. (The Polish army was subdivided into two components, one an operational force for Pact missions, the other a territorial/home defense force, the OTK, which represented a concession to Polish concern over the security of Polish territory.)[11] Thus before Poland erupted, the Soviet theater commander (with his air and naval counterparts) could reckon from the nominal Polish order of battle of 15 divisions—five tank, eight motorized rifle divisions, with an airborne and amphibious division—on at least three or four tank divisions and three motor-rifle divisions, plus specialized units, naval support and a large tactical air reserve with over 800 aircraft. One tank division and five motor-rifle divisions could well be held back as a reserve or for home defense.

POLISH CAPABILITIES

The continuing Polish crisis does not mean the total withdrawal of Polish military capability from the Pact. But with 73 percent of the Polish Army consisting of conscripts (many flaunting Solidarity badges), and all staring glumly at the prospect of extended martial law in Poland, it is hardly to be expected that Poland's force will be suffused with martial vigor. There can be little consolation in the fact that General Wojciech Jaruzelski has garnered more power (or appointments) to himself than any man since Joseph Stalin. And while much has been made of the role of the Polish Army in salvaging Polish national integrity and protecting Polish national honor, it cannot have escaped the attention of most observers that this group of Polish generals is an artificial creation. Most of them are between 56 and 60 years of age, were members of the Polish army on Soviet soil during World War II, were trained in Soviet staff colleges and were associated with the suppression of the anti-Communist Polish underground after the war in the years between 1946 and 1948.[12]

Their record does not inspire wholehearted confidence in their concern for the fate of Poland: most, if not all, of them are political soldiers, in that they held previous appointments as political officers in Polish training establishments, the royal road to reliability. In fact, so important are these associations and connections that a senior Polish general (now in the West) has asserted that the Polish Army is engaged in a Warsaw Pact operation, not the sancta simplicitas of saving Polish honor and territorial integrity.

That does not mean a dire and direct Soviet hand but a Pact complot, outflanking the Polish Army proper. Simple common sense suggests that the *stan wojenny* (state of war, technically a state of emergency) could not have been implemented without Soviet cognizance, even connivance. Senior Soviet officers maintained close contact with the Polish Generals E. Molczyk and J. Baryla, while the Chief of the Polish General Staff, General Florian Siwicki, was in Moscow not long before the military takeover. Twice the Soviet leadership reportedly mooted military intervention, reshuffling its western theater command to align commanders,[13] but in the late spring of 1981 a Polish plan was apparently developed to control the situation, and in the early summer Polish Army operational groups began to deploy.[14]

THE PRICE OF MILITARY INTERVENTION

What havoc military intervention can wreak has been shown in doleful fashion in Czechoslovakia. There, a once highly proficient and well-equipped military establishment came close to disintegration; the shortage of competent officers and the reduction in the size of the Czechoslovak army (and the virtual halving of the strength of the air force) have deflated what was previously an impressive order of battle. A few Czechoslovak divisions might be assigned to the first Soviet assault echelon. But Czechoslovak divisions are no longer assigned to a major axis of advance running along a line from Pilsen to Coblenz, which is manifestly beyond the capabilities of the Czech forces at this juncture.

By rough reckoning, the Soviet command might be able to reckon on four or five Czechoslovak divisions, split up and bonded with Soviet units, useful in the first phase of an offensive operation (possibly to "snag" the German corps in the southeast). Soviet-Czech missile brigades, artillery brigades, engineer and transport units might have their use, but the full weight of major operations would surely have to fall on the Soviet central group. With its corps headquartered at Olomouc and its heavy concentration of independent assets, the Soviet force[15] could act as a giant mobile group under direct general staff control or could operate with the southern flank formations of GSFG in cutting into United States divisions. Or it could mount its own major thrust southwestward. However, the cost of replacing Czechoslovak capability has been heavy for the Soviet command; replacing Polish capability, if that were possible, would be even higher; it would call for well over the 18 divisions deployed in recent exercise patterns.

SOVIET-GERMAN INTEGRATION

With the NVA, in East Germany the Soviet command has a well-equipped and well-trained force (though not without its morale problems); its divisions maintain 80 percent of their manpower and 100 percent of their weapons complement, all with high densities (297 tanks and 252 infantry combat vehicles per 10,000 men, higher than the Czechs and Poles). Soviet-German integration appears to have increased of late. There is greater emphasis on German officers mastering Russian, a process that might work for senior officers trained in Soviet military academies. But at division level and below—at the unit level—German is the order of the day, as is national control. German-Soviet coordination may be barely effected by utilizing the Soviet practice of assigning *napravlentsyi (Richtungs-offiziere*, operational liaison officers) to divisions and even to regiments.[16] Clearly, language is a problem in the Pact (a factor not unknown in NATO); not only operational orders but tactical instructions come down from Soviet operational staffs in Russian, and this information must be relayed to lower levels. Here Soviet training for higher staffs and commanders in the Pact plus the provision that promotion beyond the rank of colonel in Pact military establishments is subject to Soviet monitoring and control may well pay off, but the problem of efficient tactical handling at the lower levels remains, however standardized the tactical repertoires.

The "southern tier" (Hungary, Bulgaria and Romania) offer less well-equipped forces. Stolidly pro-Soviet, Bulgaria is a quiescent ally; but the Bulgarian army, organized into three army headquarters and with its armor brigaded, suffers from obsolete equipment, although the recently opened ferry route from the Odessa military district to Varna can mean the speedy shipment and transit of armor and heavy equipment. Hungary maintains a relatively low military profile, suggesting that its main contribution would be to furnish logistics support, with the Soviet southern Group of Forces providing most of the punch. However, the importance of these southern theater forces should not be wholly discounted; their significance is underlined by the shift in Soviet exercise patterns to a north-south axis.

Romania, politically and militarily wayward, resists any form of integration or the loss of national command over its armed forces. But it keeps one toe in the Pact, keeping in touch by nominal participation in staff exercises. The breach is nevertheless considerable; Romania absolutely rejects the Soviet concept of coalition armed forces committed to coalition warfare under Soviet strategic and operational direction.[17]

The nominal order of battle, though outwardly impressive, hardly reveals reality. Long gone are the days when the Warsaw Pact was viewed as a military monolith capable of hurling more than 90 divisions against all sectors of NATO in a massive, all-out, fully coordinated and sustainable assault. At the present juncture, the grand total of 85 divisions (31 Soviet, 54 non-Soviet) cannot be reckoned as the operational strength or as an indicator of the operational effectiveness of the Pact. With regard to the much vaunted "iron triangle," the "northern tier," the military core of the Pact, there also has to be some reassessment. On paper, the non-Soviet establishments should provide 30-31 divisions (6 East German, 15 Polish, 10 Czechoslovak) plus 26+ Soviet divisions (19 in GSFG [Soviet Groups of Forces], 2-3 in Poland, 5-6 in Czechoslovakia). But it would be unrealistic to assume an operational order of battle of 56-58 divisions, at once fully available, fully equipped and properly trained, to say nothing of their fighting spirit.

Turning to that vexing issue of manpower and manning levels—the great stumbling block in the Mutual Balanced Force Reduction (MBFR) talks in Vienna—a tally of 935,000 men may be estimated for the iron triangle forces, assuming that counting means anything. Speaking of counting, there is some small evidence that the Polish military was far from satisfied with the manner in which the Soviet command counted Polish troops; on the other hand, there are suspicions that combat elements are being "tucked away," hived off into separate air landing brigades and the like.[18] Come to that, the French are counted in or out of the NATO system as the politics of special counting (or discounting) requires.[19]

Possible explanations of operational patterns may be discerned outside the nominal order of battle. Assume that the in-place, unreinforced preemptive assault pattern best suits Soviet purposes, because the least attractive Soviet option would be a commitment of forces against a well-prepared and fully deployed NATO defense. Then a large-scale, cumbersome and time-consuming Pact mobilization in all its formality may be ruled out, since surprise, which is of the essence, would be wholly dispelled. Marshal N. Ogarkov recently intimated that the classic concept of forming fronts is no longer valid, since in scale (and intensity) theater-wide operations can accomplish strategic tasks for which front organization would be too restrictive.[20]

Much will depend, therefore, on the organizational and operational assignments of these theaters of operations (TVD's) and attendant strategic sectors. Cross-national task forces with select non-Soviet participation (specialized units, support, rear security) or even as part of assigned battle groups would provide useful forces, which could be readied with a form of mobilization by exercise/maneuver. In that context, the pattern of exercises, changed some time ago from large, standardized maneuvers to more specialized training, including amphibious operations in the Baltic, winter warfare in the Carpathians, armored thrusts through narrow mountain valleys, night fighting in heavily wooded country, and experimentation with mobile operations in Hungary.

Most commentary on Soviet/Pact operations presupposes the staged movement of first and second echelons, bringing large masses of armor and artillery to bear in a relatively short period.[21] This seems to imply shifting Groups of Forces forward holus-bolus, followed by reserve divisions. But this swarming into an attack zone at some distance from the battle line does not seem to fit with growing Soviet emphasis on *peregruppirovka,* not merely tactical regrouping but regrouping on a strategic-operational scale.[22] Echeloning does at least afford great flexibility, and operational patterns might envisage an initial assault without mobilization, the use of airborne units and air transport to push units forward, with dispersed forces picking up cross-national battle groups as they deploy to exploit success—none of which tactics would override the Soviet principles of deception, surprise and shock power. On the contrary, these could be studiously applied, and non-Soviet Pact military units would have considerable utility. With pre-assigned units, their capability would be known, coordination would not be an insuperable problem, and the logistics load could still be carried along separate Soviet and national lines.

This analysis would not be complete without reference to the major modernization and restructuring program of the Soviet Ground Forces (Soviet Army), the main military muscle of the Pact. This formidable catalogue includes improvements in mobility, firepower, shock power, command and control, air defense, electronic warfare (EW), logistics and sustainability. The T-64 tank now equips GSFG; the T-72 has been brought into the western military districts (and introduced in small numbers in non-Soviet Pact

armies); the BMP (infantry combat vehicle) has gone to motor-rifle and reconnaissance units (a new BMP model mounts a 30-mm gun);[23] artillery holdings have been expanded (GSFG now has 30 percent more artillery plus an increment of some 17,000 men); nuclear-capable heavy artillery brigades equipped with 203-mm howitzers and 240-mm mortars have been introduced; there are new tactical missiles (the SS-21 and SS-22) and the BM-27 multiple rocket launcher (kept under wraps for a lengthy period); and in the field of *upravlenie voiskami* (troop control, or C_3—command, control, communication) improvements include communication by satellite, radio equipment, and computerized systems for field artillery and tactical decision making.[24]

The tank battalions in the motor-rifle divisions have received more tanks (from 31 to 40), and tank regiments in tank divisions are acquiring motor-rifle battalions (in place of the previous companies) as well as artillery battalions. The net effect of these changes gives both tank and motor-rifle elements the capacity to operate in a combined-arms mode with a mix of armor-infantry plus artillery support, air defense and NBC (nuclear, biological, and chemical warfare) protection. This great influx of artillery was accompanied by a protracted and intense debate in Soviet circles, which have now concluded that the artillery battalion (rather than the battery) should be the basic organizational unit. Today, the introduction of two self-propelled guns (the M-1973 152-mm and the M-1974 122-mm self-propelled howitzer) at last provides support for fast moving advances. Both the Polish Army and the NVA have paraded these models, while the Czechoslovaks have developed a rather oddly configured vehicle of their own.[25]

Perhaps most impressive is the buildup in helicopter strength in transport, support and attack modes. What must be of great relevance to the European theater is now being tested in Afghanistan; the operational evaluation of the SU-25 (FROGFOOT)[26] close support aircraft, and the development of tactics for the integration of fixed-wing aircraft with the powerful Mil-24 helicopter. Moving from the tactical battlefield, the Su-24 (FENCER)—some 400 of which are in service but not deployed in strength beyond Soviet boundaries—provides the Soviet command with the capability to mount precision strikes throughout the depth of the NATO region.[27]

While this is usually described as a Soviet military buildup, from the Soviet viewpoint it is essentially the maintenance and the reinforcement of favorable force ratios, levels of weapons and manning required to meet operational norms. Such calculations, however, are only part of a larger equation.

If the Pact (the non-Soviet elements) contributes only marginally to overall Soviet capability, why does the Soviet Union carry "in the economic sense over 80 percent of this [defense] burden within the framework of the Warsaw Pact."[28] The military economics of the Pact are a separate and complex subject, and what is often interpreted as political difficulty in Pact circles may have much more to do with money and machines, especially when the pace of military modernization is being forced in badly battered economies.[29] Perhaps the answer lies in the Soviet conviction that this is the age of contending coalitions, where an appropriate correlation of forces is essential to security requirements; here the Warsaw Pact has undeniable utility in spite of dissatisfactions and querulousness.

The Polish crisis notwithstanding, the Pact does not appear to be on the point of dissolution, even if that crisis has visibly damaged military readiness, military-economic relations, and the general mobilization base. I have never shared the view that the Warsaw Pact is an entangling alliance for the Soviet Union; Moscow has a ruthless way with encumbrances and entanglements. As long as the Pact has a perceived utility, it will be maintained and sustained in spite of its cost and its demand for a larger slice of Soviet military resources. Most important, in an age of global coalitions—a dominant Soviet strategic perspective—the Pact cannot be allowed to wither away. For all its faults and faltering, the Pact still has its uses.

NOTES

[1]See Lawrence S. Kaplan and Robert W. Clawson, eds., *NATO After Thirty Years* (Wilmington: Scholarly Resources, Inc., 1981); also Gavin Kennedy, *Burden Sharing in NATO* (London: Duckworth, 1979). In general, disputed issues have been identified as credibility of nuclear posture, burden-sharing, and "out-of-area" problems.

[2]A two-part study, *US Strategy at the Crossroads* (Cambridge, Mass.: Institute of Foreign Policy Analysis).

[3]For a discussion of the place of coalition warfare waged with coalition military forces, see Colonel General G.F. Vorontsov, *Voennye koalitsii i koalitsionnye voiny* (Moscow: Voenizdat, 1976), pp. 340 *passim;* also V.F. Samoilenko, *Osnova boevovo soyuza. Internatsionalizm kak faktor oboronnoi moshchi sotsialist-icheskovo sodrushestva* (Moscow: Voenizdat, 1981). See also Lt. General S. Radzievskii, "Voennoe sotrudnichestvo i soglasovanie usili stran antigitlerovskoi koalitsii," *Voenno-istoricheskii Zhurnal,* no. 6, 1982, pp. 48-54 on Soviet-directed "coalition forces," Polish, Czech, Romanian, Bulgarian, and liaison with the Yugoslavs.

[4]On Pact organization, see Robin Alison Remington, *The Warsaw Pact* (Cambridge, Mass.: MIT Press, 1971); Stephan Tiedtke, *Die Warschauer Vertragsorganization* (Munich: Oldenbourg Verlag, 1978); Robert W. Clawson and Lawrence S. Kaplan, eds., *The Warsaw Pact: Political Purpose and Military Means* (Wilmington: Scholarly Resources, 1982), pp. 3-63; also Appendix A (pp. 151-156) in A. Ross Johnson et al., *East European Military Establishments: The Warsaw Pact Northern Tier* (New York: Crane Russack, 1982).

[5]See the unique and indispensable studies by Michael Che-

cinski that illuminate the hugely neglected field of Pact military-industrial/military-economic affairs, *The Costs of Armament Production and the Profitability of Armament Exports in COMECON Countries* (Jerusalem: Hebrew University Research Paper no. 10); also *Osteuropa-Wirtschaft,* vol. 20, no. 2, June, 1975, pp. 117-142. One of the most valuable studies written on the Pact is Checinski's *A Comparison of the Polish and Soviet Armaments Decisionmaking Systems,* RAND Corporation, Report R-2662-AF, Jan., 1981 (pp. 18-19, on the Pact Military-Technical Committee, organization, personnel).

[6]See Malcolm Mackintosh, "Military Considerations in Soviet-East European Relations," in Karen Dawisha and Philip Hanson, eds., *Soviet-East European Dilemmas* (London: RIIA/Heinemann, 1981), p. 138.

[7]See Lawrence T. Caldwell, "The Warsaw Pact: Directions of Change," *Problems of Communism,* Sept.-Oct., 1975, pp. 2-10. See also Colonel V. Semin, "Voenno-politicheskii oboronitel'nyi soyuz strau sotsializma i voevoe sodrushestvo ikh voorzhennykh sil kak ob'ekt issledovaniya," *VIZ,* no. 7, 1982, pp. 67-74 (bibliographical survey, useful references).

[8]See Robert W. Clawson, "Warsaw Pact Air Forces," in *The Warsaw Pact,* pp. 251-273. My own calculations give a figure of 2,644 aircraft for operational use (including the Hungarian Air Force, plus Naval Aviation and 50 bombers of LRA assigned a conventional role; going as far as the Urals, the figure rises to 4,370 combat aircraft. As for the argument over the respective positions of interceptor/Frontal Aviation, with the latter "gaining," the introduction of larger numbers of multipurpose aircraft makes this a rather artificial disputation.

[9]I am far from clear about the implications of recent restructuring in Soviet air. Air assets in MD's (military districts) have been reorganized (first in the Baltic and the Carpathian MD's), thus replacing the "air army" organization by an "air force" (VVS) designation, possibly comprising *all* wartime/operational air assets. New aircraft coming into service include MiG-25M, SU-27 interceptor/air superiority fighter, SU-25 close air support aircraft, MiG-29 (possible follow-on to MiG-23). Production of the interceptor models suggests that the Soviet command is not convinced of the overall reliability of surface-to-air defensive systems. A strategic bomber and a specialized high altitude reconnaissance aircraft are being developed; 200 BACKFIRES are currently in service.

[10]See Louis J. Andolina, "Warsaw Pact Sea Power," in *The Warsaw Pact,* pp. 195-211.

[11]Expertly discussed and analyzed in A. Ross Johnson et al., *East European Military Establishments: The Warsaw Pact Northern Tier* (RAND Report R2417/1-AF/FF), Dec., 1980, pp. 33-37.

[12]For details of commanders/actions see *Z walk przeciwko zbrojnemu podziemiu 1944-1947* (Warsaw: MON, 1966).

[13]Discussed in Richard D. Anderson, "Soviet Decision-Making and Poland," *Problems of Communism,* March-April, 1982, pp. 22-36; this is an impressive analysis but there are grounds for disputing Ivanovskii's place as a "prominent loser" in the transfers. It is equally plausible to suggest that Ivanovskii was moved to become a possible "north-west theatre commander" in the event of military action in Poland—and he is still in position.

[14]Neal Ascherson, *The Polish August* (London: Penguin Books, 1981), *passim;* Roman Stefanowski, *Poland: A Chronology of Events (February-December, 1981),* Radio Free Europe, RAD Background Report/Chronology, contd.; also J.B. de Weydenthal, *Anatomy of the Martial Law Regime: The Institutions,* Radio Free Europe Research, RAD Report no. 32, Feb. 2, 1982. The Polish steel industry and mines are now under military control and half the provinces are run by military

4. SOCIALIST STATES

commissars, with more military presence in central government.

[15]Five divisions (18 Tank, 13 Tank, 31 Tank, 48 and 33 Motor-Rifle Divisions); and a missile brigade at Jasenik: 50,000-60,000 men with a reported tank park of 10,000 with what seems to me to be a profusion of artillery, anti-tank, anti-air, multiple rocket launcher (MRL) and tactical missile assets.

[16]A. Ross-Johnson et al., *op. cit.*, footnote to p. 74. This is a system similar to that operated in the Soviet Army, and I have argued elsewhere that General Staff *napravlentsyi* are also assigned at the Soviet regimental level.

[17]See Walter M. Bacon, "The Military and the Party in Romania," in Dale R. Herspring and Ivan Volgyes, eds., *Civil-Military Relations in Communist Systems* (Boulder: Westview Press, 1978), pp. 165-80.

[18]Air landing/assault brigades have 3 or 4 air assault battalions, one heavy (weapons) battalion, helicopters for lift and fire support, and 2,000-2,500 officers and men.

[19]The NATO study of "comparative strengths" (reported in *Aviation Week and Space Technology*, May 10, 1982, p. 17) seems to me to be a singularly inane example of "counting."

[20]Marshal N.V. Ogarkov, *Vsegda v gotovnosti k zashchite Otechestva* (Moscow: Voenizdat, 1982), pp. 34-35. This is exactly the formulation he employed in his article in *Kommunist*, no. 10, 1981.

[21]In terms of gross figures, the Pact forces can mass 13,300 armored vehicles and artillery pieces in the 1st echelon on the FEBA; within 16 hours they can add a 2nd echelon of 7,100 tanks/guns; and within 48 hours they can bring 19,400 tanks/guns into action. Note, however, that this massed force must deploy along *five* axes of advance.

[22]I understand that three contexts were being considered: *peregruppirovka* in (i) intercontinental, inter-theater and inter-front terms, (ii) operational levels—inter-front and inter-army, and (iii) tactical, involving division and below (units).

[23]The BMP-80 was brought into GSFG in 1978-1979.

[24]Quite the best survey of this Soviet program was written by Donald L. Madill, "The Continuing Evolution of the Soviet Ground Forces," *Military Review*, August, 1982, pp. 52-68; it covers organization, weapons, tactical forms and tactical air, with excellent reference material.

[25]A 152-mm gun, mounted in a turret on a modified TATRA-813 chassis. This is less a turret than a truck-mounted casemate, so that the gun cannot be trained laterally.

[26]Though bearing the odd number designation applied to fighters, the SU-25 is reported as a clear-air close support aircraft (not unlike the American Northrop A-9A).

[27]According to *Flight International*, August 21, 1982, 30 SU-24 strike aircraft have been deployed to East Germany. The SU-24 is able to fight for control of the air even over NATO territory; but this strategy presupposes advances in Soviet C_3 for such air operations well ahead of the FEBA.

[28]This figure (80 percent) is supplied by O. Behounek, "RVHP a obranyschopnost Socialismu," *Historie a Vojenstvi* (Prague, 1980), no. 1;

[29]I can only make this point in a clumsy fashion, although it is expertly and vastly illuminated in M. Checinski, *op. cit.*

East Europe Instability

F. Stephen Larrabee

F. Stephen Larrabee, a former member of the National Security Council staff, is co-director of the Soviet and East European research program at The Johns Hopkins School for Advance International Studies, and visiting professor of government at Cornell University.

WASHINGTON—Perhaps the main problem confronting Yuri V. Andropov as he takes over the top post of the Soviet Union is how to manage and contain the growing forces of instability and change sweeping across Eastern Europe. In the past, Moscow has sought to do this by a policy of political and economic integration, and where necessary outright repression. It is increasingly questionable, however, whether either of these methods alone will suffice in the future. If the Soviet Union is to preserve its Eastern European empire, it will have to adopt new more flexible methods of control.

The most immediate and pressing problem facing Mr. Andropov is, of course, the unsettled crisis in Poland. Military rule has temporarily muted the most threatening forms of unrest, but it has done nothing to resolve the basic problems that gave rise to the unrest in the first place. There is little prospect for economic improvement without large-scale reform, which the regime is too fearful to implement. The party is too divided and demoralized to provide effective leadership. And the population remains sullen and defiant, unwilling to cooperate with a regime it neither trusts nor accepts. At the same time, military rule poses a direct challenge to the party's leading role and establishes a precedent that cannot help but make the Soviet leadership uncomfortable—particularly given the potential for unrest elsewhere in Eastern Europe.

After a period of relative economic prosperity in the early 1970's, the Soviet bloc has entered a period of retrenchment and austerity. The 1976-80 five-year plans showed the lowest growth rates since the end of World War II—and it is unlikely that even this relatively modest growth will be achieved in the 1980's.

Economic problems will be accentuated in the coming decade by the impending energy crunch. With the exception of Rumania, all Eastern European countries are dependent on the Soviet Union for oil and, according to Western estimates, they will have to increase oil imports by approximately 3 to 5 percent per year to satisfy domestic demand during the next five years. Yet the Soviet Union has told its allies that its exports of oil cannot be expected to exceed 1980 levels. And if Moscow cannot meet their growing requirements, these countries will have little choice but to buy oil elsewhere at world market prices, aggravating their already considerable balance-of-payments problems. Their only alternative would be to reduce imports and cut back on economic growth.

The growing energy crunch will make it increasingly difficult for many Eastern European governments to meet consumer demands in the 1980's. The Hungarian regime, for instance, has warned the public that over the next few years it must reckon with no improvement—or at best a minimal change—in its standard of living. At the same time, the growing debt problems faced by many Eastern European countries, especially Poland and Rumania, have left many Western bankers unwilling to engage in the large-scale lending that occurred in the 1970's.

Over the long run, it is quite possible that this economic decline could fuel political unrest throughout Eastern Europe—as in Poland, where the regime's inability to satisfy even minimal consumer demands was in large part responsible for increased pressures for political change.

Economic difficulties can be expected to accentuate the guns-versus-butter issue and could possibly lead to increased resistance to Soviet calls for higher defense budgets. Rumania, for example, has reduced its defense spending over the last several years. Faced with growing economic constraints, other Eastern European countries may well be tempted to follow that example, severely complicating Moscow's plans for modernization of Warsaw Pact forces.

Leonid I. Brezhnev's death may also have repercussions in Eastern Europe. Traditionally, the succession process in the Soviet Union has caused the Soviet leadership to turn inward, and Eastern European leaders have sought to exploit Soviet preoccupation with internal matters to increase their autonomy and

4. SOCIALIST STATES

experiment with domestic reforms. This was the case after Stalin's death in 1953, which led to unrest in Poland and Hungary in 1956, and it was the pattern after Nikita S. Khrushchev's ouster in 1964, which stimulated major economic reforms throughout Eastern Europe.

Eastern Europe is also facing a number of possible succession problems of its own that could add to any instability created by the Soviet succession. Czechoslovakia's Gustav Husak is 69, and the Bulgarian party leader, Todor Zhivkov, is 71. In Hungary, Janos Kadar recently celebrated his 70th birthday. The key question is whether "Kadarism"—the policy of economic and political liberalization that has been a hallmark of Mr. Kadar's rule—can survive him or whether economic constraints will compel Hungary to adopt more restrictive policies once he leaves the scene.

Mr. Andropov is no closet liberal, as has lately been suggested. He is a shrewd, tough-minded *apparatchik* who can be expected to pursue Soviet interests with firmness and vigor. But he does have extensive first-hand experience in dealing with Eastern Europe—first as Ambassador to Hungary and later as head of the Central Committee department responsible for relations with ruling Communist parties—that some Eastern Europeans may make him more flexible and sensitive to their problems than his predecessors were. Reports from both Budapest and Moscow suggest that he has been a strong supporter of Mr. Kadar's moderate course in Hungary—in large part because that course has insured political stability. He is most likely aware that a return to tighter centralized control would probably only accentuate the crisis in Eastern Europe and increase the potential for greater turmoil. Thus, in order to forestall further unrest at a time when he is facing major problems at home, Mr. Andropov may be willing to tolerate a greater degree of economic experimentation and reform in Eastern Europe as long as this remains carefully circumscribed and controlled by the party.

102

The German Democratic Republic

ARTHUR M. HANHARDT, JR.

Arthur M. Hanhardt Jr. is a visiting scientist at the Battelle Human Affairs Research Centers in Seattle, Washington. He is the author of *The German Democratic Republic* (Baltimore: The Johns Hopkins Press, 1968) and has written on German politics in the *Koelner Zeitschrift fuer Soziologie und Sozialpsychologie, The Journal of International Studies, Societas* and *Materialien zur Politischen Bildung.* He visited East Germany in 1970, 1972 and 1974 and West Germany in 1969, 1972, and 1980. Barbara Keen of Battelle—HARC provided bibliographical assistance for this article.

THE German Democratic Republic (GDR or East Germany) evokes strong responses. The Soviet Zone of Occupation in Germany, the Berlin Blockade, the Workers Revolt of June 17, 1953, and the Berlin Wall are familiar terms in the cold war vocabulary. During the era of détente, attention tended to concentrate on the treaty package that helped normalize relations in East Central Europe between the Federal Republic of Germany (FRG or West Germany), the GDR, Poland, Czechoslovakia, Hungary and the Soviet Union. Additionally, the status of Berlin was regulated in the Quadripartite Treaty of 1972. Although this period also witnessed the worldwide diplomatic recognition of the GDR, for the rest of the decade scant attention was given to internal East German affairs by the Western partners in détente. But perhaps the new cold war now going on between the United States and the Soviet Union will return attention to the GDR of the 1980's.

East Germany is a small country, about the size of the state of Tennessee, with a 1980 population of 16,737,000. It is located in a strategically vital area of Central Europe, lying between the NATO (North Atlantic Treaty Organization) forces arrayed in West Germany and volatile Poland. This exposure places a high value on close ties between the GDR and the Soviet Union; their alliance is secured by an extremely loyal Communist party, the Socialist Unity party of Germany (SED), the excellent East German National Peoples Army (NVA), and 20 Red Army divisions permanently stationed in the GDR.

Beyond the politico-military complex, the East German economy has an enviable record by East European standards. Notwithstanding imposing political and economic odds—it has few natural resources, for example—East Germany is now one of the world's "top ten" industrial states with the highest standard of living in the Soviet bloc.

But although East Germany is a self-proclaimed land of "socialism existing in reality" ("*real existierenden Sozialismus*"), all is not well in the "First Workers and Peasants State on German Soil." East German political development can be observed and assessed at the SED party congresses now held every five years in the East Berlin "Palace of the Republic." The tenth congress was staged in April, 1981, with all the pomp and ceremony associated with the rituals of an established workers and peasants party.

For the SED leadership, the tenth congress was an affirmation of Erich Honecker's unchallenged control of the party. This was Honecker's third party congress as General Secretary. On short notice, he replaced the aging Walter Ulbricht in 1971. The ninth congress in 1976 consolidated the Honecker leadership, while the 1981 meeting was a celebration of that leadership, with adulatory speeches and demonstrations. The few personnel changes in the SED hierarchy were all identified with Honecker's inner circle.

Ideologically, the tenth congress contained nothing new; no elements of genuine debate could be gleaned from the many speakers. Brotherhood with the Soviet Union in arms and economy was stressed. Speech after speech exhorted political organizations to greater efficiency and determination. Remarkably, there were few echoes of the events in neighboring Poland; and these few were sounded by relatively minor officials.

"The German Democratic Republic," Arthur M. Hanhardt, Jr., *Current History*, November 1982. Reprinted by permission.

4. SOCIALIST STATES

Essentially, the tenth congress lauded the achievements of its leadership, approved the results of the last five-year plan, and admonished the cadres to cope with the difficulties attending the 1981-1982 plans.[1]

THE ECONOMY

The economy is one of East Germany's proudest accomplishments, but now it is threatened. The economy was built in adversity. The ravages of war and Soviet reparations in the Soviet zone of occupation, plus a steady loss of population, did not augur well for the country in the 1940's and 1950's. It was not until the Berlin Wall was built and women were encouraged to join the workforce that the economic base was stabilized in the 1960's. Thereafter, economic growth was substantial and included improvements in the "quality of life" obvious even to the casual visitor to East Berlin and East Germany's inadequately supplied provinces.

The threat to the economy comes from several sources. First, economic geography sets limits to East Germany's growth. Its population has exhibited a declining trend in the past decade as a result of demographic imbalances (a large elderly population) and a trend toward one-child families. Natural resources are few: lignite (brown coal), some industrial salts, and uranium (all of which is shipped to the Soviet Union).

The East German economy is also threatened by economic developments beyond the socialist bloc. The leadership often claims that East Germany is protected from the ravages of OPEC (Organization of Petroleum Exporting Countries) price increases, capitalist inflation, and the current combination of high interest rates and Western recession. But in reality, East Germany is caught in a tightening economic vise.

The petroleum price increases of the mid-1970's were eventually reflected in higher prices for Soviet oil, which forms the vital basis for the expanding East German petrochemical industry. Soviet price increases squeezed profit margins for plastics and synthetic fibers marketed in hard currency countries. The critical situation worsened in 1980-1981, when it became clear that Soviet oil exports would level off and perhaps decline. Expanding this sector according to the 1981-1985 economic plans would be extremely difficult, forcing the East German economy to seek growth in ever increasing productivity.[2]

Western inflation has reached East Germany's otherwise carefully guarded boundaries. Rising prices for vital goods have East German economists in an agonizing double bind. Unless higher prices are paid for Western technology and materials, the quality of East German goods will suffer. Declining quality means fewer Western sales and concomitantly reduced hard-currency income. In other words, hard currency must be spent in order to earn hard currency. In response to this, East German trade functionaries have pressed for "counter-trade" agreements whereby part (usually 40-50 percent) of hard currency imports are paid for by export products.

High interest rates and recession in the West are adding to pressures on the East German economy. East Germany is not so indebted to the West as Poland and other East European countries. Nonetheless East Germany, which has enjoyed a high credit rating in the international financial community, is having trouble servicing short-term hard currency debt due in 1982. This would normally not be a problem. But, since East Germany must now borrow at high rates to roll over short-term debt, its financial problems have been drastically compounded.[3]

Finally, the Western recession makes it more difficult for East Germany to sell in the West, further restricting the incoming flow of hard currency. Markets for East German goods have been shrinking even where East Germany is competitive.

The 1981-1985 economic plan promulgated at the tenth congress indicates how East Germany intends to cope with its economic problems. First priority is accorded to heightened productivity. This has been a constant theme in the political economy since before the workers revolt of June, 1953, caused by the prospect of working longer for less to achieve plan goals.

Industrial productivity in East Germany improved steadily in the 1970's. From a 1955 base of 100, industrial productivity rose to an index level of 253 in 1970 and 407 in 1980. 1981 figures claim a five percent productivity increase.[4] There is considerable doubt that this trend can continue without increasing investment beyond affordable levels. Honecker has repeatedly warned that investment funds are virtually unavailable. The 1981 plan called for no growth investment.

A second high priority is allocated to robotics and the automated production process in East German industry. In 1980, East Germany employed 220 robots and fewer than 400 were employed in 1981. By 1985, the plan calls for the use of 40,000 to 45,000 industrial robots. In spite of beginning its own robotics industry

[1]For West German coverage of the tenth party congress (including documentation) see *Deutschland Archiv*, vol. 14, nos. 4, 5 and 6 (April, May and June, 1981). For the GDR, see, among many others, "The Socialist Unity Party of Germany—the leading force in the socialist society of the German Democratic Republic," *Panorama DDR: Dokumentation*, 1981. (These reports, in English, are available through the Ausslandspresseagentur GmbH, DDR 1054 Berlin, Wilhelm-Pieck-Str. 49.)

[2]"The Business Outlook: GDR," *Business Eastern Europe*, vol. 11, no. 8 (February 19, 1982), p. 59.

[3]"East German Debt is Worrying Lenders, Bank Economist Says," *The Wall Street Journal*, June 7, 1982, p. 25.

[4]*Statistisches Jahrbuch der Deutschen Demokratischen Republik 1981* (Berlin: Staatsverlag, 1981), p. 130.

in 1980 (production: 40), this is an unlikely goal, especially given the shortage of investment money. In addition, there is a semantic problem: East German literature applies the term "robot" to a wide range of automated production elements that fall short of the robotic standards of re-programability, multi-axis deployability and universality generally demanded by the term in the United States, West Europe and Japan.[5]

A third plan priority is aimed at aiding the economy through effective energy use. East German economists hope to improve the utilization of imported petroleum in industrial production, while accelerating the exploitation of native lignite resources. Lignite will be used increasingly for thermal energy; the petroleum thereby saved will feed the petrochemical industry unable to rely on the previously increasing but now level imports from the Soviet Union.

Finally, the party has exhorted the population to continue making sacrifices. The political risks of the 1981 plan are apparent. Measures supporting continued improvements in living standards must be bought in part with hard currency and/or investment funds, both in short supply.[6] And East Germans have become accustomed to consumption and are looking beyond dishwashers, television sets and refrigerators toward big ticket durable goods, notably autos.

THE MILITARY

Two events at the tenth congress shed light on the significant role of the East German military. First, more military personnel entered the Politburo and Central Committee of the SED. The influence of the military is as clearly increasing in East Germany as it is in the Soviet Union. Second, the Congress proceedings featured an elaborate military ceremony, symbolizing growing militarism in East German society. Evidence for this ranges from paramilitary training in the schools (now a mandatory two years in ninth and tenth grades) and the activities of the Society for Sport and Technology, a youth organization of over half a million young people pursuing "military sports" like target practice with firearms and parachuting.[7]

In spite of economic problems, East German military expenditures are steadily increasing. These expenditures support an efficient and effective military machine of about 6 divisions, closely integrated with the 20 divisions of the "Group of Soviet Forces in Germany."

THE SOCIETY

East German society has been influenced by the SED for over 30 years, but how effectively it has been transformed cannot be ascertained. The educational system and youth and party organizations have attempted to cultivate the "socialist personality." Although no firm statistics are available, results are clearly mixed. The gulf between public conformity and private views has not been eliminated in spite of party efforts to eradicate "careerism" and to turn those who "go along to get along" into sincere and enthusiastic supporters of the socialist system.

Several factors explain the limited success in transforming East German society. The most apparent is the close proximity of the Federal Republic of Germany (FRG, West Germany) and the reach of its media, particularly television. Even though the East German standard of living is high relative to Europe, the comparisons that count tend to be made with West Germany and West Europe. Images, goods and visitors from the West have the combined effect of blunting the "you never had it so good" approach of the SED.

At the same time, SED propaganda is taking full advantage of the economic downturn in the West to play on deep-seated German fears and anxieties concerning inflation and unemployment. The East German media continually contrast the labor shortages and stable prices for basic goods in the East with unemployment lines and rising prices in West Germany. The effectiveness of the appeal that East Germans should "count their blessings," as it were, is a matter of conjecture.

The bureaucratic and bureaucratized nature of East German society is another factor limiting the appeal of SED social visions and goals. Dullness, routine, literal-mindedness and doctrinaire behavior are sometimes identified with "socialism." And this has caused some concerned socialists to approach East German society from a critical Marxist perspective.[8]

Critical perspectives, even if Marxist in inspiration, are not welcomed by East German political and cultural establishments. Critics from within the SED, like Rudolf Bahro, are subject to arrest and expulsion. Controversial literary figures are treated similarly. The result has been tension between the official League of Culture (*Kulturbund*) and dissenters, many of whom have found publishers and audiences in West Germany. Intellectual *Gleichschaltung* reinforces the dullness of East German society, thereby effectively dampening support for the regime.

Finally, religion is a small but significant factor inhibiting socialist transformation in East Germany. Re-

---

[5]"GDR Looks to Robots to Save Labor, Markets," *Business Eastern Europe*, vol. 10, no. 41 (October 9, 1981), pp. 324-325.

[6]Hans Wetzek, "Politische Leitung—Oekonomische Leistung," *Einheit*, vol. 36, no. 7 (July, 1981), pp. 664-670.

[7]"VII. Kongress der Gesellschaft fuer Sport und Technik," *Informationen* (Bundesminister fuer innerdeutsche Beziehungen), no. 14 (1982), pp. 12-13.

[8]For an example see Rolf Schneider, "Der Ludergeruch wird uns anhaengen," *Der Spiegel*, vol. 36, no. 16 (April 19, 1982), pp. 131-136.

cently, the Protestant church has received growing attention, because young people are attracted to the Christian message of peace and brotherhood and to churches as places where ideas can be discussed and explored without the strictures of official doctrine.[9]

The peace and disarmament movement, "Swords into Plowshares," is now the focus of a major clash between the state and organized religion. The party will not tolerate a peace movement that urges disarmament in the East as well as the West.[10] (According to East German doctrine, threats to world peace emanate exclusively from the NATO imperialists. The East German army and the Warsaw Treaty Organization exist to guarantee peace and, if necessary, to fight a "just" war.)[11] A popular badge depicting a smith hammering a sword into a plowshare (after a Soviet sculpture) was outlawed as a dangerous manifestation of an unofficial and therefore impermissible movement. This action has not caused the movement to disappear. In fact, tensions focusing on peace and disarmament will intensify this fall when church-sponsored meetings are scheduled across the country.

Although socialist transformation may be imperfect and incomplete, it is clear that East German society is stable. Dissent and other unofficial activities constitute no threat to the Honecker regime. A partial reason for this stability, for the active and passive acceptance of the status quo, can be found in East Germany's international relations.

INTERNATIONAL AFFAIRS

Throughout its history, East Germany has viewed itself as a state that is either beleaguered, on the attack, or both. The evocation of a harsh and unfriendly international environment, the classical threat from the West, has keyed appeals to unite the citizenry. At the same time, East German doctrine holds that under the leadership of the Soviet Union the East European alliance will overcome the machinations of the imperialists by aggressively forwarding the cause of socialist revolution worldwide. In contemporary international affairs, East Germany is concerned with four areas: the socialist bloc, German-German relations, the capitalist West and Japan, and the third world.

Relations with East Europe and the Soviet Union have been problematical for East Germany. Even 37 years after World War II, a great deal of prejudice runs both east and west within the socialist bloc. Shifts within the bloc are seismically magnified in their im-

pact. This was illustrated anew in the East German response to events in Poland after August, 1980.

The prospect that Polish unrest would shake the foundations of the East German party and state apparatus was worrisome even though no serious independent East German labor movement has been evident recently. Nonetheless, finding an adequate response to the advent of Solidarity was difficult, and ultimately the leadership exploited traditional German prejudice against Poles to innoculate the citizenry against the "Polish disease."

Another factor that contained the appeal of Polish developments was the economic disruption that reverberated through the country as a result of the chaos in Polish mines and factories. East German-Polish trade dropped four percent in 1980 and even further in 1981. East Germany lost vital coal imports and was called on to provide unplanned support for the Polish economy.

East German officialdom was among the harshest critics of Solidarity and strongly supports the military regime of General Wojciech Jaruzelski. As was true during and after the Prague Spring of 1968, East Germany rode out the shock waves of threatened change in the socialist bloc more through a policy of Soviet-inspired orthodoxy than through the promise of flexibility and accommodation.

STRUGGLE AGAINST CAPITALISM

On the front line in the struggle with capitalist imperialism, East Germany confronts another German State, West Germany. The era of détente and West German *Ostpolitik* (Eastern Policy) caused severe problems for the SED. How could the GDR follow the Soviet line of better relations with the West without importing dangerous ideas that might undermine party, state and society? The answer was a policy of *Abgrenzung* or demarcation from the West. Broad categories of East Germans were forbidden to have contact with the flood of Western visitors who came to East Germany in the wake of German-German normalization in the early 1970's. As détente declined after the Soviet invasion of Afghanistan and the election of Ronald Reagan, East Germany returned to a more familiar and, perhaps, more comfortable neo-cold war mode in relations with West Germany.[12]

The most emphatic signs of a chill from East Germany came shortly after West German Chancellor Helmut Schmidt's reelection had been assured on October 5, 1980. Eight days later, Erich Honecker announced a virtual doubling in the amount of hard currency that Westerners were required to exchange for each day spent in East Germany. This change in

[9]Peadar Kirby, "The Threat of Peace. Church and State in East Germany," *Commonweal*, June 4, 1982, pp. 336-338.

[10]"Noch zu Wenig," *Der Spiegel*, vol. 36, no. 27 (July 5, 1982), pp. 51, 54.

[11]Wolfgang Scheler, and Gottfried Kiessling, *Gerechte und ungerechte Kriege in unserer Zeit* (Berlin: Militaerverlag der DDR, 1981).

[12]See my article "The Germanys and the Superpowers: A Return to Cold War?" *Current History*, vol. 80, no. 465 (April, 1981), pp. 145-148, 179-180.

policy had the desired effect of reducing the number of visitors while not radically affecting hard currency income.

No West German retaliation followed. Chancellor Schmidt's coalition is committed to a policy of avoiding countermeasures that might cause hardships for the East Germans. Sanctions in the form of cuts in the low-cost "swing" credits that finance East German imports to West Germany were thought to be an ineffective means of retaliating for the hardships West Germans faced if they visited East Germany.

In effect, German-German relations have been at a virtual standstill since Schmidt and Honecker met at Werbellinsee in East Germany in December, 1981.[13] That meeting produced no concrete results beyond clarifying the positions of the two sides. The fact that the Polish military regime was established in the midst of the German-German summit served to underline the unavoidable reality: East and West German relations are to a great extent hostage to issues and forces beyond the two Germanys. The major immediate issues between the two are the high mandatory exchange rate for Western visitors to East Berlin and the GDR; the disputed Elbe boundary; East German insistence on West German "recognition" of East German citizenship; and the East German demand that West Germany's Salzgitter Central Documentation Center (which monitors East Germany) be closed.

There was little movement between Bonn and East Berlin during the first eight months of 1982. However, Bonn has moved closer to a restriction of swing credits, with a reduction spread over the next three years. For its part, East Germany denied entry visas to two West German politicians, underlining the sometimes capricious nature of German-German relations.[14]

German-German politics can be expected to continue to reflect the chilly state of relations between Washington and Moscow. For the Honecker leadership, this is a desireable state of affairs; a hard line toward West Germany buttresses those now in control.

Relations with the market economies of the leading industrial nations represent hazards and opportunities. The major opportunity lies in hard currency trade to finance the economic expansion vital and dear to the East German political leadership. A fundamental and unsolved problem is how to offer Western markets quality goods meeting world standards of technological sophistication. Moreover, East German economic decision-makers must constantly balance the opportunities for Western trade against the demands of socialist partners and the Soviet Union.

Diplomatically, East Germany entered the mainstream of the industrialized world when normal relations were established with Western countries as a result of détente and West German *Ostpolitik*. In the mid-1970's, this led to great expectations that East Germany might take its rightful place internationally as an advanced and sophisticated industrial nation.

Economic expectations were disappointed. Despite the granting of major hard currency credits, the East German economy could not produce enough quality goods to participate fully in the give and take of international trade. Nonetheless, trade with the West (including West Germany) increased 5.5 times in the decade of the 1970's to nearly $11 billion in 1980.[15]

Major hard currency trade items offered by East Germany include steel, fertilizers, plastics, optical goods, machinery and manufactured consumer items. Yet these products must be traded with the Soviet Union and other socialist countries in order to assure supplies of petroleum, natural gas and other raw materials vital to East German industry. East Germany cannot afford to neglect either set of trading partners and therefore faces a severe dilemma. Compounding the problem are the ever rising defense expenditures, which rose 7.9 percent in 1981.

The United States has an overwhelming and consistent balance of trade surplus with East Germany. Following recognition in 1974, the volume of trade between the United States and East Germany increased about two and one-half times. Most of the dollar value of the trade today is accounted for by agricultural products (about $534 million in 1980). Feed grain for livestock comprises the largest single item and is linked to efforts to improve domestic meat supplies.

In the area of nonagricultural products, the United States sold East Germany some $26 million in goods while importing goods worth $44 million in 1980. United States-East German trade has been impeded by the fact that East German imports do not benefit from most favored nation (MFN) treatment, nor do American exports to East Germany qualify for Export-Import Bank financing. Nonetheless, there was a four-fold increase in trade between the United States and East Germany between 1974 and 1980.[16]

Disappointments in the capitalist West have led to an attempt to cultivate economic relations with Japan, the industrial giant of East Asia. In May, 1981, Erich Honecker visited Japan to explore the prospects of expanding trade links within the ambit of "peaceful coexistence." The Japanese trade presence in East Germany has gradually expanded over the past five years.

[13]Wilhelm Bruns, "After the Schmidt-Honecker Summit," *Aussenpolitik*, vol. 33, no. 2 (2d Quarter, 1982), pp. 134-144.
[14]"Bonn Protests East German Decision," *The Week in Germany*, vol. 8, no. 29 (July 30, 1982), p. 2.

[15]"German Democratic Republic: Emphasis is on Industrial Reorganization, Expansion of Economy and Foreign Trade," *Business America*, October 5, 1981, p. 10.
[16]*Ibid.*

4. SOCIALIST STATES

A Japanese trade office is now open in East Berlin, and a major luxury hotel, the Merkur, was built by the Japanese in Leipzig, home of the East German trade fairs.

The long-range impact of Honecker's visit to Japan has yet to be felt. However, it is clear that East Germany is seeking to diversify economic options beyond the United States and West Europe. In the areas of robotics and computers, Japanese technology could play a significant role in the current five year plan if financial problems can be solved.

THE GDR AND THE THIRD WORLD

Third world countries have played an important role in East Germany's foreign policy since the early 1960's. It was in the third world that East Germany sought to breach the diplomatic isolation imposed by the West German Hallstein Doctrine (a doctrine which said West Germany would break diplomatic and trade ties with any country recognizing East Germany). The third world was also viewed as a fertile field for sowing the seeds of socialist development and cultivating future markets.

The Honecker era brought renewed interest in developing countries from two perspectives: cultural and educational support, and military aid. East Germany's cultural and educational activities in the third world have concentrated on sub-Saharan Africa, with major efforts in Ethiopia, Angola, Mozambique and Guinea-Bissau. "Friendship Brigades" of young teachers and skilled workers associated with the Free German Youth organization in nine developing countries are currently practicing an "effective form of anti-imperialistic solidarity" while teaching mechanical and basic engineering skills. This effort has been extended to the Middle East (South Yemen) and to Vietnam.

Many of the same third world countries have benefited from East German military skills. When a Japanese journalist asked in May, 1981, if East German troops were stationed anywhere outside East Germany, Honecker replied that he knew of none, except, perhaps, for troops engaged temporarily in maneuvers. This was at best a disingenuous response. Although hard data are rare, it is apparent that some 2,700 military advisers were stationed in seven African countries in 1980. It is unlikely that the numbers have declined. East German military specialists are also involved in South Yemen.[17]

East German military advisers abroad are active in intelligence and internal security. These highly sensitive areas give the East German advisers a significance far beyond their numbers. In all this East Germany is carrying out a role in the socialist international division of effort with Cuba and the Soviet Union in support of national liberation movements and progressive forces.

Ideologically, economically and militarily, East Germany will continue to serve as a western anchor, securing the socialist bloc for the Soviet Union. Ideologically the SED leadership will reinforce the Soviet line without significant reinterpretation. This trend was confirmed and guaranteed at the tenth congress of the SED in 1981.

Economically, East Germany evidences problems that will intensify later in the 1980's. Still, past economic performance and the currently desperate state of the Soviet allies indicate that East Germany will produce relatively well within the socialist bloc. Economic problems in the West will highlight the apparent stability of the SED regime.

Militarily, the NVA will remain on the front line alongside the Red Army, and East Germany will play its military role in the third world, finding there a welcome and expanding outlet for traditional talents and progressive socialist solidarity.

---

[17]"Wir haben euch Waffen und Brot geschickt," *Der Spiegel*, vol. 34, no. 10 (March 3, 1980), pp. 42-61.

China's Split-Level Change

DAVID BONAVIA
ROBERT DELFS
TERESA MA
ADI IGNATIUS·

David Bonavia, Robert Delfs, Teresa Ma, and Adi Ignatius write for the newsmagazine "Far Eastern Economic Review" of Hong Kong, from which this is excerpted.

The September session of the Chinese Communist Party's Twelfth Congress showed that setbacks, shocks, and turnabouts have by no means been eliminated from China's political life. Top leaders who had been repeatedly giving assurances that they wanted to step down and make room for younger men ended by changing their minds and staying on after all. New blood has, however, been entering the party's high echelons and a way has been found to continue making use of the experience of elderly Central Committee members even after they leave the august body.

As always in China, it is a problem of political line. Deng Xiaoping and his leadership group have been working for six years to reverse the line followed by Mao Zedong in the last decade of his life, but not all top cadres in the party, Government, and armed forces can keep up with their pace or agree with their viewpoint. Nobody sticks out his neck and says, "I am in opposition," but the groundswell of discontent aroused by some of Deng's more far-reaching policies is obvious.

The People's Liberation Army (PLA) has the most grievances. Starved of new armaments technology, indicted for arrogance and privilege-seeking, and no longer particularly attractive as a career option for rural youth, the PLA has seen five of its former top commanders go on trial for treason. The more the Army grumbles, the tighter Deng takes hold of it.

Whatever its military disarray, China has heightened its diplomatic posture noticeably in recent months, with sharp responses to what its leaders see as slights to their national self-esteem. The crisis of the year has been the dispute with the U.S. over Taiwan. In August a truce was declared in the form of a vaguely worded commitment on the part of the U.S. not to raise the level of arms sales to Taiwan and to review the whole question of such sales. China indicated that a military solution to the problem would be a last recourse.

President Reagan had to consider his domestic Taiwan lobby and rightwingers such as Sen. Barry Goldwater. The Americans could be forgiven for believing they had called the Chinese bluff. Peking was not about to downgrade links with the U.S. over this issue. The essential thing was not to behave as though a bluff had been called because saving face was the real issue. President Reagan carried this off well.

China's attitude toward the Soviet threat, whether to itself or toward Europe, is more relaxed than in the 1970s. A Soviet invasion of China is no longer seen as anything more than a remote prospect, though China is still refusing formal talks aimed at improving relations with the Soviet Union until the latter "shows in deeds, not words" that it is sincere and withdraws some of its million-strong forces on the Chinese border and in the Mongolian People's Republic.

The joker in China's diplomatic deck this year has been Japan, with its tactless changes in school textbooks suggesting a desire to whitewash some of Japan's aggressive actions and atrocities in China from 1931 onward. Joining with South Korea, Peking furiously denounced this rewriting of history which at one point seemed likely to

force a postponement of Prime Minister Zenko Suzuki's scheduled visit to China. The Japanese minister of education was forced to cancel his proposed visit. Tokyo eventually mollified the Chinese by promising to review the textbooks.

The problem of Hong Kong is thornier. After years of being lectured by British and U.S. businessmen on the need for a clear statement of Peking's intentions toward Hong Kong, the Chinese Government in July produced its first recommendation: that Taiwan, Hong Kong, and Macao should be made "special administrative regions" of the People's Republic. Signs are that Peking is looking to 1997 as the date for a change of sovereignty — real or cosmetic — for Hong Kong at least. Controversy focuses on the question of how much Chinese control would be established and how international investors' confidence in the territory's vigorous economy could be sustained.

Regionally, China continues to view the Vietnamese occupation of Cambodia as the biggest problem of the 1980s. Somewhat to Peking's surprise, Prince Norodom Sihanouk did what he had hesitated to do in recent years and joined the Khmer Rouge and the forces of former Prime Minister Son Sann in an anti-Vietnam front. China continues to denounce Vietnam severely, and the Soviet Union for its support of Hanoi, and sees little likelihood of a political solution until Vietnamese troops are withdrawn. A resumption of large-scale hostilities between China and Vietnam is not ruled out.

The word went out early this year that foreigners are dangerous and ordinary citizens should have as little private contact with them as possible. Over the past few months China has been beating a retreat from its policy of opening the country to more foreign contacts at the person-to-person level.

From *World Press Review,* December 1982. Excerpted from Far Eastern Economic Review of Hong Kong. Reprinted by permission of World Press Review.

4. SOCIALIST STATES

The open-door policy now applies mainly to trading and other official links with foreign countries. The reasons for the renewed restrictions are plain. Foreigners were getting to know more about China than the authorities thought healthy, and — perhaps more disturbing to officials — Chinese people were becoming more knowledgeable about the outside world and its allures.

Until recently private friendships — most of them struck up since 1978 — had survived, but by August nearly all of them were stopped. Hotels have been ordered to be stricter about letting Chinese in without registration, and the registration form has become a lengthy questionnaire about the visitor's identity and reasons for entering the premises. Taxi-drivers now must report if a Chinese takes a ride with a foreigner.

Foreigners wishing to marry Chinese must do so in China because the Chinese partner will not be given an exit visa to marry abroad. The couple must obtain the approval of their respective work units and the Chinese person's family. Then they need the approval of the Public Security Bureau, which means the foreign partner must get a document from his or her hometown to the effect that he or she is not married already and is of good character; then a medical certificate showing no evidence of disabling or infectious disease. After further formalities a brief marriage ceremony is performed by local authorities. It is easier to get permission if the couple plan to leave China as soon as they are married.

Despite lingering race prejudice, most Chinese families seem happy if one of their offspring marries a foreigner because that is an easy path to eventual emigration, of which so many people dream. But in the event of another fanatical mass movement like the Cultural Revolution, it can be a dangerous liability. Some such marriages have arisen from acquaintanceships struck up at dances, which were becoming very popular until they were banned two years ago. Pop music is denounced as "corrupting" and young people are urged to listen instead to "healthy music" — songs about the revolution and the deeds of the People's Liberation Army, for instance.

There has been a massive increase in what the authorities call pornography — often mild by Western standards — and obscene films or TV programs. Some people have been prosecuted for operating private movie shows. None of this has checked the present wave of skepticism and cynicism, especially among students and intellectuals. It is fashionable to laugh at party activists or applicants on the grounds that they are prigs and climbers.

Nonetheless, improvements in cultural and intellectual life since the death of Mao Zedong have been massive. Hundreds of new publications have been released on a wide range of topics. Literary journals are flourishing and are sometimes topics of critical and political debate. The cinema is churning out love stories and historical films, and British TV serials and feature films are being used to speed language training.

Traditional Chinese pastimes have made a comeback. Old men are again taking their cage-birds out for walks and comparing notes with other enthusiasts at bird markets. Cities have regained a little of their old-world charm with the opening of ancient or historical sites, restoration of buildings, and archeological research. Finds in recent years include thousands of life-size pottery warriors and horses from Emperor Qin Shi Huang's tomb near Sian.

China has been made more accessible to tourists on low budgets. It is possible to get an individual visa for up to twenty cities and travel around on buses, trains, and ferries, staying at Chinese-style hotels cheaply and with minimal interference by local authorities. This contrasts strongly with the ban on person-to-person contact between Chinese and foreign residents which, it is hoped, may be only temporary.

China's foreign trade picture is more encouraging than its relations with foreign residents. Continued growth in exports and a 4-per-cent drop in imports last year led to a $3.8-billion trade surplus — the biggest ever. Modernization and economic reform programs now under way are predicated on substantial purchases of foreign technology and injections of foreign capital over the next two decades. Improvements in living standards are inseparable from continued large-scale grain imports, which have grown from 4.6 million tons per year over 1970-76 to more than 13 million tons last year. China has little arable land to grow food for so many. (Japan has twice as much per capita.)

The value of agricultural output is less than half that of industrial output — an artifact of a controlled economy that places higher value on the products of the factory than on the fruits of the field. Farmers outnumber workers in China by 3 to 1 — 300 million out of a total labor force of 400 million. That figure represents only fulltime agricultural laborers; it does not include children under sixteen, men over sixty, or women over fifty who contribute in varying degrees to farm work. Their participation has probably increased as a result of reforms reestablishing the work team and individual family as the basic agricultural production units, rather than the commune or brigade.

Those reforms, usually referred to as the agricultural responsibility system, have been dramatically successful. Since 1979 agricultural output has increased by an average of 6.5 per cent per year. Material incentives for farmers are what the reforms have been all about. In 1979 state agricultural procurement prices were raised by 23 per cent after a 4-per-cent increase the year before; in 1980 they were lifted by about 7 per cent, with a further 6 per cent last year.

The negative side effects of the new agricultural policies should not be ignored, though they pale next to the necessity of maintaining growth in production above the rate of population increase. One problem is that the return to family-based production has reinforced rural preferences for sons over daughters and threatens to reactivate the Malthusian treadmill of having more children to grow more food to have more children. Authorities have intensified rural planned parenthood programs, but it is more difficult to enforce population control measures in rural areas than in cities, where the traditional preference for large families is less powerful.

Though China's industrial growth lags behind agricultural growth, it is in line with current targets and is the most that can be attempted, given energy and transport limitations. Energy production remained stagnant last year, but important changes are under way. China is investing in advanced foreign coal-mining technology, and foreign firms will be involved in exploiting new coalfields. A changeover from oil to coal-fired electric power stations will allow China to reserve petroleum for transportation and other areas where coal cannot be substituted, and to maintain substantial levels of oil exports to Asian customers.

China's major onshore oilfields have reached peak production and will soon decline. Offshore oil remains China's best hope for an eventual return to growth in oil production, but substantial offshore extraction is not likely to begin until the late 1980s. Until then a steady decline in oil production is likely. Natural gas production is also expected to decline slightly, but increased hydroelectric output will more than offset the drop.

The very low short-term energy growth projections have direct implications for the kind of industrial growth rate China can support. Increasing industrial output means more energy. How much more is a function of the efficiency of energy use, and in this area China has recently scored some startling successes. Conservation measures have played a role, but the key factor has been the policy of cutting back heavy in favor of light industry, which requires less energy per unit of output.

Over the next three to five years any increase in industrial output in excess of the projected low energy-production growth will have to be paid for mainly by conservation measures. Upgrading the energy efficiency of existing plants or closing them down and replacing them will also produce gains. Many small factories slated for elimination in the next year are notorious energy wasters, and planners will be looking closely at the energy efficiency of all new plants and equipment. Another advantage is that China is better able to hold down residential demand for energy than most developing countries.

As part of a plan to modernize the country through economic and technological cooperation with foreign countries, China has established four "special economic zones" in Kwangtung and Fukien provinces. Now in their second year, they are still in the elementary stage.

The most unusual aspect of the ten-year plan is the commitment to involve foreign investment in building harbors, highways, waterworks, railways, and airports. Such free-trade zones in most other countries are simply industrial sites administratively outside the host country's customs barriers. China does not confine foreign participation to small-scale industrial operations but also welcomes outside investment in basic improvements.

In cooperative production the foreign investor provides technology and trains workers while the Chinese provide land, labor, and management. Investors have a say in hiring and firing — a revolutionary move in Chinese labor management.

Sino-American Relations: The Decade Ahead

Allen S. Whiting

Allen S. Whiting is Professor of Political Science at the University of Arizona, Tucson, and was formerly Director, Office of Research and Analysis for the Far East, U.S. Department of State.

February 1972: President Richard Nixon flies 11,510 miles to the People's Republic of China where he is received by Chairman Mao Zedong, thereby ending twenty-two years of conflict and confrontation between the two Pacific powers. The subsequent seven days of official toasts, banquets, and meetings are transmitted by live television around the globe. The president's opening statement, "What we do here can change the world," is translated into the closing Shanghai Communique's assertion "that the normalization of relations between the two countries is not only in the interest of the Chinese and American peoples but also contributes to the relaxation of tension in Asia and the world."

February 1982: President Ronald Reagan's letter to Premier Zhao Ziyang commemorating the Shanghai Communique goes unanswered. Beijing's public silence on the tenth anniversary is broken the next day with an official commentary that warns, "Sino-American relations have truly come to a critical point that will determine if relations improve or deteriorate." Deputy Premier Li Xiennien remarks in a Chinese New Year's interview, "The United States is not a friendly country."

Juxtaposition of these two moments in Sino-American relations obscures the dramatic improvement in political, economic, and cultural interaction between Beijing and Washington that occurred in the intervening decade. During that time, the intermittent contact based on ambassadorial exchanges in third countries and personal visits by Henry Kissinger to China finally became normalized in full diplomatic relations, complete with embassies and consulates. Trade soared from virtually nothing to $5.5 billion in 1981. That year an estimated 80,000 Americans visited China, while some 16,000 Chinese made the reverse journey. By mid 1982, nearly 1,500 Americans resided in China in various capacities, and more than 8,000 Chinese attended American universities and technical institutes.

In strategic terms, the two governments came a long way during those ten years. The United States terminated its treaty pledging to defend Taiwan and withdrew all military presence from the island. The People's Republic of China (PRC) ended its opposition to American forces in the West Pacific and supported the U.S.-Japan security treaty. Washington gradually expanded its willingness to strengthen China's military capability, ultimately agreeing to sell technology and weapons on a case-by-case basis. Beijing exchanged military visits and showed an interest in various American items, albeit without negotiating any specific purchases. Meanwhile, both countries steadily increased their consultation and coordination on points of confrontation with the Soviet Union, including the production of intelligence on Soviet missile tests, opposition to the Vietnamese invasion of Kampuchea, and support for anti-Soviet resistance in Afghanistan.

Yet the contrast between the surface atmospherics of February 1972 and February 1982 symbolizes substantive problems that deserve attention in planning U.S. policy for the next decade of the Sino-U.S. relationship. Basic assumptions that have been articulated in American statements, both official and unofficial, require examination. Areas of contention as well as cooperation must be illuminated. Variable factors that can worsen or better relations should be identified. Preoccupation with tactical or transient matters, such as arms sales to Taiwan, cannot preclude more fundamental, long-term concerns within the broader context of regional Asian affairs.

A brief article cannot presume to deal with any of these questions fully, much less cover all related questions. Despite this acknowledged constraint, however, a few observations on certain key aspects may provoke further discussion, if not necessarily final conclusions. The culmination of the Nixon-Kissinger effort—President Carter's achievement of full normalization—was a most welcome moment. But because the United States mistakenly tied itself to the fate of Taiwan in 1950 and tragically fought the People's Republic, directly or indirectly, in Korea and Indochina, it does not necessarily follow that moving to the opposite extreme of tacit alliance is correct.

Assumption: Myth or Reality?

In his Shanghai Communique commemorative article, Former President Nixon warned, "It would be the height of folly to try to 'save' Taiwan at the cost of losing China. If China slipped back into the Soviet orbit, the balance of power in the world would be overwhelmingly shifted against us."[1]

This statement succinctly embodies several assumptions, implied or explicit, that underlie much of the rhetoric that has accompanied analysis of Sino-American relations over the past decade. The notion of "losing China" suggests the alternative of "winning China." The threat of China slipping "back into the Soviet orbit" conjures up a return to the Sino-Soviet alliance of the 1950s and implies that such a development can be either prevented or triggered by U.S. policy on Taiwan. Last but not least, China is depicted as determining the global balance of power, depending on whether it is aligned with the United States or the Soviet Union.

Let us address these assumptions in reverse order. When assessing the global power balance, real or perceived, it is useful to limit one's perspective to a decade at most. Too many intervening variables, domestic and foreign, preclude confident projections beyond that time. We need only recall "The American Century" forecasts of the 1950s and the predictions made in the 1970s of Iran's future Middle East role to appreciate the hazards of forecasting over too long a timespan. This is particularly relevant for China, where the fluctuations and perturbations in economics and politics during the PRC's first three decades caution against a simple linear projection from the present to the year 2000.

Two alternative frameworks exist for evaluating China's probable weight in the global balance of power during the next ten years. The first is readily dispensed with, namely Beijing's ability to extend military force or to exert economic influence around the world. No such ability exists at present nor is it likely to appear within this time, with the exception of China's ICBM inventory. But even in this area, there are questions of vulnerability to pre-emption, survivability for second strike, reliability and other technical aspects that may limit the force to a deterrent use at best. Otherwise, China's military force will remain essentially regional, not global, in its impact.

This regional limitation also holds for Beijing's economic influence. The recurring image of one billion Chinese and grandiose visions of China's economic modernization, coupled with sweeping but still unproven estimates of offshore oil reserves comparable with those of the Middle East, has produced a highly inflated prospect of Beijing's trade and aid potential. It is true, as A. Doak Barnett has argued, that in selected areas (such as world grain supplies), China can have a significant impact on its import demand. Generally, however, the PRC economy will remain of secondary importance to most trading nations over the next ten years, as Beijing struggles to modernize—with limited capital and a limited export capacity.

The second framework within which China's weight in the global power balance can be assessed is its contribution to constraining Soviet power that otherwise might be brought to bear in Europe, the Middle East, or elsewhere. This focuses on the Soviet's fifty or so divisions arrayed against China, the growing inventory of Backfire bombers and SS-20 missiles targeted on the PRC, and the estimated one-fourth of Moscow's military budget needed to support this formidable array of power. While the total manpower falls far short of the "one million troops" ritualistically cited by the Chinese and other sources depicting the Soviet buildup, the composition and magnitude of air and ground dispositions, particularly those concentrated in the Soviet Far East, constitute an important diversion of force that could be deployed differently.

But whether a Sino-Soviet border settlement and a reduction of tensions—the sine qua none for detente between Moscow and Beijing—would release enough of these forces to shift "the balance of power . . . overwhelmingly against us" is debatable. Several points pertain here. First, the Sino-Soviet frontier is not likely ever to be totally demilitarized on the model of the Candian-American border. In the early 1960s, before the build-up began, approximately fifteen Soviet divisions at various levels of strength were distributed behind the 4,650-mile border. Given the bitterness and the bloodshed that have marked the subsequent decades, the Kremlin military planners will be reluctant to drop their guard by more than half, or twenty-five divisions, should the two sides patch up their differences and feign friendship.

Second, even if Moscow agreed to Beijing's demand that the status quo ante be restored as a condition for improved relations—leaving only fifteen divisions adjacent to China—the missile and air forces would remain for targeting against U.S. and allied dispositions on land and sea. Japan and the West Pacific would not be free of this threat in the foreseeable future, whether or not Sino-Soviet relations improve. To credit Beijing with diverting this force or freeing it for alternative use is unduly Sinocentric.

Third, the very concept of a global power balance is subject to such multifarious dimensions of measurement and such varied scenarios of hypothetical change over time that it lacks much relevance for Sino-Soviet relations, given the likely consequences of limited improvement in those relations. In this regard, the argument applies far more to Japan than China. Japan's highly trained, literate society, well endowed with concentrated capital and advance technology, could drastically change the power balance in the Pacific and thereby in the world, if the country embarked on a major military modernization, including nuclear weapons, and shifted its affiliation from the United States to the Soviet Union. China, however, lacks virtually all of the

113

4. SOCIALIST STATES

factors necessary to play the role of swing-weight between the two superpowers during the coming decade. Thus far, this analysis has rested on an objective assessment of reality—to the extent that is possible. Subjective assessments of the global power balance, however, produce very different perceptions. Insofar as they affect policy as well as public opinion, these perceptions cannot be ignored. The tendency of political figures and the media to exaggerate the import of events, particularly those associated with the Sino-Soviet-American triangle, distorts public perception, which in turn defines a new reality for policymakers. Thus, for example, reiteration of the Nixon analysis can influence how a modest Sino-Soviet detente is assessed not only in the United States but elsewhere as well. The danger of American hyperbole lies in the widespread assumption that Washington possesses the best means of intelligence for measuring and forecasting changes in the balance of power. In this sense, a worst-case interpretation of improved Sino-Soviet relations could become a self-fulfilling prophecy if reaction abroad treated this development as a genuine shift in the global power balance. This argues for keeping a cool and correct assessment of the actual weight, present and prospective, of China's ability to project military power beyond its immediate periphery.

In addition, we must address the likely relationship between Moscow and Beijing should they manage to reduce the level of military confrontation and settle the border dispute. The danger of China, in Nixon's words, slipping "back into the Soviet orbit" can be confidently ruled out for many years to come. Beijing may gradually change the degree of "tilt" toward Washington in accordance with calculations of domestic and foreign factors, but it will not reverse its relations with the superpowers so far as to tilt toward Moscow. At most, equidistance may result, although even that is unlikely.

Beijing's main consideration will be to avoid undue reliance on either superpower for national security. Such dependency flies in the face of China's bitter experience at the hands of foreign allies over the past 100 years, including the Sino-Russian entente at the turn of the century, the treatment at Versailles, and the concessions at Yalta. It also goes against the more recent memory of sensed betrayal during the Sino-Soviet alliance and continued frustration over American ties with Taiwan.

In addition to these historical facts (about which the Chinese are continually reminded in books and articles), the political sensitivity of any Soviet alliance precludes any leader in Beijing attempting it. Mao could invite Nixon to China and shake his hand while U.S. forces fought in Indochina and remain based on Taiwan. But no successor can have that power to risk rapprochement, compared with detente, with Moscow. An opposition coalition would be tempted to challenge this as having gone too far.

This in turn raises the reference to "losing China."

The term first arose in the late 1940s, when the Communist victory appeared to many Americans as the result of Washington's failure to support Chiang Kai-shek adequately. Ironically, one of the most articulate accusers of this alleged Truman-Acheson pro-Communist conspiracy was the young Congressman Richard Nixon. But we never "had" a China to lose then, nor have we now. True, there are unique buffer states, so weak as to be defenseless between the two powerful neighbors, who may literally be won or lost as a satellite. Mongolia is thus trapped between Russia and China. No such impotence constrains China, however. There is neither the opportunity nor the rise of a win-lose situation for either the United States or the Soviet Union, as far as the PRC alignment is concerned.

Whether Beijing chooses to lean more or less toward Moscow will be influenced by several factors, only one of which is the bilateral relationship on either side. Much will depend on how the trend in the global power balance is perceived in Beijing and how alignment or equidistance suits PRC interests. Third-country relations will also count, particularly in Asia, where Korea, Indochina, and the subcontinent are of immediate concern, compared with more remote arenas of competition in the Middle East, Africa, and Latin America. Domestic politics can also influence the tilt, including such indirect but politically sensitive issues as the perceived impact on Chinese Communist mores of Western economic penetration and the relative cost of Western versus Soviet training and technical assistance. To identify a single issue, such as Taiwan, as the sole determinant of China's orientation toward the superpowers is simplistic in the extreme.

Analyses of Beijing's subtle shifts of balance between the superpowers are often distorted by a tendency to describe them in such extreme terms as alliance and confrontation. The French words—*detente*, reduction of tension; *rapprochement*, coming together; and *entente*, alignment without alliance—more accurately convey the possibilities of how two powers may approach each other. Moreover, such terms may describe an actual state of being or, in the first two instances, only a process that may or may not culminate in such a state.

From 1968 to 1972, the process of *detente* between Beijing and Washington culminated in the Shanghai Communique. Thereafter, rapprochement evolved in mutual consultation concerning the Soviet challenge but failed to achieve entente, despite token steps in this direction after Moscow's invasion of Afghanistan. In far less rapid and dramatic fashion, Beijing and Moscow probed for detente after Mao's death, but negotiations that began in late 1979 were aborted over Afghanistan. The process seems to have taken on new life in 1981-1982 but still has fallen short of visible results in the Key areas of border dispute and military deployment. The possibilities of a Sino-Soviet detente are severely limited, as we have already noted, and should suffice to dampen worst-case alarm abroad. They exclude any

114

action wherein either side must rely on the other for its national security. This rules out, for instance, encouragement of North Korea to attack the south, thereby increasing the risk of a U.S. response, which in turn would require Soviet or Chinese involvement. In addition, it is impossible to make any clear division among spheres of influence. During the 1950s, Moscow and Beijing competed for influence throughout the Afro-Asian world (as it was called then), with respect to both local communist parties and bourgeois regimes. This rivalry coexisted with their alliance and would certainly remain intense in the far more distant relationship of detente.

In short, the possibility of a Sino-Soviet detente should not provoke American anxiety over a defeat, as though a zero-sum game had ended to the United States' disadvantage. Such an alliance would have important implications, particularly as it affected Beijing's freedom to deploy the People's Liberation Army (PLA) opposite Taiwan. In addition, much of the perceived impact would depend on the state of Sino-American relations at the time. If they were good, the anticipated consequences would clearly be less threatening than if relations were bad or deteriorating. In any case, a Sino-Soviet detente would not be sufficiently final or far-reaching to warrant comparison with the Nazi-Soviet pact of 1939 or the Sino-Soviet alliance of 1950.

The Future of China

During the Carter administration, official rhetoric held that America's interest lay in a "strong and secure China." Nixon's tenth anniversary article stated the corollary, "A weak China invites aggression." Either way, one assumption of recent policy has been Beijing's and Washington's apparently mutual interest in strengthening the PLA.

These propositions, however, are neither undeniably true nor universally shared in Asia. If China remains "weak" relative to stronger neighbors, who will commit aggression—and for what reason? Japan can be ruled out altogether. India is not likely to contest the disputed border's status quo militarily, given the 1962 defeat. This leaves the Soviet Union as the one conceivable source of attack. Yet only a pre-emptive strike undertaken in response to a perceived imminent Chinese attack carries any plausible threat, which in turn disappears with the implausibility of a PRC attack on the USSR.

Short of this wholly improbable scenario, Moscow has no motivation to risk war with Beijing. Territorial conquest is not worth the cost. Xinjiang's scattered natural resources of uranium, oil, and tin add relatively little to Soviet reserves, and otherwise the province is largely a wasteland dotted with isolated oases and nascent industrial centers. Manchuria's high-paraffin oil cannot be handled by Soviet refineries, leaving only its surplus of grain to reward a conqueror, hardly

enough to justify war. Finally, Japan's inability to break Chinese resistance after occupying most of the agricultural and industrial areas is a memorable caution against trying to defeat one billion Chinese, for whatever reason.

More important, however, is the question of how a strong China will contribute to peace and stability in Asia. In this regard, it is worth noting China's various territorial disputes with its neighbors. I have already referred to the border conflict with the Soviet Union that erupted in 1969. Hard evidence is lacking, but the consensus of observers sees the PLA as responsible for the initial incident. The PLA launched a major attack against India in 1962 and ultimately overran all contested territory, after which the PLA withdrew to its original position in the east while holding in the west.

China subsequently used force against South Vietnam over the Paracel Islands in 1974 and justified its "teaching a lesson" to Hanoi in 1979 partly on the basis of a disputed boundary issue. In 1978 more than 100 PRC fishing boats, some armed and equipped with electronic equipment, circled the Senkaku Islands (Diaoyutai), demanding their return by Japan. After nearly a week, they withdrew. Deputy Premier Deng Xiaoping, however, refused to abandon China's claim during his celebrated visit to Tokyo that fall to celebrate signing the Sino-Japanese treaty of peace and friendship.

China's claims in the South China Sea contest those of the Philippines, Indonesia, and Malaysia as well as Vietnam. In an informal discussion last year at the Ministry of Foreign Affairs, I asked an official why Beijing's maps portray the entire area as lying within PRC boundaries. He replied, "These lines are simply taken from the old Guomindang (Kuomintang) maps. Of course, some of the water between the islands, reefs, and shoals does not belong to China so we do not claim the entire area." His assertions offer little comfort for states bordering the South China Sea. Beijing has formally protested to Manila over Philippine concessions for offshore exploration of the Reed Bank, and the PRC's repeated insistence that the Spratley Islands are Chinese may foreshadow military action there once the PLA acquires the capability.

The East China and the Yellow seas provide a different potential for conflict. Beijing may eventually compromise its claims to the continental shelf along the median line. But so far, the PRC has acted on the basis of natural prolongation, which carries ownership to the opposite shores of Korea and Japan, short of the Okinawa Trough. On several occasions, Beijing has officially challenged Korean-Japanese joint exploration of the shelf's oil potential, warning that such a venture violates China's sovereignty.

At present, there is no risk of Beijing using force against ASEAN (Association of Southeast Asian Nations), Japan and Korea. The PRC's top priority is economic modernization, which requires maximal access to foreign capital, technology, and know-how. It also requires

4. SOCIALIST STATES

maximal markets for foreign exchange. Japan and the United States are important to Beijing on all counts, and their role in the West Pacific precludes risking their opposition. In addition, Beijing wants to block Moscow's further expansion of influence in the region. It therefore must mute its territorial claims in order to make the Soviet Union appear as the only threat to the status quo.

Nevertheless, China's neighbors remain acutely aware of the PLA's potential power should it be capable of enforcing Beijing's claims on land or sea. This concern became clear at Manila in mid 1981, when former Secretary of State Alexander Haig had just announced in Beijing that Washington was willing to sell arms to China on a case-by-case basis. This uneasiness was also evident in Japanese editorial reaction. Even South Korean officials, while publicly silent, were extremely perturbed privately over the prospect of American arms sales to China.

In short, the American judgment that a strong China will serve the cause of peace and stability in Asia is not shared by all our allies and friends there. Nor is it congruent with Beijing's explicit claims against its neighbors. While our distance from the scene may permit some objectivity on the matter, our lesser involvement can blur our understanding of how others perceive the issues at stake. In the final analysis, it is they, not we, who must live with a strong China in proximity.

This realization does not require that Asian countries agree on all aspects of our China policy. But it does require advance consultation with our allies and friends before determining policy that affects their security. It also requires consideration of our adversaries' interests; we may wish to modify a hostile relationship rather than perpetuate, or even intensify, it. In the case of Vietnam, the utility of China's "defensive counterattack" in 1979 remains subject to question. One consequence of that brief war was Hanoi's granting of facilities in Cam Ranh Bay, Danang, and Haiphong for Soviet ships and planes. Although this move fell short of creating full-fledged bases under Moscow's complete control, it significantly improved the regional Soviet force potential beyond what was traditionally available from Vladivostok. Moreover, the continued Chinese support for Pol Pot and the Khmer Rouge guerrilla resistance in Kampuchea, combined with the PLA deployments along the Sino-Vietnamese frontier, ensured the further dependency of Hanoi on Moscow for military assistance.

In the long run, Vietnamese nationalism is likely to prevail and oust the Soviet military presence from Indochina. But when and how this will occur will be influenced critically by Hanoi's perception of the Chinese threat. To the extent that China continues to pressure Vietnam, the Soviet presence seems certain to remain. Its removal, however, is a logical objective of U.S. as well as ASEAN policy. Therefore, strengthening Beijing's ability to pursue its territorial claims against Vietnam, especially in the South China Sea, is anti-thetical to our larger interests, whatever our particular problems with Vietnam, Laos, and Kampuchea may be.

I am not implying that it is in our interest or that of our Asian associates to keep China weak or to obstruct its economic modernization. On the contrary, it is important to provide no justification for PRC perceptions of a hostile outside world that wants to keep one-fifth of humanity mired in poverty and vulnerable to whatever political or economic exploitation others may impose. This is particularly true for the United States, which maintained a total embargo on Sino-American trade for twenty years and tried to block China's trade with other countries where American licensed items were involved. The more the outside world participates in China's economic progress, the less likely it will suffer the bitter backlash of China's eventual success.

If military strengthening follows economic modernization, however, sufficient time may elapse to resolve contested territorial claims peacefully, thereby relieving China's neighbors of much of the anxiety associated with these matters. There might still be concern over ultimate PRC behavior as an ascendant, if not dominant, power in Asia. This is an unavoidable fact of history and geography, though, which should not act as an operational constraint on how the world relates to China. The PRC's growth as a major actor, first in Asia and later in the world, is virtually inevitable. It is impossible to prevent and unwise to try.

Military modernization that evolves naturally from a more general economic modernization has another consequence: the absence of any American identification with the phenomenon. This addresses the Soviet Union, which will remain of concern as our primary adversary. As long as China presses its border claims, the direct sale of major weapons systems to Beijing will be seen in Moscow as a deliberately provocative, perhaps hostile, act. The PRC's border claims involve not only inconsequential pieces of wilderness. They also include two large islands at the critical juncture of the Amur and Ussuri rivers opposite the important city of Khabarovsk, and a high plateau in the Pamir Mountains adjoining Afghanistan, the Soviet Union, and the PRC. While we are in no position to judge the legitimacy of China's demands, we can calculate their consequences for Soviet security and act accordingly.

Because the Reagan administration committed itself to the sale of weapons on a case-by-case basis during Haig's visit to Beijing in 1981, the die has been cast. Reversal would inflict irreparable and unnecessary damage to the relationship. A short list of unambiguously defensive weaponry should be made available without undue concern for the reaction of allies, friends, or enemies. Such items can include antitank, antiaircraft, and antisubmarine systems, together with command and control, communications, and radar equipment. While technological transfers from these to other uses might arguably be possible, the total impact would still pose no substantial threat to China's neighbors and would provide no legitimate basis for Soviet anger.

Beyond this list, however, the "what next" problem arises. Bureaucratic inertia is difficult to control, and Chinese pressure is difficult to resist. In addition, American officials visiting Beijing appear to emulate their historic antecedents in bearing gifts, manifested by the announcement of new opportunities for expanded Sino-American intercourse. These bureaucratic, political, and human tendencies should be balanced with the recognition that restraints applied at one point in time will not necessarily persist, especially with changes in administration.

Another problem lies in the temptation to link Sino-American military relations with Soviet behavior. Events in Afghanistan and Poland provoked some Americans to favor arms sales to China as a response to present or prospective Soviet aggression. Recurring Soviet actions against our interests, however, are inevitable. Linkage risks locking U.S. policy into automatically strengthening the PLA, regardless of other factors that may argue against it.

Thus, if U.S. policy is to remain sensitive to the differing perspectives and problems posed by allies, friends, and adversaries, the case-by-case approach will require deliberate and careful application in order to control the predetermining forces that push for the incremental expansion of weapons sales and military technology transfers.

The Taiwan Issue

In 1981-1982 ineptitude in Washington and reaction by the two rival Chinese regimes caused the issue of arms sales to Taiwan to produce the most serious crisis in Sino-American relations since the relationship was established ten years before. While the joint communique of August 17, 1982, resolved the issue for the immediate future, its calculated ambiguities left longer-term uncertainties that justify a careful examination of the question.

The debate over arms sales to Taiwan involves at least four discrete frames of reference that can facilitate analysis: legal, political, moral, and pragmatic. The legal frame consists of the Taiwan Relations Act (TRA) juxtaposed against principles of international law. The political frame focuses on the president's domestic situation, particularly in the Congress, as against the U.S. relationship with China and, by implication, the Soviet Union. The moral frame rests mainly on the U.S. commitment to the people on Taiwan and to a peaceful resolution of their dispute with mainland China. Finally, the pragmatic approach assesses the feasibility of arms sales to Taiwan as a safeguard against a forcible communist takeover.

Space precludes a definitive examination of all aspects of these four frameworks. Nevertheless, summary judgments provide at least a first approximation of analyses more exhaustively presented in congressional hearings and an extensive literature that has burgeoned in recent years.

As is often true in legal argument, sufficient ambiguities and contradictions exist to justify any one of several positions. The TRA language is a morass of congressional compromise but the key article deserves close reading:

Sec. 3 (a) The United States will make available to Taiwan such defense articles and defense services in such quantity as may be necessary to enable Taiwan to maintain a sufficient self-defense capability.

(b) The President and the Congress shall determine the nature and quantity of such defense articles and services based solely upon their judgment of the needs of Taiwan, in accordance with procedures established by law. Such determination of Taiwan's defense needs shall include review by United States military authorities in connection with recommendation to the President and the Congress.

(c) The President is directed to inform the Congress promptly of any threat to the security or the social or economic system of the people on Taiwan and any danger to the interests of the United States arising therefrom. The President and the Congress shall determine, in accordance with constitutional processes, appropriate action by the United States to any such danger.

The language is discretionary, with the interpretation of what may be "necessary" left to the combined judgment of the president, the Congress, and the Pentagon. Should the White House see no credible threat, nothing is required. The language is also totally open-ended as to what constitutes "a sufficient self-defense capability." This is in fact a non sequitur if it is placed against the potential capability of the PLA. No amount of arms could be "sufficient" if the mainland were determined to invade the island at any cost.

In addition to these anomalies, the TRA could conflict with international law. Taiwan's exact status has yet to be unambiguously defined by U.S. policy or finally resolved by formal treaty. Throughout all the verbiage of joint communiques, press conferences, and unilateral statements there has never been a simple American statement clearly placing Taiwan under Beijing's sovereignty, although this status can be logically inferred from the various formulations and semantic shifts. In the carefully chosen language of the 1979 and 1982 joint communiques, Washington only *acknowledged* the Chinese position that there is but one China and Taiwan is a part of China" (emphasis added). This falls short of *accepting* the Chinese position.

Moreover, Taiwan's international status remains technically in limbo as far as its final disposition as a result of Japan's defeat in World War II is concerned. Two authoritative statements addressed this question some thirty years ago, and their validity has not been changed by subsequent developments. On July 16, 1952, the Republic of China's foreign minister addressed the Legislative Yuan concerning a bilateral treaty between Japan and the Republic of China, noting:

> Formosa and the Pescadores were formerly Chinese territories. As Japan has renounced her claim to Formosa and the Pescadores, only China has the right to take them over. In fact, we are controlling them now, and undoubtedly they constitute a part of our territories. However, *the delicate international situation makes it that they do not belong to us* [emphasis added].

On December 1, 1954, Secretary of State Dulles replied to a question regarding whether the legal position of the offshore coastal islands was different from that of Taiwan:

> The legal position is different . . . by virtue of the fact that *technical sovereignty over Formosa and the Pescadores has never been settled.* That is because the Japanese peace treaty merely involves a renunciation by Japan of its right and title to these islands. But the future title is not determined by the Japanese peace treaty. . . . Therefore the juridical status of these islands, Formosa and the Pescadores, is different from the juridical status of the offshore islands which have always been Chinese territory [emphasis added].

Given the special interest of the Republic of China's foreign minister and the legal expertise of Dulles, their agreement on this point is especially striking. These statements provided the basis for a brief prepared in the State Department legal office in January 1955.

This is the legal loophole through which Washington can legitimately pass arms to Taiwan as long as it does not agree with Beijing that the island is part of the PRC. Otherwise it has no right under international law to so act while recognizing the People's Republic as the one and only China. Were it legal for the United States to sell weapons inside China against Beijing's wishes, such support could go to rebellious Tibetans while Moscow could supply arms across the border to dissident Uighurs or Mongols. Finally, to assert the primacy of domestic over international law as justification for implementing the TRA violates the basic concept of sovereignty as it has evolved over centuries of practice.

The August 1982 communique compounded these contradictions. Beijing repeated its consistent position "that the question of Taiwan is China's internal affair." Washington likewise affirmed "that it has no intention of infringing on Chinese sovereignty and territorial integrity, or interfering in China's internal affairs." Yet despite this apparent agreement on principle, the two sides jointly acknowledged that "only over a period of time" could "a final settlement of the question of United States arms sales to Taiwan" be realized. In sum, the legal framework offers no simple solution to the problem.

The political frame is similarly fraught with complications. The China question clearly has steadily lessened in volatility over the past decade, thanks to a recognition of reality in the United States and a PRC softening

of posture in response to American concern over Taiwan's fate. Also relevant in this regard was the death of Chiang Kai-shek, removing a key symbol of the original "China lobby."

But the issue is far from dead, as shown by Senator Barry Goldwater's 1981-1982 success in mobilizing numerous colleagues to support Taiwan's appeal for arms. President Reagan rhetorically reassured this group in his press conference of July 28, 1982, when he declared, "We are not going to abandon our long-time friends and allies in Taiwan. And I'm going to carry out the terms of the Taiwan Relations Act. . . . It is a moral obligation that we'll keep." In fact, his passing reference to "the government of the people of Taiwan" as well as his use of the term "allies" went well beyond TRA terminology. While Reagan's words doubtlessly reflected his feelings, the immediate context underlined his perception of the political risk of giving in to Beijing's total demand.

The August communique adroitly compromised the issue, albeit to the ultimate detriment of Taiwan. Beijing affirmed its "fundamental policy to strive for a peaceful solution to the Taiwan question." Washington responded that "it does not seek to carry out a long-term policy of arms sales to Taiwan" and "it intends to reduce gradually its sales of arms to Taiwan, leading over a period of time to a final resolution." Nevertheless, PRC did not rule out the possible use of force nor did the United States name a specific time for terminating the arms sales. Both sides thereby assuaged the hardliners' demands in their respective capitals and ended the impasse for the time being.

It is obviously impossible to predict the politics of Washington or Beijing over the longer run. But the relative ease with which the White House muted the Taiwan lobby's criticism of the communique makes it likely that a determined presidential stance against selling arms to the island at some future time will also win acquiescence. This is particularly probable when continuation of such sales is juxtaposed against the threat to Sino-American relations in the larger context of Sino-Soviet relations. It is further facilitated by Beijing's present posture of peaceful unification based on offers embodied in the 1981 nine-point proposal and reiterated through scholarly, athletic, and commercial contact between the two Chinese regimes. The absence of any PLA build-up opposite Taiwan, together with the opening of Fujien province to foreign enterprise and joint ventures, makes credible Beijing's protestations of peaceful intent.

There is somewhat greater uncertainty about politics in Beijing in the post-Deng period. Taiwan remains an attractive issue to exploit in a struggle for power, embodying as it does territorial sovereignty, national unity, and resistance to foreign intervention manifested in "U.S. imperialism." We have already noted that the issue cannot in itself cause a reversal of Sino-American relations in favor of Sino-Soviet relations. But its potential contribution to such a trend were it already under way, combined with political opportunism in Beijing, cannot be wholly discounted.

In view of Deng's strength and success at forming a wholly new post-Mao leadership consonant with his views, the political prospects for continued acceptance of the status quo on Taiwan are favorable over at least the next three to five years. It is difficult, however, to see beyond to a time when internal or external developments may again cause Taiwan to be prominent on Beijing's political agenda.

The moral framework ostensibly rests on absolutes but, like the other approaches, offers no single, unambiguous conclusion. Principles of self-determination and human rights are central to the American ideology. Translating ideology into foreign policy, however, requires compromise at best and capitulation at worst. No possibility of Taiwanese self-determination exists as long as the refugee Kuomintang regime remains dominated by mainlander elements in the guise of the Republic of China. While they constitute only 15 per cent of the island's eighteen million population, the remaining 85 per cent are indigenous but are denied a voice in Taiwan's future.

Nor do human rights exist with respect to this issue. Martial law remains in existence since 1949, as do political concentration camps, nighttime arrests, and summary executions. There is no freedom of press, speech, or assembly for debating the regime's legitimacy or the island's fate. True, conditions are far better than on the mainland. Were the choice simply between the status quo and communism, the majority of the population would undoubtedly choose the former for socioeconomic as well as political reasons. But in terms of moral absolutes, self-determination and human rights are inadequate criteria to support arms sales to Taiwan.

This leaves the residual U.S. commitment as the sole and strongest moral referent. While keeping a commitment may be a virtue, it can be argued that this one was born in sin. By interposing the U.S. Seventh Fleet in the Taiwan Strait in June 1950, President Truman intervened in the Chinese civil war. Otherwise, the PLA would have undertaken the attack for which it had prepared, toppling the routed and demoralized Nationalist resistance after a token invasion. In 1954 President Eisenhower changed intervention by executive order into protection by treaty, effectively denying Beijing the traditionally recognized right to fight a civil war to successful conclusion. Moreover, up to the 1970s, the CIA aided Nationalist espionage, sabotage, and guerrilla teams in their efforts to undermine Beijing's authority, particularly in coastal and border areas, including Tibet.

Yet whether the moral commitment was properly conceived or not, the question remains: is it an obligation in perpetuity or until a peaceful alternative emerges? Alternatively, can it be termed sufficient and terminated? The classic realpolitik position holds that in international relations there are neither permanent friends nor permanent enemies. That this aphorism was originally associated with the concept of "perfidious Albion" does not lessen its relevance today. This is no excuse for the opportunistic betrayal of pledges made and taken in good faith. Rather, it is a reminder that over time the dynamics of change in the international system compel states to secure their own separate interests according to the dictates of the present without excessive regard for previous commitments. In short, treaties are not made to be violated but they are expected to be terminated. Provisions for such action are standard, exemplified by President Carter's delay of one year beyond the withdrawal of recognition from Taibei for terminating the U.S. defense commitment as stipulated by the Sino-American treaty.

Beyond the treaty, is there a further moral obligation to Taiwan? Seen in one perspective, the answer is negative. Of the seventy-one years since the Republic of China was founded in 1911, nearly half were derived from peace and prosperity provided by American military, economic, and political assistance. This assistance may be seen as more than fulfilling our moral obligation. Nor is the island about to be attacked. On the contrary, the TRA and statements by every administration since 1972 make explicit the U.S. concern for peaceful resolution of the situation. While Beijing persistently rejects such admonitions as interference in China's internal affairs, it clearly is responsive to them and has tempered its posture and policy accordingly. Indeed, as far as mainland military capabilities and dispositions are concerned, there is no cause for concern over Taiwan's security for at least five or more years.

Seen from another perspective, however, the moral obligation remains. It is argued that the credibility and respectability of the U.S. position internationally depends on Washington's willingness to act on behalf of threatened friends at any point. Therefore to step aside completely and to permit Beijing use of any means at its disposal to win over Taiwan is held to be a betrayal of confidence, friendship, and hope for the island's eighteen million inhabitants. This view would compel the United States to maintain its moral commitments, regardless of the treaty's termination or the removal of diplomatic recognition.

Reagan's public position specifically cites moral obligation as determining support for Taiwan. The moral dictate, however, is neither unambiguous nor unidimensional. The point can be pressed to the extreme: if the PLA were poised to use force against Taiwan, would the United States act morally by risking war with China? The consequent casualties could hardly be blamed on Beijing alone, acting as it would to achieve territorial unity against a civil-war enemy. Nonetheless, if the ultimate implications of an absolutist moral obligation are frankly acknowledged, the image of a Sino-American war over Taiwan cannot be dismissed as inconceivable.

4. SOCIALIST STATES

This takes us to the final consideration: the pragmatic approach. We have already challenged the feasibility of providing Taiwan with a "sufficient self-defense capability" as specified in the TRA, yet we have also asserted the lack of threat for at least five years. The contradiction is more apparent than real. To take the latter proposition first, it seems safe to count on the present priorities of policy persisting in Beijing for many years to come. As we explained earlier, this involves a dependence on Japan and the United States, as well as others, for economic modernization. An attack on Taiwan would jeopardize this source of capital and technology and therefore is unlikely.

Moreover, the PLA obsolescence in air power and sealift capability makes an attack problematic as far as a quick victory is concerned. Yet a prolonged war of attrition raises the island's damage potential to near unacceptable limits. For Beijing, Taiwan is not an enemy to be pulverized into submission but rather a Chinese province whose wealth of human and technological resources is to be attained intact to the extent possible. Taiwan's defenses against invasion are fairly formidable. In addition, the 100 miles of sea in the Taiwan Strait are prone to typhoons from May to November and churned by the winter monsoon for the remaining months. Last and least, Beijing's paratroop force does not exceed 75,000 men.

These factors favoring Taiwan's near-term future are enhanced by PLA preoccupations along the Sino-Soviet and Sino-Vietnamese fronts. So long as the bulk of China's land and air forces are committed there or held in reserve for one or another contingency, Taiwan need not face Beijing's full power.

Nevertheless, these conditions could change, and therein lies the impossibility of meeting the TRA terms. The population of eighteen million, on an island only 250 miles long, is almost wholly dependent on contact with the outside world for economic survival. The prospect of confrontation with mainland China is totally overwhelming should Beijing decide to apply all the resources at its command. At the simplest and lowest level of pressure, it can declare Taiwan ports closed to foreign shipping. This is within the PRC's prerogative as the putative sovereign authority over the province. The immediate impact would be felt on insurance rates, whose rise would deter some owners and raise costs for others, with negative effects on both imports and exports. Some would suspend operations; others might unload in Hong Kong, Manila, or Japan, forcing Nationalist vessels to cover the interim distance. Meanwhile, a flight of capital and people would further weaken economic and political stability on Taiwan.

Beijing could also declare all traffic closed to the offshore islands, where at least 100,000 troops, mostly of Taiwanese origin, would become hostage to the demand for negotiations on Beijing's terms. No bombardment such as occurred in 1958 would be necessary. On the contrary, Beijing would minimize the use of force

in order to avoid unfavorable repercussions abroad while building pressure on the authorities in Taibei [Taipei] from wives, mothers, sisters, and daughters of the beleaguered soldiers on Quemoy, Matsu, and smaller points.

The PRC navy is already quite capable of exercising its strength toward these objectives. The Nationalists may not be able to draw on support from the U.S. Navy, as they did in 1958. With well over 100 submarines, 15 destroyers, and 670 fast-attack craft armed with missiles, torpedoes, or guns, Beijing's ability to isolate the offshore islands or Taiwan itself is impressive and is certain to improve with time.

While this estimation does not take into account air power on either side, even under the most favorable assumptions Taiwan could not count on breaking the encirclement with those planes that survived engagement with PLA fighter aircraft. In any event, it is not the final outcome of a prolonged scenario that may determine Taiwan's fate but rather the political reverberations on the island once pressure is applied for a negotiated union, not surrender, as Beijing's explicit objective.

Here the key variables are readily identified, although their possible interaction cannot be predicted. The eventual removal of Chiang Ching-kuo from political life will leave no comparable figure to inherit the mantle of legitimacy identified with Sun Yat-sen and Chiang Kai-shek. Nor is any individual presently on the scene able to manage public appearances and private coalitions with so deft a hand. A collective leadership of Kuomintang elders, bureaucrats, and technocrats might prove quite capable of coping with the island's problems. But this does not take into account the aspirations and actions of Taiwanese who reject the Republic of China commitment to once again ruling the mainland and who resent the domination of island affairs by mainlander elements.

Thus, in addition to the danger of an eventual PLA pressure for negotiation, there is the threat of an internal crisis in anticipation of such negotiation. While the majority of the Taiwanese are primarily concerned with economic rather than political affairs, a small minority of intellectuals, journalists, and students have demonstrated a willingness to risk their lives for the sake of self-determination. A riot over alleged electoral fraud at Chungli in 1977 and a mass confrontation between demonstrators and police at Kaohsiung in 1979 revealed the potential for trouble between the Taiwanese and local authorities. Further trouble can erupt either in response to Chiang Ching-kuo's leaving the scene, as a demand for greater Taiwanese rule, or in anticipation of Taipei negotiating with Beijing, to preempt the island's coming under communist rule.

Neither the external nor the internal threats can be controlled effectively through U.S. weapons sales. An arms race between Taiwan and the mainland must eventually end in the mainland's favor. Internal stability will be essentially independent of Taiwan's military capability. Given these severe constraints on the usefulness of American combat equipment, a purely pragmatic approach must weigh the dubious benefit to Taiwan of U.S. arms sales against the uncertain cost to U.S. relations with the PRC.

It has been argued that prudent arms sales to Taiwan can sustain local morale and thereby improve the prospects for negotiation without also upsetting Beijing unduly. But Beijing challenges the motivation behind Taiwan's desire for arms on different grounds, claiming that such sales are specifically aimed at obstructing negotiations and perpetuating the island's separation from mainland China. It is very doubtful that Taiwan authorities will enter into serious discussions with their PRC counterparts under any circumstances in the near future. Yet it is logical to infer that unlimited access to arms would reduce their propensity to negotiate while a total arms embargo, now or at a specified point in the future, would prompt a political crisis on Taiwan that might result in capitulation or collapse.

These two extremes are not in the interests of Taiwan, Sino-American relations, or the stability of East Asian international relations. U.S. policy must somehow steer between the Scylla and Charybdis of military deadlock and unconditional surrender in the Taiwan Strait, to the extent that American actions can influence the outcome short of open intervention on behalf of either side.

So far, while the formula of calculated ambiguity has satisfied neither Taipei nor Beijing, it has kept the situation relatively stable. The fact that principles are involved for both Washington and Beijing, albeit with contradictory compulsions, permits a reasoned dialogue to continue in private, however uncompromising the public position may often be. The American insistence on loyalty to friends is juxtaposed against the Chinese insistence on territorial integrity and noninterference in domestic affairs. Each side therefore can respect the other while maintaining its own position.

Fortunately, the Chinese tolerance of ambiguity has proven generous on both sides of the Taiwan Strait. Meanwhile, the informal interaction between Taiwan and the PRC in scholarly, cultural, and athletic contacts has defused much of the tension surrounding past periods of confrontation and conflict. No one, least of all an American, can divine how the situation will be resolved. But it behooves U.S. policymakers to weigh their words and actions at each instance in order to minimize provocation and maximize the peaceful evolution of relations between Taiwan and the mainland.

Conclusions

I have focused on the issues of arms sales to both sides of the Taiwan Strait because they have been the cause of much contention in recent years and are likely to remain so. In addition, however, these issues illuminate more basic factors that deserve consideration in framing the larger and longer-range U.S. policy toward China. Some of these factors can only be acknowledged as relevant while remaining obscured from our vision, such as the interaction between Chinese domestic politics and foreign policy. Others, such as the evolution of Sino-Soviet relations, can be identified as critical but unforeseeable.

Yet we need not confine our decisons to those matters on which we can be confident. We have valuable allies and friends in Asia with whom genuine consultation before the fact can be mutually beneficial, compared with post hoc notification. Chief of these is Japan. No country commands a more intimate relationship with the PRC than Japan, measured in terms of economic exchange and tourism. We have much to gain from systematically developing our China policy in concert with Japan's. ASEAN members provide a different but nonetheless important perspective. They can help us to think through the implications of China's military modernization and what role we might play therein. Linkage between the Sino-Soviet-American triangle and Southeast Asia has been made complete since the Moscow-Hanoi pact of November 1978 and the Sino-Vietnamese war of early 1979.

Consultation does not require compromise or consensus. American interests will differ from those of Japan and ASEAN, and disagreements are inevitable. But interests may also overlap or converge, and in any case decisions can be more informed by the views of others whose familiarity with China exceeds or is at least equal to ours. This is particularly true given the nature of American foreign policy. It is subject not only to the vicissitudes of Congress and public opinion but also to the intervention of amateurs as the result of changing administrations every four years. To learn while doing can be costly, as proved by the period between candidate Reagan's remarks on Taiwan in 1980 and President Reagan's agreement to reduce and ultimately end arms sales to Taiwan in the August 1982 communique.

The decade 1972-1982 has not been a bad one for Sino-American relations. Compared with what went before, it has been very good. Neither side has allowed the Taiwan issue to damage seriously any aspect of the relationship. Neither side has failed to communicate its views to the other on important matters. This is the essence of normalization, a goal that eluded statesmen in the two capitals for more than twenty years. With time, successive changes of regimes in Beijing and Washington should be better able to work out the inevitable differences in order to sustain the ties that bind them as Pacific partners. But until the Taiwan issue is finally resolved, it will require the utmost caution and consideration on both sides if these ties are to be strengthened as well as sustained.

The Third World: Areas of Conflict, Crises and Problems

The term Third World was coined to distinguish the group of independent states that began emerging in the mid-1950s, from the First World (Western and capitalist) and the Second World (Eastern and Communist). In other words, these new states, most of which were former colonies, initially intended to be "non-aligned" in ideology with either the capitalist or the communist blocs. It has long been obvious, however, that few of the 120 states belonging to the Third World are ideologically neutral; they are, moreover, not even ideologically united as a "bloc." Pressures arising from the need to get military and economic aid eventually forced most to align themselves with one power or another. While the Soviets and Western aid-donors had at first respected their neutrality, both sides soon grew tired of the states' attempts at blackmail by threatening to switch sides if they did not get what they wanted. Strings, even ropes, were attached to aid. The result is that the Third World today has distinct difficulties in taking strident anti-US or anti-Soviet stances without considering the consequences for their foreign aid programs. These countries are faced with a dilemma, for example, in deciding how far to go in alienating the US over such issues as Vietnam, South Africa, and Israel. These problems—together with religious, cultural, wealth, tribal-ethnic, national, and power divisions among various Third World States—have torn away at any ties that might have united them against the industrialized states. War between Third World countries has become increasingly frequent as each side hopes that its expensive military arsenal will prove superior to its neighbor's.

Until the 1970s, the one factor that did unify these states was their poverty and underdevelopment. The response to this economic rather than ideological division came to be conceptualized as the industrialized "North" against the underdeveloped "South." The South has relied on exports of primary products for the necessary capital to modernize. But the OPEC boycott and cartel brought further fissures within the South as the wealth and development of the oil-exporting countries rapidly increased. At the same time the modernization of many of the lesser developed countries was stopped dead in its tracks since they could no longer afford the oil required even for slow growth. Further differentiation of interests arose as the "newly industrialized countries" (NICs) emerged out of the ranks of the Third World, including such countries as South Korea, Brazil, the city-state of Singapore, and the island of Taiwan.

The lesser developed countries are still hoping that prosperity is around the corner, and that aid and investment from the industrialized countries will eventually help them turn that corner. But given the problems facing the major industrial economies, there is little chance of great leaps in foreign aid and investment. The 120 countries in the so-called "Group of 77," are still attempting to establish a "New International Economic Order," that will take into consideration the serious price differentials between primary and manufactured products, establish a "Common Fund" to protect them from the price volatility of primary products, and create a new international patent law that will permit (force) a more rapid transfer of technology from the industrialized countries. The supposition underlying the position of the Group of 77 is not only that the rich are getting richer and the poor poorer. It is also that the rich cannot survive if the poor do not prosper. This is a fact recognized by the wealthier

states. But the conclusion that the poor states have drawn from this, which is that they can therefore pressure the wealthier states into new economic arrangements unfavorable to them, has so far proven incorrect. The wealthier states have looked at the other side of the picture: if the rich do not survive, the poor will definitely perish. Some of the wealthiest economies are seriously imperiled, and to take action that would further endanger them ultimately means that they have much less to offer the poor countries in terms of aid, investment, or technology transfers.

The following articles illustrate how deeply the countries of the Third World are divided against themselves. Many of the articles are concerned with the issue of great power involvement in problem areas of the Third World. Others highlight the failure of the great powers to bring political stability under acceptable political systems through foreign aid programs. Indeed, some aid programs have contributed to political instability, which has degenerated into military conflict. Altogether too much of the aid given to these countries has either been earmarked for military conflict or diverted into military expenditures. Sadly enough, a single aid-donor has often given military aid to both participants in the conflicts. Alternatively, the superpowers find themselves confronting each other through the military conflicts of their Third World proxies. And finally, military aid to the lesser developed countries has frequently been used to suppress internal dissent.

Looking Ahead: Challenge Questions

What are the major reasons for the failure of American aid programs to Latin America? What are the roots of the "Yankee-go-home" attitudes of Latin Americans toward the USA?

What is likely to be the nature of the future relationship between the People's Republic of China and Hong Kong? What are the possibilities that China will some day have a relationship with Taiwan similar to its relationship with Hong Kong? What will the British most likely do if the Chinese insist on claiming sovereignty over Hong Kong? What differentiates the Hong Kong situation from the Falklands?

What are the major issues in the sub-Sahara African continent? How did the de-colonization process contribute to today's problems in Africa? Why has the Organization of African Unity (OAU) recently found it difficult to make critical decisions relating to all its members? What issues could possibly bring the African states to overlook their differences and act as a unified group of states?

What are the interests of the Great Powers in the Middle East? How are the national interests of each best served? What type of peace plan is likely to satisfy those interests while bringing stability to the Middle East? What is the attitude of the Reagan administration toward the establishment of an independent Palestinian state?

If Middle Eastern oil loses its importance to the survival of the economies of the industrialized states, what might happen to the nature of Great Power involvement in the region? What reasons other than oil make the Persian Gulf area significant to the Great Powers?

The Iranian "Islamic Revolution" indicates that in the Middle East there are threats to American interests other than those posed by communism and the Arab-Israeli conflict. How does the Islamic revolution complicate the picture of the national interests of the Great Powers in the Middle East? How is the spread of Islam, Iranian style, viewed by the Arab states?

Central America's Bitter Wars Spread

James Nelson Goodsell

Latin America correspondent of The Christian Science Monitor

Largely obscured by events elsewhere in the past six months, Central America's political, social, and economic malaise refuses to go away.

Indeed, the bitter struggle between rival forces in the countries of the region has, if anything, escalated during these months. The prospect that fighting will engulf the whole region looms large.

"Fighting is at an all-time high," says a senior United States official recently on the scene. "The region has become the vortex of a drama that is playing itself out in an escalating confrontation between guerrillas and governments, between nations and peoples.

"It is a battle of words and bullets.

"And it is being fought out in the rugged hill country of Guatemala, El Salvador, and Honduras, in the swampy rain forests of Nicaragua, in the major urban areas of all these countries, and at the conference table as well."

Most observers agree with this assessment.

While the Falklands crisis, Lebanon's traumas, Mexico's economic difficulties, and other issues swept world attention away from Central America, contending forces in El Salvador have been locked in bitter battles. More than 1,000 Salvadorans have lost their lives in the past six months.

El Salvador remains the center of the Central American storm. Leftist guerrillas, after some months of lessened activity, are stepping up their operations. Their current 14-day-old offensive caught government forces off guard. They penetrated the capital city, San Salvador, cut the Pan American Highway in several spots, and have seized a number of towns along the border with Honduras.

But government forces—or right-wing paramilitary groups allied with the government—appear to have struck back. Last week, as guerrillas moved into several towns near the Honduran border, six top leftist politicians were kidnapped in San Salvador. The six were the leading members of the unarmed, political sector of the opposition still living in El Salvador. Their whereabouts are unknown, and their loss would leave a political vacuum for government opponents in the country.

Recent battles between government forces and guerrillas has been intense, with scores killed on both sides. The Salvadoran Army is better equipped and trained than it was a year ago. Several thousand Salvadorans have received training in counterinsurgency in the United States, others have been trained by US advisers on the scene. The Army is also adopting some tactics used by the guerrillas.

"The night is no longer in the hands of the guerrillas," says one colonel. While this may be true in some areas, it is not true in others, due to widely varying abilities and aggressiveness of Army commanders.

So far it appears that neither government forces nor leftist guerrillas have an edge. It is not quite a stalemate, but as the struggle sways back and forth across the countryside, it appears to be threatening to engulf neighboring countries.

Guatemala is potentially as volatile, perhaps even more volatile, than its southeastern neighbor, El Salvador. Government troops and leftist guerrillas are stepping up warfare. Some Indians are joining forces with leftists. Battles in the past two months have been the most violent in a decade.

Government forces have been pursuing leftist guerrillas with a relentlessness reminiscent of 1960s engagements that decimated guerrilla ranks. Now, however, the guerrillas are stronger, more sophisticated, and stealthier. They are fighting with a resolve that has "frankly surprised us," says Army Co. Hector Ramirez Soler.

"It is nip and tuck," says a US adviser on the scene, "whether the Army will win or the guerrillas will gain the edge."

That uncertainty is augmented by charges of "criminal" human rights violations by the Army under the President, Gen. Efrain Rios Montt, who came to power in March. After offering amnesty to guerrillas who would surrender, some 300 of whom did, the government launched an offensive against suspected guerrillas. In June alone, 300 suspected guerrillas were killed or captured. Amnesty International claims that 2,600

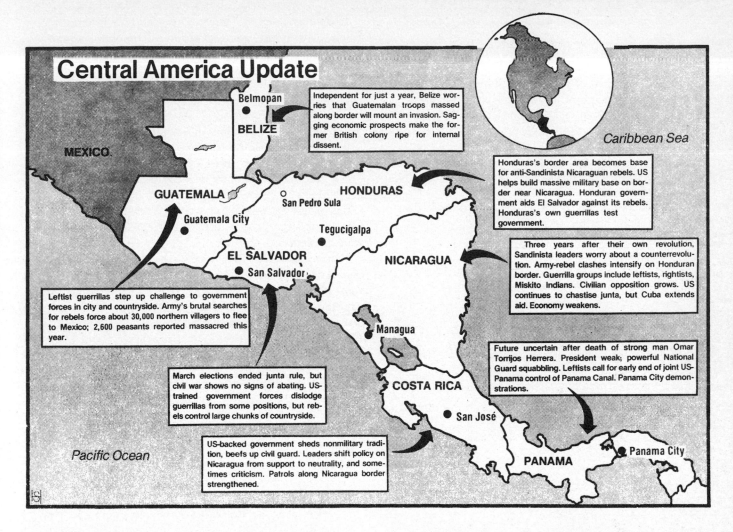

Central America Update

Independent for just a year, Belize worries that Guatemalan troops massed along border will mount an invasion. Sagging economic prospects make the former British colony ripe for internal dissent.

Honduras's border area becomes base for anti-Sandinista Nicaraguan rebels. US helps build massive military base on border near Nicaragua. Honduran government aids El Salvador against its rebels. Honduras's own guerrillas test government.

Three years after their own revolution, Sandinista leaders worry about a counterrevolution. Army-rebel clashes intensify on Honduran border. Guerrilla groups include leftists, rightists, Miskito Indians. Civilian opposition grows. US continues to chastise junta, but Cuba extends aid. Economy weakens.

Leftist guerrillas step up challenge to government forces in city and countryside. Army's brutal searches for rebels force about 30,000 northern villagers to flee to Mexico; 2,600 peasants reported massacred this year.

Future uncertain after death of strong man Omar Torrijos Herrera. President weak; powerful National Guard squabbling. Leftists call for early end of joint US-Panama control of Panama Canal. Panama City demonstrations.

March elections ended junta rule, but civil war shows no signs of abating. US-trained government forces dislodge guerrillas from some positions, but rebels control large chunks of countryside.

US-backed government sheds nonmilitary tradition, beefs up civil guard. Leaders shift policy on Nicaragua from support to neutrality, and sometimes criticism. Patrols along Nicaragua border strengthened.

Caribbean Sea

Pacific Ocean

MEXICO. GUATEMALA (Guatemala City), BELIZE (Belmopan), EL SALVADOR (San Salvador), HONDURAS (San Pedro Sula, Tegucigalpa), NICARAGUA (Managua), COSTA RICA (San José), PANAMA (Panama City)

---

peasants, including Indians, have been massacred since March. Thousands of refugees have fled across the border into Mexico.

Over the weekend Guatemalan military police are reported to have detained 24 persons, including a former agriculture minister, for plotting to overthrow Rios Montt.

Next door in newly independent Belize, there is worry about being drawn into the struggle—concern that is heightened by Guatemalan troop maneuvers along the border. Belizeans fear Guatemala will attempt to seize their country—and Guatemalans have long claimed the territory should belong to Guatemala. Several hundred British marines guard Belize. A weakening economy could lead to internal dissent, also a major concern of the government.

To the south, Honduras, which was the tranquil oasis of the region, has suddenly become home base for civilian and some guerrilla opponents of El Salvador, Guatemala, and Nicaragua. It claims to be neutral—but with thinly disguised support for government forces in El Salvador and Guatemala and for Nicaraguan exiles within its borders, Honduras can no longer honestly be called uncommitted.

Its Army beefed up with US weaponry and training,

as well as tactical support from Argentina, Honduras is "every bit as much a part of the struggle as the other countries," says a Mexico City-based spokesman for the Frente Revolucionario Democratica, political arm of Salvadoran guerrillas. The Salvadoran guerrillas claim that the Honduran Army is actively supporting El Salvador's Army "in a clear violation of its professed neutrality."

A recent hostage drama in San Pedro Sula, in which more than 100 businessmen and two Cabinet members were held by Honduran guerrillas for a week, suggests the way in which Central America's malaise is thrusting into Honduras's own political scene. Guerrillas sought the release of political prisoners and an end to support of the Salvadoran government.

The US counts on Honduras to serve as "the fulcrum," to quote a US official on the scene, of leverage against the leftist guerrillas and as a counterweight to left-leaning Nicaragua. But there is some evidence now that Hondurans are beginning to resent the growing US presence in their country.

Nicaragua appears to be drifting further left. Its war of words with the US and numerous Latin American countries is intensifying. Its Sandinista leadership, which styles itself as Marxist, came to power three years ago promising political pluralism. But that promise looks increasingly hollow.

Many original supporters of the Sandinistas, including some of the heroes of the war that toppled the archtypal dictatorship of Anastasio Somoza Debayle, have fled Nicaragua. Many of those early-supporters-turned-opponents are in Costa Rica. Others are rightists, or "Somocistas," exiled in Honduras. Sandinistas feel increasingly hemmed in. Fighting between Nicaraguan troops and Honduras-based exiles in the Zelaya swamps of eastern Nicaragua has been intense.

Bitterly attacking the US for "provocations," the Sandinistas are struggling to keep a sagging economy afloat while pushing ahead with domestic programs such as literacy and better housing. There has been progress on those two fronts. But public support for the once acclaimed Sandinistas is flagging. Some of this falloff clearly stems from growing unemployment, shortages of consumer goods, and inflation.

Economies across Central America are in trouble. Even Costa Rica—once regarded as the region's most affluent—is now in a deep recession. Urban guerrilla activities recently erupted in the Costa Rica's capital, and help explain why this traditionally antimilitary country has stepped up patrols in the Nicaraguan border region and signed an agreement with Washington for $2 million in US military aid and training.

Looming over Central America is concern that troubles here could escalate into a larger contest—like the famous domino theory in the 1960s about Southeast Asia. Mexico, whose border area has been invaded by Guatemalan forces looking for guerrillas, is clearly the most worried. Other Latin American countries are worried, too.

For Washington, the threat that the crisis could engulf the whole region, affecting operation of the Panama Canal, for example, is chilling—helping to explain why the Reagan administration has increasingly involved itself in the region.

Central America: A Potential Vietnam?

Robert Harvey

Mr. Harvey, a member of the editorial staff of The Economist, *is author of* Portugal: The Birth of a Democracy *(London: Macmillan, 1978) and of the articles on* Central America's War *in* The Economist *(27 March and 3 April 1982). This article is based on a recent talk at Chatham House.*

The Falklands conflict has helped to focus public attention upon Latin America, a continent which has long seemed peripheral to the main East-West power struggle being waged in South-East Asia, South-West Asia and the Middle East, and in the former European colonies of Africa. Yet, over the past 20 years or so, the continent has quietly undergone a gigantic and unsettling economic and social transformation that could, if mastered, allow it to become one of the engines of world prosperity or could, if untamed, cause the region to lapse into chaos.

In one part of Latin America—Central America—inner tensions are already ripping societies apart. Long after peace returns between Britain and Argentina, Central America is likely to remain in eruption, absorbing an increasing share of US foreign policy attention. The lack of familiarity most observers display towards the region has helped events there to be seen through distorting glasses. On the one hand, there is what might be called the traditional American view of the region: endemically unstable, always a prey to Communist, anti-American penetration, best governed by tough, pro-American army chiefs keeping a lid on domestic social tensions. According to this view, the methods of these rulers are regrettable, but they may be necessary.

The Reagan Administration, on coming to office in January 1981, shared that approach. At first, its policy-makers considered that the upheaval in Central America could have only one origin: a decision by the Soviet Union, through the medium of its Cuban surrogate, to light the fuse of insurrection in the region by supplying weapons, training and advisers to Marxist-Leninist guerrilla movements fighting until then hopeless battles in the hills of El Salvador and Guatemala. The Reagan Administration's initial instinct was to make an example of El Salvador as a country in which a decisive stance by the United States would frighten off outside-supported revolutionary forces, which had been allowed to succeed in Nicaragua by the weakness and indecision of the Carter Administration. Instead, when the spotlight was turned on to El Salvador, the Reagan Administration discovered, first, that the region's problems were much more complex and long-term than the simple Castroite penetration theory allowed and, second, that the sheer savagery of the conflict threatened to overwhelm the American case for involvement in the region.

The savagery is likely to be crucial to the debate about America's future involvement in Central America. Since the civil war in Nicaragua began in 1978, well over 90,000 people have been killed for political reasons in the region. Of those, about half died in Nicaragua, the overwhelming majority at the hands of the late President Somoza's national guard. In El Salvador, around 33,000 people have died since the war there began in earnest in late 1979. Again, at least two-thirds have been the victims of the Salvadorean army or of right-wing death squads. In Guatemala, around 12,000 have died over the past three years, once again very largely at the hands of the extreme Right.

Most of the victims have been non-combatants: the extreme Right's aim is usually to terrorize villagers in country areas into withdrawing their support from the guerrillas. Because Central American armies are generally ineffective at catching guerrillas, terror has been the main tactic. The killing permeates the atmosphere and moral climate of those countries. When the present writer was in Guatemala last March, the daily political death toll never fell below 20 and was often as high as 50 or 60. It is true that the guerrillas sometimes use methods every bit as ruthless as the security forces. Yet the overwhelming majority of the killings are carried out by America's apparent allies within Central America's armed forces.

This article originally appeared in the July/August 1982 Issue of *The World Today*, monthly journal of the Royal Institute of International Affairs, London.

5. THE THIRD WORLD

Simplistic Comparison

With that background, it is hardly surprising that an equally simplistic view of the conflict has been adopted by the Administration's opponents. American liberalism, which has wandered somewhat aimlessly in search of a cause since Vietnam, has reassembled around the 'new Vietnam' in Central America. The surface parallels are strong: once again, it seems that America is backing a repulsive bunch of local oppressors against guerrillas fighting on behalf of a downtrodden people. Once again, American arms, money, prestige, honour and maybe even lives seem to be engaged on behalf of a losing minority cause. Once again, America seems to have embarked upon a substantial commitment without having a clear idea of its objectives or of the depth to which it wants to pursue that commitment. Once again, America is converting a local conflict into a round in the East-West power contest, thus, it is said, forcing nationalist guerrillas to look for support from the Soviet Union and Cuba. Once again, an American administration seems to be losing the battle for domestic public opinion. Once again, it is wheeling out a discredited domino theory. Once again, in short, America has backed the wrong side.

The reality is less simple. There are four major ways in which the Vietnam analogy does not apply in Central America. First, the origins of the Central American conflict make it very difficult to compare with Vietnam. Second, the extent to which it represents a real threat to American interests is different. Third, the scale of American involvement is wholly disproportionate. Fourth, the real human issues involved are not to be compared.

Starting with the origins, the stereotype picture of Central America is of a region dominated by traditionalist landowners whose interests are defended by bloodthirsty local armies at the expense of abjectly poor landless peasants. The poverty, inequality and human misery are real enough. The stereotype fails to explain, however, how or why an explosion should have taken place just now. The answer lies in the staggering progress, in relative terms, which the region has undergone over the past 30 years.

The real value of Central America's traditional exports jumped 18 times between 1950 and 1980. In 1950, most Central American countries had been one-crop (bananas or coffee) exporting economies. By 1980, the share of exports taken by the average country's main commodity had fallen by around half, from 70 per cent to 36 per cent. Most of the wealth coming into these societies accrued through new commodity exports. But industrial growth played its part: industry grew from an average share of 11 per cent in Central American GDP to 18 per cent in 1980.

As money came in, so social structures changed. The old coffee oligarchies, for example, were shunted aside by new fortunes in cotton, cattle and industry. The old wealth did not get on with the new: the new men's methods were often more ruthless than those of the old oligarchy. But the new middle class also contained its own quota of social reformers, appalled by the inequality around them and determined to bring about change. This new educated class, which had materialized in the space of a generation, had two avenues open to it: either to seek to modify the slight traditions of republican representative government of these countries into genuine democracy, or to work for the overthrow of the system altogether.

Thus, the new middle class split three ways in most Central American countries. Part of it continued ruthlessly to support the system, using methods shunned even by the old oligarchs: that is, the part represented by 'New Right' leaders like the National Liberation Movement's Mario Sandoval Alarcon in Guatemala and Arena's Roberto d'Aubuisson in El Salvador. Part of it sought peaceful change, largely by working through the Christian Democratic and Social Democratic parties of the region, most of which attracted considerable popular followings. These moderates are represented by men like Vinicio Cerezo in Guatemala and Napoleon Duarte in El Salvador. And part chose the path of violent revolution. All challenged the hold of the old oligarchy.

Added to this, there was a dramatic change in the role of the local armed forces. Most of these, from being the paid hirelings of the old landowners, only became professional forces under the impact of American training around the middle of this century. This was true, for example, of the Nicaraguan and Panamanian national guards as well as the Salvadorean, Guatemalan and Honduran armies. As they became professionalized, the armies began to detach themselves from the old oligarchy and became suborned by the new wealth, or acquired interests and a life of their own. Lust for power very often had less to do with the decision by Central American armies to move to centre stage than the opportunity that government provided for officers of peasant background to acquire wealth.

In the space of a generation, then, Central America was transformed from a sleepy, if cruel, plantation existence to a society where four significant new social forces were competing for wealth and power. The forces could be contained as long as Central America was growing by an average of around 8 per cent during the 1960s. After the jump in oil prices and the slump in world demand in the 1970s had slowed average growth down to between 1 per cent and 3 per cent, the social strains ripped these societies apart. Conflict was translated into massacre by the awful fact that in much of Central America a frontier-style *macho* individualism dictates that most people still settle disputes with a gun.

And guns there were in abundance, not just the traditional handguns any self-respecting non-Indian Central American male carries, but Soviet- and Cuban-supplied weapons. It is not necessary to subscribe to the Reagan Administration's first view that the Central

American war was purely the product of Soviet-inspired mischief-making to accept that training and arms from Cuba have greatly enhanced guerrilla capabilities in the region.

Defining America's Interest

To what extent is this largely locally generated upheaval a threat to American interests? What, indeed, are those interests? They can be listed briefly. First, around three-quarters of America's imported oil, half of its help to Western Europe in the event of a war there, and more than half of America's commodity imports pass through the Panama Canal and the Caribbean area. Second, there is the threat posed to Mexico, which supplies around a third of American oil imports and whose oil reserves are a gigantic strategic reserve for the Western Hemisphere. There are also the strategic implications of allowing the Soviet Union a foothold in Central America: Mr. Brezhnev's recent veiled threat to station Soviet missiles in Cuba was a reminder of those implications. Fourth, and possibly most dangerous of all, is the side effect of successful Marxist-Leninist revolution in Central America. Revolution could spread to the much more highly developed, but highly unequal societies of South America, the United States's main commodity supplier.

Those are the stakes, and it was hard to disagree with the former Secretary of State, Mr. Alexander Haig, when he claimed that the threat to US security was much more obvious in Central America than it was in Vietnam, on the other side of the Pacific. It is equally hard to argue that the much maligned domino theory does not apply in Central America. The entirely unexpected success of Nicaragua's revolution brought hope to the hearts of small embattled guerrilla movements elsewhere in Central America and gave them a safe haven from which to operate and obtain arms. Disjointed guerrilla activity in El Salvador became serious in the winter of 1979, after the Sandinist victory in Nicaragua. By the following year, the Guatemalan guerrilla war was expanding; small guerrilla movements are now springing up in Costa Rica and Honduras. Only Panama and Mexico are untouched, but Mexico is more worried than it cares to admit about the trend in Central America. Its economy this year came down to earth with a bump, and severe social strains could follow.

The Central American war has already spread along the isthmus. Moreover, there is little comfort for the United States in the nature of the guerrilla movements in the region. The Sandinist movement in Nicaragua, alone amongst them, incorporated large numbers of non-Marxists; now, sadly, they are being purged. Both in El Salvador and Guatemala, the guerrillas are various shades of Marxist-Leninist or Trotskyist Left, leavened only by civilian front organizations which have secured the support of some Social Democrats and Christian Democrats.

The challenge to American interests is hardly one that the United States can realistically ignore. If the stakes are greater than in Vietnam, however, the degree of American commitment demanded is far smaller. Where in South Vietnam the United States was taking on an opponent with around 200,000 men lavishly equipped by both China and Russia, in El Salvador the guerrilla forces number around 6,000 and in Guatemala slightly fewer. The local armies are also small. In El Salvador the army has around 23,000 men, in Guatemala around 18,000. The fighting is on a tiny scale compared to Vietnam. The Salvadorean army's most effective counter-insurgency equipment, for example, consists of its helicopters—of which it has no more than 14. American aid has been on a correspondingly small scale. The total US commitment in Central America today, excluding the Panama Canal zone, is around 200 military trainers. By way of comparison, in Vietnam, under President Kennedy, before the American commitment was considered irrevocable by most, there were 16,000 American military trainers—rising, of course, to 530,000 at the height of the commitment. Total military aid to El Salvador this year will not exceed $200 m.—the cost of barely a couple of days' fighting in Vietnam.

However, the lesson of Vietnam was surely that America must look carefully at each stage in the escalation of a commitment, to see whether the price is justified. The lesson of Vietnam can hardly be that America should make no military commitment, however small, anywhere in the Third World to defend its interests for fear that the commitment may escalate. In terms of scale, Central America and Vietnam simply cannot be compared. What we actually see in Central America is a tiny-scale US commitment in defence of much more significant interests than those at stake in Vietnam against a guerrilla opposition that unfortunately is already all too committed to Soviet and Cuban interests. There remains the question of whether the United States should be standing cheek-by-jowl with murderous local soldiers.

United States policy over the last troubled few years in El Salvador and Guatemala has been to seek to coax a political centre into being between extreme Right and extreme Left—the centre represented by the Christian Democrats in both countries. Thus America ceased exporting arms to Guatemala in 1977 because of its government's persecution of the centre. In El Salvador, the United States forced the army to form an alliance with the Christian Democrats, which precariously ruled the country for two and a half years up to last May.

It is easy to dismiss the Christian Democrats as a figleaf of the extreme Right, and to point to the failure of American attempts to control army brutality, at least in El Salvador, up to now. The American attempt to find a middle way was dealt a shattering blow in El Salvador's election on 28 March, which showed that the extreme Right, led by Major d'Aubuisson, was more popular than the Christian Democratic party. Yet, what these elections also showed was that maybe one-third of El Salvador's population supported Major d'Aubuisson's call for total war to be waged against the guerrillas and the political centre. The unpalatable fact is that the extreme Right has a great deal of popular support, maybe more so than the guerrillas, in both El Salvador and Guatemala.

The United States thus finds itself in the position not just of helping local armies to defeat the guerrillas, but of holding back a large and bloodthirsty Right from going on the rampage. American policy may have helped to bring about the coup in Guatemala last March, which may have resulted in an improvement in human rights there. In El Salvador, the only thing restraining Major d'Aubuisson's followers from starting a bloodbath is a threat by the United States to deny the country military and economic aid. The first effect of an American withdrawal from El Salvador would be a horrific massacre of the Centre and Left followed by a long-drawn out civil war which either extreme might win. America has thus ended up with a humanitarian obligation to stay and seek to hold the ring in the same way, on a very different scale, that Britain has in Northern Ireland.

But that obligation disappears the moment it becomes apparent that the United States is exercising no significant restraint upon the actions of the Central American Right. If human rights start to deteriorate again in Guatemala, or if in El Salvador the activities of the death squads increase, the United States would be well advised to cut its losses and run. If open civil war cannot be avoided, better for America to be out of it. The United States should then seek to defend its interests behind the borders of civilian-ruled, civilized Mexico and Costa Rica.

Western Europe is only just beginning to sense the dimension of the Central American problem. At best, moderation imposed by the United States upon its unattractive friends may keep the fire in the isthmus isolated and small-scale. At worst, the trouble could escalate into a large and permanent diversion of American resources and attention away from the European theatre. And if the United States commits the mistake of backing killers without extracting the necessary commitments from them to reform themselves, America's image abroad could be muddied a deeper shade of black than Russia's image in Afghanistan and Poland. America has huge interests at stake in Central America; but its greatest interests are in Western Europe and in its own good name.

U.S. Policy and Africa

Alan Cowell
Special to The New York Times

DAKAR, Senegal, Nov. 17—When Vice President Bush addressed a news conference recently in Lagos, the Nigerian capital, he was asked what the Reagan Administration felt about the Libyan leader, Col. Muammar el-Qaddafi.

"We do not like what Qaddafi stands for," came the reply, and Mr. Bush spelled out the criteria by which the Libyan leader qualified for Washington's opprobium: Colonel Qaddafi was, Mr. Bush said, supportive of international terrorism; the Libyan leader was not a stabilizing factor; and, indeed, his policies disrupted neighboring countries.

The comments illuminated some differences of perception and inconsistencies that hover over the Vice President's current African tour. For, while many black-ruled African nations and others would agree with the Administration's analysis of Colonel Qaddafi, they would assert that the same standards should be applied to white-ruled South Africa—a nation toward which Washington has qualified its condemnation with what is seen by some black Africans as an evident sympathy for Pretoria's concerns about its security.

In the Case of South Africa

South Africa's forces regularly invade Angola, its commitment to the independence of South-West Africa as the black-ruled nation of Namibia is not proved and it could be depicted as an exporter of terrorism in its support for guerrilla armies opposed to the Governments of Mozambique and Angola.

South Africa, by this argument, disrupts its neighbors on a wider scale than does Colonel Qaddafi, using its economic and military powers to do so—the difference being that, on the checkerboard of geopolitics, a pro-Western regime in Pretoria, however unpalatable its domestic policies, serves Western strategic and economic interests, while Colonel Qaddafi patently does not.

The inference, from the black African perspective, is that the United States accords secondary status to individual African nations and sets greater store by a perceived need to counter Soviet influence wherever it seems to have taken root or to be in the offing. Vice President Bush's tour is clearly designed in part to counter this sentiment.

However, in its efforts to obtain Namibia's freedom from South Africa's domination, Washington's concern focuses on the withdrawal of Cuban troops from neighboring Angola as a condition, or at least a parallel development. The linkage of the two issues is publicly rejected by many black African nations for whom the United States position poses a dilemma: Moderate and Western-looking Governments such as those of Senegal and Nigeria do not see their interests served by a potentially disruptive superpower presence on African soil, particularly one that is perceived as inimical to Western-oriented democracies; yet to associate themselves with public demands for a Cuban withdrawal from Angola would invoke a loss of face for a fellow African country and offend a continent's frail sense of its own independence.

Demands for Sanctions

At the Lagos news conference, the Nigerian Vice President, Alex Ekwueme, openly opposed the American policy toward the Cubans in Angola. He also repeated Nigeria's demands for mandatory sanctions against South Africa, the richest country in Africa, to force it to dismantle its racial separation policies at home and to yield to pressure for independence of South-West Africa.

Such demands have little chance while the United States and other Western powers provide a diplomatic shield for South Africa at the United Nations. And there are complexities and inconsistencies on the black African side, Western economists say, because sanctions could not be imposed without severe economic damage to those nations still dependent on South Africa for trade and transport routes: South-West Africa itself, Zimbabwe, Botswana, Mozambique, Zambia and Zaire.

Instead of confrontation, the Reagan Administration has embarked on a policy of "constructive engagement" toward South Africa. In effect, it acknowledges a coincidence of concerns about regional security in the perspectives of Pretoria and Washington.

Senior officials in Vice President Bush's party said the aim was to enhance the stability of all nations in southern Africa. And they asserted that southern Africa's instability was caused not only by South Africa but also by those black-ruled nations that play host to the liberation movements opposed to Pretoria's domestic policies and its dominance of Namibia—movements whose very creation was rooted in Pretoria's refusal to extend democracy beyond its white minority.

5. THE THIRD WORLD

The Geopolitical Logic

Some black African officials concede in private the geopolitical logic of the argument: If the Cubans have not withdrawn from Angola by the time Namibia becomes independent, the Soviet Union will extend its influence to Windhoek, the Namibian capital, since the man now most likely to win an election there is Sam Nujoma, the Soviet-supported leader of the insurgents of the Southwest Africa People's Organization, which is based in Angola.

Mr. Nujoma has been compared to Prime Minister Robert Mugabe of Zimbabwe, the reasoning being that, like Mr. Mugabe, he will tone down his anti-Western words once independence has been won. But Mr. Nujoma's indebtedness to the Soviet Union is seen by some Westerners as being far greater than that of Mr. Mugabe, whose guerrilla army, before independence, was persistently snubbed by Moscow strategists.

Thus, the United States aim seems to be to create a sanitized Angola that will implicitly limit Soviet influence, leaving Mr. Nujoma with Namibia's long-standing and near-total economic dependence on South Africa which, in turn, may be a moderating factor. While South Africa's military forces are obliged to regroup on their own borders rather than on Namibia's to defend the Afrikaner homeland, Mr. Nujoma will be far less ready to accept Moscow-supported black South African guerrillas seeking to penetrate the Laager.

The Only Force Able to 'Deliver'

The United States insistence is that, ultimately, the players in the Namibia conflict can look to no other power than the United States because it is the only force capable of "delivering" South Africa, a caveat being that Pretoria may not yet be ready to be delivered. If the American attitude seems ambivalent, Administration officials in black-ruled Africa assert equally that Washington's influence with South Africa is greatly exaggerated.

The black African attitudes are ambivalent too, for some of those who publicly endorse the Cuban presence in Angola as being necessary for the defense of the Marxist regime in Luanda have little private liking for the Soviet Union and its allies.

Vice President Bush has frequently expressed the Reagan Administration's abhorrence of the apartheid system in South Africa. Nevertheless, some radical black African nations contend that Washington's sense of its strategic interests outweighs such preoccupations to the extent that, by failing to confront South Africa now, it is limiting its potential influence later. The United States calculation, evidently, is that the likelihood of change in South Africa does not yet constitute an imperative.

ZIMBABWE IS A SUCCESS

Jeffrey Davidow

JEFFREY DAVIDOW, *a fellow at Harvard University's Center for International Affairs, is a U.S. Foreign Service officer. He was deputy chief of mission of the U.S. embassy in Zimbabwe, 1979-1982.*

The news from Zimbabwe has assumed a distressingly familiar African tone. Interethnic tensions leading to armed banditry confront a government intent on maintaining domestic security and on consolidating its hold on power by creating a one-party state. Zimbabwe's gloss of uniqueness appears to be wearing off, and it is becoming just another of those African countries whose actions Westerners dismiss with sorrow and self-satisfying compassion.

But this view of Zimbabwe distorts the real situation there. Zimbabwe's prospects, although clouded by problems that are largely the legacy of the country's long liberation struggle, remain bright. What happens there is of great importance to America. Zimbabwe's location in the center of southern Africa, a turbulent region that has not witnessed a year without war for nearly two decades, lends it a universally recognizable geopolitical significance. The economic and political currents of the region flow through and around Zimbabwe: racial tension in South Africa; Soviet and Cuban influence in Mozambique, Angola, and other countries of the area; the search for a Namibian settlement; and efforts toward economic cooperation among the region's black states.

In the future Zimbabwe's position as a regional power, and perhaps as a leader of Africa as a whole, will increase as it becomes more willing to focus beyond its pressing domestic problems and to exert itself on a larger stage. Zimbabwe's real and potential wealth will provide additional weight to its future geopolitical role. The country possesses two-thirds of the world's known reserves of metallurgical grade chromite and ranks among the top three in the production of chrysolite asbestos. Zimbabwe is the world's second largest producer of chrome and the fifth largest producer of gold. It mines 36 other minerals including nickel, platinum, copper, and coal.

Few countries have been obliged to carry as much symbolic weight as has Zimbabwe. For 15 years Rhodesia—Zimbabwe's name prior to independence in 1980—was the pre-eminent unfinished item on the agenda of decolonization. How countries treated Rhodesia was interpreted by other African states as a measure of commitment to the continent. A 1971 amendment sponsored by Senator Harry Byrd (I.-Virginia), permitted the importation of Rhodesian chrome into the United States between 1971 and 1977 in open violation of U.N. sanctions. Many in Africa and elsewhere viewed this legislation as a reflection of America's callous attitude about the issues of racism and colonialism.

Once Zimbabwe attained independence, its symbolic value changed but did not lessen. For the West the creation of a moderate, democratic, multiracial society in southern Africa assumed great importance for the potential example it could set for South Africa. It was hoped that such an outcome in Zimbabwe would encourage South Africa to move toward black rule in Namibia and away from rigid apartheid at home. Zimbabwe has served as a symbol of Africa's conflicts, its aspirations for self-determination, and now, its hopes. It is a heavy burden for one country to carry, and today's criticisms of Prime Minister Robert Mugabe's government are often expressions of disappointment from those whose high expectations have not yet been met. In reality, however, Zimbabwe in its first two years of independence has generally succeeded in building a new society without destroying the old economic base.

Mugabe Moves Forward

In 1979, when the Zimbabwean civil war was claiming 50 lives each day, any observer who would have dared to predict the Zimbabwe of 1982 would have been dismissed as a hopeless dreamer. Few could imagine former Prime Minister Ian Smith periodically rising in

5. THE THIRD WORLD

Parliament to criticize a government led by, of all people, Mugabe; an avowedly Marxist regime acknowledging the need for a private sector and nationalizing no industry without more than adequate compensation; or an ex-guerrilla government offering only moral encouragement to South African liberation groups and in some areas working out a rocky but reasonable relationship with Pretoria.

Independent Zimbabwe is a success. The Mugabe government has moved cautiously in its stated socialist ideology and goal of bringing about the national transformation promised by the liberation struggle. Most of the government's activities have been directed toward repairing the damage and destruction caused by the long war and pacifying the country by integrating the three armies that fought in the civil war—Mugabe's Zimbabwe African National Liberation Army, Joshua Nkomo's Zimbabwe People's Revolutionary Army, and the Rhodesian security forces—into one military organization. In addition, the Mugabe government has begun to redress the vast income and status disparities that exist between white and black by increasing minimum wages, opening positions to Africans in the civil service, and implementing programs on peasant agriculture and development of rural resources.

Despite Mugabe's socialist orientation, he has not changed many of the country's social and economic patterns of development:

• The government has made primary education free, resulting in more than doubling the number of African children attending elementary school and causing overcrowding. Nonetheless, as the third academic year after independence begins, the excellent government schools in Harare's posh northern suburbs remain nearly lily white.

• The need to turn over land to the peasants is proclaimed as an article of revolutionary faith, but the Mugabe government's land reform program moves at a careful pace dictated by a perceived need for detailed planning. Yet the number of white commercial farmers, who are the backbone of Zimbabwe's domestic and export crop producers, has actually increased since independence.

• Despite revolutionary ideology that would seem to mandate increased nationalization of the domestic industrial and commercial sectors, the government has not acted precipitously to pursue those goals and has accepted U.S. aid funneled through the private sector of the Zimbabwean economy.

The list continues, revealing a government struggling with itself every day, attempting to strike a balance between revolutionary theory and rhetoric and the exigencies of the real world. For the most part, Zimbabwe under Mugabe is moving forward with the tasks of national reconstruction and development in a manner that is heartening.

Yet not all is well in Zimbabwe. The economy is shaky. Its performance in the first two years of independence was impressive. Real growth reached 14 per cent in 1980 and 8 per cent in 1981 as industry increased production to meet the rising demand for consumer goods fueled by higher minimum wages. In 1982 growth will most likely fall to zero or even show a negative rate. Increased government spending for social programs and for the maintenance of the enormous Zimbabwean army has contributed greatly to inflation, a new phenomenon for a country isolated from international trends by sanctions and South African protection for nearly 15 years.

Although significant, Zimbabwe's economic troubles are not unique and in many ways resemble problems in many underdeveloped countries: Imports, in particular petroleum, cost too much; export prices have dropped; the creation of new jobs has not kept pace with population growth. Zimbabwe may, however, find itself in a better position than most countries over the long run. International sanctions against Rhodesia prompted the creation of a relatively well-diversified economy based on agriculture, mining, and manufacturing. When the Western economy recovers, Zimbabwe, led by its mineral exports, could rebound to its healthy performance levels of 1980-1981.

Zimbabwe's most pressing problems are political, or more precisely ethnic: how the majority Shonas—80 percent of the population—handle their relations with the country's two minority ethnic groups, the Matabeles and the whites. Few countries live as close to their past as does Zimbabwe. Indeed, only 90 years separate Cecil Rhodes's Pioneer Column from Mugabe's accession to power. The compression of modern Zimbabwean history into such a short period of time has added greater intensity to the country's existence and vastly complicated relations among ethnic groups.

The black majority interprets Mugabe's policy of reconciliation to mean that Smith, his supporters, and blacks who cooperated with his regime should not be victimized for their past actions; rather they should have the opportunity to lend their energies to Zimbabwe's development without special privilege or status. But that does not suffice for most whites. The white population, less than 3 per cent of the country's population, seeks constant reassurance that it is both protected and wanted by the Mugabe government. Mugabe has made efforts—speaking to white International Rotary clubs, appointing whites to his cabinet, preserving the relative sanctity of white schools—but his own history and black self-respect will allow him to go only so far.

Whites leave Zimbabwe for many reasons, but the most significant is a generalized sense of loss of power, of insecurity about their role in the new society and the prospects for their children. The large number of whites who have left since Mugabe came to power—roughly 50,000—is countered by the estimated 150,000 who have opted to stay for the present. More would leave if Mugabe relaxed the tight controls on the remittal of capital instituted by the Smith regime. But the prime minister has no intention of doing so, and thus whites and blacks hold each other hostage. Ultimately, the white-black problem will resolve itself as the white population stabilizes and feels more secure.

A more complex ethnic problem for the Mugabe government concerns the strained relations between the country's majority Shonas, represented by Mugabe, and the minority Matabeles, represented by Nkomo. Nkomo led a national protest movement in Rhodesia during the 1950s. By the early 1960s, however, Nkomo and his Zimbabwe African People's Union (ZAPU) were being challenged by more radical elements—including Mugabe—who formed the Zimbabwe African National Union (ZANU). Relations between the two liberation groups were further strained by heavy-handed and unsuccessful Soviet attempts to force Mugabe to accept Nkomo's leadership.

During the 1970s, ZAPU's rank and file became almost exclusively Matabele, although most of the senior officials were, and remain, Shonas. This fact was confirmed in the 1980 elections when ZAPU won only 20 seats, all in traditional Matabele areas, while Mugabe's ZANU swept 57 of the remaining 60 African seats, reflecting the much larger Shona population. After his poor electoral performance Nkomo refused Mugabe's offer of the country's presidency, fearing that accepting the apolitical, figurehead position would signal the end of his political aspirations and of his party. Nkomo later accepted a cabinet position in Mugabe's government, still maintaining that the Zimbabwean people would reject ZANU for ZAPU in the 1985 parliamentary elections.

Many African countries, particularly those with newly established governments, have little tolerance for dissent. Thus far Mugabe has responded in a generally restrained manner, but Nkomo's political activities have added greater impetus to ZANU's call for a one-party state. The Mugabe government believes that such an action would limit the ability of political opponents to capitalize on ethnic and other social tensions. One-party statism, which has shown itself to be a dismal failure elsewhere in Africa, will undoubtedly come to Zimbabwe although probably not before the next general elections. A persistent siege mentality that is in part a holdover from the understandable need for self-preservation while fighting a guerrilla war has conditioned the response to Nkomo's challenge. Significant acts of sabotage—launched from South Africa, the Zimbabweans think—such as the bombing of ZANU's Harare headquarters and the national army's main ammunition depot have increased ZANU fears.

The early 1982 discovery of large ZAPU arms caches reinforced this sense of threat and suspicion of Nkomo's intentions and led to his ouster from the cabinet and the subsequent desertion from the unified army of a significant though still small percentage of former ZAPU military. Since the discovery of the caches Mugabe has maneuvered skillfully, asserting at every opportunity that he seeks only to punish lawbreakers, not ZAPU, the former ZAPU military in the national army, or the Matabele people. But he has sought to discredit Nkomo as a political leader and to split ZAPU, offering cabinet positions to known Nkomo critics and to others within ZAPU who seek to maintain the image and possibly the reality of national unity. The strategy has done little to lessen Nkomo's popularity among the Matabele.

As ex-guerrillas themselves the ZANU leadership recognizes the importance of not alienating the Matabele population of Zimbabwe's southwest where the armed dissidents operate. In practice, however, the Zimbabwean government is finding it difficult to combat the insurgents while maintaining the support of a local population firmly linked by blood, language, and political affinities to the rebels who operate within their midst. Numerous incidents of security force brutality have been reported and many more have gone unnoticed by the press and independent observers. The Zimbabwean government's insistence on maintaining political stability has resulted in an unfortunate disregard for human rights.

A troubled relationship with South Africa is

in some ways Zimbabwe's most complicated problem. The inevitable ideological differences that exist between a state committed to African liberation and another state equally committed to continued white minority rule have prompted the friction between the two countries. The tension is magnified by blocked channels of communication, lack of mutual trust, unwillingness or inability on each side to enunciate clearly what it expects from the other and the price it is willing to pay for better relations, and finally the almost total South African advantage in power, size, and geographic position.

By the end of the Smith regime, Rhodesia's economic dependence on South Africa had deepened to the point where for all practical purposes the smaller state had become an appendage of its neighbor. South Africa was Rhodesia's leading export market, offering preferential tariff rates and providing 30 per cent of Rhodesian imports. With the closing of Mozambican railways and harbors to Rhodesia after the accession to power of Frelimo—the Mozambican ruling party—nearly 100 per cent of the Smith regime's exports and imports not destined to or emanating from South Africa had to pass through South African ports.

During his first days in office Mugabe publicly agreed to honor the Smith regime's debts to South Africa and to maintain commercial relations with Pretoria. He ruled out diplomatic contacts, although the South African government continues to maintain a sizable "trade representative" office in Harare. In an effort to lessen its dependence on South Africa, Zimbabwe has been a moving force in the newly created Southern African Development Coordinating Conference—SADCC—which seeks to promote economic cooperation among the black states of the region. Zimbabwe has also diverted some of its trade through the Mozambican ports of Beira and Maputo. But that country's railways and ports are in serious decay and subject to sabotage, as is the recently reopened oil pipeline from Beira to the Zimbabwe border city of Mutare. As a result, Zimbabwe will remain heavily dependent on South Africa for its lifelines to the world for the indefinite future.

If Zimbabwe wants to decrease South Africa's economic and political leverage, Pretoria obviously seeks the opposite. South Africa intends to use its power to draw Zimbabwe into an open political relationship. The Zimbabwean government has steadfastly refused to take the bait.

Zimbabwe's new leaders recognize South Africa's strategic concerns and realize the great harm South Africa could inflict upon their country should Zimbabwean moral support for South African blacks turn into more concrete assistance. Zimbabwean officials are outspoken in their condemnations of apartheid in the Organization of African Unity and other forums. In reality, however, their position is notably restrained. Thus far, the Mugabe government has refused to allow guerrillas from the African National Congress and the Pan African Congress to use Zimbabwe as a base for guerrilla raids into South Africa. Official status has yet to be accorded to the South African liberation movement offices in Harare.

The Mugabe government believes that South Africa is intent on subversion and destabilization. Zimbabweans witness South African troops operating in Angola and South Africa's support for the armed resistance movement in Mozambique and feel threatened themselves. Incidents of sabotage and a suspected South African military presence within Zimbabwe, as evidenced by the September 1982 killing of three active duty South African soldiers in Zimbabwean territory, reinforce the sense of threat from the south.

In meeting the challenge of maintaining a stable relationship with South Africa, the Zimbabwean government has demonstrated qualities of leadership and management that bode well for the future. The recent railway crisis provides a good example. In early 1981 South African Railways informed its Zimbabwean counterpart that it would not be able to renew the lease on 25 locomotives on loan to the Zimbabwean railways. The situation was critical. The loss of skilled white manpower from the railways had already impeded Zimbabwe's ability to keep its aging locomotive fleet on the tracks at just the time when a bumper maize crop as well as other products needed transport. In response Mugabe used Canadian and American aid to order 60 new locomotives and recruited technicians from India and Pakistan to train Africans and to refurbish several older but still usable steam locomotives. The government also entered into quiet negotiations at the senior civil servant level with the South Africans to repair the damage. Ultimately an arrangement was made in which South African Railways increased the number of its locomotives on loan to Botswana and Zambia, freeing up other locomotives from these countries' lines for use within Zimbabwe.

Zimbabwe's effective handling of the railway crisis gives some hope that it can resolve its other difficulties with South Africa and its economic and ethnic problems at home in a similarly pragmatic manner. Zimbabweans themselves must confront these problems, but outside assistance, particularly from the United States, will remain important.

America and Zimbabwe

U.S. policy toward Zimbabwe since 1976 has produced one of America's few clear-cut foreign policy successes in recent years, one for which both Republican and Democratic administrations can rightfully claim credit. The failed U.S. gamble in Angola in 1975 and a perceived need to block further Soviet penetration in southern Africa drew former Secretary of State Henry Kissinger's attention to Rhodesia. The Kissinger initiative ended with the failed Geneva conference of October-December 1976. In retrospect, Smith's acceptance for the first time of the principle of majority rule, an integral element of the Kissinger package, was the beginning of the end for white rule.

The Carter administration altered the Kissinger approach considerably, eliminating both a heavy reliance on the prospect of South African good will to bring Smith along and the willingness to reward South Africa for doing so. This policy was replaced with a more cooperative attitude toward the African Front Line states—Angola, Botswana, Mozambique, Tanzania, Zambia—and the liberation groups. Policy makers in the Carter administration viewed a Rhodesian settlement as a cornerstone of the president's human rights policy.

One element of U.S. policy that remained a constant from 1976 onward was a pledge of substantial U.S. financial support to ease the transition to majority rule. The United States was first to sign a formal aid agreement with Zimbabwe, on its independence day. However, U.S. budgetary problems later complicated efforts to supply Zimbabwe with the promised funds and prompted some Zimbabwean ministers to ask where the "Kissinger billions" were. The situation improved toward the end of the Carter administration with the arrival of more aid in fiscal year 1981.

Suspicions of the Reagan administration were intense in Zimbabwe as they were elsewhere in Africa in the first months of 1981. The president's unfortunate remark referring to South Africa as an unforgettable ally in two world wars was continually reiterated to American officials and journalists as evidence of the new administration's intention to turn its back on black Africa. The response of the new policy makers in Washington surprised and relieved the Zimbabweans. In resubmitting Carter's 1982 budget to Congress, the Reagan administration did not slash the $75 million in aid for Zimbabwe initially requested. In addition, at the March 1981 Zimbabwe Conference on Reconstruction and Development (ZIMCORD) in Harare, the United States pledged similar levels of assistance for the following two fiscal years. The Zimbabwean government itself organized ZIMCORD, which succeeded in taking advantage of the good will the new state enjoyed in the international community. The Zimbabweans' appeal for approximately $2 billion in aid over a three-year period was exceeded by a small amount.

America has made the largest and most significant contribution of any country to Zimbabwe's reconstruction and development, with the possible exception of Great Britain. By 1984 U.S. financial assistance to Zimbabwe will total over $400 million, placing Zimbabwe among the largest recipients of U.S. aid in sub-Saharan Africa.

Critics have argued that the United States receives too little in return for its massive aid program. They point to Zimbabwe's voting record in the U.N.—almost always in opposition to the United States—or note its unwillingness to sign an investment agreement with the United States. In their desire to see every dollar of aid turned into immediately usable leverage, these critics lack a basic understanding of what is happening in Zimbabwe today. Zimbabwe is still in its formative stage and offers opportunities for U.S. influence in its political and economic development. Further, the openly cooperative approach adopted by the United States and the West has already produced benefits, some more tangible than others but all consistent with the West's objective of helping to create a Zimbabwe that provides stability in southern Africa. Some examples are:

> The Mugabe government has consistently turned toward the West for its commerce, maintaining markets open for Western products and assuring continued access to Zimbabwe's considerable natural resources.

> Zimbabwe's suspicion of American designs in the region have diminished, although not entirely disappeared, enabling Zimbabwe to play a helpful role in the search for a Namibian settlement.

> Mugabe's own proclivities, based on his experience during the liberation struggle, to freeze the Soviets out of any meaningful role in Zimbabwe have been reinforced.

5. THE THIRD WORLD

> By avoiding the economic and political chaos many South Africans assumed would be inevitable upon the advent of majority rule, the Mugabe government has helped create a climate in which the South African government can, if it so wishes, contemplate an internationally approved settlement for Namibia.

> A prosperous, Western-assisted Zimbabwe provides an economic core for neighboring black states needing access to Zimbabwe's agricultural and manufacturing surplus.

Not everyone would agree that these benefits have been fully demonstrated, but few could persuasively argue that the developments in Zimbabwe since independence have not been advantageous for Zimbabwe itself, for the region, and for Western interests.

Future U.S. Policy

The attitudes and actions of the Carter and Reagan administrations toward Zimbabwe have been constructive and efficacious. The following are suggested policy guidelines for the coming years:

• *Respect U.S. aid commitments.* Reneging on a commitment is hardly the best way to demonstrate American interest and constancy in international affairs. Further, observers continue to believe that $1 of assistance spent in Zimbabwe provides greater developmental return than $1 utilized in almost any other recipient country in Africa.

• *Intercede with South Africa.* The Zimbabwean government overestimates the influence the Reagan administration has on the government of South Africa, which in Zimbabwe's view is its single most dangerous enemy. Nevertheless, America's current policy of "constructive engagement" gives the United States increased opportunity—some would argue obligation—to let Pretoria know that Washington believes that it is in South Africa's own best interest, as well as that of the United States, to allow Zimbabwe to progress without further threat of destabilization.

• *Maintain a policy dialogue.* The Mugabe government neither seeks nor particularly welcomes advice. However, it is possible to engage the government in serious dialogue that might influence its decisions. Zimbabwe's acceptance of the U.S. private sector aid program—not necessarily an easy path to take for a socialist government—and the reversal of its vote in the

U.N. from abstention to affirmation on the resolution calling for the withdrawal of foreign troops from Afghanistan, for example, were both decided upon after reasoned and repeated approaches from U.S. officials.

• *Continue the search for a Namibian settlement.* The Zimbabweans are critical of American insistence on linkage between Cuban troop withdrawal from Angola and U.S. progress toward Namibian independence. However, Zimbabwe recognizes the importance and good will in the effort by the Contact Group—Canada, France, Great Britain, the United States, and West Germany—to arrive at a peaceful Namibian settlement. Whatever setbacks may confront the current negotiations, the effort should not be abandoned.

• *Bolster shared principles.* Many of the essential principles upon which the Zimbabwean government remains based—respect for human rights and related values and modes of conduct—are those that the United States also prizes. While appreciating the threats, real or perceived, to Zimbabwe's security, Americans should nevertheless encourage Zimbabwe to adhere to democratic practices and to avoid governmental abuses of power.

• *Promote investment.* The Zimbabwean government recognizes the country's critical need for investment. Regrettably, it has not yet followed up the recognition with a coherent program to attract the needed capital. Zimbabwe's leaders must realize that they compete with scores of other countries for investment dollars, francs, or pounds; a more aggressive approach is essential. In particular, the Zimbabweans will have to revamp their thinking and sign investment agreements, such as the Overseas Private Investment Corporation (OPIC) agreement the United States has been pushing and similar agreements other countries have proffered.

The H.J. Heinz Company's recent major investment in Zimbabwe may signal the end of the disappointingly low level of foreign investment since independence. The United States should continue to urge Zimbabweans to take another look at OPIC. The United States can also set the stage for further foreign investment by promoting trade and investment delegations, by providing Commerce and State Department briefings to interested businessmen, and by encouraging Zimbabweans themselves to make additional approaches to the American business community.

138

• *Recognize the limits*. Zimbabweans are grateful for the American support they have received, but their revolutionary mentality that tends to view the capitalist world as a potential obstacle rather than as an ally on the road to social justice will not be easily overcome. In this regard it is wise not to wave red flags at the bull of Zimbabwe's rampaging nationalism. Simply stated, threats—implied or real—will have even less chance of obtaining the desired actions from Zimbabwe than from other states.

The United States will not have clear sailing in southern Africa until South Africa's racial policies and the West's relations with Pretoria recede as international issues—probably a fairly long time. But even given these constraints, it is still possible for the United States to deepen a workable and amicable relationship with Africa's newest state to the benefit of both.

Sino-American Relations: Reaching a Plateau

JOHN F. COPPER

John Franklin Copper, Associate Professor of International Studies, Southwestern University, lived in Asia for more than 10 years, and is the author of China's Global Role: An Analysis of Peking's National Power Capabilities in the Context of an Evolving International System *(Stanford: Hoover Institution Press, 1980), and* China's Foreign Aid: An Instrument of Peking's Foreign Policy *(Lexington, Mass.: Lexington Books, 1976).*

IN the spring of 1982, almost ten years to the month after the so-called turning point in Sino-American relations—the signing of the Shanghai Communiqué—the period of improving relations between the United States and the People's Republic of China was apparently ending or reversing course.[1] The "Taiwan question" was at the center of the disagreement between Washington and Beijing, and both sides agreed that this was the one issue that had not been resolved during the past decade. But it is clear that the changing course in relations between the two countries cannot be explained by looking only at the last several months or, at this single issue.

United States-China relations had begun to improve almost 15 years earlier, in 1969, when United States President Richard Nixon announced in a speech at Guam (later to become known as the Nixon Doctrine) that the United States planned to withdraw from Asia militarily and that the United States was seeking improved relations with the People's Republic of China. At the time, Chinese leaders were battling the Soviet Union on their border in what amounted to a conventional war. During the fighting, Soviet military leaders advocated "taking out" Chinese atomic weapons production sites and missile emplacements or invading the Chinese capital. It was not surprising that China's leaders began to look to the only other world power that might offset the Soviet threat.[2]

A United States tilted toward China apparently helped to defuse the crisis. Washington subsequently persuaded the United Nations to admit China (or at least did not prevent this action). Beijing responded by trying to help the United States withdraw from Vietnam "with honor." Clearly, a new relationship between Washington and Beijing had been established.

In early 1972, President Nixon visited China and signed the document which was later called the "turning point." But the Shanghai Communiqué was clearly ambiguous on one major point, the issue of Taiwan. It noted that the Chinese on "either" side of the Taiwan Strait agreed that there is only one China. The context suggested that the United States assumed that both the People's Republic and the Republic of China (Taiwan) concurred on the situation; yet the use of the word "either" suggested just the opposite. The fact that the United States "did not challenge" the Chinese view that Taiwan is part of China also hinted that the two sides did not concur.[3]

In the next few years, trade, cultural exchanges, tourism, scientific and technology exchanges flourished. In the mid-1970's, however, the euphoria was dampened to a considerable extent by domestic problems in both countries: Watergate in the United States, which was followed by a non-elected President; the death of Chairman Mao Zedong in China, followed by the rise and fall of the "gang of four."

When Jimmy Carter became President, he seemed to have no special interest in pursuing markedly better relations with China, but in late 1978, he suddenly decided to grant diplomatic recognition to the People's Republic. In the process, he agreed to terminate the United States–Republic of China defense treaty with Taipei, to withdraw American troops from Taiwan and to withdraw recognition from the Republic of China.[4] He also agreed without equivocation that there was only one government of China and that Taiwan was part of China.

The timing of President Carter's move—a fortnight before Christmas when Congress was in recess—was patently designed to avoid public or congressional input. Early in 1979, however, Congress passed the Taiwan Relations Act, which gave Taipei the right to use United States courts and to be represented in the United States, and granted it most favored nation status. This action, in essence, returned sovereignty to Taiwan. Furthermore, by stating that the United States would sell Taiwan sufficient weapons for its defense needs, Congress apparently also gave Taiwan the means to preserve its sovereignty.

Both President Carter and Chinese First Deputy Premier Deng Xiaoping subsequently chose the joint recognition communiqué as the basis for United States-China relations, ignoring the Taiwan Relations Act. Beijing protested the act, but neither loudly nor repeatedly. Deng visited the United States in January, 1979—he was the first high-level Chinese leader to see Washington—and was given a reception suitable for the visiting head-of-state of an important country. He was followed by other Chinese leaders, and within a few months four members of the Carter Cabinet made the trek to Beijing. In August, Vice-President Walter Mondale joined the long list of United States officials visiting the Middle Kingdom.

In January, 1980, after the Soviet invasion of Afghanistan, Defense Secretary Harold Brown visited Beijing and hinted of United States-China military cooperation. A few months later his counterpart, Geng Biao, vice chairman of China's Military Affairs Commission, visited Washington. Again United States weapons deliveries to China were discussed. Meanwhile, Congress passed a United States-China Trade Agreement, which went into effect in February, 1980, giving China most favored nation status.

Of tangential but not inconsiderable importance were other kinds of "progress" in United States-China relations. During 1979, United States-China trade doubled. That same year 40,000 American tourists visited China, many of them reporting after they returned that they were accorded special treatment that in some ways resembled the unequal situation during the "imperialism" of the last century and that they were isolated from the masses and discouraged from making friends or establishing personal relationships. Meanwhile, 2,500 Chinese students came to the United States to study, most of them unprepared for either American life or academic work.[5]

It was in this context that Ronald Reagan campaigned for the presidency and won. President Reagan specifically stated during the campaign that he was not in agreement with the Carter administration's China policy and that he supported the Taiwan Relations Act. He declared that if elected he would upgrade United States relations with Taiwan. These statements, plus the fact that Taiwan representatives were invited to his inauguration, seemed to indicate that an immediate reversal in United States-China relations was pending.

However, once in office President Reagan notified Beijing that he wanted to continue close ties with Beijing. The first foreign ambassador to be given an official audience with President Reagan was Chai Zemin, the ambassador from China. The President also declared that relations with Taiwan would continue to be conducted on an "unofficial" basis.

In subsequent months, United States relations with China were friendly and probably improved. President Reagan publicly expressed his commitment to the normalization agreement and said little about the Taiwan Relations Act. He sent former President Gerald Ford to China in March, 1981. In June, Secretary of State Alexander Haig visited Beijing, announcing that the United States was willing to sell offensive weapons to China. This was regarded by most observers as a major change in United States policy.

During this same period, three new Chinese consulates were opened in the United States, the issue of taxation was settled, the sale of a large computer was negotiated and a joint commission on trade was established. Intelligence information on Cambodia and Afghanistan was exchanged, and (underscoring the "partnership" against the Soviet Union) it was revealed that a United States-equipped listening post had been set up in China to monitor Soviet missile tests. Meanwhile, $500-million worth of arms sales to Taiwan were held in abeyance, as was the sale of advanced fighter planes that Taipei had been seeking for some time.[6]

PROBLEMS AND DISAPPOINTMENTS

Nonetheless, behind the facade of cordiality and agreement on global issues, there were several problems. Taiwan, of course, was one. It had not been given favorable treatment by the Reagan administration; Taipei had apparently been "put on hold," although it attracted considerable support from members of the administration and the American public.

In addition, many American businessmen were disappointed in their contacts with China. False expectations were partially responsible. But the government of China also caused difficulties. It gave many business contracts to Japanese companies instead of American companies and, in many cases, it tried to take advantage of American companies. At the same time, Americans feared that China was invading the textile and small manufacturing goods market in the United States, which might eventually exacerbate American unemployment, even though the trade balance remained in favor of the United States.

China also noticeably failed to support the policies of the new administration toward the third world. At Cancún in October, 1981, the first real signs of disagreement on an international issue of importance emerged. President Reagan and Chinese Premier Zhao Ziyang held separate discussions at the meeting, and the President was apparently not happy with the tenor or the substance of the talks.[7] Some of his advisers later noted that China should not expect "aid" from the United States while it preached to third world countries about Western "imperialism" and cleavages between the third world and the West.

The most important issue in Washington, however, was the United States strategic alignment with China or, as the cliché went, "playing the China card."[8] But Washington also found its "alliance" with China against the Soviet Union wanting in several respects. In Southeast Asia, China's tough stance alienated several United States friends and allies. Regarding Afghanistan, China was able to do very little to challenge the Soviet presence and limited its help to sending small arms to Afghan rebel forces through Pakistan. In the case of Poland, China was willing to criticize Soviet policy, but it was unwilling to support Solidarity, fearing that such support might encourage a labor movement at home.

American policymakers were disappointed in the China "alliance." And they began to believe that China needed the United States much more than the United States needed China. It was widely believed, further, that the Chinese would not return to the Soviet camp;

Western trade, technology and capital were too important. Soviet leaders would not trust China and would not welcome it back into the fold until China apologized and demonstrated its loyalty. Chinese leaders apparently had a vested interest in Sino-Soviet hostilities; in the event of a significant rapprochement a leadership shakeup in Beijing would bring new leaders into positions of power. Finally, China would be an economic burden to the Soviet Union. The truth of these judgments is hardly in question; yet Washington did not fully understand the constraints the Chinese leadership felt or its attitude on several issues, most important, Taiwan.

CHINA'S PROBLEMS

In 1978, when the Carter administration had agreed to accept China's three conditions for normalization—the withdrawal of American forces from Taiwan, the cancellation of the United States–Republic of China Defense Treaty and an end to diplomatic relations with Taipei—Deng was pleased about the progress he had made in United States–China relations. And he publicized his accomplishments to bolster support for his economic programs and his leadership.

At the same time, Deng chose to ignore certain problems. He was not pleased about President Carter's arms sales policies, including sales to Taiwan. He was also less than enthusiastic about the Carter administration's human rights campaign and its generally vacillating and weak foreign policy. In early 1979, when China invaded Vietnam in order to "teach Hanoi a lesson," Deng may have expected American support of some kind. Instead, the Carter administration expressed regret about the war and hoped that it would soon end.[9]

Deng also noted that the United States expected China to support American attitudes in Southeast Asia and toward the Soviet invasion of Afghanistan while it displayed little resolve itself in dealing with these problem areas. China, in fact, may have seen itself as implementing United States policy in Southeast Asia. Regarding Afghanistan, because of the logistics and the nature of the situation, China had to follow the United States lead. Meanwhile, Washington's anti-Soviet efforts were undermined by its weak policies vis-à-vis the Kremlin in Europe.

By 1980, Deng also faced the fact that his modernization program was not proceeding as quickly as he had promised and that many projects had to be scrapped. China's war against Vietnam had been expensive, and Deng was presented with demands for budget allocations from the military that would impede his economic development plans.[10] Meanwhile, the public, given a taste of consumer goods, wanted more. In short, Deng had made promises that he could not keep and had raised expectations that were being deflated. He had alienated the military to

a considerable extent and still had to contend with former supporters of Mao and the "gang of four."

In this context, in 1981 Deng had to build a new relationship with a new United States administration. On trade, technology and other issues Deng had no cause for disappointment, yet his expectations may have been too high. Chinese leaders were not pleased with the President's stance on the issue of Taiwan, but they were pleased with the tough American stand toward the Soviet Union. Still, they may have expected too much. Deng spoke of a "united front," comprised of the United States, West Europe, Japan and China, to stop Soviet "hegemonism."[11] But while President Reagan pressured Japan to spend more on defense, made every effort to preserve Western unity, and apparently wanted to "play the China card" against the Kremlin (thus cooperating with the Chinese "united front" strategy), he also wanted (or needed) to improve relations with the Soviet Union.

Viewed another way, Chinese leaders had cause to be apprehensive about their reliance upon the United States, which had already undermined Chinese independence in foreign policy, especially toward the third world. The United States offered weapons but placed limits on its military and other help to China—just as the Soviet Union had done during the 1950's (though admittedly the United States seemed more generous). In short, efforts by China to align itself with the United States carried some undesirable burdens and some costs.

Deng also had to contend with the foreign influence that accompanied both improved relations and the efforts to attract foreign capital. While not predisposed to dislike Americans or most other Westerners, the Chinese were irritated by the fact that special privileges were extended to foreigners. This harked back to the days of foreign imperialism and was an issue Deng's opponents were quick to exploit.

In addition, Deng had overextended himself politically: reducing the military budget, purging the top leadership of former pro-Mao leaders, and purging the bureaucracy. In so doing he created new opposition. This may explain why he never promoted himself to a top position in either the party or the government even though he was clearly running both. It may also explain official statements during early 1982 concerning his retirement and his intent to relinquish power to younger leaders.

THE TAIWAN ISSUE

With regard to Sino-American relations, the Taiwan issue was the easiest for Deng's opposition to exploit. Thus, beginning in 1981, Beijing began to make an issue of Taiwan's sovereignty. It was not clear whether the normalization agreement (which conceded China sovereignty over Taiwan) was the foundation of American policy, or whether the Taiwan Relations Act (which regarded Taiwan as sovereign) was the foundation. Making an issue of this reflected Deng's need to take a tough stand toward the United States to ward off his critics.

The importance of the Taiwan problem was underscored by the fact that in October, 1981, China made apparently generous offers on unification to Taipei, which were refused out of hand. Furthermore, Beijing could argue justifiably that Taipei did not need additional weapons in view of the fact that China had withdrawn many of its forces from the province adjacent to Taiwan as a peaceful gesture, although Beijing withdrew because it needed additional forces on the Sino-Soviet border and the Sino-Vietnamese border.

Thus when the Reagan administration made the decision to sell spare parts to Taiwan in January, 1982, Beijing responded with a threat to downgrade relations with the United States. Beijing made it plain to the Reagan administration that the United States sale of spare parts to Taiwan was illegal. Yet Deng did not seem prepared to carry out his threats. His policies seemed geared to his opposition, which was making an issue of Taiwan. Or Deng was bluffing. In any event, by mid-1982 the crisis in United States-China relations had apparently passed.

CHANGING U.S. GOALS

There has been a certain inevitability in the cooling of United States-China relations, if only because of the nature of international politics. One can argue that both sides were unrealistic or at least held inaccurate perceptions about what each nation could expect of the other. Finally, there was the factor of euphoria: when enemies become friends, euphoria often leads to false hopes.

Clearly, Taiwan was not the issue that caused the crisis.[13] The real impediment to a closer relationship between the United States and China was and is the relationship between the United States and the Soviet Union. As United States-China relations improved, the United States could not resist using China as leverage against the Soviet Union, and the Chinese were certainly willing to be so used. This was especially true in the context of declining United States defense spending and a marked increase in the Soviet military budget. But Washington also knew that it had to deal with the Soviet Union separately and that United States-Soviet relations were of a different order of priority: the Soviet Union could destroy the United States with its nuclear arsenal; China could not.

This meant that ultimately the China card had to be played and China had to be "used" to promote better relations with the Soviet Union. This was made more imperative because of the Reagan administration's tough stand toward the Kremlin and its prompt efforts to redress the military balance at the cost of social programs and economic stability at home. Moscow contributed to this pressure through its successful anti-nuclear war propaganda in Europe and elsewhere.

One must also be reminded of the fact that the United States tilt toward China in 1969, when a conflict between Moscow and Beijing seemed in danger of escalating, may have prevented a war. The same cannot be said of United States-China relations now. In fact, it can be argued that the United States cannot be as tough toward the Soviet Union as China would like—lest this lead to a United States-Soviet war. To argue that China could offset the huge Soviet military buildup would reflect a premature view of multipolarity in global strategic relations and would represent a gross overestimation of China's military power. In this context, it is noteworthy that China's defense budget has been cut markedly twice in two years.

Further, United States allies are questioning Washington's relations with China. European leaders have often subtly suggested to the United States that America cannot be as militant as China would like, that it cannot be dragged into war by China, and that United States foreign policy cannot be dictated by Beijing. Washington's Southeast Asian allies have also criticized United States-China cooperation in Southeast Asia. Several countries in the region are more fearful of Chinese than of Soviet and Vietnamese influence.

Many third world countries are also concerned about the increase in United States "aid" to China in the form of advantageous trade relationships, underpriced or free technology, and credits. This is particularly true in the context of America's declining ability to grant economic assistance and trade concessions. In short, third world countries are fearful that United States-China relations will improve at their expense.

On the Chinese side there are also problems. Again, the most important is the Soviet Union. Chinese leaders are fully aware that the United States may want or need to sacrifice relations with China in order to improve relations with the Kremlin. In fact, it may be that Deng made his demands on the Taiwan issue because of this perception, thinking that once the China card is played his bargaining position will be lost or weakened. The Kremlin's foreign policy ventures seem to be exacting a heavy burden, making it more likely that Moscow will be willing to come to terms with the United States. Finally, Chinese leaders remember their past dependence on the Soviet Union and the problems that caused. The Chinese People's Liberation Army seems open now to offers of military assistance from the United States. Building such a relationship could—as it did in the past—cause problems for the Chinese leadership.

China also has a problem in terms of its relations with third world countries. Beijing already sacrificed to some considerable degree its leadership role among the more anti-status quo third world countries when

143

5. THE THIRD WORLD

it accepted a Sino-American relationship. The question now arises: is China simply to follow United States policy vis-a-vis the third world? If so, China will no longer have any basis for an independent foreign policy and thus for an important global role. China's leadership of the third world countries is the only claim China has to prominence in international politics.

The sudden opening of China to foreign influence, which seems to have been required in the pursuit of better relations with the United States, likewise seems to constitute a continuous worry. Xenophobia is still latent in China, and the leadership's opponents can take advantage of this, especially if xenophobia parallels unfulfilled expectations in terms of economic progress and material rewards.

CONCLUSION

In conclusion, while it seems unlikely that United States-China relations will deteriorate seriously, it also appears that the trend from friendship, to alignment, to alliance has ended and that the near future will be characterized more by friendship and alignment than alliance. Trade and cultural relations will probably continue to improve, while strategic relations will be frozen. Trade and other commercial relations have been little affected by disagreements between Washington and Beijing. In fact, foreign oil exploration—mostly American—has proceeded ahead of schedule, and two-way trade continues to increase. Neither side would like to see relations deteriorate; nor would either side want to resume the kind of relationship they had during the 1950's. Relations have improved and mutual interests are being served. Yet it is unreasonable to think that this relationship can continue to improve, or that it should do so.

NOTES

[1] In February, 1982, President Reagan and Premier Zhao Ziyang exchanged letters commemorating the tenth anniversary of the signing of the Shanghai Communiqué. The tenor of the letters was proper and seemed cool to some observers.

[2] See Harold C. Hinton, *The Sino-Soviet Confrontation: Implications for the Future* (New York: Crane, Russak and Company, Inc., 1976), chapter 3.

[3] See John F. Copper, "Reassessing the Shanghai Communiqué," *The Asian Wall Street Journal*, December 27, 1977.

[4] See William R. Kintner and John F. Copper, *A Matter of Two Chinas: The China-Taiwan Issue in U.S. Foreign Policy* (Philadelphia: Foreign Policy Research Institute, 1979).

[5] For a background summary of U.S.-China relations during the 1970's, see John Bryan Starr, ed., *The Future of U.S.-China Relations* (New York: New York University Press, 1981), introduction.

[6] This figure is based on the average amount of arms sold to Taiwan during several previous fiscal years. It should be noted in this context that President Carter resumed arms sales to Taiwan after a one-year moratorium following "normalization," during which time the United States-Republic of China defense treaty remained in force; and he rejected Beijing's pressure to discontinue such sales. A more advanced fighter plane would probably also have been included in these sales had it not been for domestic issues in the United States.

[7] David Bonavia, "Rich Man, Poor Man," *Far Eastern Economic Review*, October 30, 1981.

[8] Many Americans regarded United States-China ties as a marriage of convenience, to enable the United States to close the strategic gap and catch up with the Soviet Union. The alternative was to reach an arms agreement with the Soviet Union. And there was considerable pressure from European allies and the American public to do this.

[9] See Drew Middleton, "U.S. Policy Toward Moscow and Beijing in an Era of Declining Détente," in Douglas T. Stuart and William T. Tow, eds., *China, The Soviet Union and the West: Strategic and Political Dimensions in the 1980's* (Boulder, Colorado: Westview Press, 1982), p. 243.

[10] Lowell Dittmer, "China in 1980: Modernization and Its Discontents," *Asian Survey*, January, 1981.

[11] See John F. Copper, "China's Global Strategy," *Current History*, September, 1981.

[12] Most Americans regarded the sale (limited to spare parts) and the continuing agreement to coproduce the F-5E fighter aircraft as concessions to Beijing. But in any event, American pressure groups were organizing in reaction to Washington's treatment of Taiwan, and the issue could no longer be delayed.

[13] Nonetheless, the Taiwan issue is a matter on which the United States cannot capitulate. The administration has made every effort to defuse statements the President made during the campaign, especially with regard to upgrading relations with Taiwan. But no United States administration can consider abandoning Taiwan completely, because Taiwan has too much support in the United States. Nor can a United States President ignore the wishes of 18 million people—more than 99 percent of whom do not want to be "incorporated" by the People's Republic of China. Any President seeking to enforce a one-China policy would also endanger his relationship with Congress.

144

The Strategic Significance of South Asia

ZALMAY KHALILZAD

Zalmay Khalilzad is Assistant Professor of Political Science and a member of the Institute of War and Peace Studies at Columbia University. He is the author of a monograph, Return of the Great Game: Superpower Rivalry and Internal Turmoil in Afghanistan, Iran, Pakistan, and Turkey. *His articles on regional politics in Southwest Asia and international security issues have appeared in scholarly journals.*

SOUTH ASIA is in an era of historic transformation, facing multiple and interactive threats. These include the Soviet invasion of Afghanistan and the possibility that the Russian-Afghan war may spread to Pakistan; the regional rivalries and conflicts between India and Pakistan, including the possibility of a "nuclear crawl" between them; internal instabilities caused by crises of social justice, political participation and national integration; and renewed and intensified superpower competition. Although the role of the superpowers in the area is likely to remain impressive, their relations with the countries of the region are inherently unstable.

The Soviet Union has important interests in South Asia. The region has been the object of its sustained interest since the mid-1950's, not only because of the territorial contiguity of the region to the Soviet Union, but also in the context of Moscow's competition for influence with China and the United States. Moscow has approached its rivalry with China and the United States in the area as a zero-sum game. In the 1950's, as the West sought close anti-Soviet and anti-Chinese allies, Moscow took advantage of Indian and Afghan hostility toward Pakistan and developed friendly relations with both countries.

Moscow's break with China significantly increased the importance of India in Soviet calculations. The Sino-Indian war of 1962 was followed by Moscow's increased importance to New Delhi. Since the mid-1960's, India's desire to achieve regional domination in South Asia and to strengthen itself against China has coincided with the Soviet Union's anti-Chinese policies and its desire to pressure Pakistan, a country with close ties with both China and the United States. Moscow has continued to encourage Delhi to maintain a hard line against China. However, with the Soviet invasion of Afghanistan, a lively debate has developed in India about the future of Indo-Soviet relations.

In the case of Afghanistan, since 1955 Soviet policies appear, prima facie, paradoxical. The Afghan pattern may well be characteristic of Soviet policies toward small contiguous states. The Soviet Union's level of activity, including the military invasion of small countries on its borders, apparently increases as the ideology of such countries and the Soviet Union converges. This Soviet tendency has worrisome and instructive implications not only for Pakistan but also for Iran and Turkey. Although Soviet involvement in Afghanistan goes back many years, it increased substantially after April, 1978, when Khalq, a Marxist-Leninist group, carried out a coup.[1] The new government initiated radical changes in Afghanistan's external and internal policies. Externally, the new government moved decidedly closer to the Soviet Union. However, the Khalq government began to face large-scale internal opposition. Over time this opposition turned into a major anti-regime insurgency.

There have been many speculations about the reasons for the Soviet invasion. It is possible that those participating in the decision favored intervention for varying reasons. Nevertheless, on the pretext of an invitation from the regime that had allegedly overthrown the Khalqi government, the Soviet military entered the country in force. Whatever the Soviet motive, the invasion had far-reaching regional and global implications. It eliminated a buffer state and brought Soviet forces to the border of Pakistan, one of the major South Asian countries. It set a new precedent for the massive use of Soviet forces outside the Soviet satellite empire and was the first application of the Brezhnev Doctrine* outside East Europe. On the strategic level, the Soviet occupation has increased Soviet ability to project power to South Asia, the Arabian Sea and the Persian Gulf. With Afghan bases, the Arabian Sea and the Persian Gulf are within the range of Soviet tactical aircraft. This increased capability followed the great expansion of the Soviet navy in the Indian Ocean over the past 25 years.

Once in Afghanistan, Soviet leaders initiated a multipronged strategy for the pacification of the country. Efforts have been made to accommodate Islamic feelings; there has been a propaganda blitz to win support for the Soviet position both in Afghanistan and abroad; and blame for the Afghan crisis has been assigned to the Americans, the Chinese and the Pakistanis. Attempts have been made to harmonize relations between the two PDPA factions and to broaden the base of government through the formation of the National Fatherland Front, an umbrella organization representing the various elements of the population. Moscow is also trying to train hundreds of Afghans who are expected to help not only in maintaining law and order but in running the country. The Soviet-installed regime has also attempted to win popular support by undoing some of the "radical" policies of the previous government. Moscow has tried to build loyal armed forces to turn the Soviet-Afghan war into an Afghan-Afghan war. The Soviet military strategy apparently consists of holding major cities and highways and applying force intermittently against the area of resistance in the countryside. The Soviet strategy is aimed at minimizing Soviet loss of life, and Soviet leaders believe that in time they will either discourage the population from supporting the resistance or force dissidents to leave the country.[2] Moscow is also apparently counting on the international community to forget the Afghan crisis.

The Soviet strategy has not been successful so far, and Moscow is far from pacifying the country. Violent opposition to the occupation has spread. Several factors will play a critical role in determining whether Soviet leaders succeed in liquidating or neutralizing the Afghan partisans. These include the policies of Pakistan toward the insurgents, the extent of external support for Afghan partisans and refugees, the success or failure of Soviet attempts to convert divisions among the insurgents into open conflict, Soviet efforts to establish a government in Kabul that commands a large armed force and has a wide base of support, and the scope and duration of the Soviet military commitment.

---

*In 1968, following the Soviet invasion of Czechoslovakia, Soviet Premier Leonid Brezhnev declared the Soviet Union's inherent right to intervene in any "socialist" (Communist) country in order to preserve "socialism"; this statement is known as the Brezhnev Doctrine.

SOVIET POLICY IN PAKISTAN

Recognizing the importance of Pakistan in the Afghan conflict, Moscow has increased its attention to Pakistan. Soviet-Pakistani policies have traditionally been less than cordial. Pakistan's membership in Western alliances and its close relations with China have been a source of concern to the Soviet Union. In the 1960's and 1970's, Moscow encouraged Pakistan to weaken its ties with the People's Republic of China and the West and to follow the example of Afghanistan and India in pursuing a policy of Soviet-tilted neutrality. However, since the 1978 coup in Afghanistan, and especially since the 1979 invasion, the Soviet Union's desire to consolidate its position has led to a major deterioration in its relations with Pakistan. Pakistan led the international denunciation of the Soviet move, and Islamabad plays a critical role in determining the fate of the Afghan resistance. It has provided sanctuary for more than two million Afghan refugees, and it has allowed several Afghan resistance groups to operate in the country. By providing increased support for the groups fighting the Soviets, Pakistan can block Moscow's pacification strategy. On the other hand, Pakistan could help Moscow's cause if it recognized the Soviet-installed government in Kabul and moved against the partisans.

To date, Pakistan has resisted accommodating the Soviet Union; at the same time, Pakistan has not allowed a substantial improvement in the effectiveness of the Afghan fighters. The current Pakistani government does not favor the consolidation of Soviet power in Afghanistan, believing that such a development would enormously increase the Soviet Union's ability to influence developments in Pakistan. At the same time, Islamabad has not allowed a substantial improvement in the organizational and military capability of the Afghan resistance, fearing that such improvement would bring increased Soviet pressure on itself. The Pakistanis fear limited Soviet strikes against valued targets, the Soviet-Afghan occupation of Pakistani territory, and Soviet encouragement to India to increase pressure on Pakistan.

Thus far, Pakistan has allowed only a little assistance to the Afghans, so that the resistance can be kept alive; it hopes for a political settlement that would involve Soviet withdrawal from Afghanistan.[3] Islamabad is also hoping that because of the Afghan conflict it will receive substantial economic and military assistance, to increase its ability to resist Soviet or Indian pressure. President Zia ul-Haq's opponents have argued that he is using the Afghan crisis to consolidate his own position at home and to gain a greater acceptability abroad. It is possible that current Pakistani policy might bring about the very situation it most fears: the consolidation of Soviet power in Afghanistan. Meager assistance to the resistance movement and the miserable living conditions of the Afghan refugees might lead to feelings of resignation and defeat among the Afghans and to a subsequent Soviet military victory.

To gain Pakistani cooperation on the Afghan crisis, Soviet leaders have applied considerable pressure, both positive and negative, on Islamabad. On the positive side, they reportedly have offered "security," the recognition of the Durand Line,** and even nuclear power plants in exchange for cooperation. Positive incentives have been accompanied by many threats. Soviet and Afghan aircraft have frequently violated Pakistani airspace, and Kabul has threatened to support political groups inside Pakistan opposed to the current regime. Kabul has already given refuge to some of President Zia's opponents, including Mir Murtaza Bhutto, the son of former Prime Minister Zulfikar Ali Bhutto. The Soviet Union's public posture on Pakistan has at times been very threatening. For example, Soviet Foreign Minister Andrei Gromyko has warned that if Pakistan continues to serve as a puppet of imperialism in the future, it will jeopardize its existence and its integrity as an independent state.

However, while Soviet statements have been heavy-handed, Soviet policy toward Pakistan has been cautious and prudent. The Soviet military has not attacked any major targets in Pakistan; and there is no evidence of major training and infiltration of the regime's political and ethnic opponents. The Soviet Union's caution may in part be due to its preoccupation with Afghanistan, a desire to maintain a dialogue with Pakistan, and the knowledge that Pakistan could make the Soviet role even more difficult in Afghanistan.

Besides pressuring Pakistan, Moscow has tried hard not to allow its action in Afghanistan to damage its relations with India and other states. Soviet leaders have discouraged other Indian Ocean states from moving close to the United States or allowing the United States to use their facilities. As for India, in 1980 Soviet leaders gave it high priority and regarded Indian goodwill as important. The Soviet Union sold New Delhi $1.6 billion in arms at concessionary terms in 1980. Soviet Premier Leonid Brezhnev visited Delhi between December 8 and December 11, 1980, to underline the importance of India in Soviet policy; perhaps he also wanted to be seen in a major third world country in the aftermath of the Soviet move into Afghanistan, which had been condemned by most developing countries.

Soviet policy toward India has paid off. The official Indian attitude on Afghanistan has been ambivalent. On January 11, 1980, at the United Nations, India supported the Soviet position. Indian leaders believed that the Soviet move was a limited and temporary defensive move. Their response may be a function of several considerations. The Indian government may prefer the Soviet-installed government to an Islam-motivated government, which India may regard as the alternative. Premier Indira Gandhi may not have been displeased with the Soviet move, further, because it increased pressure on Pakistan. New Delhi may have hoped that Soviet pressure might make Islamabad more accommodating toward India. In addition, Gandhi probably believed that India could not antagonize Moscow, a treaty partner and partial ally. Many Indian officials believe that India needs Soviet support more than vice versa. This Indian attitude is likely to persist as long as the Sino-Indian dispute remains unresolved and Delhi sees no alternative for the type of assistance and security support that Moscow has been willing to provide. Indian leaders also believe that India can do very little to affect Soviet policy in Afghanistan because of the importance of the issue to the Soviet Union.

However, over time, India has modified its position, arguing that Afghanistan's independence, territorial integrity, sovereignty and nonaligned status must be preserved.[4] Indian officials have privately expressed concern that the withdrawal of Soviet troops from Afghanistan is becoming increasingly less likely. The perception of a toughened Soviet position on Afghanistan has been accompanied by Indian gestures pointing in conflicting directions, indicating uncertainty. On the one hand, Gandhi has tried to rationalize the Soviet position by saying that

> the outcry and feeling that everybody was ganging up against them have caused them [the Soviets] to dig in their toes.

On the other hand, she is displeased with the implications of the Soviet action. According to Indian officials, she responded negatively to Soviet invitations to visit Moscow on the occasion of the tenth anniversary of the Soviet-Indian Friendship Treaty. Indian leaders still believe that "quiet diplomacy" may encourage Moscow to leave Afghanistan. To official India, the preferred solution of the Afghan crisis apparently includes the consolidation of the Karmal regime, the phased withdrawal of Soviet troops and the suspension of United States military sales, especially F-16's, to Pakistan.

However, the Soviet invasion has been condemned strongly by non-Communist Indian opposition groups, and many articles very critical of the Soviet action and the official Indian response have appeared in the Indian press. In marked contrast to his 1973 trip when thousands of people lined the route, during his 1980 visit Brezhnev was driven to Delhi in a bullet-proof car and faced many demonstrators. Popular sentiment in northwest India is especially sympathetic to the Afghan resistance.

Many Indians have argued that the Soviet invasion marks the beginning of a strategic conflict of interest

---

**Established by British official Sir Mortimer Durand in 1893, the Durand Line is the boundary between Pakistan's North-West Frontier and Afghanistan.

between Delhi and Moscow. Many also believe that successful Soviet consolidation in Afghanistan will make the Soviet Union the dominant South Asian power. Others fear that Soviet power and influence may spread to Pakistan, threatening India directly. Indian opposition leaders argue that the Soviet invasion provided an opportunity for improved relations between India and Pakistan; they have been critical of their own government's policies. A number of analysts have suggested that if India distances itself from the Soviet Union, other states in the area, including Pakistan and the Gulf states, may move away from the great powers and work with Delhi on regional security issues.[5]

THE UNITED STATES AND SOUTH ASIA

In contrast to the Soviet Union, South Asia has seldom had high priority for the United States. Nonetheless, United States attention to the region has increased at times of crisis in the area, be it regional conflict or a heightened perception of the Soviet threat. Since the revolution in Iran and especially since the Soviet invasion of Afghanistan, South Asia, especially Pakistan and the Arabian Sea, along with the Persian Gulf, have emerged from the periphery to the forefront of United States policy considerations. Despite the common American and Indian commitment to a democratic political system, the two have often disagreed on major international issues, especially with regard to United States policies toward the region. American leaders think that Indian leaders do not appreciate global realities and the systemic conflict between the superpowers, which affect a spectrum of issues including developments in South Asia. Indian leaders believe that American diplomats do not understand regional complexities in South Asia and are insensitive to India's desires for regional dominance. These different priorities explain the Indian opposition to American efforts to seek allies in the area; and the conflict between Washington's efforts to increase the American naval presence in the region (to offset the enormous advantage the Soviet Union has in the region because of its proximity) and the Indian opposition to any outside naval presence in the area. India and the United States have also disagreed on issues of world order and North-South relations. India has opposed United States nonproliferation policies and has been an advocate of the New International Economic Order.

While India has opposed United States efforts in the area, Pakistan has been their main beneficiary, even though, like India, until recently Pakistan's concern has been almost exclusively regional. In the 1950's, United States policies toward the region were focused on containing what was seen as the joint Soviet-Chinese threat. Pakistan joined United States efforts at containment, becoming a member of two Western security pacts, the Central Treaty Organization (CENTO) and the Southeast Asian Treaty Organization (SEATO), and signing a mutual security agreement with the United States. By the early 1960's, Pakistan had become the United States' "most allied ally" in Asia. Pakistan's membership was in large part due to its desire to gain Western support to check India's regional ambitions.

But United States–Pakistani relations have run into problems of their own. In the aftermath of the Sino-Indian war of 1962, when the United States provided arms to India to contain the People's Republic of China, United States credibility with Pakistan declined. Relations between the two further deteriorated in 1965, when the United States (already preoccupied with the Vietnam conflict) imposed an embargo on arms to both India and Pakistan. United States attention to the area increased dramatically in 1971, before the Indo-Pakistani war. The United States opposed Indian war efforts and sent naval forces to the Bay of Bengal.

The American "tilt" toward Pakistan, which was serving as a middleman between the United States and China, infuriated India. Nor were Pakistanis reassured when they lost the war. Pakistan was also increasingly suspicious of the United States because it feared that Washington was accepting Indian hegemony in the area. Pakistani suspicions were confirmed when the 1976 Democratic party platform asserted that "India has now achieved a considerable hegemony over the subcontinent . . . future American policy should accept this fact."[6]

In keeping with his party's platform, United States President Jimmy Carter improved relations with India, but the two countries remained at odds over nuclear proliferation and the presence of United States naval forces in the area. While relations with India have improved somewhat, relations with Pakistan have deteriorated substantially. Like India, Pakistan opposed the United States stance on nuclear nonproliferation. Largely because of its rivalry with India, Pakistan wants to increase its own nuclear option. Thus, in 1976, Pakistan signed a contract with France for the purchase of a nuclear reprocessing plant. The United States promised to supply Pakistan with conventional weapons, including 110 A-7's, in exchange for the cancellation of the project. Pakistan refused. Many Pakistanis believe that because of this refusal the United States encouraged the turmoil in Pakistan after the 1977 election and encouraged the subsequent coup.

The post-coup government, however, has continued Bhutto's nuclear policies. Although the French government cancelled the project in 1978, Pakistan continued its nuclear efforts, clandestinely working on a uranium enrichment and plutonium separation plant. This led to the cancellation of all United States assistance in 1979.

The Carter policy of disengaging from Islamabad to deter Pakistan from pursuing a nuclear program failed to produce the desired result by the time of the Soviet invasion of Afghanistan. In the aftermath of this Soviet move, Washington offered Islamabad a two-year package of economic and military aid worth approximately $400 million. Pakistan rejected this offer as inadequate, in view of the threats the country faced. Negotiations continued between the two countries, however, and led to a five-year economic and military aid sale, including the sale of symbolically important F-16 aircraft.

The new United States policy toward Pakistan is designed to serve several purposes. Washington hopes Pakistan's ability to resist Soviet pressure will increase. It is also expected that an increase in Pakistani capability will deter a Soviet attack on Pakistan. Increased Pakistani capability is expected to increase the threshold cost for any Soviet military operations against Pakistan by making any small attack a major operation. Washington also hopes that, unlike the policy of disengagement, the current policy will give it enough leverage to influence Pakistan's nuclear program. (Pakistan has been warned that United States assistance will be cut off if it explodes a nuclear device.) Washington also hopes that closer cooperation with Pakistan will lead to the coordination of policy between the two countries for the security of the Persian Gulf.

United States–Pakistani relations have improved because the United States has made a major effort to improve its power projection capability in the area in the aftermath of the Iranian revolution and the Soviet invasion. The United States has more naval force in the Indian Ocean than the Soviet Union. In April, 1981, it had 17 combat ships, including a carrier, in the area; the Soviet Union had 5. Washington has also signed a cooperation agreement for the use of facilities with Kenya, Somalia and Oman. A United States satellite monitoring the Indian Ocean was launched in March, 1981.

From Washington's viewpoint, Pakistan has many assets in relation to the Gulf. It is part of the hinterland of the Gulf states. Pakistan itself has emphasized its relations with the Gulf states, especially since the 1971 war. It receives considerable economic assistance from the countries of the area, and several hundred thousand Pakistanis are employed there, remitting more than $2 billion annually. The Gulf provides a growing market for Pakistani goods. And Pakistan has intensified its security ties with the Gulf states, in which it has several hundred military advisers. At the start of the Iraqi-Iranian war, Pakistan reportedly dispatched some 5,000 military personnel to Saudi Arabia. There have been several reports that as many as two Pakistani divisions might be stationed in the oil-rich kingdom. It has been argued that the Saudis needed Pakistan's trained, disciplined and non-Arabic-speaking military

and nonmilitary personnel. However, the Saudis have apparently not made up their minds about the desirability of such a large Pakistani military presence.

The future of United States–Pakistani security cooperation in the Gulf is unclear. While Pakistan and several other states in the area, especially Turkey, can assist the United States in many plausible contingencies, Islamabad has ruled out any overt cooperation. Pakistani officials have stated that they will not allow United States facilities and bases on their territory and that Pakistan will remain in the nonaligned movement and a member of the Islamic conference. While some American officials have expressed interest in having access to Pakistani naval or land facilities, at present this has been ruled out.

While United States relations with Pakistan have improved, the opposite has been true in the case of India. Indian opposition to American arms sales to Pakistan and United States naval activities in the region has been more vocal than India's opposition to Afghanistan. The dominant Indian policy regards United States policy toward Pakistan as threatening Indian interests. New Delhi believes that Pakistan should accept a subordinate position to India in the subcontinent. American arms for Pakistan are regarded by many Indians as an American intrusion into the "Indian sphere of influence," and many Indians believe that the current agreement will lead to a direct United States military presence in Pakistan. It is believed that American arms make Pakistan less accommodating to Indian wishes in the region and that the United States may directly support Pakistan in a war with India. Many Indians believe that Pakistan is using the Soviet invasion as an excuse to strengthen itself against India. Even those opposed to the United States sale of arms to Pakistan, however, do not regard a Pakistani attack against India as a rational option in the near future.

While the dominant Indian view is one of hostility to United States arms and United States naval forces in the area, a vocal Indian minority does not see a conflict of interest between India and the United States in the Persian Gulf[7] and sees American arms to Pakistan as justified because of the Soviet invasion. Like the Pakistanis, Indian critics of the current government, especially the non-Communist opposition, believe that the Soviet invasion has changed the strategic environment, necessitating improved Indo-Pakistani relations. They argue that opposing a stronger Pakistan is not necessarily in the interests of Indian security. They point out that only Pakistan separates Soviet forces from India. Many Indians see this geographic noncontiguity from Soviet-occupied territories as a blessing and regard a strong independent Pakistan as an asset for long-term Indian security.

PAKISTAN AND INDIA

For its part, Islamabad has proposed a no-war pact

between the two countries. Islamabad also proposed negotiations for troop reduction on the Indo-Pakistani borders and a nuclear-free zone in the region. Initially, Indian officials dismissed the Pakistani no-war pact proposal as a propaganda ploy aimed at gaining American congressional support for proposed economic and military aid. However, domestic and international pressure has forced the Indian government to change its mind, and the two countries have agreed to hold a series of meetings on the issue.

A friendlier Indian policy toward Pakistan would include a greater expression of sympathy for Pakistan's security problems, decreased opposition to Pakistan's arms purchases and increased pressure on the Soviet Union to withdraw from Afghanistan. So far, Gandhi has signaled in both directions, talking both about "clouds of war," and a no-war pact between the two countries. It is likely that once she makes up her mind, she will have the support of most Indians.

Uncertainty is also reflected in Indian policies toward the United States and the states of the region. Despite Indian protests against United States policy toward Pakistan, India seems interested in maintaining correct relations with the United States. Both countries want an amiable resolution of the continuing disagreement over the United States refusal to supply slightly enriched uranium for India's Tarapur power plants.[8] The United States is India's major trading partner and is an important source of technology. Correct relations with the United States give India the ability to influence United States policies. They also provide a degree of diplomatic flexibility.

Superpower interest in South Asia is likely to persist. The spread of the Afghan war, leading to a limited invasion or the (unlikely) massive invasion of Pakistan, would further strain relations between the superpowers and might well alter Indo-Soviet and Indo-United States relations. On the other hand, a political settlement of the Afghan issue, including a Soviet withdrawal, would dramatically decrease tensions in the area and between the superpowers.

NOTES

[1] The coup was carried out by a coalition of the two rival factions of the People's Democratic party of Afghanistan (PDPA). Soon the Percham faction (headed by Babrak Karmal) was eliminated and the Khalqis (headed by Nur Mohammad Taraki and Hafizullah Amin) emerged victorious. Louis Dupree, "Afghanistan Under Khalq," *Problems of Communism*, July-August, 1979, pp. 34-50. Hannah Negaran (pseud.), "The Afghan Coup of April 1978: Revolution and International Security," *ORBIS*, Spring, 1979, pp. 93-113.

[2] On Soviet strategy see Zalmay Khalilzad, "Soviet Occupied Afghanistan," *Problems of Communism*, November-December, 1980.

[3] Pakistan has agreed to a dialogue with the Karmal government to look for a political settlement of the Afghan conflict through the good offices of the United Nations. In February, 1981, U.N. Secretary General Kurt Waldheim appointed Javier Perez de Cuéllar as his representative to seek a political settlement. Newly elected Secretary General Cuéllar is expected to name his own representative.

[4] Kuldip Nayar, *Report on Afghanistan* (New Delhi: Allied Publishers Private Ltd., 1981).

[5] Bhabani Sen Gupta, "The Asian Tinder Box," *India Today*, May 16-18, 1981.

[6] Quoted in Norman D. Palmer, "The United States and South Asia," *Current History*, April, 1979, p. 146.

[7] Rajendra Sareen, "India and USA: Adversaries?" *The Hindustan Times*, December 24, 1981.

[8] A. G. Noorani, "Indo-U.S. Nuclear Relations," *Asian Survey*, April, 1981, pp. 399-416.

The Tragedy and the Hope

Arthur Hertzberg

In the confrontation between Reagan and Begin, Reagan is playing the part of the sheriff, and reading his lines with conviction. He was outraged by the bombing of Beirut, and especially by the massacre in the refugee camps, and now believes that a solution for the Palestinians is not to be found at the barrel of anybody's gun. But Begin is not acting at all, even though his rhetoric and gestures are more theatrical. He has been preparing himself for such a moment as this one since he was a young man.

The Reagan initiative of September 1 was a brilliant piece of political craftsmanship and timing. My own talks in Washington and Jerusalem made it clear that those officials in the State Department who framed the new policy were not innocents. They expected that the immediate response in Israel would be defiance, that new settlements on the West Bank would probably be announced, and that Begin would try to rally the nation against being pushed around by Big Brother. Nor was it unexpected that Begin would call for early elections in Israel, though the smaller parties in his coalition may stop them.

For the Israeli government, the new American pressure is the unexpected, and unwelcome, result of the Lebanon invasion. Before the war, neither the Carter administration nor Haig and Reagan made a strong effort to encourage the negotiations for West Bank autonomy. They stood by while the Egyptians and the Israelis conducted those talks in the most desultory way for several years. During the last weeks of the campaign in Lebanon, the Americans realized that their influence in the Middle East would quickly decrease if they simply brought Philip Habib home while Israel proceeded to replace Syria

as the dominant force in Lebanon and kept increasing its settlements on the West Bank. This would be like returning a fire engine to the station to await the next alarm. To be sure, during the presidential campaign and thereafter, Reagan had several times declared these settlements to be "legal"; and he did not try to force an early end to the fighting in Lebanon. Nevertheless, by mid-July the Israeli newspapers were saying that the logic of the American position would require it to make some move, after the fighting ended, toward its Arab friends. The Jordanians obviously felt threatened by the repeated assertions of Israeli officials that "Jordan is Palestine" and by Sharon's brutally casual statements that Hussein was expendable, and that a Palestinian takeover in Amman would be welcomed by Israel.

The United States invested some of its diplomatic capital in the Middle East in ending the siege of Beirut; it put pressure on a number of unwilling Arab governments to accept a share of the PLO fighters who were to be evacuated. At the very least, even if no immediate compensation was promised, these governments had to expect some prompt American action that would be seen in their world as a redress of the balance between Israel and themselves. Everyone thus expected some gesture of "evenhandedness." If the new American initiative peters out in a few weeks or months, it will be such a gesture, but all the signs are that more than a gesture is intended. The American government will likely try to carry out its plan during the next two years, until the end of the Reagan administration.

The debates that have already begun within both the Jewish and the Arab camps can only become sharper and angrier because the American initiative has forced into the open fundamental

questions about the Jewish state. This has been immediately apparent in Israel, and, to an unexpected degree, among its most committed Jewish supporters elsewhere. Menachem Begin has never disguised his ideological commitment to the "undivided land of Israel," and he has acted consistently to defend this principle, in peace and in war. At Camp David he agreed to exchange the whole of the Sinai for peace with Egypt and, as he believed, for Sadat's indulgence of Begin's need to retain the West Bank and Gaza.

When the last strip of the Sinai, including the city of Yamit, was evacuated last April, angry and even violent scenes took place before the television cameras. It was widely held in Israel that Menachem Begin had orchestrated these events in order to demonstrate to the world how painful was the dismantling of an Israeli settlement; to the commentators in the Israeli press he seemed to be asserting, in Israel as well as abroad, that the government would never again abandon Jewish settlers. All of the present and future Israeli settlements on the West Bank were thus taken to be inalienable. By the fourth or fifth day of the war in Lebanon, it was correctly understood in Israel that one of the prime objectives of the invasion was to bring about a military defeat of the PLO that would prevent it from taking part in any negotiations over the future of the West Bank.

It was, in fact, an open secret in Israel in June and July that as Israel approached Beirut from the south, General Sharon expected the Christian Phalange army to join the war and to deal decisively with the PLO fighters in Beirut. But the Phalange was deterred, in part for the very reasons that were to keep the Israelis from storming West Beirut in August—the probable high cost in casualties of house-to-house fighting in narrow streets against heavily armed PLO forces. Perhaps even more important, Bashir Gemayel, the head of the Phalange, wanted to be elected president of Lebanon and he had to improve his brutal image. He could not be seen simply as the instrument of the Israelis, or as the unrelenting enemy of the Moslems, or even of the PLO.

His assassination, together with that of some of his top commanders, left a power vacuum in his own ranks. At the invitation of the Israeli occupiers, Phalange elements went into the two Palestinian camps on September 16 and 17 and took part in the murderous horrors that were committed there. (They may have been helped by Major Haddad's troops, some of whom are reported to have made their way into the camps, not to mention obscure Lebanese terrorist elements, who, according to some Lebanese reports, wanted to destroy the possibility of any kind of order in Lebanon.)

In advance of a thorough and unbiased investigation, it seems fair to say from the partial evidence available that the horror in the camps was mainly the work of Phalange elements—perhaps not controlled by their weakened high command—who were bent on revenge for the assassination of Bashir Gemayel, for the slaughters of Christians by the Palestinians in the Lebanese town of Damur, as well as for other horrors in the seemingly never-ending cycle of murder and retaliation in Lebanon. Apart from revenge, and inflicting sheer terror, the aim of this most recent assault was to make an end of the last vestige of PLO power in Beirut. But from reports I have heard, the attack may have had another purpose as well—to add to the fears of the hundreds of thousands of Palestinians in Lebanon so that they might start to stampede from the country.

If this were a motive of the Phalange, it would have coincided with the vision of General Sharon and, ultimately, of Prime Minister Begin. In Israel last June I heard from several well-connected sources of Sharon's hopes that the Lebanese war would start a flight of Palestinians to the eastern borders and, inevitably, to Jordan. The Israeli troops that took over West Beirut after the murder of Bashir Gemayel and let the Christians into the camps had heard again and again that not one Palestinian fighter could be allowed to remain in Beirut and that both Lebanon and Israel

would be better off without the Palestinians. The grand purpose of the war in Lebanon was to eliminate the PLO, but it was also a war that seemed intended to intimidate the Palestinians on whom the PLO drew for recruits and support.

This was the background for the disastrous behavior of the Israeli command on September 16 and 17. What happened had the earmarks of a pogrom. The czarist police and army had stood by, carelessly or purposely, while mobs of Muzhiks worked off their murderous instincts on Jews. Now Jews were the cops, or worse. Sharon's army sealed off the camps, planned the entry of the Phalange militia, failed to intervene after Israeli soldiers and journalists knew—and high officials had been told—that slaughter was taking place. Begin and Sharon then compounded their government's disgrace—first Begin, by righteously denying all responsibility, then Sharon, by a blustering self-defense that fell short of the truth. Their fixed guide was their view of the PLO and the Palestinians in the camps—there was little they would not do to keep them from Judea and Samaria, the inalienable land of Israel since Abraham's time.

Begin has thus followed his star without deviation, although he has changed tactics. The ideological issue of the "undivided land of Israel" had been largely muted for two reasons: the Camp David accords left the West Bank under Israeli control, while the final negotiations on the question of its future sovereignty were put off for five years; and Israel's supporters and friends abroad, especially in America, largely ignored the increasing number of settlements in the West Bank. They busied themselves making the case for Israel's security against PLO terrorism and emphasizing the dangers of putting sophisticated arms in the hands of the Arab states. The new American initiative has now made it clear, even to those who have preferred not to see, that if the forces of heavenly angels themselves were deployed to protect an Israel that had lost sovereignty over the West Bank, Menachem Begin would nonetheless stand before God and demand that he keep his promise to return the whole of their homeland to the Jews.

Dissociation from both the style and the substance of Begin's policy, once

rarely made public in the Jewish establishment, therefore emerged rapidly after Reagan's speech on September 1 in places as surprising as the America-Israel Public Affairs Committee—the pro-Israel lobby itself—the B'nai B'rith, and the American Jewish Committee. The spokesman from the Public Affairs Committee later changed his views; but most American Jews, even in the established organizations, clearly preferred pursuing Reagan's plan for negotiations to defiance. Begin's own rhetoric meanwhile grew more shrill. He declared that the new initiative is an American effort to push him from office in favor of the much more moderate Labor party, and that he is not Allende. When Shimon Peres, the leader of the opposition, accepted the Reagan initiative as a basis for discussion, his Likud critics, led by the prime minister, came very near to accusing him of plotting with the Americans during his visit to Washington in August, and of being prepared to be "their man in Jerusalem." But Israel's Labor party, despite its own internal divisions, has always stood for some form of "territorial compromise" on the West Bank, and it is no more ready than Begin to dismantle all the existing settlements, some of which were created by Labor governments.

If Begin's fury sometimes seems out of control, there are several reasons for this. As is now apparent, the fall of General Haig was, for him, a great defeat. George Shultz spoke on Sunday, September 12, in New York to a United Jewish Appeal audience which was attentive and divided. Haig appeared before the same group two days later and made headlines by attacking the new policy as weakening America's most powerful friend in the Middle East and as wrong-headed in asking for a stop to West Bank settlements. There is no reason to believe that Begin and Sharon shared their invasion plans in June with Haig, but it was clear then, and it is even clearer now, that they had reason to expect gratitude for the strategic benefits they were bringing to America and, in return, indulgence for their plans for the West Bank.

Begin's second reason for anger is to be found in Israel itself. The opposition now has an issue. The infighting within the Labor party may blunt its attack, but a national debate has begun. It may not lead to a quick Labor victory, but one question now dominates political discussions in Israel: is the West Bank worth the huge costs being paid for it, including the blood of continued war, divisions among Jews, a world press reaction so bad that it is helping the un-prepossessing Arafat look better, and, not least, open disapproval in Washington? Now that Reagan, in the aftermath of the Beirut massacre, is seriously demanding that the Israelis leave Beirut and Lebanon itself, Israel's government could, and should, change fairly soon. Begin has thrived on being able to call his critics illegitimate, but at this moment these critics include a probable majority of American Jews, while over half of Israel was found in a recent poll (taken after the withdrawal of the PLO from Beirut and just before the American initiative was made) to be in favor of the return of territory for peace. Some of Begin's own supporters in Israel have now joined the opposition in denouncing Israel's failure to prevent—and evasions about—the Beirut killings. This moral indignation will have political consequences.

Begin is now confronted with a seemingly impossible problem, made even more acute by the massacres. He has to prove in the United States that "greater" Israel is a good for which Americans should be willing to bear heavy political and diplomatic costs; and he has to show that this is better for America's long-term interests than a West Bank that would be demilitarized—as Shultz has promised—although not under Israel's immediate control.

This debate may, of course, be deflected, and even if the Americans do not themselves get tired, the signals that they send may be misread, or misused. The day-to-day business of helping Israel with money and arms will and must continue. But if the supply from America is not to some degree cut back, then the tough-minded political experts in Israel may deduce that Americans do not really stand by the Reagan plan, for they have put no teeth in it. If the supply is obstructed by some contrived slowdown, then Israel and its supporters, including "doves" who otherwise oppose Begin, will coalesce instantly, claiming that such pressure is unfair and dangerous, both to Israel and to America, because it weakens Israel's ability to survive in an unfriendly region.

Nonetheless, after the slaughter in the Palestinian camps in Beirut, America's leverage and responsibility have both increased. Israel may be more defiant for a while, but it is now much more difficult for it to act unilaterally on the Palestinian question. The Americans pulled out of Beirut much too soon, and took the French and Italians with them, without real assurance that the Lebanese army was in control. By doing so they acquired increased responsibility for the safety and future of the Palestinians. Thus Reagan had no legitimate alternative to saying, on September 20, that he would send back US troops.

In late September, as I write, seventy-five F-16s, which have long been promised to Israel, have not yet been formally released through notification to Congress. Israel will eventually get the planes. But if this is done in a way that appears to offer proof that the Americans are not really willing to bring pressure on Israel in order to carry out their plan, that would be a major mistake. Reagan and Shultz have staked their prestige on this initiative and they hope, in two years, to have laid the foundation for settling the main issues of the Palestinian question, both the future of the West Bank and that of the Palestinian diaspora, especially those Palestinians in refugee camps. Such an achievement would overshadow the one at Camp David, provide Reagan with a place in diplomatic history, and make Shultz a central political figure. More important, in the present view in Washington, it would make America's friends in the region, both Israel and the "moderate" Arab states, more secure in the long run and free of the threat, and need, of war.

Reagan and Shultz have been no less bold in their approach to the Arabs. In none of the documents that define the new initiative, including the State Department's published "talking points," did the American government discuss either the future of the PLO or of the Palestinians living outside Israel and the West Bank. These, and not the future of the West Bank as such, are, however, the urgent issues for the Arabs. In Morocco, the leaders of the Arab governments affirmed on September 9 that the PLO was the sole representative of the Palestinian national interest and insisted again on the right of return of the Palestinian refugees to their homeland.

29. The Tragedy and the Hope

Nonetheless, the Fez declaration was described by Arab diplomats as a movement toward the American peace plan.

On September 13, King Hussein spoke on British television and made his support for the Reagan plan fairly explicit. He reiterated the Arab formula that the PLO is the designated representative of the Palestinian cause, but insisted that the PLO is "a transition," that the Palestinians will eventually "present themselves to the world in a different way" and that he expected to be "heavily involved" in the discussions on the West Bank. Hussein is, of course, a master of survival and ambiguity (in his case they go together), but it is possible to discern without great difficulty what his real position and interests are. Hussein also certainly knows what is on the minds of the makers of the new American policy, for Nicholas Veliotes, the assistant secretary of state for Near Eastern and South Asian affairs and a former ambassador to Jordan, made a secret trip to brief him on the Reagan proposal and to get his assent to it before it was announced.

Hussein has good reason to like Arafat no better than he does Sharon. Both Hussein and Arafat remember September 1970 ("Black September") when, in order to save Jordan from what was soon to happen in Lebanon—the takeover of part of the country by the PLO for its domain—Hussein decimated the Palestinian fighters and forced the survivors out. In the recent dispersal of the Palestinians from Beirut, Hussein took the smallest number. Even though he kissed them one by one as they came off the plane, he had this relative handful quickly disarmed.

Hussein said on September 20 that he was willing to discuss with the PLO a federation of Palestine and Jordan that would be approved in a referendum. But he certainly does not want or need a semi-state on the West Bank that would be run by the PLO, although nominally under his royal authority. What he needs even less is additional hundreds of thousands of Palestinians returning to the West Bank. The likeliest candidates are the 400,000 or more Palestinians in the camps in Lebanon, perhaps the 250,000 in Syria, and the fighters from Beirut now scattered throughout the Arab world. The approximately 380,000 oil workers, highly trained technicians, and professionals in Kuwait and the other rich Persian Gulf states will not be better off if they return to Ramallah or Hebron. For those in the refugee camps, especially in the aftermath of the war in Lebanon, the move to Jordan might seem appealing. If their presence is added to that of the more than one million Palestinians who are already just about a majority in Jordan, and the 1.15 million on the West Bank and Gaza Strip, the situation will, in Hussein's view, be beyond his control.[1]

One cannot imagine that Hussein has gone as far as he has in accepting the American initiative unless he has at least some general assurance that the American plan will not result in his being flooded with Palestinians and then deposed. What Hussein knows cannot be a secret from the rest of the Arabs, notwithstanding their show of Arab unity in the Fez declaration. No doubt most of the signers believed that the Reagan initiative would eventually founder and that, meanwhile, there was nothing to be gained by denouncing it—while also giving nothing away, not even the formal recognition of Israel's existence. But the hardliners among the Arabs, especially the Syrians, probably took the very view that even Israeli moderates fear: let the Americans first separate the West Bank from Israel if they can, and put it in Arab hands. Soon to follow would be demands for complete repatriation of the Palestinian refugees, for true sovereignty, including the end of any initial demilitarization, and for the installation of the PLO, not only by votes, but also by the elimination of its various opponents. This is a catalogue of Hussein's fears as well, but he now seems more confident than he did before the Reagan initiative. In an interview on September 21, he indicated that he was eager to pursue negotiations on Reagan's proposal, but not with the Begin government. There is, at least, a fundamental identity of interest between Jordan and Israel that the status of the West Bank should not be changed in a way that could endanger either country.

---

[1] I have used the State Department's estimates of Palestinian populations throughout. None are definitive and the PLO estimates tend to be higher. The Lebanese authorities estimate there are 600,000 Palestinians in Lebanon. See *The New York Times*, July 4, 1982, section 4, p. 1.

Ronald Reagan has said nearly as much, not through emissaries, but rather in a public declaration. He added a paragraph to his speech on Wednesday, September 1, saying that he had no intention of asking Israel to return to its narrowest, least defensible border. This assurance of security for Israel has been reiterated by both the president and the secretary of state. It is not plausible that the American proposal is intended to soften either Jordan or Israel for eventual PLO control of the West Bank; the Americans know that such an outcome is what each finds most threatening. It is all the more certain that the PLO is not well regarded among the anticommunists in Washington, because of its links to the Soviet Union and to its surrogate in the Middle East, the Syrians. Moreover the accumulating accounts of the PLO's harsh control of the parts of Lebanon it occupied have been cautionary for officials in Washington; they have no intention of repeating this experience elsewhere.

Reagan could win his argument with Begin hands down, even in Israel, if he simply said publicly what he has strongly implied, by silence and indirection, about the need to exclude the PLO and the Palestinian diaspora from the West Bank. He cannot, however, come any nearer to being explicit. Except for Jordan, most of the Arab governments would have to oppose a policy that explicitly separated the future of the displaced Palestinians and of the PLO from the issue of the West Bank—and they would do so not just to save face. In their reluctance to accept the PLO fighters from Beirut, even temporarily, the Arab governments have proved that they would feel endangered by militant Palestinians within their own borders. They prefer a solution to the West Bank that promises them relief from the Palestinians at the expense of Israel and Jordan. Any premature assent by Arab states to the dispersal of some of the Palestinians and their settlement elsewhere than on the West Bank could create immediate conflict and even terrorism within the Arab countries themselves.

On the other hand, it is precisely assurances of protection against Palestinian pressure that Israel, even its moderates, require. Reagan's oblique, implied, but unstated promise to keep a PLO government and most of the Pales-

tinian diaspora out of the West Bank is at the heart of the issue. The essential question is, do the Americans mean to keep such a promise, and even if they do, could they possibly deliver on it?

Both the Israeli moderates, led by Shimon Peres, and the less forthright King Hussein are willing to take the chance that the US can make the promise stick. And Hussein could not have gone as far as he did if he did not have some encouragement from Egypt, Saudi Arabia, and other moderate Arab nations. For both Israeli and Arab moderates the American initiative has several virtues. It would deal with the two problems that have blocked a solution for the West Bank: assuring Israel's security if it gives up the territory, and assuring Jordan that it will not be overwhelmed by a PLO state into which hundreds of thousands of Palestinian refugees would flow. The initiative still offers Arab moderates hope that the Palestinian question can be solved, even at inconvenience to themselves, so that it will not plague their grandchildren. With the West Bank under Jordanian rule, and the PLO fighters sequestered under the control of the Arab countries, the problems of the diaspora Palestinians could be dealt with gradually.

For the Israelis, the reality of Lebanon after the war is even more sobering. With Bashir Gemayel's assassination their main hope of political stability in Lebanon under auspices favorable to them is gone. Arafat, in military defeat, holds the center of the stage, even at the Vatican. Israel has no assurance that occupying Lebanon for a winter, or for a year or two—if the US does not insist on withdrawal—will yield it better results than the Syrians achieved in their years of dominance in Beirut.

The ultimate aim of the new American initiative is to shore up stability in the Middle East through an exchange, a trade, in which the West Bank is detached from both Israel and the PLO; the problem of most of the refugees would then be dealt with, partially at least, by the absorption of some of them into Lebanon, the dispersal of others to other Arab countries, and by the prospect of aid as recompense for giving up the right of return. This is not an ideal solution, but it could well look better to the most concerned parties as their alternatives turn sour. To stay the course, the United States must not only split Israeli and Jewish opinion, as it has already done, in the hope that the government after Begin will be reasonable, but also split the Arab leaders who will eventually have to face up to, and disappoint, both many Palestinian refugees and the PLO as it is now organized.

Reagan may be in a position to do this. He is not likely to be a candidate for reelection, and even if he is, he may indeed win, rather than lose, Jewish votes if he persists in confronting Begin in the name of reasonableness. His government anticipated the main lines of its new policy before his speech of September 1. The United States helped Israel out of the quagmire of Beirut: it pushed unwilling Arabs into accepting PLO fighters. In Jordan, Hussein made clear his own terms for absorbing them: he would accept only those who were Jordanian citizens and would live under Jordan's laws. What Reagan has proposed, and already begun to act out, is a classic and moderate "Zionist" solution for the Palestinian question. Let there be a peaceful homeland in the West Bank for the Palestinians, with hundreds of thousands of supporters abroad who are full citizens of the countries of their dispersion but who look warmly toward their "national center."

Such full citizenship for the displaced Palestinians in Arab countries is hard now for anyone to visualize, especially in view of what has happened in Lebanon. Hussein would face a great

---

[2] *Time* magazine, September 20, 1982.

challenge in making the West Bank and Gaza a Palestinian homeland although, with many Palestinians in his government, he is now in a better position to provide a fair and workable administration than he was before 1967. A *Time* magazine poll on the West Bank last spring showed that 86 percent of those questioned wanted a West Bank state run by the PLO. But according to recent reports from the West Bank, the reception there of Reagan's proposal has not been notably hostile. A Palestinian editor commented, "It may not be what we have been struggling for, but you have to be a realist."[2] This, I suspect, may reflect the attitude of many West Bank Arabs, especially if the prospects for a deal with Hussein seem strong. What the Americans are counting on is that the hard interests and the financial resources of the moderate Arab nations will come into play to give the US initiative momentum once serious negotiations become a reality.

For the moment, with attention focused on the crisis in Lebanon, the initiative of Reagan and Shultz seems derailed or at least shifted to a siding, but it is even more necessary and urgent now. The United States took a difficult and historic opening step in early September toward settling the Palestinian question so that both Israel and Jordan might be safe. It must now add the Palestinians themselves to America's list of worries and try to ensure that they are safe from the hatred of all the factions in an all too unfriendly Middle East. Those who claim that the Palestin-

ian question can be ignored as irrelevant to American interests do not understand America's responsibilities as a world power whose vital concerns in the Middle East demand that Palestinian claims not fester indefinitely. The Palestinians have been the target of the Lebanese war yet they remain, even in military defeat, a source of embarrassment, fear, and potential political instability to all of America's friends in the region. The United States has practiced a policy of avoiding, or discounting, the Palestinian question for three decades, in concert with Israel's policy of "gaining time." The failure of these endeavors is now clear for all to see, except those who really want to justify annexing the West Bank against any odds. Such counsels are good neither for Israel nor for America. The repeated explosions in Lebanon and the intransigence of Begin and Sharon and the Arab leaders at Fez prove that neither by war nor by diplomacy among themselves are the parties to the conflict likely to solve their own problems. The US cannot avoid going further into this thicket by asserting diplomatic leadership and putting pressure on all the conflicting parties.

Reagan and Shultz have not even begun to face the intractable problem of Jerusalem except for a broad hint that Israel might allow some official Arab presence in an undivided city. They may yet founder on unexpected and unforeseeable disasters. But they are being bold, even intransigent, in the cause of moderation, and, after the bloody years of hopeless impasse, that is a venture that deserves every chance.

Moscow's Middle East

Dimitri K. Simes

Dimitri K. Simes is director of Soviet and East European research program at The Johns Hopkins School of Advanced International Studies.

WASHINGTON—There is a widely held view in Washington that the outcome of the Israeli invasion of Lebanon was a humiliating defeat for the Soviet Union and a welcome triumph for the United States. Some signs point in this direction, but the cheerleading may be premature. Obviously, the Kremlin, which is proud of its image as a superpower, was not overjoyed watching Israel, an ally of the United States, trounce Syria and the Palestine Liberation Organization. And, of course, Moscow cannot have been happy that Soviet weapons performed so poorly in Syrian hands. Still, the Politburo appears to believe that, in the long run, the Lebanese war may work to the Soviet rather than to the American advantage.

It was this belief, more than anything else, that shaped the Soviet response to the Israeli invasion. True, Russian options were extremely limited. Short of sending troops into Lebanon—an inconceivable adventure from the cautious Brezhnev regime's standpoint—there was little the Russians could do to prevent an Israeli military victory. And even the relatively limited action of landing Soviet forces in Syria would be quite risky, given Israeli air superiority and the well-known philosophy held by Menachem Begin and Ariel Sharon that the best defense is a good offense.

No doubt, the overextension of the Soviet empire and the looming succession were also restraining factors. Soviet insiders say that the Russians' continuing intervention in Afghanistan and preoccupation with Poland made the Kremlin less inclined to throw its weight around. Add to this the growing ineptness of a leadership increasingly involved in pre-succession maneuvering, and it seems clear that the Politburo's ability to act quickly and decisively may have been impaired.

Nevertheless, it would be a serious mistake to assume that senility or weakness made the Brezhnev team incapable of a more assertive response in Lebanon.

Superpowers have a variety of means at their disposal for reminding others that they cannot be ignored. The Russians could have sent their fleet close to Beirut. They could have issued warnings that Moscow's treaty obligations would permit no violations of Syrian airspace or territory. They could have put their paratroop units on more than routine alert. And it would not have cost much to proceed with a sizeable airlift to Syria. These actions would probably have made little difference on the ground in Lebanon. But the Soviet Union would now be in a position to argue that its warnings and activities had stopped Israel from even more aggressive action. It is fairly simple to claim credit for preventing ominous developments that stood little likelihood of taking place.

Why then was the Kremlin so uncharacteristically shy? Chances are that the reason for its restraint was not a lack of alternatives but a calculated assessment that it was not in Moscow's interest to play a visible role. Soviet inaction was a thinly disguised message to the Arabs that as long as they fail to put their house in order, the Soviet Union will not bail them out. Moscow has plainly lost patience with Arab inability either to fight the Israelis or negotiate with them.

There appears a strong sentiment in Moscow that the Arabs have on the whole proved to be inflexible politically, ineffective militarily and profoundly ungrateful and unreliable as allies. P.L.O. documents captured by the Israeli Army indicate that the Soviet Foreign Minister, Andrei A. Gromyko, has delicately but pointedly advised Yasir Arafat to recognize Israel's right to exist. Of course, Moscow was not being altruistic: P.L.O. acceptance of Israel with pre-1967 borders would allow the convening of negotiations in Geneva on the Arab-Israeli conflict, which would again put the Soviet Union in the driver's seat in Middle East politics. In any case, Mr. Arafat has not obliged.

Senior Soviet officials argue publicly that the Arabs have been so committed to fighting each other that they have no energy left to fight Israel. Moscow has frequently stated, both publicly and privately, that it has been made a convenient scapegoat for Arab faults. That is why the Politburo told an Arab League delegation last summer that the Soviet Union would not fight an Arab war in Lebanon while the Arabs themselves failed to display determination and unity.

Today the Kremlin is upset that all roads to an Arab-Israeli settlement now seem to lead through Washington, but it still argues that the Reagan peace initiative will not save the Americans from falling flat on their faces. The Russians openly suggest that the Begin-Sharon Government will ignore American pleas and will refuse to make even the limited concessions that would satisfy pro-Western Arab leaders. It seems clear, then, that the Politburo hopes that the United States will be no better equipped to deliver a negotiated settlement than the Soviet Union was to provide a military solution. And Moscow undoubtedly calculates that it would be a major beneficiary of the resulting anti-American mood.

Soviet tactics are designed accordingly. The Kremlin has chosen to keep a low profile and to display moderation. Despite its harsh public rhetoric, Moscow preached caution during the Arabs' recent, aborted attempt to challenge Israeli credentials at the United Nations General Assembly, and it has given its support to the moderate Arab peace plan drawn up at the summit meeting in Fez, Morocco, in September. Soviet commentators have grown fond of reminding listeners that Moscow has always advocated a peaceful settlement guaranteeing not only Arab rights but also Israeli security. And although the Kremlin is proceeding with rearming Syria, it is also making clear its willingness to build ties to Arab states that do not necessarily belong to the rejectionist front.

Moscow continues to criticize Egypt's loyalty to Camp David, but Soviet spokesmen now tend to emphasize what they feel are the constructive aspects of the foreign and domestic policies of President Hosni Mubarak of Egypt. Moscow has also put new energy into efforts to convince Cairo that an improvement in relations may be possible. Finally, the Russians strongly support the idea that Arab unity is a precondition for both confronting Israel and for talking to it. The war between Iran and Iraq is being portrayed as senseless and dangerous—something that only creates opportunities for Israel and the United States.

The present Soviet policy in the region sounds one recurrent theme: The Americans are responsible for all Israeli sins, and there is no realistic hope that Washington will significantly change its anti-Arab orientation. The United States is accused of trying to use the Camp David agreement to divide the Arabs, of encouraging Israel to invade Lebanon and of breaking its promise to the P.L.O. to protect West Beirut against incidents like the massacre in the Shatila and Sabra refugee camps. The Reagan plan is described in Moscow as totally unacceptable and deceitful—window-dressing designed to distance the Reagan Administration from "Zionist atrocities."

It is not entirely clear how many Arab leaders take these Soviet accusations seriously. Most Arab governments seem willing to give President Reagan the benefit of the doubt. They will apparently give him some time to try to work out a settlement—but more because they lack other options than because they share his views. Moderate Arabs are encouraged by America's apparent determination to see a settlement through and by Israel's new soul-searching. In short, it is not the Israelis' success in Lebanon, but rather the new emotional and geopolitical climate created by the invasion that suggests the possibility of a new beginning to America's friends in the Arab world. But rising expectations always involve some dangers. If they are not satisfied, there is bound to be a backlash against both the United States and those Arabs who risk cooperation with Washington.

A visitor to Cairo is struck by how frequently senior Egyptian officials compare what is happening in the Arab world today to the predicament of the former Shah of Iran. Boutros Ghali, the sophisticated Egyptian Minister of State for Foreign Affairs, who is known for his sympathy for the United States, told me that if no genuine progress was made on the Palestine issue, the stability of the entire region, Egypt included, would suffer as a result. The Defense Minister, Gen. Abdel Halim Abu Ghazala, linked strategic cooperation between Egypt and the United States, including facilities for the Rapid Deployment Force, with the general state of bilateral relations, and these in turn he tied to movement on the Palestine question. "Everything will be possible," if this issue is adequately addressed, he commented.

Egypt's reluctance to deepen its cooperation with the United States before seeing some softening of Israel's positions is shared by other Middle East leaders. King Hussein is said, for example, to be favorably disposed toward the Reagan initiative but not persuaded that the President will see it through. To some degree, his and other Arabs' willingness to enter negotiations with Israel is contingent on assurances from Washington that they will not be left at Mr. Begin's mercy and that there will be reciprocal concessions by Israel.

If the United States fails again to put its money where its mouth is in dealing with Israel, it runs the risk of encouraging explosions in one or more moderate Arab states. And, as the Egyptian journalist Mohammed H. Heikal wrote: "If and when these explosions occur, the Soviet Union is bound to be involved. No *Pax Americana* is going to be able to prevent that."

Israel and the Peace Process

HAROLD M. WALLER

Harold M. Waller is former chairman of the Department of Political Science at McGill University and has written extensively on Middle East issues, including articles on U.S. foreign policy in the Middle East, energy policy, and various aspects of the Arab-Israeli conflict. During the summer of 1981 he traveled widely in Israel.

IN the last year, Israel has learned more about the difficulty of converting military prowess and success into political gains. The conclusion of the peace treaty with Egypt, tied to the future of the West Bank and Gaza by the terms of the Camp David accords, required a shift of focus toward Palestinian autonomy, one of the main objectives of those negotiations. It was in Israel's interest to achieve the autonomy agreement contemplated at Camp David, which called for the participation of some of the inhabitants of the areas in question and the cooperation of Jordan. The Palestine Liberation Organization (PLO), based in Lebanon, opposed the Camp David objectives because its professed goal is to replace both Israel and Jordan as sovereign in the territory that it regards as "Palestine," which includes the land from the Mediterranean Sea to the eastern border of Jordan.[1] Whether a homeland or a state on only a small portion of that territory would ever be permanently acceptable is a matter of continuing and intense debate within and without the PLO.[2] Because implementation of the autonomy plan would be a serious political setback to its goal of statehood, the PLO pressured the residents of the disputed territories to avoid participation in the negotiating process and pressured Israel by continued military and terrorist threats from Lebanon.

The attempted assassination of the Israeli ambassador to Britain in June, 1982, offered Israel an opportunity to attack the PLO in Lebanon. From Israel's perspective, however, the results of the war were ambiguous. Israeli opposition to the war was given a boost by the reaction to the murders of several hundred Palestinian Arabs in Shatila and Sabra by Lebanese Christian militia forces in September, 1982. Israel's military presence in West Beirut, for the avowed purpose of preventing anarchy, raised questions concerning Israeli responsibility for the massacre that remain to be answered by the judicial inquiry established by the Israeli government.

But whatever the outcome of the inquiry, the war against the PLO and its aftermath in the Palestinian areas of Beirut left Israeli politics in turmoil and confusion. Although the government retains much popular support, its political effectiveness has been diminished, and the opposition, both within the Knesset and without, is fighting the government with increased intensity.

The external costs of the war have also been high. Israel's military offensive caused dismay in many quarters, especially among European governments, although the administration of United States President Ronald Reagan displayed considerable understanding and sympathy for the aims, if not always for the means. In other parts of the world, where hostility toward Israel has frequently been a cardinal principle of foreign policy (especially since 1967), the outcry was predictable. The net result was the increased isolation of Israel in the international community, a trend that was aided by world press and electronic media that were antagonistic toward Israel and seemed to single out Israel in a manner not comparable to media treatment of actors in other international crises.[3] Moreover, the positive disposition of the United States toward Israel's actions was partially dissipated by what was perceived as the excessive Israeli use of force toward the end of the war and by the debacle of the massacre.[4]

---

[1] David Bernstein, "A Friendship Renewed—Warily," *The Jerusalem Post International Edition*, October 17-23, 1982, p. 1, argues that meetings between King Hussein and Yasir Arafat, in which there was talk of a possible Jordanian-Palestinian confederation may just be a smokescreen for unchanged PLO objectives.

[2] Yehoshafat Harkabi, "The Evolution of the Palestinian Movement," in George Gruen, ed., *The Palestinians in Perspective* (New York: Institute of Human Relations Press, 1982), p. 63.

[3] Edward Alexander, "The Journalists' War Against Israel," and Melvin J. Lasky, "Embattled Positions," *Encounter*, vol. 51, nos. 3-4 (September-October, 1982), pp. 87-97 and 102-106.

[4] The decline in public opinion support for Israel is shown in "Newsweek Poll: Israel Loses Ground," *Newsweek*, October 4, 1982, p. 23.

Clearly, Israel will face very formidable challenges in the aftermath of its incursion into Lebanon against the PLO.

Israel's experience as a besieged state has prepared it to utilize military force in an era when states are at least nominally committed to the peaceful settlement of disputes. Several wars for national survival in the decades that followed the destruction of defenseless millions of Jews in Europe, along with a perception of continuing threats from neighboring countries, have led Israel to include military options as an ongoing feature of the foreign policy process.

When it launched the attack on the PLO in June, 1982, Israel had several objectives, some military and some political.[5] Its major military objectives were to achieve security for northern Israel, to destroy the PLO infrastructure of a state within the state of Lebanon, to eliminate the center of international terrorism, and to expel the PLO from Lebanon so that it could no longer threaten Israel again from that direction.

Israel's political objectives were more complex and subtle. It was most important to weaken the PLO politically in order to lessen its influence on the local Arabs of the West Bank (Judea and Samaria) and the Gaza Strip. Israeli planners believed that the prospects for progress on the stalled autonomy talks envisaged in the Camp David accords would be enhanced if the inhabitants of the occupied areas were not subject to influence, intimidation, threats, and even violence emanating from the PLO based in Lebanon.[6] Israelis believed that the people on the scene were more pragmatic than the PLO leadership and less ideologically committed to PLO goals, and that they were inhibited with respect to participation in the autonomy talks by their fear of the PLO. The Israelis reasoned that if the PLO were defeated in Lebanon and if its infrastructure were destroyed, its ability to operate effectively in other regions would be sharply reduced.

There were also less important political considerations. The restoration of public confidence in the Israel Defense Forces (IDF), reduced by the debacle at the outset of the Yom Kippur War, would be a useful by-product of a successful military operation. A military victory would also be a reminder to friend and foe alike that the military option is not really available to the Arabs and that they would see the necessity of negotiations.

Another objective was to influence the direction of political developments in Lebanon.[7] In the Israeli view, the presence of the activist PLO had destabilized Lebanon's fragile political system and had weakened the political power of the Christian communities. The Israelis hoped for the resurgence of the Christians—a possibility if the PLO could be forced out of Lebanon—because they believed that a Christian resurgence would make it possible to reestablish the peace-

ful border that existed before the PLO took over southern Lebanon. Moreover, a friendlier government in Beirut would mean a significant strategic improvement. Unfortunately, Israel relied too heavily on Bashir Gemayel, whose assassination damaged the prospects for a rapprochement between Lebanon and Israel.

For the most part, Israel's military objectives were achieved. The PLO was defeated; its political, military and terrorist infrastructure was destroyed; and the threat to Israel's northern region was removed. Israel's general strategic situation also improved.[8] But because Israel is weak politically in the international context, it is not always able to translate military victories into political gains. In all its previous wars, Israel prevailed militarily, but its military gains were at least partially neutralized by its inability to prevail in the subsequent political conflict. Thus the possibility that Israel would achieve major political objectives in the 1982 war was greeted with skepticism by many observers.

In 1982, political objectives were realized only partially while Israel incurred high political costs because of the very negative publicity connected with its conduct of the war. In particular, Israeli leaders were mistaken in their belief that it would be easier to conclude the autonomy negotiations after the defeat of the PLO in Lebanon. The introduction of the Reagan Middle East peace plan undercut what little incentive remained for the resumption of the autonomy talks, especially with the broader representation of the Palestinian Arabs and Jordan.

Another development that affected Israel adversely was a change in the role and standing of the PLO. Despite the military losses that shattered its bravado and may have undermined whatever unity of purpose it had, the PLO probably gained from the war in Lebanon. The Palestinian cause received a tremendous boost by virtue of the sharp juxtaposition of its position and that of Israel and the outpourings of sympathy that accompanied the casualties. And the PLO continued to be identified as the Palestinian spokesman. The events of the summer of 1982 made it easier for Western political elites to speak seriously about the possibility of the creation of a Palestinian state. In addition, the homelessness of the refugees (which, it might be

---

[5]There is a significant debate over whether Israel had political goals in the war. Deputy Foreign Minister Yehudah Ben-Meir flatly denied this contention in a speech at Montreal on October 22, 1982. Two views of how objectives changed as the war progressed are found in Aharon Yariv, "Unfinished Business," *The Jerusalem Post International Edition*, October 3-9, 1982, p. 15, and Robert W. Tucker, "Lebanon: The Case for War," *Commentary*, vol. 74, no. 4 (October, 1982), pp. 19-30.

[6]Tucker questions this view, *op. cit.*, p. 25.

[7]David Ignatius, "U.S. Risk in Lebanon Seen Escalating," *The Wall Street Journal*, October 11, 1982, p. 25.

[8]Tucker, *op. cit.*, p. 19.

argued, has been caused by the refusal of Arab states to integrate them over the years) was accentuated in a way that focused responsibility on Israel. Paradoxically, in this situation Israel might be able to bypass the PLO in a settlement of the Palestinian problem, if the incentives are great enough for Israel and for the Palestinian Arabs. Even if the PLO has been weakened as an organization and even if its internal contradictions begin to surface, any strengthening of the Palestinian cause will be viewed with concern by Israel.

One of the most serious effects of the war may well be political. The Labor opposition led the way; party leader Shimon Peres frequently expressed his opposition to carrying the war into Beirut, while other critics opposed the military operation altogether. In the wake of the Beirut massacre, opponents of Prime Minister Menachem Begin's regime coalesced in a call for the resignation of the government, an appeal that won a great deal of support in an already divided political system. But Labor could not win the support of a majority of the population.[9]

Insofar as Israel is concerned, the overall effect of the war against the PLO has been mixed. On the positive side are undoubted military gains at the expense of Syria and the PLO, the prospect of an improved situation in Lebanon, a weakened PLO, and enhanced security in the north. On the negative side are a further decline in Israel's international political position, increased sympathy and support for the Palestinian cause, increased internal dissent and more intense political opposition, an unwanted American initiative, and the jeopardizing of Israel's relations with Egypt and the United States.[10]

Whether the benefits outweigh the costs may not be determined for many years. If Israel's action in 1982 guaranteed its security in the north and helped to pave the way for a settlement on the central front without the involvement of the PLO, then the effort was probably worthwhile. But if increased sympathy for the Palestinian cause leads to more pressure for an independent Palestinian state, then the Israelis probably lost more than they gained.

AFTER LEBANON

Israel's long-range foreign policy goals have not changed, although the events of 1982 stimulated considerable analysis and debate.[11] Israel's primary aims are to preserve and enhance national security and to achieve peace with neighboring countries. National security has been a preoccupation of all Israeli governments since the founding of the state. But concern with matters of peace is relatively recent, because except for Egypt, Israel's neighbors have implacably opposed the idea of peace with Israel. Between 1967 and 1977, the idea of peace was seriously considered because Israeli control over considerable territory raised the possibility of the trade of territory for peace, as envisioned in United Nations Security Council Resolution 242. Once the Israeli-Egyptian peace treaty became reality, the need to consider the requirements for peace with other neighbors became inescapable, especially when external pressures for progress on the peace process became stronger.

The Likud's accession to power in 1977 led to a shift in policy. The government continued to support Resolution 242; nonetheless, the notion of a straight trade of territory for peace on the Jordanian and Syrian fronts was modified. According to the Begin administration, the long-term prospects that real peace could be achieved in this manner seemed very slim; the security risks involved in such a trade seemed too great; and the intrinsic importance of some of the areas in question received new emphasis. Consequently, the Begin government developed a new approach to peace, specifically, the autonomy plan. Begin preferred autonomy as a long-term solution, but agreed to accept it as an interim model at Camp David.

Should Labor regain power in Israel, the government would probably return to earlier positions. Although both Labor and Likud would like to achieve peace, they differ on the shape of the optimum solution, the means to achieve it, and the assessment of the possibility of obtaining genuine Arab agreement, while they concur on the dangers to Israel that are inherent in Palestinian statehood.[12]

In the intermediate term, many Israeli objectives have suffered in the past months. The bilateral relationship with the United States must be repaired. Begin has had to deal with two U.S. Presidents, Jimmy Carter and Ronald Reagan, and he has faced serious problems with both. He has taken the view that he must risk antagonizing Israel's closest friend if vital Israeli interests are at stake. The result has been a series of contretemps. Despite the official displays of United States anger (like the administration's statement in August, 1982, when Israel was bombing a besieged Beirut in order to increase pressure on the PLO), the American-Israeli relationship appears to have great resilience.[13] Whether it will remain so indefinitely is in doubt, but for the moment efforts to repair the damage seem to be at least moderately successful.

---

[9]"How Public Would Vote," *The Jerusalem Post International Edition*, October 3-9, 1982, p. 2, shows that opinion polling after the Beirut massacre still gave the Likud half the vote, with the rest split.

[10]Tucker, *op. cit.*, pp. 25-28.

[11]The goals of Israel's foreign policy are explored in greater detail in Harold M. Waller, "Israel's Foreign Policy Challenge," *Current History*, vol. 81, no. 471 (January, 1982), pp. 18-21.

[12]A fine comparison of the two perspectives is Shlomo Avineri, "Territory and Security," *The Jerusalem Post International Edition*, September 26-October 2, 1982, p. 11.

[13]Wolf Blitzer, "Back from the Brink," *The Jerusalem Post International Edition*, October 3-9, 1982, p. 3.

Israel also must be careful of its relationship with Egypt. The fragility of the ties was accentuated by the recall of the Egyptian ambassador to Israel in September, 1982, after the massacres in Beirut. The peace treaty with Egypt and the subsequent peaceful ties constitute Begin's crowning foreign policy achievement, and he can ill afford to see them deteriorate. Egypt's President Hosni Mubarak knows this and has threatened a change in Egypt's policy. But apparently Begin believes that in the absence of any direct Israeli provocation against Egypt, Mubarak will not risk the peace in order to gain favor with other Arab countries.

Israel must also try to negotiate a withdrawal of all Syrian, PLO, and Israeli forces from Lebanon and to resist external and internal pressure to settle any aspect of the Arab-Israeli conflict on terms that are perceived to be unfavorable. Despite unquestioned Israeli military superiority, the latter is a formidable task because Israel is widely perceived to be excessively stubborn regarding the substance of negotiations. Israel believes that its critics underestimate the dangers that it faces and are therefore insufficiently sympathetic to its security needs, for which it has the ultimate responsibility.[14]

Despite the close 1981 election, where Likud and the Labor Alignment were deadlocked in terms of vote percentages and parliamentary seats, Prime Minister Begin retained strong control of the political system because other parties in the Knesset preferred a coalition with him rather than with Labor. Therefore, even though the coalition held only a slim majority in the Knesset, the nature of the party and the election system gave Begin some stability, barring defections from the coalition. Still, he is anxious to reduce his reliance on the smaller parties, which exercise a great deal of leverage. Polls taken in the 18 months since the 1981 election indicate that the popularity of the Likud alliance has increased and that events in Lebanon did not have a major effect on voter preferences.[15] Whether that will change when voters have more time to reflect remains to be seen. The unease in the National Religious party, a key coalition partner, had become palpable by the fall of 1982.[16] And Begin found himself in a difficult position because of the demands of the Agudat Yisrael, another coalition partner. Thus the prospects for change seemed greater by the end of 1982 than they had a year earlier.

Begin's retirement or disability, which are impossible to predict, cannot be discounted in a man of his age and physical condition. And new elections or the replacement of Likud by a Labor government, based on shifts by smaller parties, would also spell political change. Labor, which recognizes its electoral weakness, would like to engineer the disintegration of the existing coalition and the formation of a new coalition with Labor dominant. Its efforts have come to naught, but the possibility that it might succeed cannot be ex-

cluded. Despite the reluctance of several parties, early elections may be forced on the administration. While the war was under way, there were indications that Begin was planning an election for the spring or late summer of 1983, two years earlier than required. The furor over the Beirut massacre has probably made new elections essential, even though the timing would be more difficult because of a possible connection between the report of the judicial inquiry commission and the election. However, Begin has indicated that he wants to make the next election a kind of referendum on the Reagan plan, with the Labor Alignment's Jordanian option depicted as being in accord with that plan. Until that election, Begin would certainly try to avoid any concessions in the peace process, adhering to the position that he staked out when he heard about the plan.

In the political calculus, Labor is severely handicapped by the demonstrable lack of popularity of its leader, Shimon Peres. The Alignment's electoral position has also been weakened by the ongoing feud between the Peres faction and the faction led by former Prime Minister Yitzhak Rabin. Labor should find a new leader but, in the absence of a clearly popular alternative candidate, a change in the leadership seems unlikely. The only person who has received much attention in this connection is President Yitzhak Navon, a former Labor politician who now holds the ceremonial and non-political presidency. His term expires in May, 1983, but he has given no clear indication of whether he wants a second term (which Begin might not approve), retirement, or a return to active politics. Should Navon decide to seek the leadership of the Labor party, the political situation could change significantly, especially since his Sephardic origin presumably would enable him to make inroads among voters who have been strongly pro-Begin and Likud in recent years.

Two other political issues merit attention. The first of these is the role of extra-parliamentary groups, like the Peace Now movement. These groups have their ups and downs, but they apparently revived during the protests of the summer and early fall of 1982. Insofar as they claim that the party system does not allow enough options concerning the vital issues of war

---

[14]President Ronald Reagan, in his address on September 1, 1982, went out of his way to try to reassure Israel that its security interests were paramount in the formulation of his plan.

[15]"How Public Would Vote," *op. cit.*

[16]Mark Segal, "Moral Values and the Use of Force," *The Jerusalem Post International Edition*, October 3-9, 1982, p. 13, is an interview with Education Minister Zevulun Hammer, an NRP (National Religious party) minister. See also Rochelle Furstenberg, "New Questions at the Yeshivot," *The Jerusalem Post International Edition*, October 3-9, 1982, p. 14, and "NRP's Loyalty Pledge," *The Jerusalem Post International Edition*, October 17-23, 1982, p. 9.

and peace, they could become a potential electoral threat, given the ease with which new party lists can be formed at election time. So far there is no indication that they will follow that route.

The second issue, an imponderable one, is the effect of the report of the judicial commission of inquiry. Although one cannot predict the findings, they will almost surely be injurious to the government, even if Begin successfully turns an unfavorable report to his advantage in an election campaign.

Since the completion of the Israeli withdrawal from the Sinai early in 1982, the negotiations of the autonomy plan envisaged in the Camp David accords have been deadlocked because Israel and Egypt cannot agree on the nature of the autonomy and because neither Jordan nor representatives of the local Palestinian inhabitants of the West Bank and Gaza have been willing to join the talks. If the war against the PLO was in part an attempt to diminish its veto power over the autonomy negotiations, then it was only partly successful. With Israel on the defensive politically since the war, the chances of obtaining a satisfactory agreement on the nature of the autonomy are slim, at least for a while. It was partly in response to this impasse that President Reagan launched his own initiative, a major departure from the Camp David framework; in the Reagan plan, the five-year transition period is essentially rendered meaningless and the outcome of the negotiations regarding the final status of the territories is effectively predetermined.

Regardless of the merits of the Reagan plan, it obviates the autonomy negotiations as they were envisaged at Camp David, where a key objective was to delay negotiations regarding a permanent settlement of the status of the West Bank and Gaza until a cooling-off period of five years had demonstrated that the parties concerned could live together in peace. It was assumed that after five years concessions from all the participants might be more readily forthcoming. Hence the autonomy plan was to be an interim arrangement.

The Camp David partners deliberately avoided any decision about arrangements to be made at the end of the five-year interim period. What President Reagan did last September was to short-circuit the interim autonomy plan and move directly to the outlines of a permanent solution that hinges upon the position of Jordan. It sets the President against Prime Minister Begin, whose government clearly is not prepared to concede the possibility that the West Bank and the Gaza strip might be put under Jordanian tutelage for the purpose of granting autonomy to the Palestinian Arab inhabitants. Further, despite Reagan's explicit rejection of the idea of a Palestinian state, the nature of his plan apparently does not exclude the possibility that a new Palestinian state might result. Israel is unalterably opposed to a Palestinian state in the West Bank and Gaza because it believes that a security threat could not be avoided under such circumstances.

The Likud position, articulated by the Prime Minister, prefers the Israeli retention of the disputed areas but contemplates the possibility of autonomy if Israel retains security control. The Labor opposition, in contrast, is willing to consider Jordanian sovereignty over the populated portions of the territories and demilitarization of the parts returned to Jordan. But neither of the major political groups is prepared to accept the possibility of an independent Palestinian state west of the Jordan River, one which would probably come to be dominated by the PLO; and both Israeli groups insist on retaining security control west of the Jordan in one fashion or another. Likud and Labor differ in their response to the Reagan plan because of their different assessments of the likelihood that an independent Palestinian state would emerge if the Reagan plan were to be implemented.

The initial Israeli responses to the plan were confused. The government rejected it out of hand in a move later endorsed by the Knesset. The Labor Alignment expressed support for some elements of the plan because the basic concept resembled its own Jordanian option, essentially a new partition of Mandatory Palestine west of the Jordan River but east of the 1949 armistice lines, with Israel retaining strategic control of the territory west of the river. The Prime Minister, for his part, remained steadfast in his support for the Camp David concepts, namely the five-year transitional period followed by negotiations for a definitive settlement. Although he has made it clear that Israel would assert its claim to sovereignty over the West Bank and the Gaza district, Begin would assert his claim in the context of negotiations to which Israel remains committed. It is doubtful that the other parties to those negotiations would accept such a claim; thus the negotiations might well yield an outcome other than that preferred by Israel. But for the moment, the chance that second-stage negotiations will take place seems remote because of the first-stage deadlock. To be sure, that is precisely the situation that the Reagan plan is designed to remedy.

The Arab response, whether at the Fez conference or from Jordan, tended to be somewhat vague on matters of vital interest to Israel.[18] Nothing that was said could be construed to be a sufficient inducement to get the Begin government to negotiate on the basis of the Reagan plan, which would mean abandoning Camp David.

---

[17]Israel opposes the plan for a number of reasons, including the positions on the nature of the autonomy, Jewish settlements, security provisions, the final status of the territories, Jerusalem, and the role of Jordan.

[18]Howard Adelman, "Begin, Reagan and Fez," unpublished paper.

The two sides continue to be so far apart in their public positions that it hardly seems possible that they can be brought to the bargaining table. Israel insists on proceeding with the Camp David negotiations, while the Arabs set out demands unacceptable to Israel. With the Camp David talks stalemated and the whole process undercut by the Reagan plan's implication that the Camp David negotiations are no longer necessary, the only ways to bring Israel to the bargaining table are either extreme pressure from the United States, which is not very likely, or a grand surprise gesture from the Arab side, like Egyptian President Anwar Sadat's 1977 initiative.[19] Therefore, there will probably be little progress in the near future. In fact, the cycles of Israeli and American electoral politics could conceivably delay meaningful diplomatic activity until a new American administration takes office in January, 1985.[20] However, what is now a relatively fluid situation would be much more rigid after a long delay. Consequently, the United States government, which is the only outside force able to make progress toward a peace settlement, has a strong interest in maintaining some momentum, like bringing Jordan and Israel together for negotiations.

The prevailing view in Israel is that it has waited for a long time for the Arab recognition that it believes is inevitable and that it will wait longer if necessary. When such recognition becomes a reality, serious negotiations can begin. Until then, Israel appears unwilling to shoulder the entire or even the major responsibility for concessions that might bring an agreement closer. After so many years of war, Israel clearly believes that its enemies have at least an equal responsibility to contemplate concessions. Hence a conciliatory approach by all parties concerned offers the best chance for solid progress in peace talks.

The recognition of this fact has not been consistent on the American side, a factor that detracts from the many positive aspects of the American-Israeli relationship. On the other hand, American efforts to bring one or more Arab countries into the peace process have been thwarted by attempts to achieve a unified Arab position, like the meeting at Fez last year. The pressure to subscribe to a common position (like a demand for total Israeli withdrawal or the creation of a Palestinian state) only hardens the stands of potential participants and makes it more difficult to initiate negotiations.

The dilemma for would-be peacemakers is that when stripped to the bare essentials the positions of the Arab states and Israel have been fundamentally incompatible ever since Israel was created. In the 1948-1967 period, steadfast Arab refusal to recognize Israel and accept its legitimacy precluded any possible peace negotiations. And Arab rhetoric concerning the destruction of Israel did not encourage a conciliatory Israeli attitude.

Since 1967, the focus has been on the territories that fell into Israel's hands during the Six Day War. The Arabs have always insisted on total Israeli withdrawal while Israel, under both Labor and Likud governments, has insisted that total withdrawal is impossible. It was only when Sadat made his great conciliatory gesture that meaningful negotiations became possible. The main hope for progress is either a grand gesture of some sort or a new approach that might lead to a solution without confronting some of the seemingly intractable problems.[21]

Israelis believe that someday their position in the Middle East will be normalized and that they will then be able to carry on conventional relationships with their neighbors. The experience with Egypt over the past few years, imperfect as it may be, has provided hope to those who share a vision of Arab-Israeli peace. Yet despite one signed peace treaty, a great deal of talk, and hints of peaceful Arab intentions at least from some quarters, a broadly based peace remains remote. The challenge to Arabs, Israelis, and concerned outsiders continues to be formidable indeed.

---

[19]Movement within at least part of the PLO is reported in David Bernstein, "PLO leader Hints at 'New Line'," *The Jerusalem Post International Edition*, October 3-9, 1982, p. 1.

[20]Nadav Safran, *Israel: The Embattled Ally* (Cambridge: Harvard University Press, 1981), p. 594.

[21]One solution is suggested by Daniel J. Elazar, "Shared Rule: A Prerequisite for Peace," in Elazar, ed., *Judea, Samaria, and Gaza: Views on the Present and Future* (Washington: American Enterprise Institute, 1982), pp. 211-222.

The International Political Economy: Aid, Investment, Trade, and Finance

The international economic system is in serious trouble. World trade is stagnant because the participants, suffering from unemployment, recession and hence a lack of sufficient hard currency, are unable to expand trade. East-West trade, which had been flourishing, is now plagued by the debt of the Soviet bloc in the amount of $80 billion. It can only repay the debt by paying out from its reserves, borrowing even more from the West, or producing more. None of these seem likely alternatives. Poland's debt alone ($30 billion) requires interest payments that are in excess of 100 percent of its hard-currency export earnings. Third World countries face similar problems of heavy debt services on their borrowing. Moreover, having defaulted on their loans so frequently, Western banks are reluctant to lend them further necessary capital. Foreign aid programs are, of course, suffering from bad economic times. In response to domestic pressures, fewer disposable funds, and poor returns (both political and economic) on foreign aid dollars that have been lavished on Third World countries, foreign aid programs are under scrutiny. Ultimately, however, if Third World countries, not to mention Poland, go bankrupt and essentially drop out of the international economic system, all participants in the system are hurt. It is an illustration of the "non-zero sum" nature of international economics: we may all win or all lose together.

The interrelatedness of states is nowhere so conspicuous as in the various dimensions of the international political economy. Since World War II, the international political economy has been complicated by the participation of numerous non-state actors, such as multi-national corporations, whose annual output dwarfs the size of the GNP of some nation-states. Moreover, the tripling of the number of states participating in the international economy, and the political implications of economic decisions, complicates any attempt at drafting "solutions" to problems.

Some states, for example, have attempted to influence the international economy through the use of a strategic natural resource as a tool to improve their position within the international economic system. But as the oil weapon illustrates, the results of using economic power as an instrument of foreign policy are not entirely predictable. In the case of OPEC, the member states dramatically increased the price of oil beginning in 1973 in an attempt, on the one hand, to influence the political situation in the Middle East and, on the other, to gain more economic wealth for themselves. The outcome, however, has not been altogether happy for OPEC countries. The oil boycott and increased price of oil (with the exception of Britain and Norway, three-fourths of all oil consumed in Western Europe and Japan is controlled by the OPEC cartel) led to an intensive and extensive search for domestic oil and alternative energy resources by countries whose economic security was threatened. Oil that had formerly been considered prohibitively expensive to exploit suddenly seemed far cheaper in comparison to OPEC-produced oil. The US created "strategic petroleum reserves" to protect its national security against the use of oil as a political weapon. Extensive efforts have been made to diminish dependency on foreign oil. Oil prices, which had increased from $2.40 a barrel in 1973 to $37.00 in 1981, fueled world inflation, ultimately making the finished manufactured products that the OPEC states need for their own modernization commensurately expensive. And more than the intended result of undermining the economies of the industrialized states, the increased price of oil hurt OPEC's Third World "friends," bringing their economic development to a halt. Some less fortunate ones were forced over the edge into the "fourth world." Since 1981, the oil-producing states have been faced with a crisis caused in large part by an "oil glut," with falling oil revenues cutting into their own modernization efforts. But the benefits are not totally in favor of the oil-consuming states; for now the billions of petro-dollars that were available for investment in the industrialized states are diminishing. This forces the former beneficiaries of such investments to look elsewhere.

The problem of calculating means and ends is repeatedly demonstrated when individual states take unilateral economic actions to improve their inter-

6

national position. In the 1970s, America's allies cried out in anguish that the US had to take rigorous measures to control its inflation and to redress the imbalance in its international balance of payments. America was spending more abroad than it was producing. As a result the large number of dollars that were piling up in foreign banks were rapidly losing their value. This not only made the dollar less acceptable as an international reserve currency, but also undermined American leadership in the international economic system. The US responded to this pressure (and domestic pressures) with a series of measures, not the least of which was increased interest rates. But in the process of strengthening the value of the American dollar, this action also led to a siphoning off of international capital into American investments. Thus America's allies now find it difficult to attract the necessary capital for investment in their own enterprises, leaving them distressed again. They have successfully pressured us to lower interest rates dramatically, but the end result of this measure may not be what they had hoped for either.

Such a situation indicates once again the difficulties of making adjustments on a national scale to respond to maladjustments somewhere in the international economic system: remedies for one problem lead inexorably to new problems. If no new markets materialize, protectionist measures to limit imports may mean that countries formerly depending on exports will have to cut back production. This leads to unemployment and recession, necessitating a cutback in that country's own imports. With enough contraction in world trade, the international economy itself moves toward a recession, and all countries suffer.

Thus the US and the European Economic Community (EEC) countries, while resenting Japan's success in exporting to them and the problems this creates for their international balance of payments, are in a dilemma: if they retaliate against Japan by implementing protectionist measures that succeed in slowing Japanese economic growth, it could be a major catalyst to a world economic depression. In fact, there is considerable doubt as to whether Western industrial

economies would benefit significantly if protectionist measures succeeded in cutting Japanese imports. The Japanese economy, which is totally dependent on exporting, would suffer immeasurable damage, yet it makes little sense to insist on what amounts to an economic declaration of war. The end result might well be the weakening of America's strongest and most loyal ally in Asia, and a weakened international economy that would hurt all of us. What the West really wants is an end to Japan's protectionist trade policies and its non-tariff barriers. Proposals to "share the burden" of economic hard times also include Japan's producing goods within the Western industrialized states themselves. But urging Japan to divert its capital from the economic sector in order to make greater contributions to defense and foreign aid programs must be looked at long and hard for its ultimate political and military implications.

Looking Ahead: Challenge Questions

How does the value of a currency relate to a country's international political leadership? Do those countries that now hold the five leading international hard currencies effectively control the international economic system? How does this carry over to their ability to influence international politics?

What is the significance for the international economic system and for Soviet economic and political leadership of the Russian ruble not being an internationally acceptable hard currency? How do countries that lack an internationally acceptable currency do business? Why is counter-trade growing? How does the US feel about counter-trade arrangements?

The IMF's advice to countries suffering from serious balance of payments problems is to export more and import less. How can such a solution work if many countries attempt it?

Is an "economic cold war" against the Soviet Union—withholding goods needed by the Soviet Union as a weapon to achieve political goals vis-à-vis the Soviets—likely to have its intended effect? What do the oil pipeline controversy and the sale of grain to the Soviets suggest about the results of such policies?

165

Development Strategy Distorted by Western Propaganda

Lyubov Chernorutskaya

Africa and Latin America have only 17.4 per cent of all radios, 10.5 per cent of TV sets, and 14.2 per cent of all daily papers. Almost 75 per cent of information on the developing countries themselves appearing in their periodicals is taken from news agencies in New York, Paris or London. Information reports sent from the newly-free countries but processed in the West take on quite a different colouration in conformity with the interests of big business.

The transnational corporations operating in the sphere of information consistently carry out the behests of imperialist quarters, moulding public opinion in the newly-free countries and seeking to influence the socio-economic and political processes there in the interests of world capitalism. They allot much attention to elaborating "alternative development strategies" for the newly-free countries in keeping with the neocolonialist interests of imperialism. As far as the concept of "collective self-reliance" (which the young states are striving to implement to join efforts for more dynamic development) is concerned, bourgeois scholars have recommended that this concept be aimed only at improving local agriculture and producing elementary commodities, thereby limiting the economic tasks facing the newly-free countries. This approach is based on the well-known bourgeois theory of "basic needs" which dooms the young states to permanent backwardness and dependence.

The practice of extolling the activities of the TNCs and their "partnership" with the national bourgeoisie in the young states is designed to promote private enterprise and help the emergence of local capitalists, the class allies of the TNCs. The imperialist mass media devotes a great deal of attention to the need to create a "favourable investment climate" for the TNCs, and to make greater inflow of investments dependent on the recipient countries' providing guarantees against nationalisation. At the same time, the fact of the TNCs receiving huge superprofits, their brazen interference in the domestic affairs of the newly-free countries, their "limiting business practices" and so on, are glossed over or left unmentioned.

Advertising in every possible way the "advantages" of foreign private investments in the economies of young states, which is aimed at implanting capitalist production relations there, Western propaganda gives an increasingly pessimistic evaluation of the role played by "official aid for development". This is being done deliberately to create the impression that this aid will be inevitably reduced. For example, the West German magazine *Wirtschaftswoche* wrote that the US Administration is intent on cutting government aid to developing countries by 20 per cent and will regulate it depending on each given country's "political reliability". *Inter-Economics* magazine, another FRG periodical, cites the question put by the US Administration: can the problems of development be solved by money injections made into national economies from outside, or is it necessary to take a new approach to the policy of development which provides for the growth of the private sector in the economies of the newly-free countries? The Indian newspaper *Business Standard* emphasises that the strategy of transnational corporations in all emergent countries is directed at "denationalisation of the nation-state" and is implemented along many lines, chiefly economic and ideological ones. Indian Minister of Information and Broadcasting P. Sathe censured the work of Western mass media with respect to developing countries and stressed that misinformation, glossing over some developments, and tendentious news reporting undermine the domestic political stability in those countries and have a pernicious effect on their development.

The brain-washing done by the Western mass media in the newly-free countries on the eve of the Conference in Cancun (Mexico, October 1981) is a case in point. Just before the Conference opened, the *Christian Science Monitor* carried an article which stressed that the developing countries should not hope for a success in Cancun because President Reagan insisted that the United States would grant the assistance on terms meeting its economic interests. Some time later, the

"Development Strategy Distorted by Western Propaganda," Lyubov Chernorutskaya, *Asia and Africa Today*, Moscow, Vol. 4, 1982.

New York Times also carried an article which noted the negative attitude of the White House toward any increase of government aid to the developing countries. The *Washington Post* stressed repeatedly that the USA is against the redistribution of wealth between "rich and poor countries".

A "news leak" was specially organised in the US to weaken the resistance of the newly-free countries. It followed from this "information" that changes unfavourable to the developing countries might occur in the activities of the World Bank and the International Monetary Fund. The idea was to compel the young states to reconcile themselves to the status quo in the world capitalist economy. In his speech in Cancun, President Reagan stated that "North-South" global negotiations would be possible only if they proceeded within the framework of the agenda offered by the US, which covered such issues as the development of food and energy resources of the developing countries and the improvement of conditions for private capital investments. Reagan noted that the participants in the negotiations should also respect the decisions of the existing specialised international agencies and make no attempts to set up new institutions; the negotiations should be oriented toward domestic economic policy and should not assume the nature of a political confrontation.

As a result, no constructive decisions were adopted at the Cancun Conference. The Declaration divulged after the Conference speaks in general terms of the need to work out national strategies to solve the problem of hunger. Commenting on this document, the Western press hastened to claim that the problem was not easily solved at national level. The statistics adduced to corroborate the claim show that in the 1970s, the per-capita agricultural production dropped in more than 60 developing countries, while in 15 it shrank in absolute terms. The developing world has become more dependent of food imports. Whereas in 1970 grain imports amounted to 43 million tons, of which 30 million came in as food aid, in 1980, the figure was nearly 90 million tons, with food aid accounting for only 11 per cent of the total. Such a showing would "objectively" invite the conclusion that the developing countries are unable to do without the West's "assistance", and thus the food problem becomes a powerful lever helping subjugate the newly-free countries' social and political development in accordance with imperialist interests.

The US has begun to withdraw its investments from industrial construction and reinvest in agricultural development, which, according to US reasoning, will contribute towards implementing the "basic needs" concept and reducing social antagonisms in the young states. The first to receive this "aid" are the USA's military allies and those countries that follow in the wake of US policies. Within this category, the US press is giving prominence to Middle East countries which have come to account for 41.6 per cent of American economic aid in late 1970s. Likewise it has turned

spotlights on the countries which the UN has listed as the least developed, publicising the efforts to create "adequate technology" for them capable of being geared to their specific conditions: low-skilled workforce, poor infrastructure, etc. Of definite social purport is also the US scientific and technical assistance to these countries, the training of their personnel in the USA, etc.

American propaganda believes it expedient to have state aid granted to the least developed countries lacking favourable conditions for the operation of private capital. This aid is designed to contribute toward a rapid growth of capitalism, after which it should be distributed according to the so-called gradation principle: the more ripe is a country for TNC infiltration, the more private investments it gets, and the less the state aid is.

The US press attaches special importance to the Agency for International Development forming "reconnaissance groups" which include representatives of US business and financial circles. These groups are supposed to travel on fact-finding missions assertaining the expediency of private investments in newly-free countries. The first such group has parted for Indonesia, Thailand, Kenya and Sri Lanka. Similar visits are expected in Egypt, Pakistan, Ivory Coast, Zimbabwe, Jamaica and Costa Rica, i.e. the countries which the US press has named as strategically most important for the USA.

The *Washington Post* summed up the Cancun Conference by saying that Reagan and his team came to Cancun to urge the newly-free countries to develop market economy and encourage private investments, rather than to heed their demands for more aid.

In this connection, Prime Minister Indira Gandhi of India noted that the Cancun Declaration failed to mention a major issue: the multilateral financing which would make it possible to satisfy the development needs. She also pointed out that the market forces favoured by President Reagan neglect the poorest and the weakest and, therefore, cannot serve as a means of overcoming poverty. Indian press emphasised that it is precisely the United States that is responsible for the fact that the participants in the Conference failed to work out concrete decisions aimed at rectifying the current unequal relations. This is why the developing countries should grow "political muscle" which no one can ignore.

It is no accident that the need for the establishment of a new international economic order is tied in by the developing countries to the demand for changes in the sphere of information. In 1973 at the Fourth Conference of the Heads of State and Government of Non-Aligned countries in Algeria, problems of improving mutual information communications were discussed, and at the Fifth Conference in Colombo in 1976, the non-aligned countries passed a decision to set up a pool of information agencies. The political declaration adopted at the Conference emphasised that the emancipation and development of national sources of information are an inalienable part of the common struggle for genuine independence for many peoples, inasmuch as the dependence in the sphere of information impedes political, social and economic progress.

The same idea was emphasised when this particular problem was discussed at the Sixth Conference of the Heads of State and Government held in Havana in 1979. The documents adopted at that conference stressed that "cooperation in information is an inalienable aspect of the struggle by non-aligned and other developing states for the establishment of new international relationships in general." The Conference stressed that the concerted efforts the newly-free countries make through the medium specialised agencies of the UN, which efforts are aimed at training national personnel and developing a technical and technological basis are a *sine qua non* for the establishment of a new international order in the sphere of information.

The creation of a pool of information agencies is the first attempt at organising such an international system of information which would be independent of Western information services. The pool distributes 40,000 words of information in five languages daily, issues a bulletin, and assists in training journalists for national agencies. It must be admitted, however, that technical, financial and other difficulties prevent the pool from fully solving the problems it faces.

The 20th Session of the UNESCO General Conference held in 1978 adopted the "Declaration on Fundamental Principles Concerning the Contribution of the Mass Media to Strengthening Peace and International Understanding, the Promotion of Human Rights and to Countering Racialism, Apartheid and Incitement to War" In 1970, the Soviet Union came out with the idea of such a Declaration, and after many years of efforts this document has been adopted unanimously. However, Western countries which signed the Declaration, as well as other documents concerning the establishment of a new international economic order, have not introduced any changes in their policies. Bourgeois propaganda continues to whip up political tensions and undermine detente.

In 1980 the 21st Session of the UNESCO General Conference approved a resolution which noted that the international programme of communications development should become part of the efforts for establishing a new, fairer, more efficient world order in the sphere of information and communications. The bourgeois concept of the "freedom of information" was counterposed by proposals of representatives of many young states who stressed in their speeches that today "freedom of information" is tantamount only to the freedom of Western information agencies to exploit all their possibilities in the interests of imperialism. This resolution demanded that measures be taken to change the obtaining situation. The developed capitalist countries either abstained or voted against such an approach. But nonetheless, the resolution was passed by an overwhelming majority. The Conference also approved the document on the preparation of medium-term UNESCO plan for 1984-1989 envisaging the elaboration of ways toward decolonisation and democratisation in the sphere of information exchange. It is indicative that the problem of interconnection between the new international information order and economic order was regarded as the key issue at the Conference.

Apart from the pool of information agencies, regional information associations of the developing countries have begun to play an important role in the fight against "information imperialism". Early in November 1981, the Fifth General Assembly of the Organisation of Asian News Agencies was held in Kuala Lumpur. The major issue at the conference, in which UNESCO took part, was the problem of reorganising the abovementioned association by means of a considerable expansion of its composition and setting up, within the framework of that body, of a single Asian-Pacific network of information exchange.

This body is now called the Organisation of Asian and Pacific News Agencies. It has admitted nine more national agencies, and the total membership has reached 23 agencies. It is important that the majority of new members of the organisation are the news agencies of socialist countries, including the USSR, Laos, the Korean People's Democratic Republic, Mongolia, Vietnam and Afghanistan. A number of changes have been introduced in the Charter, and today to spread information concerning the overcoming of poverty, unemployment, disease, and participation in the struggle for peace and mutual understanding between nations and against all forms of colonialism and neocolonialism has become the major trend in the activity of the organisation. The main channels will be Moscow-Delhi and Delhi-Jakarta-Manila lines based on the computer centres in Moscow, Delhi, and Manila.

In their speeches many delegates considered the creation of this organisation, as an important event. The representative of the Press Trust of India noted that Asia is becoming a continent the information agencies of which are now linked as equal partners within a single system of cooperative information exchange. A specific feature of the organisation is also the fact that information agencies of countries with different socio-economic systems take part in it on an equitable, democratic basis, and this equitable cooperation is largely predetermined by the presence of the socialist states.

At the same time, the Pan-African Information Agency set up in April 1979 is encountering grave difficulties Western information services continue to preserve their monopoly on the news "trade", inasmuch as they have a ramified network of correspondents and a modern system of telegraph and TV communications at their disposal.

The stance taken by the USSR and other socialist

states regarding the new international economic and information order is based on the Leninist principles of peaceful coexistence of countries with different socio-economic system and the support rendered to the anti-imperialist struggle waged by the oppressed peoples. The economic cooperation of the socialist states and the newly-free countries has no political strings attached and is developing along the lines of equality and mutual advantage, thereby promoting the progress of the young states. The consistent and purposeful struggle waged by the socialist countries for international detente, disarmament and the consolidation of peace also creates objective prerequisites for a further shrinking of the sphere of imperialist domination in the developing world.

The regular annual meeting of general directors of information agencies and press agencies from socialist countries held last December stressed the need for the further development of cooperation between these agencies and information services of the newly-free countries. A point was made to the effect that the expansion of such ties takes place in the spirit of the internationalist assistance rendered by the socialist states, which promotes the progress of the national mass media.

The close bonds between the demands for a fundamental restructuring of international economic relations and the need for the establishment of a new international order in the sphere of information testify to a greater significance of the political factor in the struggle against all forms of neocolonialism.

THE NORTH-SOUTH DIALOGUE: THE ISSUE IS SURVIVAL

WILLY BRANDT

Willy Brandt is Chairman of the Social Democratic Party and former Federal Chancellor of Germany. After spending the Second World War years in Scandinavia, Brandt began his career in German politics and government in the late 1940s, serving as Mayor of Berlin (1957-1966), Foreign Affairs Minister in the Grand Coalition of the SPD and the CDU/CSU (1966-1969) and Federal Chancellor (1969-1974). He was awarded the Nobel Peace Prize in 1971. As chairman of the "Independent Commission on International Development Issues," Brandt guided to completion the Commission's report, North-South: A Program for Survival, *MIT Press, 1980. This interview, conducted by Richard D. Bartel, Executive Editor of* Challenge, *took place in Bonn on June 30, 1982.*

Q. When *Challenge* reaches its readers in September, almost one year will have passed since the Summit at Cancún, Mexico in October 1981. That Summit brought together heads of state of 22 industrial and developing countries to discuss the issues of the North-South dialogue. What has happened to that dialogue? Is it continuing to make some progress? Are you optimistic for the future? Or has the industrial recession across the world brought the North-South dialogue to a standstill?
A. The Cancún Summit, of course, was the first meeting of its kind, eight heads of state coming from industrial countries and fourteen from developing countries. Most of the participants at Cancún had met before bilaterally but it was the first time they sat together on an equal basis at a summit meeting. This in itself perhaps was not unimportant. Cancún, therefore, provided a valuable focus for North-South problems and set a precedent for discussing mutual interests at the high-

est level. But it would be wrong if I gave the impression that Cancún itself and what followed afterwards made me optimistic for the future. First, I am worried that world economic conditions have worsened further, especially in the very poor countries. Since the international recession still goes on, the tendency for countries to seek relief in protectionist measures has grown. This is true not only in the trade relations between industrialized countries and the rest of the world, but even within the industrialized world itself. We all know the damage this does to world trade.

Second, Cancún did not lead directly to the kind of emergency measures our Commission had advocated—particularly a global food program, an international energy strategy and international finance arrangements. But I did take hope in follow-up meetings. The Commission members met in Kuwait in January, joined by distinguished guests from certain international institutions and national governments, to discuss the acute economic problems of developing countries. Later in February, there was a follow-up meeting—a kind of South-South summit of 34 developing countries in New Delhi. It did not carry progress much farther, but it indicated the desire for developing countries to have their own summit meetings. And why shouldn't they?

Q. What was the focus of the meeting?
A. The participants started discussions on a number of interesting issues. Could specific things be done to promote trade between developing countries? Could measures be taken to create a financial institution for the South under the responsibility of developing countries? Later, in May, the Group of 77 continued discussions of South-South issues at a meeting in Jamaica—this time not on the level of heads of government, but rather on the level of foreign ministers or economic ministers.

Finally, in June the seven leading industrial countries met in Versailles and part of their talks included North-South issues. Although I was personally not too much impressed by the overall outcome of that Versailles Summit, I was favorably impressed with the paragraph in their communiqué on North-South issues. The seven leading industrial countries agreed to take a favorable view on getting global negotiations started under the umbrella of the United Nations. They even accepted procedural proposals which had been made by the Group of 77. The Iraqi Ambassador Kittani, acting President of the General Assembly of the United Nations, played an important role in preparing these procedural proposals.

The Versailles communiqué also included a paragraph which indicated that the leading industrialized countries were willing to look into international financial institutions. Specifically they agreed to see that the World Bank's daughter, so to say, IDA (the International Development Association), which gives cheap credits to the poorest countries, does not break down. There has been a danger that this development agency would not have sufficient funds. So if these industrialized countries live up to what their leaders said in Versailles early in June—and this is especially important for the United States because of the special weight it carries and the important example it should set—the outlook for IDA at least is more promising. The heads of state agreed together with President Reagan on the replenishment of IDA for last year and this year. That is fixed now and I could not believe that the United States would not live up to that agreement. So I am rather confident that something will move in this specific field.

Q. But what about the larger question of global negotiations?

A. If you take at face value the statements coming out of Versailles, I now believe that some kind of global negotiations—which means discussions in which industrial and developing countries can all participate and on all the items involved—can possibly start sometime during the coming winter or early next year. One should be aware of the fact that these negotiations will take years. And of course this cannot be a process in which decisions are based on the principle of one country, one vote. The process will probably develop along the lines of models offered by existing institutions like the World Bank and the International Monetary Fund. But advice can be given on substantive issues, while we work on further development and perhaps some reform of these international institutions. Now, if it is realistic to assume that this will take several years, one should not only concentrate on global negotiations, but at the same time, think about how to agree on practical measures for the next few years ahead of us.

Q. Specifically, what kinds of measures do you have in mind?

A. My Commission proposed an emergency program of special urgency. A global food program must aim to raise food output in the Third World, and to provide for larger emergency food aid where needed and for longer-term international food security. An international energy strategy would work toward insuring oil supplies, encouraging rigorous conservation efforts, developing alternative and renewable energy sources, and introducing price increases in a more predictable and gradual way. In the area of international finance, we need to give immediate attention to the problems of mounting debt, especially among developing countries, and ways to relieve world liquidity pressures. These emergency programs will require some reform of international organizations. I hope by now we would be able to bring this forward in more concrete terms than we did two and a half years ago. It is also important to prepare for the global negotiations in two areas. We have to resolve the quarrel on procedural issues, which has been a stumbling block for a long time now. But at the same time we must try to make some progress on the urgent substantive problems I've just outlined. Indeed, perhaps one should give financial issues top priority today, since the indebtedness of so many developing countries has deteriorated since the *North-South* report was prepared.

Q. In moving toward more concrete proposals, as you suggest, especially in the emergency program, where do you see these initiatives being made—within the United Nations, in some other institutional arrangement, or informally?

A. I think there is an approach to be made; there is a need to strengthen, and in some cases to revitalize, existing institutions. These institutions should include in their activities some share of co-responsibility on the part of those countries which are recipients of aid or loans. I think it is a question of using the existing institutions like the World Bank or the institutions in the field of food and agriculture, and help them to work as constructively as possible. The role of the U.N. is that of an umbrella, if that is not impolite to say. It's the forum for global negotiations. If it allays the fears of my friends in the United States and in some other countries, we can speak about global *discussions* instead of global *negotiations*. Certainly even our friends in the developing countries know by now that there will be no question of ganging up against the industrialized countries. They know that there is a need for consensus, but they want to have their views included in the assessment of those discussions—or, as they are called officially, negotiations. I am not enthusiastic about the idea of creating new institutions, perhaps with the one exception of something for energy.

Q. Do you see conflict between the multilateral strategies of international institutions and the new Reagan program to stress bilateral aid using private business as the channel of investment?

A. No, I cannot see a need for a choice to be made. I think one should use both existing institutions and all the bilateral machinery which exists. We should use the regional machinery—the Lomé agreement, for example, which embodies the links between the European Economic Community (EEC) and those developing countries which had earlier colonial ties with England, France, and a few other countries. But we must develop all the possibilities and potentials of private organizations, private business, and the banks. No, there is no need to make a choice, but rather to mobilize energies wherever they can be mobilized.

But I object to another aspect of present U.S. policy: that is to link development policy too closely to foreign policy. But if President Reagan says much more should be done in the field of engaging private business in development activities, I think this is fine. I would not quarrel with him about it. If I have correct information about the Cancún meeting, some of the Presidents and Prime Ministers from developing countries told President Reagan that a role for private business would be fine, but that obviously there are some countries, and some specific development problems within developing countries, where the interest of private business probably cannot be mobilized in any considerable way. Private business won't be interested in certain kinds of infrastructure or in the very

poor countries. So we really need the participation of private business, governments, and international institutions. Public responsibility and private interests should both be mobilized.

Q. How would you respond to the viewpoint expressed by some economists and some policymakers that the best contribution industrial countries can make to the developing world is to pursue economic growth, to maintain prosperity, and to open their markets to the developing world. In other words, the complexities of global negotiations are so great that we should not pursue that route, but pursue prosperity instead.

A. Well, this would be fine but experience has shown that it just would not be enough. Depending on prosperity in developed countries alone shows that you produce for a very limited market within a developing country, for a very limited number of people. You have to develop infrastructure too—schools, roads, railways—to create the preconditions for the growth of wealth and income of larger numbers of the population. So again I think both methods have to be used.

Q. You have already spoken about the institutional arrangements of a new world order and the fact that you favor using existing institutions. I want to learn more about your impressions of the willingness of the developing world, the Group of 77, to participate in existing institutions. Are they really satisfied with their voice in the World Bank and in the International Monetary Fund (IMF)?

A. Yes, as I mentioned before, we shall have to change some of these institutions to make them better meeting places for the developing and industrial countries. For example, the process of sharing responsibility could have been speeded up, I think. I would cite one example: it did take a rather long time before Saudi Arabia was given a higher level of responsibility within the IMF and the World Bank. This happened only after it became clear how great was Saudi Arabia's role in the international capital markets. There is a good deal of criticism of existing institutions and not all of that is justified. But if you speak to responsible people in developing countries, apart from their political philosophy, what they are asking for is *not* a majority of votes for those who do not represent a majority of capital investment. What they do ask for is something along the lines of the Marshall Plan practiced after World War II. The amount of aid given by the United States was combined with an operation in which the countries receiving aid participated directly. Their people were included in the planning, the projects built on their knowledge and their experience. That made the Marshall Plan a success.

When our Commission discussed the future of international institutions, we never thought in terms of purely *formal* changes in responsibility—reapportioning voting rights, for example. What we discussed and what we still would favor, perhaps favor even more now than we did a few years ago, was to include people from developing countries to a higher degree, without introducing changes in voting systems which would not make sense. Certainly, the countries which receive aid and loans have a special responsibility to those countries which contribute the highest share of capital funds, let's say, to enter into a reasonable discussion based on sharing responsibilities. For example, the People's Republic of China not only participated in the Cancún meeting; it has also joined the IMF. Rumania and Hungary are International Monetary Fund members too, and Poland would probably by now have been a member had it not run into the crisis we all know about and deplore.

There is no doubt that even in the Soviet Union there is a discussion going on concerning these issues. When I was in Moscow last summer I spent some time at one of their international institutes to discuss North-South under the rubric of mutual interest and of global responsibility. There I found that the group of one hundred experts with whom I spoke were more or less on the same level of discussion as their counterparts in Western Europe. I also had the impression that they were very much more advanced in their thinking than their government seems to be, but I'm sure they would not like to be quoted in detail on what their thinking was concerning future developments.

Q. What about elsewhere in Eastern Europe?
A. In Eastern Europe we have experienced several times how great their interest is in global issues and the North-South dialogue. Last autumn I participated with scholars from institutes in Western and Eastern Europe in a conference, in Budapest, on North-South issues. When you discuss these topics with a leader like Hungary's Kadár, he would perhaps not use exactly the same language, but he still expresses a vital interest in the future of the international monetary system, just to take one of the important items. Eastern Europeans are also vitally interested in the future conditions of world trade and also look for answers to world energy problems for the decades ahead. The problems of international finance and energy hit them more or less the same way that they do Western Europe.

Unfortunately, the worsening of general East-West relations also pushes the questions we are discussing a little bit more into the background. Since I believe these countries act on the basis of what they consider to be their own self-interest, I thought there wasn't much use in trying to preach to them about the merits of the North-South dialogue. They will have to determine when their own interests speak more in favor of their joining not only in the North-South discussions but also in its decisions. In any case, if I am right in assuming that North-South talks will resume during the coming winter or early next year, then the Eastern bloc —more or less under the influence of the Soviet Union, of course—will play some role there. It would be good if this could be a more constructive role and not one characterized so much by rigid positions as one has experienced earlier.

Q. I sometimes hear that the Russians respond to this invitation to participate by saying that the problems of developing countries were caused by the colonial imperialists, and it is therefore the imperialists' task to solve the problem. The Russians do not want to share responsibility for a situation which they did not cause. Do you hear that kind of an argument?
A. Yes, but I think it is a rather old-fashioned argument. The responsible people, let's say in the countries between the Federal Republic and Russia, not only know that this is outdated, but I think they also express that view to Soviet leaders. In any case, I know a number of my friends in developing countries who have told the Russians that they are not interested in an interpretation of history. But they *are* interested in finding answers to the problems they face now and will face during the decades to come. Whether this "orthodox" interpretation of colonialism or the heritage of colonialism is right or not, certain practical things have to be settled and they obviously demand the participation of not only the West of the North, but of both the West and the East of the North.

Q. You have stressed in the *North-South* report the close links between the problems of economic development and the peaceful resolution of political conflicts. The crises in Central America, the Falkland Islands, and the Iran-Iraq war are just the most recent examples of resources wasted on armaments—which limits the use of resources for economic development. How can the North-South dialogue contribute to the limitations on arms and a resolution of these conflicts by means other than military?

A. I share the fear of those who say there is a danger that while the great powers start negotiations on the most serious weapons, other countries may tend to flare up and create more conflict than they have during the past. But what is critical for us in the future is what happens in the relationship between the two superpowers and the two blocs. Only if they make serious progress in limiting and perhaps even reducing armaments will we have something to build upon. Second, it would be most desirable if the superpowers of the two blocs did not wait too long to start again the discussion of their sales and delivery of weapons to other parts of the world outside the East-West bloc. This, as some of us know, was in the process of getting started not so many years ago, when the Russians and the Americans were sitting together around the table to see if they could do something about reducing the arms build-up in various parts of the world. I think arms limitation in the Third World would not occur in an isolated manner. The precondition is that the United States and the Soviet Union, or their two alliances, make progress on their items of armament. Then this could have a favorable influence on their relationships in the field of weaponry with Third World countries.

One should be alert to differences among the countries in the Third World itself. If we just look at the statistics, we can find a terrible growth of funds being used in these countries for armaments, but most of their arms build-up stems from the money which the oil-producing countries, particularly the Middle East, have been able to put into their build-up of military strength. But even beyond that build-up, with all the risk involved, we see a general tendency for poor countries to use too many resources for armaments; this will get worse if the North-South relationship continues to get even more mixed up with the East-West controversy. In the Federal Republic of Germany, we have tried to reduce this confusion: in our foreign policy in recent years we have more and more tried to apply principles which support real nonalignment wherever possible. We really do try *not* to widen the areas of East-West controversies, for ex-

ample, in various areas of Africa and other parts of the world.

Of course, both within the United Nations and in other discussions we have all considered what could be done if some of the money now used for military purposes could be directed into other channels. But the real question is how to create the preconditions for actually carrying out this ideal policy. And here I go back to my first spontaneous answer to your question, which was that unless there is a change in the relationship between the superpowers, nothing of real importance will happen in the Third World in this area. Not that I believe that the conflicts between the superpowers could be easily resolved, but the conflicts could be limited and then perhaps the disastrous consequences of the East-West conflict for the Third World could be limited, or even reduced.

Q. Does the Palme Report, *Common Security, A Program for Disarmament*, contribute some new insights into these issues of disarmament and the control of weapons?

A. I think it does in various fields. It gives some very good additional evidence on what armaments really mean for a nation's economy. People have only recently begun to realize that after a certain point, using money for armaments in itself burdens the economy and the financial system in a way that poisons the entire economic scene. I do not agree, for example, with those who, like U.S. Defense Secretary Weinberger, take the view that military spending is not too bad because in the final analysis military expenditures are investments. I believe they are investments only to a very limited degree. As the Palme Report indicates, military spending nowadays is largely a form of consumption, not investment, and it becomes dead-end, or dead-weight expenditure. The Palme Report also shows a relationship between the percentage used for weaponry and the state of a country's economy, and the health of national currencies. It is an illusion to believe that military expenditure is effective in reducing the kinds of unemployment which exist in OECD (Organization for Economic Cooperation and Development) countries today. But with all respect to my friend Palme and his Commission, even they have not been able to propose a machinery which will help us in preparing the transfer of expenditure from the military field to the field of economic development. This, in the final analysis, is not really a question for development economists or other experts to answer. It is ultimately a question of political will, particularly of the superpowers, and of what happens to the overall relationship between them and their alliances. Decisive for arms limitations are world political forces, and these are determined by the superpowers and their alliances.

Q. Do you think that the global negotiations in the North-South dialogue are an appropriate place in which to discuss these disarmament and defense issues? Or should such talks be conducted separately?

A. Arms exports and their control should obviously be discussed separately, which would mean that they could not be discussed where everyone is present. But the superpowers and their alliances should discuss these problems and how they affect their relationships with the rest of the world. Under what I call global negotiations, I think the link between armaments and economic development is an important topic for discussions. The main responsibility for action lies, however, with the leading countries. There is nevertheless a good reason to have serious discussions with colleagues from the developing countries. They too have a responsibility of their own, as they should be cautious about being drawn too much into the arms race. Developing countries should put up more resistance to arms-exporting countries who sometimes press upon them weapons beyond what they even have been asking for themselves. But certainly the growing importance of the interrelationship between armaments and development could be one of the items, in addition to the well-known economic issues, under what I call global negotiations.

Q. Moving on to another issue, Mr. Brandt, we in the United States hear much about how Western economic resources and our technology are being used directly or indirectly to help build the military system of the Soviet Union and the Soviet bloc. How do you react to the argument that we should stop the flow of our economic resources to the Soviet bloc if they are helping to build the Soviet military machine?

A. I think this is rather academic. One, because there is already a system of restrictions—the COCOM lists (the OECD Coordinating Committee on strategic equipment)—which the Western countries and Japan are already trying to live up to. The Federal Republic of Germany certainly does, has done so in the past, and will continue to do so. I am not for running away from these agreed restrictions, but I would have serious doubts that one could isolate the Soviet Union or the Soviet bloc at this point in the field of technology and even in other strategic areas of economic activity. Experience has shown us that the Soviet Union, even in past years, when there was much less contact between the West and the East, still was able to develop and become the military power it is today. Even at that time it didn't take many years for the Soviet Union to catch up with the United States in nuclear weapons, and now also in space and other areas too. The world is so interdependent today that I think it is impossible to put the Soviet Union into quarantine, beyond these limited measures such as the COCOM list. Whether one likes it or not, I think I agree with what Pierre Trudeau said when he came to Bonn for that NATO meeting just last June, a governmental system like that of the Soviet Union can force their people to accept worsening conditions of life in order to concentrate on defense whatever resources they think are necessary.

Whether we like it or not, the world has developed in such a way that the Soviet Union has relations with various parts of the world. In many cases they would find new partners in an indirect way, to overcome the obstacles imposed by Western restrictions. Any positive fruits from the approach you outline seem just too unlikely. Perhaps this seems a little bit optimistic, when you look at how things have developed in the last few years, but I still believe that if we enter into a process of negotiations in the field of limiting armaments, then a reasonable economic exchange can continue. This is all the more reason why I think the Soviet bloc should be included in discussions and negotiations on North-South issues. This would help us more than the futile attempt of trying to isolate the Soviet bloc beyond the point where it is effective.

Q. Getting back to the essential issues of economic development, you point out in the report, *North-South*, that we should not confuse the problems of growth with development. Development seems to be a much more fundamental process that includes social change and the change of values. But are the conflicts among nations really based on differences in economic capability or are they based rather on quite different values—social, cultural, political, and even religious values among countries? If this is the case, can the North respond simply with an economic program? Doesn't this imply that we are asking, or assuming, that developing countries will take on the values of Western democracies?

A. I think it would be an illusion if we had that as a goal. It wouldn't work. It would even put us into a position of arrogance. No, we don't want that. But I agree that we are faced with more than just an economic problem, even though many things in this world would be easier to achieve if we did not face mass suffering and hunger for millions of people. This alone is an additional danger to world peace and not only a challenge to our human interpretation of things. No, I do not think that we should aim to tell others to accept our Western values on a worldwide basis. I have great hesitations for the very reason that in our historical past our values have not prevented us from running into the greatest misery and rivalry. For example, various branches of the Christian religion have been the basis directly or indirectly for conflicts and wars. The common Western cultural background did not prevent the terrible catastrophe in Europe not more than forty to fifty years ago. So we should try to find some common denominator in the various beliefs and the great cultures of this world. Isn't it so that the great religions and beliefs foresee, or even ask for a peaceful life for people within a given society? Then why not within various nations and between continents? Isn't it so that some common elements of human dignity could be found in the great religious and cultural backgrounds? Of course, I am aware of the fact that it makes a lot of difference how strongly you believe in, or if you believe in, a life following the one you are just passing through. This can make a lot of difference in your approach to many social problems. Still, I think we can make some progress even if we are very modest in the field of making peace safer, in the field of overcoming mass misery and hunger. The aim should be to bring cultures with different values together on the problems of coexistence. That may challenge the vaues of our Western civilization, our social and political institutions and our churches, but it does not mean we should try to tell others that they have to accept our way of life and our philosophical or social beliefs.

Q. Looking ahead to the next North-South conference that is coming up in September, you said you would try to move in the direction of more concrete proposals and ideas for an emergency program which you have in mind. Would you elaborate on that?

A. It is a bit difficult for me to go into details now because I have just started, together with the colleagues of my ex-Commission, to work on a smaller, additional document, which if we agree, will be ready some time toward the end of this year or perhaps very early next year. Our task will be not only to spell out the areas to be covered by an emergency program, but rather to indicate the various actions which could be taken internationally, what projects could be undertaken bilaterally, which carried out regionally, and opportunities for joint business-government activity, or business backed up with government guarantees. We shall not only outline what should be done, but also *who* could undertake which projects. To indicate examples, in the field of agriculture and food, we have international institutions, and we can work to coordinate their efforts better and to make them more effective. We have a number of measures taken by now by national governments and regional organizations. And there is a good deal of work being carried on by nongovernmental organizations and the churches to fight hunger. I look at the two main churches in my own country: they have engaged in a number of activities, including activities in rural and village development in various countries. We quarrel sometimes with some of our European friends who think that one of the main areas of aid should be to ship part of our agricultural surplus to poor countries, which I believe is a rather expensive and not very effective way of fighting hunger. I believe rather in using money to speed up agricultural production in all those countries where the preconditions exist. It is just ridiculous that a country like Zambia should not be able to feed itself; all the objective conditions exist there, but you need experts, you need fertilizer, among other things. Of course, there will be areas where emergency food aid is necessary, but I am very much in favor of concentrating on speeding up agricultural production in particular countries.

Q. You have referred to energy as a special case, for which a new institution might be important in global negotiations. What do you have in mind here?

A. My Commission also believed that something should be done urgently in this critical area to prevent some future slide toward economic disaster.

The proposal is rather modest, but still important. We should look to see if the exploration and development of energy resources could be financed internationally for developing countries which just cannot do it themselves. For example, in a number of African countries, coal cannot be exploited because there are no funds for doing it. The same is true in other areas of conventional energy resources. Speeding up the process of exploration and development would be important not only for those countries who are so poor that they cannot finance the investment themselves, but it would also help the overall world energy situation. The idea is to establish a limited energy financing institution. It was discussed at Cancún, but I am sorry to report that this hasn't made much progress. I think U.S. hesitations may help explain why it hasn't.

Q. In what way is the U.S. hesitating?
A. The United States seems hesitant to participate in it, which I think is especially deplorable, because the Saudis said that they would participate, along with some other oil countries, West European countries, and Japan. Especially with U.S. participation, this could be a major operation to explore and develop world energy resources. I have even been among those who, behind the scenes, have said, let Western Europe, Japan and some of the oil countries just go ahead with the program if they still are prepared to participate, and leave the door open so that when the United States is ready, it can join. Lest there is any misunderstanding, I intended no hostile act but merely wanted to get the program started as soon as possible. Apart from this limited energy financing institution, the international community may still need something more in the field of energy. In a way it is strange that under the roof of the United Nations we should have an international organization for food and agriculture, one for health, and then the International Monetary Fund and the World Bank, among others, but none for energy, in spite of the fact that energy has become such an important international problem. But I leave that open as something to be built up for the future. The most pressing thing to do now in the energy field is to develop this international agency to help finance the exploration and development of energy resources in those countries which just do not have the capital to do it on their own. Here again it is not difficult to imagine that private international energy corporations can play a concrete role in exploration and development in close cooperation with an international energy financing institution. Such a strategy can be consistent with a U.S. policy that emphasizes the role of private business.

Foreign Aid: Reaching Bottom of the Barrel

The word is going out from Washington to the world's poorer nations: Don't count on Uncle Sam to rescue you from mounting economic troubles. Recession in the U.S. and disillusionment with past programs are causing firm resistance in Congress and the White House to big new commitments on foreign aid. This attitude is prompting America's allies to complain that the plight of impoverished nations will grow worse because the U.S. is not carrying its share of the load.

The Reagan administration is trying a different approach. It wants to supplement public dollars with private financing by encouraging banks and other businesses to invest in underdeveloped nations.

Behind the policy change is a feeling in the U.S. that, for all the billions paid out, neither the U.S. nor the beneficiaries of economic aid have much to show for it.

"Too often, aid has been used as a crutch for diplomacy," remarks Representative Ed Derwinski (R-Ill.). "The ambassador says it makes life easier if he has a goody to parcel out."

Many in Congress argue that it is hard to justify spending billions on foreign aid while the budget runs a deficit exceeding 100 billion dollars. Such reasoning has bottled up President Reagan's Caribbean Basin initiative and his plans for a modest increase in economic assistance, including funds for world development banks—from 8.1 billion dollars to 8.6 billion for the fiscal year that began in September. Instead, aid is likely to remain at last year's level.

"There is not much of a constituency for foreign aid," observes a congressional staff member. "A lot of voters are saying foreign aid is a good idea but that, in a time of recession, we can use the money better in this country."

It's not just the amount but also the workings of the program that have others, both in and out of government, concerned.

Since World War II, the U.S. has pumped 220 billion dollars into foreign aid, 130.2 billion in the form of economic assistance and the rest for mili-

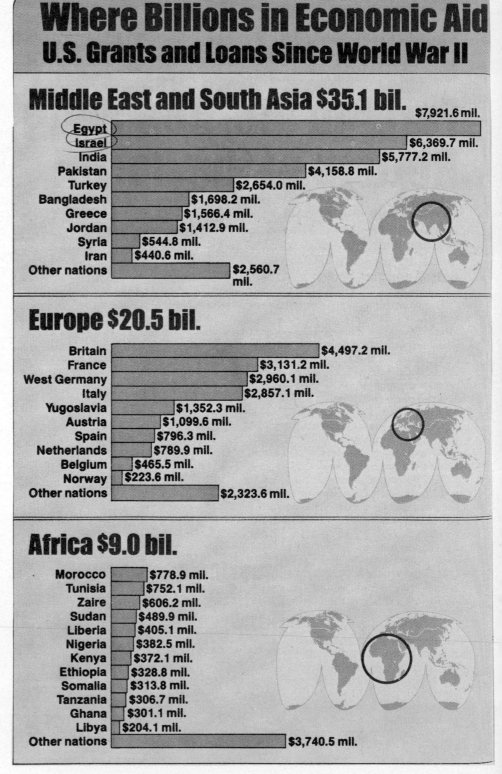

Where Billions in Economic Aid
U.S. Grants and Loans Since World War II

Middle East and South Asia $35.1 bil.

Egypt	$7,921.6 mil.
Israel	$6,369.7 mil.
India	$5,777.2 mil.
Pakistan	$4,158.8 mil.
Turkey	$2,654.0 mil.
Bangladesh	$1,698.2 mil.
Greece	$1,566.4 mil.
Jordan	$1,412.9 mil.
Syria	$544.8 mil.
Iran	$440.6 mil.
Other nations	$2,560.7 mil.

Europe $20.5 bil.

Britain	$4,497.2 mil.
France	$3,131.2 mil.
West Germany	$2,960.1 mil.
Italy	$2,857.1 mil.
Yugoslavia	$1,352.3 mil.
Austria	$1,099.6 mil.
Spain	$796.3 mil.
Netherlands	$789.9 mil.
Belgium	$465.5 mil.
Norway	$223.6 mil.
Other nations	$2,323.6 mil.

Africa $9.0 bil.

Morocco	$778.9 mil.
Tunisia	$752.1 mil.
Zaire	$606.2 mil.
Sudan	$489.9 mil.
Liberia	$405.1 mil.
Nigeria	$382.5 mil.
Kenya	$372.1 mil.
Ethiopia	$328.8 mil.
Somalia	$313.8 mil.
Tanzania	$306.7 mil.
Ghana	$301.1 mil.
Libya	$204.1 mil.
Other nations	$3,740.5 mil.

tary aid. Despite notable economic successes in such places as Western Europe, South Korea and Taiwan, critics say some countries appear to be no better off.

Bangladesh is a case in point. The beleaguered Asian country has received about 1.7 billion dollars from the U.S., yet the funds have seemed to disappear into a sinkhole. One project to provide cheap agricultural loans didn't work because farmers had to pay as much in bribes to corrupt officials as they received in credit.

Now Bangladesh must import between 1 million and 3 million tons of food each year to feed its burgeoning population. "Basically, we're here to keep the place from going down the drain," says one worker for the U.S. Agency for International Development (AID) in Bangladesh.

Another nation in which aid has fostered little economic improvement, say U.S. officials, is Tanzania. "It receives more money per capita than any country in the world, yet it's in a major agricultural crisis and balance-of-payments problem," contends Ian Butterfield of the Heritage Foundation, a conservative research organization.

He says that the 1.4-billion-dollar Food for Peace program is making things worse in Africa because cheap grain hurts farmers by depressing prices for their crops.

Failures elsewhere. Other donors have also encountered failures. France built a costly radio-TV system in Zaire, but Zaire didn't have the capacity to maintain or use the equipment. China constructed a railroad through Tanzania to permit Zambia to export copper through the port of Dar es Salaam, but now the locomotives sit rusting on the tracks, for lack of maintenance.

Mayra Buvinic, director of the International Center for Research on Women, favors more foreign aid, but she says programs need to be more sensitive to the real needs of people. In a Bolivian aid project, she says, women wanted classes on sheepshearing and veterinary technology. What they got were instructions on "crocheting, embroidery, papier-mache and paper-flower making."

Others insist that too much money is spent to prop up military allies and not enough for other needy nations. "The U.S. aid program has been sadly skewed over time to be heavily focused on the Middle East," says John Sewell, president of the Overseas Development Council. "There is now a strong military-security feel to the program."

Of the 12.2 billion dollars for all foreign aid spent in fiscal 1982, 4.1 billion went for military aid. An additional 2.7 billion came from the Economic Support Fund to bolster the economies of friendly nations, many of which are not particularly impoverished. That left 1.4 billion for Food for Peace and 3.8 billion for assistance to developing countries, plus smaller amounts to the Peace Corps and all other programs.

Israel was the largest beneficiary of the Economic Support Fund—806 million dollars—followed by Egypt with 771 million and Turkey 300 million.

Many foreign-aid supporters say it would be in this country's own interest to direct money instead to less developed countries, which buy 39 percent of all U.S. exports.

As an example of a successful program, they point to Indonesia. There, the U.S. is providing 45.2 million dollars per year in development loans, 22.1 million in technical assistance,

Have Gone

Far East $24.4 bil.

Vietnam	$6,457.4 mil.
South Korea	$5,540.5 mil.
Indonesia	$2,448.6 mil.
Philippines	$2,034.6 mil.
Taiwan	$1,879.6 mil.
Japan	$1,685.4 mil.
Laos	$902.6 mil.
Cambodia	$822.9 mil.
Thailand	$716.5 mil.
Burma	$66.3 mil.
Other nations	$1,834.1 mil.

Latin America $10.9 bil.

Brazil	$1,807.7 mil.
Colombia	$963.4 mil.
Bolivia	$730.5 mil.
Chile	$725.3 mil.
Dominican Rep.	$629.3 mil.
Peru	$587.6 mil.
El Salvador	$524.5 mil.
Guatemala	$429.8 mil.
Panama	$375.4 mil.
Nicaragua	$358.6 mil.
Other nations	$3,733.1 mil.

Oceania $0.9 bil.

Aid not allocated by region $29.5 bil.

Total U.S. Economic Aid $130.2 bil.

Note: Figures include repayments of principal and interest on loans through 1981. Figures for 1982 are estimates and do not include repayments that may have occurred. Figures may not add due to rounding.

USN&WR—Basic data: U.S. Dept. of State

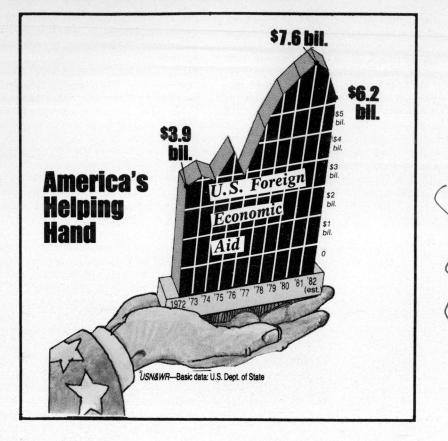

America's Helping Hand

$3.9 bil.

$7.6 bil.

$6.2 bil.

U.S. Foreign Economic Aid

$5 bil.
$4 bil.
$3 bil.
$2 bil.
$1 bil.
0

1972 '73 '74 '75 '76 '77 '78 '79 '80 '81 '82 (est.)

USN&WR—Basic data: U.S. Dept. of State

22.2 million in food aid—plus about one fourth of the 1.1 billion contributed by international organizations.

Aid to Indonesia goes to a stable government with a political and social climate that attracts foreign investment, contend supporters of the program. Agricultural aid helped bring record crop yields and self-sufficiency in rice production. The country is also a producer of oil and other raw materials the U.S. needs.

Other proponents cite India, which utilized foreign aid to build its food production to the point that it now exports wheat.

Some credit these foreign-aid pluses to a decision in 1973 to shift U.S. aid away from dams, reservoirs and capital projects with high maintenance costs and toward farming and other projects that help the poor directly. One successful approach in many countries has been to build feeder roads into relatively isolated areas to permit farmers to get their goods to market.

The security aspects. "Aid traditionally is viewed as a giveaway, and congressmen don't see it in its correct national-security dimensions," says Michael Samuels, a vice president of the Chamber of Commerce of the U.S.A. "In fact, as a share of our national out-

put, our aid program is not anywhere near the top."

Though the U.S. is still the world's largest donor of foreign aid, it contributes only one fifth of 1 percent of its total output of goods and services to development programs. Of the 18 largest industrialized countries, only Italy contributes a smaller share. Still, the U.S. is ahead of the Soviet Union, which contributes $3/100$ of 1 percent.

In September, a committee of the Organization for Economic Cooperation and Development, made up of industrialized nations, expressed "deep concern" at the size of the U.S. share. Allies have also criticized the U.S. for being 400 million dollars in arrears on payments to the World Bank, an international lending institution.

The nation at the forefront of foreign-aid programs is France, whose Socialist government argues that poorer countries can be the source of raw materials and markets for larger countries. "Causes of inequality today," asserts French President François Mitterrand, "may become causes of conflict tomorrow."

Unlike the U.S., the French give aid to such nations as Nicaragua and Grenada without regard to their political philosophies. They also make some loans

and grants to countries such as Brazil, Algeria, India and Indonesia contingent on purchases of French equipment.

West Germany, by contrast, avoids such explicit "strings," yet reports that two thirds of what goes into underdeveloped countries comes back in the form of orders. Bonn provides aid directly to poorer countries and relies on nongovernment organizations to assist nations with less pressing needs.

Policy cornerstone. The Reagan administration is making emphasis on private involvement the cornerstone of U.S. aid policy. It has established a Bureau of Private Enterprise to stimulate businesses in 10 key developing countries—Indonesia, Sri Lanka, Thailand, Pakistan, Egypt, Ivory Coast, Kenya, Zimbabwe, Jamaica and Costa Rica. The 26-million-dollar program will attempt to arrange private financing to assist agricultural firms, private banks and others.

As part of this effort, the U.S. spent $18,000 to bring Jamaican agribusiness officials on a tour of this country's food facilities. AID officials say that the new techniques learned could generate 18 million dollars in purchases of American goods and create 10,000 new jobs in Jamaica.

Another glimpse of the administration's foreign-aid approach came in Reagan's Caribbean Basin initiative, announced last March but still not enacted by Congress. Reagan sought authority to eliminate duties on all imports from the Caribbean countries except on textiles, apparel and most sugar. He also proposed a tax credit on U.S. investments in the Caribbean.

Reagan aides vow not to send U.S. aid to countries that have a bad climate for economic improvement. "The worst example is trying to help farmers in countries where the government sets artificially low food prices for the benefit of urban consumers," AID Director M. Peter McPherson says. "It just doesn't pay farmers to produce more."

The administration also plans to emphasize new technology, such as increasing the milk production of goats and improving the yield of sorghum and millet production in Africa's sub-Sahara region.

With such programs, the Reagan administration hopes to stave off big spending projects by world development banks, which receive about 20 percent of their funds from the United States. Reagan aides are vigorously fighting attempts to double the size of the International Monetary Fund's 67-billion-dollar lending kitty.

Private banks indifferent. One of Reagan's proposals—getting private banks to increase their lending in developing countries—has drawn little support from financiers because banks already are concerned about the safety of existing loans of that sort. Poor nations need more, not less, direct finan-cial help at a time when they are un-able to get loans from private banks, argues Roger Lawrence, director of finance at the U.N. Conference on Trade and Development.

Whatever the outcome of Reagan's new approach, it is clear that U.S. aid will not soon return to the scale of the 1950s and 1960s, when developing countries looked to the U.S. to bring them into prosperity.

By MICHAEL DOAN with JOHN COLLINS of the Economic Unit and the magazine's overseas bureaus

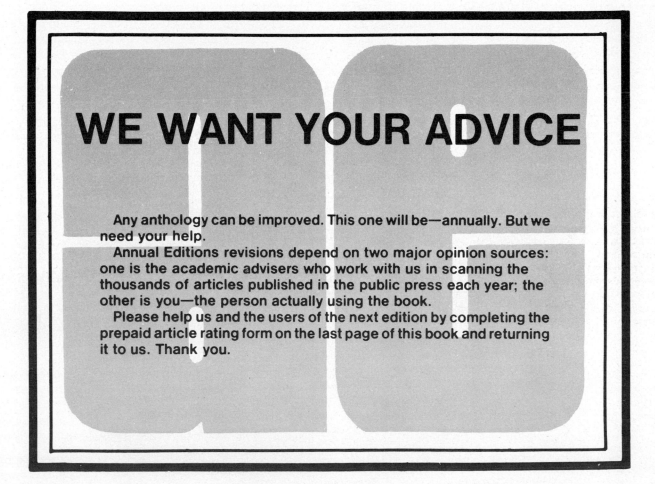

WE WANT YOUR ADVICE

Any anthology can be improved. This one will be—annually. But we need your help.

Annual Editions revisions depend on two major opinion sources: one is the academic advisers who work with us in scanning the thousands of articles published in the public press each year; the other is you—the person actually using the book.

Please help us and the users of the next edition by completing the prepaid article rating form on the last page of this book and returning it to us. Thank you.

The US Caribbean Basin Initiative

Ramesh Ramsaran

Dr Ramsaran is Senior Lecturer at the Institute of International Relations, University of the West Indies, St Augustine, Trinidad.

In a speech to the Organization of American States (OAS) on 24 February 1982, President Ronald Reagan of the United States outlined a programme of special assistance to the countries of the Caribbean and Central America. For some time previous to this, discussions had been held by the United States, Canada, Mexico and Venezuela on the scope and nature of an aid package to the region. The decision by the US to embark on its own programme undoubtedly reflected an inability on the part of the four countries to agree on a common scheme, or on the conditions that should be attached to any programme of assistance. Canada, for its part, has long been renowned for providing aid without controversial 'strings'. Mexico, too, had made it clear that it was opposed to certain conditions which the US was trying to include in the aid package. For instance, President Lopez Portillo of Mexico was adamant in his view that certain countries (e.g. Cuba, Nicaragua, Grenada) should not be excluded from any aid programme on the basis of their political ideology or economic policies. Nor did he feel that military aid should form part of any aid package. Venezuela, for its part, apparently felt it could get more political mileage by providing aid on a bilateral basis.

President Reagan's Caribbean Basin Initiative (CBI) proposals went to the US Congress in March 1982, but the financial part was not cleared until mid-August 1982, after some modification. The package as a whole survived several attempts to defeat it in both Houses. The aid component was included in a US $14.1 billion appropriations Bill, which the President vetoed on 28 August because Congress had tacked on some additional expenditures which would have increased his planned deficit for the year. The CBI thus got caught in domestic political wrangling unrelated to any particular foreign political issue. In mid-September, however, Congress overrode the President's veto, which for all practical purposes, means that the aid proposal is now law. The other aspects of the programme would require specific pieces of legislation for implementation after final approval.

The CBI programme

The reaction to President Reagan's Caribbean Initiative has been varied. Before discussing these reactions, however, it might be useful at this point to outline the proposed aid package.

The creation of a one-way free trade area

This is perhaps the most important element of the package. It is proposed that exports (excluding textile and apparel products) should receive duty-free treatment in the US. Under existing arrangements, it is estimated that some 87 per cent of Caribbean Basin[1] exports already enter the US market duty-free. The argument put forward is that some of the duties that remain in place are in sectors of special interest to Basin countries. They also limit export expansion into many nontraditional products. It is also argued that the global reasons used for excluding certain products from the US Generalized System of Preferences (GSP) are not relevant to the Caribbean Basin. The complex structures of the GSP itself militates against the ability of small inexperienced countries to take advantage of the opportunities offered.

Sugar will receive duty-free treatment but only up to a certain limit.

For goods to qualify for duty-free entry they must have a minimum of 25 per cent local value added. Inputs from all Basin countries can be cumulated to meet the 25 per cent minimum.

Beneficiaries of the proposed Free Trade Area will be designated by the President. 'Communist' countries and countries which expropriate without compensation or which discriminate against US exports will not be eligible. The countries' attitude towards foreign investment and policies employed to promote their own development will also be taken into account.

Tax incentives

In order to encourage the flow of private capital to the area, the President proposes to ask Congress to provide 'significant tax incentives for investment in the Caribbean Basin'. He also indicated a readiness to negotiate bilateral investment treaties with interested Basin countries. The purpose of these treaties would be to provide 'an agreed legal framework for investment, by assuring certain minimum standards of treatment and

This article originally appeared in the November 1982 issue of *The World Today*, monthly journal of the Royal Institute of International Affairs, London.

by providing agreed means for resolving investment disputes.' Mention has also been made of the services provided by the Overseas Private Investment Corporation (OPIC) which currently offers political risk insurance for US investors abroad. This institution is in the process of expanding insurance coverage available to eligible US investors by working with private sector insurers to establish informal consortia to deal with projects on an individual basis.

Financial and military assistance

Non-military aid to Basin countries is currently channelled through three main programmes: (i) the Development Assistance Programme (DA) which is project oriented; (ii) the Economic Support Funds (ESF) which are more flexible and can provide direct balance of payments support as well as credit for crucial imports; (iii) food aid, provided through PL 480 programmes. For countries 'which are particularly hard hit economically' the President intends to provide additional funds in the fiscal years 1982 and 1983. It is proposed to increase the 1982 ESF current budget level from US$140 million to US$490 m. or by US$350 m. The proposed ESF figure for 1983 is US$326.0 m., while the DA figure has been given as US$217.6 m. as compared to US$211.3 m. budgeted for 1982. Total economic assistance (including food aid under the 'Food for Peace' programme) proposed for 1983 is in the region of US$664 m.

It has been stressed that the ESF funds 'would be used primarily to finance private sectors imports, thus strengthening the balance of payments of key countries of the Basin while facilitating increased domestic production and employment'. Institutions like the IMF and the World Bank are to be consulted on the reforms necessary to ensure that ESF assistance has the desired impact.

Military assistance is treated separately. In the 1981 fiscal year, the US provided military assistance of US$50.5 m. to the countries of the Caribbean and Central America. El Salvador received US$35.5 m. or 70.3 per cent of this total. The figure given for the fiscal year 1982 is US$112.1 m., of which El Salvador will receive US$81.0 m. or 72.3 per cent of the total. The supplemental appropriation of a further US$60.0 m. proposed by President Reagan for 1982 would have brought the figure to US$182.1 m.[2] The 1983 estimate is US$106.25 m.[3]

Technical assistance and training

The CBI offers 'technical assistance and training to assist the private sector in the Basin countries to benefit from the opportunities of this programme'. Efforts will be concentrated in investment promotion, export marketing, technology transfer, as well as programmes to facilitate adjustments to greater competition and production in agriculture and industry.

International assistance

Under the CBI, President Reagan pledges 'to work closely' with Mexico, Canada and Venezuela, 'to encourage stronger international efforts to co-ordinate our own development measures with their vital contribution and with those of other potential donors like Colombia'. Such a co-ordinated approach, it is argued, will multiply the impact of each individual effort.

Puerto Rico and the US Virgin Islands

With respect to Puerto Rico and the US Virgin Islands, President Reagan assured that special measures would be adopted to ensure that these countries benefit and prosper from the programme. Among the measures proposed are: (a) excise taxes on imported rum will be rebated to these two countries; (b) inputs into Caribbean Basin production from the possessions will be considered domestic under the rules of origin; (c) their industries will have access to the same safeguard provisions as mainland industries; (d) a Tropical Agricultural Research Centre is to be established in Puerto Rico; (e) an Eastern Caribbean Centre for Educational, Technical and Scientific Interchange is to be set up at the College of the Virgin Islands; (f) Puerto Rican and Virgin Islands facilities, personnel and firms are to be used in technical assistance programmes and development projects; (g) special assistance aimed at making Puerto Rico and the US Virgin Islands the transport hub of the Caribbean is to be provided.

In addition to these measures, interest has been expressed in helping Basin countries to modernize their agricultural and animal-producing sectors. There is also an expressed desire to have the private sector play a greater role in the development effort of Basin countries. 'The US Government will be working with Caribbean Basin governments to design private sector development strategies which combine private, public and voluntary organisation resources in imaginative new programmes. We will also explore ways to promote assistance to comply with US health and sanitary regulations; to improve transportation links; and in general to remove public and private national and regional impediments to private sector development, with emphasis on new investment.'

Reaction to and implications of the CBI

As indicated earlier, the programme announced has received a mixed reaction in the region. The reason for this can be found as much in its context and timing as in its content. The Caribbean Basin as defined by the US President consists of some two dozen countries in the Caribbean, Central America and the northern tip of South America. Until now these countries were treated as part of the larger Latin American bloc. The decision to regard the Caribbean and Central America as a sub-region with special problems requiring special attention is a new approach which undoubtedly stems from recent developments in the area. The emergence of the Socialist-posturing government of Michael Manley in Jamaica during the period 1972-80, the forcible removal in Grenada of the Eric Gairy government by the left-leaning Bishop regime in 1979, the violent overthrow of the right-wing dictatorship of Anastasio Somoza in Nicaragua, also in 1979, and the continuing political instability in El Salvador and other Central American states, were undoubtedly major factors in the decision to formulate the CBI. The factors are perceived to be linked to the deteriorating economic conditions in the region. It is reasoned that if these conditions are improved, countries of the area would become more stable and this would make them less vulnerable 'to the enemies of freedom, national independence and peaceful development'. The programme, however, is not only aimed at improving economic conditions. 'The thrust of our aid is to help our neighbours realize freedom, justice and economic progress.' How these other objectives are to be attained is not quite clear. One strategy is to withhold aid in order to enforce the adoption of particular political and economic policies. The carrot and stick approach is quite explicit in the President's statement. Countries which pursue policies acceptable to the United States (e.g. Jamaica under Edward Seaga) would be rewarded, and those (e.g. Cuba, Grenada, Nicaragua) which embrace views and programmes which do not accord with American perceptions would be denied assistance. The question of exclusion is handled in a very subtle way. The position is taken that the US does not explicitly exclude anyone from the CBI. Countries exclude themselves by reason of the stance they adopt *vis-a-vis* United States values. 'We seek to exclude no one. Some, however, have turned from their American neighbours and their heritage. Let them return to the traditions and common values of this hemisphere and we will welcome them. The choice is theirs.'

The content of the programme itself has drawn a mixed response. Many of the politicians in the area welcomed the additional aid, though some of them (particularly in the Eastern Caribbean) expected the financial part to be more substantial. They could not hope to attract foreign investors, they argue, without improving their basic infrastructure. The business groups tend to see the opening up of the US market as an opportunity for the expansion in trade. The academics, on the other hand, have expressed grave reservations about the possible impact on the integration movement in the Caribbean and on development strategies in general. They also feel that the independence of the Caribbean states would be compromised. It would be instructive at this point to go into a little more detail into the thinking behind these various positions.

In recent years, the Caribbean Basin states (particularly the non-oil producing countries) have been experiencing serious economic difficulties. Real economic growth in many instances has been close to zero and in some cases even negative. Foreign-exchange earnings have been declining. Inflation and unemployment have taken on significant proportions. Such problems, of course, tend to generate social discontent and their persistence has led to a questioning of basic development strategies. In such circumstances, even existing political arrangements have come under attack. A major purpose of the financial assistance provided under the CBI, it is indicated, is to assist countries 'which are particularly hard hit economically'. The division of the supplemental financial assistance proposed for the 1982 fiscal year, however, does not seem to accord with this objective. Of the US$350 m. supplemental aid proposed under the ESF programme for the 1982 fiscal year, El Salvador is slated to receive US$128 m. (36.6 per cent), Jamaica US$50 m. (14.3 per cent), the Eastern Caribbean US$10 m. (2.8 per cent), Belize US$10 m. (2.8 per cent), Dominican Republic US$40 m. (11.4 per cent), Costa Rica US$70 m. (20.0 per cent), Honduras US$35 m. (10.0 per cent), Haiti US$5 m. (1.4 per cent), and the American Institute for Labour Development US$2 m. (0.6 per cent). Political considerations seem to weigh heavily in this allocation.[4] The Eastern Caribbean islands which are in serious economic difficulties and which need to develop their infrastructures in order to increase production, get less than 3 per cent of the total as compared to over 14 per cent for Jamaica (where it is hoped that the advantages of a market-oriented private enterprise economy will be demonstrated), and almost 67 per cent for three Central American countries.

As far as military assistance is concerned, the total budgeted for 1982 amounts to about 20 per cent[5] of all aid proposed for this year. (This does not include the additional US$60 m. in military aid that was proposed by President Reagan for El Salvador.) The President has stated that this expenditure is needed to meet 'the growing threat of Cuban and Soviet subversion in the Caribbean Basin'. There are many, of course, who would argue that the political instability in the region is more rooted in domestic political and economic conditions than in outside interference, and the situation is more likely to improve if these conditions are addressed directly. Failure to do this is likely to lead to annual escalations in military expenditure.

With respect to the trading arrangements, one view holds that the effect is likely to be more psychological than anything else, since 87 per cent of Basin goods already enter the US market duty-free. Another view is that the non-tariff barriers would remain a serious impediment to an expansion of exports to the US market. A third position is that the duty-free market is meaningful only if one has the production capacity. The Eastern Caribbean states, for example, would need to develop their physical infrastructure before they can significantly expand their production. There may be some merit in each of these positions. Spokesmen for the Reagan Administration, however, tend to see the effects of the free-trade arrangements in both a short- and long-term perspective. The immediate effects, they argue, would be felt in the traditional commodities area (e.g. sugar, coffee, cocoa, vegetables, raw materials etc.). This argument, however, has to be seen against the fact that in recent years, earnings from most of these items have been declining and not for lack of markets. In the medium and longer term, existing and new manufactured goods are likely to be affected. Again, it must be noted that many of the countries have not been able to satisfy the origin rule for manufactured goods to take advantage of the opportunities offered under various GSP Schemes and under the Lome Convention in which several Basin countries are participants. The point is, the provision of markets may not be the crucial thing. Structural and technical problems exacerbated by irrelevant policies may be the more important factors facing an expansion of production and exports.

In the US itself, the free-trade idea has received strong opposition in certain quarters, despite the safeguard provisions of the plan, and despite the fact that imports that would be affected by the proposals currently account for less than one-half of one per cent of the US total imports. The 25 per cent local content requirement has been criticized as being too low. Some American producers feel that the Caribbean will be used as a conduit by foreign competitors to penetrate the US market. The AFL-CIO group is concerned about the impact on jobs as investors are attracted away by the proposed arrangements.

The CBI is cast in a particular framework which has given rise to a great deal of controversy. A certain basic model is assumed in which government intervention in the economic system is played down, and a free enterprise system involving an expanded role for the private sector[6] is pushed to the centre stage of the development strategies. When we add to this measures to attract foreign capital producing for a foreign market, we have virtually all the elements of the Puerto Rican model, which has so far failed to deliver the promised goods. The ideological bias in the programme is clear. The fact that to qualify for aid, domestic policies will have to pass the scrutiny of the US Administration raises the whole question of political and economic sovereignty—a very sensitive issue on which any advantages in the programme may eventually flounder.

In the context of Commonwealth Caribbean integration, it is feared in some quarters that bilateral assistance of the kind envisaged in the CBI could seriously interfere with the process. It is widely felt that the Caribbean Development Bank should be the appropriate institution for channelling aid aimed at regional development. The CBI shows no particular concern with integration objectives, but rather addresses itself to an ideological drift and the need for the US to reassert its hegemony in the political and economic circumstances of the early 1980s. In the absence of a common policy on foreign investment, member states of the Caribbean Community may find themselves offering a wide variety of arrangements that could make nonsense of the whole integration movement. The industrial programming effort now being made could also be affected if foreign investors (with the collaboration of individual governments) decide to pay no attention to the agreements reached.

Concluding remarks

The benefits offered by the CBI are conditional. In other words, there is a cost involved, and prospective beneficiaries would have to decide whether they are prepared to pay this cost. More fundamentally, they would have to decide whether the benefits offered are significant for their development objectives, and whether the conditions are compatible with the solution to their economic difficulties as they see them. The positive aspects would have to be weighed against the negative.

The basic strategy envisaged in the CBI is not new. It has been tried and found wanting. And this may explain why more and more countries of the region are turning to new approaches that often entail political and economic reorganization of a far-reaching nature. If the CBI is supposed to constitute a response to this situation, the US has failed to understand the mood of the region or to appreciate the link between its own foreign policy and poverty and oppression in the region. No lessons seem to have been learnt from past mistakes or from the experience of the Alliance for Progress whose benefits were largely confined to privileged groups unwilling to undertake the fundamental reforms necessary to deal with the question of widespread poverty. The concern with security continues to override all other considerations in a renewed cold-war atmosphere.

NOTES

1. 'Caribbean Basin' is an arbitrary term used by the Reagan Administration to cover some two dozen countries in the northern tip of South America, Central America and the Caribbean. Taken together these countries have a population of about 39 million people and a GDP of US$45 billion.
2. In a compromise move between the US House of Representatives (which baulked at the additional military aid to El Salvador) and the Senate, the additional appropriation was rejected during congressional discussions.
3. For the figures on financial and military assistance, see State Department, Special Report No. 97, *Background on the Caribbean Basin Initiative*, March 1982.
4. In order to get a more balanced allocation, the US Foreign Relations Committee had suggested a ceiling of US$75 m. for any one country. This was rejected by the full Senate.
5. Compared to an actual of 10.7 per cent in 1987.
6. As indicated earlier, most of the US$350 m. supplemental assistance for 1982 is intended to finance imports for private sector development.

Article 36

Conditionality ...
Reflects Principle That Financing and Adjustment Should Act Hand in Hand

A country making use of the Fund's resources is generally required to carry out an economic policy program aimed at achieving a viable balance of payments position over an appropriate period of time. This requirement is known as "conditionality," and it reflects the principle that balance of payments financing and adjustment must go hand in hand.

A viable payments position has meant—especially for many developing countries—a current account deficit that can be sustained by capital inflows on terms compatible with the development prospects of the country and without resort to restrictions on trade and payments which add to, rather than correct, the existing distortions. The corrective strategy provides for a reorientation of the economy toward sustained growth and avoids purely deflationary policies that may have a deleterious effect on investment and fail to encourage the required shift of resources to the external sector.

Flexible Approach. Conditionality must be adapted to changing circumstances and specific cases; it cannot be a rigid and inflexible set of operational rules. Executive Directors have on several occasions reviewed and amended the policies and practices relating to the conditional use of Fund resources. A general review was undertaken in 1968, and since then there have been periodic discussions of particular aspects of conditionality when new facilities have been introduced or in connection with discussions of individual stand-by or extended arrangements.

Most recently, in 1979 the Executive Directors completed a second comprehensive review of conditionality. This resulted in a set of guidelines that incorporates many of the conclusions reached in previous discussions, such as the use of consultation clauses, the phasing of purchases, and the injunction that objective indicators for monitoring performance (or "performance criteria") be limited only to those variables necessary to ensure achievement of the objectives of Fund-supported programs. The revised guidelines include other elements:

- emphasis on the need to encourage members to adopt corrective measures at an early stage of their balance of payments difficulties;
- recognition that many cases require periods of adjustment longer than those normally associated with a stand-by arrangement;
- adoption of a flexible approach for the treatment of external borrowing in adjustment programs; and
- stress on the necessity to pay due regard to the domestic social and political objectives, economic priorities, and the circumstances of members, including the causes of their payments problems.

The need to keep conditionality under review is confirmed in the revised guidelines. They provide that the staff will from time to time prepare assessments of programs supported by stand-by arrangements so as to enable the Executive Board to evaluate their appropriateness, the effectiveness of policy instruments, and the results achieved. On the basis of such assessments, the Board will determine when another comprehensive review of conditionality might be necessary. No further modifications of the guidelines seemed warranted at the time of the most recent evaluation of programs, but the subject is kept under active consideration.

Managing Director J. de Larosière, in an address on July 13 before the Economic and Social Council of the United Nations in Geneva, said "the perception by some that conditionality has been tightened does not derive from any change in the Fund's policies but reflects the realities of the current situation and the scale of the payments deficits that have to be corrected." Mr. de Larosière stressed that "while we have not changed our policies on conditionality, we have sought to broaden the base of our programs so as to help member countries handle the more deep-rooted structural problems that have been characteristic of the payments difficulties for many of them in recent years. The Fund has been placing emphasis, therefore, not only on demand management but also on measures to strengthen the economy."

Basis for Conditionality. Conditionality has sometimes been viewed as a penalty for the shortcomings of past policies or a quid pro quo for the financial assistance provided by the Fund. It is rather to be seen as an essential element of the contribution that the Fund makes to alleviating the balance of payments problems of member countries and to facilitating the international adjustment process. Indeed, in practice there is a large degree of complementarity between conditionality and financial assistance. Financing without the adoption of the policy measures required by conditionality would postpone necessary adjustments and run the risk of prolonging an untenable situation. At the same time, corrective measures without financing would render the process of adjustment more difficult and needlessly disruptive.

Reprinted from *IMF Survey*, November 1982, pp. 1-3, by permission.

Normally, it is neither desirable nor feasible to finance balance of payments deficits over a protracted period without reducing or eliminating the underlying causes. If payments difficulties are merely suppressed by resorting to restrictions, or if they are merely financed, they are likely to reappear after a period of time, perhaps in a more acute form, thus compounding the severity of the required adjustment measures.

The fundamental question of whether adjustment is required depends on whether the imbalance is temporary and self-reversing in a reasonable period of time. In such cases, adequate financing on a temporary basis is all that is required. On the other hand, when an imbalance is not due to transient and self-reversing factors, there is no alternative to the adoption of measures to adjust to the changed circumstances.

Conditionality in Practice. In helping countries formulate programs that can be supported by its financial assistance, as well as in its general policy advice to members, the Fund does not rely on any particular model or approach. Given the number and diversity of Fund members, with their wide range of economic and social structures and systems, stages of development, and individual problems, it would be impossible to devise any one model of adjustment that could apply across the board to all Fund members.

Within the context of the guidelines on conditionality, Fund-supported programs do, however, emphasize a number of major economic variables, most importantly certain financial aggregates such as domestic credit, the financing of the public sector, and external debt, as well as some key elements of the price system, including the exchange rate, interest rates, and in exceptional cases, the prices of commodities that bear significantly upon the public finances and foreign trade.

The choice of the performance criteria is dictated by several considerations. In addition to factors such as the economic and institutional structure of the country and the availability of data, these include the desirability of confining the criteria to broad macroeconomic variables. For instance, limitations on overall credit expansion, which are employed in almost all programs, are consistent with these considerations in that they embrace broad policy decisions In the financial field in both private and public sectors. It would, however, be inaccurate to identify the Fund's approach as a standard "monetary approach" to balance of payments analysis. While the Fund gives due recognition to the relationship between monetary factors and external developments, its approach embraces all aspects of economic policies bearing on the supply of and demand for resources.

The impact of Fund-supported programs on other economic variables, such as income distribution, employment, and social services, depends on the manner in which the relevant policies are implemented. Decisions on the detailed execution of policy measures are naturally the sole responsibility of the government. These decisions include how credit should be allocated, the areas where public expenditures should be reduced, and the application of specific tax and subsidy measures. Any other approach would involve the Fund directly in microeconomic policy measures that are closely related to a country's social and political choices, e.g., the determination of the appropriate distribution of the burden of adjustment between various segments of the economy —an involvement which in all likelihood would be strenuously resisted by most countries and would be at variance with the conditionality guidelines.

Fund programs are designed jointly with the member country. A program involves a thorough review of the member's economy, including the causes and nature of its balance of payments problem and an analysis of the most appropriate policies within its institutional framework for achieving a sustainable balance between the demand for and the availability of resources. Depending on the particular circumstances of each case, this may include a combination of policies aimed at containing demand expansion, increasing allocative efficiency, establishing a realistic rate of exchange, and creating the conditions that will stimulate the growth of output. The periodic review of Fund programs confirms that, in the practical application of conditionality, a considerable degree of flexibility is exercised and circumstances of different members are taken into account.

Role of Supply Management. The continued exercise of flexibility in Fund-supported programs is at present all the more important in the light of the substantial changes in the world economy and in the nature of problems facing Fund members. Chief among these are the significant changes in the nature and magnitude of disequilibria, including, for many countries, a deterioration in the terms of trade that is not likely to be reversed. It is also increasingly felt that, in the formulation of adjustment programs geared to present circumstances, supply management and the structural problems of members require greater attention.

Increasingly, the success of an adjustment program will depend on eliciting an adequate response from the supply side of the economy. Macroeconomic variables such as the interest rate and the exchange rate are of singular importance in this respect, as they have a direct bearing on saving and investment opportunities and on the overall orientation of the growth effort. Moreover, in emphasizing certain aspects of members' economic problems —such as the current account of the balance of payments—the adjustment programs call attention to supply-related measures, such as export promotion policies or measures to increase the efficiency of government spending, because these contribute to the elimination of imbalances without jeopardizing growth prospects.

Conditionality in Current Circumstances. Conditionality evolves over time in order to ensure its adaptation to changing circumstances. Given the structural and deep-rooted nature of many of the payments imbalances characterizing the present world economic situation, the Interim Committee, in the communiqué issued after its May 12–13, 1982 meeting in Helsinki, reiterated its agreement that "the Fund has an important role to play in the adjustment and the financing of balance of payments deficits, and that it must be strong enough, and have adequate resources, to be able to cope effectively with the problems it may face in the

1980s.'' Such financing must be in support of appropriate adjustment policies.

These adjustment policies place additional emphasis on measures to create conditions conducive to an improvement in the supply of resources and a broadening of the productive base. Such an improvement will require supporting measures on the demand side to create an environment in which growth can be sustained and, in view of the nature of the present imbalances, the Fund must be in a position to provide larger amounts of assistance and support adjustment during longer periods than in the past.

The larger amounts and longer periods of the Fund's balance of payments financing and the structural nature of the adjustment involved in the programs now being supported make it essential for the Fund to coordinate more closely with development financing organizations, above all the World Bank. This coordination ensures that policies supported by the Fund are compatible with investment programs aimed at overcoming structural deficiencies which are often the basic cause of members' payments difficulties.

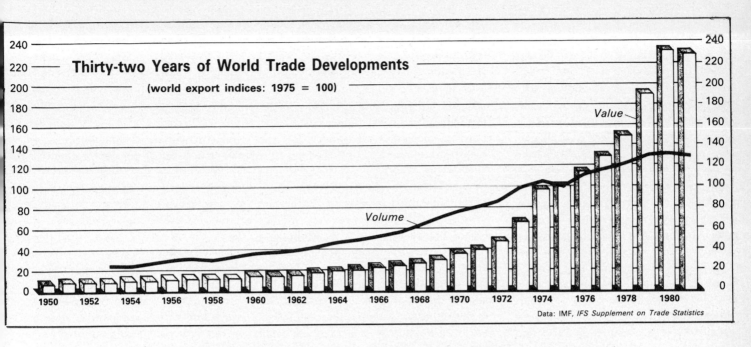

Thirty-two Years of World Trade Developments

(world export indices: 1975 = 100)

Value

Volume

Data: IMF, *IFS Supplement on Trade Statistics*

This chart indicates that although the value of international trade has increased considerably since 1950, the total volume of trade has leveled off.

Reprinted from *IMF Survey*, December 13, 1982, by permission.

De Larosière Stresses No Monetary System Can Substitute for Sound Economic Policies

Following are excerpts from remarks by J. de Larosière, Managing Director of the Fund, on "The International Monetary System and the Developing Countries," delivered on November 26 at the ESSEC (Ecole supérieure des sciences économiques et commerciales) Colloquium in Cergy-Pontoise, France.

. . . The decade that has elapsed since the breakdown of par values—a period of generalized floating and considerable exchange rate instability—has seen wide fluctuations in the growth of world trade. In the past three years, the growth of world trade has been negligible. These developments have been very harmful to the developing countries, whose economics are often heavily dependent upon international trade and, therefore, vulnerable to external disturbances. For the majority of the developing countries, growth rates during the past decade were below those achieved in the 1960s, and the slowdown became more marked after

1979. For 1981 and 1982, average growth rates for the non-oil LDCs [developing countries] are the lowest in several decades. For the first time in the postwar period, real per capita income in most of these countries is now falling.

What accounts for this highly disturbing turn of events which more or less coincided with the major changes in the international monetary system of the early 1970s? Could the tempo of growth be restored by turning the clock back and reinstituting the par value system? Let me address these two questions very briefly.

First, the roots of the present malaise in the world economy run deep. It is the legacy of many years during which the prevailing conditions of stagflation were building up in the industrial countries in large part because of mistaken policies. These economies became much less flexible and efficient. Inflation, aggravated by oil price increases, rose to successively

higher levels from one business cycle to the next, and there was a growing divergence in price performance among the major industrial countries. Inflationary expectations became entrenched. Growth rates declined, and unemployment moved up. And there was a loss of public confidence in national economic policies. Thus, the present recession in the industrial world, which is the prime factor behind the slump in world trade and the slowdown in growth in the developing countries, has complex origins. Comprehensive and sustained policy efforts will be required to correct it.

Turning now to the second question— could adaptations in the monetary system help to turn the fortunes of the world economy around? For one thing, it is widely accepted that exchange rate stability provides a far better atmosphere for world trade and economic relations than exchange rate instability. But the stability of exchange rates that was achieved during most of the 1950s and 1960s was primarily a reflection of underlying stability in the world economy, particularly the relatively low rates of inflation throughout the industrial world. When these conditions changed around the mid-1960s and countries tended to resist exchange rate adjustments, the par value system came under mounting pressure. The divergence of economic performance among the major industrial countries led to growing distortions and increasingly unrealistic exchange rate relationships among the major currencies. Meanwhile, the vast growth of international capital markets and greater mobility of capital (resulting from liberalization and the growing sophistication of the banking system) opened the way for large-scale speculation. This combination of events produced the financial upheavals and exchange rate crises of the early 1970s and eventually led to the collapse of the par value system.

Thus, exchange rate stability is not a reflection of the international monetary system. . . . To my mind, the frictions and instability that have been recently manifested in the international monetary system are, first and foremost, a reflection of adverse conditions in the world economy stemming mainly from policy weaknesses and the wide divergence of performance among the major countries. They have, of course, been aggravated by the severe repercussions of two oil price shocks during the 1970s. . . .

. . . To search for solutions to these fundamental problems through changes in the international monetary system would not be the right approach. No system can be a substitute for sound economic policies on the part of national authorities.

That is not to say that the way in which the international monetary system itself functions does not matter. On the contrary, the disruptions and instability in the world economy in recent years—stagflation, escalating energy prices, and massive shifts in the structure of international payments imbalances—have put added strains on the international monetary system, which, in turn, have aggravated the problems of the developing countries. . . .

Payments Imbalances of the Developing Countries: An Unsatisfactory Blend of Adjustment and Financing

. . . Adjustment to the enormous payments deficits that built up has, on the whole, been too slow. Many countries—and not only in the developing world—found it possible to finance their large deficits through commercial borrowings and, thus, to postpone adjustment for too long. For some, those borrowings have already proved to be unsustainable and debt servicing difficulties have arisen. . . .

The substantial increase in the burden of external indebtedness not only reflects higher borrowings, it is also attributable to the existence of stagflation in the industrial world, which—as I have already mentioned—is, in turn, the result of a lengthy period of weak economic policies in the industrial countries. Recession has meant slower growth of markets and weak export prices for the developing countries. In addition, the restrictive financial policies that have been adopted by most of the industrial countries over the past few years to tackle inflation—and which have had to be all the more rigorous because they were so long delayed—have had the short-run impact of compounding these trends. The historically high interest rates which have accompanied the policy shift are both symptoms of the maladjustment in the industrial world and a reflection of high inflation. The increase in interest rates alone has imposed very heavy costs on the developing countries. For example, from 1978 to 1981, the London interbank offered rate (LIBOR) roughly doubled, and interest payments by the non-oil developing countries on their long-term foreign debt alone rose by some $23 billion—or by substantially more than the $17 billion adverse shift in their oil trade balance over the same period.

These events have given rise to debt servicing problems in a number of countries and this, in turn, has produced uncertainty and apprehension in international financial markets. Typically, where debt problems have occurred it has been because the relatively easy access to the international capital markets has enabled countries to postpone for too long the policy steps that are ultimately needed to adjust their economies to a harsher

world economic climate. But countries cannot live beyond their means indefinitely. Sooner or later, deficits have to be brought to levels that are consistent with the country's ability to service its external obligations over the medium term. When this rule is not observed, the country inevitably finds itself in a financial crisis.

Such crises are harmful all-round. From the standpoint of the debtor country, the abrupt cutback in foreign financing that usually follows leaves the authorities with no alternative but to resort to restrictions and other inward-looking policies that can force the necessary adjustment through quickly. Action of this sort involves a sharp reduction of domestic activity and is harmful to international trade and hence to the creditor countries. At the same time, crises undermine confidence in the financial institutions involved and can lead to defensive actions by those institutions, which are also disruptive. For example, besides cutting back sharply on their lending to countries that have run into debt financing problems over the past year or so, there has also been a tendency for the banks to "regionalize" their reactions by cutting back on their lending to neighboring countries or even by seeking to cut down on their overall international exposures.

Exchange Rate Instability

Instability of the exchange rates for the major currencies has been one of the outstanding features of international financial conditions in recent years. It has become particularly pronounced over the past two years or so. To an important extent, exchange rate movements have been induced by changes in interest rates and in short-term interest differentials between major financial centers. For that reason, they have often been unrelated to, or have even run counter to, developments in relative inflation rates. The result has been frequent "overshooting" or "undershooting" of exchange rates from their long-term equilibrium levels, often for as long as two or three years. This, in turn, has produced shifts in competitive positions among individual countries which have affected current account positions, domestic price levels, and the management of domestic demand. There has also been considerable volatility in exchange rates—by which I mean erratic short-term fluctuations—with frequent day-to-day shifts of more than 1 per cent and quarter-to-quarter changes in excess of 5 per cent.

It is of course difficult—if not impossible—to measure the costs of exchange rate instability in terms of its impact on trade and growth. But there are good reasons for believing that such costs do exist and that the recent variability of exchange rates has complicated the efforts of the developing countries in managing their economies and fostering development. . . .

Fostering Stability in the System

Improving the functioning of the international monetary system would enhance the conditions for growth. But the essential route to a lasting recovery must be through improvements in the quality of economic policies in individual countries. In this endeavor, the International Monetary Fund can play an important supportive role.

Of course, the brunt of the development effort will always have to come from *the developing countries* themselves. For the most part, their policies need to be strengthened. Indeed, many developing countries have been unduly lax in their domestic economic policies in recent years, thus compounding the problems arising externally.

In a recent survey, the Fund staff concluded that the stance of policy was appropriate in only about two fifths of the non-oil developing countries. In the others, policies were considered to be too expansionary—and by a wide margin in many cases. For example, half the non-oil developing countries had budget deficits of 6 per cent of GDP [gross domestic product] or more in 1981, about double the level of the average deficit in the mid-1970s. Typically, rising budget deficits have been financed through domestic monetary expansion which has added to inflationary pressures. Recent studies in the Fund have shown clearly that those countries that have a poor record on inflation have also been lagging behind in their growth performance. Accelerating growth and development, thus, calls for lower inflation. This, in turn, requires lower budget deficits and greater monetary restraint, as well as a revamping of

policies aimed at improving efficiency and strengthening the productive base. . . .

The success of efforts on the part of the developing countries will of course depend crucially upon the *economic policies and performance of the industrial countries*. Fundamentally, the best contribution the industrial countries can make to the cause of economic growth and development is to press ahead with the agreed policy strategy, aimed at putting an end to inflation and revitalizing their economies. This is the only path toward a recovery of growth and international trade. This strategy involves a comprehensive, balanced set of economic policies comprising monetary restraint, fiscal discipline, and steps to attack rigidities in the markets for labor and goods. But these policies involve a transitional period of demand restraint, which inevitably hurts the developing countries. This makes it even more important that the industrial countries should support the adjustment efforts of the developing countries, especially through their trade and aid policies. . . .

. . . And there are no simple expedients, through adaptations in the monetary system, for example, that could ever serve to make up for the impact of adverse trends in these fundamental policies on the development prospects of the LDCs. . . .

The Fund has a crucial role to play in current conditions, not as a provider of development financing, which is outside the scope of its functions, but as a monetary institution helping to foster monetary cooperation and to promote economic adjustment in its member countries and globally. . .

. . . Surveillance [over members' exchange rate policies] has to be exercised over the policies of *all* member countries. But it is of particular importance in connection with the policies of the major industrial countries because of their pervasive effect on the rest of the world. The Fund has been vigilant in monitoring developments in the industrial countries and has sought through moral pressure, where necessary, to bring about improvements in their demand management and to encourage resistance to protectionist pressures, and dismantling of subsidies that distort international trade, and the pursuit of orderly and cooperative exchange rate policies. Recent developments clearly testify to

the need for the Fund's surveillance to be strengthened. . . .

The fact that by far the greater proportion of *Fund financing* is linked to the adoption of corrective policy measures in the borrowing country gives it a unique characteristic. In present circumstances with the compelling need for strong policies of adjustment in so many countries the world over, the Fund's conditional financing is becoming more and more important. Moreover, as I have already indicated, the days of easy access to commercial bank financing are probably over. And a more judicious blend of adjustment and financing will need to be adopted by the developing countries in managing their balance of payments positions.

Adjustment in present circumstances, however, cannot be brought about overnight without aggravating existing problems. If the adjustment process is to be orderly, financing flows will have to be maintained on a large scale. But, in view of the debt servicing difficulties that have arisen in some countries, the commercial banks, which constitute the primary source of finance in the system, will be seeking greater assurances that borrowing countries are taking the policy steps that are needed to put their economies on a sound medium-term footing. Greater emphasis on adjustment policies will make it both possible and likely that more countries will seek access to Fund financial support. For that reason, the steps now being taken to strengthen the capital resources of the Fund are both timely and important. Negotiations toward the Eighth General Quota Review are at an advanced stage. It has been agreed that the present quota increase will have to be "substantial." (Total Fund quotas presently amount to SDR 61 billion.) We are working to resolve remaining issues on the size and distribution of the quota increase by April 1983. This would make it possible for the new quotas to go into effect sometime in 1984. Quotas will continue to be the Fund's primary source of finance. However, it is likely that the Fund will have to continue to borrow from official sources to supplement its capital resources, and possible access to private sources of finance cannot be ruled out.

Over the past few years, the Fund has simplified the *SDR* which is now valued on the basis of a basket of the five major currencies, and has taken steps to give the SDR all the characteristics of a full-fledged reserve asset in official transactions. This is essential if the

6. THE INTERNATIONAL POLITICAL ECONOMY

objective of making the SDR the principal reserve asset of the system is ever to be realized....

Of course, it is not possible for me to anticipate the future evolution of the SDR. Certainly, the needs of the developing countries, particularly in the present difficult conditions, are very great. But I do not believe that these problems can be effectively addressed by transforming the monetary system according to any simple formula, new or old. I have already spoken of the policy strategy that the industrial countries must pursue both to ensure their own economic recovery and that of the world economy. The policy orientation of the industrial countries and the mix of their policies, together with the domestic policy efforts of the LDCs themselves, will be decisive for the growth prospects of the developing countries in the period ahead.

Currency Units per SDR

Currency	November 1	2	3	4	5	8	9	10	11	12	15	16
Deutsche mark	2.72181	2.71760	2.71985	2.73092	2.73305	2.74441	2.74797	2.74053	2.75513	2.75265	2.74797	2.73885
French franc	...	...	7.66540	7.70651	7.71253	7.73976	7.76138	7.79470	...	7.77685	7.75963	7.74611
Japanese yen	295.361	294.429	...	294.380	294.397	292.996	291.417	287.406	286.607	284.940	285.276	285.120
Pound sterling	0.633887	0.633361	0.633877	0.636522	0.637058	0.639582	0.640768	0.640145	0.642342	0.643200	0.651623	0.655381
U.S. dollar	1.06379	1.06677	1.06523	1.06121	1.06204	1.05966	1.06124	1.06565	1.06269	1.06321	1.06169	1.06388
Argentine peso	41461.2	41790.7	41943.4	41997.4	42242.6	42349.3	42614.1	43004.3	43097.4	43331.1	43481.5	...
Australian dollar	1.13774	1.13971	1.13673	1.13571	1.13709	1.13418	1.13635	1.13488	1.13052	1.12951	1.12934	1.13323
Austrian schilling	...	19.0738	19.0836	19.1729	19.1794	19.2593	19.2732	19.2456	19.2985	19.3121	19.2941	19.2147
Bahrain dinar	0.401049	0.402172	0.401592	0.400076	0.400389	0.399492	0.400087	0.401750	0.400634	0.400830	0.400257	0.401083
Belgian franc	...	52.5544	52.6117	52.8907	52.9480	53.1711	53.2371	53.1493	...	53.3412	53.2318	53.0504
Brazilian cruzeiro	234.704	235.361	235.022	238.231	238.417	237.883	238.238	239.228	242.782	242.901	242.554	243.054
Canadian dollar	1.30261	1.30285	1.30065	1.29754	1.30419	1.29533	1.29376	1.30073	...	1.30020	1.30015	1.30496
Colombian peso	...	...	72.1800	72.0031	72.1444	...	72.1855	72.5814	...	72.5003	...	72.6417
Danish krone	9.56932	9.53052	9.53541	9.58007	9.58491	9.62383	9.62810	9.62815	9.64923	9.64704	9.63802	9.60684
Ecuadoran sucre	35.2646	35.3634	35.3124	35.1791	35.2066	35.1277	35.1801	35.3263	35.2282	32.2454	35.1950	35.2676
Finnish markka	5.86255	5.86190	...	5.87061	...	5.89489	5.90156	5.90370	5.90324	5.90613	5.90724	5.91198
Guatemalan quetzal	1.06379	1.06677	1.06523	1.06121	1.06204	1.05966	1.06124	1.06565	1.06269	1.06321	1.06169	1.06388
Indian rupee	10.3641	10.3555	10.3639	10.3753	10.3522	10.3612	10.3804	10.3704	10.4059	10.4198	10.5563	10.4861
Indonesian rupiah	724.441	726.470	725.422	723.480	724.311	722.688	724.296	727.306	725.817	726.172	725.134	726.896
Iranian rial	92.3000	92.3000	92.3000	92.3000	92.3000	92.3000	92.3000	92.3000	92.3000	92.3000	92.3000	92.3000
Iraqi dinar	0.314152	0.331614	0.331134	0.329885	0.330143	0.329403	0.329894	0.331265	0.330345	0.330507	0.330034	0.330715
Irish pound	0.798042	0.797585	0.799122	0.802731	0.803359	0.805519	0.804518	0.804082	0.806290	0.809140	0.807983	0.804933
Italian lira	...	1556.42	1557.90	1565.82	...	1573.33	1576.47	1573.70	1581.28	1581.26	1579.79	1576.14
Kuwaiti dinar	0.312127	0.312532	0.311974	0.311380	...	0.311212	0.311559	0.312374	0.311857	...	0.311426	0.312249
Libyan dinar	0.314938	0.315820	0.315365	0.314174	0.314420	0.313716	0.314183	0.315489	0.314613	0.314767	0.314317	0.314965
Malaysian ringgit	2.51374	2.51832	2.50862	2.50870	2.51215	2.51086	2.51068	2.51366	2.52049	2.51641	...	2.52235
Malta pound	0.456053	0.455690	0.455557	0.455455	0.456850	0.457243	0.457411	0.457675	0.458115	0.457550	0.457487	0.459004
Mexican peso	...	...	...	...	...	...	...	...	...	...	...	...
Netherlands guilder	2.95574	2.95229	2.95601	2.97086	2.97371	2.98612	2.99057	2.98222	2.99466	2.99134	2.98760	2.97886
Nigerian naira	0.718631	0.720644	0.719604	0.716888	0.717449	0.715841	0.716909	0.719888	0.717888	0.718240	0.717213	0.718692
Norwegian krone	7.70716	7.70101	7.69522	7.73091	7.73484	7.76201	7.76722	7.76219	7.75870	7.77207	7.76308	7.77803
Omani rial	0.365412	0.366435	0.365907	0.364526	0.364811	0.363993	0.364536	0.366051	0.365034	0.365213	0.364691	0.365443
Portuguese escudo	...	96.4851	96.5919	96.9246	97.0269	97.3001	97.4049	97.3940	97.7271	97.7345	97.8952	97.8504
Qatar riyal	3.87220	3.88304	3.87744	3.86280	3.86583	3.85716	3.86291	3.87897	3.86819	3.87008	3 86455	3.87252
Saudi Arabian riyal	3.65412	3.66435	3.65907	3.64526	3.64811	3.63993	3.64536	3.66051	3.65034	3.65213	3.64691	3.65443
Singapore dollar	2.36427	2.35778	2.34617	2.35217	2.35401	2.35372	2.35457	2.35509	2.36130	2.35395	...	2.36128
South African rand	1.24187	1.24173	1.23850	1.22825	1.22779	1.22547	1.22277	1.22040	1.21756	1.21858	1.21614	1.21434
Spanish peseta	...	124.471	124.736	125.276	125.533	126.153	...	126.644	127.309	127.532	127.721	127.719
Swedish krona	7.92151	7.90797	7.90933	7.92618	7.95999	7.97606	7.99750	8.00836	8.01481	8.01873	8.02425	8.03229
Swiss franc	2.34566	2.33889	2.33871	2.36034	2.36060	2.36389	2.36179	2.35722	2.37033	2.36990	2.36332	2.34447
Trinidad & Tobago dollar	2.56267	2.56985	2.56614	2.55645	2.55845	2.55272	2.55653	2.56715	2.56002	2.56127	2.55761	2.56289
U.A.E. dirham	3.90517	3.91611	3.91046	3.89570	3.89875	3.89001	3.89581	3.91200	3.90113	3.90304	3.89746	3.90550
Venezuelan bolívar	4.56632	4.57911	4.57250	4.55524	4.55881	4 54859	4.55537	4.57430	4.56160	4.56383	4.55730	4.56670

Note: The value of the SDR in terms of the U.S. dollar is determined as the sum of the dollar values, based on market exchange rates, of specified quantities of the first 5 currencies shown above. The value of the SDR in terms of any currency other than the U.S. dollar is derived from that currency's exchange rate against the U.S. dollar and the U.S. dollar value of the SDR. An exception is the Iranian rial, the value of which is officially expressed directly in terms of the rials per SDR.

Data: IMF Treasurer's Department

Trade Relations Between Industrialized Countries in Times of Crisis

Roy Denman

Sir Roy Denman is Director-General for External Affairs, Commission of the European Communities.

I am very glad to speak to you today about trade relations between the world's major trading partners in today's difficult times. I shall concentrate on what we in Brussels consider at present our major problems—that is our relations with Japan and the United States.

Because today international trade is a reality to an audience like yours in a way which 30 years ago it was not. More than 20% of US industrial production is now exported. Farm produce from two of every five acres in US agriculture is sold abroad. One of every six jobs in the US manufacturing sector is created by exports. And almost one of every three dollars of US corporate profit derives from the international trade and investment activities of American firms. Every American family and every American farm has a stake in international trade. So you will know the picture is bleak. Let me tell you just how bleak it is.

The present state of world trade is at its gloomiest since the war. In volume terms aggregate world trade stagnated in 1981. It rose by only 1% in 1980. In that year cyclical downswings in the major industrial countries superimposed on the lower long term growth path since the early 1970s and the oil price increases, combined to make the growth and volume of world production and world trade to the third lowest gains in a quarter of a century. And it is clear that at present economic levels the industrial countries will not attain a rate of economic growth sufficient permanently to reduce unemployment. Both in the Community and in the United States there is some hope starting in the second half of this year for a marginal increase in GDP. But unemployment in the Community is now approaching 11 million and is likely to remain remorselessly high. Forty percent of these unemployed are under 25. And all this means not only a dangerously stagnant situation in relation to world trade but protectionist pressure and strains—in all the major trading countries of the world—on the social fabric which imperil the open world trading system on which the prosperity of the free world has been built since the war.

It is against that background that at meetings over the next few months a number of world trading nations are getting together to consider these economic problems. The Versailles Summit at the beginning of June will bring together the United States, Canada, Japan, four Member States of the Community, and the Commission—which acts for the Community in trade matters—and the Presidency of the Council of the Community. And in November this year, in Geneva, the GATT, the body which writes and polices the rule of law in world trade, will be holding its first Ministerial meeting since 1973: between 80 and 90 trade ministers will be there. It would not be realistic to think that one or two meetings can solve the trade problems of the world. And the Versailles Summit will have wider problems. But in the trade field we must hope that the GATT Ministerial meeting is also a success. A failure at the end of the year for the trading nations of the world to agree on major points would signal the end of the broad consensus on an open world trading system which has prevailed since

"Trade Relations Between Industrialized Countries in Time of Crisis," Roy Denman, *The Atlantic Community Quarterly*, Fall 1982.

193

the war and could mark the beginning of reversion to the protectionism—with all its political consequences—of the 1930s.

What are the prospects? Three elements seem to us essential if we are going to have a success in Geneva by the end of the year.

First, the problems arising in trade and economic relations between Japan and its partners and which spring for an insufficient interpenetration of the Japanese economy into the Western economic system. We need to have got to the stage where there is some real prospect of a major opening up of the Japanese market and some restraint certainly for the time being in the Japanese exports pouring into some of the sensitive sectors of our markets.

Second, there needs to be some pause in the escalating trade conflicts between the European Community and the United States notably on steel and agriculture.

Third, economic activity in the main industrialized countries needs to revive. A rising tide, said President Kennedy, lifts all boats. The lift will not be enough as yet to deal with the problem of unemployment. But without some beginning, even modest, of a rising tide few would bet on the harbor lasting much longer.

Let me take these problems one by one. The problems of the Community—and I may add the United States—with Japan are ascribed from time to time by Japanese commentators to workshy Europeans and Americans facing efficient Japanese competition to sheer protectionism, to a reluctance to adjust. The picture in reality is a different one. The Community's problems with Japan stem from a combination of three factors. Each on its own would be of limited import. Taken together, like the chemicals in a dangerous combination, they can create an explosion.

The first is the size of our bilateral deficit with Japan. In 1963, the ten present members of the European Community had a trivial 8 million dollar deficit with Japan. This rocketed to some 500 million in 1970, to 3.4 billion in 1975 and 14 billion in 1981.

At the same time Japanese exports to Europe in certain highly sensitive areas like automobiles, color television tubes and sets, and certain highly developed machine tools rose massively. At the same time European business found it difficult year in year out to penetrate the Japanese market.

Taken in isolation, these factors are not all in themselves decisive. We run bilateral surpluses and deficits in turn with our trading partners. But taken together, a massive and increasing deficit, increasing inroads on our sensitive industries and a sense that our manufacturers cannot get into the Japanese market to the same extent as they can get into other industrialized countries of the world creates an increasingly dangerous climate.

Let me give just a few figures to support what I have said. Total Japanese exports of manufactured goods in 1960 amounted to 3 billion dollars. In 1981 the figure had soared to 136 billion dollars. But Japanese imports of manufactures in 1960 at just under 1 billion dollars had risen in 1981 to only 28 billion dollars.

Again in 1980 the European Community imported manufactured products equal to just under 800 dollars per head. The figure for the United States was 547 dollars, the figure for Japan was 233. Thus Japan's imports of manufactured goods are about the same value as those of Switzerland, an economy one-tenth of that of Japan. And in per capita terms Japan is next to last among Member States of the OECD. The percentage of total imports represented by manufactured goods is equally striking—55% in the case of the United States, 46.5% in the case of the Community—only 22% in the case of Japan.

These figures demonstrate more clearly than any long argument the size of an imbalance which is putting an increasing strain on the world trading system. We have therefore over a period of years pressed the Japanese authorities to take action in a number of areas. We have asked for an easement of tariffs, fiscal charges and quotas, of what we consider to be very restrictive standards and testing and acceptance procedures as well as improvements in the conditions for financial services and investments.

We have asked the Japanese to provide tangible assurances that from 1982 onwards Japan will pursue a policy of effective moderation towards the European Community as a whole as regards Japanese exports in sectors where an increase in Japanese exports to the Community could cause significant problems, notably passenger cars, color television sets and tubes, and certain machine tools. And more broadly, we have emphasized that the essential argument concerns the need for Japan to open up its market. This related to the effect of Japanese trading and economic policies as a whole and the need to achieve a more balanced integration—commensurate with Japan's international responsibilities—of the Japanese economy with that of its main industrialized partners and notably with the European Community.

With this in mind, we have recently taken action to consult with Japan under the "nullification and impairment" provisions of the GATT. We have thus given notice that if no satisfactory adjustment can be effected between us within a reasonable period of time then we shall need to consider proceeding to take the matter for adjudication to the Contracting Parties of the GATT. This will provide the GATT with one of its biggest postwar tests, but we are faced with one of the biggest postwar problems of the world trading system. As some senior visiting Japanese politicians were recently told in Brussels "the regrettable fact is that the EEC now has trade problems with Japan of sufficient seriousness to compromise the overall economic and political relationship between us. If we cannot solve our trade problems or at any rate render them less acute then our efforts to restore prosperity and growth to our domestic economies and to the free world as a whole will be substantially set back. More than this, the tensions now prevailing in relations with Japan, not only in Europe but also in the US, risk precipitating the end of the free world trading system as we have known it in the postwar years".

Now let me turn to another somber picture. Trade relations between the Community and the United States. There are differences between us in a number of areas—export credits, interest rates, East-West trade. But the main areas of difference at present relate to steel and agriculture.

On steel we are clear that the US steel industry has launched a massive campaign of harassment against European exporters. The trading rules do not declare dumping illegal. What is at issue is whether dumping to the extent it exists is causing material injury to the US steel industry. That is where the rules bite. We think that any such claim is moonshine. The share of the American market for Coal and Steel Community products in 1981 was 4.7% compared with 6.7% in 1979. Yet on January 11 four trucks containing over a million documents drew up outside the ITC Headquarters and 85 suits were launched against European steel markets. We said at the time that these suits were enormously strong on allegations and incredibly weak on evidence. There were companies against which allegations were made who never export the product cited for the good reason that they never produce it. There were people who had exported 450 tons. Is it conceivable that 450 tons can cause a problem? In the case of one product, hot rolled carbon sheet, Community exports represented 0.31% of the US market. In the case of cold rolled carbon strip 0.35%. Who do you think is kidding whom?

It is true that ITC rejected a number of these cases in February. But the remaining cases still account for some four-fifths of the volume covered by the full number. And of course as this timetable rolls on this massive campaign of harassment is bound to have results in terms of withholding of appraisement and consequent reluctance, given the uncertainties involved, of importers to import. All this threatens trade of some 5-6 million tons, worth some 2 billion dollars a year. And to this should be added another recently launched action under Section 301 against Member States on specialty steel.

So much for one major area where grave consequences are threatened by US action for trade across the Atlantic. Let me turn to another—agriculture. Now here we should be clear from the outset that there can be no reasonable charge that the Community is a protectionist bloc. The EEC remains the biggest importer of agricultural products in the world. In 1980 we took a quarter of world agricultural imports and we had a trade deficit in agriculture of nearly 29 billion dollars. The trade deficit of the EEC in agriculture with the US increased in fact from 5.8 billion dollars in 1979 to 6.8 billion dollars in 1980. That was an increase of 17% and in the

first nine months of 1981 it continued to increase by 13%.

An argument has recently developed on our imports from the United States of corn gluten feed. Here all we have proposed to our Council is that we open consultations with the United States on the possibility of temporarily levelling on rapidly spiralling imports from the US in return for compensation as provided for by the GATT procedures.

In fact most of the argument between us is not about imports into the EC. It is about exports from the EEC to third markets. And here there is a basic difference of perception. Your authorities say agricultural subsidies are bad and must be removed. We say that this is not what the international trading rules provide. The agreement come to after long and difficult negotiations in the Tokyo Round in 1979 confirmed and elaborated a long standing rule that agricultural subsidies are permitted providing that these did not lead to any Member of the GATT obtaining more than an equitable share of world trade.

How has this worked out? First it should be borne in mind that we are not the only ones who give government aid to our farmers. In many official documents from the US we find comparisons which suggest that the cost of farm support in the EEC is 40% higher than that provided by the US Government to its farmers.

But such comparisons mean nothing. It really is almost impossible to get a precise idea of the financial support provided by governments for agriculture. You have to estimate not only the direct budget support but all the direct and indirect transfers of resources to the farm sector—not just budget subsidies, in other words, also policies affecting land, production costs, direct and indirect taxation, transport costs and so on—and in relation to the USA spending from State budgets as well as from the Federal budget. If you compare budget spending on agriculture with the value added of the agricultural industry you will find that in 1976-78 the ratio in the EEC was 39.2% and in the US it was 37.6%. In our view if you compare like with like the conclusion must be that farm spending in the EEC is of the same order of magnitude as in the US.

So, as seen by the Republican Party, we are both sinners in the eyes of the Lord. Having said this what has happened then to our shares of world trade? Mr. Block complained to the Foreign Agricultural Policy Subcommittee of the Senate Committee on Agriculture on December 16 last year that "subsidies have helped to push EC wheat exports to 14 million tons, double their wheat exports three years ago, with a depressing effect on world prices". Yes, it is true that Community export doubles between 1969-1970 and 1980-1981 to 14 million tons. But world trade was expanding even more rapidly. Our share actually fell from 16.6% to 14.9% over this period. What happened to US exports? They did not just double. They rose from 16.5 million tons to no less than 41.9 million tons—from 38.4% of world trade to no less than 44.8% of the world market. Indeed thirteen years ago the United States exported 40% of their production—now this amounts to between 60 and 70%. Let me take poultry. Community exports in 1978 took 54.2% and in 1980 54.3%. US exports over the same period remained broadly static. And in respect of total world agricultural exports between 1973 and 1980 EEC agricultural exports rose marginally from 9.5% to 11.1%; US exports fell marginally 19.8% to 18.9%. In the United Kingdom lawyers used to talk about the fount of common sense legal wisdom resting with the men on a Clapham omnibus. I think they would have difficulty in concluding from these figures that the Community was using agricultural subsidies to take an unfair share of world agricultural trade.

Let me go on to put it another way. After the hard fought agreement we reached in the Tokyo Round about "an equitable share of the world market" can we in Brussels go back to our farmers when the world market for a certain product is doubling or trebling and say to them that they cannot increase their exports because this might inconvenience farmers elsewhere? If you believe that, as the Duke of Wellington said, you can believe anything.

And let us talk not only about the past. For the future the EEC intends to continue and intensify its efforts to rationalize its agriculture. Our underlying aim domestically is to put more and more responsibility on farmers themselves to dispose of surpluses especially by making the farmers contribute to the cost of surplus disposal. Not that we consider an excess of domestic production over domestic consumption is necessarily a surplus that must be eliminated. The EEC intends to keep its place in world trade. But we consider that for some products the European Community's price guarantees to its farmers should no longer be limited but graduated. We have this system already fully in force for sugar and in part for milk products. And for cereals we intend to fix "production thresholds" in terms of quantity for our cereals for the 1980s. This means that if the threshold is exceeded then in the following year the level of support will be diminished.

So much for some elements of the record and some guidelines we are following for the future. What has been the United States reaction to all this? I would divide it under four heads. In the first place a whole number of separate cases have been brought for adjudication in the GATT by the United States—wheat flour, sugar, poultry, pasta, canned fruit, and citrus. You might say why not? If there is adjudication in the GATT let it take its normal course. But in the first place these cases each require lengthy and detailed debate. In the second place this concentration of cases is not only unparalleled; it risks blowing the dispute settlement process in the GATT and with it the rule of law in world trade just as certainly as overloading with too many bulbs an electric circuit. A desire for maximum illumination does not mean that you want the lights to go out.

Secondly, the attitude of the US authorities to the GATT seems to an outsider somewhat uncertain. With the cases I have mentioned, they seem to attest the validity of the GATT, even while overloading the circuit. At the same time, as far as the provisions of the Subsidies Code negotiated in the Tokyo Round are concerned—with which no senior official now in Washington has any first hand experience—they seem somewhat less than certain. Mr. Brock said on February 11 to the Subcommittee on International Trade of the Senate Finance Committee that if the EEC Commission is found by GATT to be in the wrong, the EEC will change its policy. If the US interpretation is wrong the US will try to change the Subsidy Code. This is what is known in the Queen's English as "heads I win, tails you lose."

Again, you will know that the Commission has recently proposed to the Council of Ministers in Brussels that the Community start consultations with the United States under Article XXVIII of the GATT to level off the soaring exports from the United States of corn gluten feed to the Community—in return for due compensation. An official statement I have here by the Public Affairs Office of the US Mission to the European Communities says, "US says corn gluten not negotiable". This is simply not in accordance with GATT procedures. International trade rules provide that negotiation must be engaged; the compensation then offered needs to be the subject of agreement. But negotiation cannot be refused.

One further example. A statement of US views on the Common Agricultural Policy handed to us and widely distributed to Congress in February this year said, "the US cannot tolerate the evolution of the CAP to a common export policy . . . EEC export subsidies are the single most harmful of EC policies. The US must seek an acceptable plan and timetable for their elimination". All this goes a million miles beyond what was negotiated in the Tokyo Round when not only the United States and the Community as two countries which subsidize their agriculture to a comparable degree agree together with nearly 80 other Contracting Parties on the "equitable share of the world market" as the limiting factor.

A third point is the tone of voice adopted by the US Administration. And this was set by Agriculture Secretary Block before the House Agriculture Committee on 18 February when he said—and I quote—"my Department is working aggressively to stimulate long-term growth of exports of US farm products". Anyone could understand a cabinet member's wish to boost the products for which he is responsible. But what worries us is this constant use of the word aggressive not just in this but many other statements. Mr. Block went on to say that "we are going to do battle with the EEC forever and whenever it is necessary".

I find it difficult not to be reminded of Mark Twain talking about Carlyle and the Americans "at bottom he was probably fond of them but he was always able to conceal it".

Fourth there are pressures on the part of the US Administration to change and broaden the rules of world trade in agricultural products. This we find surprising. For it is the United States which does not fully apply the GATT rules on agriculture. Since 1955 the so-called GATT waiver has allowed you to ignore certain rules of the GATT—to be precise, notwithstanding any provision of the GATT, the United States can impose what controls it likes on *inter alia* imports of cotton, sugar, peanuts, and dairy products. The EEC benefits from no such provision. And I mention only in passing the DISC system in force since 1972—which we consider a clear export subsidy not to be applied to exports of non primary products—exports under Section 1 of P.L. 480, the government to government agreements on milk products and the US method of applying drawback for sugar—all of which we do not consider compatible with the rules of GATT. Those who want to change the rules in any particular game should at least take care that they are accepting them and observing them.

It is difficult to avoid on the European side drawing two general conclusions from that fact I have set out. The first is that there is an attempt to shift the blame for certain difficult conditions in the United States to foreigners in general and Europeans in particular. The US steel industry is going through a difficult time. Like steel industries elsewhere—and in this the US is not unique—there has been inadequate investment, rationalization, modernization. All of you know that the troubles of the US steel industry do not in any substantial way come from European steel exporters—these represent less than 5% of the total US steel market, and ludicrously small in the case of particular products. But the OECD steel consensus of 1977 provided that the burden of restructuring should be shared equally on both sides of the Atlantic. This is what the US steel industry is now trying to throw into the waste paper basket.

Again, on US agriculture all of you know that the deep troubles of US agriculture can be ascribed to a variety of causes: interest rates—total farm debt has soared to 200 billion dollars meaning that the average farmer owes 10 dollars for every dollar he earned, five times

more than the historical rate—growing American agricultural surpluses, a strengthening dollar and a fall in the US share of Soviet grain imports since the embargo from 75% to 40%. Certainly competition in third markets has played a part. But the Community cannot and will not accept that its farmers do not have a right to make a living selling overseas providing they abide by the international trading rules. The Community is not prepared to be a scapegoat for the difficulties of US agriculture.

The second general conclusion is this. A rule of law depends nationally or internationally on those in authority being prepared to spell out what the rules are for better or for worse. No Sheriff in a Western town ever told everybody that the law would always be 100% in his favor in any circumstances. Nor nowadays does your lawyer. In the Community we had a case 18 months ago where there was massive pressure for import restrictions to be placed on American exports of petroleum chemical products because of the artificially low price in the United States for natural gas and the consequent fierce competition on the European market. On this the Commission of the European Communities stuck to its guns. We were told that the existing world trade rules were less than perfect. But they were the only rules we had. It is not to us apparent that the United States Administration is quite as ready to explain the rules of the world trading system in quite this even handed form. But unless we, all of us, do this with our clients it will become more and more difficult to keep what in the West you used to call "peace in the valley".

I have tried to set out a Community view of some of the tensions now straining world trade. Our hope would be—and we shall join in it from the Community in good faith—that the series of meetings we have over the rest of this year, our bilateral contacts and our meetings in the GATT, can contribute to resolving these key difficulties. If we do not, then what is at risk is simply the world trading system which has been responsible over the last 30 years for the biggest increase of prosperity in the free world ever recorded. The stakes are so high that we must succeed. This will require much courage, much effort and very cool heads. But we cannot afford to fail.

Delivered to the Houston Chamber of Commerce, May 18, 1982.

The Arms Race, Arms Control, Nuclear Freeze, and Arms Sales

"If you want peace, prepare for war." So said Julius Caesar twenty centuries ago and it seems his advice is still heeded today.

What distinguishes today's arms race from that of previous centuries is the advance of the "technetronic-nuclear" era, which has made weapon manufacturing and war-fighting strategy the main occupation of not only generals and admirals but thousands of businessmen and scientists as well. Together, they plot scenarios involving fantastic Buck Rogers killing devices from "smart bombs" to the neutron bomb and from Multiple Independently Targetable Re-entry Vehicles (MIRVs) to laser-equipped, killer satellites. In the efficient and sanitary war rooms of wide-screened computer chart displays, there are only targets, launchers, payloads, and statistics of "acceptable" casualties in the environs of 100 million each for the US and the USSR.

When Ronald Reagan campaigned for the presidency, he warned the American electorate that the US was slipping into the number two position vis-à-vis the USSR. The slogan of the day was to close the "window of vulnerability." When pressed, however, neither Mr. Reagan nor his aides could explain nor agree on whether such a "window" existed, what it was, or how to close it. Also eluding the general public has been the debate over theatre nuclear forces (the TNFs have such names as Pershing II and SS-20, also known as MRBMs or medium-range ballistic missiles). TNFs may be of marginal concern to Americans, but not to Europeans. When President Reagan remarked that a theatre nuclear war could be limited to Europe, and when Secretary of State Haig, a former NATO Supreme Commander, talked about a NATO doctrine of firing nuclear warning shots, the West Europeans were shaken. These remarks confirmed what the West Europeans had feared all along, namely that the US was willing to fight to the last European.

Since the latter part of 1981, anti-nuclear protests have erupted all over Western Europe and the US. The Reagan Administration has tried to dismiss their importance, alleging that the freeze movement is infiltrated by Soviets. But clearly Western Europeans and Americans do not need Soviet inspiration for advocating a nuclear freeze.

The only accord on strategic arms limitations (SALT I) was signed in 1972, and produced only two agreements: The Anti-Ballistic Missile Treaty and a five-year Interim Agreement on offensive strategic nuclear weapons. No long-term agreement on limiting offensive strategic arms could be reached. SALT II became a victim of the Soviet invasion of Afghanistan in January 1980. President Reagan then scrapped the SALT II proposals and offered a new form of arms control and disarmament in strategic arms reduction talks (START), but negotiations slowed to a standstill by early 1982. This was due in part to the imposition of martial law in Poland, and to both sides being unable (the Soviets) or unwilling (the Americans) to make new concessions in anticipation of a leadership change in the Kremlin.

Since Andropov's succession to Brezhnev's position in November, 1982, several proposals on arms control and disarmament have been put forward by both Superpowers. The Soviets have offered to reduce their 500 MRBMs aimed at Western Europe to 162, which is the combined total of French and British missiles, if the US agrees not to deploy 572 Pershing II launchers and cruise missiles in Western Europe. The latest State Department proposal is that, as an interim solution, the two states agree to having an equal number of missiles at the lowest possible level. The assumption behind this proposal is first, that the Soviets cannot be expected to destroy all their missiles as Reagan's "zero-option" would require; and second, if the US deploys no missiles in Europe as part of the NATO force, leaving all defense up to the independent nuclear forces of England and France, the credibility of the American nuclear deterrent would be jeopardized. This would be particularly distressing for the West Germans, who are deeply concerned about the US becoming "decoupled" from European defense.

In the meantime, as the following articles indicate, focussing attention on Soviet-American strategic arms may be blinding the US to the increasingly dangerous situations that could lead to military conflict between the two superpowers: nuclear proliferation, and the sharp increase in the volume and quality of arms transfers to the rest of the world. It is altogether possible that the Soviets and Americans may come to an acceptable agreement on strategic arms, only to find the world set on fire by a newcomer to the nuclear club.

Looking Ahead: Challenge Questions

The logic of strategic deterrence indicates that a state does not want its enemy to think that it is either significantly stronger or significantly weaker than itself. Otherwise, "mutual armed destruction," the basis for deterrence, is lost. If this is the case, what does it suggest about the best type of strategic balance to be negotiated with the Soviets? Is unquestioned American military hegemony really in the interest of the US? Why do countries launch pre-emptive wars?

One of the major difficulties over the years in negotiating arms control and disarmament with the Soviets is their adament refusal to permit inspection to assure compliance. Without surveillance, each side can "cheat" by building more missiles than it has agreed to. What kinds of problems does this imply for reducing the number of missiles on both sides to a very small number? Is "overkill" in some sense necessary?

If American missiles under NATO command are not deployed in Western Europe, what would be the most likely response by West Germany? How might other European countries feel about a nuclear-armed Germany? How might the Russians feel?

If Soviet SS-20s are simply moved East of the Urals, what kinds of responses can be expected from the Chinese and the Japanese? Can you foresee any new sorts of military alliances in such circumstances?

RUSSIAN AND AMERICAN CAPABILITIES

JEROME B. WIESNER

Jerome B. Wiesner, Institute professor and president emeritus of Massachusetts Institute of Technology, served as special assistant to President Kennedy for science and technology.

OVER THE PAST THIRTY YEARS, THE NUCLEAR-ARMS race has been propelled by political tensions, by technical innovations, and by rivalries inside the governments of the United States and the Soviet Union. But at the moment, on the American side one overriding concern promotes the buildup of nuclear weapons—the fear that the United States might be denied its ability to inflict a devastating retaliatory blow if the Soviet Union struck first. This fear presumes that a nuclear war, far from being an act of mutual annihilation, might be a controllable, survivable, even "winnable" encounter, and that the Soviet Union may be better equipped than the United States to prevail in a nuclear war.

Such an anxiety, if well grounded, would compel any responsible American leader to search seriously for new nuclear-weapons projects, beginning with the MX missile and perhaps extending to antiballistic-missile systems and greater efforts for civil defense, in the hope of redressing the balance. The Reagan Administration, of course, is pushing ahead on several such fronts and says that it cannot persuade the Soviet Union to negotiate for reductions in strategic weapons unless we first show our determination to increase American strength. Even if the strategic-arms-reduction talks (START) that President Reagan has proposed eventually lead to an agreement, that welcome development would not come sooner than several years from now. In the meantime, American policy need not be driven by a fear of a Soviet first strike. Instead, it should rest on a recognition of the basic reality of the nuclear age: that the only option open to either the Soviet Union or the United States is deterrence. Given today's weapons, neither side can do anything to protect itself against the retaliatory threat the other poses; by the same logic, neither side need fear that its threat to the other will be called into question. This balance hardly justifies political or moral complacency. Because of the catastrophe that would occur if deterrence failed, our best efforts must be directed to preventing the circumstances in which nuclear weapons would ever be used. But the concept of deterrence suggests a very different direction for American action from the one indicated by anticipation of a Soviet first strike.

The current era has often been spoken of as a "window of vulnerability," in which America's nuclear force is uniquely at risk. But it can instead be a "window of opportunity" in which to negotiate an end to the arms race. The most obvious and the most sensible step for the United States at the moment is to add *nothing* to our nuclear forces, and to seize this opportunity to press for a freeze on the development, testing, and deployment of all nuclear weapons and new delivery systems by each side.

As has happened before in the arms race, we have been told that technical progress has created a theoretical vulnerability for our force. The Soviet missile force has increased in size and accuracy, and supposedly poses fresh dangers to our land-based nuclear missiles. The Soviet Union's theoretical ability to destroy nearly all of these missiles in a surprise attack, it is argued, will psychologically upset the balance of deterrence, and will thereby make the United States vulnerable to Soviet blackmail. This will happen, it is further argued, even though the great majority of the American nuclear weapons are carried on bombers or by ballistic-missile submarines, rather than by the Minuteman and Titan missiles that are based in silos throughout the Midwest. An American President might be afraid to retaliate after a Soviet attack on the U.S. missiles, because the Soviet Union would then respond with a major attack on American cities. The conclusion of this line of reasoning is that the U.S. cannot contemplate any slackening of the pace until it has redressed the imbalance by building the MX missile or other systems.

I accepted this scenario myself until I made a few simple calculations concerning how vulnerable the Minuteman system actually is and what the strategic situation would be even if it were somehow totally destroyed. It emerges from any such calculation that neither side can escape the risk of devastating retaliation if it launches a pre-emptive attack. This is the only vital issue for each side—the actual capabilities for responding after attack, not guesses about what the other side's intentions might be. Intentions may change, and they are always difficult to discern. But the meaning of the capabilities is unambiguous: *under present technology, either side could devastate the other after enduring any conceivable attack.*

The U.S. has more deliverable nuclear warheads than the Soviet Union does. A 1978 study prepared for the Congressional Budget Office estimated that in the mid-1980s, when the "window of vulnerability" will allegedly stand open, the U.S. will have 13,904 warheads on its strategic delivery systems, versus 8,794 for the Soviet Union. The Soviet Union, for reasons we have never fully understood, has chosen to build missiles larger than ours, with larger warheads; and its force, though smaller in numbers, contains more "equivalent megatons" than ours does. (The measure "equivalent megaton" takes account of the fact that small nuclear warheads do proportionately more damage than large ones, since the area a warhead destroys does not increase linearly with the size of the warhead.) The same Congressional Budget Office study estimated that in the mid-1980s the U.S. force would represent 4,894 equivalent megatons, versus 8,792 for the Soviet Union. Paul Nitze, of the Committee on the Present Danger, which has been among the most strident of the groups warning about a window of vulnerability, has estimated that if both sides built up to the limits allowed by the SALT II treaty (whose ratification the committee opposed), the U.S. would have 12,504 nuclear warheads and the Soviet Union 11,728. It foresees roughly the same advantage for the Russians in equivalent megatons as does the Congressional Budget Office.

Of the 13,000 to 14,000 warheads projected for the American force, roughly 2,100 are on the Minuteman and Titan missiles. The land-based force represents some 1,507 equivalent megatons. Therefore, if every single Titan and Minuteman were destroyed in a successful surprise attack, the U.S. would be left with somewhere between 11,000 and 12,000 nuclear warheads. The submarine fleet would account for approximately 6,000 of these weapons, and the rest would be carried by bombers. All together, these remaining American warheads would represent about 3,500 equivalent megatons.

IN PLANNING AMERICAN NUCLEAR FORCES IN THE early 1960s, Robert McNamara came to the conclusion that 400 equivalent megatons would be sufficient to inflict unacceptable damage—and that the U.S. could have absolute confidence in its deterrent if it built such a retaliatory capacity three times over, once on the bomber fleet, once on land-based missiles, and once with the submarine force, for a total of 1,200 equivalent megatons. In other words, the 11,000 or 12,000 warheads, representing 3,500 equivalent megatons, that the U.S would retain even after a perfectly successful first strike against our land-based missiles would be three times larger than the force that was itself designed to be able thrice to destroy the Soviet Union. The accuracy of nuclear weapons has improved since McNamara's day, further increasing their effective power. These figures do not even count the several thousand American warheads that are left in Europe and other parts of the world, some of which could be used for retaliation.

Nearly all scenarios for a first strike assume that an attacker would have to target two warheads against each missile silo it hoped to destroy. The U.S. has 1,000 Minuteman missiles and several dozen Titans. The Soviet Union would, therefore, have to devote about 2,200 warheads to an attack. The most generous estimates put the mid-1980s Soviet force at slightly fewer than 12,000 warheads; so after launching its first strike, the Soviet Union would end up with fewer than 10,000 warheads, or several thousand *fewer* than the United States.

So far, these calculations have been based on extreme assumptions: that the Soviet Union would be able to destroy totally the force of Minuteman and Titan missiles, but that it would leave the submarine and bomber fleets intact. More realistic assumptions yield the same conclusion: that a first strike would be suicidal irrationality, which is the premise upon which deterrence is based.

Moreover, first-strike scenarios rest on the assumption that large numbers of men and machines will perform exactly as planned. The weapons used in a first strike would have to perform reliably and very accurately, and the detonations of several thousand warheads would have to be coordinated with perfect skill, or else the whole scenario becomes immediately implausible. Yet no complex system ever works as predicted when it is first used. In carefully controlled tests, involving small numbers of weapons, it may be possible to attain the levels of accuracy required for a first strike, but I am convinced that the necessary levels of accuracy and reliability are simply not attainable in an operational force. It would require many more test flights than either nation normally conducts to get enough data to establish the actual facts about these systems. How many trial runs of a surprise attack could the U.S. or the Soviet Union carry out?

Three factors make it seem especially unlikely that a surprise attack could be successfully carried out. First, the accuracy of the attacking warheads is uncertain. Because their targets, the missile silos, are so greatly "hardened," warheads must come much closer to a silo than to "softer" targets to do damage. But it may be impossible for either side to know how accurate its warheads will be when they are fired in large fleets on a trajectory that has never before been tested.

Second, the reliability of the missiles themselves is open to deep question. Optimists assume that 80 percent of the missiles that are fired will perform satisfactorily. The likely rate may be closer to 50 or 60 percent. This would mean that even assuming maximum accuracy and accepting the formula that two warheads fired at a silo will have a 95 percent probability of destroying it, the Soviet Union might fire 2,200 warheads at our missiles and destroy only 500 to 600 of them.

Third, such an exercise would require prodigious feats of timing. It would involve very precise firings of the individual missiles, so that the two warheads attacking each Minuteman would be so perfectly spaced that the detonation of the first would not destroy the second, and warheads attacking neighboring sites would not disable each other. (These very probable accidents are known as fratricide.) A successful first strike would depend on flawless communication within the Soviet command structure. It is generally recognized that the command-and-control system is the weakest link in the nuclear forces of both sides.

7. THE ARMS RACE

In principle, the Soviet Union could improve its possibilities of success by firing more than two warheads at each missile, but then the potential for destructive interference becomes even greater, as do the complications of command and coordination. Most experts believe that two warheads per target is the practical limit.

All in all, the result is this: even after a surprise Soviet attack on the American Minuteman force, *U.S. strength would actually be slightly greater than the Soviet Union's.* If the Soviet Union could carry out the worst attack that the alarmists have been able to imagine, the United States would not only retain its relative position but would have enough nuclear weapons to destroy several Soviet Unions. And by the same logic, the Soviet Union would certainly retain the capacity to inflict unacceptable punishment on the United States, no matter how large and clever a surprise first strike the U.S. were to launch. Theorists may claim that it would not be "logical" for the side that had endured the first strike to order a retaliation, since that would lead to further devastation, but such forbearance on the part of a badly wounded but still armed nation is hard to credit.

Theorists defending the first-strike hypothesis often refer to the issues of the Cuban missile crisis. In 1962, the U.S. had many more nuclear weapons than the Soviet Union, and this superiority, many advocates of the MX now say, forced Nikita Khrushchev to back down. But in the early sixties, the Soviet Union had so few *deliverable* nuclear weapons that its leaders had legitimate reason to fear that a first strike might take away their ability to threaten destructive retaliation. The imbalance *may* have affected Soviet behavior—although American superiority in conventional naval forces seems to have weighed more heavily in the Soviets' calculations. At the comparatively low levels of nuclear weaponry of twenty years ago, a difference in size between the arsenals could have political significance; indeed, much of the impetus in American policy has been to regain the first-strike potential the U.S. enjoyed for many years. But when each side has a super-abundance of weaponry, which is the case today, small differences in size no longer matter.

AT THE MOMENT, NEITHER THE U.S. NOR THE SOVIET Union has a meaningful strategic advantage. A window of vulnerability does not exist. Furthermore, it is almost impossible to imagine how either side could achieve a usable advantage. Both sides are thoroughly deterred from using their strategic forces, because a decision to use them would be a decision to commit national suicide. And this seems sure to remain true no matter what either side deploys in the way of new weapons.

Though the Soviets might theoretically increase the capacities of their missiles in such a way as to pose significant new threats to the Minuteman force, it would require a major breakthrough in both technology and production to do so. The same is obviously true for American forces. The MX and the cruise missiles based in Europe might be the American entry into such a competition. But at the moment, such capabilities do not exist and so cannot be deployed. Thus, now is the time for a disarmament agreement, one that would freeze all missile developments, leaving both sides with an unquestioned deterrent but without any plausible threat of a first strike. Now we have a "window of opportunity" for safer, saner alternatives to a major arms buildup. This might mean ratification of the SALT II agreement, whose limitations the Reagan Administration has so far chosen to observe, or a comprehensive freeze on the testing and development of nuclear weapons, which I favor.

An agreement to halt all testing of nuclear weapons, and of the vehicles that would deliver them, could dramatically change the political cloud that surrounds these weapons. Military technologists will strenuously resist the enactment of any such program. They will be reluctant to give up new weapons already in the pipeline. Moreover, they will maintain that if they cannot test-fire weapons, they cannot guarantee that they will work as planned. That is true, but scarcely a problem. While no one could be sure that the weapons would work as planned—which further reduces the certainty essential for a first strike—neither could anyone be certain that they won't work. They would not suffice for pre-emptive attack, but they would still represent a secure deterrent.

If this opportunity for arms control is not taken, the job will only grow more difficult in the future. The weapons of today are easy to count and monitor, but those of tomorrow won't be. The cruise missile, the stealth bomber, and far more accurate guidance systems would lead us to a nightmare world, one in which our fears would increase. That is why the opportunity must be seized now.

A limited solution to the arms race is not pleasing to many religious and ethical leaders who are emphasizing the immorality of relying on the very weapons that may threaten the extinction of the species. For contrary reasons, a nuclear-arms freeze irritates conservative political leaders, who imagine that this dimension of military force should somehow be made more "usable," and who object to a policy—deterrence—that places the civilian population of the nation at risk. Deterrence is unsatisfactory—except by contrast with the alternatives. The weapons that create the threat of annihilation cannot be uninvented. The sad fact of this era is that our populations cannot conceivably be protected except through political skill and courage applied to the task of minimizing the chances that nuclear weapons will ever be used.

Seizing this opportunity to freeze the arms race would be one demonstration of such skill and courage. It would free both sides from the fear of a first strike and would leave them with such security as a deterrent can provide. It would set the stage for further safety measures, including the reduction of nuclear forces. Meanwhile, the fear of unknown new weapons would be eliminated. And with less money devoted to strategic nuclear weapons, more would be available to repair the deficiencies in our conventional forces, to right the economy, and especially to work on the ever-growing set of civilian problems facing the world.

PUSHING ARMS

Barry M. Blechman,
Janne E. Nolan, and Alan Platt

BARRY M. BLECHMAN *is a resident associate of the Carnegie Endowment.* JANNE E. NOLAN *is a visiting scholar at the Georgetown Center for Strategic and International Studies. Both Blechman and Nolan served on the U.S. delegation for Conventional Arms Transfer talks.* ALAN PLATT *is a senior associate of the Rand Corporation. This article is adapted from a paper prepared for a study of U.S.-Soviet crisis management directed by Alexander George and funded by the Ford and Rockefeller foundations.*

The United States and the Soviet Union have long understood the political significance of arms sales, employing them as central instruments of their foreign policies throughout the postwar period. Often serving as the leading edge of great power involvement in regional conflicts, arms transfers to rival Third World countries have occasionally led to a serious risk of military conflict between the two superpowers.

This danger may be even greater in the years to come because all major arms producers, particularly the United States and the Soviet Union, have sharply increased the volume and quality of arms transfers to the rest of the world. Inevitably, this progressively unrestrained trade in arms will give rise to a call for efforts to negotiate some limits to the transfers. Is restraint possible?

There is an earlier effort worth studying. Recognizing the dangers of arms trade, the Carter administration in 1977 initiated the Conventional Arms Transfer (CAT) talks with the Soviet Union. The administration wanted to find a basis for cooperation in limiting arms sales. Some also saw the negotiations as a way to engage the Soviets in a dialogue about limits on the roles of U.S. and Soviet military power in the Third World and to reach a mutual understanding of the boundaries between proper and improper behavior in developing regions. Although the negotiations fared poorly, the superpowers achieved enough progress to provide practical lessons in the promises and problems of arms transfer negotiations.

Both the United States and the Soviet Union use arms transfers as levers to gain influence in the developing world. At times they secure tangible benefits such as military facilities in a Third World country. In recent years, for example, the Philippines, Spain, Somalia, and Oman have directly linked continued U.S. access to bases to sales of military equipment. More often, however, the exchange is more subtle and has little to do with either the military capabilities of the donor or the military needs of the recipient. Basically, both superpowers seem to value greater influence or steps that they see as potentially convertible into increased influence in their own right and for their own sake. The recipient's dependency on the donor for maintenance, spare parts, and replacement of major items of military equipment is seen to provide leverage in difficult situations. The arms donor need not actually threaten to curtail supplies because the two superpowers know that this dependency will influence the recipient's decisions long before the donor would need to contemplate such threats.

During crises the security commitment implied by arms transfers is tested. They therefore carry the danger that a local conflict could escalate into superpower confrontation. Once a military conflict involving the recipient begins, the donor nation must decide whether to sustain its commitment by replacing weapons lost during the war and whether to make available additional weapons so that its client might continue fighting.

A decision to discontinue supplying weapons, such as that made by the French with regard to Israel after the 1967 Six-Day War or by the United States with respect to India and Pakistan during their 1965 war, is equally if not more significant than a decision to continue to provide weapons. By withdrawing further deliveries, the donor dissociates itself from the war aims of the recipient and in many cases signals disapproval. If it decides to maintain the arms flow, the supplying nation involves itself directly in a military conflict.

When the superpowers sell arms to rival nations, each conflict that erupts between superpower client states carries the potential for involving the United States and the USSR militarily on opposing sides. During conflicts, the donor's armed forces may assist in transporting urgently needed weapons by delivering them into the war zone. Although such involvement does not actually commit the donor to fight, its armed forces are just a short step from involvement in the conflict itself.

The great powers can reach arrangements that ease the potential dangers of their arms transfers. Throughout the Vietnam war, for example, the United States and the Soviet Union avoided a direct superpower confrontation. The United States chose not to interdict the flow of military supplies to North Vietnam, avoiding targets that ran the risk of harming Soviet nationals until near the end of the U.S. involvement. Meanwhile, the USSR decided not to supply certain weapons to North Vietnam that might have threatened U.S. naval vessels operating in the Gulf of Tonkin. For example, the Soviet Union did not send North Vietnam either land-based surface-to-surface missiles or fast patrol boats equipped with antiship missiles until 1975. Yet these types of weapons were transferred to Soviet Middle East clients throughout this period.

The United States and the Soviet Union have demonstrated mutual restraint in other situations. In East Asia, for example, the superpowers did not make available to their Korean allies certain types of military equipment that they had already transferred to allies in other regions throughout the 1970s. Most important, the Soviet Union did not supply North Korea with mobile air-defense systems, which would have greatly strengthened Pyongyang's ability to mount an invasion in the face of U.S. and South Korean air superiority.

This restraint made it possible for the United States to resist domestic pressures and South Korean requests for the transfer of the most advanced models of U.S. fighter aircraft. In turn, this prudence permitted the Soviets to resist demands from North Korea for both mobile air defenses and its own advanced fighter aircraft. Also, neither the United States nor the Soviet Union has supplied surface-to-surface missiles to the Korean peninsula, except for the shortest-range weapons of strictly tactical utility. These tacit arrangements existed until 1981 when the Reagan administration decided to sell F-16s to South Korea.

Risk of Superpower Conflict

At other times and in other situations, circumstance, ambition, and perceptions of na-

tional interest have combined to expand arms sales relationships into dangerous confrontations between the superpowers. From 1967 through 1973 a clear pattern of escalating involvement emerged in four crises in the Middle East, each of which contained the potential for superpower conflict. In 1973 both superpowers took actions that brought them closer to actual involvement in the fighting than they had ever been.

Although the Soviets had denied certain types of weapons to Egypt and Syria prior to the 1973 Arab-Israeli war, Moscow quickly began massive arms deliveries when hostilities broke out. These deliveries continued throughout the war and rose to such high levels that they clearly implied continued Soviet support and encouragement to the belligerents. When Israeli air strikes on Syrian ports damaged Soviet merchant ships delivering munitions, Moscow deployed its navy along the air and sea routes between Eastern Europe and the Middle East to signal Soviet willingness to defend these lines of communication. Furthermore, when Israel threatened major strategic defeats for Soviet clients—the possibility of an attack on Damascus on October 17 and the possibility of destroying the encircled Egyptian Third Army on October 24—the Soviet Union threatened by word and by active military preparation to intervene with its own forces after the United States rejected a joint US-USSR force.

The United States delayed arms deliveries, in part because of opposition from certain Defense Department officials. Secretary of State Henry Kissinger also saw long-term advantages for the United States in maintaining distance between Washington and Israel's war aims. Eventually, however, the United States sea- and air-lifted arms to Israel, necessitating the deployment of some American military personnel at Lod Airfield near Tel Aviv and, according to some, at Sinai air bases as well. The United States Sixth Fleet in the Mediterranean supported and protected the airlift. And at the most dramatic point of the confrontation, on October 24, the United States responded to a threatened Soviet intervention by advancing the readiness of all its armed forces and by taking other actions that indicated a willingness to counter Soviet moves in a manner that could result in nuclear war.

Thus, in 1973 routine decisions to sell arms in peacetime led gradually yet inexorably to a real risk of conflict between the United States and the Soviet Union. The confrontation ended only when the United States pressured Israel to conform to the terms of the cease-fire arranged by the superpowers, relieving pressure on the besieged Egyptian army. Given the instability of politics in the Third World, the possibility that situations similar to the 1973 crisis will develop can be ruled out only rarely. Moreover, the problems caused by arms transfers during crises cannot be separated from those caused by routine, peacetime deliveries: The former follow inevitably from the latter. The kind of confrontation in the Middle East in 1973 will very likely occur again elsewhere. This prospect is particularly worrisome in the current tense state of U.S.-Soviet relations.

CAT Strategies

Steps to regulate arms transfers can help blunt the leading edge of U.S.-Soviet military competition in the Third World and thus could prevent a superpower confrontation. Such steps would complement and extend obligations the United States and the Soviet Union incurred in the 1972 Basic Principles of Relations and the more specific 1973 Agreement on the Prevention of Nuclear War. Together the documents sought to spell out rules necessary to sustain and promote cooperative relations between the superpowers and to avoid situations that might lead to nuclear war. With these considerations in mind, the Soviet Union and the United States convened conventional arms transfer negotiations in 1977 and 1978.

In March 1977, during Secretary of State Cyrus Vance's trip to Moscow, conventional arms transfers was one of eight subjects on which the United States and the USSR agreed to establish working groups. The two countries held exploratory consultations in Washington in mid-December 1977. The American delegation explained to the Soviets in some detail the new U.S. arms transfer policy. The Americans pointed out that multilateral cooperation would be required to sustain the initial Carter policy of unilateral restraint. They also emphasized the relationship of these talks to the 1972 Basic Principles of Relations. This point seemed to impress the Soviets.

The Soviet delegation listened carefully during this first round, but did not make a significant contribution to the dialogue. Later, however, the Soviets requested further talks.

In preparing for the second round of negotiations, held in Helsinki in May 1978, American officials decided that for both domestic and international reasons the talks should produce some tangible, public sign of progress. They agreed that at least a joint communiqué making certain specific points was required to encourage interest and cooperation among the major West European suppliers and among Third World recipients. This emphasis on obtaining concrete results also reflected growing skepticism within segments of the administration about Soviet motives for entering the talks.

At Helsinki the American delegation tied the CAT negotiations to the 1972 Basic Principles of Relations more explicitly; the final joint communiqué, issued on May 11, 1978, unmistakably reflected this strategy. The two sides acknowledged that "the problem of limiting international transfers of conventional arms is urgent" and that "these meetings, being a component of the Soviet-American negotiations on cessation of the arms race, are held in accordance with the Basic Principles of Relations." Soviet behavior during this round and the wording of the final communiqué convinced most American participants and many foreign observers that the Soviets—for whatever reasons—were indeed willing to pursue the negotiations seriously. Such great optimism surrounded the talks at this point that the two sides scheduled a third round for July—only 10 weeks later. While the United States was preparing for the next round, however, a crucial difference of opinion developed within the U.S. government over the approach to be pursued in the negotiations.

The Arms Control and Disarmament Agency (ACDA) argued that the strategy for CAT should minimize the political aspects of the talks, particularly in the initial stages. ACDA suggested that the talks focus on technical issues, such as detailed lists of weapons systems whose transfer might be limited or banned on a global basis and whose exclusion from international arms traffic would not be very controversial. The talks could emphasize precluding sales of weapons not typically considered for widespread transfer in any event, such as long-range surface-to-surface missiles, napalm, or small, lightweight air-defense systems that could be used by terrorists. Indeed, a whole category of such weapons—known as weapons of ill-repute—for one reason or another could probably have been banned without raising too much dissent.

Such agreements would not have had much of an impact on world arms sales. But that was not the major point. The underlying objective of this strategy was to acclimate the bureaucracies in both the United States and the Soviet Union to the idea of restricting arms transfers. In so doing, advocates of this stance hoped to develop and institutionalize the mechanisms and procedures necessary to make progress later toward the regulation of arms transfers. This approach also seemed to offer the best chance for early concrete progress, which ACDA saw as a prerequisite for West European participation and for greater interest in multilateral negotiations.

The ACDA strategy envisioned moving eventually to the more common and significant currency of the world's arms trade, such as high-performance aircraft or ground-combat vehicles. It accepted that the goal of those later discussions necessarily would be regional rather than global restraints because weapons considered technologically advanced in one area might be relatively unsophisticated in another. But the objective of the talks would be to limit specific weapons worldwide, taking into account the differences between various regions, rather than to limit all weapons transfers to individual regions with exceptions for specific weapons.

The State Department favored a different approach. It viewed CAT more as a political than a technical negotiation. Through these talks, it hoped the United States and the Soviet Union might begin to discuss and reach mutual understandings about their rivalry in the Third World and begin to regulate that competition. At a minimum, the two sides might reach implicit agreement about appropriate norms of behavior in the Third World. Furthermore, State Department officials argued, the talks would have to focus on specific regions or subregions to permit consideration of the full political and military scope of U.S.-Soviet competition. Weapons systems would be discussed, but only as conduits. State feared that the ACDA approach would drag on for years and distract attention from the real issue behind arms transfers: the political struggle between the superpowers for influence in the Third World.

A Political Negotiation

President Carter ultimately endorsed the State Department's approach to the talks. He was increasingly concerned about Soviet inroads in the Third World and the effects of these inroads on his political standing. CAT was to be viewed largely as a political negotiation. It would attempt to achieve parallel U.S. and Soviet initiatives designed to lessen tensions and reduce the risk of military confrontations in certain regions of the Third World by restraining arms transfers.

Accordingly, in the third round of talks the United States emphasized the need to discuss arms transfers to specific regions. It suggested the establishment of a working group on regions and proposed early discussions on Latin America and sub-Saharan Africa, given the relatively low level of arms transfers by either side to these areas. Although the U.S. approach also envisioned negotiating guidelines for weapons transfers around the globe, its principal aim was to achieve restraint agreements for particular regions.

During the third round the Soviet delegation emphasized the need for legal principles governing global arms transfers and, in particular, establishing eligibility criteria for potential recipients. For example, the Soviets argued that a guideline should permit arms transfers to countries that needed arms for self-defense but not to countries that used them to violate another state's territorial integrity. The American delegation accepted the need for such legal guidelines but emphasized the concurrent requirement for more technical criteria defining the permissible levels and types of weapons that could be transferred to legitimate recipients.

During these talks the United States gained explicit Soviet agreement that the legal and technical guidelines should receive equal attention. Some U.S. officials considered Soviet concentration on general legal principles a sign of the essentially propagandistic Soviet motives in CAT. Yet Soviet agreement to hold the two sets of discussions and active participation in both working groups was a clear indication of Soviet seriousness. In the end both sides proposed language and joined in detailed negotiations on common language for both types of guidelines.

Most important, however, the Soviets agreed to the U.S. proposal to discuss restraint in specific regions. The Soviets even accepted the possibility that interim regional restraint agreements could be concluded in advance of any final decisions on overall criteria. They indicated that these interim agreements could consist of lists of specific weapons that would be restrained, the position hoped for by the United States to insure rapid progress. Accordingly, a working group on regions began to meet and discuss Latin America and sub-Saharan Africa.

By the end of July both sides had agreed on a three-part arms transfer restraint framework. It included political-legal criteria to determine recipient eligibility, military-technical criteria to govern types and quantities of arms that could be transferred, and arrangements to implement these principles and guidelines in specific regional situations.

In preparing for the fourth round of the talks, scheduled for December 1978 in Mexico City, American officials again concentrated on regions. Preliminary diplomatic contacts indicated that the Soviets would want to discuss what they called East Asia—China—and West Asia—the Persian Gulf. Some American officials thought that discussing these regions with the Soviets would be a risky undertaking, particularly at the end of 1978. In East Asia, normalization of relations with China was in its delicate final stages. In West Asia, the stability of the government of Shah Mohammad Reza Pahlavi in Iran was deteriorating daily.

A number of senior American officials, particularly in the National Security Council (NSC) and the Department of Defense felt that to talk with the Soviets about these regions could lead to problems in U.S. relations with key nations and damage U.S. security interests. The NSC argued that the American delegation should break off the negotiations if the Soviets broached these regions in the talks and that Washington should inform Moscow of U.S. intentions before the talks began. Others felt that the United States was obliged at least to listen to Soviet proposals about these regions, even if rejection of the proposals were preordained. Never before, they noted, had one side refused to listen to the other's presentation at a U.S.-Soviet arms control negotiation. Moreover, in gaining Soviet agreement to discuss Latin America and sub-Saharan Africa, the U.S. side had explicitly pledged to discuss any legitimate geographic region suggested by the Soviet Union. In the end, Carter accepted the NSC arguments. The delegation was instructed to discuss only Latin America and sub-Saharan Africa and, if the Soviets brought up other regions, to walk out of the talks.

In Mexico City, Leslie Gelb, the chief U.S. delegate and director of the Bureau of Politico-Military Affairs in the State Department, presented the U.S. position to his astonished Soviet counterpart before the formal opening of the talks. After nearly one week of procedural meetings regarding an agenda for the negotiations, the two sides reached a compromise. The regional working group was not convened, and no regions were discussed at any of the sessions. Both sides subsequently proposed lists of political-legal and military-technical criteria, worked on common texts, and agreed on the need to establish a consultative mechanism to oversee the implementation of the guidelines. But the talks had foundered on the regional issue, and subsequent diplomatic exchanges did not resolve it. For all practical purposes, the CAT talks ended in Mexico City in December 1978.

Flying Pigs

CAT failed primarily because the talks were conducted against a backdrop of deteriorating U.S.-Soviet relations, a volatile Middle East, and an increasingly difficult political situation for the Carter administration at home. Bureaucratic confusion, personal rivalries, and tactical errors complicated these problems. Most important, in 1978 Carter made two contradictory decisions: first, that CAT should be a political rather than a technical negotiation; second, that the international political relations upon which it would impinge were too sensitive to discuss with the Soviet Union. This contradiction, above all, insured the failure of CAT.

A tolerable level of cooperation between the United States and the Soviet Union is a basic requirement for success in such an effort. But by 1977 the spirit of U.S.-Soviet détente, which had spawned the 1972 Basic Principles of Relations and other forms of superpower cooperation, had seriously waned.

The CAT experience also demonstrates that any U.S. administration that wishes to pursue such negotiations must be unambiguous about its purposes and must build domestic political support behind them. If the purpose is to limit actual arms transfers, then a relatively non-controversial, technical approach, such as that proposed by ACDA in spring 1978, seems most appropriate. Such an approach can accomplish the possible and delay or otherwise de-emphasize the tasks that would impinge on sensitive political relations.

If the purpose, however, is to begin to manage U.S.-Soviet competition in the Third World, thus reducing the risk of confrontation between the superpowers, then both sides must face the essentially political nature of the problem. The effort should not begin before the U.S. government has developed the necessary political constituencies at home and abroad. Both sides must make it clear that the talks involve the identification of respective interests in specific regions and the discussion of what each side perceives as acceptable and unacceptable behavior. Such a forthright declaration could not be made lightly. It would worry foreign leaders dependent on U.S. support. But only by facing these potentially adverse international consequences directly can bureaucratic and political opponents be pre-empted and domestic support sustained.

For the moment, in light of the current state of U.S.-Soviet relations and the continuing pressures to counter Soviet military initiatives, any proposal to negotiate restraints on arms transfers would have the credibility of flying pigs. Moreover, the failure of the CAT experiment has no doubt increased skepticism about the utility and feasibility of negotiated restraint in arms transfers.

Nevertheless, the continuing escalation of arms transfers to increasingly autonomous Third World countries threatens both global stability and U.S. national interests. Both the United States and the USSR have learned that the results of arms transfers are at best unpredictable.

Ironically, the arms suppliers themselves undermine their ability to dominate certain Third World conflicts partly by this very effort to secure political advantage by the transfer of increasingly sophisticated weapons. The diffusion of advanced military capabilities will increasingly circumscribe the influence and diplomatic flexibility of the superpowers.

Moreover, sound military reasons exist to limit the export of certain types of military equipment, in particular, those incorporating advanced technologies whose export could compromise existing American—or Soviet—military advantages. Important elements of the U.S. policy community, more often in the military than in the diplomatic corps, have recognized the potentially serious long-term threats to U.S. security from efforts to gain short-term political advantages by exporting advanced weapons. Without a coordinated multinational approach to arms transfers, however, this threat is frequently overshadowed by pressing political decisions, especially during times of political crisis.

In principle, US-USSR arms transfers consultations could have a stabilizing effect on U.S.-Soviet rivalry. Actual agreements to restrict some types of weapons transfers, at least to certain regions, could have even more dramatic effects. At the very least, any approach that began to establish norms for arms transfers would facilitate national decision making by providing more complete information on the recipients' security requirements since it would be known which kinds of weapons no recipient in the region could receive. Norms would lend some measure of predictability to what is at present an area of great uncertainty.

Possibilities for Restraint

For now, arms transfer limitations would best be pursued in a multilateral context in which the influence and problems of recipient states could mitigate the superpower rivalry. Negotiations of this type would focus first on technical issues of arms restraint—for example, the characteristics of weapons systems included in a restraint regime. This approach would allow the parties to put aside the more politically volatile issues until a durable infrastructure for negotiation were developed. The talks would initially seek to establish guidelines for global restraint without confronting the highly contentious issues involved in applying those rules to specific regions or countries.

An attempt to regulate superpower competition more explicitly could reinforce these efforts. At first it could take the form of concurrent bilateral discussions on weapons restraint guidelines, again largely technical in nature. Because generalized codes of conduct for arms restraint might be effective or in fact desirable for only the most technologically advanced or militarily insignificant types of weapons, more effective restraints would ultimately require more ambitious guidelines. Over time, specific measures could supplement initially broad global guidelines.

To this end, the two sides might initiate a bilateral dialogue that identified mutually acceptable patterns of behavior and types of restraint either during negotiation of or after initial agreement on broad guidelines. Such an approach could lead to diplomatic understandings tailored to specific areas. Although arms transfers would be only one element in these exchanges, they could reinforce and even facilitate multilateral comprehensive restraint agreements.

Another possibility for arms limits would be the sort of self-restraint the United States and the USSR have previously exhibited in other sensitive areas. Whether pursued as alternatives to or as supporting guidelines for explicit restraint measures, such tacit agreements could help mitigate superpower competition significantly, regardless of the success of future CAT efforts or even without resumption of formal arms transfer efforts.

None of these strategies is mutually exclusive, but multilateral efforts are presently more likely to succeed. The Committee on Disarmament in Geneva would provide a convenient forum to establish a working group for arms transfer negotiations. The talks would include not only all major suppliers but also major

Third World arms purchasers. If other nations chose not to address the problem directly, responsibility for a continuation of the current situation would not rest solely with the superpowers.

Although the discussion would grow more complex with the larger number of participating countries, the benefit of avoiding some of the political frictions that would emerge from a strictly supplier-oriented framework would far outweigh that disadvantage. Any discussion among only the United States and other suppliers on conventional arms transfers would invoke intense suspicions and fears of paternalism among recipients, especially because of the necessary secrecy and cartel-like structure of a suppliers' conference. Some recipients would fear a loss of flexibility in their relations with supplier countries if the talks seemed to be leading to a supplier condominium. Others would resent any suggestion of limitations on their ability to determine their own self-defense requirements. Recipients, of course, also realize that suppliers may become less sympathetic to demands for weapons based on exaggerated security perceptions that recipients frequently foster by manipulating one superpower against the other.

Another political problem concerns the role of West European arms suppliers. Without the support of Western Europe, no significant arms transfer limits negotiated by the superpowers could survive. A U.S.-Soviet agreement could be undermined quickly by continued opposition from other suppliers despite the superpowers' interest in monitoring each other's high technology exports and in developing guidelines for their competition. At the same time, the United States would have to decide whether the potential benefits of an arms restraint initiative were worth engendering frictions in the NATO alliance.

Conversely, some West European reasons for resisting multilateral arms restraint should be questioned. Motivated by a fear that such an agreement would penalize their export-dependent industries, Great Britain and France have tended to dramatize the negative impact that such agreements could have. But restraints that aimed most directly at selective types of weapons would not cause major economic dislocation in Western Europe.

In addition, multinational efforts to share advanced technology among NATO countries may provide an avenue for greater coordination of arms export guidelines in the Western alliance. Regardless of the political climate, the United States will continue to place restrictions on West European exports of advanced, coproduced equipment. In essence, this arrangement is a diplomatic tradeoff involving West European compliance to U.S. export restrictions in return for access to advanced U.S. technologies, a high priority for most NATO countries. West European sharing in state-of-the-art technology will always be contingent on such an arrangement. Although this issue has already led to considerable political friction in the alliance, it has not been unmanageable. Mutual interests among NATO countries in this area could lead to more explicit cooperative measures for arms export restraint.

A multilateral discussion would focus on selecting candidate weapons for global restraint and developing guidelines to govern their transfer. Although these talks might be linked eventually to the effort to develop consultative channels between the superpowers for crisis prevention, the multilateral arms transfer negotiations must not be expected from the outset to moderate U.S.-Soviet rivalry in the Third World. In keeping with the traditional logic of arms control, these initial efforts should be assigned only modest objectives.

Specifically, the strategy most likely to develop momentum in these negotiations would probably focus on weapons systems whose transfer was not central to either side's foreign policy and that both sides considered particularly dangerous—for example, long-range surface-to-surface missiles or weapons that could be diverted by terrorists. Weapons that have been the subject of international attention for their indiscriminate effects and that have marginal military utility, such as incendiary or fragmentation weapons, could also be discussed. These weapons could begin a list of arms whose transfer would be banned globally or that would require consultation among the suppliers before transfer took place.

Serious definition and verification problems would plague global arms transfer restrictions. Even if these problems were successfully resolved, such multilateral efforts would have modest results. Even if an agreement prohibited the transfer of all weapons that could conceivably be regulated on a global basis, weapons flow to the Third World would not be significantly slowed. Still, regulation could ease some specific problems, such as terrorists' access to advanced military technologies, and prevent the introduction of destabilizing new technologies into Third World arsenals. Moreover, it would demonstrate the practicality of negotiated restraint and create the procedures and institutions necessary to implement it. From such a base, more ambitious efforts could be contemplated, such as regional conferences to limit the more-common currency of the Third World arms trade—aircraft and ground-combat vehicles—and broader initiatives between the superpowers to discuss regional issues.

For such negotiations to have a chance for success, the domestic and international constituencies necessary to sustain them must be developed. This task will not be possible unless the participating governments explain carefully the importance of the subject and the potential national security benefits of both bilateral and multilateral negotiations. Otherwise, the risks might seem much greater than the benefits, and the potential short-term damage to U.S. relations with traditional clients in the Third World would obscure whatever long-term political and security benefits might be derived from the discussions.

Building a constituency for arms restraint and for crisis prevention generally is not a precondition for undertaking initiatives. Rather, such a constituency will result from a coherently conceived and carefully articulated foreign policy. The sensitive and controversial nature of arms transfer limitations invites opposition and sometimes sabotage. Without consistent and firm leadership from the highest levels of the U.S. foreign policy apparatus, CAT and all related efforts to mediate the U.S.-Soviet rivalry risk becoming the domain of arms-control advocates—correct in vision but flawed in any operational sense.

Conventional Arms Transfers in the Third World, 1972–81

FIGURE 1

Dollar Value of Arms Agreements

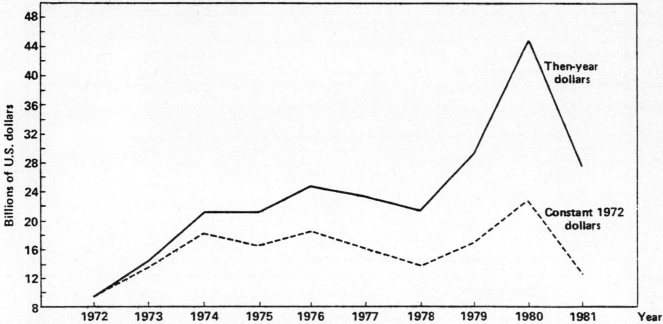

FIGURE 2
Total Arms Deliveries

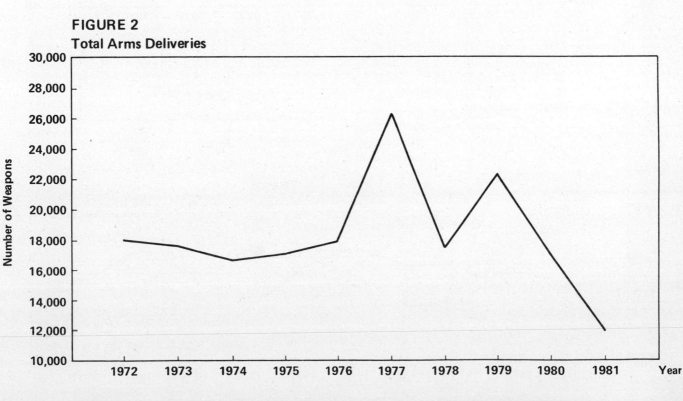

"Conventional Arms Transfers in the Third World, 1972-1981," Special Report No. 102, *U.S. Department of State,* August 1982.

211

7. THE ARMS RACE

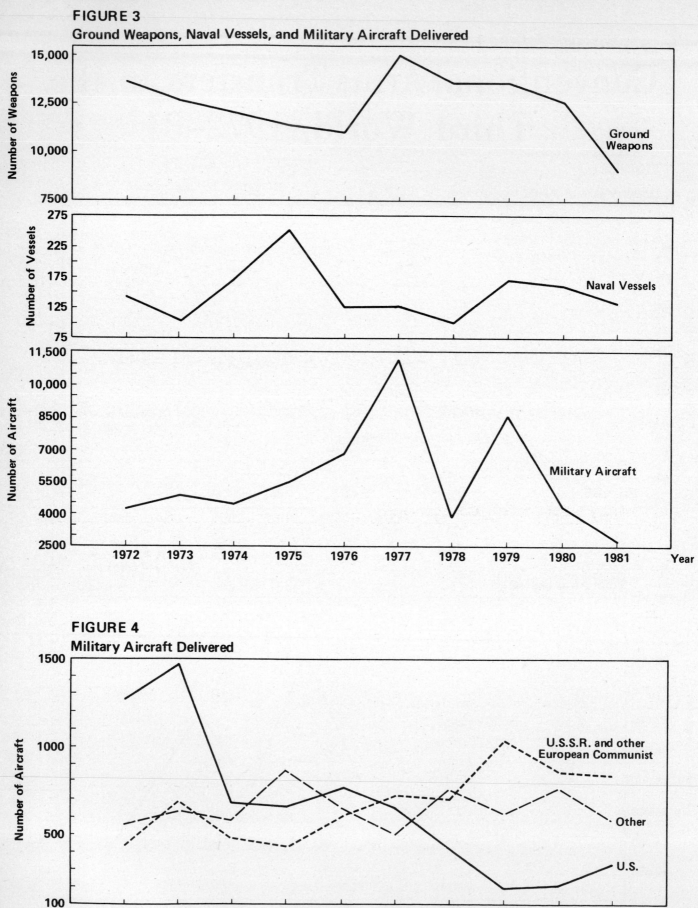

FIGURE 3
Ground Weapons, Naval Vessels, and Military Aircraft Delivered

FIGURE 4
Military Aircraft Delivered

FIGURE 5
Major Ground Weapons Delivered[1]

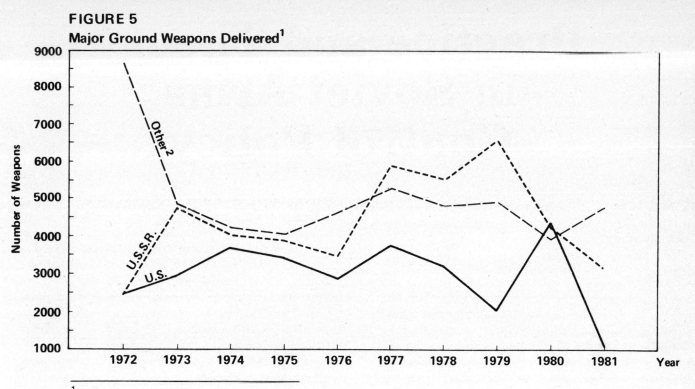

[1]Tanks, self-propelled guns, light armor, and artillery.
[2]Includes European Communist countries excluding U.S.S.R.

FIGURE 6
Tanks and Self-Propelled Guns Delivered

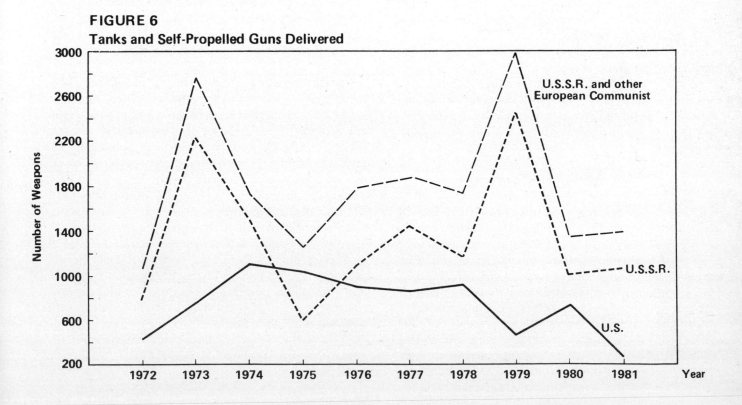

Practice and Theory in Soviet Arms Control Policy

Otto Pick

The author is Professor of International Relations at the University of Surrey.

The present Soviet Constitution, dating from 1977, defines the purpose of Soviet foreign policy in clear and unambiguous terms: 'The foreign policy of the USSR is aimed at assuring international conditions favourable for building Communism in the USSR, safeguarding the state interests of the Soviet Union, consolidating the position of world socialism, supporting the struggle of people for national liberation and social progress, preventing wars of aggression, achieving complete and universal disarmament, and consistently implementing the principle of peaceful co-existence of states with different social systems.' (Article 28). The mention of disarmament in this catalogue of virtues could be dismissed as empty rhetoric, but its inclusion at the time was projected as a response to 'popular' demand and it certainly mirrors one of the major preoccupations of Soviet foreign and defence policy. The Soviet leaders must know that 'complete and universal disarmament' lies outside the realm of practical politics today, but they are naturally keen to control the weapons at the disposal of potential enemies, even if that means that they might have to negotiate about the levels of their own arsenal.

The Correlation of Forces

Although Soviet foreign policy may claim to derive its aspirational targets from the allegedly scientific generalizations of Marxism-Leninism, its operational guidelines are theoretically rooted in the much more realistic concept of the 'correlation of forces'. This is little more than an elaboration of the traditional balance of power, with one very fundamental difference. While the theorists of the balance of power at least pretend that the aim is to create an equal distribution of power in the international system in order to maintain an equilibrium, the practitioners of the correlation of forces act in the expectation that the base of the global order is inexorably tilting in favour of the 'socialist' world because of the predetermined self-destructive features of capitalism. Soviet statesmen therefore merely have to pursue policies designed both to benefit from and to serve the inevitable historical process predicted by Marxist analysis. To achieve this end, the correlation of forces must be maintained at a reasonable level from the Soviet point of view and all available opportunities for manipulating and adjusting it must be seized. Soviet policy planners are therefore very aware of the need to reconcile essentially long-range goals with short-term interests, and their task is made much more difficult by immediate problems such as their country's economic deficiencies and, in the military sphere, by the Nato decision to modernize the alliance's long-range theatre nuclear forces in Europe.

It is conceptually pointless to discuss Soviet foreign policy in terms of either offensive or defensive characteristics, but it is much more useful, particularly when examining Soviet arms control proposals, to draw distinctions between short-term and long-term goals. The control of nuclear armaments represents an area where talks are both necessary and possible, and where the present correlation provides the Soviet Union with an advantageous baseline for negotiations.

Negotiating About the Strategic Nuclear Balance

As long ago as 1961 it was argued in Washington that all aspects of co-operation and agreement with the USSR should depend on Soviet good behaviour. The delusion of linkage was immediately rejected by the Soviet Union and it could never be applied in a consistent manner by the United States. President Carter's decision to withdraw the SALT II Treaty after the Soviet invasion of Afghanistan prevented its rejection by the Senate, but the move was also seen as an exercise in linkage. However, President Reagan, despite the emphasis on linkage during his election campaign, has had to concede that the question of nuclear arms control is so important that it must be dealt with regardless of other issues.

It took the Reagan Administration ten months to make up its mind to negotiate about nuclear weapons in Europe, and even longer to go into the Strategic Arms Reduction Talks (START). Nevertheless, the tacit abandonment of linkage, underlined by the lifting of the US grain embargo and directly expressed by the decision to start talking about nuclear weapons in Europe despite the deteriorating situation in Poland, has given

This article originally appeared in the July/August 1982 issue of *The World Today,* monthly journal of the Royal Institute of International Affairs, London.

the Soviet Union a considerable psychological advantage. More significantly, the USSR is negotiating at a time when the correlation of forces in nuclear terms appears to have moved in its favour. It is therefore in a better position to court public opinion on both sides of the Atlantic with apparently constructive and sensible proposals.

Since 1964, the nuclear balance has been moving in favour of the Eastern bloc and the West's technological lead has been reduced. In 1972, the USSR disposed of 2,500 warheads against America's 5,700. Ten years later the gap has been narrowed to 8,040 Soviet warheads as against 9,480 on the other side. More significantly, the USSR has made considerable technological progress in deploying multiple and independently targeted re-entry vehicles. In terms of overall nuclear destructive force, Soviet capability is now, more than double that of the United States—almost 8,000 megatons as against 3,500 megatons. Both super-powers have the means to destroy each other and most of the world many times over and yet it has been the Soviet Union which has been much more skilful in exploiting the position of nuclear absurdity in which they find themselves.

Soviet policy and propaganda, operating from a possibly illusory base of perceived advantage, has benefited from the remarkable growth of an essentially populist movement in the West stimulated by widespread horror at the prospect of nuclear conflict and nourished by loose talk in the United States of being able to fight, win and survive a limited nuclear war. The leaking of a recent Pentagon strategy paper in June, which stated that 'US nuclear capabilities must prevail even under the condition of a prolonged nuclear war' has not helped to reassure public opinion in Europe and has provided the American advocates of a nuclear freeze with fresh ammunition.

On the other hand, little has been said about Soviet war-fighting doctrine. Following Khrushchev's fall from power in 1964, the Soviet military press carried a spate of articles which emphasized the capacity of the Soviet armed forces to fight and survive a nuclear war. For a time, some Western commentators were able to frighten themselves with accounts of Soviet war-survival doctrine, based on absurd Soviet claims about the efficiency of their civil defence programmes and their ability to evacuate some of their major cities in face of threatened nuclear strikes. After 1973, Soviet declaratory policy underwent a complete change, and in public statements for consumption abroad the stress was again placed on the defensive nature of Soviet foreign policy and military doctrine.[1] But the military handbooks continue to press the old line. Thus, the Soviet Military Encyclopaedia, published between 1976 and 1980 well after the start of détente, called for 'military technological superiority over the enemy[2] and again argued that the Soviet Union could win and survive a nuclear war.[3] Indeed, in July 1981 Marshal Ogarkov, the Chief of Staff, even

repeated this claim in *Kommunist*. This contradiction has been largely ignored by the more vocal critics of the American positions, but it is not illogical when viewed in the context of the opportunistic doctrine of correlation of forces. The manipulation of public opinion is used to maintain short-term advantages, but this does not imply any abandonment of fundamental policy goals such as the pursuit of technological superiority. Of course, Soviet statements that the USSR could survive a nuclear war are as preposterous as similar views expressed elsewhere, but if these ill-founded beliefs were to dominate the thinking of the decision-makers in the Kremlin, the risk of nuclear war would be greatly increased.

European movements opposing the proposed deployment of Pershing II and cruise missiles have had a profound effect on the attitudes of the Belgian and Netherlands governments[4] and have helped to create a serious crisis within the Social Democratic party (SPD) in the Federal Republic of Germany. In the United States, these fears, combined with alarm at the mounting cost of the Reagan Administration's rearmament programme, have given rise to a co-ordinated groundswell of opinion favouring a nuclear freeze, which has begun to affect the grass roots of American politics.

On 9 May, President Reagan finally announced that the United States was prepared to negotiate about phased reductions of strategic nuclear weapons. This proposal envisaged that, at the end of the first phase, warheads would be reduced to equal levels at least one-third below their current total and that no more than half these warheads would be deployed on land-based missiles. In the second phase, equal limits on missile throw-weight would be sought. A final agreement would have to contain proper verification measures.

This American initiative may have come rather late in the day after many months of delay, during which the Soviet Union was allowed to encourage the build-up of a vociferous and politically significant 'anti-nuclear' movement in Western Europe and North America. The tardiness of the American response was symptomatic of the false sense of priorities which characterized the early months of the Reagan Administration and is seen by many as an attempt to catch up with public opinion instead of leading it. The Soviet Union was, in fact, allowed to seize the initiative and even Brezhnev's rejection of the American plan was regarded as reasonable by many critics of US policy. Addressing the Congress of the Communist youth organization, the Komsomol, on 18 May, the Soviet leader described Reagan's proposals as 'absolutely one-sided' because they excluded the missiles which are of most urgent concern to the Soviet Union—the long-range theatre weapons which Nato hopes to deploy in Europe to balance the potential of the Soviet SS-20. Nevertheless, President Brezhnev welcomed the American offer to start negotiations on strategic arms control as 'a step in the right direction'.

7. THE ARMS RACE

The long awaited START talks which began in Geneva at the end of June, have produced another paroxysm of propaganda in Moscow. 'Peace' rallies, organized by the official 'peace' campaign, which certainly does not represent a true counterpart to Western movements calling for nuclear disarmament and merely exists to support official policies, have multiplied. In late May, Soviet officials received a CND delegation from Britain, and at the beginning of June, a ship carrying members of the Greenpeace environmentalist group was welcomed in Leningrad. Finally, on 15 June, the Soviet Union made its bid to outdo President Reagan on his home-ground. Speaking in New York, at the special United Nations session on disarmament, the Soviet Foreign Minister, Andrei Gromyko, pledged unconditionally that his country would never be the first to use nuclear weapons. The United States has consistently refused to join in similar declarations on the ground that such a promise would deprive Nato of its main deterrent against a conventional attack, and the Americans continue to adhere to this logical, though emotionally unappealing, position. It would appear, however, that in psychological terms the Soviet Union enters the START talks with a definite advantage.

The SS-20

President Brezhnev's announcement at the 17th Congress of Soviet Trade Unions in March that the Soviet Union was immediately suspending its deployment of SS-20 missiles west of the Urals, and that this freeze would last until an arms agreement was concluded with the United States or until the start of the positioning of Pershing II and cruise missiles in Western Europe, had been precisely calculated to reinforce the anti-nuclear movements in the West and to maintain the superiority in nuclear weapons which the USSR has achieved in the European theatre. The Soviet Union now has 300 SS-20s targeted against Western Europe; in 1979, there were 100. The SS-20 is a solid-fuel missile system, equipped with three multiple independently targeted warheads; it is very accurate and, because it is mobile, it is less vulnerable and more versatile than the weapons it has replaced. In short, it represents a significant qualitative advance in medium-range nuclear weaponry, and in conjunction with the Soviet Union's conventional superiority, it has profoundly affected the European balance. Nato, on the other hand, has no land-based missiles in Europe capable of hitting Soviet territory. The Soviet leaders' apparent dedication to the status quo is not unreasonable from their point of view, as it would simply freeze the momentary advantage they hold at present in the correlation of forces. Their nuclear superiority in Europe seems even to have encouraged them to offer concessions in conventional terms. The draft proposal, tabled last February by the Warsaw Pact at the balanced arms reduction talks (MBFR) in Vienna, calling for initial cuts of 20,000 Soviet and 13,000 US troops in Europe with the aim of ultimately bringing down manpower levels to 900,000 on both sides in Nato and the Warsaw Pact, is again designed to present the Soviet Union in the best possible light—although it ignores its much greater reinforcement capability.

It can, of course, be held that there is a sufficiency of nuclear weaponry located outside Europe capable of decimating the USSR and that this should be enough to deter any Soviet military moves against Western Europe. Yet, this view overlooks the argument that local Soviet superiority in Europe, in addition to providing immediate political advantages by creating an environment conducive to the pursuit of aggressive diplomacy, also places additional strains on the American nuclear guarantee. If the only possible response to the SS-20 were to be an American strategic bombardment of the USSR, it is more than probable that any US President would be deterred from exercising this option by the increased vulnerability of his own country in face of the remarkable technological progress the Soviet Union has been able to achieve since the mid-1970s. Europe would thus become an expendable hostage in the nuclear game and America's freedom of action would be severely curtailed. The long-term Soviet aim of de-coupling Western Europe from the United States would be greatly advanced.

The well-rehearsed arguments about the credibility of the American nuclear guarantee are academic in the worst sense of the word. At present, the Soviet Union has the psychological advantage of being able to make superficially attractive proposals, while being free from the strains imposed on the Western Alliance by the proposals to modernize theatre nuclear forces in Europe. President Reagan's 'zero-option' has done little to reduce this position, for it does not come to grips with European doubts about the credibility of the American guarantee, although more could have been done to develop its potential to influence public opinion.

The Leninist Analysis of Capitalism

The Marxist concept of revolutionary development is firmly based on the dialectic analysis of the internal contradictions of capitalism which, according to Lenin, is predetermined to begin to disintegrate at the imperialist stage. Despite the spate of revisions to which Marxist and Leninist dogma has been subjected since 1917, Lenin's successors have never abandoned this particularly Utopian belief. The arms race may not be irrelevant in this context—as long ago as May 1953, President Eisenhower warned that the Soviet Union would try to 'force upon America an unbearable security burden leading to economic disaster'. It is at least arguable whether the sudden increase in defence spending, leading to vast deficits, high interest rates, social insecurity and economic tension within the Atlantic Alliance, really serves the best interests of Western

Correlat
of forces

43. Practice and Theory

societies. In particular, US demands for a rise in European defence contributions to Nato are bound to cause new difficulties.

The Pentagon's financial requests for 1981 and 1982 represent an increase of 56 per cent after inflation over 1980. The five-year forecast of US defence expenditure amounts to 1.5 trillion dollars.[5] Furthermore, the West suffers from structural disadvantages in comparison with Soviet practice. A disproportionate share of defence expenditure is eaten up by the cost of salaries and retirement payments. Western procurement procedures, involving constant changes during the development stage of new-weapon systems, are markedly less efficient. The Soviet Defence Ministry appears to exercise much tighter control over design changes. Command economies have certain advantages in this respect and the cut-throat competition which distorts Western defence procurement would seem to confirm the Leninist analysis of the self-destructive tendencies affecting capitalist societies.

Although Western estimates of Soviet defence spending based on sometimes doubtful criteria, such as estimating Soviet manpower costs on the basis of US pay rates, it is clear that the Soviet economy is not really able to cope with the demands of the Soviet military. An arms race can be a double-edged sword. Moscow's frantic efforts to maintain the status quo may stem partly from an awareness of the Soviet Union's economic weakness. The USSR's military effort has also to take account of the long-standing dispute with China and Brezhnev's recent overtures to Peking must owe something to this consideration. The per capita GNP of the Soviet Union is still only half of the US level, and the prodigious rise in military expenditure during the Brezhnev years must be seen against the background of declining economic growth rates and an increased emphasis on secondary industries intended to satisfy some of the rising expectations of Soviet consumers.

Brezhnev's Peace Offensive

The ideological justification of Soviet foreign policy has remained unchanged since the Revolution. The Soviet Union is always for peace, but peace on its own terms—a state which can only be achieved by the universal victory of the proletariat, for the 'imperialist' powers are allegedly always impelled towards war by the internal contradictions of the social system they profess. In the meantime, the national interest of the USSR, as well as the Utopian blueprint outlined by Marx and Lenin, demand that the correlation of forces should be continually adjusted. This conception of international relations allows for considerable flexibility, for in the final analysis almost all short-term policies can be rationalized by reference to an unchanging ideological premise: the Soviet Union, while it has to act like any other state in the international system, remains fundamentally different because of its long-term mission and

purpose. It may, of course, be true that the confusion between ideology and pure national interest in the making of Soviet foreign policy has become more pronounced as the memory of the Revolution has receded, but the present generation in the Kremlin still has to think within the constraints imposed by doctrine and dogma, because it has no other conceptual framework to which it can refer.

In waging his current peace offensive, Brezhnev is manipulating the correlation of forces with skill and finesse. His primary aim is to head off the modernization of Nato's nuclear arsenal in Europe and to delay and possibly reduce President Reagan's rearmament programme. Brezhnev's modus operandi furthermore serves to tighten the psychological tensions which have so often disturbed the transatlantic relationship at a time when the United States finds it increasingly difficult to cope with this challenge. There might even be other beneficial spin-offs in reducing the military burden the Soviet economy has to bear and in reshaping relations with China.

In the short term, the doctrine of the correlation of forces places a premium on the exploitation of opportunities and here, at least, Brezhnev would appear to be a worthy successor to Lenin, perhaps the most polished opportunist of them all. The present policy acknowledges the changes in the international environment which have occurred in recent years. The economic expectations nurtured by the early years of détente have been disappointed and the Polish experience has certainly given rise to doubts about foreign economic ties. An arms freeze would therefore help to underpin the precarious foundations of the Soviet economy, while preserving the USSR's relative military strength. This last factor is all the more important because of the Soviet Union's use of military power as an instrument of foreign policy, exemplified by the invasion of Afghanistan and by Soviet actions in the Horn of Africa in 1978. Despite the cautious attitude Moscow has so far displayed towards the Polish crisis, military power obviously also plays an important role in maintaining a reasonable degree of Soviet control over Eastern Europe. Brezhnev naturally wants to have his cake and eat it, and for the time being he appears to be succeeding, at least as far as his dealings with the Reagan Administration in the field of arms control are concerned.

NOTES

1. E.g. General M. A. Milstein in an interview with the *New York Times,* 25 August 1980.
2. *Sovetskaya Voyennaya Entsiklopedia* (Moscow: Voyenizdat), Vol. 6, p. 500.
3. *ibid.,* Vol. 2, pp. 308-9.
4. See J. A. Emerson Vermaat, 'Neutralist tendencies in the Netherlands', *The World Today,* December 1981.
5. *Strategic Survey, 1981-2* (London: International Institute for Strategic Studies, 1982), p. 39. See also Press Release by Department of Defense, Washington, D.C., 8 February 1982.

Limits and Cuts:
SALT and START

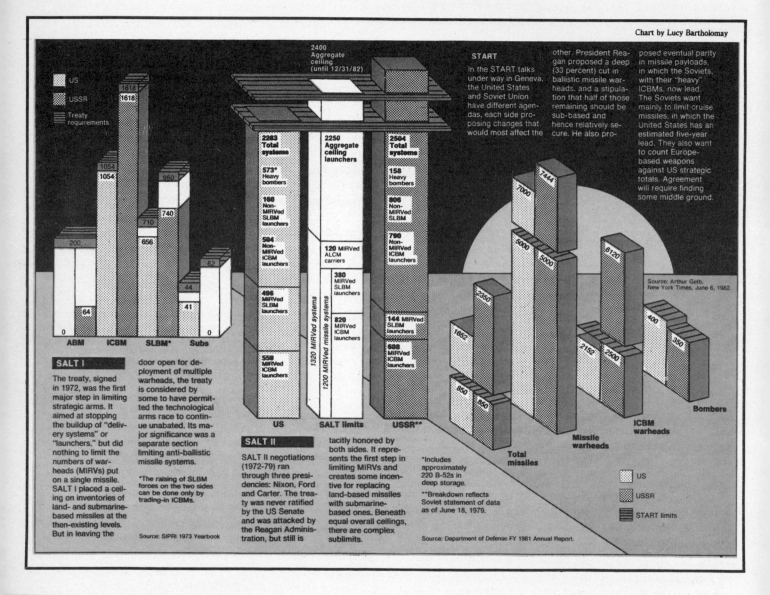

Chart by Lucy Bartholomay

US
USSR
Treaty requirements

2400 Aggregate ceiling (until 12/31/82)

1618
1618
1054
1054
950
740
710
656
200
64
62
44
41
0
0

ABM   **ICBM**   **SLBM***   **Subs**

2283 Total systems
573* Heavy bombers
160 Non-MIRVed SLBM launchers
584 Non-MIRVed ICBM launchers
496 MIRVed SLBM launchers
550 MIRVed ICBM launchers

1320 MIRVed systems

2250 Aggregate ceiling launchers
120 MIRVed ALCM carriers
380 MIRVed SLBM launchers
820 MIRVed ICBM launchers

1200 MIRVed missile systems

2504 Total systems
158 Heavy bombers
806 Non-MIRVed SLBM
790 Non-MIRVed ICBM launchers
144 MIRVed SLBM launchers
608 MIRVed ICBM launchers

US   **SALT limits**   **USSR****

START
In the START talks under way in Geneva, the United States and Soviet Union have different agendas, each side proposing changes that would most affect the other. President Reagan proposed a deep (33 percent) cut in ballistic missile warheads, and a stipulation that half of those remaining should be sub-based and hence relatively secure. He also proposed eventual parity in missile payloads, in which the Soviets, with their "heavy" ICBMs, now lead. The Soviets want mainly to limit cruise missiles, in which the United States has an estimated five-year lead. They also want to count Europe-based weapons against US strategic totals. Agreement will require finding some middle ground.

7444
7000
5000
5000
2350
6120
1652
2152
2500
400
350
850
850

Source: Arthur Gelb, New York Times, June 6, 1982.

Total missiles
Missile warheads
ICBM warheads
Bombers

US
USSR
START limits

SALT I

The treaty, signed in 1972, was the first major step in limiting strategic arms. It aimed at stopping the buildup of "delivery systems" or "launchers," but did nothing to limit the numbers of warheads (MIRVs) put on a single missile. SALT I placed a ceiling on inventories of land- and submarine-based missiles at the then-existing levels. But in leaving the door open for deployment of multiple warheads, the treaty is considered by some to have permitted the technological arms race to continue unabated. Its major significance was a separate section limiting anti-ballistic missile systems.

*The raising of SLBM forces on the two sides can be done only by trading-in ICBMs.

Source: SIPRI 1973 Yearbook

SALT II

SALT II negotiations (1972-79) ran through three presidencies: Nixon, Ford and Carter. The treaty was never ratified by the US Senate and was attacked by the Reagan Administration, but still is tacitly honored by both sides. It represents the first step in limiting MIRVs and creates some incentive for replacing land-based missiles with submarine-based ones. Beneath equal overall ceilings, there are complex sublimits.

*Includes approximately 220 B-52s in deep storage.

**Breakdown reflects Soviet statement of data as of June 18, 1979.

Source: Department of Defense FY 1981 Annual Report.

The Falklands
and the Law

J.E.S. Fawcett

Until recently President of the European Commission of Human Rights and Professor of International Law, King's College, University of London, 1976-80.

I

Answers to questions about the status and future of the Falkland Islands and Dependencies will vary with who is asked—lawyers, ministers, parliamentarians, or the public—though answers may sometimes coincide. To confine the discussion to the response of lawyers and ministers, we shall find, on the one hand, that the law governing the status, disposal and defence of the Islands has changed over time, that there is some new law, and that law, whether international or national, is often uncertain—the House of Lords and US Supreme Court are each often divided; and, on the other hand, it is plain that ministers concerned with the future of the Islands, while sometimes making a tactical use of law, consider primarily what courses of action will both serve national interests, as they are seen, and satisfy their public.

The Islands consist of the Falklands and four other groups of islands: South Georgia and Shag Rocks; South Sandwich; South Orkneys; and South Shetlands. By Letters Patent (1908) these groups of islands and Graham Land, a coastal stretch of the Antarctic peninsula, were made Dependencies of the Falkland Islands, subject to the Governor-General and Executive Council. By Letters Patent (1917) 'all islands and territories between 20° West and 50° West and south of 50° South, and between 50° West and 80° West and south of 58° South' were declared to be British territories. This area then included not only the Falkland Islands and Dependencies, but also a sector of the Antarctic continent pointed from the South Pole. The sector as defined overlaps similar sectors claimed respectively by Chile and Argentina. In 1962, British Antarctic Territory was established as a 'separate colony' by Statutory Instrument 1962/401, which defined this territory as 'all lands and territories between 20° West and 80° West and south of 60° South'. The southern latitude limit was taken from the Antarctic Treaty (in force from June 1961), to which Argentina, China and the UK are among

the parties, and which brings the whole area south of 60° South under an international regime: this then embraces the South Orkneys, South Shetlands and Graham Land. But Article IV of the Treaty provides that nothing in the Treaty shall be interpreted as:

> a renunciation by any Contracting Party of previously asserted rights of, or claims to, territorial sovereignty in Antarctica,

or

> prejudicing the position of any Contracting Party as regards its recognition or non-recognition of any other State's right of, or claim or basis of claim to, territorial sovereignty in Antarctica.

The Treaty in effect then places in suspense territorial claims to the South Shetlands and Graham Land, claimed by Argentina, Chile and the United Kingdom, and to the South Orkneys, claimed by Argentina and the United Kingdom. They have therefore not been brought into the present dispute, which is limited to the Falkland Islands, South Georgia, and South Sandwich Islands, though the last do not appear to have been given much attention.

II

The history of the Falkland Islands and Dependencies is fragmentary, not surprisingly perhaps given their remoteness. Principal events leading to the occupation of the Falkland Islands by Britain were the revolt of Argentina, a vice-royalty, against Spanish rule, beginning in 1810 and bringing the province to virtual independence over the next decade; the establishment of an Argentine administration in 1829, under a Hamburg merchant as Governor, of the Falkland Islands; the seizure of three American fishing vessels for breach of fishing regulations in the area, which led to protests by both the United States and Britain. There being no response, Britain moved in in force in January 1833, expelling the Argentine soldiers and settlers. British occupation and administration, extended to the Dependencies, endured without any interference until 2 April 1982.

Argentina has asserted title to the Falkland Islands and Dependencies on various grounds from the end of the Second World War. In the prevailing mood of anti-

This article originally appeared in the June 1982 issue of *The World Today*, monthly journal of the Royal Institute of International Affairs, London.

219

colonialism, the British seizure of the Falkland Islands by force in 1833 is seen by Argentina as no different in form, and worse in character, than the Argentine intervention in 1982. In 1947, the United Kingdom proposed that the status of the Dependencies be referred to the International Court of Justice, which would have necessarily entailed some determination of the status of the Falkland Islands themselves. Argentina refused to take part in such a reference. It is reasonable to suppose that the Court would have found that the taking of the Islands in 1833 was not contrary to the law applicable at that time; but that, in any case, their continuing and undisturbed occupation and administration by Britain for a century and a half established a valid title.

The law has, in fact, changed. The taking of the Falkland Islands by force in 1833 was not contrary to such law as was applicable at the time. Comparable were the British occupation of Ascension Island in 1815, and the capture of Aden by a naval force of the British Government of Bombay in 1839. But the intervention by Argentina by force in the Falkland Islands is plainly an armed attack contrary to its obligations under the UN Charter, Article 2(4), which provides that:

> All Members shall refrain in their international relations from the threat or use of force against the territorial integrity or political independence of any State, or in any other manner inconsistent with the Purposes of the United Nations.

British territorial integrity has been broken, and the UN Purpose, stated in the Charter, of 'suppression of acts of aggression and other breaches of the peace' has been impaired. Security Resolution 502 confirms this conclusion.

III

What then of the United Kingdom reaction in force? What has just been said is qualified by Article 51 of the UN Charter, which provides that:

> Nothing in the present Charter shall impair the inherent right of individual or collective self-defence if an armed attack occurs against a Member of the United Nations, until the Security Council has taken the measures necessary to maintain international peace and security...

The right of individual self-defence can certainly be invoked by the United Kingdom against the armed attack by Argentina. But, as for all broad concepts, limits have to be found and set to self-defence, if it is not to become an open door to any action. Measures and action taken in self-defence must be then confined to the reversal of the armed attack and its effects, and must in the scale of, for example, weapons used, targets attacked, and effect on civilians, be proportionate to the achievement of that aim. How far does the declaration of a maritime exclusion zone around the Falkland Islands come within the right of self-defence? Extended up to 200 miles from these Islands, it is in great part an

area of the high seas, and also overlaps an area of the 200-mile territorial sea claimed by Argentina. Is the declaration contrary to international law, as the USSR suggests?

The high seas are free and open to all vessels, surface or submerged, as is the airspace to all aircraft. The High Seas Convention, in force since 1962, is carefully silent about the exercise of the right of self-defence on the high seas, while Article 8(1) states that:

> Warships on the high seas have complete immunity from the jurisdiction of any State other than the flag state.

But Article 2(1) also states that

> Freedom of the high seas is exercised under the condition laid down by these articles and other rules of international law.

It can then be said that the inherent right of self-defence, recognized in the rule set out in Article 51 of the UN Charter, will, if properly exercised, prevail over the freedom of the high seas: that is to say, its exercise would be strictly limited to the policing of, and when clearly necessary, the use of arms against, vessels or aircraft supporting the original armed attack.

Where the maritime exclusion zone overlaps part of the territorial sea claimed by Argentina, it could be said that international law does not recognize a territorial sea extended to 200 miles from coastal baselines. While it is true that all the South American countries, except Colombia and Venezuela, claim territorial seas up to 200 miles, and the Territorial Sea Convention, in force since 1964, does not prescribe a particular limit, state practice in recent years has taken 12 miles as the acceptable limit, and this has been specified in the negotiating text of UNCLOS. It can then be concluded that states can refuse recognition of a 200-mile territorial sea, as being an impermissible intrusion into the high seas. The maritime exclusion zone, itself not a claim of territorial sea, would not then be an infringement of the territorial sea of Argentina; and it appears that a subsequent order has extended the zone up to 12 miles from the coast of Argentina.

IV

Another rationale advanced by United Kingdom Ministers to justify the use of force around the Falkland Islands is that it is designed to make aggression ineffectual and unprofitable, so warning and discouraging other potential aggressors. This is plainly not an exercise of the right of self-defence; further, Article 51 of the UN Charter makes it clear that the suppression of aggression, as a UN purpose, is the exclusive responsibility of the Security Council. But where the Security Council does not take the necessary measures, prescribed in Chapter VII of the UN Charter, against an unlawful armed attack against a UN member—it has so far only called for the withdrawal of Argentine forces from the Falkland Islands—the question arises whether exclusive responsibility passes to the UN General Assembly, or whether countries may, individually or collectively, take economic measures or use force to restrict or punish the aggression. Such a question can be answered only within the UN itself, to which Argentina must refer it, if it seeks an answer.

V

A new development in the law of the sea has been the recognition of the right of coastal states to explore and exploit the natural resources of their adjacent seabed on the continental shelf up to a depth of 200 meters or beyond that to the limits of exploitability: Continental Shelf Convention, in force since 1964, Articles 1 and 2. Where such areas of continental shelf of two or more countries overlap, boundaries must be determined by agreement between them. Article 6(1). Such agreements have been reached over the North Sea. The Falkland Islands stand on the continental shelf of South America; it would therefore be necessary, if they are to remain British, for an agreed boundary to be drawn between the continental shelves assigned to Argentina and to the Falkland Islands. This could be, perhaps, a positive element of common interest that might help to resolve the dispute, or take the place of arid claims to sovereignty.

International Organization and International Law

The United Nations is ineffective, impotent, and increasingly irrelevant to the problems confronting the international system—or so say its critics. It is true that the UN is suffering from serious problems created by the new power structure that has emerged since its formation in 1945. At that time, it was structured to reflect the current balance of power. There was no Third World group of nations, a group which now constitutes more than two-thirds of the entire UN membership. But the UN has had to face the problems created by changes from the old power configuration to an entirely new one. Among its failures have been its inability to do anything about the spiraling arms race; the refusal of UN members involved in a conflict to respond positively to UN resolutions; the use of the veto by one of the five permanent members of the Security Council to obstruct an action by the United Nations that might jeopardize its interests somewhere in the world; and the Third World use of the General Assembly and many of the UN Standing Committees as rhetorical platforms and for carrying out vendettas against such unpopular countries as South Africa and Israel.

To focus on its failures, however, denigrates the value of the United Nations, as well as of regional organizations (although the past year has been an unhappy one for both the OAS and the OAU). These have become increasingly important fora for airing publicly the viewpoints of the various member states, and for offering an organization through which they can cooperate to resolve regional problems. Moreover, numerous international agencies and organizations, many of which are products of the United Nations itself, have been remarkably successful in dealing with specific issues in environments less susceptible to national political pressures. One of the presumptions of the "functionalist" theory of international relations is that, by breaking down the world's problems into separate "functions," solutions can be found. In addition, states will discover that they have more to gain through cooperation than through conflict and war. It is only through such cooperative efforts in the framework of international organizations that, for example, international disease control and health services have been established (WHO); world-wide meteorological information is collected that is relevant to discovering more about such issues as world food production, pollution, climate, and weather modification (WMO); children in desperate situations can be cared for (UNICEF); international postal rates have been set (UPU); and information about the best types of crops, seed development, and plant and disease control

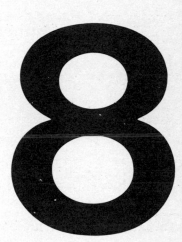

(FAO) are dealt with on an international basis. These efforts have been successsful at solving fairly non-political functional problems because states have been willing to relinquish enough of their national sovereignty, and perhaps agree to compromises, so that all participating states may benefit.

The short-sightedness of abjuring participation in such functional international structures in order to be able to pursue national interests, unfettered by agreement to a set of related international law, may soon become apparent for the US (as it did with its non-participation in the League of Nations). In April, 1982, the US was the only Western industrialized state to reject the final treaty adopted by the Third United Law of the Sea Conference, and the US may also choose not to become a part of the new International Seabed Authority. As Leigh Ratiner (Deputy Chairman of the US delegation to the Third UN Conference of the Law of the Sea) has noted in *Foreign Affairs* (Summer 1982), we have clung to our defense of the values of free enterprise and the rights of American companies at the potential expense of having mining rights claimed by American flag companies rejected, whlle those of our industrial competitors are protected. Indeed, by not participating in the Treaty, the US risks challenges to what it believes are its national rights to navigational freedom, exclusive economic zones, jurisdiction over the American continental shelf, fisheries, and carrying out of scientific research in the oceans. The history of international organizations and international law has shown that in the long-run, more is gained by relinquishing some degree of national sovereignty for the sake of pursuing common objectives through international organizations and international law than is gained by an insistence on absolute sovereignty.

Looking Ahead: Challenge Questions

In what ways has the UN changed since its founding in 1945? What kinds of further changes are necessary to accommodate the different power configuration in the UN in the 1980s? How can it be made more effective in dealing with such important issues as arms control and military conflicts?

Is a supranational institution desirable? Who would control such an institution? How would such concepts as "human rights" and "aggression" be defined by such a supranational institution?

What types of states, with what types of power, would be most likely to control a world police state?

What is "international law"? Why do most states obey international law? Why is it in their interest to respect international norms and laws?

The UN: keeping alive a withering dream

Forty years after the UN's birth as a winning military alliance, diagnoses and prognoses of its ills are hopelessly vague and inadequate. Not surprisingly, proposals for reform are patchy and piecemeal. Eduardo Crawley surveys the leading arguments against the backdrop of the changing face of the UN.

As the 37th General Assembly of the United Nations begins its session, which will overlap the North-South Summit at Cancún, Mexico, there is a growing feeling that *something* must be done to make the UN respond more adequately to the demands placed upon it by a complex, crisis-ridden world. However, there is little agreement either on what is wrong with the organisation or on what, precisely, should be done to set it straight.

It is hard to find anyone, politician or scholar, who will come out with an outright condemnation of the UN and all its works, and a call for the creation of an entirely new organisation. Indeed, those concerned tend to insist there is nothing amiss with the basic structure of the organisation and its ruling principles, but . . At this point criticism forks out into two main streams. One maintains that the UN would function perfectly if only its member states would abide by their commitments and use the UN more consistently. The other holds that the UN has grown too big (though there are two subvariants of this position; one holding that bigness refers to membership, the other directing its attention to

the proliferation and size of UN agencies). In fact, critics often switch from one line of criticism to the other almost imperceptibly.

Kurt Waldheim (see interview on page 18) is perhaps the best exponent of the current view that all that is needed is for UN member states to put their money where their mouth is. Thailand's Thanat Khoman, a former Foreign Minister, sums up the case against enlarged membership even better than the most outspoken of United States government spokesmen: "It is necessary," he says, "to restore the balance between the democratic principal of 'one country — one vote' and political considerations; a country's responsibilities should correspond to its means, resources and contributions". And in case anyone does not get the message, he adds: "Power linked to numbers only leads to mob rule".

S. Rajaratnam, Singapore's Deputy Prime Minister for Foreign Affairs, rep-

resents the line that criticises bigness in the UN's offspring. "A lot of agencies," he says, "are really a waste of money. Often we have no choice but to send a man just to keep up appearances. Agencies like the World Health Organisation or the International Labour Organisation can be very small outfits, which can carry on basic technical tasks instead of having endless rounds of big meetings". In Rajaratnam's view, the overstaffing of UN agencies only adds to the brain-drain already suffered by the South. His solution is "to cut down on some of these agencies; not to send more people from the Third World but to get them back into their countries".

France's André Lewin, a one-time spokesman for Kurt Waldheim and a 20-year veteran chargé of UN affairs for the Quai d'Orsay, echoes Rajaratnam's plaint when he states: "Since its creation in 1945 the number of member states has increased from 51 to 154 and there has been a great proliferation of organisms and mechanisms, which complicate both its functioning and its funding. In my view the most urgent task is a radical rationalisation of structures and methods."

"The UN: Keeping Alive a Withering Dream," *South, The Third World Magazine*, October 1981. South Publications, Ltd., London, England.

Implicitly, Sri Lanka's ambassador to the European Economic Community, Lal Jayawardena, agrees with this outlook when he proposes the creation of small negotiating groups, both within Unctad and during the forthcoming Global Round of negotiations in New York. These groups "of manageable size" (up to 30) would include countries particularly interested in the issues under discussion and would agree to negotiate on behalf of the other countries who choose them.

Among those who sidestep the bigness issue there tends to be a return to the first position — that the UN is not adequately used by its members. Brazil's Foreign Minister, Ramiro Saraiva Guerreiro, translates this as a lack of informed political will. His formula is threefold: "First, there should be a focal point that could be the General Assembly itself, whence would converge the political will of states to act in unison, and whence would flow political directives according to a global vision of problems in the basic areas of energy, finance, credit and technology. Second, there must be a recognition of the priority and importance of the North-South dialogue. Third, there is an urgent need for the member states to abandon a short-sighted economic and political outlook, protectionist and isolationist in essence, to find new ways to reach a New International Economic Order".

A slight shift of slant is found in people like Nigeria's Leslie Harriman, former representative of his country at the UN, who calls for "democratisation" and a reform of the veto system. "The idea of having five nations dictating the tune at the UN," he says, "is not only obsolete but also negates the principles of democracy". Harriman would like to see an enlarged permanent membership of the Security Council, with Nigeria, hardly surprisingly, occupying the African seat.

This potpourri of reactions and proposals reflects, to a large extent, the confusion created by the rapid growth of an organisation which came to life almost 40 years ago as a military alliance, led by the Big Four (USA, USSR, UK and China), with a following of 46 nations from which "enemies" (Germany, Italy, Japan, Hungary, Austria, Romania, Bulgaria, Finland and Thailand) and "neutrals" (Switzerland, Spain, Portugal, Sweden, Ireland, Afghanistan, Iceland and Yemen) were excluded. Even when it became a permanent organisation in 1945, the Third World countries were nominally a majority (31 out of 51), though at the time at least 20 of the 31 voted almost automatically according to the lead given by the US State Department.

Numerically, the UN grew much like those geometric progression charts with which Doomsday lovers show the world's resources running out soon after the year 2000. By 1950 membership had expanded to 55; by 1955 to 71; by 1958 to 78; by 1964 to 112; by 1971 to 132. Today it stands at 154. But numbers are only part of the story; the proliferation of so-called "microstates" was already worrying Secretary-General U Thant in 1967, when he called for future incorporations to be limited to those who could at least face the immediate expenses of UN membership. Incidentally, Luxembourg, a micro-state if ever there was one, was a founder member.

Like most processes of democratisation in history, UN rhetoric claimed from the outset that the organisation was for everyone. "The Organisation is based on the principle of sovereign equality of all its Members," says Article 1 of the UN Charter. But in practice, again echoing the history of nations, the franchise was only slowly, and often accidentally, extended beyond the privileged few.

Mirroring the political development of the North, the UN was designed with a universal Lower Chamber (the General Assembly) and a Senate. Indeed, it was designed with senates-within-senates, as illustrated by the Security Council, and within that, the permanent members.

Moreover, the UN was created with two parallel functions: preserving the peace and administering the peace. Much as in Northern societies, again, the "senates" devoted to administering the peace assume the mantle of technical independence from the political authority: they are the IMF and the World Bank, where exclusiveness of real power-wielding is enshrined in weighted voting rights.

It is easy, with hindsight, to claim that the UN was involved ab initio with the process of decolonisation that would eventually give the Third World its present personality. But it is frequently forgotten that the UN's initial preoccupation was with "good government" for dependent peoples, and not with independence. The latter, wrested more than conceded, became a central UN theme only when the General Assembly took over this area from the original specific organisations dominated by the big powers.

A look back over the UN's first 37 years shows an apparent correlation between a growing membership and the increasing assertiveness of the General Assembly, to the point that the United States, under both Democratic and Republican administrations, has complained bitterly about the tyranny of numbers in this body.

Yet the shift of power, inasmuch as it has taken place, grew out of a crack in the edifice created by the superpowers themselves.

Born in the enthusiasm of a wartime alliance that felt the imminence of victory, the UN, perhaps naïvely, was set up on the assumption that the Big Four would continue to act in harmony. But by the time the final details were hammered out at the Yalta Conference, it was evident that US-Soviet rivalry would dominate the immediate postwar scene. The organisation felt the impact on several fronts; when the US engineered the exclusion of the People's Republic of China from the Chinese permanent seat on the Security Council, and when the liberal use of the Soviet veto threatened to paralyse the UN completely.

It was to overcome the obstacle of the Soviet veto that the US, during the Cold War, pioneered an enlargement of the General Assembly's faculties, most notably in the "Uniting for Peace Resolution" of 1950 which allowed the Assembly to recommend action, including the use of force, "if the Security Council, because of lack of unanimity of its permanent members, fails to exercise its primary responsibility". But the US attitude assumed continuing support for Washington's policies from a majority of member states. The growth of the Non-Aligned Movement and increasingly independent postures of Third World states has destroyed this assumption and, not surprisingly, dulled the early North American enthusiasm for a strong General Assembly and the supremacy of one country — one vote.

The criticism that member states refuse to abide by, or make use of UN mechanisms and principles has usually focused on the organisation's "primary" task of peacekeeping. The chart on page 12 shows how few major crises since 1945 merited attention in special or emergency sessions of the UN, and the even smaller number in which the UN was asked to perform a peacekeeping role.

What does not emerge from that retrospective view is that, behind very many of the decisions not to appeal to the UN lay the reality of superpower conflict, directly or by proxy, and the implicit or explicit threat of either a veto or the flouting of UN resolutions by one or another superpower. This same background goes a long way to explaining why the UN has taken 29 years to come up with a commonly accepted definition of aggression.

Defenders "in principle" of the UN system can, however, point to a fair number of cases (apart from the direct use of UN peace-keeping forces) in which "quiet diplomacy", usually through the good offices of the Secretary-General, has helped to defuse or prevent the spread of conflict. And they usually add that, on balance, there are far more areas in which the UN "works" than those in which it does not.

Indeed, if one looks at the entire range of UN organisms and agencies, it is quite evident that in an overwhelming majority of cases they perform their tasks almost automatically, with little visible "political" interference. This is especially true of agencies and organisms concerned with economic and social issues — the part of the UN devoted to "administering the peace". It has even been said that in this area the UN, through the General Assembly, has become an effective factory of "instant customary international law".

True though this may be, first appearances do not tell the whole story. Many of the leading agencies, such as the World Bank, the IMF, the High Commission for Refugees and even the Food and Agriculture Organisation were originally created to solve problems created by the war in the northern hemisphere, or for the countries of the northern hemisphere. Their adaptation to the needs and demands of the remaining two-thirds of the world has been slow, often patchy, and increasingly opposed by the nations that conform the UN's "senate".

The automatic functioning of the UN's economic and social activities was implicitly based on acceptance by all of the rules of the game, as expressed in the governing principles of the IMF, the World Bank and GATT. These organisations still reflect, in essence, the interests of the western members of the founding alliance (plus their former enemies, Germany and Japan). The competing interests of the Third World began, on a parallel track, to seek their expression in Unctad (see story on page 75), and finally entered on· a collision course with the IMF-World Bank-GATT system in 1974, when the General Assembly issued the declaration and programme for the establishment of a New International Economic Order and the Charter of Economic Rights and Duties of States.

The late 70s (see chart on page 12) has witnessed a slowing down of UN action comparable only to the pause imposed by the Cold War (1952-56). The United States has been at the forefront of a campaign against what it calls the "politicisation" of UN agencies. In that spirit it withdrew from the ILO (whose history can be traced back to the attempt to prevent the spread of "social revolution" in Europe) and has lambasted Unesco (for a couple of items in its "cultural" agenda, which absorbs only 8 per cent of its budget). In the same spirit it attempts to do away with the very concept of the Third World and discredit the very notion of the New International Economic Order.

Most of the diagnoses and prognoses of the UN's shortcomings tend to overlook the fact that the large area of harmony and automatic functioning has come up against its limits with the demand for the NIEO. Almost inevitably, these limits will emerge more clearly from the North-South summit at Cancún. Less evidently, the future of the international community will be affected by Washington's strategy to separate the lesser developed Third World nations from their more industrialised neighbours.

The Third World, as yet, has no counter-strategy, and will not have one as long as its attention is distracted by vague generalisations about "bigness" and complacency with a supposedly perfect organisation which would work properly if only "all member states" willed it to do so.

Interviews and research by Marcel Barang, Clarence da Gama Pinto, Raana Gauhar, Shada Islam, Peter Okoro, Enrique Oliva, Lucia Rabello de Castro, and C. Raghavan.

The Common Heritage

An Overview of the International Laws That Call For Sharing Global and Celestial Wealth

FRANCIS X. CUNNINGHAM

Francis Xavier Cunningham joined the Foreign Service in 1973, following 15 years of industry experience in solid-rocket propulsion project management. He was assigned to Brussels in 1974, Manila in 1976, and is currently in the Bureau of International Organizations Affairs, with primary responsibility as action officer for the United Nations Environment Program. The views in this article are the author's and do not necessarily reflect Department of State policy.

The concept of "The Common Heritage of Mankind" is a challenge that has been thrown before the developed countries. It is a continuous thread running through the Third World's demands for a global redistribution of wealth. The oceans, the seabed, outer space, and the electromagnetic spectrum are examples of resources said to belong to no state, corporation, or individual but rather to all mankind.

The Common Heritage philosophy surfaced as an element in the North-South dialogue in 1970. The Maltese ambassador to the United Nations, Arvid Pardo, on behalf of the developing countries requested the General Assembly to create a seabed committee. The committee declared a moratorium on all seabed exploration, ruled the seabed lying beyond national coastal jurisdiction the "Common Heritage of Mankind," and convened the Third United Nations Conference on the Law of the Sea in Caracas in 1974.

In the Common Heritage philosophy, any country, corporation, or consortium that undertakes to exploit what is said to belong to mankind should do so for the benefit of all. Much of the reward from the activity should be used for meeting the needs of the developing world. This idea was also raised in preparations for the World Administrative Radio Conference, and it is contained in the U N. Outer Space Treaty of 1967 and the so-called Moon Treaty, which is open for signing.

The moral and philosophical arguments of the Common Heritage idea are difficult to refute, but many capitalist nations in the North believe it strikes directly at the free enterprise system. After ten years of pressure by the developing world, these countries are on the defensive and may eventually agree to it as a basic principle in future negotiation.

Moral Consciousness

The civil rights revolution of the Sixties, and the anti-war movements, have awakened many Americans to a need to reassess their ethical and moral assumptions. The Common Heritage concept does seem morally right, and consonant with our traditions. It of course greatly antedates the North-South confrontation, being found in the English principle of the common area and American national parks, for example. Thus the South is recalling a doctrine that has had long standing in the North. More recently, federal regulation of the domestic broadcasting industry began with the belief that the airwaves belonged to everyone and that therefore their use should be regulated to ensure the public interest. Internationally, our policy toward Antarctica, for example, has been one of opposition to staking claims, even though several other countries have done so. We neither claim Antarctic territory nor recognize the claims of others. When Admiral Byrd flew over the South Pole in 1947, he dropped the flags of all U.N. members to dedicate the continent to "the ideal of brotherhood among peoples."

The United States Senate may have endorsed the concept of the Common Heritage by passing Resolution 49, introduced in 1978 by Senator Claiborne Pell, Democrat of Rhode Island. Resolution 49 "expresses the sense of the Senate that the United States government should seek the agreement of other governments to a proposed treaty requiring the preparation of an environmental impact statement for any major project, action, or continuing activity which may be reasonably expected to have a significant adverse effect on the physical environment or environmental interests of another nation or a global commons area." One might read the "global commons area" of Resolution 49 as referring to a "Common Heritage area," and the implication might be that no nation or corporation or consortium should act unilaterally to reap the benefits of exploiting what is the Common Heritage.

At present, exploitation of resources often leads to problems. Spreading desert-like conditions due to overgrazing and other factors claim an area about the size of Maine each year. By the year 2000, desertification and erosion could destroy a significant portion of the world's cropland, and as much as 40 percent of the tropical forests may be gone. But when we urge the developing countries to husband these resources, they respond: "You didn't worry about natural resources during your development. Does your new-found concern reflect a desire to keep us from catching up?" Perhaps our unqualified acceptance of the Common Heritage concept could give validity to our demand that developing countries act as responsible stewards of their portion of the Heritage.

The Role of Science

The Club of Rome, in its recent report "No Limits to Learning—Bridging the Human Gap," is very critical of science: science has departed from its objective ideals; it is a victim of "maintenance learning," which conforms to old assumptions about how the world works. "Science and technology, whose original purpose was the reduction of complexity, now count among the causes for its increase," says the report. And it adds: "Where the relevant sectors of pure and applied science are needed most—in health, food, shelter, and education—they are least available. And where science is most available it is employed for destructive ends—defense and arms." Science, the report says, needs a new direction: it should be aimed in an innovative way toward human needs.

This would appear to be a strong indictment of science and technology. But, apparently unbeknownst to the club, science *has* been moving in an "innovative way toward human needs." And there is reason to believe that science has brought mankind to the threshold of an era in which we will find solutions to the overwhelming problems of resource

and energy shortages, overpopulation, and global pollution. It is for this very reason that many fear the impact of the Common Heritage concept. While recognizing its moral imperatives, many feel the idea can blunt the spur of incentive, the reward for risk, the basis of the free enterprise system that has brought a high living standard to the West. They fear it could smother the driving force behind the new thrust of science. The arguments of those who oppose the Moon Treaty show that this is not merely an academic concern, and they were able to persuade Congress last year that the treaty could chill any commercial interest in space.

Using science and technology as a springboard, industry will be heading outward into the solar system in the next 50 years, because space is an exciting environment for industrial operations. It offers a range of gravitational accelerations from zero up to as fast as you want to spin a centrifuge, various gravity gradients, a very high vacuum available just by opening the door, a temperature range from near zero up to solar temperatures, and a broad spectrum of electromagnetic radiation. These characteristics and their corollaries—absence of separation caused by density differences, ability to mix materials in a precise manner, and opportunity to grow perfect crystals as well as very large ultra-thin membranes, for example—have excited industrial researchers. Space industry will give mankind many new products.

The nearby moon offers vast supplies of raw materials for space industry. There is also abundant energy from the sun that will permit almost any manufacturing operation. And space industry cannot pollute the Earth's biosphere or, for that matter, the solar system. Almost any commercial process that can be done on Earth can also be carried out in space. And many processes can be done only there.

Space industrialization offers a solution to the problems which are rapidly encroaching on our world of the 1980s—overpopulation, insufficient energy, scarce resources, global pollution. It suggests that perhaps we need not give up hope for

the future of free enterprise; perhaps our economic system has an untapped potential bounded only by our imagination and optimism. According to G. Harry Stine:

The risks are high, but the entire 21st century may hinge on what we manage to do in space in the next 20 years. Without the [space] shuttle and its progeny to open up the closed system of Spaceship Earth, we may indeed be faced with a future in which we chase our tails endlessly in a closed cage with limited resources, a dwindling supply of fossil fuels, a growing population, real or politically contrived shortages of everything imaginable, and the famous Club of Rome "Limits to Growth" staring us bleakly in the face. We may even find ourselves headed down into a new Dark Age—this time with our fingers on the nuclear triggers.

And all the while, a hundred miles above our heads lies a new frontier with abundant energy, a solar system full of raw materials, and an opportunity for us to test the hypothesis that we are not insignificant beings.

This generation may be the first and last capable of recognizing that the human race can, within a century, spread throughout the solar system, performing activities of great value and changing its lifestyle for the better.

We should not dismiss this vision as exaggerated or impossible. Remember that at the end of World War II the jet airplane was a new device, full of bugs, surrounded by emergent technologies, and requiring the best possible people to operate. To suggest that a grandmother would be able to fly around the world aboard a jet in armchair comfort at nearly the speed of sound within 15 years would have been an unbelievable forecast. As it turned out, *great*-grandmothers could do this, and within 25 years it was the only way a grandmother could visit her grandchildren because the jet airplane spelled the demise of the ocean liner and most of the long-distance passenger trains.

The private capital investment to create the international airline network was staggering. It involved not only aircraft, but great new airports, incredibly complex control systems, complicated navigational systems, fuel storage and distribution, ground transportation, maintenance organizations, food handling operations, and an entire chain of subsystems to support these.

The vast resources of the sea and the seabed offer similar potential. The oceans themselves contain large amounts of minerals in solution or suspension, and the seabed is literally littered with nodules containing important elements that are relatively scarce on the surface. Interestingly, the resources of the sea could help us exploit the resources of space and celestial bodies, for the nodules are rich in manganese and cobalt, which are used in rockets. Like the exploitation of space, mining the sea is a relatively new concept made possible by a relatively new technology whose possibilities are only now becoming visible.

Incalculable Resources

The potential of these resources is incalculable. The seabed comprises nearly twice the area of the continents, and the solar system contains a resource base perhaps the equivalent of a thousand earths. In both areas, international treaties call for a sharing of the wealth among all nations while recognizing that only a few have the capital and technology to exploit it. The latest draft of the sea treaty calls for the establishment of an international authority to regulate seabed mining and to distribute its fruits, and a similar regime could arise out of the Moon Treaty clause that calls for "an equitable sharing by all states parties in the benefits derived from those resources." Though the Moon Treaty cleared the General Assembly for signing in 1979, the Law of the Sea treaty is hung up in conference on the issue of seabed resources.

The practical interpretation of these clauses will be task for lawyers and judges in years to come, of course. But the question can be asked as to whether there will be incentive for private enterprise to manufacture moon mining equipment, for example, when control and profit from such technology will be shared with Third World countries that have not shared the risks. As space-law expert Arthur Dula says, "Resources that are owned by everybody are developed by nobody." Treaty backers, on the other hand, say that prospects for private enterprise in space will be enhanced by mutual cooperation under the treaty. The "international regime" does not have to be a profit-eating dictatorship. It could work like Intelsat, in which nations and companies jointly own and operate the international network of communications satellites.

The free enterprise system offers the potential of great reward to those who take large risks, and there will be great technological and financial risks involved in achieving the promise of space industrialization and seabed mining. But many of the socialist countries emphasize redistribution of the world's wealth, rather than production of new wealth. Will exploitation of these resources be pursued under a system where rewards must be shared with those who have not shared in the risks of the ventures?

This is a practical, not a philosophical, question, and it addresses an issue concerning the future of our race. It illustrates the fact that the Common Heritage of Mankind is an idea with extremely far-reaching implications, in the areas of ethics, science, economics, politics, and diplomacy. Could acceptance of this concept by the North actually frustrate man's attempt to bring to reality the vast promise which can be foreseen for the future of his species? If such a question about the Common Heritage can be seriously asked, a serious answer must be given. And one wonders whether such answers can be reached through position papers or task force reports.

Perhaps the answer should come from a great national debate—a debate which would involve our best minds in economics, political theory, ethics, science, the unions, homemakers, students, farmers. And perhaps it should address such questions as the moral and ethical demands of the Common Heritage concept, the future of free enterprise and capitalism, and the mutual obligations of North and South. If we believe in democratic principles, we owe it to ourselves to arrive at a real consensus before making decisions, implicit or explicit, on issues which might have a fundamental impact on the future of mankind.

Law of the Sea: The Next Phase

Elisabeth Mann Borgese

Introduction

In April 1981, the *Third World Quarterly* published a report on the Third United Nations Conference on the Law of the Sea and an analysis of the Draft Convention by Dr S P Jagota. The report traced the history and origin of the Conference, described the position of various interest groups on the major issues involved, and assessed the emerging compromise solutions.

Since Dr Jagota finished his report, two further Sessions of the Conference have taken place; the Tenth Session was held in New York from 9 March to 17 April 1981, and resumed in Geneva from 3 August to 28 August 1981. The Eleventh Session opened in New York on 8 March and culminated on 30 April 1982, with the adoption of the Convention by a vote of 130 States in favour, four against, and 17 abstentions.

The changes made in the text of the Convention since Dr Jagota's report are of secondary importance and his analysis remains as valid today as it was when it was written. What has changed—in some aspects, dramatically so—during the last year and a half, are the circumstances surrounding the text of the Convention, and, without repeating what has already been stated in Dr Jagota's excellent analysis, this article will simply begin where he ended.

We shall briefly discuss the events of the Tenth and Eleventh Sessions and the background against which they arose, and then try to assess the importance of the Convention as a whole, in the context of the present world situation. Within this perspective, we shall attempt to examine the role of ocean mining and of the International Seabed Authority (ISA) in international and national development strategy.

Chronology of Events

The Tenth Session

The Ninth Session ended in a mood of euphoria. A major breakthrough had been achieved on one of the most intractable questions that had still remained unresolved; that is, the mode of decision-making in the ISA's powerful executive body, the Council, one of the great innovative features of the emerging Convention. The solution to this problem had been largely engineered by the leader of the US delegation, Ambassador Elliot Richardson, who, at the end of that session, expressed the confident hope that the Conference was now ready to adopt the Convention, an event which he described as the most important since the foundation of the United Nations itself.

Instead, the Tenth Session was overshadowed by the United States' decision to undertake a comprehensive review of the Draft Convention, questioning the very principles on which it was founded, and to withdraw from the negotiations at the Conference until this review was completed. The gaps between 'Reaganomics' and the new philosophy of the common heritage of mankind were all too evident. Major changes, affecting the basic principles of the Convention, could not be considered without risking the unravelling of the whole 'package'. It soon became clear that the choices were not between *this* Convention and another or better one, but between *this* Convention or none at all; not between a Convention with or without the US, but a Convention without the US or no Convention at all. What effect the US withdrawal would have on the other industrialised countries and, in particular, on NATO allies and the EEC, was not too difficult to predict. It was clear that Europe's interests differed substantially from US interests and that Europe's relations with Third World countries were considerably more important than those between Reagan's America and the developing countries. It was clear that countries such as Canada, Australia and Norway, had too much to gain from the Convention to be willing to give it up, while the socialist countries could not be displeased by a demonstration of political isolation of the United States as the Cold War temperatures kept sinking. If the Tenth Session began with deep concern about the practical utility of a Convention to which the major maritime powers would not be parties, it ended with the unquestionable determination to go ahead and conclude this monumental work, even at the cost of abandoning the principle of consensus and proceeding to a vote. In spite of the overwhelming political difficulties looming in the background, the work of the Tenth Session was productive.

Of the five major issues left unresolved—listed by Dr Jagota on p 291 of his article—two were solved: the question of the location of the ISA and its organs and, simultaneously, the location of the International Tribunal for the Law of the Sea; and the question of the delimitation of economic zones and continental shelves between States with adjacent or opposite coasts.

The question of the seat of the Authority was a politically sensitive one, since it was divisive within the Group of 77 itself. Malta, which had played a leading role in laying the foundations for UNCLOS III, officially renounced this role during the Second Session in Caracas in the summer of 1974. 'The path indicated by Malta in the past remained open', Mr Bellizzi, the Maltese representative, said on 11 July, 1974, 'but my delegation would not be acting as guides.'[1] In accordance with this policy, Malta did not put forward its candidacy for the seat of the Authority. Filling the vacuum, Jamaica stepped forward and promptly secured the support of the Group of 77. It was only thereafter that Malta changed its mind and placed its candidacy. The competition between the two developing island states was fierce, and often bitter, and not defused by the advent of a third competitor, Fiji, which joined the contest in 1976 without, however a serious chance of displacing the two senior rivals.

When it became clear that the Conference could not reach consensus on the question of the seat, it was decided to put the question to a vote during the Tenth Session—together with the equally strongly-contested seat for the International Tribunal for the Law of the Sea, coveted by Portugal, Yugoslavia, and the Federal Republic of Germany.

Jamaica won the vote, on the second ballot, with 76 votes, while Malta obtained 66 votes, and there were five abstentions. Fiji, having received only fourteen votes in the first ballot, was eliminated in the second. To have failed, actually only by five votes, after starting the race with such an unfortunate handicap, was really a moral victory for Malta and attested to the perseverance and diligence of the Maltese delegation, working, as they did, under very difficult circumstances. Malta conceded her defeat graciously, with sincere recognition of Jamaica's valour in the contest. Fiji's somewhat jesting conclusive observation, that 'Jamaica has the seat of the Authority, but we have the nodules' may have more significance than may have been apparent when it was made. The seat of the International Tribunal for the Law of the Sea went to the Federal Republic of Germany. May the Hanseatic city of Hamburg, with its long maritime tradition and its independent spirit, provide a suitable home!

The question of delimitation had eluded satisfactory solution through nine sessions. The advocates of the two opposing schools of thought—one relying on 'equi-distance' (median line) as the decisive criterion for delimitation, the other, on the principle of 'equitable principles'—were entrenched in two separate interest groups. Both held out, unwilling to make concessions which might have entailed losses in case UNCLOS should fail and there was no Convention. On this issue, involving territorial rights and questions of sovereignty, there was no difference between developed and developing countries. Both the 'equidistance' group and the 'equitable principle' group—one led by Ireland, the other by Spain—contained both developed and developing countries.

The eventual compromise, very simple, and embodied in Articles 74 and 83 of the Draft Convention, provides that delimitation between States with opposite or adjacent coasts 'shall be effected by agreement on the basis of international law as referred to in Article 38 of the Statute of the International Court of Justice, in order to achieve an equitable solution. The articles also contain a formula on an interim solution which should not prejudice the final delimitation. That the Tenth Session saw hardened positions softening and a compromise solution emerging, was a clear indication of the political mood of the Conference.

Substantial progress was made on the discussion on 'participation', that is, the question of who may sign the Convention and be a member of the ISA. Was it to be States only, as under traditional international law, or other entities as well, responding to the fact that the structure of international relations is changing? The status of the Draft Convention was altered by dropping the subtitle 'Informal Text'; and, finally, an iron-clad schedule was adopted for the completion and adoption of the Convention at the Eleventh Session.

The achievements of the Tenth Session were substantial, considering the difficulties engendered by the US withdrawal and the general deterioration of the world political climate which might even have led to the break-up of the Conference.

The Eleventh Session

The agenda for the Eleventh Session was heavy. Three of the five issues listed by Jagota were yet to be resolved: the establishment of a Preparatory Commission and its functions and powers in relation to the future ISA; the proposal, by the industrialised countries, for a 'Preparatory Investment Protection' (PIP) pending entry into force of the Convention; and the issue of participation. The Drafting Committee had yet to complete its work, particularly on Part XI and annexes. Beyond these technical questions loomed the political problems arising from the fact that the US had completed its fundamental review, and was ready to discuss a set of amendments. These were first presented in the so-called 'Green Book'—an almost complete rewrite of Part XI of the Convention, taking the Conference back to pre-Caracas days—and subsequently, in somewhat attenuated form in a set of formal amendments sponsored by seven industrialised states (Belgium, France, Federal Republic of Germany, Italy, Japan and UK).[2] Some of this material found its way into an alternative set of amendments, sponsored by a group of neutral 'Friends of the Conference' consisting of medium-sized and small industrialised countries (Australia, Austria, Canada, Denmark, Finland, Iceland, Ireland, New Zealand, Norway, Sweden, and Switzerland).[3] This group tried to mediate between the US on the one hand and the Third World on the other, but only three minor points of their proposal survived in the final text of the Convention as adopted by the Conference.

In accordance with the timetable adopted at the end of the Tenth Session, the first three weeks (8-26 March) were devoted to informal consultations and negotiations. The results were presented on 29 March in a series of documents (Report by the President on participation in the Convention by entities other than States, *Doc. A/Conf. 62/L.95;* Report by the Chairman of the First Committee, Paul Bamela Engo of Cameroon, indicating lack of agreement on proposed changes in the text, *Doc. A/Conf. 62/L.91;* Report by the Co-chairmen of the Working Group of 21 on seabed issues, offering two draft resolutions, one on preparatory investment protection, the other on the establishment of the Preparatory Commission, *Doc. A/Conf. 62/C.1/L.30;* Report by the Chairman of the Second Committee, Andres Aguilar of Venezuela, stating that sufficient support had been indicated for only one minor amendment, proposed by the United Kingdom and regarding the duty of coastal States to remove abandoned or disused structures to ensure safety of navigation).

The introduction of these reports was followed by nine plenary meetings during which 112 speakers were heard. On the basis of this discussion, the Collegium completed the final revision of the text. The recommendations of the Chairmen and of the President were all incorporated, with very minor changes.[4]

After receiving the final revised text, the Conference was ready for the introduction of formal amendments by States who were dissatisfied with the compromises reached. A spate of amendments came forth, affecting almost every part of the Convention. Six meetings were devoted to hearing 87 speakers on these proposed amendments. During this period, however, Tommy Koh, the President of the Conference, succeeded in convincing the sponsors of most of them not to press for a vote. The adoption of amendments, which could have upset the balance of the Conference package as a whole, might have endangered the adoption of the Convention. On 23 April the Conference determined that all efforts of reaching general agreement had been exhausted, and that the Conference was ready for decision-making. The amendments were then disposed of on 26 April. All but 12 of the 31 sets of formal amendments had already been withdrawn, and more disappeared during that day. In the end, only three were put to the vote. Two (by Spain) concerned minor points with regard to passage

through straits used for international navigation; one was put forward by Turkey and would have cancelled Article 309, provided that 'No reservation or exception may be made to this Convention unless expressly permitted by other articles of this Convention.'

The defeat of these amendments demonstrated that the Conference wanted to conclude and adopt the Convention such as it was, and no chances were to be taken by opening a Pandora's box of amendments, wherever they came from. On the other hand, the rejection of these amendments was paid for with the loss of three votes. Spain abstained in the final vote, while Turkey and Venezuela voted against the adoption of the Convention which to them was unacceptable, unless they had the right to make reservations, especially with regard to the question of delimitation. Only one amendment proved to be sufficiently uncontroversial to be adopted, and it concerned a Resolution rather than the Text itself. This amendment enabled Namibia, through the UN Council for Namibia, to sign the Convention and thereby qualify for participation in the Preparatory Commission.

The next two days were marked by hectic activity, to make ready the final package for adoption or rejection on the appointed day, 30 April. 'Consensus' was still possible, inasmuch as it was clear that the overwhelming majority of the Conference was in favour of the Convention, but it was anybody's guess whether the United States, and perhaps some of its allies, would raise a 'formal objection'. Last-minute changes were conceded, to better the odds, but in vain. On 30 April, the United States demanded that a roll-call vote be taken. Had the Conference gauged the mood of the US correctly, it might have refrained from last-minute compromises which could not soften the US position, while frustrating the Group of 77 and alienating, and finally losing, the East European socialist states.

The Resolution

The Resolution on the Protection of Preparatory Investments

The major confrontation, at this time, was not over the Convention itself, but the Resolution on the Protection of Preparatory Investments (PIP) the one important innovation emerging from the work of the Eleventh Session.

A first draft for a text on PIP had been introduced by the United States on 2 April 1980, at the end of the Ninth Session. It was not discussed during that session but formed the basis for discussions outside the Conference, on the so-called 'Mini-Treaty' or reciprocal agreement among States which had already enacted unilateral mining legislation. The US proposal was officially withdrawn from the Conference early in 1980.

Upon the urging of the Conference, a new text was introduced, so-sponsored by Belgium, the Federal Republic of Germany, Italy and the US.[5] The proposal amounted to a Mini-Treaty. It carved up the international seabed into enormous blocs and totally emasculated the ISA, obliging it to rubber-stamp the production plans presented by the 'pioneer investors' who would proceed with their plans without that rubber stamp, in case the Convention was not ratified ('Nothing in this resolution shall be construed to prohibit commercial production after 1 January 1988 if the Convention has not entered into force by that date'.)

An alternative proposal was introduced by the Group of 77. In fourteen points it stressed strict conformity with the provisions of Part XI of the Convention and demanded that training and technology transfer would be undertaken on a scale that would make it possible for the Enterprise to initiate exploitation simultaneously with the 'pioneer operators'. In the meantime, the co-chairmen of the Group of 21 had introduced a draft which subsequently went through a number of revisions incorporating suggestions in the above-mentioned documents. The final draft was introduced on 20 April[6] and was accepted by the Conference on 30 April 1980.

In essence, Resolution II defines and recognises a number of 'pioneer investors'. It obliges them to register their claims to an exploration site not larger than 150,000 km², and to pay a registration fee of $150,000, after they have ensured that there are no overlapping claims among themselves and, in case of conflicting claims, accepted a system of mandatory dispute settlement (this, really being the essence of the 'Mini-Treaty'). It carefully circumscribes their right to the exploration of polymetallic nodules in the international area, and to research and development of the pertinent technology. It further imposes on them the duty (a) of turning over to the Preparatory Commission a 'reserved site' in accordance with the terms of the Convention; and (b) of assuming the responsibility for training and technology transfer for the future Enterprise. Finally, it guarantees priority to the pioneer investor with regard to a contract for exploitation and a production authorisation, once the Convention has entered into force and the 'pioneer investor' has ratified it (assuming the 'pioneer investor' is a State), or in the case of a consortium, its 'certifying State' or States have ratified it.

The importance of this resolution is considerable. It establishes immediately an interim regime for an indeterminate time, which may be quite long. Although it is almost certain that fifty States will be found to sign the Convention and establish the Preparatory Commission, ratification and entry into force may require several years, depending on circumstances other than the interests of seabed miners.

On the one hand, this regime does incorporate the principle of 'the common heritage', or at least, pays lip-service to it. It should be noted, however, that the term 'common heritage of mankind' does not occur in the Resolution. The Resolution, nevertheless, recognises that the principle can be deduced from the assertion

(para. 1(e) (iii)) that 'area . . . shall have the meanings assigned to [that term] under the Convention', since, in the Convention, the Area and its resources are defined as 'the common heritage of mankind'.

On the other hand, the regime practically creates a 'grid system' as proposed, e.g., by the UK in pre-Caracas days. It effectively divides the common heritage and turns it over to a limited set of operators functioning on the basis of reciprocal agreement, licensed by a Commission with little operational capacity of its own.

The 'pioneer investors' as defined by the Resolution, are eight, consisting of (i) France, India, Japan and the Soviet Union with their state companies; (ii) of six private consortia (Kennecott, Ocean Mining Associates, Ocean Management Inc., Ocean Minerals Co., Association Francaise pour l'étude et la recherche des nodules, and Deep Ocean Minerals Association) associated with one or more of the following eight States: Belgium, Canada, Federal Republic of Germany, Italy, Japan, Netherlands, UK and US. The door is also left open to newcomers from developing countries, provided that they meet the financial criteria by 1 January 1985. Depending on wider political and economic circumstances, one could envisage three more 'pioneers' emerging within this period: Brazil, Mexico, and perhaps a regional African consortium, as proposed by the Tunis Symposium in May 1982. Also possible is the emergence of three regional, private/public enterprises: an African, a Latin American, and an Asian, which might influence the development of the ISA in unexpected ways once the Convention is in force.

This division of the actual or potential 'pioneer investors' into three groups—two of which, (i) and (iii) are States which are obliged to sign the Convention to qualify, while the one group (ii) consists of non-state entities (consortia, most of which are multinational)—caused great difficulties and the eventual withdrawal of the East European socialist states. The East Europeans had two basic objections. First, they maintained that private corporations had no place in an international convention which is concerned with the conduct of States not of non-state entities; secondly, and, more important, the provision was discriminatory inasmuch as the States enumerated under (i) and indicated under (iii) were bound to sign the Convention in order to qualify as pioneers, whereas the phrasing of (ii) provides a loophole for States to benefit from the activities of their associated companies without signing. Thus, for example, the United States could benefit (without signing) from the work of a consortium, some of whose components were domiciled in the US but which was 'certified' by other (signatory) States.

On the first point the socialist states were overruled by the Legal Advisor of the UN whose advisory opinion had been sought at the request of the Soviet Union. The advisory opinion was that international law was not being violated by the provision in question. On the second question, the discriminatory character of the provision was conceded. It was pointed out, however, that a subsequent paragraph (para. 8 (c)) ensures that 'no plan of work for exploration and exploitation shall be approved unless the certifying State is a party to the Convention. In the case of entities referred to in para (a) (ii), the plan of work for exploration and exploitation shall not be approved unless all the States whose natural or juridical persons comprise these entities are parties to the Convention.'

The Soviet Union and its allies demurred, for the situation remained that during a first phase, of indeterminate length, discrimination remained. Thus the eight members of the socialist bloc abstained in the final vote. How the question will eventually be resolved, depends on the Soviet policy in a broader context. It may be that the Soviet Union will prefer not to sign, if the US insists on non-cooperation—especially in consideration of the fact that, for the Soviet Union, its signature will be almost tantamount to ratification; and entry into force, without the United States, has substantial financial implications. If the Soviet Union wants to sign and to participate in the work of the Preparatory Commission, there are two possible scenarios. First, a loosening of the Conference package; perhaps, in Caracus (in December, 1982) it may be possible to sign the Convention while maintaining one's disapproval with regard to one or more of the Resolutions. Should the Conference insist on maintaining the integrity of the 'package', there still might be a second way open to the Soviet Union and its allies. That is, they could sign the Final Act of the Conference, implying an observer status in the Commission, with a statement that they will accede to the Convention as the 53rd to 60th State; for, upon the deposit of the sixtieth instrument of ratification or accession, the Convention enters into force, and the discriminatory provision lapses.

The second important aspect of the Resolution is that it recognises that 'activities in the area' in the foreseeable future shall not consist of commercial exploitation and that contracts for 'integrated mining operations' (such as envisaged, with such lavish detail, by the text of the Convention) shall not be applicable for the foreseeable future. It will be the task of the Commission to concentrate its attention, for the time being, on exploration, research and development and ensure the fullest possible participation of developing countries in these activities. This could be achieved in one of several ways. There is nothing in the text of the Resolution that prevents the Commission from establishing a joint venture, or joint ventures, for exploration, research and development, financed jointly by the private sector, States, and international funding institutions in the field of development cooperation. Such arrangements would be highly beneficial to the industrialised countries, by cutting investment costs and sharing risks. They would be equally advantageous to developing countries, enabling them to participate on an equal

footing in an enterprise of high-technology management. Whether there would be one such joint venture, composed of those industrialised States and companies who wish to participate, together with a certain number of Board Members from developing countries who might be appointed by the Commission, or whether there would be several such ventures, taking into account eventual regional developments as suggested by the Africans, depends on the actual course of events over the next two or three years. In any case, concentration on such a venture or ventures would scale down the cost of the ISA and the Enterprise to a non-utopian level, in line with economic and technological realities.

The proposal was first introduced by the Austrian delegation in a statement on 31 March[7] and is very much in line with the proposal launched by President Mitterrand at the opening of the Versailles Summit in June 1982. 'Ocean exploration', together with space technology, biotechnology, electronics, nonconventional energy technologies, make up the 'Third Industrial Revolution'. It is in the area of new technologies that the French President proposed the launching of a 'concerted programme', by establishing 'international commissions for research and development and for technological cooperation between private and public firms and states.' In this proposal he stressed the importance of the participation of developing countries in 'joint ventures' (initiatives conjointes) to assure acquisition by them of these new technologies.[8] Nothing could be more in line with the French proposal than this suggestion that the Commission concentrate its early efforts on establishing a joint venture for exploration, research and development in ocean mining.

The Preparatory Commission

A third important aspect of Resolution II is its impact on developments which will have to follow implementation of Resolution I which calls for the establishment of the Preparatory Commission. Discussions during the Eleventh Session clearly demonstrated that this Commission had to be different from other preparatory commissions established within the UN system in the past. The Commission had to have executive and operational powers if it was to discharge the tasks imposed on it by Resolution II, that is, to recognise pioneer investors, register claims, choose reserved sites, and arrange for training and technology transfer for the ISA. So important, indeed, are the functions assigned to the Commission that it may become essential to devise a system of balanced representation and decision-making. One delegation went so far as to propose that the Commission itself should be composed along the lines of the future Council of the Authority, and that it should appoint various subcommissions and committees.

The final text, as adopted, provides that the Commission shall be composed of all signatories to the Convention, and all signatories to the Final Act may participate as observers. The Commission shall establish a special subcommission 'on the problems of land-based producers likely to be most seriously affected by the production of the Area'. A second subcommission is to be established to 'take all necessary measures for the early entry into effective operation' of the Enterprise.

There is nothing in the Text to prevent the Commission from appointing or electing a smaller executive council, which might be organised on a regional basis. The Resolution, in fact, provides (para. 7) that 'The Commission may establish such subsidiary bodies as are necessary for the exercise of its functions and shall determine their functions and rules of procedure'. The establishment of an executive council might increase the efficiency of the Commission and guarantee a fair balance in decision-making which could be lacking in the larger body.

Other Resolutions

Not much need be said about the remaining Resolutions in the 'package'.

Resolution III reaffirms, but separates from the body of the Convention, what was previously a Transitional Provision. It guarantees to those people who have not yet obtained full independence the enjoyment of the rights and benefits of the Convention.

Resolution V, introduced by the Group of 77, calls on Member States, the competent international organisation, the World Bank, and the UN Secretary-General to assist developing countries in training, education and assistance in the field of marine science and technology and ocean services. These two resolutions were uncontroversial, but considerable controversy was caused by Resolution IV, which provides that the national liberation movements, which have been participating in UNCLOS III, shall be entitled to sign the Final Act of the Conference, in their capacity as observers, and that, in that capacity, they may participate in the Preparatory Commission. The adoption of this Resolution as an inextricable part of the 'package' induced Israel to vote against adoption of the Convention.

The Convention on the Law of the Sea

Introduction

As already mentioned, the changes made in the text of the Convention itself are minor, and the reader is referred to Dr Jagota's analysis which remains valid. It is on the basis of that analysis that we will attempt to assess the importance of the Convention for the international community in general and for developing countries in particular.

There can be no doubt that the adoption of the Convention is a landmark. It signifies a breakthrough in the structure of international relations introducing, as it does, a number of concepts into international law which, taken together, offer a new platform from which to launch a new international order. These innovations

were stressed, in the final statements of the President of the Conference, Tommy Koh, and the Chairman of the Drafting Committee, Ambassador Beesley of Canada:
a) The concept of the common heritage, transcending the traditional notions of sovereignty and ownership.
b) The concept of a public international institution (the Seabed Authority) that is operational, capable of generating revenue, imposing international taxation, bringing multinational companies into a structured relationship; responsible for resource planning on a global scale as well as for the protection and conservation of the marine environment and scientific research. An institution linking politics, economies and science in new ways—a model, potentially, for international organisations in the twenty-first century.
c) The concept of the Economic Zone, adding a new dimension to development strategy.
d) The concept of international environmental law.
e) New concepts such as the archipelagic State or transit passage, adjusting the traditional law of the sea to the requirements of the situation as it emerges from UNCLOS III.
f) A regime for marine scientific research and technology transfer.
g) The most comprehensive, and most binding system of international dispute settlement ever devised.
There has never been a document like this.

Needless to say, progress is never linear. History manages to move forward and backward at the same time. The Convention is the result of political compromises, reflected in ambiguities, loopholes, and even contradictions. Solutions of some problems give rise to new problems. Perceptions of interests keep changing. Circumstances surrounding problems supposedly solved keep changing. Agreed solutions may turn out to have unforeseen implications and consequences.

Thus, while the Conference was crossing the last 't' and dotting the last 'i' of this law for the future, symbolically, and as though to remind the world community of the persistence of the old order, navies were girding for battle in the South Atlantic, to decide a question of 'sovereignty', imperial style. At stake was not just the domination of a far-flung tiny colonial holding, but the hub of an ocean area larger than the continent of Europe, probably rich in untapped resources, and a bridgehead to the last continent, Antarctica, where the next conflict is looming between the principle of national sovereignty and the principle of common heritage, between the past and the future.

The Common Heritage, ISA and Ocean Mining

The concept of the common heritage of mankind, proposed by the delegation of Malta in 1967, is one of the great contributions of the twentieth century to political theory and international law. Resource depletion, technological and economic developments transcending the boundaries of nation states, and the degradation of the marine environment on which all life depends, were beginning to play havoc with the application of the traditional principles of sovereignty and ownership to the new medium of the ocean. While not negating the old principles, the new concept of the common heritage transcends them by asserting that certain resources, and, inseparably linked with them, certain technologies, and certain financial resources cannot be owned in the traditional sense; they must be managed in common, for the benefit of all mankind, with particular consideration for the needs of the poor and of future generations and are to be used for peaceful purposes only.

The principle of the common heritage, first applied to the resources of the seabed beyond the limits of national jurisdiction, has implications far wider than the oceans. Ideally, it could become the foundation of a new economic order. It should become the basis of a new economic theory, which the world so badly needs to replace the worn-out and evidently bankrupt economic theories applied today.

True, the Convention does not fully define the new principle: but the gist is there. True, while proclaiming the new principle, States, both developed and developing, hastened to contravene and abridge it as far and as fast as possible by stretching the limits of their national jurisdictions. These jurisdictions are, however, permeated by the new principle of *functional sovereignty* (sovereign rights over uses) that is taking the place of *territorial sovereignty* and absolute ownership. True, the mechanism embodying and articulating the principle of the common heritage (the ISA) is far from perfect, and reflects conflicts and contradictions that the Conference was not really able to overcome.

Thus, industrialised countries, having spent many millions on developing technologies that should have increased their independence from supposedly unstable foreign producer countries, found themselves slipping, through the ISA, under the control of the very same countries that they had sought to avoid individually. Developing countries, on the other hand, who had hoped to gain collectively from sharing in the management of the common heritage, found their economies threatened by the competition between marine resources and land-based resources.

The very nature and scope of the ISA remains somewhat uncertain; between the aspirations of the developing countries, who wanted to build a first piece of the New International Economic Order in the shape of an operational Authority with broad and comprehensive powers and functions ranging from scientific research and environmental policy to resource management, technology transfer and a redistribution of wealth, and the conservatism of the industrialised world wanting the Authority (if any) as narrow in scope (restricted to nodule mining) and as powerless as possible. To reduce its discretionary powers to the minimum, they insisted that every administrative and financial detail be spelled out in advance: and, this, for an industry still

at the experimental stage and on the basis of economic projections that had to be purely conjectural.

Thus, with every session that passed, the compromise text became more complex, more ambiguous, more unwieldy, and more remote from the real world, for the assumptions of the 1970s, on which the whole edifice (including systems of production, production limitations, *etc.*) is based were never questioned. While they remained immobile, however, the real world kept moving, so that a gap opened, and began to widen, between the construct and the economic and political reality.

The assumptions of the 1970s, basically, were three: first, that seabed mining would be fully operational on a commercial scale by the 1980s, and that the revenues accruing to the Authority, both from licences and from the operations of the Enterprise, would be substantial. Secondly, that seabed mining would in practice be restricted to the mining of polymetallic nodules, and that other deepsea minerals would be without economic interest for the foreseeable future; and, thirdly, that nodules were to be found only in the 'international area', far beyond the limits of national jurisdiction, so that the Authority would have a monopoly position enabling it effectively to control production.

All three assumptions have turned out to be wrong: economic depression, a glut of land-based minerals, and volatile prices on the commodity market, are not conducive to the launching of a new mining industry. Before the beginning of the next century, there is unlikely to be a commercial, integrated mining project of the kind considered by the MIT Model,[9] on which the convention has lavished such an abundance of legal minutiae. Thus, no revenues are in sight for the ISA. Instead of being an instrument for the redistribution of wealth, it needs large-scale international funding to defray administrational costs and assist the Enterprise to become operational.

This reappraisal of the financial potential of the ISA raises the fundamental question of the relevance of ocean mining for developing countries, and, on this, opinions are divided. The more traditional view of the development economist is that ocean mining is of no interest, since the technologies involved are highly complex and highly capital-intensive rather than labour-intensive. I have always held the opposite view. Ocean-mining technologies belong to those listed by President Mitterrand as part of the Third Industrial Revolution. If developing countries fail to join this revolution 'on the ground floor'—at the present stage of research, development, and exploration—the development gap will widen to the point at which 20 years from now it may become unbridgeable. Furthermore, ocean-mining technologies can be disaggregated into systems and subsystems which range from the highly complex to fairly simple. At the less complex end of the spectrum, even the least industrialised countries could make some contribution. Participation in an international venture in ocean mining will accelerate technology transfer and enhance industrial diversification. If, in the long term, over the next fifty years, there is going to be a large-scale displacement of land-based mining by ocean mining—a development that appears to be very probable—then land-based producers should be the first ones to join the new industry. Just as the oil companies are eager to buy into alternative energy industries, in view of the anticipated shift from a petroleum-based energy economy to one based on other energy resources and technologies.

The second assumption, on which Part XI of the Convention is based, is that the only commercially interesting form of deep-sea mining would be nodule mining; recent scientific discoveries have altered this picture. The discoveries of sulphide deposits offshore the Galapagos Islands and off the West Coast of the United States, with metal contents in concentrations far superior to those of the manganese nodules, have defused interest in the manganese nodules which are the only type of resources covered by the text and thus the Convention, is already obsolete in this respect. Rules, regulations and procedures will have to be drafted, not only for manganese nodule mining but for other forms of deep-sea mining as well.

The most serious consequences, however, will derive from the collapse of the third assumption—that the ISA has a virtual monopoly over the resource it is to manage. Apart from the metalliferous muds of the Red Sea (under the jurisdiction of Saudi Arabia and the Sudan), and the sulphides (under the jurisdiction of Ecuador and the United States), nodule deposits of considerable commercial interest have been identified in the Economic Zones of Chile and Mexico. It is probable that additional deposits have already been discovered and will be explored by French Polynesia and offshore Hawaii.

It need not be emphasised, because it is self-evident, that the ISA's position is of one kind if States and companies have no choice but have their activities organised, carried out and controlled by the ISA on behalf of mankind as a whole; and quite another kind if States and companies have a choice between working under the ISA or under bilateral agreement with some coastal State in areas under national jurisdiction. It is well known, and documented, where the preferences of the companies lie.

Production limitation under the Convention has always posed problems which have not really been resolved. It was only during the Tenth Session that the land-based producers among the developing countries became aware of the fact that a limitation formula based on the projected nickel demand would not really protect the producers of cobalt and manganese. But even supposing it has been possible to devise a formula safeguarding these countries; it is one thing to base such a formula on the assumption of monopoly by the ISA, and it is quite another thing to apply such a formula, if

production is out of the ISA's control and takes place in areas under national jurisdiction. For what cannot be produced by or through the ISA—because of the application of production limitation—may be produced, unchecked in areas under national jurisdiction.

Thus, there arises the spectre of an Authority incapable of performing the functions for which it was created, and useless, because ocean mining, if and when it comes, will take place in areas under national jurisdiction. Thus arises the spectacle of a whole bureaucracy 'Waiting for Godot'.

But it need not go that way. Curiously enough, those very actors, who through the kind of PIP resolution that they proposed at the Conference, clearly manifested the intention of postponing the common heritage regime *ad kalendas Graecas* and, for all practical purposes, of replacing it with a registry system based on mutual agreement among the seabed mining states, have opened the possibility of initiating activities in the right direction. Part XI being inapplicable in the present situation, the Convention might have been by-passed if ratified, or not ratified at all. The PIP resolution confers powers and functions on the Preparatory Commission that it might not have had otherwise. Yet the Preparatory Commission, unlike the rigid structure erected in Part XI, is flexible enough to adjust the concepts of the 1970s to the realities of the 1980s. Furthermore, the establishment of the Commission when a mere fifty States will have merely *signed* (not ratified) the Convention, is a goal that is undoubtedly far easier to reach than the sixty *ratifications* needed for the establishment of the ISA. Whether the Commission will succeed in adjusting and preparing the activities of the ISA in such a way that, rather than waiting for Godot, it may render tangible and immediate services to the world community and especially to developing countries, depends on the trends of history, the political will and the leadership capacities of those who will be called to serve. The foundation has been laid. Never before has the international community had at its disposal an instrument with a development potential such as that of the Commission.

The Exclusive Economic Zone

One need not be Hegelian (assuming that whatever happened had to happen) to realise that the extension of national jurisdiction into the oceans was inevitable. The territorial sea of three, or of six, or even of twelve miles was an anachronism, unable to respond to the needs of military as well as economic security as shaped by technological developments. Industrialised countries had to regulate and manage the penetration of the industrial revolution into deeper and wider offshore zones. Developing nations had to defend their coastal waters against the depredations of modern distant-water fishing fleets and factory-ships. No country could tolerate the emplacement of spying devices or the conduct of polluting activities near their coast. The time of *laissez-faire* in the oceans was over.

Systems of management were required, and jurisdiction was needed to build them. Even Arvid Pardo, the father of the common heritage concept, proposed (as early as 1971) in his Draft Convention submitted to the Seabed Committee, the recognition of 'national ocean space' up to a limit of 200 miles from clearly defined baselines. Nor was he over-concerned that the establishment of such a zone would detract from or conflict with the concept of the Common Heritage.

In principle, the EEZ concept is the most benign, the most flexible, and the most innovative way in which the inevitable trend towards the extension of national jurisdiction could have been met. In the Convention, however, it is flawed by ambiguities which, as in the case of seabed mining, open the possibilities of increasing inequality, conflict and chaos as well as those of rational management and international cooperation.

If the hope had been that the new limits would be such as to forestall further expansion of claims which might entail conflicts and further increase inequalities among States, this hope has been deluded. There are three major loopholes through which expansion could proceed unchecked.

The first is the inadequate definition of *straight baselines* in Article 7, which does not specify the maximum *length* of these baselines from which the territorial sea, the EEZ and, in some cases, the breadth of the continental shelf are measured. Nor does it define the 'appropriate points' to be connected by the baselines which need not be on land but may be defined by coordinates on the map. Thus, States have the possibility of including considerable ocean spaces as 'internal waters' and extending their EEZs, the breadth of which is measured from the baselines, well beyond 200 miles from the shore.

The second loophole is the lack of a proper definition of *islands* in Article 121. It may turn out to be difficult to draw the line between an 'island' defined as a 'naturally formed area of land, surrounded by water, which is above water at high tide' (which is entitled to an EEZ and a continental shelf) from a 'rock which cannot sustain human habitation or economic life of its own' (which is *not* entitled to an EEZ or a continental shelf of its own). The acquisition of tiny islands, or rocks claimed to be islands, may bestow vast ocean spaces and their resources. The Falkland Islands conflict, may, alas, be one in a long series of similar conflicts.

The third loophole is the definition of the limits of the Continental Shelf in Article 76. The 'Irish formula' of Byzantine complexity, on which it is based, is practically open-ended, and competent geologists from the Soviet Union as well as from the Intergovernmental Oceanographic Commission of UNESCO, and others, have not failed to point out that it is inadequate as a basis for actually drawing boundaries. I do not hesitate to define it as pseudo-scientific. Beyond that, I would seriously challenge the validity of invoking geophysical criteria for the drawing of political boundaries. Such criteria have long since been abandoned on land, and there is no reason for this relapse into romantic geopolitics at sea.

The Soviet amendment, incorporated in the final text of Article 76, limiting any claims under the Irish formula to no further than 350 miles from the above-mentioned baselines, is undoubtedly an improvement. But even this limit is as elastic as the baselines from which it is measured.

The continental shelf doctrine might have been deemed superseded by the economic zone doctrine, as was proposed by Arvid Pardo and advocated by a number of countries, especially African and Arabic, at the Conference. To have a single boundary, from the surface through the water column to the ocean floor and its subsoil, at 200 miles from clearly defined baselines would have been simple and tidy. Only a few countries would have lost rights they might have claimed, beyond 200 miles, under the Continental Shelf Convention of 1958 and they might have been compensated.

As long as present political winds prevail, it is to be feared that expansion will continue, and the discovery of any significant resource anywhere in the oceans will immediately be followed by claims by the nearest coastal island or archipelagic State. Further expansion of claims will further increase inequalities among States and increase tension and conflict. But, again, the glass is half-empty as well as half-full. The Convention, while yielding to, and further encouraging, expansionist and nationalistic tendencies, also responds to other needs and has triggered off different trends. The extension of national jurisdiction itself, and the transition from a *laissez-faire* system to a system of management requires more, not less international cooperation and organisation. Three developments, all initiated by the Convention even before its adoption, are clearly discernible.

New Trends, Triggered by the Convention

National Legislation

The first is the adjustment and updating of national legislation and the building of national infrastructure as a response to the opportunities offered and responsibilities imposed by the new Law of the Sea. This is a complex process. Old laws have to be pulled out of a great number of government departments. Activities that did not exist, areas over which the State had no jurisdiction, have to be covered by new laws. Boundaries have to be determined, out at sea, or negotiated with neighbours. Hydrographers, geologists, and experts in marine biology, fish population dynamics and fisheries management, in the protection of the marine environment in all its ramifications, in ocean mining, and in energy, are needed; also, lawyers, trained in the most recent developments in public and private international law, collecting, collating, updating, and harmonising the old law, internally and with international law.

Ocean Development departments and ministries for Ocean Affairs have to be built and their interaction with other government departments, at the national, at the local, as well as with international agencies, have to be articulated. In no other area are internal and international affairs so inextricably linked as in ocean affairs.

Regional Integration

Pollution, as is well known, does not stop at national boundaries. Fish cross political frontiers without submitting to passport control. If, in a *laissez-faire* or freedom-of-the-seas system, it was possible for each nation to fend for itself, and the strongest nations fended best, a system of management, instead, requires attention to interlinkages. If Nation A wants effectively to manage a certain fish stock, it depends on Nations B and C for cooperation, for this stock may migrate between two or more EEZs, or between EEZs and the high seas. And it is not only with regard to this one stock that cooperation is necessary—it is for the stock that this fish feeds on, as well as the predators that may feed on the fish in question; it is the environment in which it breeds; it is the whole ecosystem, which in most cases cannot be contained within national boundaries.

Scientific research, on which stock assessment and management must be based, must extend over the whole ecosystem, and, if management is to be effective, the political system will have to be adjusted to it. Oceanographic research is too costly to be carried out by individual nations and necessitates international cooperation, not only because the ecosystem to be researched is transnational but also as a cost-sharing mechanism.

Thus, we see an emerging trend towards regional integration of marine activities. The Convention foresees such developments, Article 123, of Cooperation of States Bordering Enclosed or Semi-Enclosed Seas, and in the sections dealing with the management of living resources, in the EEZ as well as on the high seas; with the protection and preservation of the marine environment; with marine scientific research; and with the transfer of technology.

The real push, however, came from the Regional Seas Programme, initiated and coordinated by the United Nations Environment Programme (UNEP) and involving the cooperation of over a hundred governments, intergovernmental organisations and nongovernmental organisations. Ten regional sea programmes are presently in action, covering one area after another with networks of regional cooperation, with laws and regulations, plans of action, monitoring and enforcement systems, and financial arrangements to carry the cost. The Regional Seas Programme would be unthinkable without UNCLOS III and the principles it has been evolving. On the other hand, the Convention on the Law of the Sea might have remained a dead letter, had it not been for the Regional Seas Programme, which is beginning to articulate, at a practical, regional level; to

implement and complement; to give 'teeth' to the new Law of the Sea.

The Evolving Basic Ocean Organisations

The third development, closely related to the first two, is the restructuring and strengthening of the UN agencies and institutions, engaged in marine activities. 'Basic organisations', in this respect are: the Intergovernmental Maritime Organisation (IMO—formerly, IMCO), the Intergovernmental Oceanographic Commission of UNESCO (IOC), the United Nations Environment Programme (UNEP), and the Committee on Fisheries of the Food and Agriculture Organisation of the United Nations (COFI).

The text of the Convention imposes new responsibilities and enlarges the scope of activities of each of these. There are no less than sixty-two references to the 'competent international organisations' whose cooperation is prescribed in determining shipping-lanes, in managing living resources, in monitoring pollution, in advancing scientific research and facilitating technology transfer, in establishing regional centres, and in harmonising national laws, standards and regulations. 'Competent international organisations', identified here as FAO, UNEP, IMO, and IOC, have to play an entirely new role in dispute settlement. They have to establish and maintain a register of experts from which special arbitration commissions may be drawn, and which may also be entrusted with functions of fact-finding in disputes.

Resolution V, adopted by the Conference as part of the Convention package, recognises 'the special role of the competent international organisations envisaged by the Convention on the Law of the Sea,' and recommends 'that all competent international organisations within the UN system expand programmes within their respective fields of competence' for assistance to developing countries in the field of marine science, while Article 278 of the Convention itself prescribes that 'the competent international organisations referred to in this Part (XIV) and in Part XIII shall take all appropriate measures to ensure, either directly or in close cooperation among themselves, the effective discharge of their functions and responsibilities under this Part.'

A study, released by the Secretary-General of the UN during the Tenth Session in 1981, on 'The Future Functions of the Secretary-General Under the Draft Convention and on the Needs of Countries Especially Developing Countries for Information Advice and Assistance Under the New Legal Regime', points out that 'The emphasis in the present study has necessarily been placed on the interrelationship among 'problems of ocean space' and on *the need to establish effective linkages among marine activities particularly for the establishment of sufficiently comprehensive policies.*' (emphasis added). While this is beyond the scope of the Conference itself, it may be expected, the study concludes, 'that the "cross-organisational programme analysis" on marine affairs to be conducted for the Committee on Programming and Coordination in 1983 will be helpful in this respect as will the various studies that have been made or are planned by individual organisations with respect to the effects of a new legal regime on their technical cooperation activities and the effects of the relevant provisions of the Draft Convention on their functions.'

Looking at the Convention in a wider historical perspective, one notices a curious discrepancy. 'Conscious that the problems of ocean space are clearly interrelated and need to be considered as a whole', the Convention covers all uses of the oceans. In this sense, the Convention is truly 'a Constitution for the Oceans'. At the same time, however, it provides an institutional framework only for one specific use of ocean space— and not the most important one—that is, deep-seabed mining. With respect to the other uses of the oceans, the Convention is satisfied with more or less nebulous references to 'the competent international institutions'.

The Maltese Draft of 1971—the prototype of this Convention—provided an institutional framework for all major uses of ocean space. It was way ahead of its time.

Rather than doing the whole, overwhelmingly complex, job in one revolutionary swoop, the international community has chosen a more gradual approach, both building on the past and utilising existing structures within the UN system. They are now busy analysing the effects of the Convention on their own structures and functions and studying how they can adjust to the new requirements. It is more than likely that the ISA, the institutional model provided by the Convention, will exercise some influence in the various areas in which restructuring is required.

The first requirement is a transition from a coordinating to an operational stage. As long as membership of these organisations was restricted to a small number of countries with highly developed marine capabilities of their own, coordination of their activities was a proper function. Now the task is not only to coordinate and harmonise, but to create marine capabilities where they do not exist, especially in the developing countries. This clearly requires operational capacity.

There is indeed no reason why *mutatis mutandis* the basic 'competent international organisations' should not, over time, develop 'Enterprises' or 'joint ventures' of their own, just like the ISA, on a regional or on a global basis. Just as in seabed mining, such ventures would offer the most direct, effective, and economical way to bring developing countries into the mainstream of ocean management. The regional marine scientific centres prescribed by the Convention could be conceived as joint ventures in research and development. A first such venture, with the IOC or the ISA or both, for research and development in ocean energy (OTEC, tides, waves, salinity gradients) would be of direct and immediate benefit to developing countries. A joint venture with FAO for the exploration and exploitation of Antarctic krill, which should be declared part of the common heritage of mankind, could provide a very large source of protein to developing countries. An International Sea Service, in joint venture with IMO, could perform not only useful international functions with regard to emergency situations, disaster relief, or training, but it could provide an economically effective way to strengthen Third World shipping capabilities.

Secondly, what is needed is an expansion of financial resources. Here, again, the innovative principles already adopted with regard to the ISA could serve as an example. The ISA has the power to impose taxation. There is no reason why the other basic organisations should not equally have a right to tax.

If they are operational, they ought to be able to generate revenue, just as provided for the ISA. If they render tangible services to the international community, these services ought to be paid for. Nothing could be more equitable than a progressive tax on the major commercial ocean uses or users, the beneficiaries of the activities of these 'competent international organisations.' An Ocean Development Tax was proposed by the International Ocean Institute as early as 1970. The Maltese Draft provides for it in Article 61. In the evolving ocean economy, such a tax would go a long way towards securing the kind of 'automaticity of transfers' that has been sought by development economists in the World Bank and elsewhere.

Thirdly, there is the requirement of close cooperation and integration of policies between all the basic organisations, including the ISA. The existing inter-Agency coordinating mechanisms are evidently inadequate for the new job as indicated by the Secretary-General's recommendation that new ones be established. What is needed is an effective integrative machinery, comprising the ISA, IMO, UNEP, FAO and COFI—perhaps through a joint Assembly where problems of ocean policy and management can be debated in a comprehensive, trans-sectoral manner.

All these developments will undoubtedly take time— perhaps the next 25 years. Let us assume a time-table could be agreed on to complete them by the time of the review conference of the ISA.

Taken together, the signing of the Convention and the establishment of the Commission as an effective interim regime; the adjustment of the functions of the ISA in accordance with the terms of the Convention but in accordance, also with the economic and technological realities of the 1980s; the development of national legislation and infrastructures in accordance with the provisions of the Convention and interacting with international law and organisation; regional integration and cooperation; the evolution of the 'competent international institutions' and integration of their policies with those of the ISA through an appropriate integrative machinery; and, the introduction of a functionally-based 'ocean development tax' could contribute much towards transcending the unwanted and unforeseen implications of the Convention. Such a development, based on cooperation rather than conflict, on redistribution of income rather than on unilateral aggrandisement, on the concept of the common heritage of mankind rather than on obsolete concepts of the absolute sovereignty and ownership, would also greatly diminish the importance of where the 'boundaries' are and would facilitate the participation of landlocked and geographically disadvantaged countries in regional and global joint activities, as well as the participation of developing countries in the new ocean industries.

The establishment of a New International Economic Order is not a one-time happening at a given place on a given date. It is an ongoing process and will never quite be completed. Within this process, however, the adoption of the Convention on the Law of the Sea is undoubtedly a milestone. The Convention is imperfect, as are all things human. It is ambiguous, it is ambivalent. It does not by itself solve the problems it set out to solve. Neither security of boundaries nor economic justice nor the integrity of the environment are necessarily enhanced. Given certain political trends, the further escalation of national claims, increased inequality among States, the degradation of the environment, the exhaustion of fish stocks, will go unchecked. The Convention cannot prevent it. Mankind may destroy itself at sea as on land and in outer space.

But it need not be so. The Convention on the Law of the Sea, more than any other international instrument, offers to all countries and all persons of goodwill the possibility of an alternative development, the realisation of new principles, the emergence of new economic theories and solutions. It offers a forum, a platform on which to stand a framework within which to act creatively, innovatively. Without the Convention we would not have had these possibilities. With the Convention, we have at least ambivalence: the path to destruction is not closed, but a path to construction has been opened.

It is, therefore, of the utmost importance that at least fifty States sign the Convention this year, so that the Commission can be established and the next phase can begin. Clearly, this decision is in the hands of the Third World.

NOTES

1. UNCLOS Official Records, Vol. 1 p 158.
2. *Doc. A/Conf. 62/L. 121*
3. *Doc. A/Conf. 62/L. 104*
4. *Doc. A/Conf. 62/L. 93 and corr. 1*
5. *Doc. A/Conf. 62/L. 122*
6. *Doc. A/Conf. 62/L. 141. Add. 1.*
7. *Provisional Summary Record of the 160th Plenary Meeting, A/Conf. 62/SR 163, 6 April 1982.*
8. Reported in *Le Monde* (Paris), 6-7 June 1982.
9. J D Nyhart *et al, A Cost Model of Deep Ocean Mining and Associated Regulatory Issues.* Cambridge, Massachusetts: MIT, 1978.

Sea Law Convention Battle

Wang Shifang

The third UN Conference on the Law of the Sea concluded in Montego Bay, Jamaica, on Dec. 10 with the signing of a new Law of the Sea Convention after nine years of arduous negotiations. The representatives of 117 nations and two other organizations signed the new convention, far more than the 60 countries needed to make it effective. This is a great victory for the world, especially for the third world countries who united to successfully confront the repeated attempts of the superpowers to weaken the convention.

Third World Stand Upheld

The new convention is fundamentally different from the four conventions adopted at the first UN Conference on the Law of the Sea in 1958. At that conference, of the 80 countries attending, only half were Asian and African countries. This represented the limited historical conditions of the time. The four conventions adopted under the manipulation of the big powers were entirely advantageous to the maritime hegemony of the superpowers and were disadvantageous to the just struggles of the developing countries attempting to defend their sovereignty and safeguard their national economic interests.

The new convention embodies the long-held demands and principled stand of the third world countries: coastal territorial waters extending 12 nautical miles off shore and an exclusive economic zone up to 200 nautical miles out to sea. Beyond that point, the seabed and its resources are the common heritage of all mankind. The new convention does not consider just the interests of the developing countries, but it also considers the interests of the developed countries. It embodies the interests of both coastal and landlocked countries. Therefore, this is the most reasonable and acceptable convention for most countries to date.

However, there are still shortcomings and even serious defects in the provisions of quite a few articles in the new convention. As the Chinese representative pointed out, the articles relating to innocent passage through territorial waters contain no clear provisions regarding the passage of foreign warships. In addition, the convention also fails to adequately define the continental shelf, or the principle for delimiting the exclusive economic zones and continental shelf between opposite or adjacent states. Thus a number of articles of the convention will undergo further refinement as they are implemented in the future.

The new convention is a hard-won victory over many difficulties and obstacles.

The third UN Law of the Sea Conference officially opened at the UN in December of 1973. It held many sessions over several years. After years of revisions and corrections, the overall draft convention on the exploitation of maritime resources was adopted in April of 1980. After further revisions it became the official draft convention. The revised draft convention adopted at the 10th Session of the UN Law of the Sea Convention in August of 1981 made possible the official sea law convention.

Task Not Yet Ended

After the conclusion of the 10th Session of the Third UN Law of the Sea Conference, the United States roped some developed countries into agreeing on a "mini-treaty" alternative to the Law of the Sea Convention. The United States refused to sign the convention on the excuse that the deep-sea mining provisions do not conform to US interests. At the US initiative, the United States, Britain, France and West Germany then signed an agreement on deep-sea mining, i.e., the "mini-treaty," aiming at using their abundant capital and advanced technology to divide among themselves the ocean resources belonging to the whole of mankind.

At the Jamaica conference the United States not only refused to sign, it also urged as many countries as it could not to sign. Its attitude has been criticized by the third world countries. Prime Minister of the host country, Edward Seaga pointed out that the "mini-treaty" signed by the United States and some West European countries has no legal status. "It is contrary to the provisions of the Law of the Sea Convention." Actually, one member of the "mini-treaty," France, has signed the new convention. This shows that the US attempt to enlist the support of others for its boycott of the new convention was not easy.

The new convention stipulates that as of Dec. 10, 1982, the convention will remain open for signature in the Foreign Ministry of Jamaica for two years. It also may be signed in the UN Headquarters, from July 1, 1983 to Dec. 9, 1984.

The birth of the new convention marks a great change in the balance of the international political forces. Its implementation will undoubtedly face many obstacles which will demand continued joint efforts and steadfast struggles on the part of the participating countries, particularly the third world countries, to protect the gains already achieved and finally turn the sea into a real asset of all humanity.

Problems and Prospects for the Future

International relations have an uncanny resemblance to human relations in an important respect: they are able to tolerate an inordinate amount of abuse, conflict deterioration, and challenge if it occurs in small increments. In both the international and human dimension, relationships ordinarily adjust to these negative inputs and come up with a modus operandi, until one day, someone suddenly discovers that the relationship is intolerable. To continue it requires rethinking and restructuring. This need not be seen as the end but rather as a beginning of a healthier relationship.

Such a situation has evolved countless times in international relations. As an example, détente was only seriously considered when the Soviet-American relationship deteriorated to a crisis point. On the other hand, the international economic system has had one bandage after another applied to it because it has not yet reached the level of world wide depression. Some may argue that at this point it is already too late. But in many cases, it is only when all parties at last realize that they too are losers in the existing relationship, that

they will at last come up with the compromises and the proposals necessary for improving it.

In several areas of international relations, we are at a critical turning point: either distressed relationships will be rescued by rethinking and restructuring them, or they will collapse. This is the case in the present adversarial Sino-Soviet relationship, the Soviet-American confrontation, and in the critical area of strategic weapons. Within the context of alliances, it may also soon be the situation in America's relations with Europe and Japan. Population, hunger, energy, ecological deterioration, and world resource problems are rapidly moving toward crisis proportions, and efforts are being made to cope with them. Here, however, the solution encompasses more than national efforts, and may require major changes in the international economic and political system before other than temporary solutions can be achieved. Moreover, those states in a position to take positive actions lack motivation: their political constituencies do not believe their stake in a solution justifies any sort of compromise or sacrifice on their part. This is the case also with refugee flows—another problem that

will confront the international community as long as military conflicts, human rights suppression, and poverty continue. And it is still unclear whether anything will be, or can be, done about nuclear proliferation or terrorist groups with access to atomic bombs before it is too late. This is not to suggest that things must hit rock bottom before they can get better, but only to say it is unlikely that action will be taken on many of these issues until crisis looms.

As the following articles indicate, there are many ideas for how to restructure the future of the international system in ways that are directed toward international rather than national action, and addressed toward fundamental causes rather than symptoms of the malaise. New international institutions and structures seem called for. But which ones can prevent a collapse of the world order? Will states perceive it as in their self-interest to act according to new international regulations and under new structures? One thing is clear; the interrelatedness of problems and the interdependence of states has become so complex, and the "globalization" process so powerful, that no state can remain safely insulated in a prosperous

cocoon while the rest are mired in poverty, conflict, and despair.

Looking Ahead: Challenge Questions

Why are there predictions of "global disaster" within the next 20 years? Do you think these are unduly pessimistic predictions? Have such scenarios been conceived of before?

What do you believe are the best means of solving some of the problems that presently threaten the international system? Is it realistic to think that there can ever be a "world authority"? Is it realistic to think that the world can continue for another hundred years without a "world authority"? Is it likely that the nation-state will some day not be the major actor in the international system?

Are most of the problems faced by the international system the result of conscious acts by humankind, or are they the result of "inexorable forces" about which little can be done? Even if they are the result of human decisions, does that mean that they can be dealt with any more easily?

GLOBAL FUTURE: TIME TO ACT

New ideas for action to avert global disaster in 2000.

The *Global 2000 Report to the President*, issued eight months ago, offered a gloomy view of the world 20 years from now if governments fail to act. The result of three years' analysis of probable changes in world population, resources and environment through the end of the century, the report warned that unless nations do something now to alter the trends, the earth's capacity to support life will decrease while population growth continues to climb; there will be a steady loss of croplands, fisheries, forests, and plant and animal species; and there will be degradation of the earth's water and atmosphere—all in the next 20 years.

The *Global 2000 Report* identified the problems; it did not attempt to find solutions. *Global Future: Time to Act* is the next step. Published in January, and prepared by the Council on Environmental Quality and the State Department, this latest report answers how—how to change course and reach a different end.

Global Future is a collection of new ideas for actions the United States could take, along with other nations, for a vigorous response to urgent global problems. For example, by doubling the use of family planning services in the developing world before the end of the decade, the world could hold its population in 2000 to half a billion lower than the projected 6.3 billion.

Another idea: Sufficient reserves of basic food should be available for prompt response to a major shortage. The United States ought to join in this year's effort by the International Wheat Council to agree on the concept of nationally held reserves with international coordination at times of market strain.

The report points out that foreign assistance, while vital, is only a part of the complex pattern of trade and monetary issues, domestic policies and needed investment that influences economic development in developing countries. To improve the U.S. ability to respond to global resource, environmental and population issues, the report recommends that development and coordination of U.S. policy on these issues be centralized in one agency, preferably in the Executive Office of the President.

The study also calls for establishing a "hybrid public-private institute" to supplement the government effort, to stimulate independent analysis and discussion among industrial, labor, environmental and academic groups and the government. The Population, Resources and Environmental Analysis Institute that it recommends would have several roles, all designed to enlist private sector groups in the solution of global problems. A major part of the institute's program would be to supplement the government's capability to make accurate projections. This capacity appeared lacking in the *Global 2000* study. The institute would also further analyze government policy and "stimulate independent analyses of long-term global problems."

Why should the United States or other comfortable countries, with a seeming wealth of resources at their command, take an urgent interest in global resource impoverishment and environmental degradation? "First, the resulting poverty and misery for hundreds of millions of people is a matter of serious moral concern," *Global Future* answers. "Then, there is a profound human interest in protecting the earth's resources for generations to come. Finally, there are impelling reasons of national self-interest. U.S. political and economic security, broadly defined, is already being affected by global resource, environment and population problems—more so than is commonly understood. The effects will become far greater with time, if present trends continue."

Here is a summary of recommendations:

"Global Future: Time to Act," Council on Environmental Quality and U.S. Department of State, *Agenda,* U.S. Agency for International Development, April 1981.

Population

Problem: By the year 2000 there will be almost 2 billion more people in the world. Ninety percent of the growth will occur in low-income countries, where most people are young and have their child-bearing years ahead of them. At the very least, explosive population growth makes it harder to provide decent conditions. In some areas, it is already overwhelming efforts to provide education, housing and jobs. And the attempts of growing numbers of people to wrest a living from the land is eroding the very soil, water and forests on which long-term stability and improvements in standard of living depend. Population growth in richer countries, though much slower, is also of concern because consumption per capita (especially of energy and other unrenewable resources) is much higher.

Recommendations: The United States should:

• Together with other donors and international organizations, intensify family planning over the next decade, by doubling resources and improving maternal and child health care.

• Provide more government assistance for research in contraception, suited to the needs of individual countries.

• Develop a national population policy that includes attention to stabilizing population; making family planning programs available; drafting just, consistent and workable immigration laws; improving information; and ensuring continued attention to domestic population issues through institutions.

Food and Agriculture

Problem: Population increases will strain the world food supply. While food production may expand 90% (that is optimistic) by the year 2000, the per capita increase will be less than 15%. This global estimate disguises regional disparities; food availability and nutrition levels may scarcely improve in South Asia and the Middle East and may actually decline in the poorer parts of Africa. Of particular concern is the ability to improve world agricultural yields in the face of degradation of soil and water resources and the conversion of some of the best cropland to other uses.

Recommendations: The United States should:

• Expand development assistance in the area of food in low-income countries.

• Establish an Interagency Task Force on World Agricultural Lands (on the model of the Interagency Task Force on Tropical Forests) to assess world trends affecting agricultural productivity; review current national and international responses; recommend a coordinated U.S. strategy, as part of international efforts; provide the foundation for an international plan of action.

• Lead by example in protecting and managing U.S. agricultural lands; elements in the program should include:

—Federal technical and financial assistance to state and local governments wishing to develop land preservation policies and soil and water conservation programs.

—An Agricultural Land Conservation Fund to help finance state and local conservation programs.

—Financial incentives to help preserve farmland and encourage conservation.

—Examination by federal agencies of programs affecting agricultural lands (for example, federal loan and loan guarantee programs, sewer, water and highway programs) to ensure that their actions do not unnecessarily encourage farmland conversion.

—Examination and use by state and local governments of growth management tools to discourage farmland conversions.

• Propose an international technical conference on conversion of agricultural lands.

• Strengthen national and inter-national programs to preserve crop germplasm.

• Through assistance, cooperation and research programs, domestic and international, encourage the use of sustainable agricultural management techniques, including integrated pest management, more efficient use of commercial fertilizer, and biological fixation of nitrogen.

• Work actively toward a better international food reserve system.

Renewable Energy Resources and Conservation

Problem: While most of the world, rich and poor, must adjust to soaring oil prices, developing countries without their own oil are hardest hit. They are now spending $50 billion a year to buy oil—almost twice the amount they receive collectively from all outside sources for development assistance. At the same time, the world's poorest half, most of whom rely mainly on firewood and agricultural waste for fuel, face another energy crisis: dwindling supplies of firewood. This combination is aggravating already severe economic and ecological problems and adding to the difficulty of achieving economic growth.

Recommendations: The United States should:

• Support recent World Bank proposals for a major increase in assistance for growing and conserving fuelwood. AID should substantially increase its assistance for planting trees.

• Encourage the World Bank to accelerate lending for renewable energy and conservation activities and support the idea of a new World Bank energy facility.

• Develop mechanisms by which developing countries can take advantage of new energy technologies developed by the U.S. government and, so far as possible, by corporations.

• Study ways to make U.S. government technical experts in renewable energy and conservation more readily available to developing countries, including a voluntary program of short-term technical assistance that would tap the private sector.

• Participate actively in the 1981 U.N. Conference on New and Renewable Sources of Energy.

• Establish an interagency task force to develop a realistic strategy for achieving the goal of 20% of U.S. energy from renewable sources by 2000.

Tropical Forests

Problem: The conversion of forests to farm land and the demand for fuelwood and other forest products are depleting the world's forests at an alarming rate—as much as 18-20 million hectares (one hectare = 2.5 acres) each year (or an area half the size of California). Most of the loss is in the tropical regions of developing nations, where some 40% of the remaining forests may disappear by 2000. Hundreds of millions of people are already directly affected by this extremely serious and growing global environmental problem.

Recommendations: The United States should:

• Press for an international plan of action on tropical deforestation.

• Provide financial and technical assistance to enable the U.N. Food and Agriculture Organization to fulfill the international leadership role.

• Coordinate U.S. programs closely with the FAO and World Bank to make the best of resources.

• Designate and support the Forest Service's Institute of Tropical Forestry (Puerto Rico) and Institute of Pacific Islands Forestry (Hawaii) as "national centers" for tropical forest research, education and training.

• Call upon the World Bank to design and support an international program on reforestation of large watersheds.

• Expand the tropical forest management ability of AID and the Peace Corps.

• Pursue, through the U.S. Interagency Task Force, a new partnership of government and private industry to broaden the base of U.S. planning and improve U.S. technical contributions to international programs.

Biological Diversity

Problem: The accelerating destruction and pollution of the habitat of wild animals and plants means that in the next 20 years many species will disappear—on an unprecedented scale, as much as 15 to 20% of all species on earth. About half would go because of the loss and degradation of tropical forests, the rest principally in freshwater, coastal and reef ecosystems. Estimates of species loss often include only mammals and birds, or all vertebrate animals. The estimate here also includes insects, other invertebrates and plants.

Recommendations: The United States should:

• Establish a federal Interagency Task Force on Conservation of Biological Diversity to develop a long-term U.S. strategy to maintain biological diversity.

• Increase U.S. support to ongoing international programs to set priorities for protecting biological diversity.

• Consider establishing an international fund to help developing countries protect and manage critical ecological reserves, especially in tropical forests.

• Increase support of national and international efforts to inventory the world's plants and animals and to collect species and germplasm.

• Increase training assistance for wildlife management and conservation professionals in developing countries, especially at selected institutions in those countries.

• Expand its ability to offer technical expertise in conservation of biological diversity.

Coastal and Marine Resources

Problem: Urban and industrial development leading to destruction of productive coastal wetlands and reefs; pollutants washed from the land, dumped or discharged in the ocean or deposited from the atmosphere; and exhaustion of world fisheries are growing threats to coastal and marine ecosystems. Fish harvesting—a major component of the world's food supply—has leveled off and by the year 2000, fish may be contributing less to the world's nutrition, on a per capita basis, than it is today. Adding to the concern is the lack of data regarding the degree of pollution and disturbance in the open oceans.

Recommendations: The United States should:

• Set up a U.S. technical conference to review and improve ecologically sound strategies for fishery management.

• Expand support of fishery management in developing countries bilaterally and through increased funding to FAO.

• Inventory and map coastal resources and assess the amount and the effects of major pollutants spilling into coastal and marine areas from land; cooperate with other countries to do the same.

• Increase efforts to establish marine sanctuaries and seek an international agreement on protection of habitats of migrating species.

• Support a moratorium on all commercial whaling until the continued survival of whales can be assured.

• Do the research needed to implement the Antarctic Living Resources Treaty; continue efforts to assure that Antarctic minerals will not be exploited until a decision has been made on the basis of sufficient information that such development is acceptable.

Water

Problem: The need for water will greatly increase over the next 20 years; in half the countries of the world population growth alone will cause demand to double. Information on water availability and quality is exceptionally poor, but it is clear that problems of water supply will be serious in many regions. Parts of the world, especially the Third World, already are suffering severe water shortages and drought, and water-borne disease is endemic. Unless a concerted effort is made to preserve water, reliable supplies will continue to disappear.

Recommendations: The United States should:

• Establish an Interagency Committee on Global Water Supply and Management to assess monitoring of the world's water, identify potential areas of conflict and propose ways for the United States to cooperate with other nations to share knowledge.

• Improve bilateral technical assistance in water management and increase financial support of FAO for training in water management.

• Increase research to reduce the need for water for irrigation.

• Take part in international efforts to assure safe drinking water as a major development goal.

• Encourage arrangements to anticipate and resolve international disputes over water.

Global Pollution

Problem: Certain by-products of economic development and industrial growth threaten the earth's life support systems. Hazardous substances, nuclear waste, the buildup of carbon dioxide in the air, damage to the stratospheric ozone layer, and acid rain all could harm virtually every aspect of the earth's ecosystems.

Recommendations: The United States should:

• Work toward improving international agreements to control hazardous substances and waste.

• Improve its system for notifying countries that hazardous substances banned for all or most uses in the United States are being exported to them, and, in cases of extremely hazardous substances, control their export.

• Improve its ability to handle hazardous wastes.

• Develop procedures for regulating the export of hazardous wastes.

• Take national and international measures to reduce amounts of nuclear waste and control their disposal.

• Protect against radioactive material.

• Analyze alternatives for the future with special emphasis on action to reduce carbon dioxide build-up.

• Support further research on acid rain, continue work with Canada on air pollution, and intensify legal efforts to control acid emissions.

• Support more research on ozone depletion and encourage action by international organizations to protect the stratospheric ozone layer.

• Improve national and international climate programs.

Sustainable Development

Problem: Many of the world's most severe environmental problems are in part a consequence of extreme poverty: deprived people are forced to undermine the productivity of the land on which they live. They plant crops on poor soil, graze stock on marginal land, causing it to turn to desert, cut trees that are needed to stabilize the soil and the water supply, and burn dung needed to fertilize and condition agricultural soil.

Recommendations. The United States should:

• Make up its overdue obligations to the World Bank and other development funds and contribute its share to the World Bank's general capital increase.

• Expand its development assistance targeted to food, energy, population and health, and coordinate it with programs of other countries and international organizations.

• Urge the World Bank and other international organizations to integrate resource and environmental considerations more fully into their planning.

• Increase resource management expertise in AID programs and encourage all U.S. agencies with significant activity abroad to further integrate resource and environmental considerations into their decisions.

• Develop ways to use the scientific, technical, resource management and environmental expertise of U.S. government agencies more effectively both in AID programs and in other international cooperation programs.

Institutional Changes: Improving Our National Capacity to Respond

Problem: The U.S. government currently cannot adequately (1) project and evaluate future trends; (2) take global population, resource, and environmental considerations into account in its programs and decisions; and (3) work with other countries to develop international solutions to these problems.

Recommendations: The United States should:

• Establish a government center to coordinate data collection. This will ensure that policy analysis on long-term global population, resource, and environment issues will rest upon sufficient information.

• Improve the quality of data collection and modeling for global issues and promote wider access to data and models.

• Establish a federal coordinating unit, preferably in the Executive Office of the President, to develop federal policy and coordinate ongoing federal programs concerning global population, resource, and environment issues. Activities should include coordinating data and modeling described above; issuing biennial reports; assessing global population, resource, and environment problems; and serving as a focal point for development of policy on long-term global issues.

• Adopt devices that force action, such as budget review procedures, a presidential message, a blue-ribbon commission, offices in each federal agency to deal with long-term global issues, or legislation ordering federal agencies to address long-term

9. PROBLEMS AND PROSPECTS FOR THE FUTURE

global issues, a federal coordinating unit, and a public-private institute.

• Create a public-private Global Population, Resources and Environment Analysis Institute to strengthen and supplement federal government efforts on long-term global analysis.

• Improve the budget process to make technical expertise of U.S. agencies more readily available to other countries.

• Assure environmental review of major U.S. government actions that significantly affect natural or ecological resources of worldwide importance; designate tropical forests, croplands, and coastal wetland-estuarine and reef ecosystems as globally important resources.

• Continue to raise world population, resource, and environment issues in appropriate international forums; work with and support appropriate international organizations and other countries in formulating solutions.

• Enlist business in formulating responses to long-term global problems.

• Increase public awareness of global population, resource, and environment issues.

Global Future: Time to Act calls both for fresh starts and for continuing efforts. It emphasizes our special strengths—especially scientific and technical—and it looks to others for leadership in *their* areas of special strength. The report stresses that international cooperation is imperative in maintaining a productive and habitable earth. No one nation can tackle the problems alone.

In general, the recommendations in the report are the first steps in what needs to be done, efforts that must be duplicated, enhanced, repeated, and expanded upon many times over by other nations and international organizations, by private institutions, by business, and by industries. A guiding hand at the center of the U.S. government's share of the response is critical—not only for coordination but for staying power.

Copies of Global Future: Time to Act *are available from the Council on Environmental Quality, 722 Jackson Place NW, Washington, DC, 20006. Please enclose a self-addressed mailing label.*

The Establishment of a World Authority: Working Hypotheses

Silviu Brucan

Professor, University of Bucharest, Bucharest, Romania.

This paper diagnoses the present-day global disorders and upheavals—social, political and economic—as symptoms of a transition set in motion by the incapacity of existing international arrangements to contain and mediate tensions and conflicts, both actual and potential, in international affairs. They point to the need for the creation of a new international institution that would take into account the widespread aspiration and urge for restructuring of the international power system. It finds in history, especially since the emergence of modern nation-states (coincidentally with the expansion of the capitalist mode of production and its global thrust for the creation of a market global in its sweep) evidence of attempts at setting up international order-keeping institutions. The last such attempt in the shape of the United Nations, although more universal and democratic than its predecessors, mirrored the power structure that existed at the time of its birth. The world scene has changed enormously since, thanks to the emergence of many more new nation-states following decolonization, all conscious and assertive of their rights and all grappling with the complex problems bequeathed to them by colonialism. The UN has time and again demonstrated its incapacity to cope with the various problems— even in such a crucial sphere as war-prevention and peace-keeping. The article proposes, as a solution, the creation of a world authority that would facilitate the transition to a new world order. It then defines the functions of such a world authority and the powers it will have to be armed with to perform its functions.

I. Introduction

As we approach the end of the twentieth century, the world is entering a stage in which every major development—whether an essential resource becoming scarce, a social or political upheaval—seems to acquire such magnitude and involve consequences so ominous that new international arrangments are required to contain, control, and direct them. The globalization of the phenomena, processes, and problems besetting our world has turned the establishment of an international institution capable of controlling and managing them into the central question of world order.

An earlier version of this paper was presented at the Lisbon Conference of the World Order Models Project, 13-20 July, 1980.

In the 1960s, a world institution was proposed with the exclusive purpose of preventing a catastrophic nuclear war. Very soon, however, it became clear that such a partial approach is thoroughly inadequate. To build a new international institution one must deal with the *whole*, not with its parts; even the elimination of war is preconditioned on the solution to global economic and social problems that have proved unmanageable under present international organizations.

In fact, the general disorder prevailing now in various international activities informs us that we are on the threshold of a new era in the history of international relations. As I view this, we are going through a period of transition—from the *international state-system* to the emerging *world-system*. Whereas in the former, the nation-state is the prime mover and its inputs are predominant in shaping the system and determining its behavior, in the latter, it is the reverse effect of the world system that is beginning to prevail over its subsystems, adjusting them all to his own motion. No longer is the nation-state functioning as a self-contained social system whose decisions are determined inside; outside factors now increasingly participate in national decisions and governments are totally inept in coping with them.

Apparently, international relations and transnational activities are growing so interdependent, so systemic, that the world system acquires a drive of its own. And since such a drive has no conscious direction and rationality, it is imperative that a world authority control and direct its motion. It is in that historical perspective that I intend to deal with the issue of the new world institution.

II. The Historical Case

Throughout history, international organizations or institutions have always mirrored the contemporary world power structure and the respective stage in the evolution of international relations. The issue now involves chiefly the management of power in international society and the ways and means of securing the smooth functioning of relations among its political units. Here, one must proceed from the fact that in the international arena there is no center of authority and power like the state in national society. Over the ages, this vacuum has been filled by various schemes substituting for a central power and endeavoring to perform in the international sphere order-keeping and integrative functions—if possible, through international organizations.

Such a necessity became particularly critical with the formation of the modern international system in the historical period in which the expansion of capitalism coincided with the making of nation-states in Europe—a symbiosis that left its mark on the whole system and its behavior. The capitalist mode of production gave an impetus to the extention of trade and to the creation of the world market, overcoming the isolation of countries and continents typical of the Middle Ages and feudalism. Nation-states provided the basic political units that would constitute the structure of the system.

Although not an international organization, the Concert of Europe (1812-1914) was the first comprehensive scheme for coordinated management of world order. It was based on the premise that each of the four or five participating European powers could enforce common decisions in its own sphere of influence. A classical balance-of-power scheme, the Concert of Europe was hailed as the "golden age of diplomacy" stretching over a century of "international order and stability." Yet, if one looks deeper into the matter, one finds that this Golden Age witnessed the imperialist conquest of Africa, Asia, and Latin America that kept the colonial powers so busy overseas that Europe remained necessarily peaceful for a while.

The League of Nations, endowed with a Covenant, an Assembly, a Council, and a Permanent Secretariat, constituted a radical departure from previous arrangements. It was a real organization with a legal personality, a structure and agencies of its own. The League was a step forward in international society, responding to the growth of international activities after World War I. Its membership reached more than 30 nations, for the first time providing small nations with an opportunity to participate and be heard in an international forum. Yet, the League reflected the predominant position of Britain and France, allowing them to control the organization and to use it for their imperialist ends. Hence the Covenant did not specifically outlaw war—an expression of an epoch in which force was still considered the final arbiter of international conflict.

The United Nations is an organization much more democratic and universal in membership and more advanced in its principles. However, while most of the principles and purposes of the UN Charter reflect the new openings in world affairs after World War II, the mechanism of the governing structure of the UN bears the imprint of the power realities of 1945. The Big Five of the victorious coalition were given a privileged position as permanent members of the Security Council with a right to veto any resolution that did not suit their particular interests. The practical consequence has been that the UN is unable to take effective action whenever one of the great powers is directly or indirectly involved in a conflict. Thus, very few military outbreaks can be resolved by the UN, for we live in a world in which power is ubiquitous. What is more, as one author puts it: "In relations among the Great Powers, decisive for the maintenance of world peace, international organizations stand exposed to perpetual defeat."[1] The total impotence of the UN in halting the insane nuclear race is a case in point.

Since power relations are never static, the evolution of the UN has followed postwar shifts in the worldwide distribution of power. For the first 15 years, the United States, as the leader of both the Western world and of the Latin American nations, controlled more than two-thirds of the votes and could easily prevail over the group of socialist states in the General Assembly. By the end of the 1950s, a new political factor began to assert itself in the UN: as Latin American nations joined the Third World, the voting pattern within the UN shifted dramatically. In this respect, then, the UN has come a long way—from the "blunt truth that far more clearly than the League, the UN was essentially conceived as a club of great powers"[2] to the present state of affairs in which the great powers complain about the "tyranny of the majority."

From a strictly juridical angle, power simply does not exist in the UN. Article 2, paragraph 1 of the Charter solemnly proclaims: "The Organization is based on the principle of the sovereign equality of its members." The same principle is implicit in Article 18 which gives each member of the General Assembly one vote. To be sure, there are political analysts who take these provisions at face value as though world politics were guided by legal criteria and rules. Actually, international power relations are marked by great discrepancies, and the distribution of power in the real world merely points up the gap between juridical principles and power realities. Hence the theory of the "weighted vote" is essentially an attempt to eliminate this gap and to duplicate in the UN the power relations prevailing on the international scene.

The contrast between world law and world reality may well be the underlying reason why in recent years issues involving the great powers have been gradually removed from the UN. The major protagonists feel they are in a better position to promote their interests outside a setting that has become too egalitarian and democratic for power politics. Apparently, the nuclear stalemate outside the UN has been compounded by a political stalemate within the organization. On the one hand, to be effective, key UN decisions require the agreement of the great powers; on the other, neither the United States or the Soviet Union nor any combination of the major powers can any longer move the UN to act against the interests of the Third World.

This is a structural crisis that must be carefully examined. To begin with, while the drafters of the UN Charter recognized the state of international relations after World War II and decided to codify it as an international state-system functioning according to the principle of national sovereignty, their underlying assumption was that such a system could be run by an organization in which the great powers could act as coordinate managers of world order on the premise that each one would enforce UN decisions in its own sphere of influence. This basic constitutional assumption reflected the ideology of an epoch in which power realities were skillfully disguised in the liberal rhetoric of international law.

At the time of the Concert of Europe, four or five powers were able to apply such a scheme because there were actually very few sovereign states in the other continents: the colonial empires of the European powers practically covered the whole planet. Such a scheme, though gradually altered, continued to function in the years of the League and seemed still workable at the time when the UN was set up. It was not until the 1960s, when the political configuration of the world radically changed, that it became obvious that such a scheme could no longer work. Social revolutions in Eastern Europe, China and elsewhere had considerably enlarged the number of countries dropping from the capitalist system. The national liberation movement expanded rapidly: almost 20 Arab states appeared, while in Africa and Asia dozens of new states arose over the ruins of the French, British, Dutch and, lastly, Portuguese empires. Indeed, the number of sovereign political units around the world has multiplied to well above 150, and so has the membership of the United Nations.

And it is not only the map that looks different. Though the new states started with a backward economy and therefore have had to retain economic links with their former metropoles, the political activation of the mass population stimulated by independence, increasing education, and touches of modernization and industrialization, has resulted in a powerful thrust of national resurgence that has swept world politics. While it is true that this resurgent movement does not involve power in the traditional sense of the term, it has nevertheless produced a new international setting in which it is no longer possible for the major powers to run the world, or even to exercise effective control over their allies, partners or clients. Actually, we are witnessing the most decentralized international system in modern history.

Perhaps the greatest merit of the UN lies in its capacity of accommodating the decolonization struggle and the support it gave the new nations in achieving statehood. In fact, the UN has helped extend the state-system to all continents, making the system truly international. The UN Charter proved well drafted for this historical task while the organization displayed flexibility in adapting to its requirements.

Having accomplished this mission, the UN seems to have reached its historical limits. Apparently, the UN was neither conceived nor equipped to deal with the global problems that have come to the fore in recent years (the nuclear arms race and proliferation, development, world resources and the energy crisis, ecological deterioration, etc.), or with the economic and financial disorder trouble the world today. These problems and tasks actually belong to new historical conditions so different from those which produced the UN. The very principle of sovereignty that made the UN system work and enabled it to successfully carry out the internationalization of the state-system is now the single greatest barrier in coping with the problems now confronting the international community.

To sum up the historical case with the extension of the state-system all over the world, international organizations can no longer work as instruments of great powers, nor can international organizations substitute for a center of authority whilst their activity depends on the political will of 150 member-states with conflicting interests, objectives, and views. A new type of international institution must now be established having the authority to plan, to make decisions, and to enforce these decisions.

III. Why a World Authority?

Ours is a world in which changes on the international scene are so rapid that decisions made today must be necessarily conceived in terms of tomorrow. This is even more so when the issue is a world institution designed to accommodate world developments in the decades to come.

The world of the next decades will be a "small world" in which the per capita GNP of the developed nations will still be 12 times that of the developing nations, even if the growth rates set by the UN for the year 2000 were achieved. The population of the developing nations, however, will be five times that of the developed world. Anyone who puts these two sets of figures together must realize that the explosion will not be limited to population. We will live in a world in which it will take about two or three hours to fly from Caracas to New York or from Lagos to London, a world in which the Bolivian or the Pakistani will see on television every night how people live in the affluent societies, a world in which there will be no suburbia for the rich to insulate themselves from the poor.

While the insane nuclear arms race will continue generating its own perilous moments in the drive for first-strike capability and military superiority (whatever that means in overkill terms), the world of the next decades will live and sleep with a balance-of-terror in the hands of 20 or so ambitious nations armed with atomic weapons, not to mention terrorist groups using atomic bombs for blackmail or ransom. With the shift of the superpower confrontation to the battlefields of the Third World, the arms race will continue to be exported to Africa, Asia, and Latin America, infecting a growing number of developing nations with militarism, dominance appetites, and regional policeman roles. As the pillars of the old order crumble one after the other, the world of the coming decades will look like New York, Tokyo, or Paris, without traffic regulations and policemen.

The present dislocations in the world market and the recurring disruptions in the monetary system, compounded by the chaos of oil prices, are but signals of the pounded by the chaos of oil prices, are but signals of a long period of instability ahead for the world economy. We can thus expect an equally long period in world affairs that will involve great dangers of military adventurism and neofacism caused by the desperate attempts of finance and corporate capital to hold on to its challenged positions. It is the belief of this writer that the remaining two decades of this century may go down in history as its most critical and explosive period. For never before have so many social and political contradictions requiring structural changes converged in a world so small and so capable of destroying itself.

Surely, the United Nations is not equipped to deal with problems of such nature and magnitude. A decision-making system with 150 independent participants is in itself a prescription for ineffectiveness in dealing with global problems. A strong and effective world institution is *the only rational solution* to the kind of global problems confronting us today. What else could break the war system by halting the arms race and reversing its trends while planning and managing the conversion to a peace economy without serious disruptions? Twenty years of disarmament negotiations have resulted in a complete failure. Military expenditures have reached monstrous proportions while nations, starting with the great ones, feel less secure than ever.

Within present international arrangements, nothing can stop the escalation of the nuclear arms race, the most aberrant product of power politics. The nuclear arms race seems very little affected either by rational economic arguments or by moral standards; it remains untouched by the most terrifying prospects and is stronger even than man's instinct for self-preservation. To keep the war system going, even "peace agreements" like that of Camp David are supposedly buttressed by arming to the teeth the two partners—Egypt and Israel; so-called arms control treaties, like SALT II, are actually used as a springboard for a new escalation in armament expenditures.

Equally inefficient are the efforts by present international organizations to deal with development. Two "Development Decades" have elapsed under the UN's aegis, and the abysmal gap between the haves and the have-nots is growing wider. In the years since 1974, when the UN adopted the historic resolution on the establishment of a New International Economic Order, it has become all too clear that no significant headway will ever be possible without some sort of global planning and management designed to ensure that the transition toward a new order is not marred by disruptive competition and chaos for industrial nations and developing ones alike. Such global planning is inconceivable without a world authority.

Furthermore, even a partial agreement in North-South negotiations will come up against the issue of enforcement. *Who* will make sure that all the parties involved will observe the terms of the agreement? The real choice is between a world authority and the laws of the market, which systematically work in favor of the rich. As for the latter, global planning is also imperative if the industrial nations are ever to come out of their present economic and financial crises. Thus a world authority is a *must* for both.

In recent years, international UN conferences have brought to the fore the enormity of such world problems as the human habitat, population growth, transfer of science and technology, ecological deterioration and pollution, food, etc. They all point in the same direction: the need for global planning and management. To cite but one such problem, merely to build the physical infrastructure of the human habitat—houses, schools, hospitals, factories, new cities, etc.—required before the end of the century entails a construction job similar in scope to that accomplished since the Middle Ages. And what about the task of providing work for the 350 million able-bodied men and women currently underemployed or unemployed, the one billion or more new jobs that will be needed for children now being born?

Finally, while people are worried about the depletion of nonrenewable resources, the so-called renewable ones face more imminent dangers: the rapid degradation of the tropical rain forests, the advance of desertification, and an accelerating extinction of animal and plant wildlife. If these processes are not halted, we are bound to lose drastically in terms of health, habitat, and quality of life.

IV. The World System

I submit that neither the convergence in time of global problems, nor the commonality of their nature and scope are accidental. Although they seem to be products of a chaotic amalgamation of factors, processes and phenomena, there is a certain logic in their appearance, manifestations, and magnitude. I think they actually inform us about something fundamental taking place in the very system of international relations: the emergence of the world system.

Here I must point out that there are various approaches to studying the world system and the timing of its appearance. Immanuel Wallerstein, in a monumental work, relates it to the expansion of capitalism, starting with the fifteenth century, when the origins and early conditions of the world system, then exclusively European, appeared.[3] Other authors stress the role of great powers (starting with Portugal) in the formation of the world system since 1500. Although I agree with Wallerstein's focus on the role of capitalism in the formation of the world economy, I consider that political developments did not necessarily parallel the economic ones, as illustrated by the Absolutist State—the maker of modern nation-states in Europe. What followed was essentially a state-system, then exclusively European, extending only lately to all continents.

I suggest that the watershed in the creation of a global system encompassing the whole world and functioning with sufficient regularity to impose certain recognizable patterns of behavior on all its subsystems is primarily related to the scientific-technological revolution. It is this revolution that has made communication universal, information instantaneous, transportation supersonic, and modern weaponry planetary, and that has allowed for a global sphere of multilevel interdependencies to emerge and function with a unifying and integrating force. Therefore, I place the appearance of the world system at the middle of the twentieth century, when major breakthroughs in science started to be applied on a large enough scale to become consequential in world politics. Previously large sections of the world had remained isolated and practically unaffected by central events—even by the two world wars.

The important point is that 'world-system' is the conceptualization best suited to explain the new global problems that have arisen in recent decades. Certainly, development, ecological equilibrium, nuclear proliferation or the energy crisis cannot be dealt with adequately in the context of the "world system of the 1500s" or, for that matter, of the 1800s, for the very simple reason that they were not world problems then. And they were not problems then because there was no world system to account for their global scope.

As I mentioned earlier, what distinguishes the world system from the present international state-system is to be found in the relationship between the two levels of systemic motion—the national and the world level. The first level covers the nation-state as the basic political unit of the international system; the second takes the world-system and global dynamics as its starting point. To be sure, there is constant interaction between the two. But, whereas in the present international system, the nation-state is still the prime mover whose decisions and performances eventually produce the functioning principles and prevailing patterns of behavior, in the world-system, it is the reverse.

A typical effect of the world system upon nation-states is being felt in military policy. Since nuclear missile weapons are planetary both in destruction and delivery capability, nuclear policy acquires a global scope that transcends alliances and overrides all other considerations, including ideological ones. Globalism has led the US and the USSR to stubbornly preserve their monopoly of basic decisions on war and on nuclear strategic weapons. The two nuclear treaties (test-ban and non-proliferation) jointly drafted by American and Soviet experts, as well as SALT I and II, reflect this basic policy. China's advocacy of a strong Western

European defense is also inspired by the nuclear logic and the power game it regulates.

The global power rivalry, continuously fed by the arms race, makes for a war system with a drive of its own. This may well explain why the nuclear arms race goes on and on in spite of that fact that already, in the late 1960s, the arsenals of the superpowers were sufficient to destroy the world and kill everybody many times over. The overall effect of the world system is apparent in the active participation in the nuclear arms race of all great powers, irrespective of their domestic system, and in the tendency it generates in other ambitious nations—some of which are still in a pre-industrial stage—to go nuclear.

It is in international economic relations and activities that the world system is at its best in influencing nation-states. International trade has been converted from an exclusive club of the big exporting nations into a real world activity. The rate of growth of world exports is rising faster than the growth rate of either production or average GNP. Thus, national economies are increasingly dependent on foreign sources of raw materials and modern technology, and on foreign outlets for their products. The energy crisis highlighted the dependence of most powerful states on oil imports; indeed, interdependence is the law of the world.

The globalization process powered by modern technology is a basic feature of international economic relations. It is a factor so strong that it overpowers even ideological prejudices: joint ventures between socialist states and multinational corporations are cropping up every day. The current economic and financial disorder is truly global with all nations, including socialist ones, feeling its effect.

The attempt of the industrial states to plan their economic development (OECD Scenario for 1980) as well as the strategy set by the regular summit meetings of the seven rich have both ended in complete failure, proving once more that the industrial nations cannot overcome the crises by planning in a closed circuit. Equally self-defeating are the barriers raised by these countries against industrial goods of developing nations; thus, the very purchasing power of the latter for buying industrial equipment from the West is reduced. Only by global planning could the present crises be overcome. Gone are the days when economic policies of nations were decided inside; now even major industrial nations, such as Great Britain and Italy, have to develop their annual budget in accordance with the instructions of the International Monetary Fund. Outside factors are now integral to the major economic policies of all governments.

Briefly, in both the military and economic domains, *the world-system causes nation-states to make adaptive decisions that they would not make in response only to domestic wants.* The impact of the world-system upon its basic units, the nation-states, is thus felt in all major areas of foreign policy, and, as far as we can tell, the

9. PROBLEMS AND PROSPECTS FOR THE FUTURE

tendency of these external stimuli in determining the behavior of nations is going to grow.

V. A New System—A New Institution

Historically, the case for a world authority rests on the emergence of the world-system eroding the present international state-system. It logically follows that a new system of international relations requires an adequate institution to establish its corresponding world order and secure its smooth functioning during the long transition period from the old system to the new one. To be explicit in what we are talking about, by world order I mean a pattern of power relations among states capable of ensuring the functioning of various international activities according to a set of rules—written and unwritten.

Thus far, the discussion of a new international or world order has been dominated by moral, religious, ideological, and, lately, juridical and economic principles and values. Surely, none of these criteria should be overlooked since each provides some of the motivations underlying large-scale human actions so essential to such an undertaking. What is still lacking is conceptual clarity and scientific groundwork, particularly in bringing into focus the fulcrum of politics which is and remains decisive in settling the issue of world order.

A serious intellectual effort is required to fill this gap. Here are my suggestions regarding the direction of such research work and how to go about it.

1.   Since the issue involved is chiefly the management of power in international society, I submit that the first thing that must be worked out is the ways and means for the establishment of an international institution wielding power of its own. In practical terms, this means that a transfer of power—a partial and gradual one, to be sure—would have to take place from nation-states to the new institution. The transfer of power to the World Authority being assumed to be gradual, it follows that during the transition period world order will be maintained by a *duality of power*: the nation-state retaining most of its sovereign prerogatives and the World Authority exercising power in international affairs to the extent of its delegated authority and competence.

2.   The concept of World Authority is different from that of world government. The latter presupposes the dissolution of nation-states and the creation, instead, of a single governing body designed to run the whole world, whereas the World Authority requires the nation-state to be maintained with only a partial transfer of power to the new institution so as to enable it to operate effectively within its limited area of competence.

3.   It is assumed that the World Authority will be initially entrusted with two major tasks: *peace maintenance* with a view to enforcing general disarmament and eventually abolishing war, and the *restructuring of international economic relations* with a view to overcoming the present economic crisis and eliminating the glaring inequality between the developed and developing nations. Securing peace actually means breaking the war system by halting the arms race—its specific form of movement—and reversing its momentum. This also involved the gradual dismantling of military forces and organizations parallel with the establishment of a *world police force* and a *world tribunal*, which are needed to make sure that the decisions of the World Authority are enforced, to intervene whenever the law is violated, and for the peaceful settlement of disputes.

4.   The choice of government, of its economic, social and political system will remain the unalienable right of each nation. The World Authority will see to it that no foreign power interferes with such internal affairs of member-states. As the existence of a national police force does not prevent citizens from exercising their constitutional rights, so will the World Authority and police force not prevent nation-states from exercising their sovereignty in all spheres of domestic activity, nor will they be able to interfere with the struggle of exploited classes or oppressed minorities for a better society. Briefly, it is only the *use of force* in interstate relations that will fall within the competence of the World Authority.

5.   While we live at a time when nationalism is stronger than ever and nations are extremely sensitive about their sovereign rights, experience shows that nations are nevertheless prepared to transfer some of their prerogatives, provided they are impressed by the advantages deriving therefrom. Recognizing that it is in their best interests that foreign airplanes should fly over their territory and across their frontiers, national governments have accepted the establishment of the International Civil Aviation Organization, and have abided strictly by its rules. Also, such activities as weather control, shipping, control of contagious diseases, have been entrusted to international organizations wielding some power of their own. Therefore, a thorough study should be undertaken to examine the kind of requirements to be met before governments would be willing to hand over national prerogatives to the World Authority in such activities as peace maintenance and economic relations. Since we are dealing with nations having conflicting views, both as to objectives and as to methods, such a study must find compromise solutions to accommodate everyone.

6.   Confidence-building measures are essential in the case of a supranational institution, particularly on matters of national security, disarmament, and a world police force—where fears and suspicions reach their highest intensity.

7.   *Economics of a warless world:* the question of conversion to a peace economy must be reexamined in the context of the present economic crisis and strategy of development.

8.   *Politics of a warless world:* what kind of restrictions and pressures are necessary to apply to the nation-states, particularly great powers, in order to prevent

them from using force, and eventually to abolish war. Given the dynamics of power politics, how can the World Authority contain and control it?

9. *The law of a warless world:* a totally new legal framework must be formulated, keeping in mind the conceptual novelty of a supranational institution and allowing for a gradual process toward that goal. The new constitution must spell out clearly what kind of authority and power and over what substantive areas, will be entrusted to the World Authority; also what kind of safeguards will be necessary to prevent organs of the new institution from encroaching upon areas remaining under the authority of nation-states. Finally, the jurists will also have to examine the creation of a world tribunal to establish ways and means for settling disputes.

10. *The new institutions:* The World Authority with its enforcement agencies must be conceived and spelled out functionally in terms of membership, structure, organizations, distribution of power and representation, deliberative and executive bodies, secretariat, rules of procedure, etc. Here the authors will have to devise the new institutions in such a way as to allay the fears that the World Authority once constituted may abuse its powers and become a Frankenstein monster that will terrorize us while we are unable to control it. This issue is paramount in terms of political feasibility; for, unless we assure people that they need not fear abuses from the World Authority, the political will for establishing the institution is not likely to be forthcoming.

Equally important in this respect is to convey the feeling that in the organization of the World Authority there will be fair and equal opportunities for all nations, irrespective of size, power and wealth. Experience has implanted in the small and poor nations fear and suspicion against misuse and manipulation of international organizations by the powerful and rich nations. A fair system of representation and distribution of power should allay such fears.

In practical terms, the UN could be instrumental in the initiation phase of the new institution, providing the proper forum for discussion of its principles, organization and structure. What is more, the new institution will probably have to make use of the experienced staff and vast facilities of the UN, once the latter would cease to exist.

VI. Conclusion

Let me frankly admit that a world authority, however rational its establishment, and however persuasive its historical case, is far ahead of present political and ideological realities and, therefore, its very idea is bound to encounter formidable resistance. Paradoxically, those who need it most, fear it most.

In fact, the changes that require the setting up of such an institution have come so rapidly in international life—quicker than a generation's span of time—that political thought and practice have been left well behind. In no other domain is there a contrast so great between the speed of change and the nature of problems, on the one hand and the political institutions supposed to deal with them, on the other hand. And yet, horrendous problems are piling up threatening our jobs, the peace we cherish, the air we breathe, the cities we live in, the planes we fly in, and, in the last analysis, our very existence as human beings.

In a world divided by power, wealth and ideology, probably the most difficult assignment will be the building of a model for the World Authority equally attractive and reassuring for all nations. While citizens of great and developed nations should look at the World Authority as the safest way of avoiding a nuclear catastrophe, the citizens of the Third World should look at it as the best way of building a more democratic and equitable world order. As for the socialist nations, who are interested in both the maintenance of peace and the establishment of a more equitable economic order, surely 'peaceful coexistence,' however noble a principle, is still an "armed peace," and as such is no guarantee whatever against the outbreak of wars—not even among socialist nations themselves. It is only a world authority that can provide such a guarantee. For a Marxist, it should be clear enough that imperialism will never give up its privileged positions without resorting to the "biggest bang" at its disposal, nor will the advanced capitalist states willingly renounce their commanding positions on the world market. What could socialism mean on a radiated planet?

Apparently, with the emergence of the world-system, everybody must think anew and act anew.

Notes

1. Stanley Hoffmann, *Organisations Internationales et Pouvoir Politique des Etats* (Paris: Armand Colin, 1954), p. 412.
2. George Ball, "Slogans and Realities," *Foreign Affairs* **47**, 4, July 1969, p. 625.
3. Immanuel Wallerstein, *The Modern World-System* (New York: Academic Press, 1974), Vol. 1, Introduction.

Let the Old Order Die

Altaf Gauhar

Dr Ralf Dahrendorf used the phrase 'intellectual pause'[1] to explain how he was trying to understand the world all over again: 'Ten years ago I thought I knew what the main reforms were that were needed.' Now, he said, it would take him years of study and travel to make some sense of the world: the West was engaged in a reappraisal of its own fundamental values and if the politicians did not appear to be interested in such a reappraisal it was because 'The politicians are always late. They administer the past rather than define the future, and that is more true today than it has been for a very long time.'

In Beijing last May, Zhang Wenjen, a veteran Deputy Foreign Minister of the People's Republic of China, said in a private interview that the superpowers wanted nothing but power. Asked what they would do with power if there was no world, he replied: 'What is the world to them, if they don't have the power?' Supremacy was the only logic which governed superpower conduct: they were not concerned with what kind of a world it was, subservient or free, so long as it was their's.

A week later, in Rome, President Sandro Pertini told me his main worry was that the destiny of the people was controlled by those who could 'act independently of the will of the people.' A man of 84, Pertini has seen two world wars and three Italies—pre-fascist, fascist and post-fascist. He found little evidence that mankind had learnt anything from the two world wars. 'Mankind', he said, 'has always been at war—with intervals of peace.' Except that now the intervals of peace are getting shorter all the time.

Is the world order in a state of collapse? Is Yalta now a relic of the past and the international institutions which were devised to reflect the post-war power realities no longer capable of responding to the pressures of the present and the challenges of the future?

Stanley Hoffman's *Primacy or World Order* (New York, 1978) was published a year before the Soviet Union's troops moved into Afghanistan. Even then he was conscious of the stresses to which the international system was being subjected. He could see 'all the conditions for chaos, all the elements of disaster' and little chance of the gradual emergence out of 'the present cacophony' of the sense of obligation 'which would give to agreement on rules of the games greater solidity than is provided by their present foundations.' Such a sense could only come out of a single, world-wide ideology and since such an ideology was not on the horizon, 'the dampening of the ideology' might help to save the system. Hoffman identified two major factors of restraint which could save the world from regression: the desire to survive which, though not new, was important because 'for the first time it is directly connected to the performance of the international system, not merely in the matter of physical protection from violent annihilation, but also in that of starvation, pollution, and an end of vital resources'; and 'the common imperative of development—the race to welfare.' If it was not possible to have a central power, then we should at least strive to maintain 'effective international institutions', and if a social or political consensus on a broad range of values was not available the system might at least develop 'a dense web of ties signifying the prevalence of mixed interests over adversary relationships and a code of behaviour corresponding to a minimum of common values.'

Whatever bonds of mixed interests may have existed in 1978 had disintegrated by the end of 1979. Hoffman's 'incomplete tapestry' of the world is today totally unravelled.

Harold H Saunders, sees the United States as the defender of a 'disintegrating status quo'[2], but he does not see the need for change. Instead, he recommends that the status quo (which he calls a new security system) should be preserved by strengthening key countries (meaning those who support the status quo) against external attack or internal subversion.

The international system survived the adventures of the cold war and the misadventures of detente. The thaw in the cold war started in the early 1960s when voices of moderation and restraint began to assert themselves in the corridors of power. Despite several flashpoints, a global conflagration was avoided, primarily because the core area of superpower interests was clearly defined, while the periphery remained relatively restricted and dormant. The superpowers were able to protect their vital interests in the core area and did not allow the tensions in the periphery to push them over the brink.

It is instructive to remember that during the 1956 Suez crisis the US and the USSR voted together in the Security Council to demand the withdrawal of Israeli troops, despite the fact that the Israelis had invaded Egyptian territory under a prior arrangement with Britain and France. This was also the time when the Soviet Union was engaged in suppressing a rebellion in Hungary. Despite US support for Israel and her partnership with Britain and France, the United States

---

1. 'North South Dialogue', *Third World Quarterly* 2(1) 1980, pp 1-13.

2. *The Middle East Problem in the 1980s,* Washington DC: American Enterprise Institute, 1981.

sided with the Soviet Union to contain a situation which could have resulted in a major war.

The process of detente started around 1955 when President Eisenhower met the Soviet Union's leaders at Geneva in July 1955 and told them that 'We have come to find a basis for accommodation which will make life safer and happier, not only for the nations we represent but for the people elsewhere.' The cold war period finally came to a close with the Cuban missile crisis in 1962 when President Kennedy told Kruschev that if he was 'prepared to discuss a detente affecting NATO and the Warsaw Pact, we are quite prepared to consider with our allies any useful proposals.' Then followed the Hot-Line Agreement between the superpowers in 1963; an Accidents Measures Agreement to improve safeguards against accidental or unauthorised use of nuclear weapons in 1971; a Prevention of Nuclear War Agreement in 1973; the Partial Test Ban Treaty in 1963, followed by the Threshold Test Ban Treaty in 1974 and the Peaceful Nuclear Explosions Treaty in 1976. SALT I was ratified in 1972 and SALT II was negotiated in 1979. In retrospect, the years 1972 and 1973 appear as the apogee of detente.

According to Henry Kissinger (*Years of Upheaval*, London, 1982) both the US and the USSR 'were gambling on certain trends' when they opted for detente. During his second visit to Beijing in February 1973, he told the Chinese Premier, Zhou Enlai: 'The Soviet Union believes that it can demoralise Western Europe and paralyse us. We believe . . . that through this policy we are gaining the freedom of manoeuvre we need to resist in those places which are the most likely points of attack or pressure.'

Kissinger classifies the agreements negotiated by the US with the USSR during this period into three categories: (a) those of particular interest to the US; (b) those of mutual and general interest, *eg* limitation of strategic arms; and (c) those of technical interest but of no major political significance, *eg* scientific and cultural exchanges and trade.

The early years of detente created certain misapprehensions in the Western Alliance. The Western leaders were all for coexistence but too close an understanding between the two superpowers could result in a 'super Yalta' and another world carve-up. The Americans, on their side, wanted 'to discourage the Europeans from unilateral initiatives to Moscow.' The Europeans should know 'that in any competition for better relations with Moscow, America had the stronger hand.' Kissinger anxiously tries to explain what detente was and what it was not. This anxiety is understandable for he was the one attacked for taking the Americans to a wife-swapping party from which they had returned home alone. He succeeds only in establishing that 'the American strategy of detente . . . was never an end in itself.' The policy sometime served to create conditions of coexistence, but most of the time it was pursued as a necessity for mastering 'self-destructive domestic con-

vulsions'. Kissinger lists four major achievements of detente: (1) the US succeeded, through better relations with the USSR (and China), to isolate Hanoi. 'In 1972 Moscow acquiesced in the mining of North Vietnamese harbours and the bombing of Hanoi and Haiphong.'; (2) the US succeeded in compelling Hanoi to settle 'for terms it contemptuously rejected for years.'; (3) in Europe, 'the knowledge that the Americans, too, could talk to the Russians reined in the temptation to blame tensions on the United States and to seek safety in quasineutralism.'; and (4) it helped the United States 'to bring about a diplomatic revolution in the Middle East'. The reference is to the expulsion of Soviet troops from Egypt which, according to Kissinger, was the price the Soviet Union paid for detente.

The first is unsupported by any evidence except Kissinger's word; the second will find few buyers; the third is a personal statement of dubious value, and the fourth, though partially correct, is a simplification. But, whatever the value of these statements, detente was seen as an arrangement of mutual benefit.

As the process of detente developed, a certain lack of cohesion and loss of direction became noticeable in the Atlantic community. At one point in his narrative Kissinger complains, 'a whole generation had grown up who knew nothing of the perils of the 1940s that had produced the Alliance or of the vision of man that had shaped their political institutions' (p 136). He can see that the post-war institutions no longer command the allegiance of the early years. In a similar vein, Richard Nixon, under criticism from the French, said in 1973: 'There must be some underlying philosophy that animates all of us. Otherwise those shrewd and determined men in the Kremlin will eat us one by one. They cannot digest us together but they can pick at us one by one. That is why it is so important that we maintain the Atlantic community . . .' (p 176).

The election of Ronald Reagan as President of the United States officially marked the end of detente. SALT II, which President Carter failed to refer to the Senate for ratification, was reopened and the arms reduction talks were all but forgotten. The US expressed its determination to develop a whole range of nuclear weapons to eliminate what was called 'Soviet superiority'.

Today the popular assumption is that with the end of detente the world has reverted to the cold war era. This assumption is highly questionable because, as has been indicated above, the principal feature of the cold war period was the existence of a fairly well-defined core area of superpower interests, in which no transgression was attempted, and a hemmed-in and dormant periphery where the superpowers could, by mutual arrangement, contain tensions and conflicts. Also, the lines were clearly drawn and there was unanimity within the Atlantic Community and the Warsaw Pact. This unanimity was the result of common perceptions and common approaches to world problems. Now the core area has shrunk and the periphery is becoming enlarged and highly activated. In the 1950s and 1960s it was not possible for a superpower to grab strategic advantage or territory. Now 'grab' has become the rule so long as you can get away with it.

The unanimity within the two camps is badly fractured. Events in Poland have shown the profound tensions in the Warsaw Pact. The Atlantic Alliance is faced with growing contradictions in the fields of defence, trade and in relations with the Third World.

Lawrence Freedman, writing in *International Affairs* (Summer 1982), discusses the Atlantic crisis. He does not foresee the Community heading toward a breakup: 'The real risk may be of a drifting apart, fuelled largely by indifference and introspection, rather than some dramatic and decisive breach in the Alliance bond.' It is also becoming increasingly clear 'that in any given trouble-spot it is not likely that American and European interests will directly coincide'. And this absence of coincidence of interests has robbed the Alliance of much of its original purpose.

The present period is neither one of cold war leading toward a thaw, nor one of detente leading towards peace. It is a period in which the superpowers have allowed themselves to get trapped into a state of immobility like two muscle-bound giants. This super-power immobility has been repeatedly demonstrated in the last three years. The Soviet Union grabbed Afghanistan but could not swallow it, while the US made a great deal of noise but took no retaliatory action; now the two giants are caught in a stalemate where their policies are determined by the events on the ground. The superpowers watched like dazed bystanders as the Iranian Revolution unfolded—not only during the hostage crisis but even when Iraq invaded Iran—and now when Iran has marched into Iraqi territory, neither side made any move to contain or resolve the conflict in a meaningful manner. In the Falkland Islands, the United States found that it could not deter the Argentinian junta from invading the islands, despite growing political understanding between the United States and Argentina. When the British retaliated by despatching a task force to recapture the Falklands, the Americans found they could not influence the British decision, despite identity of political positions on most international matters.

But the most dramatic instance of superpower immobility is Israel's June 6 invasion of the Lebanon. For weeks Israel held the world and the world powers a hostage to terror. What the Nazis did during the Second World War remained unknown for a long time but the Beirut holocaust is flashed across the globe hour after hour, day after day, night after night. Yet the superpowers have been unable to make an effective move to put an end to this barbarism.

The United States failed to intervene, leaving everyone to wonder whether Israel was acting with US support or in defiance of US policy. The USSR failed to act because they saw no role for themselves.

This superpower immobility is reflected in the bewilderment and inability of the United Nations to put a stop to the war in the Lebanon or to bring about a withdrawal of forces from that hapless country. The Security Council is a mirror of the superpowers' failure to agree on any initiative which could bring the crisis to an end.

It is not only the United Nations which appear to have been affected by this superpower immobility—other international institutions are similarly affected.

The Islamic Conference comprising 44 member-states, could not be convened because the minimum number of states required for the quorum was not available. What was a matter of the highest importance and urgency failed even to attract the attention of the membership, not because they were unconcerned, but because they had no indication from the superpowers how to act. They waited for some signal, none was forthcoming. The Arab League could not meet because there were not enough member-states ready to sit together and consider what action should be taken to counter the Israeli aggression. The Organisation of African Unity which was to meet in Tripoli in early August failed because of the lack of a quorum. But was that the reason? There were suggestions that the Americans exercised great pressure through their friends to prevent the required number of Heads of State going to Tripoli. Whatever the reason, none of these organisations could even meet to discuss the situation arising out of the Israeli invasion of the Lebanon. The superpowers, unable to act themselves, would not allow anyone else to act. Here was a policy of inaction compounded by a policy of pre-emption.

Statesmen and scholars are not afraid to admit that there is something fundamentally wrong with the present international system: they talk of the need for reappraisal, they discuss the imperatives of survival and development, they even acknowledge that the status quo is disintegrating, but they will not recognise the obvious—that the world order has been pulled down and cannot be rebuilt on old foundations. We should recognise the new realities of power and submit to the demands of the masses to build a new world order—based on equality and justice, with every nation having the right and capability to live in peace without having to submit to internal or external social, economic or political domination. Without such a recognition, the superpowers will remain indefinitely trapped in a moment of immobility, allowing neither the old order to die nor the new to be born.

U.S. Nuclear Strategy and World Order Reform

An Interview with Louis René Beres

Louis René Beres is Professor of Political Science at Purdue University. He received his Ph.D. from Princeton University (Politics, 1971) and is the author of numerous books, monographs and articles on international relations, international law, and world order studies. His recent writings on nuclear strategy and nuclear war include: *Nuclear Strategy and World Order: The U.S. Imperative* (a new WOMP Working Paper); *Apocalypse: Nuclear Catastrophe in World Politics* (University of Chicago Press, 1980); *Terrorism and Global Security: The Nuclear Threat* (Westview Press, 1979) and the just completed *Mimicking Sisyphus: America's "Countervailing" Nuclear Strategy*. His other books include *People, States and World Order* (F.E. Peacock, 1981); *Reordering the Planet: Constructing Alternative World Futures* (Allyn and Bacon, 1974); and *Planning Alternative World Futures: Values, Methods, and Models* (Praeger, 1975).

In the following interview, Professor Beres discusses current U.S. nuclear strategy and different paths to nuclear war avoidance and world order reform.

In recent years, you have written widely on various aspects of the nuclear arms race and the growing danger of nuclear war. Your most recent work has focused on U.S. nuclear strategy. In what ways has current U.S. nuclear strategy contributed to the problem?

► Current U.S. nuclear strategy is enormously dangerous and misconceived. In rejecting minimum deterrence, it has produced a "counterforce syndrome" that gives unprecedented legitimacy to the idea of nuclear warfighting. Coupled with preparations for "victory" in a nuclear war, this strategy actually makes nuclear war much more likely.

At a time when myriad medical and scientific analyses point to the conclusion that nuclear war can never be tolerated, the Reagan Administration counsels a policy based on preparations for "rational" nuclear warfare. At a time when the Soviet Union reiterates its continuing rejection of the idea of "limited nuclear war," U.S. leaders codify a nuclear targeting policy that accepts such an idea as a critical starting point. At a time when the Commander-in-Chief of the U.S. Strategic Air Command openly doubts the prospects of launching an effective "countervailing" attack in the wake of a Soviet first-strike, the Reagan Administration reaffirms a "selective" nuclear strategy that is designed to fulfill military tasks at a level far exceeding the requirements of "assured destruction." And at a time when the need for collaborative de-escalation of the arms race must override all other considerations, the administration makes plans to deploy new strategic weapons with hard-target kill capabilities, a new generation of intermediate-range ballistic missiles that would threaten the Soviet homeland itself, and the neutron bomb.

If these plans were not enough to increase instability, President Reagan has gone ahead with the MX in a fashion that will have no bearing on the alleged problem of ICBM vulnerability. Taken together with planned programs for ballistic missile defense (BMD), civil defense, C³I (Command, Control, Communications and Intelligence) improvements, and anti-satellite weapons, the MX decision (with the resurrection of "linkage") is bound to make the Soviets increasingly fearful of a U.S. first-strike. Naturally, this means that the Reagan nuclear strategy *contributes* to the prospect of Soviet preemption.

How do you respond to those strategic experts who argue that these new weapons are needed to make deterrence more credible?

► To meet our deterrence objectives, we need to ensure that our strategic forces are sufficiently invulnerable and penetration-capable to assuredly destroy an aggressor after riding-out a first-strike attack. We do *not* need to take steps to threaten the other side's retaliatory forces in a manner that is exceedingly provocative. With this in mind, all of the administration's ongoing "improvements" in U.S. nuclear forces will have the effect of *undermining* this country's deterrence posture. This is the case because they will add nothing to the invulnerability/penetration capability requirements while they *will* heighten Soviet incentives to strike first.

Under President Reagan, this country's search for a "margin of safety" in strategic capability vis-a-vis the Soviet Union is making the world much less safe. After all, this search has now gone far beyond the reasonable requirements of reduced vulnerability and minimum deterrence to an institutionalization of unrestrained nuclear competition. Based on an exaggerated expectation of Soviet intentions, it has led to the expression of all the poison and impotence of U.S. foreign policy in the post-war period. In its drowning of any remaining hopes for long-term cooperative security with the Soviet Union, it offers a routinization of humancide that may ultimately project Armageddon from imagination to reality.

The Reagan administration's argument seems to be that the Soviet Union has developed a first-strike capability and that the U.S. must match them to keep the Soviets from gaining the upper hand in any conflict situation?

► Supporters of the MX counterforce targeting qualities argue that there is no reason to make such Soviet targets safe from U.S. ICBM's when comparable targets in this country are at risk from Soviet ICBM's. But this argument is based entirely on the confusion of survivability and targeting objectives, and substitutes "monkey - see - monkey - do" logic for a well-reasoned de-escalation of strategic competition. It may be true that Soviet modernization has placed U.S. ICBMs at some risk—although there is disagreement about this. But it is not true, even if our "worst case" assumptions are correct, that our assured destruction capability is in jeopardy or that U.S. security is best served by acting in an equally provocative or more provocative manner.

Curiously, nothing in our current nuclear strategy suggests a plausible relationship between nuclear war and politics. Why, exactly, are the Soviets believed to be getting ready to "fight and win" a nuclear war with the United States? What conceivable post-war prospect can be associated with alleged Soviet plans for a first-strike against the

"U.S. Nuclear Strategy and World Order Reform," an interview with Louis René Beres, *Macroscope,* No. 11, Spring 1982.

261

United States? Why should the Soviets be expected to disregard Clausewitz's principle that war should always be conducted with a view to sustaining the overriding "political object"?

The dangers of assessing Soviet nuclear intentions *in vacuo* are considerable. By assuming that their *Staatspolitik* offers no homage to plausible relationships between nuclear war and national political goals, our own nuclear policy creates a bewildering expectation of first-strike scenarios that in turn produces a staggering array of provocative tactics and deployments. The net effect of such United States strategic thinking is a heightened prospect of escalation and irrevocable collision.

The reasonableness of a second-strike counterforce strategy (i.e., America's current nuclear strategy) is contingent upon the expectation that a Soviet first-strike would be limited. This is the case because if the Soviet first-strike were unlimited, this country's retaliation would hit only empty silos. Yet, there is no reason why the Soviets would ever choose to launch a limited first strike against the United States. It follows that our current search for increasing hard-target kill capabilities may be geared to achieving a first-strike capability against the Soviets.

In response, of course, the administration argues that the Soviets have a refiring and reconstitution capability with their missiles and that even an unlimited first-strike would take place in several successive stages. Hence, United States counterforce-targeted warheads, used in retaliation, would not necessarily hit only empty silos. They would also hit silos that might otherwise spawn weapons to enlarge the damage of the Soviet first-strike.

Even here, however, the administration argument is devoid of intellect and understanding. Most obviously problematic, this argument is oriented entirely to issues of nuclear war *fighting*. Accepting the likely prospect of a nuclear war and the probable failure of nuclear deterrence, it concerns itself (in conjunction with plans for multi-layer ballistic defense, air defense, and civil defense) exclusively with *intra-war* damage limitation. Yet, there would be very little of the United States left to protect after the first round of Soviet attacks had been absorbed (we must remember, in this connection, that we don't even target SLBMs). And the countervailing strategy makes such attacks more likely in the first place by undermining stable deterrence (i.e. by signaling U.S. first-strike intentions). Looked at in cost-benefit terms, therefore, it is abundantly clear that the alleged damage-limitation benefits that would accrue to the United States from its countervailing strategy during a nuclear war are greatly outweighed by that strategy's deterrence-undermining costs.

Finally, I must mention that current U.S. efforts for nuclear force "improvements" derive from an assumed need to be able to fight a nuclear war to victory. But why should this be correct? Is there any reason to suppose that the Soviets can be deterred effectively only by the prospect of all-out nuclear war? And even if there were such a reason, don't the Soviets (given their ideas about the implausibility of limited nuclear war) already calculate on the basis of total nuclear effort on both sides? The only consequence of the administration's new emphasis on nuclear warfighting potential as essential to deterrence is heightened Soviet insecurity concerning U.S. first-strike intentions. Moreover, the shift to an increasingly provocative configuration of counterforce targeting is apt to further *erode* our deterrence posture, since it is clear that a U.S. strategic second-strike against hard targets would produce substantially less damage to the Soviet Union than would extensive countervalue attacks.

The Reagan Administration's thinking on this issue, then, is a significant departure.

▶ Yes. In fact, the idea that the concept of "victory" has no place in a nuclear war is as old as the nuclear age. Yet, the administration's policies display no understanding of this idea. Even before the nuclear age, philosophers and military strategists probed the idea of victory with far greater sensitivity and prescience. Machiavelli, for example, recognized the principle of an "economy of violence" which distinguishes between creativity and destruction. Lacking Machiavelli's more insightful brand of *Realpolitik*, the administration is unable to grasp the difference between violence and power. This is the case, incidentally, not only in terms of nuclear strategy, but also in terms of our nation's increasingly insipid and simplistic approach to insurgency and human rights.

Still another problem with the idea of "victory" in a nuclear war is the arbitrariness or unpredictibility intrinsic to all violence. Contrary to the anesthetized expectations of strategic "thinkers" who anticipate near-perfect symmetry between human behavior and their own rarified strategic plans, violence harbors within itself an ineradicable element of the unexpected. Entangled in metaphors and false assumptions, and unable to cope with the intellectually-demanding problems of synergy, the president and his strategic mythmakers display a singular failure to understand the non-rational springs of action and feeling, and an indefensible degree of faith in game-theoretic systems of rational explanation. If only our leaders could learn to appreciate how little humankind can control amidst the disorderly multitude of factors involved in war. If

only they could learn to understand what presumptuous hazards are associated with a strategy that seeks to impose order on what must inevitably be a heightened form of chaos.

You mentioned that the Soviets have rejected the idea of "limited nuclear war." Yet, there has been a lot of talk about it and its place in U.S. nuclear strategy. Is there any reason to believe a nuclear war can be kept limited?

▶ As we have already seen, the United States now labors for security by founding its nuclear strategy upon an incomprehensible set of assumptions. Among these assumptions none is more dangerous or indefensible than the idea of a limited nuclear war. Curiously, the Soviets have never shared our view of controlled nuclear conflict—an asymmetry in strategic doctrine that could give rise to very dangerous U.S. moves. What is developing in Washington today is a counterforce doctrine that understates the effects of limited nuclear war while it ignores the antecedent fact that such a war makes no military sense.

Once the nuclear "firebreak" has been crossed, it is most unlikely that conflict could remain limited. Ironically, this point was accepted by Henry Kissinger when, in 1965 he wrote: "No one knows how governments or people will react to a nuclear explosion under conditions where both sides possess vast arsenals."

While the prudent course for the United States would be to assume that any onset of a nuclear exchange must be avoided lest it become total, current U.S. nuclear strategy underscores counterforce targeting and its corollary recognition of limited nuclear warfighting. Although it is clear that once a nuclear exchange had begun it would be impossible to verify yields, sizes, numbers, and types of nuclear weapons employed, current policy reaffirms the notion of limited exchanges conducted in deliberate and controlled fashion.

There are also some ironies involved. While U.S. nuclear strategy is premised on the plausibility of limited nuclear war, it also assumes that the Soviet Union is preparing to "fight and win" a nuclear war. Clearly, these two central assumptions of American nuclear strategy are at odds with one another. The strategy contradicts itself.

Another irony lies in the fact that the unreasonableness of limited nuclear war has been articulated not only by major Soviet military planners, but also by Professor Richard Pipes, one of the Reagan Administration's own strategic mythmakers. In the fashion of Soviet General Mikhail A. Milshtein and General-Major R. Simonyan, Richard Pipes has derided the idea of a limited nuclear war. "In the Soviet view," wrote Pipes in his now famous *Commentary* piece ("Why the Soviet Union Thinks

It Could Fight and Win a Nuclear War"), "a nuclear war would be total . . . Limited nuclear war . . and all the other refinements of U.S. strategic doctrine find no place in its Soviet counterpart. . . ,"

Aren't many of the risks you mentioned in current nuclear strategy also inherent in minimum deterrence?
► Yes, even a return to "minimum deterrence" would represent a continuation of grave danger. *Any* system based upon the threat of nuclear retaliation is fundamentally unstable. At one time or another, in one way or another, the manifestly catastrophic possibilities that now lie latent in nuclear weapons are almost certain to occur, either by design or by accident, by misinformation or miscalculation, by lapse from national decision or by unauthorized decision. The encouragement of a "counterforce syndrome" by the United States, however, is making a dangerous system even more dangerous.

What do you see as necessary for bringing this growing nuclear danger under control?
► There is a story by Jorge Luis Borges in which a condemned man, having noticed that expectations never coincide with reality, ceaselessly imagines the circumstances of his own death. Since they have thus become expectations, the man reasons, they can never become reality. Understood in terms of the overriding imperative to prevent nuclear war, this story points to the need for further confrontations with the imagery of extinction. Only by trying to understand and imagine the full import and likelihood of a nuclear war (and there is, already, an enormous literature on what would be involved) can we begin to take steps back to a durable peace. To do otherwise would be to accept the role of actors in a Greek tragedy who have lost command of their destinies, and who have foresaken the hope that human intervention can still be purposeful. In this connection, the motto for the Enlightenment, *sapere aude!*, dare to know!, suggested by Immanuel Kant, acquires a special meaning in the late twentieth century study of nuclear war. Just as repression of the fear of death by individuals can occasion activities that impair the forces of self-preservation, so we can impair our prospects for preventing nuclear war by insulating ourselves from reasonable fears of collective disintegration.

But isn't there the danger that the public is being prepared for nuclear war with routine discussions of civil defense, limited nuclear war, etc.?
► The growing prospect of nuclear war is tied very closely to the language that has been adopted by strategic mythmakers. Such euphemisms as "crisis relocation," "limited nuclear war," "countervalue"

We must come to understand that the growing number of formulations of livable post-apocalypse worlds are both nonsense and dangerous.

and "counterforce" strategies and "enhanced radiation warfare" are insidious to the cause of peace because they tend to make the currency of nuclear warfighting valid coin. Just as the barbarisms of the Nazis were made possible through such linguistic disguises as "final solution," "resettlement," "special treatment," and "selections," so do the euphemisms of the nuclear age make nuclear war more likely. To counter the current euphemisms that may etherize an unwitting humanity into accepting nuclear war, humankind must come to understand how much it has already lost in its own gibberish.

We must also come to understand that the growing number of formulations of livable post-apocalypse worlds are both nonsense and dangerous. This is the case because they interfere with the essential task of cultivating "end-of-the-world" imagery—imagery that must precede a durable peace. Without a fuller awareness of the effects of nuclear war, we will continue to stand outside the arena of mortality, unable to picture ourselves as victims.

Fortunately, the Administration's loose rhetoric about nuclear war has had quite the opposite effect and has prompted great public concern. The need to avoid nuclear war, only a few years ago a marginal tic of consciousness, is now the basis for a growing movement. Of course, heightened *awareness* is only the first step to preventing what the physicians now call "the final epidemic." Once such awareness has been generated, it is up to us to encourage the establishment of a new nuclear regime—one based upon such immediate measures as a return to minimum deterrence, agreement on a no-first-use pledge, a nuclear weapons "freeze," a comprehensive test ban, and additional nuclear weapon free zones. Each of these measures is described at some length in my WOMP working paper and in my forthcoming book, *Mimicking Sisyphus*. What I must stress here is that the essential arena of world reform must be *intra*national, with a special responsibility falling upon the United States to accept vital de-escalatory obligations. This means a rapid and far-reaching disengagement from developing patterns of counterforce targeting and preparations for nuclear warfighting.

These are mostly short term goals. As you have pointed out, we cannot expect nuclear deterrence to work forever. What

type of long-range changes should we be exploring?
► Without necessarily seeking fundamental changes in the prevailing state-centric structure of global authority, the two superpowers must learn to associate their own security from nuclear war with a more farreaching search for worldwide stability and equity. To prevent nuclear war between the superpowers, the prescribed nuclear regime must be augmented by a new awareness of the "connectedness" of states.

Ultimately the chances for a successful detachment from strategic arms competition will depend upon the specific steps needed to underscore the total disutility of a nuclear threat system. Implementation of these steps will require an early world summit of leaders from both rich and poor states to deal with international development and other pressing security issues. And these steps will depend upon a prior understanding, by the superpowers, that their own security interests are inevitably congruent with the security interests of the world as a whole. The balance of power between the Soviet Union and the United States can never be more stable than the balance of power in the whole of international society.

To prevent nuclear war that might occur through proliferation requires a nuclear regime that extends the principles of superpower war avoidance to the rest of international society. The centerpiece of this universal regime must be the cosmopolitan understanding that all states, like all people, form one essential body and one true community. Such an understanding, that a latent oneness lies buried beneath the manifold divisions of our fractionated world, need not be based on the mythical attractions of universal brotherhood and mutual concern. Instead, it must be based on the idea that individual states, however much they may dislike each other, are tied together in the struggle for survival.

Ultimately, then, what we should seek are more than the customary restraints offered by institutional and juridical modifications. Although such modifications are essential, they must be surrounded by a new field of consciousness—one that flows from a common concern for the human species and from the undimmed communion of individual states with the entire system of states.

Living at this juncture between world order and global disintegration, states must slough off the shackles of outmoded forms of self-interest. With the explosion of the myth of realism, the global society of states could begin to come together in a renewed understanding of the connection between survival and relatedness.

In your book *People, States and World*

263

Order you explore two broad paths to world order: what you call institutional and behavioral. Many of your proposals here stress the behavioral path to world order reform. Why?

► As I point out in my book, there are essentially two basic paths to the conceptualization of alternative world futures: institutional and behavioral. The first path focuses on improved norms and procedures for global regulation, while the second path emphasizes the transformation of human and state conduct in world affairs. The first path has a long history in the search for a more harmonious configuration of planetary life, either through recommendations for reforming international law within the existing decentralized system of international relations, or through recommendations for the replacement of balance of power world politics with some form of central world government. The second path, which emphasizes the need for alterations of individual and national behavior, has a much shorter history.

While there is much to be said on behalf of institutional paths to world order reform (they are, to be sure, specific, precise, and relatively unambiguous), the time is at hand to *augment* these paths with attention to behavioral paths. These behavioral paths of transformation might be examined at the level of individual human beings and at the level of states. *Taken together,* the institutional and behavioral paths to world order reform can define the modus operandi of a greatly improved strategy of global transformation.

For example, students of world order reform may now begin to consider modifying the characteristic ways in which human beings structure their interactions with each other. The principal theme of such consideration must be maximal individual development balanced by the demands of interpersonal harmony. While a continuing antagonism seems to exist between the search for personal progress and the requirements of social accord, it needn't be an irremediable sort of antagonism. We might explore the desirability and the feasibility of certain compromise "trade-offs" between these competing claims and begin to set forth the basic behavioral underpinnings of a new world order.

Paradoxically then, a better system of world order must rest upon both personal development and on the willing renunciation of certain features of such development. To assist in binding this "partnership," humankind must renew its awareness of "oneness" or "connectedness." Each person's future is tied intimately to the whole. All people are linked to their fellows and to the larger universe of which they are a part. There are no unrelated beings.

These holistic and cosmopolitan ideas seem rather novel to most people, even those engaged in world order studies. Is there a developed body of thought to which we can refer?

► Actually, the tradition of human unity and cosmopolis has a long and persuasive history. We know that the great Roman stoic, Marcus Aurelius, understood the universe as one living being with one substance and all people as actors within a web of single texture. By the Middle Ages, the idea of universality had fused with the idea of a *respublica Christiana,* a Christian Commonwealth, and Thomas, John of Salisbury and Dante were contemplating Europe as a unified Christian community. This whole universe was tidy and orderly. At its center lay the earth, at once both a mere part of creation and a single, unified whole unto itself. Such a conception of human oneness ultimately set the stage for the cosmopolitanism of the Enlightenment.

Recently, the writings of Pierre Teilhard de Chardin appear in this tradition. As he has stated in *The Phenomenon of Man,* "Each element of the cosmos is positively woven from all the other . . . " There is no way in which the network of cosmic matter can be sliced up into distinct, isolable units.

With respect to the potential evolutionary future and prospects of the human race, we are born into a world of inconscience. But we are capable of an upward development of consciousness and an ascent into reaches wherein personal growth is easily harmonized with the good of the whole. To unloose this capability we must appreciate that a oneness lies hidden beneath the diversities of a seemingly fractionated world. People are cemented to each other not by haphazard aggregation, but by the certainty of their basic likeness and by their increasing interdependence.

You are currently working on a book tentatively entitled the *Principles of World Order Design.* How does this book relate to other work that you and others have done on world order modeling?

► As we have already seen, scholars must begin to respond to humankind's growing incapacity for biological and and cultural adaptation with "blueprints" for a new global community. Yet, it is not widely understood that such blueprints, if they are to be genuinely promising, require an expanded awareness of world order design principles. With this in mind, my current efforts are geared to answering the question: "How should 'preferred world' models be designed?"

In confronting this question, I have begun to try to answer a number of subsidiary questions. For example: What philosophical, epistemological and methodological issues need to be considered before the trajectory of our collective decline can be reversed? What problems of normativity, conceptualization, hypothesis formation, modeling and analysis need to be grappled with before we can move toward creative planetary renewal? What are the ethical and moral elements of the world order design process that will augment systematic inquiry with a concern for dignity or *humanitas*?

As you know, my earlier writings have considered these questions at the level of *utility.* That is, they have responded to the antecedent issues of design with particular prescriptions for "doing world order." What these writings have not yet considered—and what I am now considering in *Principles of World Order Design*—are the specific connections between world order design and the refined insights of philosophic/epistemologic investigations. Since the adequacy of any plan for world order reform depends upon an understanding of these connections, *Principles of World Order Design* seeks to contribute to both the stature of world order studies as a disciplined field of inquiry and to the prospects for peace, social justice, economic well-being and ecological balance.

Now, perhaps I should be more specific. My book links the prospects for a new world politics to an extensive and intensive awareness of the nature and function of conceptualization, the heterogeneity of world order values, approaches to world order analysis, intellectual operations, alternate modes of inference, analytic tools, and multiple meanings of theory. Here, special attention has been directed to the ideas and insights of such thinkers as Carl Hempel, Thomas Kuhn, Karl Popper, Morris Cohen, Hannah Arendt, Arthur Koestler, and Michael Polanyi.

My book also ties the actualization of new forms of world politics to different ways of "knowing," including not only the customary modalities of social science, but also religion, myth and certain forms of mysticism. Here, particular attention is being paid to the ideas and insights of such figures as Doris Lessing, William Irwin Thompson, Robert Jay Lifton, Herman Hesse, W. Warren Wagar, Pierre Teilhard de Chardin, Sri Aurobindo and various elements of the Talmudic and Kabbalistic literary universe.

Taken together, these complementary features of *Principles of World Order Design* may assist other teachers and scholars to produce newer and more promising archetypes for a just and durable global society. By combining millenial imaginations of the future with the long-ignored insights of philosophical, epistemological and fictional speculation, this book seeks to broaden public consciousness of the intransigence of nationalism and the futility of *realpolitik*.

Abbreviations

ABM: Antiballistic missile
ACDA: Arms Control and Disarmament Agency (USA)
ACP: African, Caribbean, and Pacific Countries
AID: Agency for International Development (USA)
ALCM: Air-Launched Cruise Missile
ANC: African National Congress (South Africa)
ANZUS: Australia, New Zealand, and the United States
ASAT: Anti-satellite
ASEAN: Association of Southeast Asian Nations
ASW: anti-submarine warfare (DOD)
AWACS: Airborne Warning and Control Systems
bbl: barrel
BMD: Ballistic Missile Defense
C³ (C-cubed): command, control, communications
C3I: command, control, communications, and intelligence
CBW: chemical and biological weapons
CCD: Conference of the Committee on Disarmament (UNO)
CCP: Chinese Communist Party
CD: Committee on Disarmament (UNO)
CIA: Central Intelligence Agency (USA)
CIEC: Conference on International Economic Cooperation
CMEA: Council on Mutual Economic Assistance
COCOM: Coordinating Committee for Multilateral Export Control
COW: Committee of the Whole (UNO)
CPE: Centrally Planned Economies (communist industrial)
CPSU: Communist Party of the Soviet Union
CSCE: Conference on Security and Cooperation in Europe
CTB: Comprehensive Nuclear Test Ban Treaty
CW: Chemical warfare
DC: developing country
DIA: Defense Intelligence Agency (DOD)
DOD: Department of Defense
DTA: Democratic Turnhalle Alliance (Namibia)
EC: European Community
ECDC: Economic Cooperation among Developing Countries
ECOSOC: Economic and Social Council (UNO)
ECU: European Currency Unit
EEC: European Economic Community
EFTA: European Free Trade Association
EMS: European Monetary System
END: European Nuclear Disarmament
FAO: Food and Agriculture Organization (UNO)
FBS/FOBS: Forward based systems (strategic)
FDR: Revolutionary Democratic Front (El Salvador)
FMLN: Farabundo Marti National Liberation Front (El Salvador)
FRG: Federal Republic of Germany (West Germany)
G-77: Group of 77
GATT: General Agreement on Tariffs and Trade
GCC: Gulf Co-operation Council
GDP: Gross Domestic Product
GDR: German Democratic Republic (East Germany)
GLCM: Ground-launched cruise missile
GNP: Gross National Product
GWP: Gross World Product
IAEA: International Atomic Energy Agency
ICA: International Communication Agency (USA)
ICBM: Intercontinental Ballistic Missile
ICJ: International Court of Justice
ICNT: Informal Composite Negotiating Text (UNCLOS)
IDA: International Development Association (World Bank)
IEA: International Energy Agency (OECD)
IFC: International Finance Corporation (World Bank)
IGO: Inter-governmental Organization
IISS: International Institute for Strategic Studies (London)
ILO: International Labor Organization
IMF: International Monetary Fund
IRBM: Intermediate Range Ballistic Missile
JCS: Joint Chiefs of Staff (DOD)
KT: Kiloton
LDC: Less Developed Country

LLDC: Least Developed Countries
LOS: Law of the Sea
LRTNF: Long-range theatre nuclear forces
MAD: Mutual Assured Destruction
MARV: Maneuverable Re-entry Vehicle
MBD: Million of barrels per day (oil)
MBFR: Mutual and Balanced Force Reductions
MDB: Multilateral development banks
MFN: Most Favored Nation
MIRV: Multiple Independently Targetable Re-entry Vehicle
MNC: Multinational Corporation
MRBM: Medium-range ballistic missile
MSA: Most Seriously Affected Countries
MTN: Multilateral Trade Negotiations
MX: Missile Experimental
NATO: North Atlantic Treaty Organization
N-bomb: Neutron bomb
NGO: Non-governmental (international) organization
NIC: Newly Industrializing (industrialized) country
NIE: National Intelligence Estimate
NIEO: New International Economic Order
NIO: New (international) Information Order
NPT: Non-Proliferation Treaty
NSC: National Security Council
NSM: National Security Memorandum (NSC)
NTB: Non-tariff barrier
OAPEC: Organization of Arab Petroleum Exporting Countries
ODA: Official development assistance
OECD: Organization for Economic Cooperation and Development
OPEC: Organization of Petroleum Exporting Countries
OSD: Office of the Secretary of Defense
PD: Presidential Directive
PGM: Precision-guided munitions
PLO: Palestine Liberation Organization
PQLI: Physical Quality Life Index
PRC: People's Republic of China
PZPR: Polish United Workers (Communist) Party
RDF: Rapid Deployment Forces
RV: Re-entry vehicle
SAC: Strategic Air Command (DOD)
SALT: Strategic Arms Limitation Talks
SDR: Special Drawing Rights
SIPRI: Stockholm International Peace Research Institute
SLBM: Submarine-Launched Ballistic Missile
SLCM: Submarine-launched cruise missile
SRBM: Short-range Ballistic Missile
SSBN: Submersible Ballistic Nuclear (Nuclear Ballistic Submarine)
START: Strategic Arms Reduction Talks (Reagan)
SWAPO: South-West African People's Organization
TCDC: Technical Cooperation Among Developing Countries
TNE: Transnational Enterprises
TNF: Theatre Nuclear Forces
UN: United Nations
UNCLOS: UN Conference on the Law of the Sea
UNCTAD: UN Conference on Trade and Development
UNDP: UN Development Programme
UNEF: UN Emergency Force
UNEP: UN Environment Programme
UNESCO: UN Educational, Scientific, and Cultural Organization
UNGA: UN General Assembly
UNHCR: UN High Commissioner on Refugees
UNICEF: UN Children's Fund
UNIDO: UN Industrial Development Programme
UNITAR: UN Institute for Training and Research
UNO: United Nations Organization (the whole UN system)
UNRWA: UN Relief and Works Agency for Palestine Refugees
UNSC: UN Security Council
UNU: UN Security Council
WHO: World Health Organization
ZPG: Zero population growth

Glossary*

This Glossary contains primarily technical,
economic, financial, and military terminology not
usually defined in most World Politics textbooks.

—A—

Absolute poverty: The condition of people whose incomes are insufficient to keep them at a subsistent level. If affects some 800 million people who are without adequate food intake (calories and proteins), water safe from disease-carrying organisms and toxins, minimum clothing and shelter, any kind of education, health care or employment. They are concentrated in certain areas such as the Sahel and the Horn of Africa, and Bangla Desh, but they also exist in almost all LDCs, including *middle-income countries.*

African, Caribbean, and Pacific Countries (ACP): Fifty-eight countries associated with the European Community through the *Lome Convention.*

Airborne Warning and Control System (AWACS): Flying radar stations that instantaneously identify all devices in the air within a radius of 240 miles and detect movement of land vehicles.

Air-Launched Cruise Missile (ALCM): A cruise missile carried by and launched from an aircraft.

Antiballistic missile (ABM): A missile that seeks out and destroys an incoming enemy missile in flight before the latter reaches its target. It is not effective against MIRVs.

Apartheid: A system of laws in the Republic of South Africa that seeks to preserve for the white minority population the absolute political, economic, and social control over non-whites who are variously classified as Coloureds (of mixed blood), Asians and Bantus (native Africans). Bantus are forced to settle in reservations known euphemistically as homelands or Bantustans. They must always carry passes to be appropriately stamped for work outside their area of domicile.

Appropriate technology: Also known as intermediate technology. It aims at using existing resources by making their usage more efficient or productive but adaptable to the local population.

Arms control: Any measure limiting or reducing forces, regulating armaments, and/or restricting the deployment of troops or weapons.

Arms race: The competitive or cumulative improvement of weapons stocks (qualitatively or quantitatively), or the build-up of armed forces based on the conviction of two or more actors that only by trying to stay ahead in military power can they avoid falling behind.

Association of Southeast Asian Nations (ASEAN): A regional regrouping made up of Indonesia, the Philippines, Singapore, and Thailand.

Atomic bomb: A weapon based on the rapid splitting of fissionable materials thereby inducing an explosion with three deadly results: blast, heat, and radiation.

Autonomy talks: Intermittent negotiations between Egypt and Israel, as provided in the *Camp David Agreements,* with the USA as intermediary and with as an objective the development of self-rule among Palestinians of the West Bank and the Gaza Strip. These autonomy talks are considered a sham by the Arab world, as Israel rules out a national homeland, not to say a state, for Palestinians.

—B—

Backfire: US code name for a Soviet supersonic bomber that has a range of 5,500 miles and can carry nuclear weapons. US experts disagree as to whether or not Backfire should be classified as a strategic weapon.

Italicized terms are defined elsewhere in the glossary.

Balance of Payments: A summary of the international transactions of a country over a given period of time, including commodity, service, capital flows, and gold movements.

Balance of trade: The relationship between imports and exports.

Ballistic missile: A payload propelled by a rocket, which assumes a free-fall trajectory when thrust is terminated. Ballistic missiles could be of short range (SRBM), intermediate range (IRBM), medium range (MRBM), and intercontinental (ICBM).

Barrel: A standard measure for petroleum, equivalent to 42 gallons or 158.86 liters.

Basic human needs: Adequate food intake (in terms of calories, proteins, and vitamins), drinking water free of disease-carrying organisms and toxins, minimum clothing and shelter, literacy, sanitation, health care, employment, and dignity.

Bilateral: Between two nations.

Binary (chemical) munitions/weapons: Nerve gas canisters composed of two separate chambers containing chemicals that become lethal when mixed. The mixing is done when the canister is fired. Binary gas is preferred for its relative safety in storage and transportation.

Biosphere: The environment of life and living processes at or near the earth's surface, extending from the ocean floors to about 75 kilometers into the atmosphere. It is being endangered by consequences of human activities such as air and water pollution, acid rain, radioactive fallout, desertification, toxic and nuclear wastes, and the depletion of non-renewable resources.

Brandt Commission: An independent commission on international economic issues created in September 1977 and headed by former West German Chancellor Willy Brandt.

"Broken arrows": Pentagon code word for accidents involving US nuclear weapons.

Buffer Stocks: Reserves of commodities that are either increased or decreased whenever necessary to maintain relative stability of supply and prices.

—C—

Camp David Agreements/Accords: Agreements signed on September 17, 1978 at Camp David—a mountain retreat for the US President in Maryland—by President Anwar al-Sadat of Egypt and Prime Minister Menachem Begin of Israel, and witnessed by President Jimmy Carter of the United States of America. They are "A Framework for Peace in the Middle East" and "A Framework for the Conclusion of a Peace Treaty between Egypt and Israel."

Cancun Summit: World leaders' meeting on October 22-23, 1981, in the Mexican resort of Cancun to discuss global economic issues—a major event that could make or break the North-South dialogue. The agenda item: whether to launch a new round of *Global Negotiations.*

Centrally Planned Economies (CPEs): As distinguished from free-market economies, countries generally included in this category are industrialized Communist countries: the USSR, East European countries, and the PRC.

Circular error probable (CEP): The radius of a target circle within which half of the enemy weapons are projected to fall.

Cold war: A condition of hostility between the USA and the USSR in their struggle to dominate the world scene since the end of World War II.

Commodity: The unprocessed products of mining and agriculture.

Common Fund: A fund to finance 18 commodity buffer stocks as proposed in the 1976 Nairobi *UNCTAD* IV integrated program for *commodities.*

Common Heritage of Mankind: 1970 UN declaration states the "seabed and ocean floor, and the subsoil thereof, beyond the limits of national jurisdiction. . ., as well as the resources of the area, are the common heritage of mankind."

Common Market: A customs union that eliminates trade barriers within a group and establishes a common external tariff on imports from nonmember countries.

Compensatory Financing Facility: An IMF program established in 1963 to finance temporary export shortfalls, as in coffee, sugar, or other cyclically prone export items.

Concessional loans: Loans given to LLDCs by MBDs which can be repaid in soft (non-convertible) currencies and with nominal or no interest over a long period of time.

Conditionality: A series of measures that must be taken by a country before it could qualify for loans from the International Monetary Fund, such as: (1) devaluing its currency, in an attempt to boost exports and restrain imports; (2) controlling the rate of expansion of the money supply in order to dampen inflation; (3) reducing government spending, especially human services expenditures; (4) imposing wage controls, while eliminating price controls; (5) raising interest rates in order to encourage savings; (6) increasing taxes; (7) reducing or dismantling barriers to foreign private investment and to free trade in general.

Conference on International Economic Cooperation (CIEC): A conference of 8 industrial nations, 7 oil-producing nations, and 12 developing countries held in several sessions between December 1975 and June 1977. It is composed of four separate commissions (energy, raw materials, development, and financing). It is the forum of the *North-South dialogue* between rich and poor countries.

Conference on Security and Cooperation in Europe (CSCE): See *Helsinki Agreement.*

Confidence-building measures (CBMs): Understandings (called for in the Final Act of Helsinki) to give advance notice of NATO or Warsaw Pact military maneuvers and major troop deployments.

Consensus: In conference diplomacy, a way of reaching agreements by negotiations and without a formal vote.

Contact Group: See *Western Five Contact Group*

Coordinating Committee for Multilateral Export Controls (COCOM): Composed of representatives of 14 NATO countries and Japan, it sets restrictions on the transfer of Western technology to communist nations with direct or "end use" military applications.

Council on Mutual Economic Assistance (CMEA OR COMECON): Founded in Moscow in 1949 as a counterpart of the Marshall Plan (European Recovery Program), today it is comprised of the USSR, the countries of Eastern Europe, Mongolia, Cuba, and Vietnam.

Counterforce: The use of strategic nuclear weapons for strike on selected military capabilities of an enemy force.

Countervalue: The use of strategic nuclear weapons for strike on an enemy's population centers.

Cruise missile: A small, highly-maneuverable, low-flying, pilotless aircraft equipped with accurate guidance systems that periodically readjusts its trajectory. It can carry conventional or nuclear warheads, can be short-range or long range, and can be launched from the air (ALLUM), the ground (GLCM), or the sea (SLCM).

Declaration of Talloires: A statement issued in 1981 by Western journalists who opposed the UNESCO-sponsored *New World Information and Communication Order,* at a meeting in Talloires, France.

Delivery systems or Vehicles or Launchers: Land-Based Missiles (ICBMs), Submarine-Launched Missiles (SLBMs), and long-range bombers capable of delivering nuclear weapons.

Democratic Turnhalle Alliance (DTA): A party in the Namibian dispute, set up by South Africa as a political alternative to SWAPO. The DTA is considered as a puppet creation of South Africa by the United Nations. Its leader is Dirk Mudge.

Denationalization: A policy of the government of South Africa to declare certain reserved areas as "homelands" or "Bantustans" which it then recognizes as separate "national states." The black population is forcibly transferred into one of these "independent homelands" and declared to be its citizens, whether they like it or not. Once that is done, Blacks are no longer considered as citizens or nationals of South Africa, and thus become, in effect, foreigners in their native land.

Detente: A French term meaning the relaxation of tensions or a decrease in the level of hostility between opponents on the world scene.

Deterrence: The prevention from action by fear of the consequences.

Developed Countries: (DCs): Countries with relatively high per capita GNP, education, levels of industrial development and production, health and welfare, and agricultural productivity; 24 OECD members and 6 centrally planned economy countries of Eastern Europe, including the USSR.

Developing Countries (LCDs): Also *Less Developed Countries;* these countries are mainly raw materials producers for export with high growth rates and inadequate infrastructures in transportation, educational systems, and the like. There is, however, a wide variation in living standards, GNP's, and per capita incomes among LCDs.

Development: The process through which a society becomes increasingly able to meet basic human needs and assure the physical quality of life of its people.

Disappearance: Government kidnapping of individuals without leaving a trace. A violation of human rights occurring in alarming proportions under various dictatorial regimes, whereby individuals would be taken away by government agents, unbeknownst to their family, friends, or co-workers. Where they are detained, what they are charged with, whether they are still alive or are dead is not known. Usually attempts to inquire about their fate are futile or result in the disappearance of those making inquiries.

Disinformation: The spreading of false propaganda and forged documents to confuse counter-intelligence or to create political confusion, unrest, and scandal.

Dumping: A special case of price discrimination, selling to foreign buyers at a lower price than that charged to buyers in the home market.

Duty: Special tax applied to imported goods, based on tariff rates and schedules.

East (as in the East-West Struggle): (a) A shorthand, nongeographic term that includes non-market, centrally planned (communist) countries; (b) In a more restricted sense, the Warsaw Pact (military)/ CEMA (economic) bloc of the USSR and Eastern European countries under its sway.

East-West conflict: The military, economic, political, and ideological worldwide struggle between the communist countries and the industrial democracies. Also known as the Cold War.

Economic Cooperation among Developing Countries (ECDC): Also referred to as intra-South, or South-South cooperation, it is a way for LCDs to help each other with *appropriate technology.*

Escalation: The stepping up of the level of conflict, either qualitatively or quantitatively.

Essential equivalence: Comparing military capabilities of two would-be belligerents, not in terms of identical mix of forces, but in terms of how well two dissimilarly organized forces could achieve a strategic stalemate.

Eurodollars: US dollar holdings of European banks; a liability for the US Treasury.

Euromissiles: Shorthand for *long-range theatre nuclear forces* stationed in Europe or aimed at targets in Europe.

European Community (EC): Composed of the nine European Economic Community (EEC) members; it has a Council of Ministers, an elected European Parliament, a European Court of Justice, a European Investment Bank, and a European Monetary System.

European Currency Unit (ECU): The common unit of valuation among the eight members of the European Monetary System (EMS).

European Economic Community (EEC): Also known as the European Common Market. Founded in 1957 by France, West Germany, Italy, Belgium, the Netherlands, and Luxembourg for the purpose of economic integration. It was joined in 1973 by the United Kingdom, Ireland, Denmark and in 1981 by Greece. Spain and Portugal have also applied for membership. Its main features include a common external tariff, a customs union on industrial goods, and a Common Agricultural Policy. Full economic and monetary union remains an objective.

European Free Trade Association (EFTA): Austria, Finland, Iceland, Liechtenstein, Norway, Portugal, Sweden, and Switzerland. Each member keeps its own external tariff schedule, but free trade prevails among the members.

European Monetary System (EMS): Established in 1979 as a preliminary stage toward an economic and monetary union in the European Community. Fluctuations in the exchange-rate value of the currencies of the participating countries are kept within a 2¼ percent limit of divergence from the strongest currency among them.

Exclusive Economic Zone: As proposed in *ICNT,* a belt of sea extending 200 nautical miles from coastal state. In this area coastal state would have rights and jurisdiction with respect to the resources of seabed, subsoil, and superjacent waters.

Exports: Products shipped to foreign countries.

Export subsidies: Special incentives, including direct payments to exporters, to encourage increased foreign sales.

—F—

Farabundo Marti National Liberation Front (Frente de Liberacion Nacional Farabundo Marti; (FMLN): The unified guerilla command of El Salvador, comprising five groups; Popular Forces of Liberation.

Finlandization: A condition of nominal neutrality, but one of actual subservience to the Soviet Union in foreign and security policies, as is the case with Finland.

First strike: The first offensive move of a general nuclear war. It implies an intention to knock out the opponent's ability to retaliate.

Fissionable or nuclear materials: Isotopes of certain elements, such as plutonium, thorium, and uranium, that emit neutrons in such large numbers that a sufficient concentration will be self-sustaining until it explodes.

Foreign policy: The process and the substance of preserving one's national interests in the tangled maze of global relations that are constantly changing.

Forward based system (FBS or FoBS): A military installation, maintained on foreign soil or in international waters, and conveniently located near a theatre of war.

Fourth World: An expression arising from the world economic crisis that began in 1973-74 with the quadrupling in price of petroleum. It takes the least developed countries (LLCDs) and the most seriously affected countries (MSAs).

Front-line states: As regards to Namibia, the expression refers to Black African states immediately adjacent to it, namely Angola, Zambia, Zimbabwe, Mozambique, and Tanzania. Nigeria and Kenya, being leading states of Black Africa, also consider themselves part of this anti-South Africa group, even though they are located over 1,500 miles away from Namibia.

—G—

General Agreement on Tariffs and Trade (GATT): Created in 1947, this organization is the major global forum for negotiations of tariff reductions and other measures to expand world trade. Its 83 members account for four-fifths of the world's trade.

Generalized System of Preferences (GSP): A system approved by GATT in 1971, which authorizes DCs to give preferential tariff treatment to LCDs.

Glemp, Archbishop Jozef: The Primate (top leader) of the Roman Catholic Church in Poland.

Global: Pertaining to the world as a whole; worldwide.

Global commons: The Antarctic, the ocean floor under international waters and celestial bodies within reach of planet Earth. All of these areas and bodies are considered the common heritage of mankind.

Global Negotiations: A new round of international economic negotiations started in 1980 over raw materials, energy, trade, development, money, and finance.

Golan Heights: Syrian territory adjacent to Israel that occupied it since the 1967 war and that annexed it on Decemer 14, 1981.

Gross National Product (GNP): The total value of all goods and services produced by a country in a year.

Gross world product: The sum of all gross national products.

Group of 77 (G-77): Initially a group of LDCs which issued a "Joint Declaration of 77 Developing Countries" at *UNCTAD I* in 1976 in Geneva. Now, made up of 122 countries, it remains the caucus of LCDs. Synonymous with the "South" in the North-South dialogue.

—H—

Hegemonism: Any attempt by a larger power to interfere, threaten, intervene against, and dominate a smaller power or a region of the world.

Hegemony: Domination by a major power over smaller, subordinate ones within its sphere of influence.

Helsinki Agreement: A declaration adopted on August 1, 1975 by 35 nations, including the USA and the USSR, participating in the *Conference on Security and Cooperation in Europe* that started in Helsinki, Finland, on July 3, 1973. Its main document is the Final Act in which signatories pledged to respect each other's sovereign equality and individuality, to promote detente, fundamental human rights, economic and social progress and well-being for all peoples. They also pledged not to use force or the threat of force and subversion in relations among themselves and with other nations. Three follow-up conferences took place in Belgrade in 1978 and in Madrid in 1980 and 1982. They have provided a forum for diplomatic confrontation between the USA and the USSR.

Horn of Africa: The northeast corner of Africa which includes Ethiopia, Djibouti, and Somalia. It is separated from the Arabian peninsula by the Gulf of Aden and the Red Sea. It is plagued with tribal conflicts between Ethiopia and Eritrea, and between Ethiopia and Somalia over the Ogaden desert. These conflicts have generated a large number of refugees who have been facing mass starvation.

Human rights: Rights inherent to human beings, including but not limited to the right to dignity; the integrity of the person; the inviolability of the person's body and mind; civil and political rights (freedom of religion, speech, press, assembly, association, the right to privacy, habeas corpus, due process of law, the right to vote or not to vote, the right to run for election, and the right to be protected from reprisals for acts of peaceful dissent); social, economic, and cultural rights. The most glaring violations of human rights are *torture, disappearance,* and the general phenomenon of *state terrorism*. The basic documents of human rights are: the Universal Declaration of Human Rights (1948), the Genocide Convention

(1951), Convention on Political Rights of Women (1952), the International Covenant on Civil and Political Rights (1966), the International Covenant on Economic, Social, and Cultural Rights (1966), the International Convention on the Elimination of All Forms of Racial Discrimination (1909), the European Convention for the Protection of Human Rights and Fundamental Freedoms (1954), the [Inter-]American Convention on Human Rights (1969), and the Declaration on Protection from Torture (1975). An international covenant against the use of torture is near completion in 1981.

Hu Yaobang: Chairman, Chinese Communist Party, succeeding Hua Guofeng.

Imports: Products brought into a country from abroad.

Informal Composite Negotiating Text (ICNT): Prepared in July 1977; officially only a procedural device serving as basis for negotiations, but functions as draft law of the sea treaty.

Innocent Passage: In a nation's territorial sea, passage by a foreign ship is innocent so long as it is not prejudicial to the peace, good order, or security of the coastal state. Submarines must surface and show flag.

Intercontinental Ballistic Missile (ICBM): A land-based, rocket-propelled vehicle capable of delivering a warhead to targets at 6,000 or more nautical miles.

Interdependence: An increasingly obvious characteristic of current world politics and economics whereby no country, however powerful, is totally immune from the consequences of actions and events happening in other countries, no matter how small and weak.

Intermediate Range Ballistic Missile (IRBM): A missile with a range from 1,500 to 4,000 nautical miles.

International: Between or among sovereign states.

International Development Association (IDA): An affiliate of the World Bank that provides interest free, long-term (50 years) loans to developing countries in support of projects that cannot obtain funding through other existing sources. Its lending may be curtailed if the USA, as announced, reduces its contribution from $3.2 to $2 billion for the 1983 fiscal year.

International Energy Agency (IEA): An arm of *OECD* that attempts to coordinate member countries' oil imports and reallocate stocks among members in case of disruptions in the world's oil supply.

International Finance Corporation (IFC): Created in 1956 to finance overseas investments by private companies without necessarily requiring government guarantees. The IFC borrows from the *World Bank*, provides loans and invests directly in private industry in the development of capital projects.

International Monetary Fund (IMF): Conceived of at the Bretton Woods Agreement of 1944 and in operation since 1947, its major purpose is to encourage international cooperation in the monetary field and the removal of foreign exchange restrictions, to stabilize exchange rates and aid in balance-of-payment problems.

Interstate: International, intergovernmental.

Intra-South: See *Economic Cooperation among Developing Countries.*

Jaruzelski, General Wojciech: Succeeded Jozef Pinkowski as Poland's Prime Minister, then succeeded Stanislaw Kania, as First Secretary of the Polish United Workers (Communist) Party. A pragmatic and moderate leader, he was caught in the middle by hardliners within the party's Central Committee on one side, and by the hard-liners in the Solidarity independent trade union on the other. Due to the ultimatum adopted by the Executive Committee of Solidarity on December 12, 1981, Jaruzelski imposed martial law on Poland on December 13.

Kampuchea: The new name for Cambodia since April 1975.

KGB: The Soviet security police and intelligence apparatus, engaged in espionage, counterespionage, anti-subversion, and control of political dissidents.

Khmer Rouge: Literally "Red Cambodians," the communist organization ruling *Kampuchea* between April 1975 and January 1979 under Pol Pot and Ieng Saray.

Kiloton: A thousand tons of explosive force. A measure of the yield of a nuclear weapon equivalent to 1,000 tons of TNT (trinitrotoluene). The bomb detonated at Hiroshima in World War II had an approximate yield of 14 kilotons.

Launcher: See *Delivery Systems*

Least Developed Countries (LLDC): Countries that in 1979 had a per capita income of $370 or less and where the basic human needs cannot be met for the bulk of the population.

Less Developed Countries (LDC): (Previously called underdeveloped countries, and later, developing countries.) Countries where the basic human needs are not fully met, yet are well on their way to development.

Linkage: Putting together two separate issues in diplomatic negotiations.

Lome Convention: An agreement concluded between the European Community and 58 African, Caribbean and Pacific countries (ACP), allowing the latter preferential trade relations and greater economic and technical assistance.

Long-Range Theatre Nuclear Forces (LRTNF): Recently developed nuclear weapon systems with a range greater than 1,000 kilometers (or 600 miles) such as the US Pershing II missile or the Soviet SS-20.

Low-income countries: According to the World Bank there are 36 such countries with per capita income ranging from 80 to 370 US dollars per year. They account for 2.26 billion people, of which 1.62 billions are in China and India.

Maneuverable Re-entry Vehicle (MARV): A ballistic missile re-entry vehicle equipped with its own navigation and control systems capable of adjusting its trajectory during re-entry into the atmosphere.

Medium-range Ballistic Missile (MRBM): A missile with a range from 500 to 1,500 nautical miles.

Megaton: The yield of a nuclear weapon equivalent to 1 million tons of TNT (approximately equivalent to 79 Hiroshima bombs).

Microstates: Very small countries, usually with a population of less than one million.

Middle-income countries MICs): According to the World Bank, there are 60 such countries, with annual per capita income (PCI) ranging from 380 to 4,380 US dollars. Twenty-five of these countries have an annual PCI of less than $1,000; 23 of these countries have a PCI ranging from $1,000 to $2,000; and 12 countries have a PCI ranging from $2,000 to $4,380. This is a most unsatisfactory classification, as the highest PCI of MICs is $4,380 while its lowest PCI is only $380, which is only $10 more than the highest PCI in the low-income country group.

Ministates: Small countries, usually with a population of less than five million.

Missile experimental (MX): A mobile, land-based missile that is shuttled among different launching sites making it more difficult to locate and destroy.

Most Favored Nation (MFN): In international trade agreements, a country granting most-favored-nation status to another country undertakes to make available to that country the most favorable treatment in regard to tariffs and other trade regulations that it makes available to any other country.

Most Seriously Affected Countries (MSA): Low-income countries that import their energy needs and that were hurt the most by the OPEC price increases in 1973.

Multilateral: Involving many nations.

Multilateral Development Banks (MDBs): These are the World Bank Group that include the *International Development Association* (IDA) and the *International Finance Corporation* (IFC), the Inter-American Development Bank (IDB or IADB), the Asian Development Bank (ADB), and the African Development Bank (AFDB).

Multinational: Doing business in many nations.

Multinational corporation: *See* Transnational enterprise.

Multiple Independently Targetable Re-entry Vehicle (MIRV): Two or more warheads carried by a single missile and capable of being guided to separate targets upon re-entry.

Mutual and Balanced Force Reductions (MBFR): The 19-nation Conference on Mutual Reduction of Forces and Armaments and Associated Measures in Central Europe that has been held intermittently since 1973.

Mutual Assured Destruction (MAD): The basic ingredient of the doctrine of strategic deterrence that no country can escape destruction in a nuclear exchange even if it engages in a pre-emptive strike.

Namibia: African name for South-West Africa.

National Intelligence Estimate (NIE): The final assessment of global problems and capabilities by the intelligence community for use by the National Security Council and the President in making foreign and military decisions.

Nautical mile: 1.852 kilometers.

Neocolonialism: A perjorative term describing the economic exploitation of Third World countries by the industrialized countries, in particular through the activities of multinational corporations.

Neutron bomb: Enhanced radiation bomb giving out lower blast and heat but concentrated radiation, thus killing people and living things while reducing damage to physical structures.

New International Economic Order (NIEO): The statement of development policies and objectives adopted at the Sixth Special Session of the UN General Assembly in 1974. NIEO calls for equal participation of LDCs in the international economic policy-making process, better known as the *North-South dialogue.*

New World Information and Communication Order: A highly controversial proposal made in 1980 by the UNESCO-sponsored Commission for the Study of Communication Problems (McBride Commission) to promote a "free and balanced flow of information and news" through "effective legal measures designed to circumscribe the action of transnationals by requiring them to comply with specific criteria and conditions defined by national development policies." The "transnationals" referred to here are the West's Big Four news agencies, namely the Associated Press and the United Press International (USA), Reuters (UK), and Agence France-Press, plus major Western broadcasting companies. This attempt to legitimize state censorship of foreign media by Third World countries provoked a response by Western journalists known as the *Declaration of Talloires.*

Nonaligned Movement (NAM): A grouping of nations that have deliberately chosen not to be politically and militarily associated with either the West or the Communist bloc. Started with Bandung in 1955, six nonaligned summit meetings have been held—Belgrade (1961), Cairo (1964), Lusaka (1970), Algiers (1973), Colombo

(1976), and Havana (1979). Interim leadership of the nonaligned countries rests with the country that last hosted a summit meeting. There were 94 members in the NAM in 1981.

Non-alignment: The concept or policy of remaining neutral in the cold war; not taking sides with either the USA (West) or the USSR (East).

Non-nuclear (weapons) state: One not possessing nuclear weapon.

Non-proliferation of Nuclear Weapons Treaty (NPT): Under this Treaty, the non-nuclear-weapon states pledge not to manufacture or acquire nuclear explosive devices and agree to international verification. Nuclear-weapon states, party to the NPT, pledge not to transfer nuclear explosive devices to any recipient and not to assist any non-nuclear-weapon state in the manufacture of nuclear explosive devices.

Non-tariff barriers (NTBs): Subtle, informal impediments to free trade designed for the purpose of making importation of foreign goods into a country very difficult on such grounds as health and safety regulations. Japan as of 1981 had 99 categories of NTBs.

Normalization of relations: The reestablishment of full diplomatic relations, including de jure recognition and the exchange of ambassadors between two countries that either did not have diplomatic relations or had broken them.

North (as in North-South dialogue): (a) A shorthand, non-geographic term for the industrialized countries of high income, both East (the USSR and Eastern Europe) and West (the USA, Canada, Western Europe, Japan, Australia and New Zealand.) (b) Often means only the industrialized, high-income countries of the West.

North Atlantic Treaty Organization (NATO): Also known as the Atlantic Alliance, NATO was formed in 1949 to provide collective defense against the perceived Soviet threat to Western Europe. Its members are Belgium, Denmark, France, the Federal Republic of Germany (West Germany), Greece, Iceland, Italy, Luxembourg, the Netherlands, Norway, Portugal, Turkey, the United Kingdom, Canada, and the United States. France has an independent striking force not integrated into NATO. Greece intends to withdraw militarily from NATO.

North-South dialogue: A wrangling between the industrial Western countries (North) and the LDCs (South) for trade preferences, and economic and technical assistance taking place in Conferences on International Cooperation (CIEC). The Soviet Union and its allies generally remain aloof from the North-South dialogue, arguing that LDC problems are the result of past colonialism and capitalism and, therefore, are the sole responsibility of the West. It was started in 1974 with the *Third World's* call for a new international economic order.

Nuclear free zone: A stretch of territory from which all nuclear weapons are banned.

Nuclear Non-Proliferation Treaty (NPT): A treaty that, among other things, binds those non-nuclear countries adhering to it to forego the acquisition or production of nuclear weapons and forbids the transfer of such weapons to a non-nuclear state.

Nuclear proliferation: The process by which one country after another comes into possession of some form of nuclear weaponry, and with it develops the potential of launching a nuclear attack on other actors.

Nuclear reprocessing: The separation of radioactive waste (spent fuel) from a nuclear-powered plant into its fissile constituent materials. One such material is Plutonium, which can then be used in the production of atomic bombs.

Nuclear terrorism: The use (or threatened use) of nuclear weapons or radioactive materials as a means of coercion.

Oestpolitik: Literally, Eastward politics, it is the West German foreign policy of *detente* aiming at cooperative relations with the Soviet Union and East European communist countries, with the intermediate goal of normalization of relations with East Germany and the ultimate goal of reunification of the two Germanies.

Official Development Assistance (ODA): Government contributions to projects and programs aimed at developing the productivity of poorer countries. This is to be distinguished from private, voluntary assistance, humanitarian assistance for disasters, and most importantly from military assistance

Ogaden: A piece of Ethiopian desert populated by ethnic Somalis. It has been a bone of contention between Ethiopia and Somalia, a war that contributed significantly to the refugee and starvation problems in the Horn of Africa.

Organization for Economic Cooperation and Development (OECD): Composed of 23 Western countries plus Japan. All have democratic political systems and, except for a few, have high-income industrial economics. Also referred to as the "North" as in the North-South dialogue.

Organization of Arab Petroleum Exporting Countries (OAPEC): A component of OPEC, with Saudi Arabia, Kuwait, the United Arab Emirates, Qatar, Iraq, Algeria and Libya as members.

Organization of Petroleum Exporting Countries (OPEC): A producers' cartel setting price floors and production ceiling of crude petroleum. It includes members of OPEC plus Venezuela, Iran, Ecuador, Gabon, Nigeria and Indonesia.

Osirak: Site of the Iraqi nuclear power plant near Baghdad that was destroyed by Israeli bombings on June 7, 1981. The site was constructed with the assistance of France, which has pledged to rebuild it.

Overkill: The capability of the USA and the USSR to kill not only each other's population several times over, but the world's population as well.

—P—

Palestine: "Palestine" does not exist today as an entity. It refers to the historical and geographical entity administered by the British under the League of Nations mandate from 1918 to 1947. It also refers to a future entity in the aspirations of Palestinians who, as was the case of the Jews before the founding of the State of Israel, are stateless nationalists.

Palestine Liberation Organization (PLO): A coalition of Palestinian groups united by the dedication to the goal of a Palestinian state through the destruction of Israel as a state.

Payload: Warheads attached to delivery vehicles.

People's Republic of China (PRC): Communist or mainland China.

Perez de Cuellar, Javier: The fifth Secretary General of the United Nations. His 5-year term began on January 1, 1982.

Pershing II: US MRBMs to be deployed in Western Europe to counteract Soviet SS-20s.

Petrodollars: US dollar holdings of capital-surplus OPEC countries; a liability for the US Treasury.

Physical Quality of Life Index (PQLI): Developed by the Overseas Development Council, the PQLI is presented as a more significant measurement of the well-being of inhabitants of a geographic entity than the solely monetary measurement of per capita income. It consists of the following measurements: life expectancy, infant mortality, and literacy figures that are each rated on an index of 1-100, within which each country is ranked according to its performance. A composite index is obtained by averaging these three measures, giving the PQLI.

Polisario: The liberation front of Western Sahara (formerly Spanish Sahara) that is fighting against Morocco claims over that territory. The USA supports King Hassan of Morocco in this war in return for staging rights of Rapid Deployment Forces in the Middle East/North African area.

Polish United Workers Party (PZPR): Poland's communist party's name since 1948.

Post-industrial: Characteristic of a society where a large portion of the work force is directed to non-agricultural and non-manufacturing tasks such as servicing and processing.

Precision-Guided Munitions (PGM): Popularly known as "smart bombs." Electronically programmed and controlled weapons that can accurately hit a moving or stationary target.

Pre-emptive strike, attack. To attack an enemy before one is attacked. A nuclear attack launched in the expectation that an attack by an adversary is imminent, and designed to forestall that attack or to lessen its impact.

Proliferation: Quick spread, as in the case of nuclear weapons.

Protocol: A preliminary memorandum often signed by diplomatic negotiators as a basis for a final convention or treaty.

—Q—

Quota: Quantitative limits, usually imposed on imports or immigrants.

—R—

Rapprochement: The coming together of two countries that had been hostile to each other.

Recycling: As used in recent international finance, it means the flow of money from capital-surplus OPEC countries (Saudi Arabia, Kuwait, Libya, and Iraq) into private or *multilateral development banks* (MBDs) for relending to poorer countries. Recycling resulted from the capital surplus accumulated by certain OPEC countries due to the quadrupling of oil prices in 1973-74 and subsequent price hikes.

Re-entry Vehicle (RV): That portion of a ballistic missile designed to carry a nuclear warhead and to re-enter the Earth's atmosphere in the terminal portion of the missile trajectory.

Regionalism: A concept of cooperation among geographically adjacent states to foster region-wide political (OAS, OAU), military (NATO, Warsaw Pact) and economic (EEC, EFTA) interests.

Rejectionist Front: In the context of the Arab-Israeli conflict, the front consists of Arab countries that reject any solution to the Palestinian question short of the establishment of a Palestinian state in place of the state of Israel. It is made up of the PLO, Syria, Libya, Algeria, and to a lesser degree all other Arab states except for Egypt and the Sudan. They also rejected the Camp David Agreements.

Reprocessing of nuclear waste: A process of recovery of fissionable materials among which is weapon-grade plutonium.

Resolution: Formal decisions of UN bodies; they may simply register an opinion or may recommend action to be taken by a UN body or agency.

Resolution 242: Passed by the UN Security Council on November 22, 1967 calling for the withdrawal of Israeli troops from territories they captured from Egypt (Sinai), Jordan (West Bank and East Jerusalem), and Syria (Golan Heights) in the 1967 war, and for the right of all nations in the Middle East to live in peace in secure and recognized borders.

Resolution 435: Passed by the UN Security Council in 1978, it called for a cease-fire between belligerents in the Namibian conflict (namely SWAPO, Angola and other front-line states on the one side, and South Africa on the other) and an internationally supervised transition process to independence and free elections.

—S—

SALT I: The discussions between the US and the USSR on the limitation of strategic armaments that have been under way since 1970. They have resulted in (1) a treaty limiting the deployment of anti-ballistic missile (ABM) systems; (2) an agreement setting ceilings on intercontinental ballistic missiles (ICBMs) and sub-marine-launched ballistic missiles (SLBMs) for a five-year period; and (3) the Vladivostok Accord, setting ceilings on all strategic nuclear delivery systems (including heavy bombers) and on MIRVs (multiple independently-targetable reentry vehicles).

SALT II: The SALT II agreement consists of three parts: (1) A treaty, to last through 1985, which, inter alia: sets initial equal aggregates of 2,400 on the total of strategic nuclear delivery vehicles; mandates further reductions in the overall ceiling down to 2,250 before expiration of the treaty; sets equal subceilings on several key categories of systems; restricts the number of warheads that are allowed on each missile; and limits each side to one new type of ICBM. (2) A protocol to last through 1981, which covers issues not ready for longer term resolution. (3) A joint statement of principles and guidelines for subsequent SALT negotiations. SALT II never went into effect, as it was not ratified by the US Senate.

Second strike: A nuclear attack in response to an adversary's first strike. A second-strike capability is the ability to absorb the full force of a first strike and still inflict unacceptable damage in retaliation.

Shatt al Arab: The body of water located between Iran and Iraq, and claimed by both. The dispute over Shatt al Arab was one of the causes of the Iran-Iraq war.

Short Range Ballistic Missiles (SRBM): A missile with a range up to 500 nautical miles.

Solidarity: Independent self-governing trade union movement started in Poland on August 22, 1980 and terminated on December 13, 1981 after radical members of its Presidium passed a resolution on December 12 calling for a national referendum to see whether the communist government of Poland should continue to govern. Individual members of the Presidium also called for the establishment of a provisional government.

South (as in North-South dialogue): A shorthand, non-geographic term that includes economically less developed countries, often represented by the Group of 77.

South-South: see *Economic Cooperation among Developing Countries*

South-West African People's Organization (SWAPO): The guerilla organization fighting against South Africa's illegal occupation and exploitation of Namibia. SWAPO is recognized by the United Nations as the authentic representative of Namibia.

Sovereignty: The ability to carry out laws and policies within national borders without interference from outside.

Special Drawing Rights (SDRs): Also known as paper gold. A new form of international liquid reserves to be used in the settlement of international payments among member governments of the International Monetary Fund.

SS-17, 18, 19: Soviet ICBMs.

SS-20: New mobile Soviet medium-range nuclear missiles aimed at Western Europe.

Stabex Program (stabilization of export receipts): An EEC program that provides financial assistance to selected developing countries that experience temporary export earnings shortfalls.

State: Regarding international relations, it means a country having territory, population, government, and sovereignty, e.g. the US is a state, while California is not a state in this sense.

State terrorism: The use of state power, including the police, the armed forces, and the secret police to throw fear among the population against any act of dissent or protest against a political regime. Such state power includes extraordinary measures such as martial law (military rule), revolutionary or military tribunals ("kangaroo courts"), summary executions, mass killings either by face-to-face firings or indiscriminate use of artillery, and bombings against wide areas that contain civilian settlements. It also includes the use of physical, biochemical, medical, and psychological torture on political prisoners or prisoners of conscience. State terrorism is a phenomenon of modern technology, practiced by totalitarian and authoritarian regimes, by communist and non-communist regimes alike.

"Stealth": A code name for a proposed "invisible" aircraft, supposedly not detectable by hostile forces, and that would be the main US strategic fighter-bomber of the 1990s.

Strategic Arms Limitation Talks: See *SALT I* and *SALT II*

Strategic balance or parity: A concept used in nuclear planning and debate to determine the equivalence of forces between two armed blocs, e.g. the US vs. the USSR, NATO vs. the Warsaw Pact. Opposite of strategic imbalance that could be either superiority or inferiority.

Strategic consensus: An elusive objective of forging an anti-Soviet alliance pursued by the Reagan administration in the Middle East. It would link together such entities as Israel, Egypt, and Saudi Arabia, except that Israel and Saudi Arabia consider themselves enemies. Jordan, which was also courted by the Reagan administration, would have no part of it.

Strategic minerals: Minerals needed in the fabrication of advanced military and industrial equipment. Examples are uranium, platinum, titanium, vanadium, tungsten, nickel, chromium, etc.

Strategic nuclear weapons: Long-range weapons carried on either intercontinental ballistic missiles (ICBMs) or Submarine-Launched Ballistic Missiles (SLBMs) or long-range bombers.

Strategic stockpile: Reserves of certain commodities established to assure that in time of national emergency such commodities are readily available.

Submarine-Launched Ballistic Missile (SLBM): A ballistic missile carried in and launched from a submarine.

Superpowers: Countries so powerful militarily (USA, USSR), demographically (PRC), or economically (Japan) as to be in a class by themselves.

Supranational: Above nation-states.

—T—

Tactical nuclear weapons: Kiloton-range weapons for theatre use. The bomb dropped on Hiroshima would be in this category today.

Tariff: A tax levied on imports.

Technetronic: Shorthand for technological-electronic.

Technical Cooperation Among Developing Countries (TCDC): A clearinghouse and a coordinating body through which less developed countries (LDCs) may help each other solve similar problems by low-capital, appropriate technology applications.

Territorial Sea: The territorial sea, air space above, seabed, and subsoil are part of sovereign territory of coastal state except that ships (not aircraft) enjoy right of *innocent passage.* As proposed in ICNT, a coastal state's sovereignty would extend 12 nautical miles beyond its land territory.

Terrorism: The systematic use of terror as a means of coercion.

Theatre: In nuclear strategy, it refers to a localized combat area such as Europe, as opposed to global warfare involving a US-USSR nuclear exchange.

Theatre Nuclear Forces (TNF): Nuclear weapons systems for operations in a region such as Europe, including artillery, cruise missiles, SRBMs, IRBMs, and MRBMs.

"Thinkables": Nuclear strategists who believe that one should plan in terms of nuclear war actually occurring, and for its aftermath.

Third World: Often used interchangeably with the terms *less developed countries, developing countries,* or the *South,* its two main institutions are the *nonaligned movement* (which acts primarily as the political caucus of the Third World) and the *Group of 77* (which functions as the economic voice of the Third World).

Tokyo Round: The sixth and latest in the series of GATT trade negotiations, begun in 1973 and ended in 1979. About 100 nations, including nonmembers of the GATT, participated.

Torture: The deliberate inflicting of pain, whether physical or psychological, to degrade, intimidate, and induce submission of its victims to the will of the torturer. It is a heinous practice used frequently in most dictatorial regimes in the world, irrespective of their ideological leanings.

Transnational: An adjective indicating that a non-governmental movement, organization, or ideology transcends national borders and is operative in dissimilar political, economic, and social systems.

Transnational Enterprise (TNE) or Corporation (TNC): Synonymous to *Multinational Corporation* (MNC). An enterprise doing business in more than one country.

Triad (nuclear): The three-pronged US strategic weapons arsenal, composed of land-based *ICBMs,* underwater *SLBMs,* and long-range manned bombers.

Trilateral: Between three countries or groups of countries, e.g. USA, Western Europe and Japan; USA, USSR, and China.

Unilateral: One-sided, as opposed to bilateral or multilateral.

United Nations Conference on Trade and Development (UNCTAD): Was convened in 1964 in response to growing concern among LDCs over their effort to bridge the standard-of-living gap between them and DCs. Meetings were held in 1968, 1972, 1976, and 1979 and have focused on North-South economic issues.

"Unthinkables": Nuclear strategists who believe that a nuclear war, once begun, is likely to create a disaster of such magnitude that it is not meaningful to plan in terms of its actual occurrence.

Venice initiative: The Declaration by the European Community foreign ministers, on June 12, 1980, backing Palestinian "self-determination" and participation in Middle East negotiations; calling for an end to Israeli occupation of the Gaza Strip and the West Bank and to Israeli settlements there; and condemning Israel's proposed change in the status of Jersualem.

Verification: The process of determining that the other side is complying with an agreement.

Vulnerability: As used in strategic planning, it refers to the condition under which US silo-based ICBMs can be targeted for pinpoint hits by Soviet missiles.

Walesa, Lech (pronounced vah-wen-sah): Leader of the independent trade union movement known as Solidarity, which came into existence in August 1980 and was dissolved in December 13, 1981 by the martial law decree imposed.

Warhead: That part of a missile, projectile, or torpedo that contains the explosive intended to inflict damage.

Warsaw Pact or Warsaw Treaty Organization: Established in 1955 by the Soviet Union in response to the inclusion in NATO of the Federal Republic of Germany (West Germany). The members are the Soviet Union, Bulgaria, Czechoslovakia, the German Democratic Republic (East Germany), Hungary, Poland, and Romania.

West (as in the East-West conflict): A short-hand, nongeographic term that means (a) in economic matters, the *OECD* countries; (b) militarily, *NATO,* France, and *ANZUS.* Basically the market-economy, industrialized, and high-income countries that are committed to a political system of representative democracy. The three main anchors of the West today are North America, Western Europe, and Japan, also known as the Trilateral countries. Australia and New Zealand are also parts of the West.

Western economic summits: Annual meetings of the leaders of seven Western industrialized nations (the USA, the UK, France, West Germany, Japan, Italy, and Canada) with the president of the Commission of the EEC in attendance. These meetings were first held at Rambouillet, France, in 1975. The latest was the Ottawa Summit in 1981.

Western Five Contact Group (re Namibia): Five Western countries acting as intermediaries between South Africa, SWAPO and Front-line States to work out procedures for the independence and future government of Namibia. They are Canada, the Federal Republic of Germany, France, the United Kingdom, and the United States. The European nations are more pro-SWAPO while the USA is more pro-South Africa.

"Window of vulnerability": An expression often used, but not consistently defined, by Ronald Reagan and his associates since the Presidential campaign of 1980. Military specialists use the word to refer to a period of time in the future (in the late 1980s) when US silo-based ICBMs can be accurately hit by Soviet missiles while the mobile MX system (now scrapped) will not yet be operational, and when the aging B-52 bombers are no longer serviceable while the *Stealth* aircraft will not yet be operational. Mr. Reagan approved a plan to close this "window" by MIRVing the silo-based ICBMs, by hardening their concrete covers, and by building B-1 bombers.

World Bank (International Bank for Reconstruction and Development-IBRD): Makes loans, either directly to governments or with governments as the guarantors; and through its affiliates, the International Finance Corporation and the International Development Association.

World Politics: The sum of all those actions and interactions of some 160 nation states and scores of non-national and trans-national actors in terms of political, diplomatic, military, and economic policies.

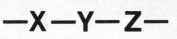

Yield: The explosive force, in terms of TNT equivalence, of a warhead.

Zero option: President Reagan's proposal made on November 19, 1981, that the US would cancel its plan to deploy MRBMs (Pershing II and GLCMs) in Western Europe if the USSR agreed to remove those it has already emplaced in Eastern Europe and Western USSR.

Zhao Ziyang: Head of government, People's Republic of China.

Zimbabwe: Formerly Rhodesia.

INDEX

Credits/Acknowledgments

Cover design by Charles Vitelli

1. **The US in an Interdependent World**
Table of Contents (TOC)—United Nations/photo.
2. **Revival of the Cold War**
TOC—U.S. Air Force/photo.
3. **Allies of the US**
TOC—United Nations/photo.
4. **Socialist States**
TOC—United Nations/photo by Saw Lwin.
5. **The Third World**
TOC—United Nations/photo.

6. **The International Political Economy**
TOC—EPA/Documerica.
7. **The Arms Race**
TOC—U.S. Air Force/photo.
8. **International Organization and International Law**
TOC—United Nations/photo.
9. **Problems and Prospects for the Future**
TOC—WHO/photo.

WE WANT YOUR ADVICE

ANNUAL EDITIONS: WORLD POLITICS 83/84

Article Rating Form

Here is an opportunity for you to have direct input into the next revision of this reader. We would like you to rate each of the 53 articles listed below, using the following scale:

1. **Excellent: should definitely be retained**
2. **Above average: should probably be retained**
3. **Below average: should probably be deleted**
4. **Poor: should definitely be deleted**

Your ratings will play a vital part in the next revision. So please mail this prepaid form to us just as soon as you complete it.
Thanks for your help!

Rating	Article	Rating	Article
	1. Defining the National Interest		31. Israel and the Peace Process
	2. Concepts and Communications in American Foreign Policy		32. Development Strategy Distorted by Western Propaganda
	3. Chain Linkage in American Foreign Policy		33. The North-South Dialogue: The Issue Is Survival
	4. Human Rights and the Refugee Crisis		34. Foreign Aid: Reaching the Bottom of the Barrel
	5. Foreign Policy: Outmoded Assumptions		35. The US Caribbean Basin Initiative
	6. Human Rights: The Bias We Need		36. Conditionality: Reflects Principle That Financing and Adjustment Should Act Hand in Hand
	7. Changing Soviet Conceptions of East-West Relations		37. Thirty-Two Years of World Trade Developments
	8. Excerpts, from *Whence the Threat to Peace?*		38. De Larosière Stresses No Monetary System Can Substitute for Sound Economic Policies
	9. Changing of the Guard		39. Trade Relations Between Industrialized Countries in Times of Crisis
	10. Reagan's Foreign Policy: New Dangers		40. Russian and American Capabilities
	11. The Russian Connection		41. Pushing Arms
	12. A New Course for Britain and Western Europe		42. Conventional Arms Transfers in the Third World
	13. Is NATO Obsolete?		43. Practice and Theory on Soviet Arms Control Policy
	14. French Diplomacy: A Two-Headed Sphinx		44. Limits and Cuts: SALT and START
	15. West Germany's New Chancellor: The Thoughts of Helmut Kohl		45. The Falklands and the Law
	16. America and Japan: A Search for Balance		46. The UN: Keeping Alive a Withering Dream
	17. Japanese Perception of America: Evolution from Dependency to Maturity		47. The Common Heritage
	18. Stability in the Warsaw Pact?		48. Law of the Sea: The Next Phase
	19. East Europe Instability		49. Sea Law Convention Battle
	20. The German Democratic Republic		50. Global Future: Time to Act
	21. China's Split-Level Change		51. The Establishment of a World Authority: Working Hypotheses
	22. Sino-American Relations: The Decade Ahead		52. Let the Old Order Die
	23. Central America's Bitter Wars Spread		53. U.S. Nuclear Strategy and World Order Reform
	24. Central America: A Potential Vietnam?		
	25. U.S. Policy and Africa		
	26. Zimbabwe Is a Success		
	27. Sino-American Relations: Reaching a Plateau		
	28. The Strategic Significance of South Asia		
	29. The Tragedy and the Hope		
	30. Moscow's Middle East		

(continued on back)

About you

Name _____ Date _____
Address _____
City _____ State _____
Zip _____ Telephone _____

1. What do you think of the Annual Editions concept?

2. Have you read any articles lately that you think should be included in the next edition?

3. Which articles do you feel should be replaced in the next edition? Why?

4. In what other areas would you like to see an Annual Edition? Why?

WORLD POLITICS 83/84